BASKETBALL

Building The Complete Program

By Norm Stewart
and George Scholz

Library of Congress Catalog Card
Number 80-52197

This book printed and published by

WALSWORTH
PUBLISHING
COMPANY
MARCELINE, MISSOURI 64658

ISBN No.
0-9605092-0-8

ACKNOWLEDGEMENTS

To our parents, Ken and Leona and Richard and Ellen, for their tremendous love and support.

To Barney and Florence and Tom and Emily for providing us with the real inspirations in our lives.

To Cleo, Ola, Riff, Tom, Beth, and Joe. Thanks for everything.

To C. J. Kessler, W. N. "Sparky" Stalcup, Lute Olson, and Dick Kuchen for ideas contained in this book and for supporting us in our chosen profession.

To Don Walsworth for everything.

To Bobby Knight for writing a foreword for our work.

To Dwight Thompkins and Dave Murray for countless hours of editing and advice.

To Bob Sundvold for his help in reviewing the manuscript.

To Mark Fitzpatrick for his help with the final chapter.

To Terry Dittman and Sue Mordt for their help in preparing the manuscript and to Lynda Juergens for providing the artwork for our diagrams. Thanks also to Beth Welch and Thane Wilson and to Pat McKee for his photographs.

To Shirley Padgett, switchboard operator at Walsworth Publishing Company, for taking and making hundreds of calls concerning the publication of this book.

To all of the dedicated teachers at Shelbyville High School, the University of Missouri, Christian Brothers High School (now Notre Dame), Jacksonville University, and the University of Iowa. Especially the late Mrs. Gladys Kessler and Ms. Louise Goodson for their dedication to their students and the training that made this book acceptable.

For unequaled family support and the actual fighting of the wars, this book is dedicated to:

Virginia
Jeffrey Cole
Lindsey Scott
Laura Elizabeth

Lynne
Corey

FOREWORD

Basketball as it is played at the University of Missouri under Coach Norm Stewart serves as an excellent guide to the game for coaches at all levels of play. Norm is one of the finest fundamental teachers in the game today. George Scholz is a fine young assistant with a bright future. Their concept of basketball is one that encompasses all phases of the game with the development of overall play being uppermost in mind rather than a particular emphasis on specific segments of offense or defense.

This book covers the development of a basketball program from the establishment of a philosophy of how to teach basic skills through the most intricate phases of the game. Each chapter is an indepth look at a specific phase of basketball. These areas are thoroughly covered from the development of concepts and the teaching of fundamentals to the cohesiveness of five man play. The thing that I enjoy most about the book is that its purpose is not an all-encompassing look at the game of basketball. Instead Norm and George have given us a very comprehensive analysis of the various facets of the game utilized in their program at Missouri.

In addition to talking about the game itself, an extensive look is taken at the mental approach to the game. This will include such things as: player selection, player-coach relationships, conditioning, off-season work, the proper approach to the season as well as individual game preparation.

You are about to begin a study of a most revealing look at one of America's most successful basketball programs. You will find this book to be one of the most valuable additions that you have made to your library in a long time.

Bobby Knight

Table Of Contents

The Trap, Teaching Three on Three Defense (First Stage), Three on Three Full Court (Second Stage), Five on Five Full Court Pressure, Two-Two-One Zone Press, Drills for Developing our Full Court Pressure.

7. Team Defense in the Half Court Area

Defensive Philosophy in the Half Court, More on the Objectives of Defense, Half Court Situations, Two on Two Help and Recover, One Man Removed Principle, Two on Two Influence, Western Roll, Reaction Drill, Inside Cut, Screen Away, Influence (3 on 3), Forward Cut, Help and Recover (3 on 3), Post Split Coverage, Three on Three Survival, Reaction Drill (4 on 4), Vertical and Horizontal Screens, Collapse on the Post, Reaction Drill (5 on 5), Baseline Help, Congesting the Middle, Five on Five Survival, Converting from Offense to Defense, Five on Five Defensive Game, Half Court Team Defensive Drills.

8. Rebounding

Six Crucial Areas in Rebounding, Defensive Rebounding, The Block Out, Helpside Rebounding, Ballside Rebounding, Offensive Rebounding, Organization of Our Offensive Rebounding, Post Pass Series, Corner Pass Series, Fourth Man Across Series, Reverse Pass Series, Rebounding Drills.

9. Practice Planning and Conditioning

Preliminary Planning, Ideas on Practice Planning, Player Rating System, Master List of Drills, Flexibility and Stations, Practice Schedules, Emphasis of the Day, Additional Player Evaluations, Final Points on Practice Planning, Philosophy on Conditioning, Mental Approach, Training Evaluations, Letters to Players During the Off Season, Complete Flexibility Program, Summer Conditioning Program, Fall Conditioning Program, Strength Development, Individual Programs, Agility and Conditioning Drills.

10. Special Situations

The Lay Up Game Philosophy, Principles Involved in Teaching the Lay Up Game, Alignment and Personnel, Basic Pattern, Movement on the Ballside, Weakside Action, Getting Behind the Defense, Additional Points of Emphasis, Strategies Employed in the Lay Up Game, Practice Hints, Out of Bounds Plays, Under the Offensive Basket, From the Offensive Sideline, From the Defensive Sideline, From the End Line, Free Throw Situations, Jump Ball Situations, Techniques Important for the Jumper, Defense Versus the Four Corners, Final Points on the Special Situations.

11. The Silent Nine

Concluding Chapter, Highlights of the 1979-80 season.

Basketball Coaches' Creed

George R. Edwards
University of Missouri

I BELIEVE that basketball has an important place in the general educational scheme and pledge myself to co-operate with others in the field of education to so administer it that its value never will be questioned.

I BELIEVE that other coaches of this sport are as earnest in its protection as I am, and I will do all in my power to further their endeavors.

I BELIEVE that my own actions should be so regulated at all times that I will be a credit to the profession.

I BELIEVE that the members of the National Basketball Committee are capably expressing the rules of the game, and I will abide by these rules in both spirit and letter.

I BELIEVE in the exercise of all the patience, tolerance, and diplomacy at my command in my relations with all players, co-workers, game officials and spectators.

I BELIEVE that the proper administration of this sport offers an effective laboratory method to develop in its adherents high ideals of sportsmanship; qualities of cooperation, courage, unselfishness and self-control; desires for clean, healthful living; and respect for wise discipline and authority.

I BELIEVE that these admirable characteristics, properly instilled by me through teaching and demonstration, will have a long carryover and will aid each one connected with the sport to become a better citizen.

I BELIEVE in and will support all reasonable moves to improve athletic conditions, to provide for adequate equipment and to promote the welfare of an increased number of participants.

BASKETBALL COURT DIAGRAM

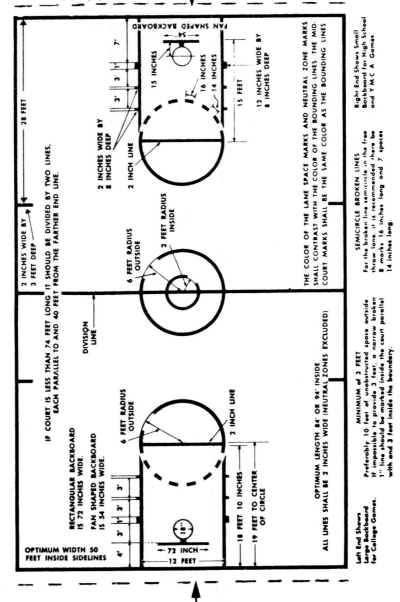

RECOMMENDED LIMIT LINE

SIX (6) FEET FROM EACH END LINE

RECOMMENDED LIMIT LINE

We would like to thank all of the following players for helping us to make this book possible.

UNIVERSITY OF MISSOURI

Bob Allen	Rod Denman	Felix Jerman	Charley Palmer	Dave Stallman
Carl Allrich	Tom Dore	Bob Johnson	Calvin Patterson	Steve Stipanovich
Carl Amos	Mark Dressler	Clay Johnson	Charles Payne	Jerry Stock
Kim Anderson	Larry Drew	Doug Johnson	Ron Pexa	Kenn Stoehner
Mark Anderson	Brad Droy	Richie Johnson	Larry Pierick	Ed Stoll
Rich Atzen	Lex Drum	Tom Johnson	David Pike	Jon Sundvold
Reid Bailey	John Duft	Gene Jones	Gene Pinkney	Shawn Teague
Dave Bennett	Al Eberhard	Ron Jones	Ernest Poe	Tom Thoenen
Curtis Berry	Greg Flaker	Jim Kennedy	Ken Pollitz	Don Tomlinson
Steve Blind	Bill Flamank	Kevin King	Stan Ray	Sam Tucker
Greg Boone	Theo Franks	Chuck Kundert	Steve Rea	LaMont Turner
Bob Boston	Gary Frazier	Barry Laurie	Glenn Robinson	Danny Van Rheen
John Brown	Ricky Frazier	Gary Link	Robert Roundtree	Jay Vocke
Richard Brune	Mark Fredrickson	Mike Love	Orv Salmon	Steve Wallace
Dick Buxton	Bill Foster	Marvin (Moon)	Ron Selbo	Carl Williams
Jim Chapman	Mike Foster	McCrary	Sam Sewell	Kevin Williams
James Clabon	Mike Griffin	Bob McDaniel	Kirk Shawver	Gail Wolf
Vaughn Colbert	Kevin Hay	Barry Maurer	Scott Sims	Scott Wolfe
Rocky Copley	Pete Helmbock	Tom Miltenberger	Henry Smith	
Jeff Currie	Brian Hochevar	Doug Ommen	Willie Smith	
Steve Dangos	Mike Jeffries	Tim Osborne	Al Sparman	

STATE COLLEGE OF IOWA
(Now University of Northern Iowa)

Paul Balcom	Tom Franklin	Duane Josephson	Bob McCool	Randy Schultz
Russell Barney	Gene Fuelling	Herb Justmann	Stan Mallin	Lyle Schwarzenbach
Ivan Bilbert	Patrick Gabriel	Craig Kneppe	Paul Martin	Pete Spoden
Roger Bock	Larry Goodrich	Dick Lange	John Moore	Larry Timion
Gary Brower	Don Hein	Bruce Lein	Charles Nolting	Bill Van Zante
Dick Christy	Jerry Holbrook	David Lister	Gerry Payne	Jim Videtich
Larry Clausen	Ken Huelman	Dick Lowe	Dennis Przychodzin	Bob Waller
Ray Cull	Rich James	Larry Lust	Steve Raver	Ed Ware
Harry Daniels	Daryl Jesse	Dan McCleary	Barry Remington	Jerry Waugh
Marvin DeWaard	Ron Jessen	Jerry McColley	Mark St. Clair	Rick Wilson
Larry Dusanek	Phil Johnson	Randy McColley	Dick Savage	

BASKETBALL

Building The
Complete Program

By Norm Stewart
and George Scholz

General Philosophies 1

Coaching Philosophy

Coaching, like many other professions, can at times seem so complex that the answers you are seeking are nowhere in sight. At other times, everything may be going right for no particular reason. The important thing to remember is that coaching is what you make it. You will get no more out of the coaching profession than you put into it. The ultimate success or decline of your program will be in direct proportion to the amount of time, organization, and hard work you and those around you are willing and able to provide.

There are virtually no secrets in the coaching profession and there are many ways of doing things to reach the same objective. Those that work the hardest will always reach their objectives and their goals more successfully and with more consistency. Establishing a winning program does not just happen nor will the hard work you have accomplished in the past sustain a winning tradition. It is an ongoing proposition which must be a part of your personal philosophy as well as your coaching philosophy.

The game of basketball has had a direct bearing on the major portions of our lives. It is now our vocation. It is conceivable then that much of our personal philosophy will be ingrained in that which we apply to coaching. We feel it is vitally important not only to develop a sound coaching philosophy, but also that we must give it repeated exposure to our players. Hopefully, the same ideals that we have developed will seem worthwhile and valuable to them, now and in the future.

We tell our players that our first responsibility, with regard to our philosophy as coaches, is to the players and others immediately involved in our program. We are there to help and we will do all that is possible to meet their needs during and after their four years at the University of Missouri. We stress the fact that we are in a supporting role. We can help them to get to where they want to go, but the bulk of the work they must do themselves.

The players must be made aware that our second responsibility is also a very important one and that at times it may put us in a position of direct conflict with the first. That responsibility is to conduct a basketball program that will represent or be a means of advertising the University of Missouri, its faculty, students, alumni and friends throughout the United States. When our team takes the floor, we want everyone of these people to be able to say, with pride, ''That is Missouri University!'', ''That is the way I conduct my class.'', ''That is my school playing,'', ''That is where I went to school,'', ''That is how I would do it.

With this in mind, our players are told that we want each man to be an integral part of **our** team. We let them know that, as a group, we are expected to achieve success in a certain percentage of our games. It is our feeling, however, that by playing with extreme intensity and playing together, we will be successful in some situations where the odds seem almost impossible. We want to be sure that each of our players can face up to this type of challenge for each particular game and during the course of the entire season. It is important that the players learn to play the games one at a time. There can be no looking ahead to a future opponent or we will stumble over our present opponent. If we have prepared ourselves mentally and physically for each particular opponent then the conference race or any post season play will fall into place. Any coach would do well to include this emphasis in his coaching philosophy. It is easy to prepare the team and individual players for the big games. The games that may seem easy to the players count just the same in the won-lost column.

There is no doubt in our minds, that each year as our economy and social values change, it becomes easier to adopt an attitude that is not competitive. We find it easier to achieve a certain degree of success whether it is social, professional, or financial. This is not to say it is wrong to accept these things which we are fortunate to have available, but is is important to recognize the conditions under which we are living. It is also important to recognize that it remains difficult to ''become one of the best.'' Since our players are involved in keen competition at a very high level, we must make them aware that to be as successful as possible or to become one of the best, we must properly motivate, stimulate, or possibly force them to use their full potential.

It is our belief that you should never be critical of anyone or anything until you have tried to help the person or the situation. To interpret this into our coaching philosophy produces the following formula.

  1.) Show the individual what you want him to do and how to do it. If he listens and attempts the skill in the manner prescribed, then give him praise, regardless of his talent and regardless of his ability to produce success with his level of talent at that time.

  2.) If he does not attempt the skill as directed, he should be corrected. Anyone can execute physical skills to a certain degree. Whether they can execute with enough quickness to be successful is incidental at first. If the individual does not attempt to execute the skill as directed the second time, he is leaving himself open to deserved criticism.

  3.) When the player has been exposed to this procedure and reacts in a negative manner that suggests he has been treated unfairly or that he needs a different instructional approach, then he is not accepting his share of the responsibility.

What we are attempting to create for the individual is an atmosphere that will develop self-discipline. Self-discipline is something that can be developed and it has a definite carry-over value from one area to another. If an individual can learn to discipline himself at this age, he can call on this quality to use at a time in his life when it may well be more important than a game of basketball. It may be needed during some of the most crucial and difficult decisions of life. If he is prepared, he can make those decisions knowing in his own mind that he has been placed in "pressure situations" before and has reacted in a manner that shows knowledge, intelligence and judgment. Basketball in itself is not an end. Learning to play within the rules and extending full effort becomes a means to an end. If our players can approach a level using a high percentage of their potential, they will find much in life that is pleasant and satisfying.

The game of basketball offers many challenges, experiences, thrilling moments, some heartaches, but above all, it offers a chance to compete in a small phase of an athlete's life that will never come again. Many people, throughout the community, the state, and the nation watch our players and use them as an example. Awareness of this position and acceptance of the responsibility it entails can help develop each player as an individual. The players must be taught to always be respectful of other people and their feelings.

This is what we will emphasize to our players both verbally and in writing at the beginning of the school year. We will continually point out these ideas to the team. They encompass sketches of our personal philosophy together with the ideals we have set up for our program to comprise our coaching philosophy.

In addition, we give our players the following advice.
> If you want to be happy, successful, accepted, and recognized, take advantage of your opportunities. Seek them out. Live and play within a framework of rules that are your own beliefs and conscience. Work hard and be patient. Do not become discouraged if it seems others are achieving more by doing less. It is your life and you alone have control over it. Hard work as well as excellence will be rewarded. When you are rewarded, accept it graciously and with pride.

Many Roles of the Coaching Profession

Coaching is a multi-faceted profession. It is imperative that we develop some expertise in all of the following roles. We must stress again that work will be the common denominator. As a coach, you can always go through the motions of acting out the various roles. Your success or lack of it, however, will be determined by your ability to recognize these roles and continually strive to improve your performance in each and every area.

Teacher-Coach. The first and most obvious role that we all have been trained for is that of the teacher-coach. Foremost among our responsibilities in this area we have touched upon briefly in discussing our ideals and philosophies with our players. We are referring to setting a good example, both directly, by the way we behave and indirectly, by pointing to good models in the past or present. The following excerpt explaining the role, purpose and process of the teacher is taken from **Teaching Physical Education in Secondary Schools** by Clyde Knapp and Patricia Leonhard. Its applicability to the coaching profession is obvious.

> "Teaching centers about the organization of learning experiences. Its purpose is to make learning more efficient. Teaching is the process of helping other individuals to learn. A teacher (coach) plans the learning experiences of his students (players) in order that the learning process becomes as efficient as possible. He encourages learning by providing means of motivation which promote initial interest in learning and maintain a necessary level of interest until the student achieves the learning outcome. He also guides the learner through the learning experience, reducing to a minimum the amount of random or trial-and-error effort. He further serves as diagnostician, noting where progress toward goals has been misdirected; and he assists the learner to recognize acceptable progress and accomplishment of desired goals."

Organizer-Planner. Organization and planning is the second important area that must be considered in undertaking the many roles and responsibilites of the coach. The definition we like best pertaining to organization is extremely fitting in application to any basketball program. It is, "an administrative and functional structure arranged by systematic planning and united effort." The head coach must set the pattern and be responsible for the overall organization of his program. However, that "united effort" must come from everyone directly involved in the organizational process—assistant coaches, players, managers, secretaries, trainers, etc. Again, you as a coach have been put in the position of setting the example. And again, the amount of work put into the organization and planning of your program will or will not produce the desired results.

Leader. Leadership is an important quality in most any profession, but even more so in coaching. The coach must give direction and provide leadership to a diverse group of young, impressionable, highly spirited athletes. The first important aspect of a leadership role is mutual respect. The coach must be respected by his players and he, in turn, must respect them as a group and as individuals. A healthy respect is earned, not given; commanded, not demanded.

Leadership by example will again set the tone for your program. A good example should insure a respectful and loyal following among your players and should inspire an emergence of additional leaders from within the team. At no time should we ask more of our team than we ask of ourselves. To command from them a high standard of conduct in matters we deem important, we must ourselves be always conscious and abiding of those same high standards.

A third important aspect of leadership is the ability to get the most out of your players while they fully understand and even enjoy the work that goes into meeting that goal. This is truly an inspirational quality that must be dealt with if a team is to be successful over the long haul of the season.

Motivator-inspirator. Later on in this chapter, we will elaborate on the importance of motivation in coaching and discuss some procedures designed to help inspire our players. We feel that the role of a motivator is a very important and often neglected aspect of the coach's job. Coaches understand its importance but don't really work at improving their ability in this area. The attempt to develop self-motivation in the player is of paramount importance in our program.

Guidance counselor. We would be wrong to claim any large amount of expertise in the field of guidance counseling. (We are in no way qualified for that title.) And yet, we must always be vitally interested in the well-being of our players off the basketball floor. We must have the time and the inclination to help where help is needed. In most cases, we are the parent-substitute for our athletes during a four-year period where remarkable growth and maturation are taking place. They come in as seventeen or eighteen-year-old-freshmen to a strange town, meeting new friends, in an entirely different situation than what they are used to. For perhaps the first time, these young people will be exposed to others from entirely different backgrounds. There will be many choices as to proper dress, proper behavior, whom to associate with, etc. Before the mode of living had been relatively the same and they knew what was expected of them.

In some cases we may even be looked up to as a father-figure. This is a large amount of responsibility for anyone to assume. Our role in a young person's life then must not be taken lightly Of utmost importance will be our ability to give our players direction. We must help them to understand the opportunities they will have before them. We must help them to select worthwhile and attainable goals, and once this is accomplished, it is our task to properly direct them toward those goals.

Disciplinarian. Discipline is an extremely important element in the make-up of any team. As we have mentioned previously, the development of self-discipline in our players is a constant goal. The value of self-discipline in all areas of life cannot be underestimated and we want our players to realize the importance of this concept with regard to the team and with regard to their own future. With this in mind, we visit with the players on an individual basis before fall practice begins. We ask them to give us their feelings and ideas concerning squad training rules. Almost without fail, their suggestions are more restrictive than what the coaching staff may have already discussed. This points up the fact that the players want discipline. Whether or not they have the maturity to discipline themselves regarding the training rules and suggestions depends upon the individual. The responsibility rests mainly with the players. We stress this fact to them, and we point out that their regard or disregard for proper conditioning and training will show up in their performance.

The following list is an example of our training rules for a given year.

Player Training Rules
1. Refrain from the use of all smoking materials.
2. Refrain from the use of drugs, except those prescribed by the trainer or a doctor.
3. Use good judgment in regard to alcoholic beverages. Understand the social pressures and also be aware of the responsibilities. This type of rule places the responsibility on you. Be willing to accept it.

Coach's Squad Rules
1. Have enough pride in your team to be a gentleman at all times.
2. Be on time or early when time is involved.
3. Us the equipment provided by the University in a prescribed fashion.
4. Keep an appearance that shows you in your best light. This applies to your dress, hair, etc.

General Training Suggestions
1. Keep regular hours.
2. Eat balanced meals with a minimum of eating between meals. Drink an adequate amount of liquids including water, milk and fruit juices.
3. Try to allow enough time to eat so that you can relax afterwards for at least a few minutes.
4. Be proud and confident of your conditioning-physically, mentally, and morally. This is definitely an area in which, as a college student and athlete, you could have an improved performance by giving it more attention.

On the floor, it is essential that we be firm but fair with each player and with the team as a whole. We must use good judgment as to how and when to make corrections. Our players realize that because of the diverse personalities on a fifteen man squad, each player may be treated a little differently. The important thing is that each is treated equally when there is an action that warrants correction or discipline.

Public Relations Advocate. As coaches, we should be constantly aware of our exposure to the public eye. It has been said that we sometimes get too much credit when we win and too much blame when we lose. Nevertheless, the scrutiny is there. We are, without a doubt, a mode of entertainment for the people within our given area. As we mentioned in the discussion of our coaching philosophy with our players, many of these people identify our program as their team, their university, their state school. They will identify not only with our performance on the floor, but with our total program. To ignore our role in the area of public relations would undermine our maintenance of a successful program. It would also exhibit disregard for the responsibilities we have to the many people important to our success.

Qualities of the Coach. Many of the important qualities or characteristics of the successful coach we have already discussed in relation to the roles of the coach. The qualities desirable in the coaching profession have also been detailed many times in previous books on coaching. In our program, there are five primary traits that we feel are important above all others. These are outlined every fall in a letter to each staff member and are constantly emphasized throughout the year. It is imperative that we develop these qualities if they are not already a part of our make-up. We must also continually evaluate ourselves to determine if we are displaying these characteristics or if we have neglected a certain area.

1. A coach must be **loyal**. You must first be loyal to yourself and then to the team, the coaching staff, the athletic department and to the University. This loyalty will, of course, extend to the community as well as to the entire state.
2. A coach must be a **leader**. You should be industrious, enthusiastic, encouraging and positive. You must be ahead of the players—leading at all times.
3. A coach must be **knowledgeable**. This includes knowledge in all phases of your own program and all phases of the game of basketball.
4. A coach must be a **hard worker.** You must be dedicated and willing to work in all areas, to do all you can toward achieving a successful program.
5. A coach must be **natural** and yet you must always be seeking to improve as an individual. Don't imitate someone else. Be yourself and your positive aspects will always come to the front.

Enthusiasm we include in our emphasis on leadership. This could perhaps be a sixth all-important characteristic. There is no doubt that enthusiasm, or the lack of it, is contagious. The players will recognize the fact that you love what you are doing, that you are totally interested in your profession, and that you are excited about the prospects for another season. They will also recognize a lack of enthusiasm and interest in your work and a lack of anticipation for the coming season. That your attitude will then have a direct effect on the attitude and spirit of the team is obvious.

| ENTHUSIASM IS CONTAGIOUS—START AN EPIDEMIC! |

Basketball Philosophy

Of major importance upon beginning a career in coaching is the development of a basic philosophy on basketball. To clarify our terminology, let us say that this basic philosophy is separate and distinct from the development of a style of play and our overall system. It is crucial in any program to have a set terminology that has been defined and is understood by coaches and players. In our basketball program, we begin with a basic philosophy, determine our style of play, and incorporate or sometimes design an overall system. We define style of play as those methods of playing the game of basketball that we put special emphasis on in our execution (i.e., fast break as opposed to slow-down, aggressive defense as opposed to passive.) Our overall system consists of the established procedure by which we will organize, teach and carry out the game of basketball (i.e., the actual organization and teaching of the fast break, offensive and defensive sets, etc.). Both of these will be detailed thoroughly in succeeding chapters dealing with the teaching of the game.

Just as your coaching philosophies and ideals will serve as a strong base for a successful program off the floor, your basic basketball philosophy will be the foundation for all that pertains to the game itself. For example, a part of your basketball philosophy would deal with the question of one set style of play or a style that will change according to your material in a given year. If you are at the high school level where there is no control over the type of players from one year to the next, it might be wise to adapt your style to fit the personnel. It is interesting to note, however, that many very successful high school coaches have been able to establish a strong community basketball network that teaches their particular philosophy, style and system of play from the grade schools on up.

At any rate, your style of play, system, coaching methods, practice planning, game organization, etc., should evolve from and be directly related to your basic basketball philosophy. At Missouri our basic basketball philosophy is outlined in six fundamental principles.

   1. **We want to play a brand of basketball that is exciting and fun for our players and for those attending the games.**

2. **We want our players to be extremely well-conditioned. They will be confident in the knowledge that they have paid the price and will be in better shape than any team they face.**
3. **We want our players to be well-versed in the fundamentals of the game of basketball.**
4. **We want our team to exhibit a high degree of spirit and aggressiveness that will enable them to out-hustle the opposition.**
5. **We will insist that our players play with the idea of the team above the individual. Teamwork and unselfishness are a must when developing a winning attitude and a winning record.**
6. **Our style of play and our basketball system have remained basically the same for a number of years. Every year, we make adjustments and refinements in these areas according to the strengths and weaknesses of each team.**

Motivating the Players

The single most important factor in the game of basketball, as well as the game of life, is our mental approach. Some term the game today as ninety percent mental, ten percent physical. We would be naive to downplay the importance of pure physical ability, but time and time again we have seen teams and individual players out-perform opponents with far greater physical skills because of their outstanding mental approach. Competitiveness, intelligence, mental preparation, dedication, intensity, alertness, poise, team orientation—all of these qualities are important to the development of a proper mental approach. The one element, however, that precedes and exceeds all of these is motivation. Is the player motivated to compete? Is he motivated to prepare himself mentally for each and every challenge? Is he motivated enough to place the team above self?

Psychological Needs of the Players. To have the ability to help motivate or to stimulate self-motivation in your players, you must first recognize the basic psychological needs of an individual. We are cognizant of the fact that our players are seeking to attain four specific areas of fulfillment through their participation in basketball.

1. **Adventure—doing something very few people have the opportunity or skill to attempt. Something out of the ordinary.**
2. **Acceptance—by a group (the team).**
3. **Achievement—accomplishing set or perceived goals through the mastery of the skills involved in basketball, plus hard work, and persistence.**
4. **Recognition—by people outside the group (i.e., the students, peers, people in the community, etc.).**

In analyzing our players, the degree to which these needs are being met will have a great influence on their personal or self-motivation. Additionally, we will be able to recognize areas where there is a problem and determine avenues to alleviate the situation.

Perhaps we have a player who is one of our top six or seven athletes, is happy with his role on the team, but doesn't get along well with many of his teammates. His needs are being met in the areas of adventure, achievement and recognition, but he is not sufficiently accepted by the team. Many times we will be aware of the possible reasons the player has trouble being accepted. It is easy then to counsel the player and attempt to advise him on ways to make progress in this area. If we are unaware of the problems, individual talks with some of the players on the team can enlighten us. We would be sure to talk about many things so as not to focus attention on this one player. Most of us have been in this situation before and are not surprised to find that there is no problem at all or if there is that the player has greatly exaggerated it in his own mind. At any rate, we are aware of the needs of our players. We recognize when and where they are not being met. Therefore, more times than not, we can lessen or resolve the problem with beneficial results for the individual and the team as a whole.

Self-motivation. We strive for the development of self-motivation for a few obvious reasons. One, motivation from within will be a stronger and more consistent incentive than that which we may apply from the outside. Two, a self-motivated player will serve as an example to the younger player or to those who need improvement in this area. Three, the ability to motivate oneself is a trait that will be beneficial throughout life. The rewards of adventure, acceptance, achievement and recognition are acceptable as stimulants toward self-motivation. However, the person who plays the game purely because he enjoys it is practicing the highest form of intrinsic motivation and this will have an ideal effect on his performance.

Emphasis on success is an important form of motivation. Through our ideals, our conversations, letters to the players, handouts, etc., the players should have no trouble determining the importance we place on working hard and playing to our potential. Realizing this goal will lead to success. We have formed an axiom, in this regard, based on something we heard George Lehman say in one of his talks on shooting. We call it the "Competitive Cycle."

**PRACTICE LEADS TO SUCCESS . . .
SUCCESS LEADS TO CONFIDENCE . . .
CONFIDENCE LEADS TO MORE SUCCESS
AND THE CYCLE GOES ON.**

Confidence. Confidence is one of the areas where we can do much to help motivate. This has to be one of the most ignored or neglected apects of the coaching profession. It is our responsibility to instill confidence in our players. We must especially recognize those players that lack confidence and seek ways to develop this attribute. A player who doubts his competence will be adversely affecting his performance. Morevoer, a player feeling doubt on the part of his coaches or his teammates regarding his ability will certainly be hesitant about performing aggressively. His performance will suffer as a result.

False confidence should not be developed. However, the player can be shown that we have extreme confidence in his ability to do certain things. It is his responsibility to accept and understand the skills that are not a part of his game. Accentuate the positive but make him aware of his limitations. In life, all of our actions, feelings, behavior, etc., are consistent with our self-image. This idea holds true in basketball. Each individual will perform according to how he perceives himself as a basketball player. If a player thinks he is good, then he will play well and vise versa. It would be advantageous for our team and for our coaching success to develop in our players a belief and confidence in themselves and their teammates. It has been said many time before but it really is a state of mind game.

The following is a handout we issue to the players to help motivate. We do not know the author but these thoughts have proven valuable in the motivation of our players.

THINK LIKE A WINNER

What are the traits that make one man a winner and another man a loser? The big difference is in how a man thinks. His attitude will govern his actions.

For instance....

☆ A winner is always ready to tackle something new ... a loser is prone to believe it can't be done.

☆ A winner isn't afraid of competition ... a loser excuses himself with the idea that the competition beat him out.

☆ A winner knows he's sometimes wrong and is willing to admit his mistakes ... a loser can usually find someone to blame.

☆ A winner is challenged by a new problem ... a loser doesn't want to face it.

☆ A winner is decisive ... a loser frustrates himself with indecision.

☆ A winner realizes there is no time like the present to get a job done ... a loser is prone to procrastinate with the hope that things will be better tomorrow.

☆ A winner thinks positively ... acts positively ... and lives positively ... a loser usually has a negative attitude and a negative approach to everything.

☆ So, if you want to be a winner, think like a winner ... act like a winner ... and sooner than you think, you will be a winner.

MIZZOU

Team Morale. Another area of importance is to continually strive to make each invididual a vital part of the program. This is especially important for each team member, but can be extended to include all those involved (managers, secretaries, statisticians, etc.). The following has been important in getting across this idea to the team. It has been helpful to us in motivating those players that are not among the starting five. Additionally, it can serve to give the star players or the starting five a clearer picture of the team as a whole.

THE PLAYERS ON THE BENCH

It takes more than five players to make a winning team. The starting five may win a game, but it takes the whole team to win the championship—to go all the way. The team is really like an iceberg. You see the starting five, but underneath it all is that big, wide, strong base—the rest of the team. This is the part of the team that builds the character of a lasting winner. The more dedicated the man on the bench, the harder he works, the more he pushes and strengthens the starting player—the higher he pushes this iceberg out of the water— the bigger it gets—the better the team. If he quits, doesn't give his all, or becomes complacent in his position, he erodes that strong base and erodes the character of the team. He contributes to the error in a tense, one point game, he is partly to blame for that mental lapse with four minutes to play in the big rivalry, he undermines the total effort necessary for the team to come back from a ten point deficit in a championship game. And yet this player on the bench must be there—watching, waiting, and hoping—sometimes agonizingly—for that chance to use his special skill to better the team effort—to make the base of that iceberg stronger—to help build the character of the team. Yes, agonizingly because he knows there is a chance he won't play because he may be the smallest man waiting to break open a press or he may be the big man called in an instant to shut down the unusually big center who is hurting the team inside. He may even be the man that's hurt, but working twice as hard to be physically fit in time to play in the playoffs. He may be the man on the bench who demonstrates to the fans that this team really has character from the bench to the basket. But even more important he may be the whole bench that the player looks to late in the game when he is hurting, out of breath, and burning inside for that spirit, that push, and that enthusiasm, and that love necessary to make the big play and win the game for the whole team.

When the game is over, when the season ends and all the fans and sports writers are talking about the top of the iceberg, the stars and heroes, the players will know that the real winner is the team, the whole iceberg, especially the base—the men on the bench who build the character to make the team a lasting winner.

Compliments of Missouri Basketball

Fire-up Program. We use handouts to our players as a continuing source of motivation and inspiration. They will again emphasize our ideals and philosophies—those things that we deem important to a successful basketball program. While we initiate our Fire-up Program in the summer before each season, the motivation at Missouri has to be a traditional thing that is passed on from year to year and from class to class. Each team, class, and individual we hope will build on that tradition so that it gathers momentum for every new season.

As a rule, we will send at least two letters during the summer. These letters will go to all those directly involved in our program. The first will be short and will deal primarily with the playes themselves—what they are doing, etc. Mention of basketball will be kept to a minimum. The second will be sent sometime toward the end of the summer. With this letter, we will begin to prepare our players mentally for the upcoming season. Below is an example.

Dear _____:

In approximately two weeks, we will be back for another outstanding year and we hope you have had an enjoyable and profitable summer.

Although we have not had a final grade check, everyone seems to be in good shape scholastically. Some of the people who were here this summer worked out, and I am sure have helped themselves become a better basketball player and, in doing so, will give us a better basketball team.

I am writing to say that the coaches are looking forward to another successful year and to emphasize one area that will be the most important *factor* in our *success* as a group—YOUR ATTITUDE. We have had three outstanding seasons, five winning years; and a good attitude has been the single most important factor. Dedication and our desire to make an all-out effort have been the other areas that are very important for Missouri Basketball. We are going to re-emphasize these ideals all year long. We are going to be in the best physical condition of any Missouri team, and play together better than any Missouri team. We will need a stronger defense than last year and this will be a point of emphasis.

We want every man to return with these thoughts uppermost in his mind. That he is going to obtain a quality education and become a better basketball player on the best basketball team possible. There will be no place for anything else.

Sincerely,

NORM STEWART
Head Basketball Coach

We have already discussed the fact that when the players arrive in the fall, we make them initially aware of our coaching philosophy and the ideals of our program. The following are two examples of thoughts we will issue to our players as the beginning of preseason practice nears. It is important to note that both of these examples are from years following a conference championship. We had excellent players coming back and much was expected.

SEASON ATTITUDE AND UNDERSTANDING

Next week we officially begin our practice sessions for the 1972-73 season, and we will have many new phases. With several men returning from a Big 8 Tournament Championship and NIT team you will be ranked in the top 20 at the beginning of the season for the first time in the history of the University. You will be playing in a facility that in many respects is the finest available in this entire country. You will be guaranteed a capacity crowd before the season is opened. Enthusiasm is at its highest level for this basketball season.

You should be proud of this position. At the same time, what a great opportunity and challenge for every member of this group! Many of the upperclassmen have stated what they think you are capable of accomplishing this year as a team. As a coaching staff, we agree that your goal should be the highest and that each game should be played and won one at a time.

You must realize that it will require great dedication, desire, concentration, perseverance, and confidence. THE MOST IMPORTANT SINGLE FACTOR, HOWEVER, WILL BE YOUR ATTITUDE! As we have often said, "It is now what happens to you that counts, it is your reaction to it." All of you possess the mental ability to conduct yourself and react positively in almost all situations.

Every man is an important part of our team at all times. Your actions and words should always reflect credit to your teammates. Your responsibility is great and you must be aware of your position and show good sound judgment in all phases of life.

Your first responsibility is your school work, and you should take pride in attendance and your grades. You will miss class due to trips; and therefore, cannot afford absences while on campus. Establish good study habits and you will achieve a goal that will remain meaningful throughout your life.

When you report to practice October 15, you are expected to be a loyal member of our group. You should realize how dependent we are upon one another, how much you can help, how much you can be helped. The team comes first and will not be sacrificed for any individual.

Everyone wants to win—the true champion realizes the steps to be taken and his first consideration is training and conditioning. You are blessed with a sound mind and healthy body and should discipline yourself in regard to regular hours for sleep, a basketball diet, and sound training habits. This step allows you to give your best effort which in turn will let you enjoy success. We expect every man to come to the floor eager to learn and with a desire to expend a 100% effort.

We have outstanding leadership in our seniors as well as talent. Our juniors have also made an excellent contribution. We have three new groups this year since freshmen are eligible along with the sophomores and transfers. New men should be patient with yourselves and the situation to allow for the adjustments that will have to take place. Each of you can help and will be given the opportunity that you must earn.

We will be playing another outstanding non-conference schedule that includes six teams that either won or finished second in their conferences. You should have two immediate goals; be in better condition, both mentally and physically, than any of your opponents and out-hustle each team that you play.

CHAMPIONSHIP CHATTER

On Friday, October 15, we will begin our practices at 3:45. We want each man to know that he can be an important part of this group at all times. To be an important part, you must accept the responsibility that goes with your position. You have enhanced your position by virtue of your successes and particularly by winning the Big 8 Championship last year.

1. Realize that we condition ourselves to play a game that requires a great deal of endurance. This conditioning applies not only to physical but mental training as well.

2. We have stressed that you *MAY* play against a team that has more ability and that may be larger, faster and quicker, but you should play against *NO ONE* as an individual or as a team who would be superior in team spirit, determination and enthusiasm.

3. We know that it is a team game and our overall success depends upon our ability to play together. Realize that we are always striving to improve. To do this we must continue the enthusiasm with which we practiced and played last year. We must improve upon our relationships as individuals and as a team to the point that we understand that each of us is an individual but that we are willing to accept one another and live with one another without undue stress or conflict.

As a team on the basketball floor, we want to improve one specific area—*DEFENSE.* We want you to have the aggressiveness to play your man the entire length of the floor. We want you to have the confidence that you will receive help and influence from your teammates. At the outset, everyone should understand that the makeup of our squad is the team aspect with leadership, in contrast to a dominant player and team aspect. The challenge this year is to repeat. As we have stated previously, you have an advantage by having been there before. To repeat will require the same or more dedication and effort. Any other positive additions that you can make as an individual are welcome. Each of you realizes that this type of success is best attained in a relaxed and confident situation. You can make a tremendous contribution by working hard to develop your own confidence and showing confidence in your teammates.

As I have mentioned to you in the past, and particularly last year, I hope that you will look upon this challenge with enthusiasm. During the season, I hope that you can find yourself accomplishing a task that here-to-fore you thought impossible and that when the season is completed you will find yourself wishing that you had another game to play.

Another example of this letter is from a year when we were just starting to come into our own as a program based on success and tradition. As you can see, it carries a somewhat different theme while still drawing on some of the same all-important ideals.

TOP TIGER TALK

In the past four years, your teams have brought themselves, the student body, the University, and the State a basketball program that everyone points to with great pride.

In just two days we begin a challenge that will test your every ability and emotion. Win the Big Eight.

Every man will play an important part in the success of this team. To be a member of this squad gives you a great responsibility and sound judgment in all phases of life is required. Everything you do should reflect credit on this group.

The Good Lord has blessed each of you with athletic ability. Naturally, as individuals we possess different degrees of potential skills. You must work hard to perform at the top of your level.

You will play relaxed as you develop your confidence on the practice floor and this confidence will be expressed during the most difficult times in the games. Each of you will have this true confidence in your ability, in your teammates' abilities, and your coaches' abilities. Confidence breeds confidence. Believe in yourself and others—they will believe in you and themselves.

All of us want to win—the champion possesses the will to prepare to win. Your determination must be outstanding and in the crucial phases of the game you will be at your best. There may be a time when you feel tired or even pain but instinct and willpower will carry you to skill accomplishment that you think impossible at this time. The true champion realizes that in order to perform in this manner he must respect his good health and physical fitness at all times. Discipline yourself in regard to diet, rest, and training habits.

Practice will begin at 3:45 and we know that every man will be loyal to our group and recognize that he is dependent upon his teammates. We must live together without extreme conflict, undue stress or strain, and know that in every phase of life there is much that is pleasant and satisfying.

Your education is your most important goal and therefore your class attendance is mandatory. You will miss class due to trips and cannot afford cuts when you are on campus. Establish regular study hours and maintain the schedule. You won't regret it.

This year's team will be more experienced and will play with greater poise. We will extend our game over more of the court both offensively and defensively. As in the past, we want you to maintain the tradition you have helped build - fundamentally sound and mentally tough.

While we do not require that our players keep a notebook, we do ask them to keep these player handouts and to refer to them often. As fall practice begins, we want our players to ask themselves a few pertinent questions. At times, we have had each individual put their answers in writing, for their own benefit and that of the team. We don't check their answers, but want them to have their commitment to themselves and to the team on paper. When times get tough, many players have gone back to these answers and reaffirmed that commitment.

Ask yourself these questions and consider the statements.

1. Do I have complete control of myself? Do I adjust quickly to adversity and success?
2. Am I truly confident in my ability. Confidence breeds confidence. Believe in yourself, your teammates and in your coaches, and others will believe in you.
3. Loyalty is devotion to the cause. Am I loyal?
4. DO I HAVE THE VICTORY SPIRIT? You must have a tremendous desire to win and endure pain with courage. Wait for rewards, work for success and take an interest in the welfare of this group.
5. Religion—The man who has faith is more relaxed and has more freedom from worry and strain. Do I have faith?

Copies of the following are also issued to our players. We ask them to weigh the advantages and disadvantages presented before they make a firm commitment to being a dedicated member of our basketball program.

ADVANTAGES AND DISADVANTAGES OF BEING A MEMBER OF THE UNIVERSITY OF MISSOURI BASKETBALL TEAM

ADVANTAGES	DISADVANTAGES
1. Scholarship—Provides financial aid to attain an education.	1. It requires time that if used properly and channeled in a different direction, could provide another meaningful experience.
2. To represent yourself, the University, and the state through competition with teams throughout the nation.	2. It requires that each individual subject himself to a single authority as well as group rule. You will be conforming to one group that may be in contrast to other individuals
3. To learn the principles of dedication, cooperation, loyalty and perseverance.	

4. To be accepted and recognized on campus as a leader and steadying influence on your society.

5. To place yourself in a position of responsibility. When you meet with success, you will be given undue praise. Conversely, when you meet with adversity or failure you will be given undue criticism.

6. To learn success patterns, positive thinking and actions. To learn that the adventure of applying yourself and your good talents is a pleasure and that the hard work and efforts are met with self-satisfaction.

7. To be in a positon that individuals and groups are sincerely interested in you and your welfare as a person while at the University and upon leaving the University.

and groups that are conforming to other standards.

A few of our squads have required that we give them a more thorough understanding of the competition involved at this level of participation. The competition in college basketbll is much different than what the players have been used to in their own hometown at the high school level. They are now faced with the challenge of vying for a position with players of equal or greater ability. A player's reaction to this challenge can sometimes be negative and therefore have an adverse affect on his behavior and/or performance. We have found it necessary in that case to give to the team these ideas and questions.

UNDERSTANDING SUCCESS AND WHAT IT TAKES

Each of us wants to have success as a team and as an individual. To each of us success means different levels of achievement.

For some of us team success might mean:

Undefeated season	NIT
Big Eight Champs	Winning season.
NCAA	

For some of us success as an individual might mean:

All American	Starting five
All District	Top seven or eight
All Big Eight	Traveling squad.
All Tourney	

Each goal is difficult to achieve. Have you set your goal properly? Is it high enough? Are you willing to work in accordance with the level of your goal? Do you really want it bad enough to hurt for it? Are you just saying it is something you would like, but you are not willing to pay the price?

In high school each of us has been involved in a demanding program. We wanted to—we enjoyed the hard work. How many of you did? When we come to college our attitude changes for some of us. Why?

In high school you were top dog. Success came every day. Once in a while you might be corrected, but overall it was you who received the attention. No one could stop you completely every night. (Was it this way always or just your last year or two?)

Now you come to college. Now you are not top dog. Now you aren't the most popular. Now you don't get all the attention. Now someone can stop you. Now it is a bigger world.

What is your reaction? Is it positive? Do you look and say, "This is tough, but I have done it before and I will do it again. I like the challenge that comes with the opportunity?" Or do you consciously or unconsciously say or react negatively by not doing what is necessary to become successful at a higher level?

Such things as report as late as possible to practice to show that you really don't have to be there until 3:45.

Not work hard all the time because it is just too tough and you don't want to be tired for other activities.

Keep everyone informed as to your dissatisfaction with anything that has not gone your way. Of course, none of these incidents have been your own fault.

What do you want? Is it the adventure of being blessed with enough talent to do what only a few are chosen to do? Is it the acceptance to a group in which you can find pleasure and pride in belonging? Is it the success that comes from hard work, discipline, and dedication? Is it recognition that comes as a reward for the person or group that is patient and understands that many times the reward is not in proportion to the deed involved? That most of the time, it is too great? Ask yourself - What are you eager to do for our team?

The Self-Motivated Player

To further develop our emphasis on self-motivation among our players, we would like to draw on the experiences of three of our players, who played on our most successful teams at the University of Missouri from 1972-1976. Each of these players played at a somewhat different level with regard to their individual ability. And yet, while playing at these different levels and achieving different levels of success, they should be, and are, equally proud of their accomplishments. Why? Because each motivated himself to come as close as possible to realizing his full potential in college basketball.

Kim Anderson (Fig. 1-1), in 1977, was named the Most Valuable Player in the Big Eight Conference. He was our leading scorer and rebounder, and he was named to numerous All-America Teams. Kim played in the Coaches' East-West All-Star Game, the Pizza Hut All-Star Game, and participated in the Aloha All-American Classic in Honolulu, Hawaii. Kim was drafted and played for the Portland Trailblazers of the NBA, and continued his career in Italy. Kim is originally from Sedalia, Missouri, an hour's drive from Columbia and the University of Missouri campus. In 1973 when Kim graduated from Sedalia High School, he never would have dreamed of some of the honors that have been bestowed upon him. Kim earned these awards by becoming one of the most dedicated individuals ever associated with our program. He combined this dedication with a tremendous amount of character and pride. All of these attributes came as a result of Kim's ability to properly motivate himself. This motivation, pride, character and dedication enabled Kim to represent himself, his family, the team, his community, the University of Missouri, and the State of Missouri in excellent fashion.

Scott Sims (Fig 1-2) is another example we would like to draw

FIG. 1-1

FIG. 1-2

FIG. 1-3

upon. Scott, in his sophomore and junior season at Missouri, averaged three points per game and was only a part-time starter during both of those seasons. Not many people expected Scott's senior year to be anything different. Scott was the exception. He made up his mind that whatever ability he did have — not a Kim Anderson perhaps — but wherever his ability did lie, he was going to do all he could do to make the most of it. He promised himself that he would not let a day go by that he didn't push himself to give the maximum effort. To give just one example of his commitment, Scott promised that during the season he would win every sprint that was run in practice. He would let no one beat him. And he didn't. As a result of this self-motivation, Scott went out that season and became our second leading scorer, averaging sixteen points per game. He led the team in assists and was named to the All-Tourney team in all three of the tournaments in which we participated. In two of those tournaments, he was chosen the Most Valuable Player. Scott capped off the season by being selected second-team All-Big Eight and was the first guard drafted by the NBA San Antonio Spurs. This tremendous season was accomplished only through Scott's hard work and his total desire to make himself a better basketball player.

Danny Van Rheen (Fig. 1-3) is a player who didn't quite have the type of season we have just described. We were only able to give Danny a limited amount of playing time. Danny could do a lot of things for us, but there were too many talented players ahead of him. Danny realized his role on the team; he took pride in doing the things we asked of him, and he always gave his best. One of the things we asked Danny to do was give 120% in practice because we felt this could help our team in many ways. It was inspirational the way Danny pushed our starters and set an example for our younger players with his hustle and hard work during practice. While Danny's statistics were not as spectacular as those of Kim Anderson or Scott Sims, his ability to motivate himself under trying circumstances was remarkable.

Inspiration. We distribute many other motivational ideas throughout the year. One which we use that has been transcribed in numerous books on coaching is the poem entitled "It's all in a State of Mind." The important thing is to find those inspirational ideas that are meaningful to you and then incorporate them into your program.

The quotations and slogans mentioned in the next few pages we have found suitable for basketball and beneficial to our players at one time or another. They are both original and borrowed.

Character

It isn't what you used to be; it's what you are TODAY.
Pride is the same in all men. The difference is the method of displaying it.

What you are speaks so loudly that people cannot hear what you say.

What you practice, not what you preach, is what you spread.

Strong men criticize themselves.

Act well at the moment, and you have performed a good action for all eternity.

There is no right way to do a wrong thing.

A man's body is remarkably sensitive. Pat him on the back and his head swells.

Don't let your parents down; they brought you up.

Be humble enough to obey. You will be giving orders yourself someday.

Life is a grindstone. Whether it grinds you down or polishes you up depends on what you're made of.

When you sing your own praises, you may sound out of tune to your listeners.

The great are always kind and courteous.

Attitudes are caught, not taught.

Attitudes are contagious—is yours worth catching?

The moral fiber of a man stands out when he is under the extreme pressure of competition.

Ability will get you to the top, but it takes character to keep you there.

We have all the time there is; our mental and moral status is determined by what we do with it.

Work

The will to win is the will to work.

Only the PAIN of hard work can save the AGONY of defeat.

After all is said and done, there is usually more said than done.

All work that is worth anything is done in faith.

Wishing will never make it so, but work will fix it so that if you think you can, **you will.**

What counts is not the number of hours you put in, but what you put into the hours.

The harder I work, the luckier I get.

Unless a man undertakes more than he possibly can do, he will never do all he can.

Determination

The will to win is not nearly so important as the will to prepare to win.

Never be satisfied with your present development; make all improvement possible commensurate with your physical ability.

If I don't stand for something, I will fall for anything.

Too many itch for something they are too lazy to scratch for.

If you are good, be better. Be an over-achiever.

One-half of knowing what you want is knowing what you must give up before you get it.

There is no limit to the heights a man can attain, as long as he doesn't care who gets the credit for it.

Be determined to be a good player—don't desire to become one.

You can be the athlete you want to be if you practice regularly with determination and persistence.

Success-Failure

Success is spelled W-O-R-K.

Nature gives us talent, but it is for man to make it work.

You will be ready mentally if you are thinking success.

A man may fail many times, but he's not a failure until he begins to put the blame on someone else.

It is easy to avoid criticism; say nothing, do nothing, be nothing.

Our greatest glory consists not in never falling, but in rising every time we fall.

A first failure is often a blessing.

It is hard to fail, but it is worse never to have tried to succeed.

A hard fought failure is a noble thing.

On Winning

There is lots of room in the world for a winner, but the "standing room only" sign is always up for the loser.

Visualize it, dream it, and get into the habit of thinking victory.

The only difference between a good team and a championship team is that the champions don't give up! Let's be champions!

A champion wants to be a champion, believes he can be a champion, works like a champion and becomes a champion! Assume a value if you want to attain it.

No matter what has been happening to you or what competition you have to meet, never think you are going to lose. Think victory. Your own psychology will wholly decide how you compete and largely decide whether you are to win or lose.

The winning is to those who believe.

Loyalty . . . truth . . . perseverance . . . drive . . . sacrifice . . . physical conditioning . . . high goals . . . superior capacity . . . great skill . . . hard training . . . outstanding performances . . . all go into the making of a champion.

Hustle is one of the indispensable qualities of a champion.

Happiness

To lose one's temper because of somebody else is to punish one's self for another's shortcoming.

Happiness is a habit—cultivate it.

Those who bring sunshine to the lives of others cannot keep it from themselves.

Leadership

Avoid "following the crowd." Be a leader!

The imprudent man reflects on what he has said; the wise man reflects on what he is going to say.

Leaders are ordinary people with extraordinary determination.

Miscellaneous

If you are not playing well, ask yourself first, and then ask your coach. Nothing will ever be attempted if all possible objections must be overcome.

He who asks a question is a fool for five minutes; he who does not ask a question remains a fool forever.

Before you louse it up—THINK. After you've loused it up—SMILE.

Natural ability can only take you to a certain level—whether or not you go beyond that level depends on **Sound Fundamentals.**

Even if great thoughts come from the heart, it is better that they should emerge through the head.

Learn from the mistakes of others. You can't live long enough to make them all yourself.

There are two ways of treating gossip about other people, and they're both good ways. One is not to listen to it, and the other is not to repeat it.

Correct your own mistakes before criticizing others.

The thing usually labeled "luck" is merely an alert team taking advantage of the mistakes made by opponents.

With proper care, the human body will last a life time.

A good coach appreciates the mistakes his players don't make.

A player's mind, like his body, must be in condition.

Plays come and go but the right way to play the game goes on forever.

The most important responsibility of being good is that you must prove it every day.

Important thought—three months to play, a lifetime to regret.

If I advance, follow me. If I stop, push me. If I fall back, inspire me.

Ninety percent of defensive play is intestinal fortitude.

The Eight Fundamentals 2

Stress the Fundamentals

John Wooden stated that he "discovered early that the player who learned the fundamentals of basketball was going to have a much better chance of succeeding and rising through all levels of competition than the player who was content to do things his own way. A player should be interested in learning why things are done a certain way. The reasons behind the teaching often go a long way to helping develop the skill."[1]

Fundamentally sound basketball players have been the trademark at the University of Missouri for a number of years and we are extremely proud of this reputation. The fundamentals are the main elements that go into the development of an offensive or defensive system. Without proper execution of the fundamentals, the greatest offense or defense in the world would not be effective.

We place a great deal of emphasis on teaching the fundamentals to our younger players. After one or two seasons at Missouri, it is a matter of constantly watching the players to make sure they are executing the fundamentals as they have been taught. We will work on the fundamentals every day, before and during practice. The players become ingrained with our teachings and philosophy in this area. Many times, we have observed a junior or senior helping a new player with a particular fundamental, using the same teaching methods and almost the exact words we used with him only a few years before. Our players pride themselves on their ability to carry out the fundamentals of the game. They accept the hard work and drills that go into the perfecting of these skills as part of the Missouri tradition. With that pride and tradition comes a confidence that as a team we are prepared for any situation that could occur in a game.

By our way of thinking there are eight fundamental skills that must be taught in the game of basketball. We analyze and evaluate our players as to their performance in these areas. Thus we are able to identify weaknesses and work to correct them. The eight fundamental skills are running, jumping, pivoting, sliding, passing, catching, dribbling and shooting. Before teaching these skills, however, we introduce and emphasize two fundamental aspects of the game that we feel are very important — flexibility (stretching) and basketball position. Flexibility and basketball position are especially important in teaching the first four fundamentals mentioned.

FLEXIBILITY AND BASKETBALL POSITION

We show our players some stretching exercises and ask them to use them before they do anything else out on the practice floor. The implications for preventing injuries are obvious. We are also great believers in the part that flexibility plays in the development of the outstanding athlete or the outstanding basketball player. Before the official beginning of each practice session, we will stretch, and do some strengthening exercises, as a group. Our flexibility routine will be discussed thoroughly in Chapter Nine on Practice Planning and Conditioning.

Basketball position is important in that a player should *never* stand straight up while play is in progress. He should be alert and ready to move in either direction whether on offense or defense. We teach basketball position early in the practice season and go back to it if our players become lax during the season. The points of emphasis are (Fig. 2-1):

1. Feet are shoulder-width apart or slightly wider. They are staggered.
2. Knees are slightly flexed. They are directly over the feet.
3. Hips are in so that the rear does not stick out.
4. The back is relatively straight.
5. The head is up so the player can see the whole floor.
6. The hands are above the waist. They should be ready to react, but not tense.
7. Weight should be evenly distributed but slightly forward. We want our players always on the balls of their feet.

RUNNING

The players are now taught running, beginning from the basketball position. We point out the importance these two fundamentals will have in our ability to convert from offense to defense and vice-versa. In running from the basketball position, the emphasis is on:

1. Big first stride.
2. Push off with the back foot.
3. Staying low throughout the start.
4. Seeing where the ball is.
5. Stopping in basketball position.

JUMPING

Next from the basketball positon, jumping is taught. The emphasis is on:

1. Dropping the rear even lower (slightly).
2. Swinging the arms up (when rebounding, the hands and arms will already be up).
3. Jumping quickly and with strength.
4. Planar flexion of the feet.
5. Being able to jump three and four times.
6. Returning to basketball position.

PIVOTING

Pivoting off both feet is the next basic fundamental we will drill our players on in the early practices. It is surprising the number of players who are unable to execute a proper pivot. Many are adept using one particular foot, but are unable to use the other foot when pivoting. We emphasize:

1. Staying low throughout the movements.
2. Making the pivot on the balls of the feet.
3. Both hands up and elbows out (to protect ball).
4. Four quarter pivots. Both front-turn and back-turn, first using the left and then the right as the pivot foot.
5. Returning to basketball position.

Wooden etal., *The Wooden-Sharman Method,* Macmillan Publishing Co., Inc. New York, 1975, p. 53.

FIG. 2-1

Eight Fundamentals 25

FIG. 2-2

SLIDING

We have been almost exclusively a man to man team at the University of Missouri. The first step in coaching the man to man defense is to teach your players how to slide. Stance is important. We want our players to assume a crouched position with the knees bent, rear low, and the back relatively straight. Their weight should be distributed evenly to create good balance. The feet should be staggered — not parallel — and the head should be directly over the midpoint between the two feet. We like the hands about waist high and palms up. They are ready but never reaching. The stance we have described is illustrated in Figure 2-2. From this stance our players are taught to:

1. Move at 45 degree angles.
2. Lead with the foot in the direction of where the offensive player is going and push off the back foot. Point the lead foot in the direction of the slide.
3. Never bring the feet together or crossed. The players should act as if there is a 6 to 9 inch board between the feet that prevents them from coming together.
4. Keep the head level. No bobbing.
5. Rear end in — not protruding out.
6. Remaining in defensive position or returning to basketball position (after reacting to pass).

These fundamentals should be taught in a group formation with the captain or a senior leading the squad. To provide more space or more individual attention, the squad can be divided into two groups at each end of the floor, utilizing two leaders. These are very important fundamentals early in the practice season and should be stressed at that time. Less time can be devoted to them as the season progresses, but the coaches should be constantly checking the players so that they do not develop bad habits.

Accuracy is emphasized early. After accuracy has been achieved, the drill is made into a reaction drill. The team is divided into two groups at each end and spread out. The leader moves them through each fundamental with quick reactions by his group. Other movements (i.e., hand movements) can be added. Both accuracy and speed are emphasized here.

The Pass

The ability to pass the basketball is cherished by every coach at every level. The unselfish and clever passing team is admired by all those who come in contact with the game. We think it is vitally important to instill in all of our players, not only an unselfish, team-oriented attitude, but an appreciation for the art of passing. We like John Wooden's idea of acknowledging a good pass from a teammate. The players must understand that passing is the most important fundamental in our system of play. Our ability to pass the basketball will determine the flow of our offense. If the passing breaks down, the offense will be ineffective. This is true in any offense.

The distance between the passer and his defensive man should be small, not more than three feet, and preferably less. The offensive player must have poise and confidence in his ball handling and passing ability. He must realize that it is practically impossible for the defensive man to take the ball away from him, as long as he maintains his poise. The closer the defensive man plays, the less time he has to react to the passer's actions — providing the passer recognizes what the defense is doing. This principle of good passing is violated more than any other.

Our players are taught to eliminate all unnecessary movements in their ball handling and passing. Slow winding up actions should be avoided. Players **at this level** should eliminate stepping with the pass and should cut the action of the pass off as short as possible. This is accomplished by quick wrist and finger action on all passes.

The offensive player should see the passing lane and the receiver without looking directly at him. The exception is when the pass has been preceded by an effective, positive fake. We are not advocating blind passes. The passer can avoid turning to face a receiver by the use of split vision. There is a big difference between seeing and looking.

Recognition of what the defense is doing and purposeful fakes are essential to an outstanding passing team. However, the player who fakes excessively, moving the ball constantly, is unable to determine what the defensive man is doing with his hands. He cannot see the passing lane and it is impossible for him to make an accurate pass to his teammate because he has lost his poise. The passer should be taught to size up his opponent's hands and make the pass quickly away from them. The "halo" around a defensive man's head offers the passer an excellent passing zone (Figure 2-3).

It is vitally important that the players learn to pass to the teammate's open side. This is a principle that is frequently violated, even by experienced players. This could be the result of the passer's inability to see, not only his own defensive man, but the passing lane and the defensive man playing the receiver. It becomes a matter of recognition — realizing what the defense is doing, and then doing the opposite. The receiver also has some responsibilities along these lines. He must "shape up" in such a manner that he presents a good target. He must keep the defensive man away from the passing lane by maintaining a relative position between the ball and the defense. Once the pass is made, he must "play the ball" as it comes into reach. It is the receiver's responsibility to meet the ball at all times.

It is a common habit among players to hold the ball too long, to not be ready to make a quick, accurate pass to an open teammate. We call it "massaging" the basketball. Our players are told that it is a good basketball player who can receive a

FIG. 2-3

Eight Fundamentals 27

pass from a teammate and make his play (pass, shot, drive) within two seconds after receiving the ball. For every fraction of a second under two seconds it takes him to successfully execute the play, the better basketball player he becomes. For every fraction over two seconds it takes him to make the play, the poorer player he becomes. The ball has to be moved. Moving the ball keeps the defense occupied, thereby creating passing lanes and scoring opportunities. Watch any great passing team play the game, and you will be impressed, above all else, by how quickly the ball is moved.

The fundamentally sound basketball player should anticipate when he may receive the ball and develop the instinct to know where the ball should go from there. He should see the whole floor and have an idea of where the open men are before he ever receives the ball. A knowledge of his teammates and a thorough understanding of the offensive pattern are essential in this regard. Also important, is the ability of the players to move without the basketball. This is why some professional teams are effective even though they appear to have very little definite team pattern. The players are of such outstanding caliber that very little team pattern is needed to create scoring opportunities. The outstanding players are those who have learned to play without the ball, as well as with the ball.

Accuracy is the most important element of the pass to be developed. When we talk about accuracy, we want our players to be accurate both in timing and in direction. They must be able to deliver the pass when the receiver is open, ready, and in a position to do something once he has possession of the ball. At that time, the pass must be thrown at about the chest level, away from the defense.

Quickness must also be stressed but not over accuracy. In other words, the players should develop accuracy with maximum quickness. In a game situation, a deflected pass or steal can be a matter of inches and fractions of a second. The speed of the pass is important in this regard. The speed of the pass must be appropriate to the situation. The pass cannot be so hard that it is difficult for the receiver to handle, but it must be firm enough so as not to be picked off by the defense. We instruct our players to make a crisp, firm pass. Not too hard and not too easy. The playmaker who has the knack of delivering the ball just right is extremely valuable and in great demand. He literally makes his teammates more effective players. In addition to the obvious advantage of giving his teammates a good shot a high proportion of the time, this kind of passer instills confidence in other players that the ball will be there, in a comfortable position, when they do get free. Knowing this, the players will be more apt to move without the basketball and create more and greater scoring opportunities.

CHEST PASS

When throwing the two hand chest pass, the wrists should be

straight, neither flexed or cocked, when holding the ball. The thumbs should be on the top half of the basketball to provide the proper backspin. The fingers should be spread and although the ball can be resting or touching the first part of the hand, the fingers will be controlling the pass. When first learning to execute the chest pass, the arms should be completely extended out in front of the body. The palms and fingers should turn out with the wrists pronated and the thumbs pointing down. As the players advance in their development and in their ability, an attempt should be made to eliminate the long extention and follow through with the emphasis shifting to quickness. There should be a medial rotation of the shoulders and a slight extention of the knee during the execution of the pass. The pass should not be made too quickly. Many players make the mistake of attempting to pass when they are not ready to execute the pass properly. These are usually picked off by the defense or thrown away. The player should remember to lead the moving man and to try to make the pass at a distance of not more than twelve to fifteen feet.

BOUNCE PASS

This pass should be thrown mainly on the inside area. It is extremely dangerous in the front court and on the side. The same fundamentals that are used in the chest pass are applied here. The proper underspin and force on the pass should be stressed so that the receiver catches it at or above waist level. The players should be taught to throw the ball to a spot just beyond the mid-point between the passer and the receiver. A bounce pass should never be thrown so that it bounces between the passer and a defensive man in a positon to intercept the ball. If that should happen, the defensive player has a good chance of intercepting the ball as it comes up off the bounce. The ball must hit the floor beyond that defensive player. Again, it is important to lead the moving man.

BASEBALL PASS

The baseball pass is important for advancing the ball up the court as quickly as possible and for limited and cautious use against a pressing defense. It can also be a very effective means of outletting the basketball after a defensive rebound. The players, because of the extended distance the ball will travel, must be careful when making this pass. However, it has proven itself to be a valuable offensive weapon especially for fast-breaking teams. We instruct our players to place the ball at the side of their ear with both hands. This will provide better protection of the ball from the defense. More importantly, both hands on the ball will allow the players to stop the pass should the receiver or receivers be covered. The hand and the fingers of the throwing arm should be spread to give greater control. The ball should be thrown straight overhand with a good follow through. The overhand motion, follow through, and a slight pronation of the wrist will help to avoid sidespin on the ball. Again, it is important to throw the ball at the receiver's chest and to lead the moving man. The player executing the baseball pass should turn sideways and step with the pass — much like a quarterback in football.

OVERHEAD PASS

The two hand overhead pass has proven effective in three primary areas. One, as an outlet pass after a defensive rebound. Two, as a pass into the post. Three, as a pass from the high post area to players cutting to the basket or to an open spot on the floor. The outlet pass is a little different from the others in that more force must be made on the pass, thus the arms and shoulders are put to greater use. For outlet purposes the ball can go back over the head with a bending of the elbows to provide greater impetus.

When making this pass to the post or to cutters in the offensive end of the court, the wrists and fingers provide most of the force. The ball is held straight up over the head with the hands on the side and slightly toward the back. The elbows are flexed, but not bent. A quick snapping motion is made with the wrists and fingers and the ball is passed at a downward angle. At times it will be helpful or necessary to extend up on the toes as the pass is executed.

PUSH PASS (Fig. 2-4)

The one hand push pass is another valuable weapon for getting the ball into the post. The same principles mentioned for the chest pass are used except that the pass is made with one hand dominating the other. When a player is being closely guarded in his offensive end, it is extremely hard to make a penetrating pass from the two-handed chest position. The one-handed push pass is quicker and easier to throw through or by the defensive man. The pass is made with a quick pushing motion toward the intended receiver. A good wrist snap will again provide much of the force and the opposite hand will help to protect the ball as it is being released (See Fig. 2-4). Quickness is the key.

PASSING THE BALL IN GAME SITUATIONS

The passes we have explained are the primary passes our players are going to use in a game situation. In addition to the fundamentals involved in making the pass, we want them to follow a few other offensive guidelines. The first line of defense the offensive player with the ball will face is his own defensive man. In getting the ball by this first line of defense, we teach our players the concept of the "passing halo" (see Fig. 2-3). The offensive player should hold the ball at chest level where he is in position to quickly shoot, pass or drive to the basket. The players head should be up, enabling him to see the whole

FIG. 2-4

30 Eight Fundamentals

floor and recognize where the open man is and how the ball should be delivered. The ball should then be thrown on the down arm side of the defensive man or over his head. The passing halo concept gives our players an idea of how to pass the ball through or by their defensive opponent. An offensive team that is content to pass the ball around the defense is playing soft, non-aggressive basketball. We want our players to be aggressive and to make things happen. A final rule with regard to the passing halo has to do with faking and moving the basketball. As mentioned previously, we want our players to have a purpose in mind when they make a fake. After a fake is made and the pass is not delivered, we want the ball brought back to the original chest position. Too many mistakes are made by players who try to make a pass from an unnatural or off balance position.

Another important guideline for the offensive player is to not become alarmed or lose his poise because of the pressure his defensive man may be applying. The closer the defensive man is to the passer, the less reaction time he will have to block or interrupt the ball. If the defensive man is applying some extreme pressure the passer should drop to a slightly lower position, protect the ball, and be prepared to either dribble back from the defensive man or drive to the basket. The offensive player should understand that he is entitled to his upright position. From this closely guarded position, the passer should realize that a quick cut to the basket after he has made a pass will often catch the defense off stride.

In passing the ball into the second line of defense, it is essential for the passer to recognize the open area and the open side of his teammate. That would, of course, be away from the defense. This will lessen the chance of iterception and also key the offensive man as to his best scoring opportunity.

Catching the Basketball

Proper spacing is an extremely important and often neglected principle in teaching the fundamentals of passing and catching the basketball. The receiver must work to get open. He must set his defensive man up, but again he must have a definite purpose in mind. If he is running all over without purpose, there is no way he can maintain proper spacing. In our offense, 15-foot spacing is ideal. By disregarding this principle, the receiver will cause too much congestion in one area or he will allow one defensive man to guard two offensive men. Interceptions and turnovers will be the result. Equally important is the receiver's responsibility to seal off the defender. He must step with the foot nearest his defender and maintain body position between that defender and the ball. As the ball leaves the passers hands, the receiver must move to meet the pass.

The following guidelines for catching the basketball have been helpful to our players.

1. Work to get open, set your defensive man up. Have a purpose in mind.
2. Meet the basketball — keep coming out.
3. Eyes on the ball until the catch is made.
4. Look in and face the basket after every catch.
5. The ball is protected by the body.
6. If the pass cannot be made because the defensive man is overplaying, the receiver should go to the basket or to the center of the floor.

Dribbling

While passing proficiency should be exphasized to all players and teams, dribbling is a fundamental that most coaches today would like to de-emphasize. Every player, and especially the guards, should work hard to become a competent dribbler. The idea, however, is not to overuse the dribble. This is a common fault of young players and is not too uncommon at higher levels.

The overriding concern among coaches is that excessive dribbling focuses on the individual rather than the team concept. The four corner offense, which has been brought back and popularized by Dean Smith at North Carolina, is a notable exception. While the four-corners usually features one particular great ball handler, it is certainly a team-oriented offense. The middle-man in this offense must be an adept one on one player but even more important, he must have the ability to keep his head up, spot the open cutters and pass quickly off the dribble. Additionally, more than one player can be used at different times in the middle. This would depend on the match-ups against a particular team. Nevertheless, in most offenses, too much dribbling will take its toll in missed scoring opportunities.

We find two basic faults in the dribbling technique of most of the players who come to us on the freshman level. First of all, the players are trying hard to keep the head up, but they are not using their vision to see the whole floor. The two teammates closest to the dribbler may be in his vision, but in most cases, the other two teammates are not. We stress the idea of not only keeping the head up, but using peripheral vision to see the whole floor. Constant work on ball handling is a must. The idea of keeping the head up is not difficult in itself. The key is that the ball handler be so confident in his dribbling and his ability to handle the basketball that he can concentrate on what is taking place out on the floor rather than the defensive pressure that is being applied.

The second area we find our players having difficulty with is in staying down over the basketball. They are dribbling the ball too high which gives the defense excellent opportunities for the steal. It also allows the ball to be handled too far away from the body, decreasing control and increasing the chance of error. We want our players dribbling the ball very low while keeping their body down and over the basketball (Fig. 2-5). This is especially important when handling the ball in traffic.

In our program there are five different types of dribbling that we incorporate into our drills. They are listed and the techniques described below.

Control Dribble

1. Knees bent, down over ball, arc in back.
2. Fingers control the ball, but top part of hand can touch.
3. Do not pound the ball, but push it firmly with the fingers and wrist.
4. Relax arm and fingers and flex wrist slightly.
5. Keep head and eyes up for down-court vision.
6. Keep the leg, arm and body between the ball and the defense.
7. Dribble below the belt or lower depending on the situation.
8. Be ready to pass and have body always under control.
9. Once the dribble has begun, keep it going until there is an open man or it is evident you could lose it.

Speed Dribble

1. For use in the open floor or out in front of everyone.
2. Same techniques as control dribble except ball may be dribbled higher and the body is more erect.
3. If out in front, push the ball as far as possible while still maintaining control.

Stop and Go (Change of Pace) Dribble

1. Stop with foot nearest defensive man in front — when defensve man closes distance, then go.
2. Combine control and speed dribble.
3. Utilize head and shoulder fakes.

Reverse Dribble

1. Stop with foot nearest defensive man in front. Stop quickly and be sure to **plant** front foot.
2. Drop the back foot — pivot on front foot and *pull* the ball with original dribbling hand.
3. Be careful not to palm the basketball.

Crossover Dribble

1. Ball must cross in front of body from outside to outside.
2. Stop with the foot corresponding with the dribbling hand slightly in front.
3. As the ball is crossed in front, bring it back closer to the body.
4. Simultaneously lower the ball as you push it across the body and lower your body position (center of gravity).
5. Must be a quick move initiated when defensive player is at a distance where he cannot interfere.

By our way of thinking, there are four general rules that must be followed in shooting. After a player has developed the proper technique, these rules are essential for the good shooter.

1. **Confidence** — The player should know each time he shoots that it is going to be two points. If there is doubt, there is no reason to shoot the ball.

FIG. 2-5 Willie Smith protecting the ball against UCLA.

Shooting

Straight Lay up   FIG. 2-6

Back-hand Layup   FIG. 2-7

2. **Control** — The body must be under control and on balance on all shots.
3. **Consistency** — The players must develop the same method on every shot. Constant practice will develop this "shooting groove".
4. **Concentration** — The target should be picked up at the very beginning of the shot and the concentration should be there until the ball is through the net.

In developing good shooters and good shooting habits, we insist that our players: 1) practice the shots that are designed for them in our offense and; 2) practice their shots off a move to get open, thus simulating game conditions. We do allow our players at times to shoot without a defense. This is beneficial early in the practice season in that the players can develop confidence in their ability to score from the various spots on the floor. They can also take free shooting for a period before practice starts. This again will serve to instill confidence and quite possibly to develop a "shooting groove." The players must always take their shot after a move to free themselves. We do not want them to stand and shoot with no concentration and no movement. That type of opportunity will not present itself in a game situation so we do not allow any haphazard unconcentrated shooting practice.

Even against a zone we want our players stepping into a "pocket" or an open area. We want them to develop quickness while still maintaining accuracy that will carry over in a game situation. This cannot be accomplished by bouncing the ball once or twice and shooting from a set position. Nor can it be accomplished by moving at half speed. Quick cuts or movements that will be successful in a game must be used in practice.

Basically, we want each of our players shooting right off the pass from a teammate while practicing. It is fine for the player to take one or two dribbles to free himself for the shot. We do allow some one on one movement in our team offense, but we do not want one player dribbling the basketball while the other four are wondering what he is going to do. We make sure that each player is aware of where his scoring opportunities will come from in our offense. We will teach the players the movements that need to be made to get open off that particular option. Also the one or two quick moves that may be made after he receives the pass and according to how the defense has reacted. The player then must practice the shots and the moves for the shot from those positions on the floor.

When free shooting is taking place, concentration must be stressed. Competitive shooting drills and recording the percentage of shots made can accomplish this end. In addition to this type of pressure, we like our players to envision themselves in a game situation while they are shooting. Every shot should be taken with the idea that two points are needed to keep us in the game. In our program, concentration and confidence are the two most important characteristics of the good shooter.

In most of our shooting drills, we will incorporate a "token" defensive player. Many high school players come to us with great ability to shoot the wide-open uncontested shot. They must increase their ability to shoot well when defensive pressure is applied. Again, concentration is the key. Constant practice with a hand up or in the shooter's face will develop that concentration. This is a practice concept that should be applied in any program. The results of a study conducted by Bob Burcholder, an assistant at Ohio State under Fred Taylor, will bear this idea out. Coach Burcholder had **all** shots that were taken during Ohio State games over a five year period charted as to whether they were contested or uncontested. The study showed that of the shots that were uncontested, 66% were successful. Only 29% of the shots were made where there was a hand in the shooter's face. This is a tremendous differential that should not be taken lightly. It has strong implications regarding our offensive shooting philosophy as well as our defensive strategy which we will discuss later.

One other practice idea that we ask our players to follow is that they practice the close in shots first and progress out to their particular range. This serves both as a warm-up procedure and as a confidence builder. We liken this to the idea of the golfer who when practicing putting, starts at a short distance and gains a confidence and a feeling for the ball dropping in the cup. We feel it can serve the same purpose in basketball and can be very helpful toward developing that "shooting groove."

THE LAY UP

From the basic right hand and left hand lay up, we teach four different types of driving shots. Because of the relative differences in a player's strong and weak hand, this gives them eight shots to master. The four types of lay ups are the straight lay up from the 45-degree angle, the back-hand lay up, the over the top lay up, and the lay up from the baseline drive. These shots are demonstrated using the right hand in Figures 2-6 through 2-9. Another possible variation is the drive down the middle. Our players are taught to veer off to either side so this shot actually becomes a straight lay up. We should note that this is not a hard and fast rule because at times the opening might be straight to the basket. When this is the case, we want our players to lay the ball up over the front of the rim with a minimum amount of spin on the ball.

There are some basic fundamentals that are the same for all of these shots. We have already mentioned that the body must be under control on all shots. This rule takes on special significance on any drive to the basket because of the possibility of a defensive player stepping in to draw the charge.

FIG. 2-8   Over The Top Lay up

FIG. 2-9   Baseline Lay up

Eight Fundamentals 35

When our players see a driving lane, they are encouraged to take the ball hard to the basket. If the opening is there and our player is driving hard but under control the defensive player would be hard pressed to gain the proper position for an offensive foul. In keeping with this same idea, we want our players to take off with the opposite foot planted inside the lane. This will give them much better control of their bodies than if they started their jump from a great distance. It will also insure a strong drive that will carry them right up to the basket in a position of strength. Too many times a player will start his jump from outside the lane and end up way short of the basket throwing up a hope shot.

On the lay up shot, the player has usually gained great momentum either from a full court run or from a hard drive. The player must be sure to transfer this momentum up toward the basket as he jumps off the opposite foot. The lay up must result from a high jump rather than a broad jump. The eyes should be fixed on the target. Many of our younger players, especially the guards, are concerned with the defensive players in the basket area. They want to make sure that they can dish the ball off if a big man picks them up. They can and should be concerned with this possibility but not to the point of missing the lay up or being intimidated. We tell them to eye that target and let their instincts and peripheral vision tell them when to dish off. Again, the idea is that if there is a driving lane open, we want a good, hard drive to the basket.

When the player is making a drive to the basket, the ball should be dribbled with the hand away from the defense. When the lay up is being attempted off the pass, the ball should be carried to a position outside the body away from the defense. The ball should then be moved upward with both hands. The ball should be released softly, at the peak of the player's jump and with full extension of the arm. The shooting hand should be at the side of the ball. On the straight lay up, there should be no spin or english applied to the ball and there should be as little as possible on the other lay up shots.

When shooting the back-hand, over the top and baseline lay ups, the players should be instructed to go toward the basket and not away. The transfer of momentum from out to up is very important on these shots. We instruct our players to turn their stomach in toward the target as they are making the shot (see Figures 2-10 and 2-11). The closer they can come to having their stomach and chest areas parallel to the target area the easier the shot will be. It is important to note that on these shots, a spot on the backboard and not the basket is the target.

THE HOOK SHOT

While the long hook has been de-emphasized in today's game, the short hook has become increasingly popular. This shot actually incorporates the basic fundamentals of the hook shot and ends up very similar to the over the top lay up. The ball can either be banked off the backboard at the proper angle or layed up over the top of the rim.

The long hook is recommended only for the big men and an occasional forward. In fact, we will not teach or work on the long hook to any great extent except under two circumstances. One, if the player has had the hook shots in his repertoire for a number of years and has developed a certain amount of ability and accuracy. Two, if the player is in need of developing more shots to make him a more effective player. Basically, however, we want our post people turning the ball in and playing facing the basket, learning the power moves inside and taking the ball to the basket via the short hook. We feel that the long hook is not a high percentage shot (unless as mentioned above, a player has developed a certain amount of skill). It is a shot that will not leave your big man in a good, balanced position to get to the offensive board. Finally, the mechanics of the shot will not allow the post man to make an effective pass to a teammate whose defender may have dropped off to help defend against the big man. This is a vital element of our offense as we will see in Chapter Three.

If it is to be utilized, the long hook shot should be taught from a position with the players back to the basket. His knees should be bent slightly in a ready position. As the ball is caught or the move initiated, the head and eyes should turn over the shoulder to quickly pick up the target. The leg opposite the shooting hand should take a step that is comfortable yet will free him somewhat from the defense. We do not want our players to make this step away from the basket. It should always be at least parallel to the target area. The foot should be placed on the floor so it is parallel to the target area and there should be a bend in the knee to provide the proper lift. As the step is made, the corresponding shoulder will turn and should point directly at the target. Note that the target area is the basket from the middle of the floor and a spot on the backboard when shooting at a 30-45 degree angle from the baseline. The leg corresponding with the shooting hand should be raised to a position where the thigh is parallel to the floor.

The ball is held at a little above waist level with both hands. Protection from the defense is vital at all times. The ball is placed in the line of flight by fully extending the shooting arm. The opposite arm folds and is used for defensive protection. The ball is delivered by soft wrist action with the index finger pointing toward the target and touching the ball last as it leaves the hand.

As mentioned, the short hook uses virtually the same fundamentals as the long hook shot. However, the differences that do exist are noteworthy. While quickness is extremely important in most phases of the game, we especially

FIG. 2-10   Incorrect - Momentum away from basket.

FIG. 2-11   Correct - stomach turned in.

Eight Fundamentals 37

FIG. 2-12

FIG. 2-13

38 Eight Fundamentals

emphasize quickness of movement in the post area. Too many big men rely on their size and can be beaten repeatedly by a player with greater intensity and quickness. Once a big man or a forward has made a quick move to the basket and is in position for the short hook, he is extremely hard to stop without a foul being committed. A long first step is the initial difference between the two hook shots. This will, of course, depend on the player's positioning on the floor, but a step should be made that will both clear the defense and carry the player to the basket. Instead of the foot being placed in a position parallel to the target area, it should turn in to the basket as far as comfortably possible. This will provide further extension up to the basket. It is also advisable to bend the shooting arm as much as needed to make for a strong shot closely related to the over the top lay up. The turning in of the stomach is again helpful with regard to balance, strength and accuracy. Notice in Figure 2-10, the player has not turned his stomach in and thus his momentum is carrying him away from the basket. The correct technique for turning the stomach is illustrated in Figure 2-11.

THE JUMP SHOT

We feel one of the most important and least taught fundamentals of the jump shot is the opening of the player's opposite shoulder so that his shooting side is in line with the basket. For many years, players have been taught to "square up" to the basket. That is, to position their feet and shoulders directly parallel to the target area. We want our players opening up to allow more freedom of movement and to help align, not only the elbow, but the entire shooting side of the body to the basket. Figure 2-12 shows a player that is squared to the basket and is trying to position his elbow, as well as his right side, in line with the target. This is much too rigid a movement. We are not looking for a pronounced opening of the body, but a slight opening up that will vary according to the individual.

When working with our players, we refer to right side alignment. Most of our players are right handed. It would, of course, be left side alignment for the left handed player. We want to take the opposite side almost completely out of the shot. Just as the opposite hand provides balance in holding the ball, we want the opposite side of the body helping to maintain balance while not getting involved in the shot. In this way, all of the motion involved in the shot is in a direct line to the target area. Basically, we are just taking the fundamental of keeping the elbow in line with the basket a few steps farther.

Two final important points on the shooting side alignment theory. One, it is a concept that is easily digested by the very young player (youngsters just learning to shoot) — there is nothing hard about it. Two, it can be used as an excellent check point when shooting problems develop. Figure 2-13 shows a player with the proper right side alignment as he begins his shot. His right side will then be in a direct line to the basket throughout the shot.

BEGINNING THE JUMP SHOT

The jump shot starts from the ground up. The feet should be staggered slightly (right in front for right handed shooters) and should remain reasonably close throughout the shot. We recommend just inside or at shoulder width. As the player initiates the jump shot, his front foot should point directly at the basket and his rear foot should open slightly (see Figure 2-13). From the very beginning of the shot, the player is opening up and creating the proper shooting side alignment. As previously mentioned, balance must be maintained on all shots and balance starts with the proper positioning of the feet. The flexing of the knees will also help to insure a firm, balanced position. A common fault among player is an over-emphasis on bending the knees in an attempt to get up as high as possible on the jump shot. Quickness rather than height should be emphasized. The height of the jump should be attained without an extreme amount of effort so that the player will be comfortable throughout the shot. We do realize the importance of the legs in providing power for the shot. In fact, we want the legs to generate as much power as possible so that the player can develop the same easy motion on all of his shots. The power, however, should come from the combined action of the flexing of the knees, the quickness of the flex, and the planar flexion of the feet.

When developing balance, the players should imagine they are in a circle three feet in diameter when they start the shot. As the shot is completed, their feet should land on balance within that circle. There is no way a player who started his shot while off balance will be able to land on balance within that area. If the player sways or does not maintain his balance during the shot, he will also land outside the circle. Ideally, when executing the jump shot, the shooter should land just forward of the spot from which he took off upon completion of the shot. Because his shooting side is aligned with the basket and his opposite side is opened up, this will allow all parts of the body to flow naturally up toward the basket.

THE ELBOW

The proper positioning of the elbow is the most important step in shooting. As the shot is initiated, the ball should be carried from the starting position to the release always in the line of flight. The elbow should be directly under the ball and pointing to the basket on a line drawn from the underside of that arm (see Fig. 2-13). I would like to again utilize an example from George Lehmann to explain the importance of keeping the elbow in line with the basket. There are four ways a shot can miss the target; left, right, short or long. Have your players

FIG. 2-14   Jon Sundvold exhibits perfect shooting form versus Notre Dame in the NCAA Tournament. Notice the right side alignment and the opening up of the left side.

FIG. 2-15

Eight Fundamentals 39

FIG. 2-16

FIG. 2-17

shoot one-handed from a short distance at the side of the basket (Fig. 2-15). Ask them to concentrate on lining up the elbow properly and following straight through on the shot. If they do this they will find that their shots will never miss to the right or left. Thus, by keeping the elbow in line with the basket and following straight through, a player can eliminate two of the four ways a shot can be missed. Now he needs only to guage the proper distance.

In following through the shooter must be careful not to over-extend his elbow to a stiff or unnatural position. The elbow is for accuracy and should not provide any power for the shot. Figures 2-16 and 2-17 show the incorrect and correct techniques for following through with the elbow. In the first photo the elbow is extended too far while in the second the shooter exhibits a nice, easy motion to the basket that is natural — almost effortless.

THE BODY, HEAD AND EYES

One of our four general rules in shooting is that the body must be under control and on balance at all times. We have already discussed the importance of the feet and legs in maintaining proper balance. Also very important in this regard is the position of the shooter's upper body and his head.

As the shot is initiated the upper body should be slightly forward with the shoulders out over the knees. However, as the shot is executed, the body becomes straight with no lean in any direction. The head will be directly centered at the mid-point between the two feet and will also be out over the knees. The head is extremely important in maintaining the proper balance for the shot. If the head were to be tilted to any of the four sides, the shooter would begin his shot slightly off balance to that side. It is also important to note that the head and shoulders remain over the knees throughout the shot. The body straightens simultaneously with the action of the knees in the jump. Thus, the knees, the head and shoulders remain in the same plane. The smoothness of this action will have much to do with developing consistency in the shot. By straightening the knees before the body or visa versa, the shooter will need to compensate somewhat on his shot and inconsistency will result.

As soon as the shot begins, the eyes must pick up the target and remain there throughout the execution of the shot and the flight of the ball. Total concentration with the eyes on the target will help the shooter overcome the defensive pressure or distractions caused by the man guarding him. We tell our players that when they catch the ball in one of their shooting areas, they are to turn, and if open, shoot the ball down. The eye focus and total concentration are on the basket or backboard (if that is the target). Their natural instincts and peripheral vision will tell them when someone else has a better shot.

When not utilizing the backboard, our players are taught to shoot for the center of the basket. They are to look at the whole basket while concentrating on an imaginary spot at the exact center. If some of our players have been taught differently and are having trouble with this concept, we tell them to imagine there is an egg sitting on the rim. Their purpose should be to shoot the ball with a nice, medium arc that will land just over the egg and into the center of the basket. Again, we will not drastically try to change a player's shot if he is having a good amount of success. However, we do not advocate shooting for the front of the rim or the back of the rim. The argument for each of these theories involves the margin of error. The fact is that shooting for the front of the rim allows for a great deal of error long, but little short. The reverse is true when shooting for the back of the rim. Shooting for the center of the basket will allow for an equal amount of error in every direction.

THE POSITION OF THE BALL

The ball is placed just above the right eye (for right handers) with the backs of the index finger and middle finger of the shooting hand almost resting on the forehead (Fig. 2-18). We instruct our players as to the idea of a vertical plane extending straight up from their forehead. We want the ball held within that plane. If the plane is broken by putting the ball too far back on the head, then the attempt at the basket becomes more of a throw than a shot. If the plane is broken too far in front, then the player is probably aiming the ball.

HANDS, WRISTS AND FINGERS

In holding the ball, the opposite hand (left for right handed shooters and visa versa) is used strictly for balance. The non-shooting hand is placed on the side of the ball in a holding position. Many players come to us with the non-shooting hand more to the front of the ball. This is a habit that has been developed since childhood. We will not try to change the habit if the player is having success. However, if the hand is too far in front, we try to explain that the player is, in effect, pitting his right hand against his left. Two opposite forces are working against each other. Figures 2-19 and 2-20 show the correct and incorrect position of the non-shooting hand. It is easy to see in the incorrect photo that the left hand would be fighting the right hand in the release of the shot.

Ideally, the shooter should let the holding hand fall away on the release. The ball is pushed up through the target line and the fingers give way, then the hand. In this way, the holding hand does not interfere with the proper release of the ball nor does it attempt to provide any power for the shot (see Fig. 2-19).

The fingers of the shooting hand should be spread equally and comfortably behind the ball. There should only be slight pressure on the ball. The wrist is cocked so that just prior to the release of the shot it forms a "U" with the hand, forearm,

FIG. 2-18

FIG. 2-19   Correct hand position. The fingers will fall away—then the hand as the ball is pushed up toward the target.

Incorrect   FIG. 2-20

and elbow (see Fig. 2-19). The fingers and wrists will propel the ball to the basket easily and naturally. We do not like the term wrist snap because it implies too much of an abrupt action that is unnatural. The shooter should not consciously try to put backspin on the ball. This will come naturally with the proper hand, finger and wrist action.

THE FOLLOW THROUGH

We briefly discussed the follow through earlier, in relation to the elbow. The most important aspect of the follow through is that of pushing the hand and arm straight through to the basket. The shooter must keep the right side alignment that has been established from the very beginning of the shot. We allow for a very slight pronation of the wrist on the release. As mentioned above, we do not want a pronounced snapping of the wrist. In his very complete book, **Techniques for Great Outside Shooting**, Dick Baumgartner calls this a thrusting motion. We like that descripiton of the hand, finger, and wrist action. From this thrusting motion, we want our players to extend their hand to the basket, to seemingly cover the basket as shown in Figure 2-22. Figure 2-23 shows an incorrect follow through that will not produce the soft touch that is desirable on all shots. A full arm extension without stiffening the elbow is also a must. (See Fig. 2-17).

We encourage our players to let their head follow through forward and up toward the target on every shot. This will eliminate any falling away (two forces working against each other) and provide further emphasis on the proper follow through toward the basket. Remember, the shooter should land just forward of the spot from which he took off upon completion of the shot.

We should mention that when teaching the set shot to younger and beginning players, most of the aforementioned fundamentals are applicable. The jump shot is just an extention of the set. An important teaching point for the set shot is to have the young player come up on his toes and allow his feet to leave the floor when completing the shot. This will enable the young shooter to increase his range considerably while still maintaining a smooth, natural release. Additionally, it will make for an easier transition from the set to the jump shot when the player becomes older and stronger.

Additional Shooting Points:

1. The ball should be released just prior to or at the peak of the player's jump.
2. When receiving a pass for a possible shot, the shooter should come in low, ready to go up for the shot.
3. Quickness with accuracy should always be emphasized.
4. When shooting from any angle, the inside foot will plant and pivot, bringing the outside foot around to the proper position.
5. The elbow of the shooting hand straightens in coordination with

the straightening of the shooter's body and knees.

6. A medium arc is recommended to produce a nice, soft shot.

7. The same, easy motion on all shots should be developed.

8. Offensive players should turn and face the basket every time they receive a pass.

9. The shooter should jump straight up and come straight down with no sway.

10. All players should practice shooting with the same intensity that goes into other drills.

THE FREE THROW

We have expressed our emphasis on concentration and confidence with regard to shooting. These two characteristics are probably even more important when shooting the free throw. While the free throw is a much easier shot than most, the pressure involved and the idea of standing alone can sometimes cause problems for the player that lacks concentration and confidence. The concentration is mental, but can be stressed in practice with competitive free throw shooting. After the proper technique is mastered, the confidence should come with repeated practice.

The first idea the players must learn regarding technique is to line up and shoot the basketball exactly the same way each time. The free throw is made easier because the variables (defense, distance from the basket, etc.) are either non-existent or they are constant. The player must take advantage of this by taking the same position and shooting with the same consistent motion on every foul shot. The players can develop this consistency by shooting a good number (at least 25-50) of free throws in succession. The player must concentrate on his form and his technique.

In shooting the free throw, the right handed shooter positions himself in a direct line to the basket, facing slightly to the left of the target. The right foot is directly below the shooting arm and shoulder. The left foot is placed at an angle so that the knee, hip and shoulder open to the basket. This gives us our right side alignment, as defined in the section on the jump shot, and allows for the desired freedom of movement. Like the jump shot, the feet should be positioned just inside or at shoulder width. The right foot should be close to the line, but with no chance of a violation.

The player should take a look at the basket and then bounce the ball a few times to relax himself. The ball should then be brought to the chest level, the head should be up toward the target with the eyes concentrating on the basket. The non-shooting hand is at the side of the basketball and slightly underneath. The fingers are spread comfortably. The shooting hand is behind the ball with the index finger through the middle of the ball.

The eyes are aimed over the top of the ball with the concentration on the whole basket or a spot just over the

FIG. 2-21   Correct

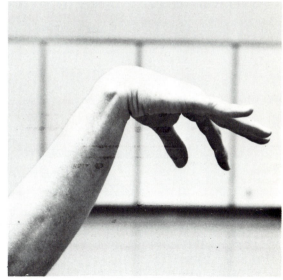

FIG. 2-22   Incorrect

Eight Fundamentals 43

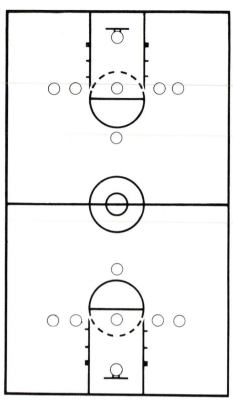

DIA. 2-1

front of the rim. The aim continues fixed on this spot as the ball is raised for delivery. The shooting motion always begins with the ball poised at this position.

The motion starts with a slight flexing of the knees. The body moves down and then up in the delivery. The shot is made in one continuous motion with no break or hesitation. The arm is extended fully and the wrist flexes with a slight pronation of the hand as the ball is released. The hand will cover the basket just like the follow through motion on the jump shot. The shooter should extend up on his toes but return comfortably to his original position to ensure the proper balance. There should be no thought of following the shot because the shooter is confident that it will be on target.

Our players are taught to stop the ball at the chest level to begin the shot. Once the shot has started, however, there is no hesitation whatsoever in the motion. The shot should be fluid and a successful rhythm should be developed.

John Wooden suggests that early in the practice season each player should shoot at least fifty free throws each day. This is to develop that "shooting groove" and consistency that we discussed earlier. Coach Wooden further suggests that as the season progresses, the players should take fewer shots until they seldom take more than two at a time. We feel this is highly important in simulating game conditions so we incorporate this idea when planning our practices.

Remember that the fundamentals of the game will be the basis for the development of your offensive and defensive system. We feel that our attention to the fundamentals has been one of the biggest reasons for our success over the past decade at Missouri. The fundamentals remain important at the college level and yet are even more crucial in developing players at the younger levels.

Drills for Teaching the Eight Fundamentals

Leader Drill (Dia. 2-1)
Objective: To teach the players to remain in basketball position and from there to teach the basic fundamentals of running, jumping, pivoting and sliding in a group situation.

Organization: We will involve the entire team or divide the squad into two groups at each end of the floor. A leader will be designated at each end and he will take the players through the basic fundamentals mentioned above and discussed thoroughly earlier in this chapter. The coaches will be watching closely to make any necessary corrections. Accuracy must be emphasized early. Technique must come first. After awhile, we will make the drill a reaction drill emphasizing quickness and technique in following the leader. Hand movements and quick feet movements will be added here.

Points of Emphasis: (see the points on basketball position, running, jumping, pivoting, and sliding discussed earlier.)

Two Line Passing Drill (Dia. 2-2)
Objective: To teach and develop the technique and accuracy required on all the basic passes.

Organization: Two lines facing each other twelve to fifteen feet apart. The players pair up with one ball for each pair. The passes are covered in this order: chest pass, bounce pass, baseball pass, overhead pass, push pass. The players merely pass the ball back and forth with the coaching making corrections when necessary. Again, technique and accuracy are emphasized first with quickness coming later.

Points of Emphasis: (see the sections on the passes mentioned above.)

Full Court Passing Drill (Dia. 2-3)
Objective: To develop the ability of the players to see the floor and execute the chest pass on the move.

Organization: The players pair up and form two lines facing each other at one end of the floor. Each pair of players advances to the other end of the court passing the ball back and forth without the ball touching the floor. At the opposite end, one of the players will take the last pass and execute the lay up. The players return in the same manner and the next group advances up the floor.

Points of Emphasis: 1. Look ahead. See the floor.
2. Lead the receiver.
3. Make the passes firm but easy to handle.

Machine Gun Passing Drill (Dia. 2-4)
Objective: To further develop the passing skills of the players. Quickness and increased strength and endurance are the prime areas of improvement.

Organization: The team is divided into groups of four players each. There are two balls to a group. One player steps out to face his three teammates. The two balls are passed back and forth continuously for a designated time period. We start with thirty seconds and advance to one full minute of continuous passing.

Points of Emphasis: 1. Quickness.
2. Pronate the wrists and the fingers. Snap the pass off.
3. Maintain accuracy.
4. Push yourself when fatigue begins.

Star Drill (Dia. 2-5)
Objective: A combination drill to develop the passing, dribbling and pivoting skills of the players.

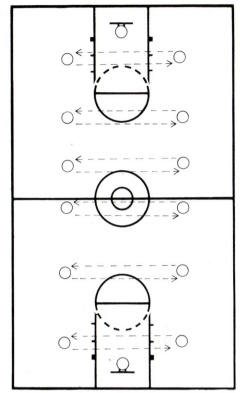

DIA. 2-2

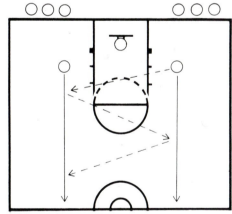

DIA. 2-3

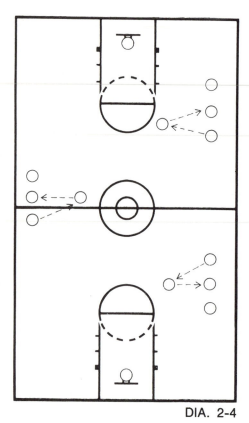

DIA. 2-4

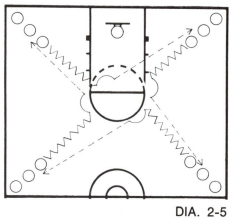

DIA. 2-5

Organization: Four lines as shown with the players facing in toward the free throw line and middle of the floor. The first player in each line has a ball. He will dribble into the center of the floor and come to a jump stop just inside the circle. Each of the ball handlers then executes a reverse pivot off a designated foot and throws the chest pass to the player standing in the next line. After making the pass, the players follow the ball and move to the end of that line. The new ball handlers continue the drill in the same manner. When reversing off the left foot, the passes and rotation will be to the left. When using the right foot as the pivot foot, the passes and rotation will be to the right.

Points of Emphasis: 1. Head up.
2. Pivot on the balls of the feet. Stay low.
3. Protect the ball.
4. Make the chest pass accurately and with the proper technique.

Halo Passing Drill (Dia. 2-6)
Objective: To teach the players the concept of the passing halo and to develop their abiity to make the pass through or by the defense.

Organization. The players form groups of three as shown in the diagram. The wing player starts with the ball and makes the pass by the defender into the post. The defensive man should apply as much pressure as possible. Each player should make a set number of passes or the coach should rotate the players on command.

Points of Emphasis: 1. Head up. Recognize the open man and make the pass to his open side.
2. Fake purposely. Do not wave the basketball.
3. After making a fake, bring the ball back into the chest area.
4. Make the pass through the passing halo.
5. Learn to execute the push pass.
6. Maintain poise.

Toss Backs
We are great believers in the toss back machines and utilize many passing, quickness and intensity drills that have been devised by the company that manufactures toss backs. These can be obtained in booklet form by writing Toss Back, Inc., Dorrance, Kansas. The three primary drills in which we utilize the toss backs to develop our passing skills are very simple. We have the players work on their chest pass into the toss back from a distance starting at fifteen feet. In the second drill, the players work in until they are right against the toss back and then work their way back out again. The players will be

working on the chest pass and the closer they get to the nets, the more strength development will be taking place in the fingers and wrists. The third drill is the same as the second except the players utilize the overhead pass instead of the chest pass. This is excellent for developing strength not only in the fingers and wrists but also in the arms and shoulders of the players. Work on this drill will improve our ability to outlet the basketball for the fast break. The nets can also be beneficial in improving the hands of a player who lacks the good hands necessary to excell in the game of basketball.

Basic Dribbling Drill (Dia. 2-7)

Objective: To work on the dribbling ability of our individual players in a group situation. We emphasize the development of the weak hand.

Organization: Three lines at one end of the court. The first player in each line dribbles to the opposite end and then returns and hands the ball to the next player in line. The control, speed, stop and go, reverse and crossover dribbles are introduced and taught in that order. The diagram shows the angles utilized to execute the reverse dribble and the crossover dribble. In working on the control, speed, and stop and go techniques, the players will advance and return in a straight line.

Points of Emphasis: (see the techniques described earlier in this chapter.)

Chase The Dribbler Drill (Dia. 2-8)

Objective: To work on the speed dribble the length of the floor with a defensive player in pursuit. This drill is also valuable for helping the players concentrate on making the lay up at the end of a full court drive with the defensive man applying pressure.

Organization: Two lines are formed in opposite corners. The first player in each line has a ball. The second player in each line and each alternating player thereafter assumes defensive responsibilities. The players reverse roles at the opposite end. The drill starts with the ball handlers dribbling hard for a lay up at the opposite end. After about a two or a three stride head start, the coach will instruct the defense to pursue. The chaser should apply as much pressure as possible to the ball handler.

Points of Emphasis: 1. Push the ball out in front as far as possible while still maintaining control.
2. Keep the head and eyes up.
3. Be aware of the pursuing defender but concentrate on getting to the basket.
4. Once into the drive, concentrate fully on the basket.

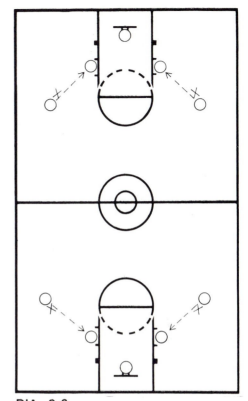

DIA. 2-6

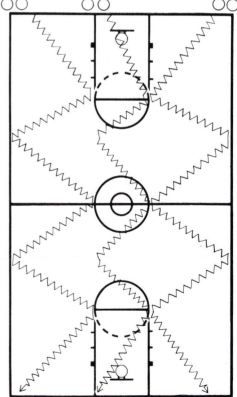

DIA. 2-7

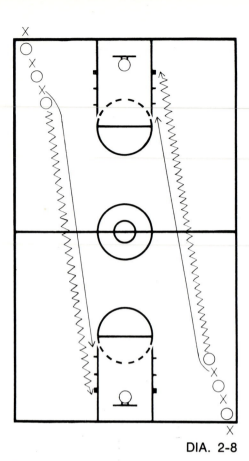

DIA. 2-8

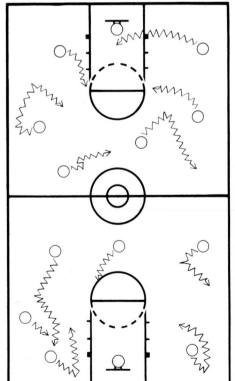

DIA. 2-9

5. Transfer your momentum up to the basket.

Dribble Tag (Dia. 2-9)

Objective: To develop the dribbling ability of the players. To improve their quickness and ability to change directions on the dribble.

Organization: The squad can be divided into six players at each end of the floor or the entire squad can execute the drill in the half court area. Everyone has a ball. One player is designated as "it". The other players try to avoid being touched by the designated dribbler while keeping their dribble alive at all times. A variation of this drill is to require that the players dribble with their weak hand only.

Points of Emphasis: 1. Head up.
2. Stay down over the ball.
3. Change hands (except when required to use the weak hand only).
4. Work on your change of direction and change of pace with the ball.

Cock Fight (Dia. 2-10)

Objective: To develop in the players the ability to handle the basketball under pressure. This drill is very beneficial in teaching the players to keep the head and eyes up.

Organization: The players pair off with a teammate of equal size. In each of the three circles, a cock fight will take place. Each player in the circle has a ball. The players try to deflect or steal the opponent's ball while still maintaining their dribble. To win the ball must be deflected outside the circle. Best two out of three wins and two new players step in. A variation here is to allow the players a certain amount of contact. This will help the players to develop their ball handling strength and ability to handle the ball under severe pressure.

Points of Emphasis: 1. Head and eyes up.
2. Learn to use both hands.
3. Learn to concentrate on the opponent's ball. Your ball-handling should be second nature.
4. Ignore contact.

Two Ball Lay Up Drill (Dia. 2-11)

Objective: To work on the lay up shots and the ability of our players to take the ball hard to the basket on the dribble drive. This drill is also effective as a warm up drill and develops the dribbling skills of the players through the execution of the dribble drive.

Organization: The players each pick up a partner and each group of players has a ball. The initial ball handlers will execute the straight lay up from the right hand and the left hand side of the basket. The partners will follow and rebound each shot. The players now reverse roles and the drill continues in this manner until each player has executed all of the eight lay up shots (four with the left hand, four with the right). As a variation, we will often times position a coach in the basket area to apply pressure on the shot. We will vary the pressure and will even deliberately foul the driver to help the players develop their concentration on the basket.

Points of Emphasis:
1. Go hard to the basket.
2. Plant the take-off foot inside the lane. Transfer your momentum up toward the basket.
3. Concentration and eyes on the target.
4. Bring the ball up away from the defense and with both hands.
5. Turn the stomach in on the backhand, over the top, and baseline lay ups.
6. Ignore the pressure. Make the three point play.

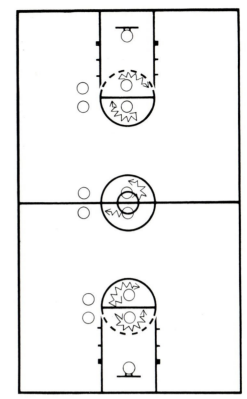

DIA. 2-10

Competitive Lay Up Drill (Dia. 2-12)
Objective: The same as the previous drill with an emphasis on the competition factor. Quickness and concentration are essential.

Organization: Squad equally divided at both ends of the floor. Each group forms a lay up line at a designated spot and angle. On signal, the first player in each line drives to the basket and executes the lay up shot. If a miss occurs the shooter must rebound the ball and put it back up until he is successful. After the made lay up, the shooter rebounds his own shot and passes the ball out to the next man in line. He then moves to the end of the line. The first group of players to reach a designated number of points is declared the winner. Dividing the groups according to position always adds for some excellent enthusiasm and concentration.

Two Ball Shooting Drill (Dia. 2-13)
Objective: To develop the shooting ability of the players and to increase their ability to get the shot off quickly while still maintaining accuracy.

Organization: Use as many baskets as possible with three men at each basket. A coach or manager can be utilized as the passer. One player stands under the basket and acts as the retriever. When the shot is executed, he rebounds the ball and gets it out quickly to the passer. The passer then relays the pass to the shooter. With two balls, the shooter must return to the floor and get ready for the next shot. We are trying to increase quickness but we do not want to increase quickness at the expense of accuracy. Concentration is extremely

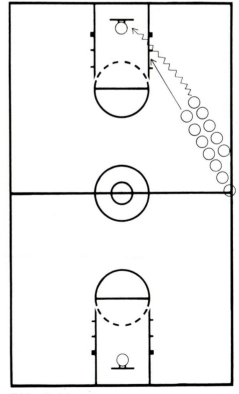

DIA. 2-11

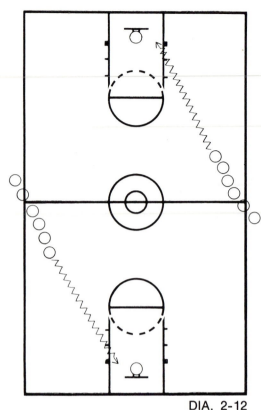

DIA. 2-12

important. We want the players to develop a shooting groove. A set number of baskets or a time limit can be the goal. The players exchange positions and responsibilities when the goal is reached.

Points of Emphasis: 1. Concentration and accuracy.
2. Quickness.
3. Develop consistency on the shot. Proper shooting form.
4. As fatigue sets in, make sure the legs are providing power.

One Minute Shooting Drill (Dia. 2-14)
Objective: Same as the previous drill with additional emphasis on movement.

Organization: Two balls and a rebounder are again utilized but now there are two passers delivering the ball from two different directions. The shooter must move across the lane continuously and execute the shots after receiving the pass from each direction. The shooter should try to make as many shots as possible within the one minute time period. We will keep a record and have players competing against each other to provide even more pressure. The players will rotate after each one minute segment.

Points of Emphasis: 1. Keep moving.
2. Come in low with the knees bent for the shot.
3. Plant the inside foot and face up to the basket each time.
4. Concentration, accuracy, quickness.
5. Proper shooting form.

Shooting Partners
Objective: Same as the previous drills with token defensive pressure added.

Organization: The players pair up and shoot from the positions they will be shooting from under game conditions. The partner hands the ball to the shooter and applies token defense. He then rebounds the ball, brings the ball back out and repeats this procedure. The shooter can execute the shot off the dribble or after a good fake toward the basket. The players reverse roles after ten shots. Depending on the time allowed, the players will shoot from a number of different spots on the floor. Pressure and competition can be added by recording the percentage of shots made from each spot and pitting the players against each other.

Points of Emphasis: 1. Ignore the defensive pressure. Concentrate on the basket.
2. When shooting off the dribble, transfer your momentum straight up

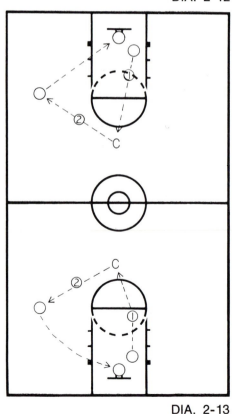

DIA. 2-13

50 Eight Fundamentals

in the air. Do not float.

3. Make an excellent fake toward the basket when shooting from the set position.
4. Proper shooting form on all shots.
5. Accuracy then quickness.

Competitive Shooting Drill (Dia. 2-15)

Objective: To develop the players shooting and to place them in a shooting drill situation involving the entire team.

Organization: Teams are divided equally at each end of the floor. Again, it adds to the enthusiasm to let the guards compete against the front line players. You can even designate three lines and let the guards, forwards and centers compete against each other. On a signal from the coach the first player in each line shoots and then retrieves the basketball. He passes the ball to the next player in line and the drill continues in that manner. The shooter must rebound his own ball. Each basket scores one point. A designated number of points can determine the winner or the coaches can set up a time limit.

Points of Emphasis: 1. Proper shooting form.
2. Do not overemphhasize speed at the expense of accuracy.
3. Concentration.

The following are shooting drills that apply directly to our offensive pattern. They can be executed with one or more players and are important in showing the players the scoring opportunities that can be derived from our offense. The players must then work on these scoring options, along with spot shooting drills, so that they become proficient in the areas where their shot will be produced. It is important to note that most of these drills can be executed with a coach and one individual player or with a group of players. We use them as individual drills before and after practice and as group drills. How these drills apply to our offense will become more clear in the following chapter.

Spot Shooting From The Point (Dia. 2-16)

Objective: To work with the guards on the options that are available upon execution of the point pass. The first option is the jump shot with no dribble. The second option is a fake to the weakside and one or two dribbles back against the grain for the jumper (shown in the accompanying diagram).

Organization: The players line up near the top of the key with the participating player stepping up to assume the point position. A coach or manager has the ball at the diagonal or wing position. He executes the point pass and the point man either shoots immediatley or makes the fake and drives back against the grain. The shooter rebounds his own shot and moves to the end of the line. The next player steps in and the

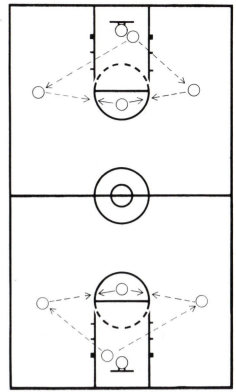

DIA. 2-14

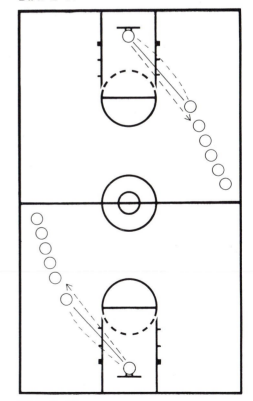

DIA. 2-15

DIA. 2-16

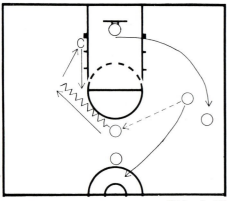

DIA. 2-17

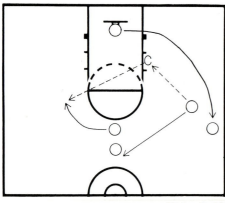

DIA. 2-18

drill continues. It is most advantageous for each player to have a ball, but two or three balls are sufficient. After awhile, we will add a token defensive player.

Points of Emphasis: 1. Read the defense in selecting the best option available.
2. Catch the ball ready to shoot.
3. Move into the shot smoothly.
4. Make a purposeful fake if the first option is not open.

Shot Off the Pinch Post (Dia. 2-17)

Objective: To work with the guards on the scoring opportunities that result from the point pass and execution of the two man play on the weakside. This is a natural progression from the previous drill.

Organization: The coach simulates the weakside forward coming up to establish himself in the pinch post. The ball can either start from the opposite wing (if enough players are available) or the point player can start with the ball. With the ball at the wing, the point pass is executed and the coach reacts up the lane for the two man play. The point player can either dribble off the pinch post or make the pass and cut off the screen set by the forward (coach) coming up the lane. The two scoring options are a shot off the screen or a drive all the way to the basket after a good head and shoulder fake. The shooter then rebounds the ball and rotates to the line at the wing. The wing player moves to the point line.

Points of Emphasis: 1. Dribble or make the cut in a straight line and rub shoulders with the screener.
2. Stop immeditely behind the screen for the jump shot.
3. Work on a good head and shoulder fake as if to go up for the jumper and then take the ball hard to the basket.
4. Lower the inside shoulder on the drive.

Flare Pass And Shot (Dia. 2-18)

Objective: To work with the guards on executing the flare cut and shooting the ball after the flare pass. The point player will be required to make this cut on the pass into the post from the wing and the pass to the four man coming across.

Organization: The same formation that was shown for the previous drill is utilized here. The coach merely moves from the weakside forward position into the post. Again, the drill can be initiated from the wing or directly from the post (coach) depending on the number of players available. As the coach receives the ball in the post, the point man will flare to an open position on the weakside looking for the pass and shot in an open area. The rotation is the same as in the previous drill. After a time, we will add a token defensive player in the drill. He will drop to help on the post and then try to recover to his man executing the flare.

Points of Emphasis: 1. Flare to a position on the free throw line extended. Find the open spot.
2. Extend the area of recovery for your defender but do not decrease the percentages of the shot by going too wide.
3. Time the cut properly and receive the pass in a position to shoot. Plant the inside foot, bend the knees.
4. Go straight up and down on the shot. Do not float.

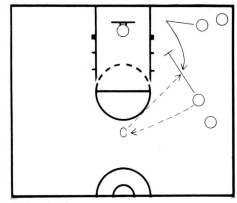

DIA. 2-19

Shot Off The Downscreen (Dia. 2-19)

Objective: To work with all of the players (especially the forwards and guards) in shooting the ball out of the corner after accepting the downscreen from the wing or diagonal. This action comes after execution of the point pass or the pass to the four man coming across.

Organization: The players form two lines at the diagonal and corner positions. The ball starts at the diagonal where the point pass is made to the coach assuming the point position. The wing man executes the downscreen as the corner player cuts into the basket to set up the screening action. After awhile, we will add a defender and the corner player must take him into the basket to set the play up properly. The coach makes the pass to the man coming out of the corner and he executes the shot off the screen. The screener rebounds the ball and the two players change lines. The next two players step in and the drill continues.

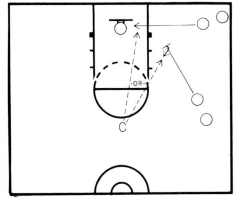

DIA. 2-20

Points of Emphasis: 1. Corner man must fake into the basket area.
2. Rub shoulders with the screener.
3. Plant the inside foot. Come into the shot low and hard. Knees bent.
4. Transfer your momentum up to the basket. Do not float.

Note: A variation of this drill and cutting action results from a failure of the defender to honor the cut to the basket by the corner man or from the execution of a switch by the two defenders coming together. In that event the corner player would continue his cut to the basket and the screener would pop out for the possible shot (Dia. 2-20).

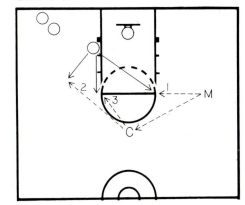

DIA. 2-21

Four Man Shots (Dia. 2-21)

Objective: To work with the frontline players (especially the

DIA. 2-22

DIA. 2-23

forwards) on the shots that can develop from the weakside forward play.

Organization: The players form two lines at the weakside forward position and at the wing or diagonal. The coach is at the point and the drill starts with the ball at the wing. The weakside forward first has the option of coming across the lane for the shot on the four man across series. If he does not elect to make this cut the wing player makes the pass to the point. The four man now has two options. He can pop out to the wing for the pass and quick jump shot or he can move up the lane to receive the pass on the two man play. If the forward comes up the lane, he is looking for his shot before or after the cut from the point player (coach). The wing player will rebound the ball and move to the weakside forward line. After shooting, the weakside forward moves to the wing line and the drill continues. A token defensive player will also be added to this drill.

Points of Emphasis: 1. Proper cuts.
2. Face up to the basket completely when shooting.
3. Come into the shots low and hard with the knees bent.

Individual Moves Off The Post (Dia. 2-22 and 2-23)
Objective: To work with the frontline players (especially the post players) on the individual moves and the scoring opportunities that are generated in the post position.

Organization: We will generally work with three players in this situation, although we can work with more or less depending on the numbers. We will establish an offensive player in the post with a token defensive player. The third post man will start with the ball at the wing and the coach will line up either at the point or in the corner. With the coach at the point the drill will concentrate on turning the ball in after the post pass from the wing and rolling to the basket upon execution of the point pass. With the coach in the corner the post pass from the wing is still in effect along with the corner pass. The post player will step up to screen and then step toward the corner man for the shot jump shot. Each offensive post man will take five shots and then rotate. The offense will move to defense. The defense will move to the wing position and the player originally at the wing will be the next offensive player.

Points of Emphasis: 1. Release to meet the pass.
2. Read the defender.
3. Learn to turn it in both ways.
4. Pin the defender when rolling to the basket.
5. After screening on the corner pass, step in tight for the shot.

There are four phases to our offense: fast break, transition, press attack and half court. Chapter Four will be devoted to the fast break and transition while in this chapter we will be concerned primarily with getting into and executing our offense in the half court area and the zone press attack.

Our half court offensive system is based on five basic principles: (1) that we have five men in shooting position; (2) that each player has the opportunity to shoot his shot; (3) that all five men are working so that these high percentage shots can be produced; (4) there is some freedom and opportunity for individual movement within the team concept and; (5) that we end up with optimum rebunding strength on any shot taken. Most of what has to do with rebounding is discussed in Chapter Eight including the rebounding principles out of our man to man offense. We did explain in this chapter the rebounding responsibilities when facing a zone defense so that they could be diagrammed right from the offensive plays shown. We will come to this shortly but first the man to man offense.

We diagram and show to our players the scoring opportunities that will develop from the proper timing and execution of our man to man offense. We ask them if the offense seems to be taking anything away from their game or if they feel there are not enough scoring opportunities designed for their position. Invariably, they will see that if they work hard at perfecting their individual skills during practice and execute properly during the game, the openings will be there.

It is important to note that our man to man offense breaks down into a series of two-man, three-man, four-man, and five-man plays. There is always the possibility of a good quick one-on-one move also. This is not to say that while a two man play is going on, the other three are standing and watching. On the contrary, each man has a job to do and he must do it effectively if the offense is to run smoothly. The strongside (ball side) is where the primary options are developing. The weakside men are moving so that the weakside defense cannot sag and help. The weakside options are very important and will be utilized according to how the defense reacts.

We teach our offense using a whole-part-whole method. In our breakdown drills, we want our players to realize the purpose for each drill, how they relate to the offense and how they relate to their scoring opportunities. We start by giving the players a thorough understanding of the principles underlying our offensive system. Then by showing them the offense as a whole and explaining the various scoring opportunities, the players get a basic idea of the entire picture and how it works. Additionally, the explanation and diagramming of the scoring opportunities gives each player an idea of how the offense will work for his and each of the other positions. All of our half court offensive drills are designed from specific plays in our offense.

3 Team Offense

DIA. 3-1

DIA. 3-2

It is easy then for our players to relate what they are doing in practice to actual game conditions and to recognize their own individual strengths and weaknesses. The players are encouraged to work on their weaknesses during practice and to go to their strengths during the games.

It is imperative that our players learn to recognize what the defense is doing and react accordingly. Too many players stereotype themselves and the offense by running to designated spots irregardless of how the defense is playing them. We do not want to force any one option. If the defense has taken one option away, then they will have left another one open. For example, if we were going to execute a simple split the post maneuver (Diagram 3-2) how many players would recognize if the defense was anticipating that cut and make the split second decision to cut behind the defense for the lay-up? Or how many would force the action by "fighting" the defensive player over the top of the post? Diagram 3-1 shows the corner player (O_2) **reading the defense** and making the proper cut to the basket. The second diagram (3-2) shows a player not taking advantage of the opening the defense has given him. There are not enough players that are adept at reading the defense. Experience is the best teacher, however, and after constant repetition of this concept and a thorough understanding of our offense and the options available, our players show great improvement in this area.

Spacing and timing are two very important elements in the execution of a successful offense. The players must be made to understand that purposeful movement is highly advantageous while movement without purpose only tends to disrupt the flow of the offense. In our offense, it is essential that the players learn when to hold their position to let a particular play develop. It is possible to keep the defense occupied because all five of our players are in a position to shoot the basketball. They are also in a position to see the ball, the basket, and the middle of the floor. If their defensive player relaxes or looks to help somewhere else, they will immediately recognize the open area whether it be at the basket or elsewhere.

The timing will come only with constant repetition of the offense in breakdown drills and five on five situations. Proper timing requires not only excellent knowledge of the offense, and the ability to read the defense, but also recognition of the individual habits, tendencies, strengths and weakness of teammates.

There is one more very important concept we would like to introduce before beginning to detail our offensive system in full. We feel it is a concept that teaches each of our players to play aggressively and with confidence. We see many teams that go to one, two, or sometimes three players as their scorers. When this happens the players that do not tend to shoot as much play very passively, thus allowing the defense to give considerable help on the leading scorers.

Any time one of our players receives the basketball he is to turn and "play the basket." We want to put pressure on the defense from all five of our positions. This cannot be accomplished by a player who is content to pass to the scorers and get back on defense. An offense that does not involve all five players, each looking for his scoring opportunities, will, in effect, be playing four on five.

The pressure that we put on each defensive player keeps them honest and creates help and recover situations that break down the defense. When we instruct our players to "play the basket" they realize that we mean with or without the basketball. A great example of playing aggressively or "making something happen" is the give and go cut. The player who makes a sharp give and go cut is putting extreme pressure on the defense and creating situations. The man playing him had better react quickly or the offensive player will be laying the ball up. Maybe the defensive player didn't react and one of his teammates has to pick up the cutter. This creates an opportunity for someone else. Quite possibly the defensive man on the ball may drop off a little to try and discourage the pass. If our offensive player is "playing the basket" like he should he now has a high percentage shot, depending on his position on the floor.

Figure 3-1 shows a player with the ball, "playing the basket". He is in a position facing the basket where he can shoot, pass, or dribble. We call it the triple threat position. While eyeing the basket the player is still able to see the floor so that he can hit the open man or continue the offense.

Figure 3-2 is an example of a player "playing the basket" without the basketball. The ball has been fed into the post and the post player has turned looking for his shot. Our weakside forward (the 4 man in our offensive system) is faced in and ready to "play the basket". If his defensive man should step to help or turn his head he should be ready to step behind to the basket. The post player, while looking for his shot, should have the instinct to see the open man and deliver the ball. Again, recognition of what the defense is doing is highly important.

When we take the ball out of the basket after a made shot on our defensive end or after a turnover by our opponents we will advance the ball into the half court area in a 2-3 set. Our players are made aware of some general principles and specific rules on inbounding the ball. These are issued in the form of a handout. We also do not allow our players to carelessly inbound the ball in practice situations. Pressure can be applied any time during a basketball game and we

FIG. 3-1

FIG. 3-2

Inbounding the Ball

want our players prepared to handle that type of pressure before a full house on game day.

Principles On Playing The Ball In Bounds After A Successful Basket Or Free Throw

1. In taking the ball out of bounds, you should face the court and survey the situation before stepping out of bounds.
2. If you are unguarded, you should signal a teammate to step out of bounds. Pass the ball to him and step to a position that will allow a safe return pass (depending on the defensive pressure, situation, etc.).
3. If you are guarded, step out of bounds and pass the ball to an open teammate.
4. You should see the entire court area, not just 15 or 20 feet. Safe passing distance is usually no longer than 1/3 the court, however.
5. The ball should be played to areas on either side of the basket. It should not be thrown across the lane.
6. After making the pass to a teammate, immediately step in bounds and in a position to take a return pass so that the ball will not hit the rim, net, or backboard.

Rules That Apply For The Throw In After A Successful Basket Or Free Throw

1. Five seconds to make the throw in.
2. Time starts when you are in position for the throw.
3. Time ends when the ball touches a player in bounds.
4. You can move along the full length of the baseline.
5. If you hit the back of the backboard or the supports, the ball will be awarded to the opponents.
6. If the ball is thrown in and slapped back at you, you should avoid the ball until it touches out of bounds; otherwise, it will belong to the opponents.

Principles On Playing The Ball In Bounds After A Violation

1. Give yourself room to make the throw in.
2. Accept the ball from the official when you are ready to make the pass.
3. If it is under your basket, know the game situation. Do you need a quick basket or just a safe pass to start your regular offense?

Rules That Apply On Playing The Ball In Bounds After A Violation

1. You must establish a pivot foot and you are only allowed one step in either direction. It is a violation if you move more than one step in an effort to throw the ball in bounds.
2. The five-second situation is in effect and same rules apply in hitting the backboard or supports.

Advancing the Ball

After a successful basket or a turnover we are not looking primarily for the fast break opportunity. However, our guards are instructed to get the ball to the center line as quickly as possible. This will of course depend on the situation and whether or not we want to speed the game up or slow it down. Usually we want the ball at the center line in four seconds or less. Even from the backcourt the guards are "playing the basket". Obviously they are not going to shoot but the man with the ball should always be attempting to drive by any defensive pressure and take the ball to the basket. By "playing the basket" the players are looking up, seeing the whole floor, and putting pressure on the defense.

We want the off guard to always be in reverse pass position in relation to the guard with the ball. He will also cheat toward the middle to cut down the distance of the guard to guard pass (Dia. 3-3). This will help relieve pressure from the defense and provide the ball handler with an outlet pass if trouble develops. The off guard must be sure that when the ball crosses half court he also steps into the offensive end so as to avoid an over and back violation.

The ball handling guard should cross half court at the mid-point between the sideline and the center of the floor (See Dia. 3-3). This spacing will provide the proper angles for each of the three passes that are available in this situation; the pass to the wing or diagonal, the post pass, or the reverse pass to the opposite guard.

The guard is not to pick the ball up until he is ready to pass and has found an open man. However, contrary to most offenses, we do not teach the guards that they must penetrate to a certain area before initiating the offense. We want the ball delivered as soon as an opening occurs and the chance of interception is minimal. We feel that the guard's ability to play the basket will take care of any needed penetration. We are looking for the open man. If the wing and post pass are being denied then more than likely the reverse pass to the off guard will be open. If all three passes are being denied, then our guard must be able to take his man one on one. Total denial by the defense is a tough proposition at the college level unless one team is completely over-matched.

We discussed at the beginning of this chapter the importance of spacing in our offense. This is one of the reasons we can have our guard deliver the ball anytime an opening occurs. When full court man to man pressure is being applied, the strong forward will run the sideline and face in so that he can see the ball, the basket, and the middle of the floor. As the guard advances to the center line area, the forward will maintain 15-18 foot spacing. If the guard slows up, the forward slows up. If the guard encounters difficulty, then the forward is there ready to help. The weakside forward, like the weakside guard, will cheat in **slightly** toward the middle of the floor. If the ball is reversed, then the responsibilities immediately change. The weakside forward now becomes the stronside forward and runs the sideline. The forward who was on the strongside now cheats in toward the middle of the floor.

The post man is positioned in the middle of the court and, in effect, we have spread our 2-3 offense the entire length of the floor. We believe, as you shall see, in a passing and cutting offense. From these positions, we are looking to pass the ball ahead and cut to the basket. Again, our primary objective is

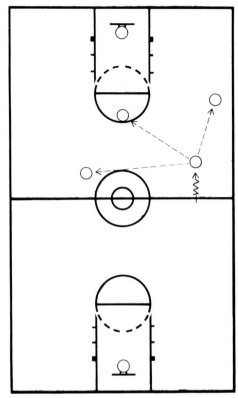

DIA. 3-3

DIA. 3-4

FIG. 3-3

FIG. 3-4

to put extreme pressure on the basket. Because the defense must be concerned with the basket and the basket area, this has to minimize the defensive pressure our opponent will be able to apply.

The three front line players are taught to break for the basket and come back to the ball as it is being brought up the floor. If the defense fails to react to a cut to the basket, the ball can and should be delivered at any time. Our guards must be able to play with their heads up, seeing the whole floor. Our players are taught further that if a pass is made, they should immediately look to break behind their defensive man as the defensive man is trying to change position. The receiver should always turn and face the basket to see what develops. An example is illustrated in Diagram 3-4. As the guard advances the ball near the center line, the strong forward loses his defensive man while the post pass is being denied. Every player should immediately recognize this situation. The ball should be delivered to the forward and the post should break to the basket. Even if the pass is not quite there we have relieved the defensive pressure. This rule applies in all phases of our offense and is just a matter of reading the defense and taking the option that is available.

Once our offense is into the half court area, our forwards are still out relatively wide and facing in toward the middle of the floor (Fig. 3-3). From this position, the forwards are taught to start the defense in and plant the inside foot at the 21' mark (Fig. 3-4). This will seal the defense off and maintain a strong receiving position between the defensive man and the ball. The guard to forward timing is extremely important because the forward should never make this move when the guard is not in a position to pass the ball. Practice and repetition will develop in both players the ability to read each other and recognize the best time to make the play. Eye contact can sometimes be a signal between the two players. We want our forwards to be aware of the guards off hand. When the guard brings his off hand to the ball the forward knows he should step hard and seal the defense because the guard wants to deliver the basketball.

If the defense is applying pressure we have many ways to get into our offense, such as; dribbling the forward out, sending a guard through and starting with one guard, etc. These will be diagrammed shortly. Before we examine our half court offense, however, we would like to show our favorite and most effective means of discouraging or beating pressure in the half court area. It is extremely simple, calling for a quick reversal of the ball and the proper footwork from the man positioned in the middle of the floor. Diagram 3-5 shows the offensive and defensive alignments. The defensive men on the ball side are denying the pass to their respective men. The weakside or helpside defense is off and toward the ball but really up on the line between their man and the man

60 Team Offense

with the ball. O_2 has the ball and has crossed the center line at the midpoint between the sideline and the center of the floor. The stronside forward (O_4) is out wide, facing in and ready to start his defensive man in toward the middle of the floor. The opposite guard (O_1) is in reverse pass position.

In Diagram 3-6, we see the ballhandler unable to initiate the offense with a pass to the forward or post so he reverses the ball quickly to the off guard. As this pass is made, the post (O_5) should step with his outside foot to seal his defensive man off or take him higher. The weakside forward (O_3) will pop out wide for a possible guard to forward pass. The original strongside players will hold position to keep the floor spread. From here we have several options, all dictated by how the defense reacts. Primarily, we are looking for the guard to forward pass, who then looks for the post breaking down the lane if X_5 has been slow to react (see Dia. 3-6 continued). If X_5 tries to cover over the top, then this option is made that much easier. Depending on the position of the defensive forward (X_3), the pass can sometimes be made directly from the guard. The post looks to step behind and to the basket if his defensive man makes the quick adjustment behind him (Dia. 3-7).

If the defensive forward reacts quickly on the reverse pass to a strong overplay on the guard to forward pass, we should be able to make the post pass. The post will immediately look for the forward cutting backdoor (Dia. 3-8). The third option that is usually made available is keyed by the defensive post man (X_5) moving behind our post on the reverse pass. The post would then step out higher to catch the ball, and the same option explained above (the forward cutting backdoor) would be available.

On all passes to the post the guards will utilize a splitting action with timing. By this we mean they will set their man up while the primary pass (to one of the forwards on the backdoor) is being considered. Also, many of our players playing the middle position have the freedom to drive by their defensive man if the opportunity presents itself. The guards would then veer off to take away the help. At any rate, with the forwards going backdoor and the guards splitting, it is easy to get into our regular offense from this type of action. By the same token, when the pass is made to either of the forwards with the post breaking behind, we teach the players how to immediately get into the offense if the pass is not there or the high percentage shot is not executed.

Some general rules that we incorporate into our offense are listed on the following page. A few have been mentioned before but are worth repeating. These ideas are helpful as handouts or perhaps part of a player's notebook. They should also be constantly stressed in practice situations. We feel it

DIA. 3-5

DIA. 3-6

DIA. 3-7

DIA. 3-8

Team Offense 61

is important for the entire coaching staff to be vocal in making coaching points and corrections. We try to discuss daily what areas need special attention in our team and individual work. We will then designate specific areas for each coach to observe and make the necessary corrections. With continued repetition many of our ideas become second nature to the players. This is what we are striving for.

Offensive Ideas

1. Any time your man turns his head — go to the hole.
2. Change your speeds. Go hard when you go.
3. Vary your moves, don't do the same thing all the time.
4. Keep head up! Always! See the open man!
5. Dribble only when necessary. There are four times to dribble:

   A. When you are going for the basket.
   B. To improve a passing angle.
   C. When you can't pass.
   D. On the end of a fast break.

6. In bringing the ball up the court — hit a man if he is in front and not covered.
7. Carry the ball up on lay ups — all the way!
8. ALWAYS BE BALANCED for your shots!
9. Watch the man with the ball. Know what he is doing so you will know what to do.
10. If a man dribbles at you — cut to the basket or to the open area. **Don't stand!**
11. READ THE DEFENSE AND ACT ACCORDINGLY!!

In our offensive system, we go from a basic 2-3 set to what we term our offset. We will generally bring the ball up the floor in the 2-3 set and get to the offset on our initial movement. However, we can instruct our players to just go to the offset.

Offset Positions VS Man to Man Defense

The offset positions are diagrammed as follows:

Point

1. One step off the top of the circle.

2. Directly in the middle of the floor.

3. Must hold this position to maintain spacing.

POINT (1)

DIA. 3-9

Diagonal

1. Positioned at the intersection of two imaginary lines. One, drawn from the free throw line extended. The other an imaginary arc drawn from the top of the circle to the corner from the basket.

2. Equidistant from the corner and point positions.

DIA. 3-10

Corner

1. One stride from the baseline and one stride from the sideline.

2. Leave baseline lane for cut.

3. Should be on an exact line with the basket.

4. Must stay out of corner.

5. The disadvantage of this spot is that many players, especially the younger ones, will not hold position. Spacing will suffer.

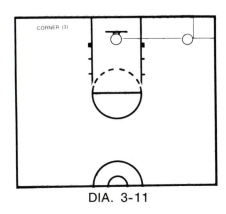

DIA. 3-11

Four Man

1. Should be in a position where he can reach and not quite touch his defensive man.

2. Usually between the blocks.

3. Facing in (see ball, basket, middle of the floor).

DIA. 3-12

Post

1. Stay on a line between the man with the ball and the basket.

2. Must learn to hold position and release on pass.

3. Spacing **important.** Don't let one defensive man play two offensive men.

DIA. 3-13

Any three of our front line players can play the post position. In fact, due to the continuity and movement of the offense the front line players must be able to play four of the five positions. The only offset position they are not responsible for is at the point. The guards must know the point, the diagonal, and the corner positions. This concept gives us much flexibility with regard to running the offense and matching up personnel. We can easily take advantage of a defensive mismatch or work to get a particular player or players open from a variety of positions.

We mentioned that we diagram the scoring opportunities for our players so that they understand the purpose of the offense and what we are trying to do. Following are the scoring opportunities from each position. As the offense is explained it will become clear where these shots will come from and how they can be produced most efficiently.

Scoring Opportunities From the Point Position:

DIA. 3-14

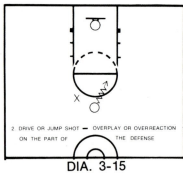

DIA. 3-15

3 PINCH POST (2 MAN PLAY)
A DRIVE
B JUMP SHOT
C BASKET CUT ON
   OVER PLAY

DIA. 3-16

4 FLARE ON POST PASS - STRONG SIDE SPLITTING

DIA. 3-17

5 FOUR MAN ACROSS
A BACK DOOR
B FLARE IF BACK
DOOR IS COVERED

DIA. 3-18

6 FLARE WHEN MAN DRIBBLES TOWARD YOU

DIA. 3-19

Scoring Opportunities From the Diagonal Position:

1 SHOT- SAGGING DEFENSE

DIA. 3-20

2 DRIVE EITHER WAY FOR
A LAY UP
B JUMP SHOT

DIA. 3-21

Team Offense 65

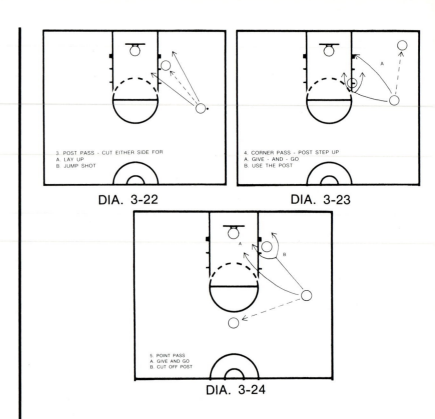

DIA. 3-22

3. POST PASS - CUT EITHER SIDE FOR
A. LAY UP
B. JUMP SHOT

DIA. 3-23

4. CORNER PASS - POST STEP UP
A. GIVE - AND - GO
B. USE THE POST

DIA. 3-24

5. POINT PASS
A. GIVE AND GO
B. CUT OFF POST

Scoring Opportunities From the Corner Position:

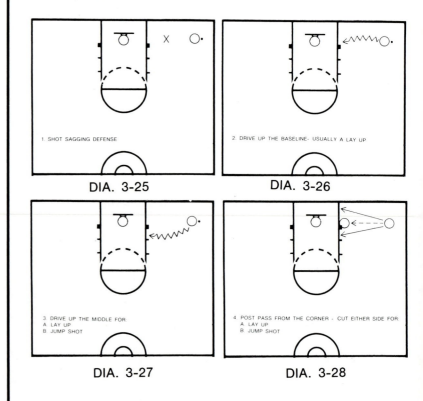

DIA. 3-25

1. SHOT SAGGING DEFENSE

DIA. 3-26

2. DRIVE UP THE BASELINE- USUALLY A LAY UP

DIA. 3-27

3. DRIVE UP THE MIDDLE FOR:
A. LAY UP
B. JUMP SHOT

DIA. 3-28

4. POST PASS FROM THE CORNER - CUT EITHER SIDE FOR:
A. LAY UP
B. JUMP SHOT

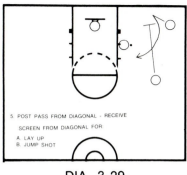

5. POST PASS FROM DIAGONAL - RECEIVE
   SCREEN FROM DIAGONAL FOR:
   A. LAY UP
   B. JUMP SHOT

DIA. 3-29

6. POINT PASS - SAME CUT AS 5. BUT WITH MORE AREA
   TO WORK WITH AND THE OPTION OF MAKING
   A BASKET CUT

DIA. 3-30

Scoring Opportunities From the Weakside Position:

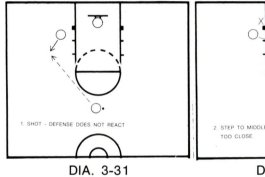

1. SHOT - DEFENSE DOES NOT REACT

DIA. 3-31

2. STEP TO MIDDLE IF DEFENSE PLAYS BEHIND AND
   TOO CLOSE.

DIA. 3-32

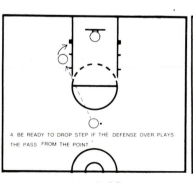

4. BE READY TO DROP STEP IF THE DEFENSE OVER PLAYS
   THE PASS FROM THE POINT

DIA. 3-33

5. FOUR MAN ACROSS
   A. DROP STEP IF DEFENSE IS OVER PLAYING
   B. TURN AND FACE IF DEFENSE IS TRAILING

DIA. 3-34

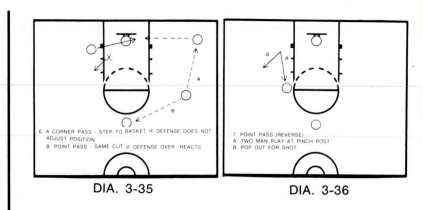

6. A CORNER PASS - STEP TO BASKET IF DEFENSE DOES NOT ADJUST POSITION
   B POINT PASS - SAME CUT IF DEFENSE OVER REACTS

DIA. 3-35

7. POINT PASS (REVERSE)
   A TWO MAN PLAY AT PINCH POST
   B POP OUT FOR SHOT

DIA. 3-36

Scoring Opportunities From Post Position:

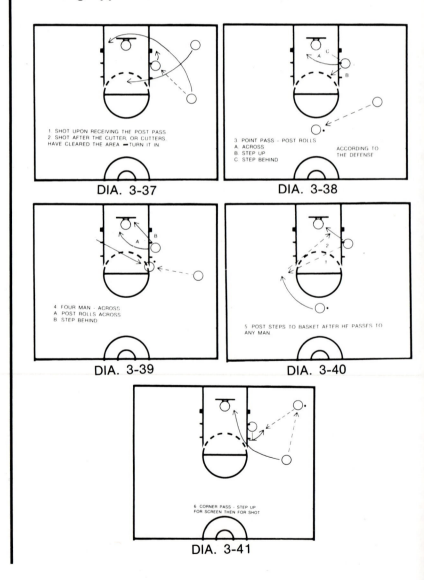

1 SHOT UPON RECEIVING THE POST PASS
2 SHOT AFTER THE CUTTER, OR CUTTERS, HAVE CLEARED THE AREA — TURN IT IN

DIA. 3-37

3 POINT PASS - POST ROLLS
A ACROSS
B STEP UP   ACCORDING TO
C STEP BEHIND   THE DEFENSE

DIA. 3-38

4 FOUR MAN - ACROSS
A POST ROLLS ACROSS
B STEP BEHIND

DIA. 3-39

5 POST STEPS TO BASKET AFTER HE PASSES TO ANY MAN

DIA. 3-40

6 CORNER PASS - STEP UP FOR SCREEN THEN FOR SHOT

DIA. 3-41

We have ten different possibilities for getting into the offset from our basic 2-3 set. These will be reduced in any given season according to the strengths and weaknesses of our personnel. We would never teach all ten options in one season. We might use only two or three options in any one game. Again, flexibility is the key. We might play an opponent whose guards are much smaller than ours. In that case, we could run our guards through and give them the opportunity to post up for an instant. To carry that further, we might have one particularly big guard who is very adept at posting down low. We would then send him through most of the time.

The many possibilities allow us to make adjustments during a game or during the course of the season. Furthermore, the means by which a team can get into the offset is certainly not limited to the ten possibilities we utilize. We have applied some passing game principles in the initiation of our offense to take advantage of special situations. There are unlimited options that can be devised according to your own philosophy and personnel.

Guard to Forward Pass — Option #1 (Dia. 3-42). This is the initial cut that we have probably used most over the years. O_2 makes the guard to forward pass and executes the give and go if his defensive man did not react to the pass (A). If the defensive guard does adjust his position off and toward the ball, then O_2 makes a basket cut behind the defense. The first look, of course, is to the guard cutting through. Secondly, depending on the situation, the match-up, etc., we can post the guard for an instant. From there the guard moves to the corner and establishes himself in the corner position. O_1 has moved to the point position and O_3 becomes the weakside player.

On the guard to forward pass, O_5 either steps behind the defense or rolls over the top to his post position. All cuts and passes should be based on the position of the defense, but they must be made instinctively. As we stressed earlier in this chapter, only constant practice and repetition will enable the players to recognize what the defense is giving them and instinctively make the right move. On this play, for instance, O_5 would time his cut if the defense is vulnerable to O_2 posting up. He would not want to establish his post position while O_2 is still in that area. Likewise, we might send O_2 through and immediately out to the corner if we feel our post player can consistently beat his man.

Diagram 3-43 shows us in the offset after sending the strongside guard through.

Guard to Forward Pass — Option #2 (Dia. 3-44). We will use this option to change the cuts and also to take advantage of defensive lapses by the opposing guards. O_2 makes the guard to forward pass and cuts in front or behind O_4 to the corner position. If no handoff is made the offset positions

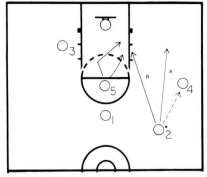

DIA.3-42

DIA. 3-43

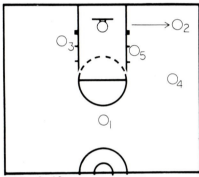

DIA. 3-44

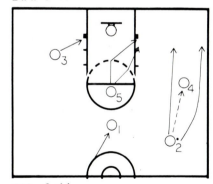

DIA. 3-45

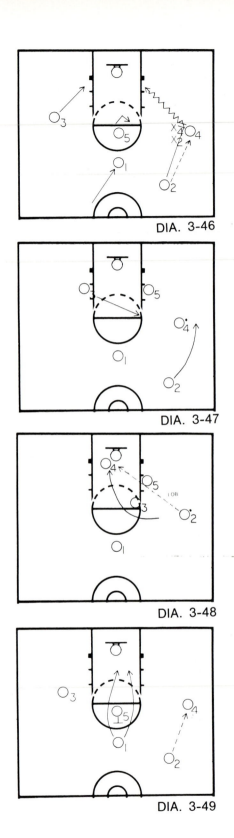

DIA. 3-46

DIA. 3-47

DIA. 3-48

DIA. 3-49

are established basically the same as they were in the first option. O_1 moves to the point position, O_3 steps into the weakside position and O_5 steps behind or rolls over the top to set up on a line between the basket and the ball.

There are three things that can happen when the guard cuts by the forward, if the defense does not react properly. When two men cross outside the shooting area, the defense should cross using the one-man removed principle (discussed in Chapter Seven). If our guard goes behind the forward and his defensive opponent stays with him man for man, the outside drive to the basket should be open. Diagram 3-45 shows this action. The offensive guard should lower his center of gravity especially his left shoulder. The left shoulder should rub the outside shoulder of the forward so that the defense cannot slide between them. The guard receives the handoff and cuts off his inside foot on the dribble drive. If the defense executes a switch then the guard can corner up with the ball and the forward maintains the diagonal position. We would then immediately react as if we had made the corner pass with the forward on top (explained in Diagram 3-73) to take advantage of the mis-match.

If our guard cuts in front of the forward, then the defensive guard, using the one-man removed principle, should slide behind his defensive teammate. However, if he neglects this principle and stays man for man, the offensive guard executes an inside steal as shown in Diagram 3-46. The handoff is made on the inside, but O_2 has the same basic dribble drive utilizing the defensive forward as a screen.

The third option is usually called for verbally in a timeout or while play is stopped. If the defense is pressuring the ball this will sometimes lead to one or more quick baskets and will open things up considerably. We will usually try to go to the side where our best jumping forward is positioned. Clay Johnson, a tremendous leaper, was especially effective on this option.

The guard cuts behind and receives the handoff from the forward. Simultaneously, O_3 the weakside player will break to the high post area looking for the pass. We now have the weakside completely open (Dia. 3-47). After handing off, O_4 would cut around a screen at the high post by O_3 and look for the lob in front of the basket from O_2 (Dia. 3-48).

Guard to Forward Pass — Option #3 (Dia. 3-49). When initiating our offense with the guard to forward pass, the off guard (in this case O_1) should always step to the point position as quickly as possible. From here, he can effectively cut off a screen by O_5 if the strongside guard holds. Again, we can call this play to take advantage of situations or we may use this as our primary cut against a particular team. It is important that the guards cut from the point position to make proper use of the screen by O_5. In this way, they will be dangerous cutting on either side. The defense will

DIA. 3-50

DIA. 3-51

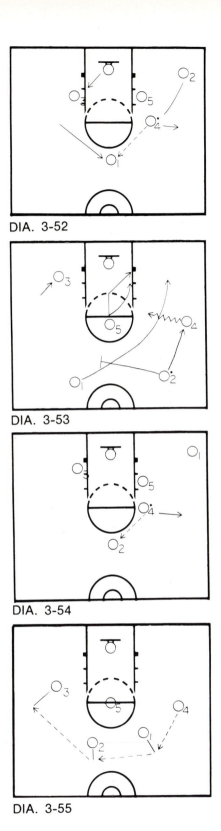

DIA. 3-52

DIA. 3-53

DIA. 3-54

DIA. 3-55

dictate which cut to make. If the defense stays weakside then the guard should cut ball side and vice-versa.

It is obvious that this action can be especially effective for a big guard taking a smaller guard inside. We can either post the guard up or take him right to the corner if he is not open on the cut. Diagram 3-50 shows the offset positions if the guard cutting through exits out the ballside.

The guard also has the option to exit away from the ball which would key a two man strongside play by 0_4 and 0_2 (Dia. 3-51). 0_4 would dribble in to the pinch post. 0_2 would cut off his shoulder for a possible dribble drive. 0_3 would screen down for 0_1 coming out and would also be in rebound position on the weakside in case of a shot. 0_5 would make his same move to the post position. If no shot is taken, the offset positions would be filled as shown in Diagram 3-52.

Guard to Forward Pass — Option #4 (Dia. 3-53). The final option on the guard to forward pass involves the strongside guard going away from his pass. This is simply to provide more action out front and to put greater pressure on slower defensive guards. After making the guard to forward pass, (0_2) will screen away for the opposite guard (0_1). 0_1 can use this screen for a cut down the middle if that is open or he can sometimes step right into the key area for the shot. Usually, we won't want the shot taken this quickly. Depending on what is open, 0_4 will dribble into the pinch post for a possible handoff to 0_1.

0_1 continues to the corner to shape up in the offset. He can either go the inside or the outside route. 0_4 can handoff to 0_1 or pass back out to 0_2 and reshape the triangle (Dia. 3-54).

We will also use this option to move the defense or emphasize movement to our players. For instance, after the screen away, we would step 0_1 out to 0_2's original position. 0_2 would pop out to where 0_1 has been and we would reverse the ball quickly to 0_3 and start our offense from there. The movement of our men and crisp passing of the basketball should provide additional problems for the defense (Dia. 3-55).

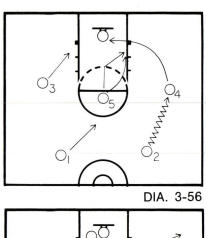

DIA. 3-56

DIA. 3-57

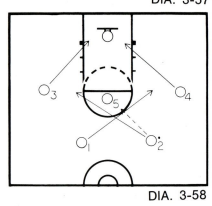

DIA. 3-58

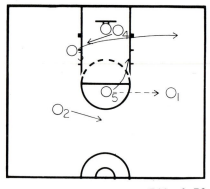

DIA. 3-59

Dribble Out — Option #5 (Dia. 3-56). An additional way we can initiate into our offense at the diagonal position is by dribbling the forward out. We will go to the dribble out to change the pace, set up the two-man play between our guard and post, or to relieve pressure on the guard to forward pass. O_2 dribbles right at O_4 and puts pressure on both defensive players. O_4 immediately goes backdoor and O_2 has his head up ready to hit him if an opening occurs. The bounce pass is usually the best pass in this situation.

O_4 must go all the way to the basket and clear out to the other side. After he has cleared, O_5 will roll over the top or step behind to the post position. O_1 will move to the point and O_3 will move to the weakside position momentarily. We now have the right side cleared for a two-man play. If nothing is there, O_5 will pop out to the corner position, O_3 will fill the post, and O_4 will assume the weakside position (Dia. 3-57). This is a great option for creating movement for the front line players that will put additional pressure on the defenders.

Post Pass — Option #6 (Dia. 3-58). We discussed this option earlier in relation to beating pressure. There are two basic ways we can get into the offset from this action. O_5 is to turn and face as soon as he catches the ball. His first look is for his own shot. Simultaneously, he sees and considers O_4 and then O_3 on the backdoor. Finally, he looks for the two guards splitting by him or flaring to either side. If we want to look primarily for the guards splitting we will have O_5 remain with his back to the basket and look over his shoulder for the backdoor. The post man must be like a quarterback on the option play. He is ready to hand the ball off if one of the guards has beaten his man, but he must also pull the ball back if it is too congested down the middle.

The first way for us to establish our offset positions from this option is shown in Diagram 3-59. After splitting the post, O_1 moves to the diagonal position and receives the pass from O_5. O_3 continues from his backdoor cut out to the corner position. O_4 moves to the weakside position and O_2 steps back out to the point. After passing to O_1, O_5 looks for the give and go down the lane and sets up in his familiar post position.

The second way to establish the offset from the post pass calls for a mobile post man who can handle the ball. It is a very effective means of pulling the opposition's big man away from the basket. As shown in Diagram 3-60, the post man dribbles from the high post area out to the diagonal position. O_1 moves directly to the corner position and O_2 again steps to the point. O_3 would step in to the post position and O_4 would align himself on the weakside.

Guard Through — Option #7 (Dia. 3-61). At times we have felt is advantageous to start in the offset as soon as we enter the half court area. If we wanted a guard in the corner position and a forward on top (diagonal), we would simply send the guard through to the corner. 0_2 would make the initiating pass to 0_4 and then move to the point. 0_3 and 0_5 would already be moving into their offset positions.

Forward Corners Up — Option #8 (Dia. 3-62). If we want to start in the offset with a guard on top and a forward in the corner, we dribble to the point and push everyone down. 0_2 takes the ball to the point. 0_3 would move down to the corner position while 0_1 would replace him at the diagonal. 0_5 fills the post and 0_4 assumes the weakside position.

1-4 to Offset

We have also utilized a very simple 1-4 offense with movement into the offset. The purpose is to isolate the guard out front and to take advantage of bigger, slower players inside. After the initial thrust, we move to the offset positions and run our regular offense. However, we have now given the offense a different look and attempted to take advantage of a particular situation.

We should note here that any time there is confusion or the floor is unbalanced the players know immediately to get into or return to offset positions. We drill them on this and they are able to recognize quickly when a spot needs to be filled. Remember that the diagonal and corner positions can be filled by any of the five players. We will always have a guard at the point and a front line player in the post and weakside positions. In the 1-4, we allow the point player, who is an excellent ball handler and driver, to dribble the ball more than usual. This can sometimes cause the floor to be unbalanced and lead to a breakdown if our players cannot quickly adapt to their positions. The guards can also call verbally for the offset if some of the players are slow to react.

The 1-4 set is diagrammed below (Dia. 3-63). We place our two biggest people in the post and they can either start low and come up or start at the high post areas. 0_3 would be our smaller forward and 0_2 would be the second guard. Primarily, we are looking to hit 0_4 breaking into the high post. Keep in mind that we are in this offense because our three frontline players, or two out of the three, are being guarded by slower people. As soon as the pass is completed, 0_4 is to turn and play the basket. 0_2 is breaking backdoor. 0_5 is stepping out to screen for 0_3, who will take his man in either direction off the screen (Dia. 3-64). 0_4 has the freedom to drive around his man at any time, and 0_1 should be ready to flare to the open area if his man drops off to help. 0_2 must recognize quickly if he is not open on the backdoor and clear out to the corner on his side.

To get to the offset, 0_4 would dribble to the diagonal position. 0_2 would corner up. 0_3 would step into the post and 0_1 and 0_5 would take a few steps to the point and weakside positions (Dia. 3-65).

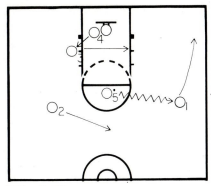

DIA. 3-60

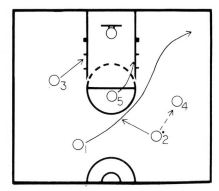

DIA. 3-61

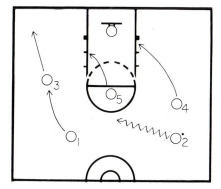

DIA. 3-62

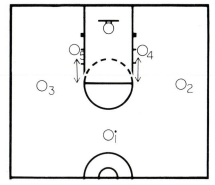

DIA. 3-63

Team Offense 73

Offset Passing Options

DIA. 3-64

DIA. 3-65

DIA. 3-66

The only other option we are looking for out of the 1-4 is the point man driving by his defensive opponent and breaking down the defense. You will remember that one of our offensive rules states that if a teammate dribbles at you — cut to the basket or an open area. The point man is taught to look for the cutter for a possible bounce pass and lay up.

The offset and the options into the offset are designed to start the ball at the diagonal position. By no means does the ball have to start there and of course it can be moved there from another position. The player at the diagonal can deliver the ball to all four of the other players as long as our spacing is correct. The cuts are keyed by which pass is made. Therefore, our offense is broken down into four series of movements and are identified as:

1. Post Pass Series
2. Corner Pass Series
3. Fourth Man Across Series
4. Reverse Pass Series (Point Pass)

As in most offenses, anytime we can get the ball inside to our post man, we want the pass to be made. We do not, however, want four spectators watching the post man do his thing. Nor do we want movement for movement's sake. Purposeful movement and a recognition of what our teammates are doing are two of our desired offensive goals. The post man certainly has the freedom to turn the ball in at any time to beat the defense. If the defense is playing him properly, however, he should look for his cutters and see what develops. Many times after the cutters have cleared the post player, he can turn the ball in and a better opportunity has presented itself. Movement has caused defensive breakdowns. Again, everything is determined by what the defense is doing. The players cutting off the post must be ready to veer off should the post man begin a scoring move in their direction. They are taught to go opposite that move. Likewise, the post must recognize where the defensive pressure is coming from and where the open man should be.

In splitting or cutting by the post, spacing is very important. The cutter cannot get too close to the post man because there will be too much congestion in a limited area around the ball. Nor can the cutter leave too much room between himself and the post man so that the defensive man can easily slide through and play the ball. We instruct our players to imagine a three-foot cylinder around the man with the ball. That cylinder extends all the way from the floor to the ceiling and is the ball-handlers area in which to manuever. The cutters should not break that plane but should learn to split the post on the exact outline of that imaginary cylinder (Dia. 3-66).

Post Pass Series — Pass From Wing. When the pass is made into the post from the diagonal that player has the option of splitting the post with the corner (Dia. 3-67) or setting a baseline screen for the corner player (Dia. 3-68). Our players are taught always to look for the give and go if the defense does not react to the pass. If the player on top does execute the give and go, he can cut on either side of the post man. The post must be ready to hand the ball off if the opening is there. The corner player would continue his splitting action off the post.

It is important that the man cornered up recognizes what the diagonal man is doing and what options have developed. If the diagonal starts to screen down the corner man must immediately set his man up with a hard move to the baseline and the basket. If the defensive man does not honor this move, then he continues to the basket and looks for the bounce pass from the post. Otherwise, he comes off the screen low and hard, brushing the shoulder of his teammate.

The guard at the point position (O_1) will flair to the open area on the weakside of the floor. This will usually be approximately three feet off the lane at the free throw line extended. If the center feels pressure from the weakside guard dropping in to help, the flare pass should be made and the shot will be there. The guards must be taught to flare so that they extend the defensive player's area of recovery. If the pass is made to the open man at the vertex of the free throw lane and free throw line, the man who has sagged to help will be close enough to recover and stop the shot. Diagram 3-69 further delineates this concept. If the guard's defensive man does not drop to help, O_1 has the option of flaring or holding position to see what develops.

Figure 3-2 and the accompanying dialogue on page 57 helps to explain the responsibilites of the weakside position (O_3 in this case) when the ball is at the post. The weakside forward is holding his position, facing in, and playing the basket. He is ready to step behind to the basket if his man helps in the middle or he is ready to step to the middle if his man drops to the basket area. If the post player turns it in and goes to the basket, O_3 is taught to move opposite. If the post man turns it in on the baseline, O_3 steps to the middle of the floor for the offensive rebound or a possible dish off. If O_5 turns into the middle of the floor, O_3 steps behind to the basket.

If no shot is taken, we must quickly reset our triangle and our offset positions (Dia. 3-70). O_5 can either dribble out to the diagonal position or pass to O_1, who must get to the corner position if nothing has developed on the first thrust. If O_5 passes to O_1 in the corner, he pops out to fill the diagonal position. O_2 would step in to fill the post from the weakside. O_2 and O_4 would move to the point and weakside positions respectively.

Post Pass Series — Pass From The Corner. We prefer the

DIA. 3-67

DIA. 3-68

DIA. 3-69

DIA. 3-70

DIA. 3-71

DIA. 3-72

DIA. 3-73

DIA. 3-74

post pass to be made from the diagonal position because of the better passing angle involved. The pass will usually come in from the corner when the post man has his defender pinned up high for a move to the baseline. If this does not materialize we have our same splitting action as diagrammed in 3-67 except that the corner man makes the first cut. The second option involves a backpick for the man at the diagonal (Dia. 3-71). O_4 starts his man away as if to interchange with O_1. O_2 steps high to set the screen and O_4 brings his man off, making sure that he brushes shoulders with O_2. After using the screen, O_4 makes a hard cut to the basket or looks for the baseline jumper. O_2 continues to the middle of the floor or he may break to the basket if the defense attempts to switch. O_1 and O_3 have the same responsibilities whenever the ball goes into the post. O_1 is flaring and O_3 is holding position, playing the basket. The point player can sometimes beat his man on a straight cut to the basket, but this cut must be wide open or it will only serve to congest the middle. The post player must be aware of what is going on behind him while the splitting action is taking place. To return to the offset, we would use the same movements as shown in Diagram 3-70.

An additional movement that is very effective in creating opportunities for our post player can be set up in the game plan or called from the bench. It simply involves a same side cut by the man cornered up and the diagonal. As shown in Diagram 3-72, O_2 makes a baseline cut putting pressure on X_5 to help if he even has a slight advantage on X_2. O_4 then cuts to the same side and they both must clear the lane. O_5 is looking for the possible hand-off to O_4, again putting a little pressure on X_5. O_5 is also ready at anytime he feels the opening to turn the ball into the middle and take it to the basket. By making the same side cut, we have relieved the congestion in the middle and given O_5 a better opportunity to beat his man. We can do the same thing to open up the baseline side by making the cuts to the middle. In both instances, we would have to reset the offense if no shot is taken. This option can be utilized on both the post pass from the corner and from the diagonal.

Corner Pass Series — Forward on Top (Dia. 3-73). With the ball on top (diagonal position), and a forward at the diagonal, we will try to set his man up for a cut to the basket on the corner pass. As O_4 makes the corner pass, O_5 steps up, just on the outside of the lane and makes himself wide. His back should be exactly parallel with the baseline and he should be about one step below the foul line extended. O_4 takes his man directly above that screen and then makes his cut to the basket on either side. O_2 must be playing the basket and must be able to deliver the ball to O_4, should he clear his man. O_1 and O_3 are holding position.

At times we will give the forward cutting through the opportunity to post low for an instant. 0_5, after setting the screen, will make a tight step with his left foot (on this side of the floor) and turn to the ball looking for the shot. If his defensive man has been forced to help on 0_4, the shot should be there. If no pass is made, 0_5 will pull out to the diagonal position, 0_4 will move to the weakside, and 0_3 is the new man in the post (Dia. 3-74).

We will also drop 0_5 to the low post position right behind the forward cutting through. 0_2 will look inside and if the pass is made, execute a wide angle split with 0_1 (Dia. 3-75). If no shot is taken, 0_5 would pull out to the diagonal either dribbling the ball or passing to 0_1 in the corner and stepping out. 0_2 would fill the point position (Dia. 3-76).

Corner Pass Series — Guard on Top. When the guard is on top with the ball and the corner pass is made, we can run the same pattern that has previously been described for the forward. However, the smaller guard cutting through is not quite as effective as a bigger forward. An option that has been effective for the guards and is also open to the forwards is keyed by the defense over-reacting to the cut to the basket. Diagram 3-77 shows 0_2 starting through the defense. His defensive man (X_2) reacts by jumping behind the screen set by 0_5. 0_2 steps back and looks for the pass from the corner man for the jumper. This is just another example of reading the defense and reacting accordingly.

The primary option that we run with the guard on top is a guard to guard interchange with a possible wide angle split if the post pass can be made from the corner (Dia. 3-78). If the post pass cannot be made, 0_1 and 0_2 have simply exchanged positions and we are still in the offset.

Fourth Man Across Series — No Pass (Dia. 3-79). The weakside player (four man) is taught to come to the ball on only two occasions; (1) if he is needed, and (2) if it is open. He does not come across the lane to try and make a play. The ball must be at the diagonal position when the four man comes across. If no pass is made, then we exchange the post and remain in the offset. It should be noted that the weakside player is positioned so that he can get to the basket and to the ball as quickly as necessary. Proper timing is essential. If the weakside player were further out, he would be too long in coming to the ball when needed.

Fourth Man Across Series — Guard Backdoor (Dia. 3-80). This option would become available when the ball is being pressured on the strongside of the floor. It can be called because of our observation from the bench or may have already been in the game plan as a result of scouting the opponent's defense. At any rate, it is keyed by X_1 overplaying the pass back to 0_1 at the point. 0_3 would come across taking

(DIA. 3-75)

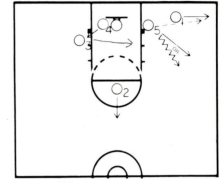

DIA. 3-76

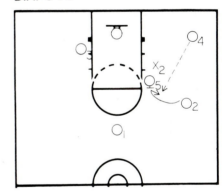

DIA. 3-77

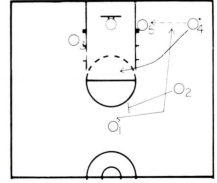

DIA. 3-78

DIA. 3-79

DIA. 3-80

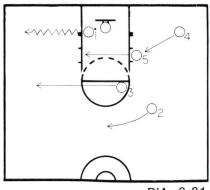

DIA. 3-81

DIA. 3-82

away the help on the weakside and leaving that side completely open. O_1 would break for the basket with timing and O_2 would execute the lob pass or a high direct pass if possible.

It is essential that all of the players become proficient at throwing the lob pass or a high direct pass on this play. We have all of our players drill on it, but like to have the guard at the diagonal because they are usually more adept at executing this pass. The players are taught to lob the ball so that it passes right in front of the rim. The play can obviously be made more effective by the use of a bigger guard going backdoor from the point position. During the 1976-77 season, James Clabon, at 6'8", played some guard for us and was especially effective running this option.

If no pass is made, O_1 must come back out to the point position and O_3 and O_5 would exchange the same as in Diagram 3-79. If the pass is made and no shot is taken, we would reset as diagrammed (Dia. 3-81). O_1 would dribble to the corner. O_5 would fill the post position on the opposite side. O_3 would move quickly out to the diagonal with O_2 and O_4 stepping to the point and weakside positions as shown. If O_4 was on top and O_2 in the corner they would still fill the same positions.

Diagram 3-82 shows an extention of the guard-backdoor option. This play is made when X_1 reacts by turning his back or helping too much on the pass to the four man across. This action is also a little safer than the lob or pass from the diagonal position. The pass would be made from the wing to the four man coming across. O_1 holds position until his man turns his back and then breaks hard for the backdoor. The four man executes a bounce pass while dropping his inside foot toward the cutter.

Another possible option that is created by the movement of the defense is shown in Diagram 3-83. X_3 is trying to overplay and deny the pass to O_3 coming across the lane. In this case, O_3 would start his man on that route and then step back to the basket with one or two steps as shown in the diagram, or by a reverse pivot method after planting the foot closest to the ball. O_2 would then execute the lob. Clay Johnson and James Clabon both made good use of this maneuver. It is an excellent way to keep the defense honest.

Finally, we can use this movement to open the post for a lob when the defense is overplaying or totally denying the post pass (Dia. 3-84). O_3 would come across. O_1, as well as all other players, would hold position and O_5 would open to the basket extending his hand for the lob. He must keep his defensive opponent on his hip without using his hands or pushing off. We teach our post people to hold their position — hands off — until they release for the ball. It helps to have both hands in the air so that there can be no question of a push-off.

Fourth Man Across Series — Pass From Wing (Dia. 3-85).
We have already mentioned that the four man comes across when he is open or when he is needed. His first look once he catches the ball is for 0_5 rolling across the lane. This is because we are always looking for that high percentage shot inside. The fact is, however, that he is turning and looking for his shot and should simultaneously and instinctively recognize if 0_5 is open or is about to become open. The third option is the guard (0_1) flaring on the weakside and the fourth is the corner man (0_4) coming off a deep baseline screen by the man who made the four man pass (0_2).

The footwork involved in the Four Man Across Series is very important for all of the front line players to learn and apply. As the weakside player comes across the lane, he must read the defense and anticipate what options would be open. If his defensive man is trailing him, then he should automatically have "shot" in mind. His last step should be with the foot closest to the defender (sealing the defense off just like our guard to forward pass) and he should be coming in low and ready to pivot off that inside foot to turn and shoot the ball down. This is the same action as shown in Figure 3-4 with the forward sealing the defender at the vertex of the free throw line and free throw lane instead of out on the floor. Again, his instincts will tell him when to dump the ball off to 0_5.

If the defender is overplaying the pass our four man must plant that inside foot hard to seal off the defense and catch the basketball. As he plants his foot and catches the ball, he should execute a reverse pivot with the back foot (or drop step, depending on your terminology) trying to get as much of the defensive man on his hip as possible. A good, quick drive to the basket should result. The post (0_5) must recognize what is taking place and step behind his man or to an open area. Likewise, the guard wouldn't want to cut backdoor and bring his man into the play.

The four man has come across because we were unable to enter the ball into the post. Usually, this will be because X_5 is overplaying the post pass on the low side. Our post players are taught then to open up to the ball (0_3 at the high post) and to try to keep their defensive man on their hip or backside — without fouling. He then extends his hand as a target and rolls to the basket.

The screen set by the diagonal man for the corner player is deeper than usual. It is set up by the corner player (0_4) taking his man in close to the basket (lane area) and then coming back off the screen. Because this is the fourth option proper timing is essential. We sometimes vary this cut for a particular game plan or for periods during the game. Instead of screening down, we step the corner man (0_4) up to backpick for the diagonal (0_2). 0_2 then has the option of going either way off the screen (Dia. 3-86).

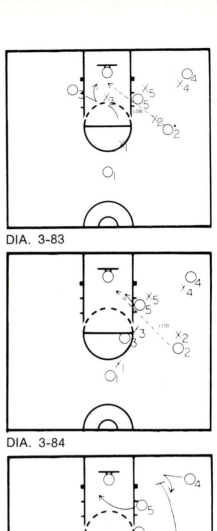

DIA. 3-83

DIA. 3-84

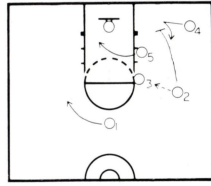

DIA. 3-85

DIA. 3-86

Team Offense 79

DIA. 3-87

DIA. 3-88

DIA. 3-89

DIA. 3-90

Another variation involves a two man play between the man on top and the four man across. After passing to the four man, the diagonal would set his man up and come off the high post for a possible jump shot or drive down the middle (Dia. 3-87).

On all of the aforementioned options (Diagrams 3-80 thru 3-87) we would reshape to the offset with the same basic movements (Dia. 3-88). O_5 would assume the weakside position and O_1 would move back to the point. O_2 or whoever was at the diagonal, would reset in the corner position and the corner player (in this case O_4) would come back out on top. O_3 would drop to the post. The only exception to this would occur if the ball were handed to the guard on the two man play and the shot was not taken. In that case, we would reverse the floor. This is explained in Diagram 3-89.

If the pass was made to the guard flaring with no shot taken, we would go to the offset in the following manner (Dia. 3-90). O_1 would dribble to the wing or diagonal position. O_5 would pop out to the corner with O_3 replacing him in the post. O_2 would establish himself at the point and O_4 would become the four man.

Reverse Pass Series — Point Pass (Dia. 3-91). When the ball is reversed to the point guard the weakside forward will come straight up the lane to position himself for a possible two man play with the guard. This will also serve to clear the area for O_5 rolling into the lane. That is the first option that O_1 should consider. A quick move by the post man should catch the defensive post (X_5) still on the low side. O_5 has two shots that he can derive from this action. If X_5 has reacted well to the pass and discourages the post from rolling right to the basket, O_5 should step up into the lane for the pass and a short jump shot. If O_5 is able to make the quick move and seal X_5 off on the outside, he should roll all the way to the basket.

The second option that can present itself is a shot from the key area by O_1. If X_1 is collapsing to help inside (Dia. 3-92) this will be the scoring opportunity that is most likely to occur. O_1 can also incorporate a ball fake and a drive back into

DIA. 3-91

DIA. 3-92

the grain for his jumper. X_1 will sometimes overcompensate when recovering from his help position. A good ball fake to the weakside forward coming up and one or two dribbles for the jump shot should free O_1 in this situation (Dia. 3-93).

In executing the two man play, O_1 has the option of dribbling off the screen for; (1) a drive to the basket, (2) the jump shot, (3) a pass to O_3 rolling to the basket (Dia. 3-94). We prefer the pass rather than the dribble because it creates better movement of the ball and our men. When the pass is made to O_3 at the vertex of the free throw line and the free throw lane, he has four options that are developing (Dia. 3-95). If it has been a quick reversal of the ball the timing is such that he can look for O_5 swinging through the lane. Secondly, he is looking for his shot after a front turn. By reading how his defensive man is playing him, he should know immediately if the shot is there. The two man play with O_1 is his third option. O_1 sets his man up and comes off the screen for a possible hand off and the same options that were available when he dribbled off of the screen. After making the point pass, O_4 moves to screen for O_2 on the baseline and also moves into rebound position. O_2 sets his man up on the baseline and comes off the screen looking for a pass from O_3 and the shot. O_3 may want to improve his passing angle by the use of one or two dribbles into the middle. The pass to the corner man coming off the downscreen can also be made directly from the point with slightly different timing.

On the two-man play, the point guard (O_1) must react to what the defense is giving him. If X_1 plays the screen, then O_1 should make a basket cut looking for the return pass from O_3 (Dia. 3-96).

There is one other possibility on this pattern that is again dictated by the defense. O_3 is taught to pop out for a quick reversal and a quick shot should his man be playing too far off of him or totally collapsing on the post, (Dia. 3-97). O_5 should still roll the post. If X_3 recovered quickly, the pass could still go into O_5. O_5 might want to hold position if we feel O_3 can beat his man on the drive.

Reshaping to the offset with no pass, and with a hand-off

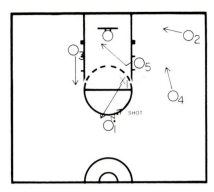

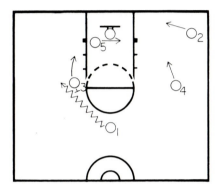

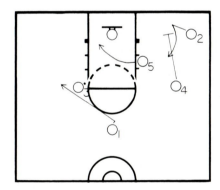

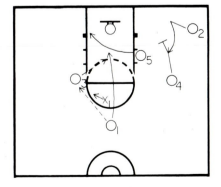

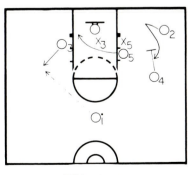

Final Points on the Man to Man Offense

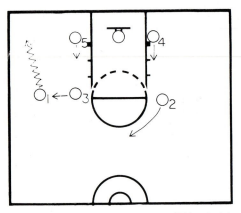

DIA. 3-99

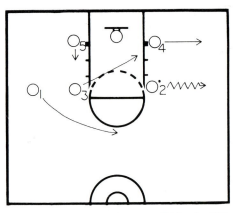

DIA. 3-100

Cutting by the Post

to the point guard and no shot are shown in diagrams 3-98 and 3-99 respectively. If the weakside forward passed to the corner man coming off the screen and no shot was taken, the offset would be fomed as shown in Diagram 3-100.

When considering our entire offense and all of the options available, it seems there is much to learn. The fact is, however, that all of the cuts incorporated into our offense are basic to the game of basketball. Our players have been making these same movements since they started organized play and many of the cuts are frequently utilized in free lance or pick-up games. As mentioned when introducing our offense, not all of the options will be taught or used in a given year. We further simplify the offense in our week to week preparations for each opponent. Practice time is devoted to the options that we think will be most effective against each particular team. This is based on the defensive philosophy exhibited by our opponent, the personnel involved, and what has worked in previous games against that opponent. Also important are the options that have or have not been working for us against other opponents.

If our offense still seems like a lot, remember that we can call for certain options from the bench or designate certain areas to be attacked during time-outs. Because of the versatility of our offense, we are able to attack a particular player or players, or an area of the floor that we feel is vulnerable. It is easily recognizeable from the bench what the defense is attempting to stop and, therefore, what they are giving us in our offense. We will immediately adjust our attack to take advantage of any weaknesses we discover.

At the risk of being redundant, the ability to read the defense is the most important element of the offense that our players must learn. Once they have a basic understanding of the cuts involved and have become adept at reading the defense, it is only a matter of executing the offense. They must then learn to execute the offense under pressure.

We issue to the players the following ideas regarding individual offensive play in our half court offensive system.

Driving Play

1. Run to daylight — always make your cut to the open side of your defensive man.
2. The defensive man should be close enough to allow you to get past him in one step.
3. Your leading shoulder should be low.
4. Make your first stride as long as possible to maintain good running balance.
5. Avoid running an arc or a circle. Cut in a direct line.
6. You have now cleared the first line of defense.

Clearing the Post

1. This is the second line of defense.

2. Run the cylinder. Cut close enough to the post to allow him to return the pass comfortably. You also use him to screen.
3. Avoid running at a distance that might cause your defensive man to interfere with the play.
4. Avoid running so close that you and your teammate will be entangled with the defense (run the cylinder).
5. Be under control so that you can stop and jump shoot or make your drive to the basket.
6. The post man does **not** shoot or manuever while the cut is being made.

1. A good guard anticipates the situation. He sees if a break is possible, or if he must set up a play.
2. He quickly recognizes whether the defense is set in a man to man or zone.
3. He knows if it is a sagging defense or a pressure defense.

Action

1. Against a sagging defense, run screening plays.
2. Against a pressure defense, run cutting plays.
3. Against a zone defense, move the ball.

Passing

1. Deliver the ball to the forwards, center, or opposite guard when they are ready and in a position to catch it.
2. Be ready to move all the way to the basket.
3. Be prepared at all times to pass to a teammate anywhere on the floor.

Shooting

1. Develop your shot from the outside so that the defense cannot sag and help on another man.
2. Develop your drive so that a defensive man can't stop your shot or interfere with your pass.

Floor Position

1. Normal position is one stride in from the sideline and at the free throw line extended.

Body Position

1. Assume the classic bent-knee basketball stance. This allows you to move quickly to the ball or to the basket.

Receiving the Ball

1. Catch the ball with the inside foot in front of the defensive man. Seal him off.
2. Meet the pass and look the ball into your hands.

Moving the Ball

1. Make a front turn and look for your shot.
2. Front turn and drive if your man is playing you closely.
3. Front turn and cross-over — then drive.
4. If your man overplays the pass, look for the drop-step or reverse pivot with your back foot and the drive to the basket.

Screener — Without Ball

1. Set screen within shooting distance.
2. Position to see basket and defense. Keep head up.
3. Hold position as the defense closes.

4. Make defense stop or change direction.
5. Be ready to roll to the basket.

Shooter — With ball

1. Manuever defensive man into screen.
2. Dribble with hand away from defense.
3. Make a long last step on the inside foot.
4. Be prepared to shoot, drive, or pass to screener.

Screener — With Ball

1. Same manuevers as screener without ball.
2. Handle ball at waist level.
3. Hand off firmly with both hands.

Shooter — Receiving Ball

1. Accept ball with long inside step.
2. Be in line with basket and screener.
3. Be prepared to shoot, drive, or return pass to screener.

Post Play Strategy

Floor Position

1. Assume a position on a direct line between the ball and the basket.
2. Maintain floor spacing that will not let a defensive man stop the shot and prevent a pass at the same time.
3. When the ball moves, assume a new direct line position and maintain floor spacing.

Body Position

1. Bent knee basketball position.
2. Make your body a big target for the passer. Extend arms, spread feet, and crouch only slightly.
3. Signal with hand away from the defensive man the line on which the ball should be passed. Give a good target.

Receiving the Ball

1. Your first obligation is to catch the ball! As the post man, you are in the center of our defense.
2. Meet the ball in such a way as to prevent your defensive man from intercepting.
3. Step in the defensive player's path as you move to receive the ball.

Shooting and Moving the Ball

1. Pivot and face the basket for a jump shot.
2. Practice turning in either direction and from both sides of the playing floor.
3. Spin and drive for the basket. Drop the back foot and step toward the basket.
4. Learn to make moves without a dribble. One low, quick dribble is the maximum for center play.

Zone Offense

We teach two simple zone offensive attacks that are set up depending on the type of zone the defense employs. Our guards, as well as all of our players, must be able to recognize immediately what type of zone they are up against. To establish that the opposing team is actually in a zone, we will send the guard through to the corner as we do in our regular offense. If the defense does not follow him through, then we will quickly adjust to one of our two zone attacks. This transitional time is sometimes vitally important regarding the flow of the offense and the confidence of the defense. The team that is well prepared will move quickly and confidently into the proper zone attack. If there is confusion and uncertainty on the part of the offense, they will be unable to execute properly and the defensive team will gain confidence and momentum.

A zone, like a man to man, must be attacked aggressively. Pressure should be put on the basket at all times and every man must be a threat when he receives the basketball. Our players are taught to make something happen, to force the defense into a mistake. This is not to say that we are looking for a quick or forced shot. On the contrary, we are moving the basketball and playing the basket in an attempt to break down the defense for the best shot possible. We simply do not want our offense to be passive, waiting for the defense to make a mistake. Too many zones are attacked with the ball moving around rather than through the defense.

In attacking a zone defense, the offensive players must: (1) recognize that the defense has set up in a zone; (2) identify the type of zone and; (3) be knowledgeble of the passing lanes that will be open and the movements that will be successful against that particular zone. The first two points have been discussed with the exception of how we are going to identify the zone and set up our attack. The two offensive sets we will utilize are the 1-3-1 and the 2-1-2. Which particular attack will be used is determined by the front men in the zone defense. If our opponents have set up with an even number of men out front we will attack with an odd number on offense (1-3-1). If the defense is in an odd man front (1-3-1, 3-2) we will initiate an even-numbered offense (2-1-2). We must be careful to recognize if the if the defensive man on the 3-2 drops back into the middle as the ball is advanced. We would then be, in effect, playing aganst a 2-1-2 and our offense would change.

Preparation in practice is important regarding the first two points mentioned above, but is even more important when considering the third mental aspect involved in attacking the zone defense. The players must understand the various defenses and where they are most vulnerable. This is simplified because our zone attacks are designed to take advantage of the weaknesses that are inherent in each particular defense. The players, therefore, should be well drilled in the offensive systems (1-3-1 and 2-1-2), but should also be well aware of **why** we are making certain passes and certain movements off those passes. The players should thoroughly understand why these actions are taking place and why they will be successful. This knowledge will enhance the team's belief in the offense and instill confidence in their ability to get the job done.

The ball must be moved rapidly in attacking the zone, especially when the ball is reversed to the weakside of the defense. At the same time, each and every player must play the basket and not be content to pass the ball around the outside of the zone. The key is to look inside and look for the shot simultaneously. If nothing is there, the basketball must be moved. Our players are taught to play the gaps. This will theoretically put two defensive men on one offensive player. An open area and an open man should result. If nothing else, the defense will have been forced to move and we have attempted to make something happen. If enough opportunities are created by an aggressive offense, and that offense is not careless with the ball, the defense will eventually break down.

Ball fakes opposite the man we want to set up are effective in getting the defense to move. They should be used frequently but always with a purpose in mind. The same holds true regarding the movement of our men. Just as we stressed in relation to our man to man offense movement for movement's sake is wasted motion. This is especially important against a zone defense because a zone reacts for the most part to ball movement rather than player movement. Again, realization of what we are trying to accomplish offensively will set the tone for purposeful player movement.

The following zone offensive principles are issued to our players. They are expected to know them and to refer to them in their offensive thinking when working against a zone defense.

Zone Offense Principles

1. If there is an even number of men on defense in front, we go to the 1-3-1. If there is an odd number of men on defense in front, we go to our 2-1-2.
2. When you catch the ball, face the basket — look in. Be a threat.
3. You can drive one defensive man — then be prepared to shoot or pass.
4. Maintain spacing of 12 to 15 feet between each offensive player.
5. Move the ball and yourself, quickly and with a purpose.
6. Play the gaps. Make two men play you. Hit the open man.
7. Get a man to the basket area and a man to the ball.
8. Baseline men — be ready to play behind the defense.
9. Get the ball inside. Protect the basketball.
10. Keep your passing lanes open. Use ball fakes.
11. Hit baseline man with the ball — post steps through — passer to middle.
12. Hit post — baseline man steps across — passer to baseline. Look to the weakside.
13. Play in triangles.
14. Reverse the ball to move the defense.
15. Treat zone, half-court zone press, and full-court zone press the same. They are the same defense employed in different-sized areas.

Zone Offense Against Two Man Front

As we advance the ball into the half court area, we should recognize whether the defense is in a zone or a man to man.

If necessary we can send a cutter through. However, if we have determined the defense is a zone with an even-numbered front, we will go from our 2-3 set into our 1-3-1. The 1-3-1 can be formed by passing or by dribbling. The formation of the 1-3-1 is determined by what is open and by how we want to place our personnel. Ideally, we will position our two best shooters at the wing positions with our best passer playing the point. The point player should also be able to handle the various fast break situations at the defensive end. In this offense, he is designated as the safety and must be back on all shots. The high post player should be our best all-purpose front line player. He should be a good shooter from the high post area and an excellent passer, adept at spotting the open man and delivering the basketball. Good hands and the ability to perform in a congested area are prerequisites for this position. The baseline player should be a strong, rugged inside player who is at his best playing around the basket.

Diagrams 3-101 and 3-102 show the two movements into the 1-3-1 set by way of the pass. The ball can be initiated to either side of the floor so we actually have four ways to enter into our offense after the first pass.

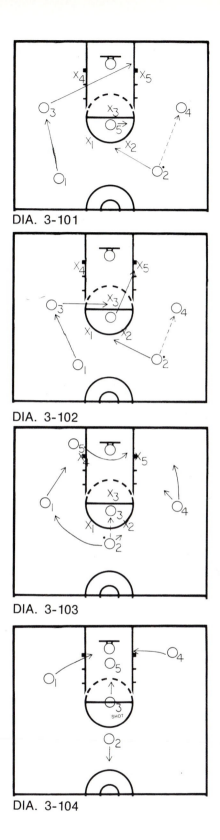

DIA. 3-101

DIA. 3-102

DIA. 3-103

DIA. 3-104

High Post Pass vs. Zone (Dia. 3-103). Once the defense has established themselves in a zone, we will bring the ball into the half court area in our 1-3-1 set. More times than not, we will initiate the offense with a pass to either wing. However, any time we can get the pass to the high post area without forcing anything, we want the pass made. Again, we are concerned with playing the ball to the open man. The high post is an excellent area from which to attack any defense. Especially if you are able to place a multi-talented player in that position. With the ball in the middle against a zone, the defense must collapse in on the ball and leave open spots within excellent shooting range. In our movement, O_3 and O_5 will be putting extreme pressure on the basket. The perimeter players must move to the open areas and be ready to shoot upon receiving the basketball. O_3 will usually turn in the direction he feels the least pressure, but he must recognize which side the baseline man is on so that he can pick him up right away. He is looking for O_5 rolling across the lane and for his shot. Very seldom will we want the shot taken this quickly. We want to make the defense work. We should make them move their zone and attempt to create a high percentage, uncontested shot.

The wing player (O_1) on the same side of the baseline man will break toward the area vacated by O_5 rolling across the lane. O_1 should pull up and set himself to shoot at an open area. The opposite wing (O_4) moves to an open area toward the baseline or pinches in a few steps also setting himself for the shot. The point player (O_2) can move to either side of the key area, but will usually fill the spot vacated by the wing player on the same side as the baseline man.

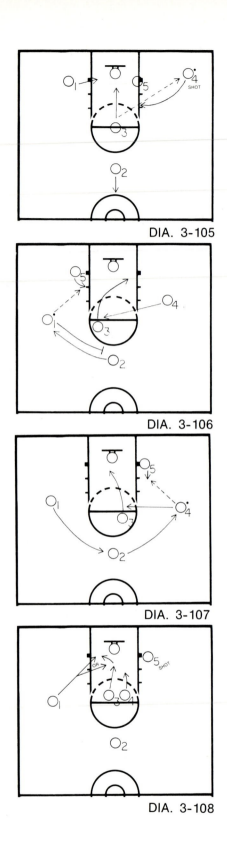

DIA. 3-105

DIA. 3-106

DIA. 3-107

DIA. 3-108

If the shot is taken by 0_3 we have 0_1, 0_5, and 0_4 moving into rebound position. 0_3 is the half rebounder and 0_2 must get back for safety responsibilities (Dia. 3-104). If the shot is taken by either 0_1 or 0_4 they must come down comfortably and then move to the middle of the floor to assume half rebounder, half defense responsibilities. 0_3, 0_5, and the wing opposite the shooter would form the rebound triangle. 0_3 goes to the side the ball was shot from or moves to the middle if 0_5 is at that side. 0_2 is back (Dia. 3-105).

Pass to Wing — Zone Option #1 (Dia. 3-106). For the most part, we want the ball initiated to the wing on the same side as the baseline man. From here the wing is playing the basket and has three passing options. His first look is to the baseline man working to get open. When the baseline pass is made the high post player (0_3) will step through looking for the open seam in the defense and a possible shovel pass from 0_5. 0_3 must be quick to move opposite to rebound position if 0_5 is open for the shot. If the pass has been made by a guard at the wing, he will simply exchange positions with the point player. The opposite wing (0_4) will step into the post.

We should note that all players have the option of holding position if **that** is the open area or if we are looking primarily for ball movement. 0_1 does not have to exchange positions with 0_2 and 0_3 does not have to step through if the middle is highly congested. 0_5 can return the ball to 0_1 and we can continue the offense from there. However, if the men are not moving, the ball must be moved. We can never hold position and hold the ball at the same time.

Diagram 3-107 shows the same option off the baseline pass except that the pass has been made by a forward at the wing position. In that case, the passer steps in to fill the post and the two guards rotate one position.

If 0_5 takes the shot, the wing opposite 0_5 should be moving quickly to weakside rebounding position. 0_3 will cover the middle and the strongside wing takes the long rebound. The weakside rebounder should recognize the position of 0_3. If 0_3 has already cleared the basket, he may assume weakside responsibilities and the wing should move to the middle. 0_5 would stay in to rebound and 0_2 would be the safety. 0_4 is the long rebounder. The same responsibilities would be in effect if the pass was made to 0_3 for the close in shot (Dia. 3-108).

Pass to Wing — Zone Option #2 (Dia. 3-109). The second option available at the wing is the pass into the high post. As the wing pass is made, 0_3 steps to the ball and is ready to face the basket if he receives the pass. The movements from this option are basically the same as in Diagram 3-103; the high post pass from the point. The one difference is that we have now determined a strongside and a weakside. Against a zone, we always want to attack the weakside so the high post player (0_3) should be aware of 0_4 moving into an open area on the blind side of the defense. O_2 should be reading the defense because he will, on most occasions, want to flare to the weakside also. **We teach O_3 to play the basket, the baseline and the other side.**

The rebounding responsibilities have already been discussed in relation to this type of action. We should stress again that this movement does not have to take place. Remember, we want movement that has a purpose. If O_2 has no advantage that would lead to a shot off the flare, he should hold position or only move slightly. The same holds true for all positions. In this way, if there is no advantage, we are basically still in our 1-3-1 set and can move the basketball in our attempt to make the defense shift.

Point Pass — Zone Option (Diagrams 3-110 and 3-111). When the pass is made back to the top, the point player is looking down through the defense for an opening inside. He is also looking for his shot or a quick reversal to the opposite wing. We like to reverse the ball as often as necessary to get the defense to move. We can rotate our men in two ways. We will designate which rotation, depending on the matchups and what has been effective during the course of the game. The first option shown, we refer to as **X-ing the Post.** On the reverse pass to the wing (O_4) the high post player will slide down the lane and look for the pass inside from O_4. The baseline player will fill the high post position ready to catch the ball and turn and face. The opposite wing (O_1) punches down in case of a high post pass to O_5 or a baseline pass to O_3. When the ball is still at the point, O_3 is at the spot marked with the small dot and O_5 is starting up the lane. They are both following the ball waiting to see what develops.

The movement diagrammed in 3-111 would be used primarily when the ball is reversed to the guard on the wing. It involves stepping the post man out and bringing a new man in. On the point pass everyone is holding with the exception of the inside players moving slightly to follow the ball. When the reverse pass is made, the baseline player flashes across the lane looking for the open area and a quick pass. O_3 immediately breaks away from the ball to fill the opposite low post. O_4 breaks in to become the new post. In resetting the offense O_3 would step out and assume the wing position. In this option, we have combined crisp passing with purposeful player movement and are still in our 1-3-1 set against the 2-1-2 or 2-3 zone defense.

The proper rebounding position is not hard to picture. If O_2 takes the shot after receiving the point pass, the passer assumes the half rebounder, half defense position. The opposite wing gets to the board on the weakside. O_3 goes to the middle of the rebounding triangle and O_5 tries to get inside from his position on the lane (Dia. 3-112).

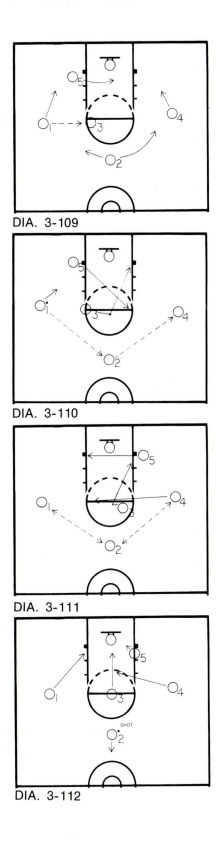

DIA. 3-109

DIA. 3-110

DIA. 3-111

DIA. 3-112

DIA. 3-113

DIA. 3-114

DIA. 3-115

DIA. 3-116

Zone Offense Against Odd Man Front

We will run a 2-1-2 offense against a defense with a one-man front (1-3-1, 1-2-2) or a three-man front (3-2). We have already discussed the possibility of the defense dropping the point man back in the 3-2 to become a 2-1-2 defense. In that case, we would run from our 1-3-1 set. If, however, they are playing with three men out front the defense will be similar to the 1-2-2.

Our 2-1-2 zone offense is even simpler than the 1-3-1. The key again is that the players recognize the different passing lanes and the weaknesses in the particular defense they are facing. Against the 1-2-2 or 3-2, the middle is the area that we would want to attack. The 1-3-1 defense is vulnerable at the baseline and at the key area. We would be primarily attacking the baseline because the highest percentage shots would be coming from there or from passes into the middle from the baseline. Also, when the ball is at the baseline, the defense flattens and the ball can be passed out to the key area for a possible uncontested shot.

In our zone offense, the players must maintain their spacing in close to the basket. Remember, we are attempting to pass the ball through rather than around the defense. The players must have confidence in their ability to handle the basketball in traffic. They must keep their poise when they are being double-teamed so they can hit the open man. The 2-1-2 zone offense stresses movement of the basketball rather than movement of the men. We instruct our players to take the ball into the defense at the gaps. The idea is to make two defensive men play the same offensive man with the ball.

As we move into the half court area in our regular 2-3 set, the forwards will simply move down to the block on their respective sides of the floor (Dia. 3-113). If we want to place O_3 or O_4 in the high post and set O_5 down low, we rotate as shown in Diagram 3-114.

The baseline players set up one stride off the lane area from the block and face in toward the basket. They are playing the basket at all times and are ready to step in front of the defensive man in their zone to catch the basketball. They must learn to stay in tight. This is hard at first, but comes with experience. We do not want to extend our offense. The high post player sets up facing the ball. As mentioned, we will usually place our best all-purpose front line player in this position. He will follow the ball except on one occasion; that being the low post flashing to the ball and the high post going opposite (see Dia. 3-111). The guard opposite the ball is always in reverse pass position but ready to step into the gap for his shot if an opening develops.

High Post Pass — 2-1-2 Zone Offense (Dia. 3-115). On the pass to the high post, the two baseline men will move to get open in their respective areas. O_3 will turn and play the basket while at the same time recognizing if O_4 or O_5 is open for the pass. The guards will flare to the open areas vacated by the zone. If nothing is open on the inside O_3 will bring the ball back out to O_1 or O_2 for the shot, continued movement of the ball, or a resetting of the offense. **The rule again is for the high post player to play the basket, the baseline and out the other side, in that order.**

For rebounding and defensive purposes out of our 2-1-2 offense, we will designate either O_1 or O_2 as the safety. It will then be his responsibility to be the first man back after every shot. Let's say that we have named O_2 as the safety in these explanations. If the shot is executed by O_3, O_5 and O_4 would have obvious rebound responsibilities. O_1 would move to form the middle of the triangle and O_3 would be the half rebounder (Dia. 3-116).

Diagram 3-117 shows the rebounding responsibilities should the close-in shot be taken by either of the baseline men. O_3 would automatically come to the boards and O_1 would move to the middle looking for the long rebound. If one of the baseline players shoots from an area away from the wing, he will become the half rebounder and O_3 and O_1 (always) will form the triangle with the opposite baseline man. If O_4 is the shooter, O_3 will rebound on his side with O_1 moving to the middle (Dia. 3-117). If O_5 is the shooter, O_3 would remain in the middle and O_1 would quickly get to the side of the triangle (Dia. 3-118).

When O_1 is the shooter the rebound triangle is already basically formed by O_5, O_3, and O_4. O_1 would have half rebound and half defense responsibilities. O_2 is again back. Whenever our designated safety is the shooter (O_2 in this case) the other guard switches roles and becomes the safety. The shooter is free then to come down comfortable from his shot and react to a possible rebound.

Pass to Wing — 2-1-2 Zone Offense (X-ing the Post). There are two movements off the pass to the baseline man stepping out to catch the ball. The baseline man is not actually stepping out all the way to the wing, but just far enough to free himself for the pass and a possible shot. The first movement involves another X-ing of the post (Dia. 3-119). The first look is to O_3 stepping to the basket, the second to O_5 stepping across the lane and filling the high post. O_4 can also make the skip pass to O_1 on the weakside if the defense has totally collapsed to the inside and left that option open. The only difference in the rebounding positions already discussed is that if the shot is taken from the strongside and the weakside rebounding is completely open, O_1 must anticipate the shot and get to that rebound position quickly, (Dia. 3-120).

Pass to Wing — 2-1-2 Zone Offense (Guards Exchange).

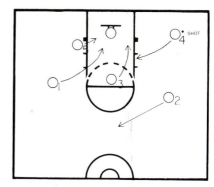

DIA. 3-117

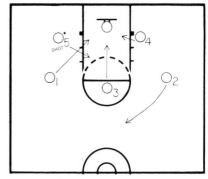

DIA. 3-118

DIA. 3-119

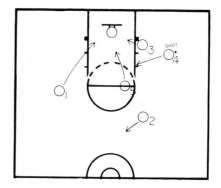

DIA. 3-120

Team Offense 91

Offense VS. Zone Press

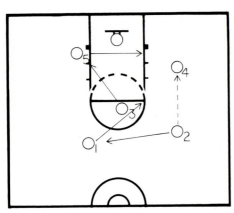

DIA. 3-121

DIA. 3-122

The second movement that we will run off this pass calls for the baseline man (O_5) to flash across the lane looking for the low post pass and a close-in shot (Dia. 3-121). The high post player (O_3) will drop to the low side opposite the ball. The off guard (O_1) will step into the vacated high post area for a possible pass from O_4. O_2 moves away to exchange positions with O_1. If no pass is made O_1 steps out to the strongside guard position and receives the pass back out from O_4. O_4 steps into the high post and we are back to our original set (Dia. 3-122). The ball can come from the high post down to the wing or from the guard to forward pass for these options to be in effect. The rebounding positions have been discussed previously. Remember that we do not have to constantly move our men. Too much movement will cause confusion and will change the placement of our personnel. As long as we are moving the ball through the defense we do not **have** to move our men.

To simplify things in our zone press attack, our players are numbered according to their responsibilities in helping to break the press. The guards are numbered 1 and 2. #1 is our best ball handler and the man to whom we want the ball inbounded on the initial pass. #3 would be our best ball handling forward and is numbered as such because he is the third man to come up to help offset the defensive pressure. The fourth man up (#4) is usually our second best ball handling forward and #5 will, for the most part, be our strongest inside player and best rebounder. These positions, however, are interchangeable according to the type of zone press we are facing. We may want to bring our big man up to catch the ball in the middle and look for the cutters breaking by him and down the sides. We may want to place a quick forward, who is also a good inside player, down near our basket to work against their big man should we break through the press quickly. To change an assignment all we have to do is tell the player his new number. This system also makes it much easier when we are making a substitution against a team that is utilizing the zone press.

When we talk about ball handling versus the press, we are concerned not only with dribbling, but with each player's ability to pass the basketball and their ability to recognize the open man and the open spots on the floor. Poise and confidence are two essential ingredients of the zone press attack. It has been our philosophy that proper preparation will go a long way toward instilling these two ingredients.

One of our principles regarding our zone offense is that the zone presses (half court or full court) are to be considered in the same manner as the half court zone defense. The press merely extends the areas that need to be covered by the defensive men. If the players can grasp that idea — they will surely not lose their poise or show a lack of confidence when faced with a press situation.

In addition to the zone offensive principles that apply against a pressing defense, our players must be aware of three specific rules that are vital in successfully attacking the zone press. Before the guard (#2) takes the ball out of bounds, he is to survey the floor: (1) to look for an opening down the court; and (2) to try and determine the type of zone press that is being set up. The inbounder must be aware of the entire floor and must never predetermine where he is going to make the first pass. We are looking for #1, but are always ready to take advantage of an opening down the floor that will force changes in the defensive alignment. Secondly, the inbounder must be sure to clear the area of the backboard so as to free himself for a pass to any area of the floor. This was previously mentioned in our principles for playing the ball in bounds.

The third rule is quite similar to the first one mentioned above and corresponds with the second idea in our zone offense principles. After every pass, the player who receives the ball must keep his head up and take a look down the court. If there is a player open and the ball can be delivered comfortably the pass should be made. If no one is open down the floor the ball must be reversed or the dribble must be utilized with good judgement. We do not totally discourage our players from dribbling against the zone press. However, the players must be mindful of our third zone offensive principle — drive one defensive man, but then be prepared to pass. The dribble escape can be a valuable tool in defeating the zone press, provided the dribbler has his head up ready to stop and hit the open man and that he is under complete control at all times.

Our philosophy versus any zone pressure is not only to move the ball through the defense, but to attack the basket and score against the press. We want to use the press to our advantage. Because the defensive players have spread themselves the entire length of the floor and because they are aggressively playing the ball we should be able to create 2 on 1 and 3 on 2 situations. Our players understand that if the advantage is not there, they are to pull the ball back out and work for the shot from our set offense.

The three primary zone presses that we are going to face are: the 1-2-2, the 1-3-1, and the 2-2-1. We very seldom see a 2-1-2 press and the 1-2-1-1 is just a variation of the 1-2-2. Our alignment against the press will be the same as in our half court zone offense. If the defense goes with a one-man front, we will attack with a two-man front. If the defense sets with a two-man front, we will attack with basically one man out in front. We say **basically** one man because in manuevering to our 1-3-1 attack, the #2 man will cheat back and will be ready to help #1 if he is in trouble or in need of an outlet. When we are advancing the ball with a two-man front, the guard

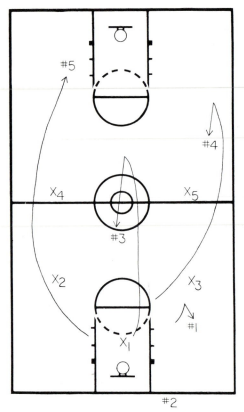

#5

#4

X₄   X₅

#3

X₂   X₃

                #1

X₁

#2

DIA. 3-123

#5

#4

X₄   X₅

#3

X₂   X₃

        #1

X₁

        HERE   NOT HERE   #1

#2

DIA. 3-124

without the ball will always be in reverse pass position. He will be ready, however, to move quickly once the ball has been passed ahead.

Versus the One Man Front

Diagram 3-123 shows the initial offensive and defensive alignments in our zone press attack versus a one man front. Remember that #2 must take a look down the court even before he steps out of bounds. #5, #4, and #3 are to turn and sprint down the court as soon as the ball is through the net. #3 and then possibly #4 will come back to the ball, but their first responsibility is to go long. If X_4 and X_5 do not honor these cuts to the basket, then #2 is prepared to throw the baseball pass to the open man. He must clear the backboard to facilitate this type of pass. We are again putting pressure on the basket to help break down the defensive pressure. #1 will start toward our offensive end and come back to meet the inbounds pass from #2. He should receive the ball in as advanced position as the defense will allow, without setting himself up for a quick trap between X_1 and X_3. We want our #1 man to start the press attack away from the sideline and toward the middle of the floor (Dia. 3-124). If we let the defense force us into the corner or sidelines area, we are playing into their hands. Remember, when #1 catches the ball, his first action is to turn and look down the court. He does not put the ball on the floor.

After inbounding the ball #2 will step into the backcourt away from his pass. He must hold in the middle of the floor for a brief instant to be ready for a possible return pass from #1. If X_1 and X_3 spring a quick trap, we do not want #2 moving away from the ball unaware of what is developing. If the pass is not made #2 will continue away from the ball and set himself in reverse pass position with about fifteen foot spacing in relation to the ball. His vision will be on #1 and he will be able to react quickly to whatever situation develops. We are now in our basic 2-1-2 alignment (Dia 3-125). #5 is to stay long so that the defense is forced to cover the entire length of the floor, but he can come up if needed.

2-1-2 Press Attack — Option #1 (Dia. 3-126). The first look against this type of defense is the #3 man working the middle. If the third man receives the pass from either #1 or #2 he immediately turns and looks for #4 or #5 downcourt. #4 will try to break behind the defense while #5 will go to the basket or come back to the ball depending on the open area. #3 is free to put the ball on the floor but he must use good judgement in doing so. In most instances he will look to #1 and #2 breaking by on their respective sides. The weakside is the area that is usually most vulnerable. Therefore, if the pass came from #1, #2 is the most likely to be open and vice-versa. All players must be careful to protect the ball against defensive men running them down from behind.

2-1-2 Press Attack — Option #2 (Dia. 3-127). The second option that is available is the pass from #1 to #4 stepping up on the sideline. When this pass is completed, #3 would make a diagonal cut toward #4 and in the direction of the basket. #5 is still playing the basket and #2 would hustle to the middle of the floor and look for the pass from #4. #1 would go away from his pass and set up in reverse pass position in relation to the #4 man. If the press is still on, we are back to our basic 2-1-2 set. #4 and #1 are playing the front, #2 is working the middle and #3 and #5 are on the wings or baseline. This option illustrates how our numbering system works. The third man was unable to receive the pass from #1 or #2 so the fourth man flashes up to help. He must go to the open spot in that sideline area or work to get open for the pass from #1. We can also vary this action by #1 executing the give and go with #4. If #1 does not receive the return pass, he fills the middle of the floor and #2 aligns himself in reverse pass position.

2-1-2 Press Attack — Option #3 (Dia. 3-128). The third option is simply a variation of the third man out-fourth man in action. The ball is reversed to #2 and the pass to the middle is still covered. #3 would then break to the sideline area and #4 would follow and fill his spot in the middle. #2 is looking for #3 to crack a seam in the defense and #4 flashing into the center of the floor. Diagram 3-128 shows our movement when the pass is made to #4. #5 plays the basket while #3 continues into the half court area and reads the situation. On the pass to #4, #1 immediately breaks down the sideline and looks for the pass out on the weakside.

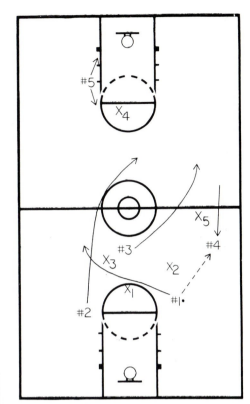

DIA. 3-127

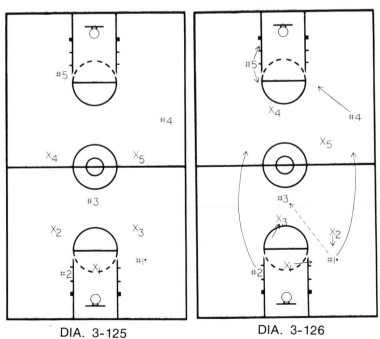

DIA. 3-125   DIA. 3-126

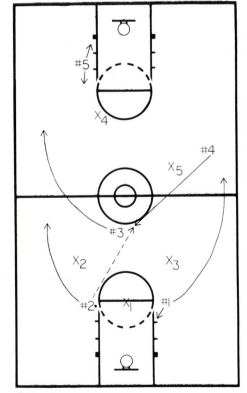

DIA. 3-128

Team Offense 95

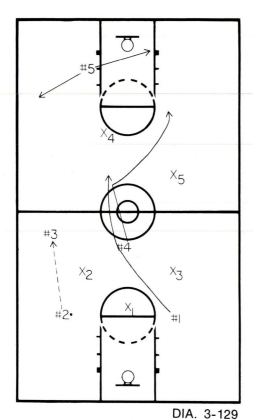

DIA. 3-129

Option #3 cont. (Dia. 3-129). When the pass is made from #2 to #3 breaking to the sideline, #3 should be completely under control but ready to dribble the ball into the forecourt if the opening develops. There should be only one man to drive around in this situation. If #3 elects to look for the pass, #4 will stay in the middle for an instant and then fill the opposite sideline. #3 would look for the quick pass into the middle but should never force this pass. The middle will be somewhat congested especially with the front men in the press running from behind. After #4 clears the middle our #1 man will step in and work to get open. #5 will read the action. If #3 brings the ball hard on the dribble, #5 will step away to the opposite lane. This will allow #3 to bring the ball on the strongside and for #4 to fill the middle lane. If #3 is looking to pass the ball, #5 can step up and to the wing to make himself available. #2 would trail the play and assume safety responsibilities.

2-1-2 Press Attack — Option #4 (Dia. 3-130). The #5 man will only come up when it is absolutely necessary or if we have called for this action from the bench. We will call for the #5 man if he is being guarded by a big, relatively immobile player or if we are having trouble getting the #3 man or #4 man open. This should not be the case. When the #5 man comes to the ball he will always work to get open in the middle of the floor if at all possible. As soon as #5 catches the ball he turns and looks for #3 and #4 sprinting down the sidelines. #1 and #2 will break right behind the forwards on their respective sides of the floor. #5 will pass to any of these four cutters.

Versus the Two Man Front

Diagram 3-131 illustrates our alignment in taking the ball out

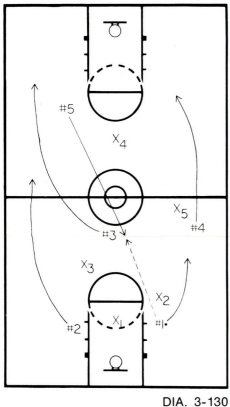

DIA. 3-130

96 Team Offense

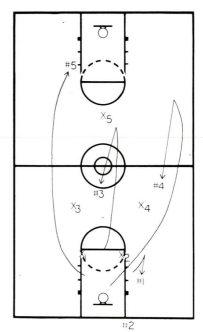

DIA. 3-131

of bounds versus the 2-2-1 press or any of its variations. This alignment is to be used when the defense is letting us make the inbounds pass. If there is pressure on the inbounds pass and help is necessary, we will bring the third man up to form a tandem on the free throw line with #1. The initial responsibilities after the basket has been made are basically the same as we have shown earlier. The fifth man is to break out of the pack and go long. The third and fourth man do the same, but are aware of the situation and are ready to come back to the ball. The #4 man will come back farther than he did in our previous zone press attack. He will basically be in the same line with #3. The #1 and #2 men have the same responsibilities, except that the #1 man will attempt to catch the ball even more in the center of the floor.

1-3-1 Press Attack. There are two ways that we can shift to our 1-3-1 attack after the ball has been inbounded. In the first movement, #2 will simply move away from his pass to become the wing in the 1-3-1 (Dia. 3-132). Remember, he will cheat back somewhat to provide an outlet if trouble develops. #1 is now the point man and he attacks the press looking for the open man.

In the second movement (Dia. 3-133) #2 will step in bounds and receive the quick return pass from the #1 man. #3 and #4 will rotate away from the side that #1 has established himself and #1 will assume the vacated wing position. Now he will be cheating back and #2 will be attacking the press from the point position. #2 should have his head up, seeing the whole floor. He should be prepared to pass to #3 or #4 as they break into their new areas.

1-3-1 Press Attack — Option #1 (Dia. 3-134). As in our half

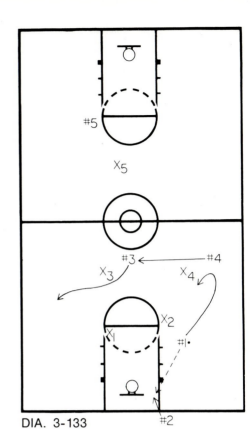

DIA. 3-133

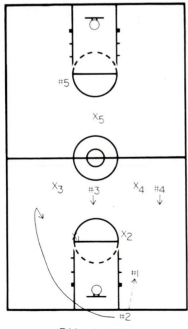

DIA. 3-132

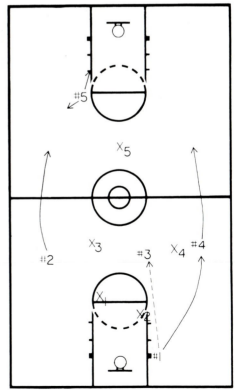

DIA. 3-134

Team Offense 97

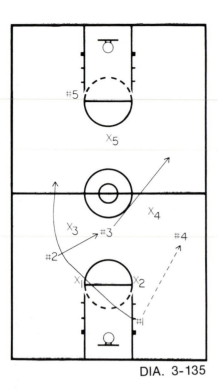

DIA. 3-135

Final Points on the Zone Press Attack

court offensive attack, the point man in our 1-3-1 has three primary targets—the two wings and the man in the middle. The #5 man is also a potential target if the defense does not properly cover in our offensive end of the floor. When the pass is made to the middle man both wings will immediately sprint for the basket looking for the possible pass from #3. The point man will flare to his side of the floor with the opposite guard (#2 in this case) ready to come back to help if needed. #5 will be ready to play the basket depending upon the situation. If #4 receives the pass and brings the ball #5 must be ready to step to the basket. If #2 brings the ball #5 can step out to the wing or clear to the other side. If the #3 man brings the ball up the middle the lanes should be formed by the #5 man and the #4 man. #2 would become the trailer and #1 the safety.

1-3-1 Press Attack — Option #2 (Dia. 3-135). On the pass to either wing the middle man will make a diagonal cut to the ball side, the opposite wing will fill the middle, and the point man will go away from his pass. The movement in attacking the basket is relatively the same that has been discussed. The ever present key is our ability to read the situation. If the pass is made from #4 into #2 filling the middle, #2 should be aware of #1 cutting down the weakside of the defense. A pass out from this position is usually very effective (Dia. 3-136).

In developing our zone press attack we start by running five offensive men against no defense. We teach the movements in a five on none situation and then repeat the options in the same situation until all players are completely familiar and comfortable with the offense. Along with the repetition we also stress concentration on the part of our players. There is a tendency for players to lack concentration when they are working without any defense. They are able to go through the motions because there is no defensive pressure to force a mistake or a steal.

When the players have a thorough knowledge of the movements required against the different zone presses and of the passing options that will be available, we will add a token defense. The token defense will help our players to recognize the type of defense they are facing and will give them an idea of why the cuts we are using will free them against a particular zone press. Repetition against a token defense will enable the players to realize the weaknesses in the zone presses and thus enhance their confidence and poise when facing full court pressure.

Most all of our work on the zone press attack is done full court. The 2 on 1 and 3 on 2 situations that we hope to create are practiced in a half court situation but are actually fast break drills. The only other exception would be on the inbounds pass. If we are expecting to face extreme pressure, or if we have had trouble inbounding the ball, we will work on this aspect in a breakdown drill. What we are building for, however, is the five on five competitive situation. When we are working on our press attack, whether we are facing a defense or not, the offense will continue the entire length of the court. If no advantage is gained in attacking the basket and we do not produce an opening during the transition, we will blow the whistle and head back the other way. However, if a scoring opportunity presents itself we want to take the ball to the basket. Play will continue until the defense gains possession of the ball on a rebound or a turnover. This is important for two reasons. First of all, we want our players to learn to attack the basket at the end of a successful zone press attack. Good judgement is a must but it is our philosophy to score against the press if the proper opportunity presents itself. Secondly, we want our players prepared to go to the boards when a shot is executed at the end of a zone press attack or fast break opportunity. We have seen too many teams stand and watch because they were not prepared to go to the offensive boards. Many times we will have three lanes filled, a trailer, and a safety so we have natural rebounding positions.

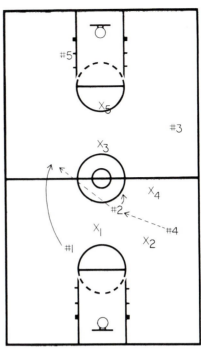

DIA. 3-136

Team Offensive Drills

Guard to Forward Timing Drill (Dia. 3-137)
Objective: To develop the timing between the guard and the forward that is necessary to successfully initiate our offense.

Organization: We divide the squad into six groups of two players each. The groups are divided so that each contains one guard and one frontline player. The guards bring the ball across half court and make the guard to forward pass as shown in the diagram. We will begin with no defense and with the guard executing the give and go cut. The forward has the option of dropping his back foot and driving to the basket or making the front turn to play the basket and look for the cutter. If the forward does not make the return pass to the guard, he can either dribble to the free throw line for the jump shot or cross over and execute the dribble drive to the basket. The guard will move to the corner position unless we are working on posting the guards. We will add the defense to this drill when the players have developed the proper timing. We will also rotate the players so that everyone becomes familiar with each other. After awhile we will add a post player and work on the guard to forward pass and guard to post pass coming into our offense. The post player has the same responsibilities as the forward except he will look for the backdoor play upon receiving the pass.

Points of Emphasis:

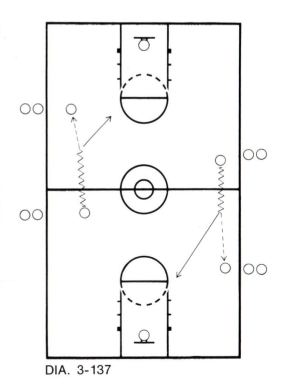

DIA. 3-137

GUARD	FORWARD
1. Do not pick up your dribble until you are ready	1. Maintain spacing.
	2. Look for the off hand of the

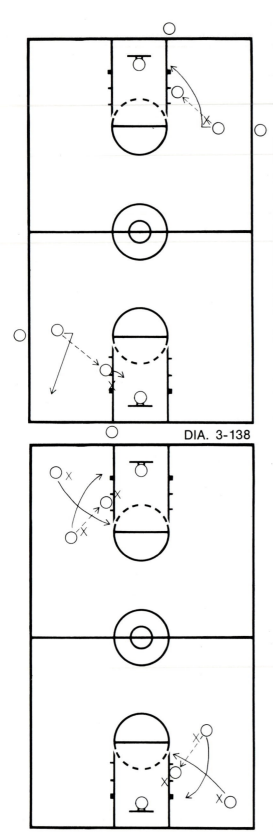

DIA. 3-138

DIA. 3-139

to pass.

2. Make the pass away from the defense.
3. Cut hard to the basket.
4. Hit the forward as soon as he comes open.

guard to go to the ball. This will tip you off that the guard is ready to make the pass.

3. Seal off your defender by stepping with the inside foot.
4. Make the proper pivot to execute the drive (drop step) or play the basket (front turn).
5. Both players have a responsibility to time the play properly.

Post Pass Offensive Drill (Dia. 3-138)

Objective: To develop in our players the ability to get to the basket or get open for the outside shot after executing the pass into the post. Also to work on the individual moves of the post player upon receiving the post pass.

Organization: The drill starts with an offensive wing player at the diagonal and a post player established directly between the diagonal and the basket. These are two of the positions that will be established as we form the triangle in our offset. We will place a defensive player on the post or on the wing player depending on which of the above objectives we are working on at the time. With the defender on the wing, the post player will look to hit the cutter when he's open and then will establish position for the rebound. If the shot is attempted from out on the floor, we want the post man to reverse out and get to the other side of the basket. If the shot is attempted off the drive, the post man must react away from the driver. With the defensive man assigned to the post, the player executing the penetrating pass will still work to get open for the return pass. The post player is taught to turn the ball in and read the defensive pressure. This drill naturally evolves into a two on two situation and then a three on three Split the Post Drill which we will diagram and explain shortly.

Points of Emphasis:

DIAGONAL

1. Halo Pass
2. Cut hard to the basket.
3. Jab step and then make the straight cut. Do not make three and four fakes because the timing is not there.
4. Cut on the cylinder.

POST PLAYER

1. Release to catch the pass.
2. Keep the ball up and maintain a position of strength.
3. Make an accurate and effective pass.
4. Get inside position for the rebound.
5. Turn the ball in and read the defense when executing your individual moves.

Triangle Split Drill (Dia. 3-139)

Objective: To develop in the players the ability to cut effectively off the post after the post pass is executed from the wing.

Organization: The players are divided into two groups of six at each end of the floor. The offensive players form the offset triangle and execute the post pass from the wing position. The wing and corner players split the post and the post man looks for the open man or his own shot. We generally run this drill with a defense although it can also be effective as a dummy drill. After three possessions the offense and defense reverse roles.

Points of Emphasis:

1. Halo Pass.
2. The cutters must go hard.
3. Straight cuts.
4. The post player turns the ball in immediately upon receiving the pass or after the cutters have gone by.

He does not turn it in while the split is being executed.
5. The cutters must clear the post to avoid congestion.

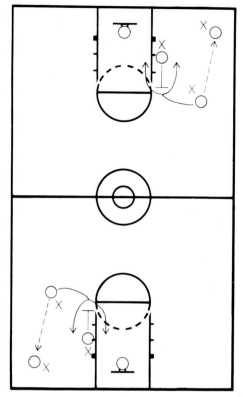

Corner Pass Drill (Dia. 3-140)

Objective: To concentrate on the cutting action required when the corner pass is executed.

Organization: Squad is again divided equally at each end of the floor and the offensive group forms the triangle as shown. The corner pass is executed and the wing player makes the appropriate cut with the post man stepping up the lane for the screen. The corner player plays the basket and looks for the cutter breaking off the screen. The post player will make a tight step toward the ball for a possible shot after the initial cut is made. The groups will reverse roles after three possessions. On the next time around the wing player and the corner player will exchange positions. This rotation will continue so that the players are required to play each of the positions. The frontline players will also rotate in the post.

Points of Emphasis:

WING	POST
1. Take your man to the top of the screen. Learn to use the screen.	1. Move quickly up the lane to set the screen.
2. Cut either side. Read the defense.	2. Set the screen parallel to the baseline just outside the lane and just below the free throw line.
3. If the defender drops behind the screen look for the shot on top.	3. Do not move on the screen.
	4. Step in tight for the jump shot after the cutter clears you.

DIA. 3-140

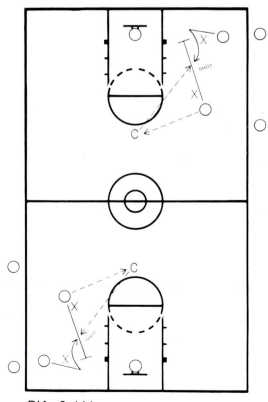

Point Pass Drill (Dia. 3-141)

Objective: To concentrate on the screening action and the shot off the screen that takes place in the point pass series.

Organization: The players align themselves at the wing and corner positions with a manager or coach at the point. The drill can be executed with or without a defense. The point pass is made from the wing position and the player making the pass immediately moves to set a vertical screen for the player coming out of the corner. The players exchange positions each time if only two players are involved in the drill. If more than two players are involved the players move from offense to defense or to the end of the opposite line.

DIA. 3-141

Team Offense 101

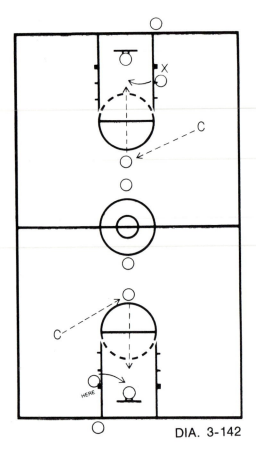

WING

1. Set the screen at the proper angle.
2. Headhunt on the defensive player.
3. Forward rebounds after setting screen. Guard drops back for defensive purposes.

CORNER PLAYER

1. Take your man into the basket.
2. Rub shoulders with the screener.
3. Plant the inside foot and come in low and hard for the shot.
4. Square up completely for the shot.

Point Pass - Post Rolls (Dia. 3-142)

Objective: To concentate on the actions of the guard and the post player after the point pass is executed.

Organization: A coach or manager makes the pass to the point player from the wing. The point player immediately looks for his shot. The post player pins his man and rolls into the middle to the basket. These are two man drills that are very beneficial as breakdown drills before or after practice. This particular drill is more effective with a defensive player on the post.

Points of Emphasis:

GUARD

1. Look first for your shot. Instinct will tell you if the post player is open and if the pass should be made.
2. Do not force the pass.

POST

1. Pin the defender on your hip.
2. Roll to the basket with timing.
3. Give the point player a good target.
4. Take the ball to the basket strong.

Two Man Play (Dia. 3-143)

Objective: To concentrate on the actions of the weakside forward and the guard in the execution of the two man play.

Organization: A coach or manager is positioned at the wing with the ball. The point player and the weakside forward are in their normal offset positions. The point pass is made and the forward comes directly up the lane to execute the two man play with the guard. The forward can also be given the option of popping out to the wing for the quick jump shot. This drill is effective with or without a defense.

Points of Emphasis:

GUARD

1. Learn to use the screen.
2. Make a sharp cut without the ball and rub shoulders with the screener when utilizing the dribble.
3. Stop on top of the screen for the jump shot or continue all the way to the basket.
4. Learn to use the head and shoulder fake and drive hard to the basket.

FORWARD

1. Set the screen exactly where the free throw line and the free throw lane intersect.
2. Come set for the screen.
3. Learn to face up to the basket with the ball if no handoff is made.

DIA. 3-142

DIA. 3-143

Four Man Drill (Dia. 3-144)

Objective: To concentrate on the moves of the four man in coming across to catch the ball in the four man series. Similar to the four man shots we work on in the shooting drills.

Organization: This is basically an individual breakdown drill that should be run before or after practice. A post player and a post defender can be added to execute the roll to the basket on the four man pass. A coach is at the wing position with the ball and a frontline player sets up at the weakside forward ready to come across for the four man play. We start the players working without a defense to concentrate on the technique and footwork involved in coming across and making a play. Later on we will add the defense.

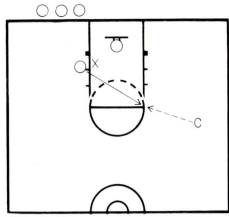

DIA. 3-144

Points of Emphasis:
1. Plant the inside foot to seal off the defender. Come in low and hard.
2. Read the defense coming across.
3. Three options.
   a. front turn-shot
   b. drop step-drive
   c. front turn-crossover.
4. Look to shoot the basket-ball

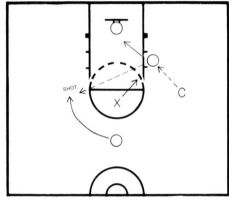

DIA. 3-145

Post Pass-Flare Drill (Dia. 3-145)

Objective: To work with the guards on executing the flare properly and with the post players on making an accurate pass with timing.

Organization: Two guards and a post player are all that are needed to run this drill. More guards can be added if available. With three players involved a coach or manager will execute the pass into the post. The defensive guard will drop to help in the middle. The point player will flare to the wing position away from the post for the possible pass and shot. The guards take a set number of shots and then reverse roles. The defender should make every effort to recover to pressure the shot after helping in the middle.

Points of Emphasis:

GUARD	POST
1. Flare to the free throw line extended.	1. Keep the ball up.
2. Plant the inside foot and square up for the shot.	2. When you feel pressure from the sagging guard, you should make the flare pass. Read the defense.
3. Extend the area of recovery for the defender but do not get too wide.	3. Make an overhead pass with the arms extended.
	4. Make the pass firm and accurate.
	5. Step to the basket for a possible return pass.

Five On Five Situations

After a certain period of time much of our team offensive work will be accomplished in dummy drills (no defense) or five on five situations. We will still utilize the breakdown drills during the regular practice time but they will be emphasized primarily before and after practice. In our initial dummy work, we will emphasize getting into the offset from our basic two-three alignment. We will work on forming the triangle and the weakside positions through the cutting action we described in this chapter. Once the players have developed a feel for coming in and getting into the offset, we will begin to apply what we have been covering in the breakdown drills. We will break the squad into two groups and have them run through the offense at each end without a defense. We will call out the passes to be made and make corrections when necessary. The players will also be developing the ability to reset the offense when a particular option does not produce a shot. After work on the dummy phase of our offense, we add the defense and execute the offense concentrating on one particular series at a time. In other words, we will work in a half court five on five situation but will designate the series that we want to run. These are further extentions of the breakdown drills that will lead up to the successful execution of our offense. When the players learn the offense sufficiently, we will progress to a live five on five situation.

Another phase of our offensive development is teaching the players to get into the offset from the fast break. We want the players to learn to get to the offset as quickly as possible once a fast break attempt is thwarted. We will simply run the break and instruct the players to get into the offset if we are unable to generate a good scoring opportunity at the end of the fast break.

Our zone offense and zone press attack are developed exclusively in the five man dummy or five on five situations. We teach and work on each in a dummy situation and then add the defense when the players learn their responsibilities. We will then work against the various zone defenses (half court and full court) to perfect our zone attack. The one variation we will utilize in preparing to face zone pressure is to add a sixth and sometimes seventh defensive player. This follows our philosophy of developing practice situations that are more difficult than what we will face under game conditions.

There is one final teaching method we will utilize to develop our half court offenses. All of the breakdown drills and five on five situations are leading up to controlled and full scale scrimmaging. Before that point, we will have the players run the offense for extended periods of time against a defense without shooting the basketball. We refer to this as "turning" the offense or "turning" the ball. The players learn through repetition. This type of continuous repetition will help the players to act instinctively in executing the offense. It will also aid the players in learning to handle the basketball and execute the offense without making mistakes or forcing the action. We will employ this teaching method in developing both our man to man and zone offenses.

The Fast Break 4

Fast Break Philosophy

Fast break basketball is exciting basketball. It is fun for the players and enjoyable from a spectator's standpoint. We have made good use of the fast break here at Missouri and will continue to incorporate the running game into our offensive philosophy and thinking. This attitude is in keeping with our desire to teach aggressive basketball.

We don't want our players to limit their aggressiveness to a particular aspect of the game. We want them to rebound aggressively, play aggressive defense and aggressively attack the basket. An emphasis on fast break basketball will allow the players to capitalize on their ability to play aggressively at both ends of the floor. An aggressive, hustling defense will develop the opportunities that will lead to fast break advantages. Likewise, the fast break scoring opportunities will help to motivate the players toward better concentration and effort with regard to their individual and team defense.

Our fast break philosophy begins with our mental and physical approach to the running game. Mentally, the players and coaches must be completely sold on fast breaking basketball. Additionally, the players must have a complete understanding of what we are trying to accomplish in generating fast break opportunities. We are teaching an aggressive fast break attack and are always looking for the quickest way to advance the basketball into our scoring area. However, the players must always be under control and must be able to recognize if we are in an advantageous situation or if the defense has the advantage. Forced passes and low percentage shots are mental errors that can quickly lead to a decrease in the success of a fast break offense. It will be important for everyone to realize the difference between race-horse basketball and controlled fast break basketball. Finally, it must be understood by coaches and players alike that fast break basketball, due to the increased tempo of play, will create more chances for error. Patience will be of extreme importance in teaching the fundamentals and the proper execution of the fast break. The number of turnovers can be minimized, however, and that leads us to our physical approach to the fast break.

Keeping in mind that the chances for turnovers are going to be greater, we must always strive for perfection, especially with regard to the fundamentals. Our players' ability to handle the basketball while on the move will be one of the main factors in determining how successful we will be in utilizing the fast break. Constant drilling, with and without defensive pressure, will be necessary to properly develop these fundamental ball handling abilities. Physical conditioning will also be of the utmost importance in teaching the running game. We have already discussed the value we place on conditioning in our basic basketball philosophy. Suffice it to say that the conditioning and endurance of the players will be even more important in a running style of play. We have found this to be expecially true in the latter stages of each half. It has been said before that all else being equal, the better-conditioned team will win.

Physical aggressiveness and quick reactions are two important ingredients in the makeup of a fast breaking team. The aggressiveness will serve to force the action at the defensive end and will create opportunities when possession of the ball is gained. As soon as the ball does change hands, the fast breaking unit must react quickly in initiating the break. On a rebounded shot the quickness of the outlet pass will have much to do with determining the success of that particular fast break. At the same time, however, the players other than the rebounder must react quickly to make available the proper outlet man and to fill the lanes to start the break. This conversion is even more important if the ball changes hands as the result of a steal or a loose ball situation with the ball remaining in play. Coach Knight at Indiana has been quoted in recent years that, in his estimation, conversion (from defense to offense and vice-versa) is more important that either offense or defense. This points up the fact that basketball is a fast moving game in which reaction time and a player's ability to size up situations quickly are vitally important. Whether or not conversion is that important to your philosophy it is something that certainly should not be overlooked. Quick conversion from defense to a fast break attack is constantly stressed in our drill situations.

In our drills and teaching situations we emphasize the concept of "controlled speed" in running the fast break. We see many players who like to play the fast break, wide-open type of game. They feel that their speed and quickness are well suited to this style of play. That same speed and quickness can be a detriment if the player cannot control his body or the basketball while on the move. This becomes especially true at the offensive end of the fast break where a player's ability to deliver the basketball to the open man is a very valuable characteristic.

We do not run a patterned or organized fast break when taking the ball out of bounds after a made shot. Our players are taught to run certain lanes and the inbounder should look up the floor even before he steps out of bounds with the ball. If the opposing team has not made the conversion from offense to defense, we will hit the open man and generate a fast break opportunity. There must be a definite advantage and the chance for interception on the long pass must be at an absolute minimum. When inbounding to the short receiver we will still push the ball up the floor as quickly as possible. If the defense or a particular defensive player is slow getting back, we will again try to take advantage of the situation that has been presented. Many times a team will have problems in converting quickly or possibly will have one or two players who are negligent in getting back and lack concentration at the defensive end. This should be noted in the scouting report and the team should be prepared to take advantage of these weaknesses. A mobile, hustling center can especially profit from the conversion and defensive lapses of his opponent. Centers can sometimes get bogged down in heavy traffic under the basket area. These big men are running the entire game from baseline to baseline. More specifically, some big men are notoriously ineffective at pushing themselves during the transition from offense to defense. Recognition of this ineffectiveness can result in two or three easy baskets a game and an increased pressure on the opponent.

The Beginning of the Break

The fast break from a missed shot begins with a rebound and a quick outlet pass or a dribble outlet. Ideally, we will have formed a rebound triangle with our front line players with the two guards positioned so that they can receive a quick outlet from whichever side the ball is rebounded. This is the perfect set-up from which we can execute our fast break offense. This is not always attainable, however, because of the particular floor balance or positioning that the offense is in at the time of the shot. The first responsibility for each player is to establish inside position for the rebound. A guard who is defending his man in the corner cannot leave that man to position himself for our fast break offense. An understanding of our break organization will help to teach our players how to start the fast break from different positions on the floor. The players must be able to react to the situation on the move. There will be certain responsibilities so the task is not that difficult. The ability to anticipate will be of great importance.

The players are coached to follow the flight of the ball and anticipate its direction upon rebounding. To accomplish this the players must understand and bear in mind the rebound percentages involved in a missed shot. Approximately 70% of the shots attempted from one side of the floor, with a medium or high arc, will rebound to the opposite side of the floor. Most shots attempted today employ a medium or high arc. A line drive shot will rebound toward the middle or come back toward the shooter depending on the touch applied. A shot from the center of the floor can bounce to either side or come back toward the shooter depending on the touch applied and which side of the rim the ball hits first. The ability to anticipate the path of the rebound will come with experience and an understanding of the above percentages. This anticipation will be important for the actual rebounder and for those who will be out of position for the rebound. The non-rebounders cannot vacate their positions early, but they can begin to cheat in preparation for the start of the fast break. As the ball comes off the rim and/or backboard the non-rebounders should recognize instinctively our chances for possession. If a teammate is going up for the ball and seems to be assured of gaining possession the other four players can immediately begin to fill spots for the break. The rebound triangle or inside players will be required, for the most part, to hold position until this happens. The guards can usually leave earlier. They should especially recognize the situation and cheat as much as possible toward their fast break positions. They are responsible for any long rebounds but the "touch" on the shot can usually indicate whether or not a long rebound is a possibility. Additionally, at least one of the guards will have limited responsibility for boxing out because his man will be required to be the first man back. This will ideally be our best ball handler and passer, the man we would like to have handle the ball the majority of the time. He will have some freedom in getting to the outlet areas and he should take advantage of this freedom by establishing himself in the best position possible to expedite the fast break. We accomplish this by having our guard move to the top of the key as soon as his man takes himself out of rebound position. From here he can survey the entire rebound area and eight of the nine other players. He also must be very aware of the man behind him so as to avoid a possible interception or charging foul upon initiating the fast break. This guard now occupies one of our two primary outlet areas (Dia. 4-1) and is in a position to fill the other area depending upon the direction of the rebound and the position of our other guard.

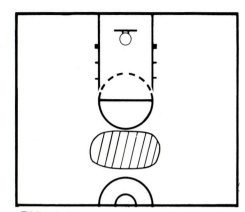

DIA. 4-1

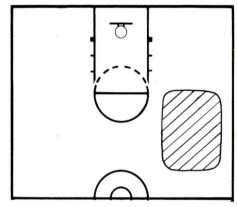

DIA. 4-2

The second outlet area is shown in Diagram 4-2. It starts just above the free throw line extended on the side the ball is rebounded and can extend almost to half court in certain situations. The farther we can safely make the initial pass, the better chance we will have in securing a fast break advantage. The side outlet area can be filled by either guard. As mentioned, our ball handling guard must be aware of not only the direction of the rebound but the floor position of our other guard. If the ball is rebounded opposite our second guard (Dia. 4-3) the ball handling guard (G_1) breaks quickly to fill the side outlet. The second guard (G_2) moves to the top of the key and looks for the outlet to the middle of the floor. If the ball is rebounded toward the side of our second guard (Dia. 4-4) he is responsible for the side outlet area and G_1 remains in the middle. If G_2 is caught in traffic or for some reason can't make it to the outlet area, G_1 hunts an open area. At times the guard may be under the basket with a forward out on the floor. When this happens the forward can fill the outlet and look for the guard or bring the ball himself. We like all of our players to have the ability and the confidence to bring the ball the length of the floor. This is not to say that a front line player should handle the ball when a guard is available. Nor should they force a break that is not there. Possession is much more important than forcing the action. The point is, we do not want to lose a fast break opportunity because of a player's inability to put the ball on the floor or handle the basketball on the move. There is no excuse for that at this level.

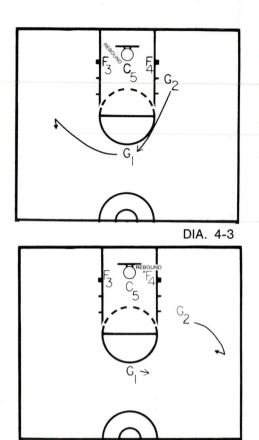

DIA. 4-3

DIA. 4-4

The outlet areas are flexible to a certain extent. The key is for the guard to find the open area and for the rebounder to choose an open passing lane to facilitate an uninterrupted outlet pass. The outlet areas serve as a guide so the rebounders know where to look for the breaking guards. We allow our guards to cheat toward the offensive end as far as possible but they must be aware of intercepters and they must be prepared to come back to meet the ball. Many fast break mistakes are made with the receiver running away from the ball when there is a defensive player playing for the interception or waiting to draw a charge. In this situation the guards must come back to meet the ball and then go with it. We definitely want to take advantage of the opportunity to hit the guards on the fly but the circumstances must be exactly right for this type of pass. The man making the outlet certainly has some responsibilities in this regard. Both the outlet men and the rebounder should be reading the defense but the rebounder is facing up the floor and has a better view of the defensive transition taking place. He can help the guard by the type of pass he throws, the placement of that pass or by some type of eye communication. So we do not jump ahead of ourseves, we will discuss these ideas shortly. Right now we will continue to concentrate on the actions and responsibilities of the outlet men.

We have already mentioned that the guards, in establishing themselves in the most advantageous outlet position, must be extremely conscious of the position of the defense. We don't mention this to be unnecessarily repetitive, but because it is so important and so often the reason for careless mistakes. This type of error can cost you a possible fast break basket and gives your opponent another opportunity to score. A four point deficit can be the result. Mentally, our guards must understand and put into practice this concept of awareness. There are some physical principles we teach that are based on the need for court awareness and which we feel are very helpful toward realizing that goal and minimizing costly errors.

We teach our players moving to the outlet areas to always be turned toward the basketball, to be on their toes ready to change direction, to accelerate or decelerate quickly and to keep their hands up ready to catch the basketball. The hands up and out also serves as a means of identification and a target for the man making the outlet pass. We call this "floating", and the emphasis we place on it has had a very sound effect on the success of our fast break and the rate of our turnovers. Floating is something that most players do instinctively, but not without mistakes. It is not something we invented, but merely something we named, defined and placed an emphasis on in initiating our fast break. In essense, we are again stressing the control factor. We want a controlled fast break, we want a controlled outlet pass, and we want our guards to be under control when they receive the ball for a potential fast break opportunity.

In initiating the fast break the guards must be mindful of numerous responsibilities. They must make themselves readily available to the man making the outlet pass. They must be reading the defensive and offensive situation before and after receiving the pass. After receiving the pass the guards must be able to move quickly into the execution of the fast break. Before all of this takes place at least one of the guards will have some boxing out responsibilities. While most of these actions are instinctive and will become second nature through constant drilling and playing experience, we feel the concept of floating helps the player place an equal emphasis on each area. This is important and extremely hard to do without using the floating technique. For instance, an outlet man can concentrate on making himself available to the rebounder and totally neglect the positions of the defense and the lanes being filled by his teammates.

The first principle involved in the floating technique states that a player should never turn his back to the basketball in moving to an outlet area. The outlet pass can be made at any time; it does not have to be made directly into the outlet area. If the rebounder is ready to make the outlet, the guard is in an open area and there is an open passing lane, there is no reason why the pass cannot be made. The break will be that much quicker if the guard is floating properly. The second principle states that the player should move to the outlet area as quickly as possible with both hands up and out—ready to catch the basketball. The hands must go up when the rebounder gains possession. This will not only help the guard to catch the ball but will enable the rebounder to quickly identify the outlet man. The third principle is that the outlet man is always on his toes whether he is moving into position or if he is actually floating in the outlet area. In this way the player is ready to move quickly in either direction. He can come back for the pass or head up court if there is a lane open with no defensive interference.

We teach the players exactly how we want them to accomplish these principles from the various positions on the floor. The ball handling guard has the easiest responsibility and this is the way it should be. He is already in an outlet area and has minimal responsibilities for boxing out. The guard at the key area should anticipate where the ball will come off and shade that side of the floor. This will be important in three ways: (1) he will be shading the side of the rebound in case it comes off long; (2) if the rebound is opposite the second guard he is closer to the side outlet; (3) even if his responsibilities remain in the middle he should shade that side to make himself available to the rebounder. As the ball is shot our primary ball handler must make sure his man is not a threat on the offensive boards. He then moves to the key area and shades a particular side of the floor as he anticipates a rebound in that direction. The player should be ready to react in case of a long rebound and he should check the rebound positions of his teammates,

FIG. 4-1

FIG. 4-2

especially the opposite guard. Lets imagine that the ball comes off to the right side and that the opposite guard is positioned on that side of the floor. The second guard must move quickly to the side outlet area. As the ball comes off the rim the middle man begins floating in the center of the floor. He should open his body almost parallel to the sideline and take a quick look to note the position of the defense. He then gets up on his toes and actually bounds into what he has determined to be an open area. The point man can proceed as far upcourt as the defense will allow or he can meet the pass in the key area and continue the fast break from there. Figure 4-1 shows the exact floating technique of the guard as he positions himself in the middle area looking for the quick outlet to start the fast break. There is a little more movement required for the primary ball handler to establish himself at the side outlet. This becomes necessary if the ball has rebounded to the left with his teammate still positioned on the right side of the floor. The guard should take a quick look up the floor as he sprints to the sideline. Other than the quick look up the floor, he is looking at the rebounder while utilizing his peripheral vision to size up the floor situation. His hands go up as soon as the rebounder grasps the ball. As the guard enters the outlet area, he plants his outside foot and turns into the court (Fig. 4-2), again opening his body almost parallel to the sideline. His vision and awareness will now tell him whether he can float upcourt, or whether he needs to meet the ball at this point because of defensive pressure. It is now up to the guard to read the situation, especially the defense, and seize the opportunity for the fast break. This technique, though, will allow him to do all of this most effectively. If the guard were to concentrate primarily on making himself available for the outlet he could miss the opportunity to catch the ball further up the floor or he could be totally unaware of a defensive man moving up for the interception. Likewise, if the outlet man was concerned only with the defenders or with receiving the outlet further up the floor it would be difficult for the rebounder to make an accurate outlet pass. There must be an equal emphasis on all elements in the initiation of the fast break. As soon as there is a breakdown in the defensive transition the guard can take advantage because he is aware of all of the possibilities.

The second guard's technique for moving to the side or middle outlet area is basically the same as we have described. He must never turn his back on the ball and must really hustle to make himself available as an outlet man. There are two additional areas of concern in regard to the guards' responsibilities on the outlet. If the second guard is in the middle of the floor on the rebound there should be no indecision as to which outlet area to cover. The ball handling guard should recognize his position and will always take the side outlet with the second guard coming up the middle. The only exception to this would be if a front line player is near the side outlet and assumes this position. The ball handler would then remain in the middle and the second guard would fill the open lane or become a trailer. Finally, there may be times when we have four rebounders and only one outlet man. The congestion may be too heavy for the guard or the front line players to quickly move to an outlet area. Again, the ball handling guard should recognize this. There is really no change in his responsibilities except that he should realize he now has a combination of the outlet areas. In other words, he has the whole side of the floor in which to float. Instead of remaining in the middle or moving to the side outlet, he should concentrate even more on making himself available in an open area that will be most advantageous for beginning the fast break.

We have discussed many things that are important in the execution of a fast break offense. None are any more important than the ability to get the ball off the boards. No one has ever been able to run without first gaining possession of the basketball. Our philosophies regarding boxing out and defensive rebounding will be examined in Chapter Eight. What is important here is the rebounder's ability to make the outlet pass as quickly and accurately as possible once possession has been gained.

In going after a defensive rebound, we want our players to make a one quarter turn to the outside if at all possible during their jump. We certainly want our players in a position of strength when rebounding so if this manuever jeopardizes that position then the turn should not be employed. Many times, such a turn will actually help the rebounder because he will be turning away from pressure. At any rate, the one quarter turn will facilitate a quicker outlet because we have eliminated one of the steps involved in making the outlet pass. We have formerly been taught to come down with the rebound and then pivot or turn to the outside looking for the outlet men. By turning in the air this step is eliminated and the rebounder also has additional time to see the floor and spot the proper outlet man.

At times the rebounder may be able to release the ball to one of the guards before coming down with the rebound. This is the ideal way to start a fast break. While difficult, it is made easier by the quarter turn during the jump. We drill our players on this manuever and expect the front line players to especially develop a certain amount of skill. Anytime a rebounder can make an accurate outlet pass before coming down with the ball we are almost assured of a fast break advantage at the other end. Possession of the ball is the most important essential, however. A quick outlet must be made but should never be forced or hurried. An important point to remember is that the rebounder can look for this type of pass but can always come down with the basketball should the pass prove

The Outlet Pass

FIG. 4-3

FIG. 4-4

too dangerous. We will still have a chance for a quick outlet and possible fast break if the opportunity presents itself. Figure 4-3 shows a player going up for the rebound and executing a quarter turn to the outside. This places him in a position to make the proper outlet as soon as he hits the floor or while he is still in the air, if the situation is favorable for that type of pass. It is obvious in Figure 4-4 that the player executing the quarter turn comes down in excellent position to get the ball out quickly.

To simplify things for our players we do not differentiate between the two outlet areas. They are not designated as primary or secondary outlets. The rebounder should be aware of both areas as he is looking to initiate the break. The overriding concern is that the ball be delivered to an open man as quickly as possible. All of the players will be made aware of our principal ball handler. Any time he is open we prefer that the ball goes to him. We do not feel anything is lost, however, by outletting to the second guard. He can make the next pass to the ball handler, if it is available, or he can bring the ball himself.

The actual outlet pass can be executed with the arms extended above the head (two hand overhead snap pass) or with the ball held at the outside ear in preparation for a baseball type pass. After the rebound is controlled the ball is immediately brought to one of these positions. Both hands firmly grasp the basketball at all times. This is a dangerous area for a quick steal because our other four players are making the transition from defense to offense. A steal in this area usually leads to a quick two points for the opposition. The rebounder should never windup to make the pass. This movement is too slow and increases the chances of a mistake in the basket area. The outlet pass should be thrown with authority. The pass should not be thrown so hard that the guard will have trouble handling the ball but the distance between the passer and receiver should allow for quite a bit of speed on the pass. A good, hard outlet will reach the outlet man quicker and thus speed up the development of the fast break. It will also decrease the chances of a defensive interception or deflection.

We instruct our players to make the outlet pass to the head of the intended receiver. The guard or outlet man will have both hands raised and this makes an excellent target for the passer. The exceptions to this rule are a possible lead pass with the guard moving up the floor or a pass to the guard's outside hand in case of defensive pressure from the inside. A pass aimed at the head area is easy for the outlet man to handle and leaves room for a considerable margin of error in any direction.

We mentioned briefly in the preceding pages that the rebounder can help the outlet man read the situation by his actions in making the outlet pass. When there is defensive pressure being applied, the guard should see this and he should feel that pressure even while focusing on receiving the basketball. If the rebounder makes a quick pump fake (short—never extended) and looks up the floor, the guard knows he should break behind the defender for a lead pass. Similiarly, if the rebounder immediately throws a lead pass further into the outlet area the guard must know then that the defensive pressure is minimal or non-existent. This gives him a better start on the break. Eye contact is important between the passer and the receiver. Basically we are talking about the players getting to know each other so they can develop the proper timing and communication that is essential in any team situation. This will be accomplished in drill and scrimmage sessions that emphasize the fast break.

Many teams will defend the fast break by swarming the rebounder to try and prevent a direct outlet pass. This should not present too much of a problem for our players if they have made the quarter turn and are prepared to outlet quickly. If the defensive pressure being applied does hinder the chances for a successful outlet, we allow the rebounder to execute a dribble outlet. Ideally, we want the front line players to utilize one or two dribbles toward the sideline in an effort to free themselves for an accurate outlet pass. The guards should be reacting to this pressure by floating to the open areas on the floor. Only in rare (and wide open) situations do we want the ball advanced up the middle of the floor by way of the dribble (from underneath the basket). If a guard or excellent ball handling frontliner has rebounded the ball they are allowed to bring the ball up the middle as a last resort or if the lane area is wide open for some reason. Generally, this will be the most congested area on the floor. Any time a forward or center utilizes the dribble he is to look for one of the guards and advance the ball to that guard as soon as possible.

We should discuss two final points regarding the actions of the front line players in rebounding the missed shot and initiating the fast break. The successful completion of the outlet pass is almost wholly the responsibility of the rebounder. The guards must find the open areas on the floor and make themselves readily available but the player outletting the ball must decide if he has a clear lane in which to complete the pass. If the ball is deflected or intercepted before reaching the outlet man, the passer is in error. He must recognize the open passing lanes and he must have the patience to hold the ball when there is no advantage to be gained from pushing the ball ahead.

Finally, as a rule of thumb for our fast break, we try not to outlet the ball below the free throw line extended. The guards are taught only to come below that line to receive the basketball when the rebounder is in need of help. If the rebounder is unable to make the proper outlet he should clear himself by the use of one or two dribbles (dribble outlet) and look for the guard moving to an open area. If there is still no high percentage pass the rebounder can hold the ball until the

The Middle
of the Break

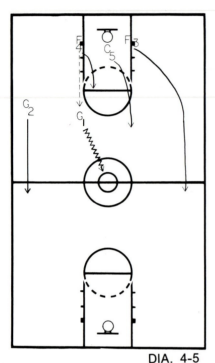

DIA. 4-5

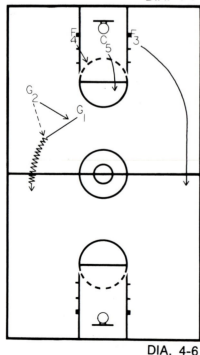

DIA. 4-6

guard breaks back to help. This is in keeping with the idea that possession of the basketball is more important than forced action on the fast break.

Our goal in continuing the execution of the fast break is to develop a three man or three lane attack that will catch the defense with only one or two defenders. Our fourth player up the floor will become the trailer and the fifth player has defensive or safety responsibilities until the ball is safely into our offensive end. The three lanes in our initial thrust consist of the two outside lanes (approximately three feet in from each sideline) and the middle lane (in the center between the two sidelines). The players occupying these lanes should stay spread throughout the middle part of the fast break.

Most teams employ, almost exclusively, a fast break pattern with the ball moving up the middle of the floor. In emphasizing a quick hitting, fast break offense we don't want to limit ourselves to a particular section of the floor. The idea is to advance the ball as quickly as possible. This is accomplished by utilizing all of the full court space and moving our men and the ball into the open areas. Thus, we use the middle of the floor, sideline, or a combination of the two in our fast break attack. Remember that the opposition will be converting from offense to defense. If the ball is at the side outlet a pass back into the middle can result in interception or deflection by the defense in transition. Additionally, the sideline break will allow for one less pass in the scoring end much of the time. Instead of the wing man receiving the pass and moving the ball back to the middle on the adjustment of the defense, the wing has the ball and can pull the defense out and execute only one pass.

Whenever the outlet is made directly to the middle of the floor the guard will take the ball up the middle until he meets too much opposition or is able to advance the ball to a wing man in a better position for a break opportunity (Dia. 4-5). We do not discourage the guards from dribbling by the first defender and continuing up the middle with the ball. This move must be accomplished quickly or we will lose any advantage that we had gained. We drill the players on this situation and encourage them to use their natural quickness and ball handling ability to blow by the defender. If the middle man is slowed up or about to be stopped by the defender he must look ahead. If at all possible the middle man should hit the wing men on the move with the pass but the wings should be prepared to break back to the ball if necessary.

When the rebounder initiates the break to the side outlet the guard at the top of the key makes a diagonal cut for a sideline lane. The ball can be advanced to this guard or the man who received the outlet can dribble into the middle and become the middle man on the break. The option selected depends for the most part on the position of the defense and the position of our offensive players filling the lanes. However, we can also take into consideration the relative ball handling and fast break abilities of the two guards. For purposes of explanation, let's designate our playmaking guard as G_1 and the second guard as G_2. If G_2 receives the outlet on the side (Dia. 4-6) we like him to make the pass to G_1 on the diagonal cut. On the other hand, if G_1 receives the outlet (Dia. 4-7) we would like G_2 to fill that outside land and G_1 to dribble behind him into the middle lane. As mentioned, the position of the defense will primarily dictate which option to choose.

On the diagonal cut the guards should never make the pass when the opposite guard is moving directly away from the passer (Dia. 4-8). This mistake leads to more turnovers and charging fouls and is the reason we place a heavy emphasis on the diagonal cut by the guard. The pass has to be made short and crisp while the guard is cutting diagonally. If the pass is not made then the guard on the side must bring the ball to the middle. The next pass can be made after the first guard turns up the floor as explained below. Keep in mind also that either guard in the side outlet position can bring the ball with the opposite guard remaining in the middle. An excellent variation of this option is shown in Diagram 4-9. The defender is playing the pass to G_1 on the diagonal cut so G_2 dribbles behind the cut by G_1 and draws the defender to him. G_2 then looks ahead to pass the ball to G_1 who has entered an open area on the floor between the two defenders.

Generally, the first two lanes on the fast break will be filled by the guards. Even after receiving the outlet and passing ahead the guard can usually fill one of the two remaining open lanes faster than any of the front line players. The third lane is then open to one of the front line players. The forward opposite the rebounder has the best chance to run this lane. He and the other non rebounder should turn and sprint for that third lane as quickly as possible. As soon as it becomes evident that a teammate has successfully filled the third lane the other player should look for another possible lane. Perhaps one of the guards has been held up in traffic and there is still a lane to be filled in the initial thrust. If all lanes are filled the player becomes the trailer. To again simplify things in our fast break pattern the trailer will always trail the play on the right side of the floor. He will be approximately eight to ten feet behind the ball and will split the area between the middle man and the wing man on the right side. The safety will assume responsibility for the left side of the floor and will move quickly into the offensive end when there is no longer the opportunity for a quick break the other way. Based on our previous diagrams the fast break pattern should look something like we have illustrated (Dia. 4-10) as we move into the crucial scoring end of the fast break.

The scoring end of the break is where the players must really come under control. They must show poise and must be able

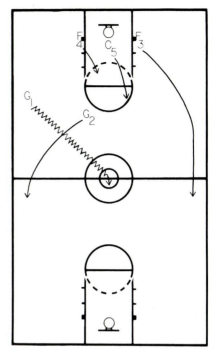

DIA. 4-7

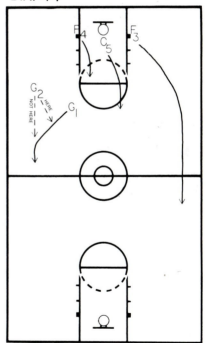

DIA. 4-8

The Scoring End of the Break

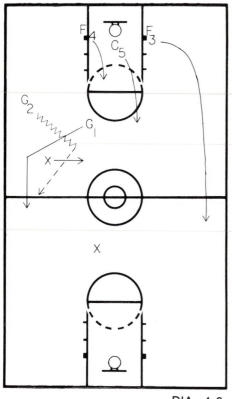

DIA. 4-9

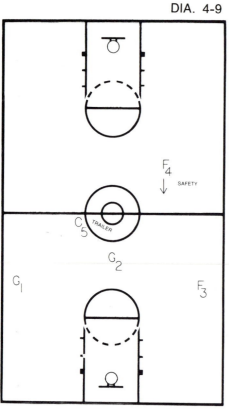

DIA. 4-10

118 The Fast Break

to recognize the difference between a good scoring opportunity and a forced shot. A well executed fast break can be negated by a poor shot. The players should have enough confidence in our half court offense to pull the ball out and work for the shot within that system. We strive for simplicity throughout the break and especially here at the end when a simple pass or movement can get the job done. Unnecessary faking and over-handling of the ball make it difficult for the players to anticipate the actions of their teammates. Often times, it is wasted motion and will just increase the chances of a mistake. We are not saying that we discourage individual creativity. We have had some fine ball handlers who were able to create scoring situations with great individual moves and passes. These players worked hard to develop these talents and certainly they were an asset to our teams. What we are saying, however, is that a player should have a good understanding of what his limitations are and should never make a difficult play when a simple one will lead to the same result.

Two On One

The ideal situation at the end of a fast break is to isolate two offensive players on one defender. This coaching point is stressed to our players from the very beginning of our fast break organization. We show them how to develop a two on one advantage from the defensive alignments that will occur during a fast break attempt and we explain to them exactly why the two on one is the most effective play. Simplification of the attack is the main reason. In the two on one the ball handler only has to concern himself with two things; the driving lane (Dia. 4-11) and the passing lane (Dia. 4-12). The driving lane is the route on a direct line to the backboard that the ball handler will take on a hard drive to the basket. The passing lane is on a direct line between the two offensive players. As the offensive players near the basket the ball handler must read the defender. If he is in the passing lane then the man with the ball executes a hard drive to the basket. If the defensive player closes off the driving lane the passing lane has to be open and F_3 (in this case) has a clear lane for the driving lay up. The offensive players must be prepared for the fakes of the retreating defensive player. Drilling in the two man situation and proper ball handling should offset any tactics utilized by the defender. Once a decision has been made to take the driving lane the driver must go hard and carry himself right up to the basket in a position of strength. If the defender has recovered and has a chance for a block the driver can always lay the ball back to his teammate for an uncontested lay up.

We teach our players to make a good fake to their teammate without interrupting their momentum for a hard drive. It is a manuever we call "taking the flash" and it is illustrated in Figure 4-5. The ball handler, as he plants his foot for his take off, gives a quick look and possible ball fake to his teammate in the other lane. This will serve to keep the defender thinking and possibly tie him up completely. Again, there is no loss of momentum or any indecision by the driver. He is simply executing a fake at the same time he is generating power for a strong drive to the basket. If the defender does not honor the fake the decision can be made to go ahead with the pass. However, if the fake is effective (Fig. 4-6) the ball handler continues his drive up to the basket for the lay up shot.

Naturally, the two on one advantage is developed whenever the defense is caught with only one man back. Any time this occurs in our three lane attack the ball handler should veer off (ball in middle) or angle in (ball on sideline) to a driving lane just outside the free throw lane area. The teammate in the best position to fill the other lane will do so and the third offensive player will trail the play and react according to what develops. The third player must be sure to take himself out of the play to relieve any congestion and/or confusion. We definitely do not want to continue a three on one attack. A three on one will allow the defender to drop back almost under the basket to cover a pass from the middle man to either wing man. The middle man is then forced to shoot from the outside when a lay up could have easily been generated by a two on one attack.

The two on one break can also be developed from an initial three on two alignment. Any time the front defender in a three on two situation tries to stop the ball, the ball handler can either blow by the defender and form a two man attack with the most likely teammate or he can pass the ball ahead and take himself out of the play (Dia. 4-13). This play is especially effective when the first defender tries to stop the ball out on the floor as shown in the diagram. As soon as this option develops the two wing men should angle in to form the proper two man relationship.

If the defender retreats to the key area the two on one situation can still be created. Excellent close in ball handling will be required and the players must be aware of the top defender dropping back quickly after the ball has penetrated his position. One aspect of this play is illustrated in Figure 4-7. The guard in the middle has faked and driven by the first defender on the right side. Seeing this, the wing man on the right is stopping to take himself out of the play. The guard and the left wing now have a two on one advantage on the back defender. If the defensive man closes off the driving lane the ball handling guard must lay the ball off before the front defender has time to recover.

When the ball is being advanced up the sideline in a three on two alignment the ball handler should drive the ball hard to the free throw line extended. He should be trying to draw the top defender out to the side so the middle man and opposite wing can isolate on the remaining defender (Dia. 4-14). If the first defender does not honor the ball handler on the side,

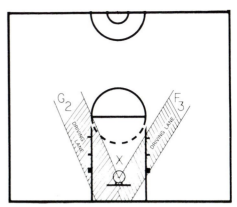

DIA. 4-11

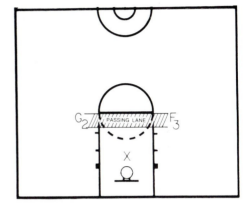

DIA. 4-12

FIG. 4-5

The Fast Break 119

FIG. 4-6

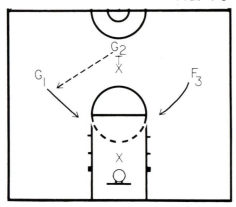

DIA. 4-13

FIG. 4-7

there is always the possibility that he can take the ball all the way to the basket for his own two on one with the opposite wing man (Dia. 4-15).

Three on Two
When the ball is in the middle the two players running the outside lanes should stay spread until they come to the free throw line extended. All players must run the proper lanes because good spacing will have much to do with the timing and, thus, the overall success of the fast break. We like both of the outside men to be slightly ahead of the middle man in a three on two situation. If the wing men are too far ahead they should let up slightly so they go into the scoring area with the proper alignment and timing. If the middle man is out ahead of the wing men, they should run all out to make up the difference and move in front. The middle man should delay slightly, but not enough to be caught from behind or to lose the fast break advantage. The players are taught to "time it up" by the use of the crossover dribble and/or a change of pace. They can also feint the defense by starting to the right side, crossing over and coming back left or vice versa. The idea is to keep the defense guessing and to remain on the offensive. The ball handler should never stop and wait for the lanes to fill; nor should he completely turn his head to look for his teammates. Peripheral vision, a knowledge of his teammates, and court awareness should enable the player to develop the proper timing essential for the success of the break.

In the three on two break the two wing men should cut for the basket at a forty-five degree angle as soon as they reach the free throw line extended. They should be under control and beginning to gather themselves for a hard drive to the basket or to pull up and shoot the soft jump shot from just outside the lane area at the forty-five degree angle. Both potential receivers should be reading the defense and the actions of the ball handler in anticipation of the pass. There is no time to catch the ball and then react to the defense. The players must be thinking ahead and planning the course of action that will lead to a quick score.

Ideally, the middle man will be right at the top of the key when the wing men begin their cuts to the basket (Dia. 4-16). He also should be coming under further control and preparing himself to make the simple pass to the best potential scorer. His goal is to make the second defensive man commit to one side or the other. If the defensive man does commit himself the middle man should deliver the ball to the opposite wing. The pass should be made high (above the chest and below the chin) and slightly in front so the receiver can catch it in stride for a strong drive to the basket. The reason we say slightly in front is because we don't want the wing man to have to reach or strain for the ball and lose some of his body control. The back defensive player still may have time to step back over for a possible offensive foul. The ball cannot be thrown behind or low to the receiver because these passes are hard to catch and control while running. We do not rule out the use of the bounce pass because under certain circumstances it is a very effective pass at the end of a fast break. It is the most difficult pass for the defense to reach but can also be troublesome for the receiver if not perfectly thrown.

If the back defender fails to commit himself to either side, then the ball handler must deliver the ball to one of the wing man in a position that will allow him to pull up at about nine feet for the soft jump shot. While we are looking for the lay up at all possible times, this is certainly a high percentage shot that with practice and the proper technique can be successful a great majority of the time. The shooter should come to a full stop and make sure that his feet and legs are underneath him as he begins the shot. If not, his momentum from the run will cause him to be off balance during and after the shot attempt. The shot requires a very soft touch. We instruct our players to try and "fluff" the ball off the backboard and into the basket. Equally important is the players' ability to run the proper lanes. If the wing man is above or below the forty-five degree angle to the basket, his shot will be that much more difficult.

The wing to wing pass in this type of situation is very difficult to complete. While we do not eliminate the wing to wing pass as an offensive posibility, we do encourage our players to throw the pass only when there is a wide open lane and an excellent chance for a resulting lay up. This will occur when the top defender fails to drop back quickly after the pass from the middle man to the wing. A good, accurate bounce pass can come into play in this situation. It must be thrown so that it bounces beyond the remaining defender and it must have sufficient force to bounce up to the opposite wing in a position to be easily handled. The back defender must be totally committed to the driving lane or to the ball for this pass to work. If he is faking or playing games, the wing man with the ball is advised to make the hard drive to the basket (if the opening is there) or to pull up for the soft jumper. By bringing the ball to the defender and still looking for the opposite wing man, the ball handler will allow the defensive man to play both of them and delay for help. This will give the top defender time to drop back to pick up the opposite wing man which will allow the back defender to put more pressure on the ball. The decision for the execution of the shot must be made prior to this time to facilitate an uncontested opportunity. Again, we must emphasize the importance of anticipation. The offensive players must be thinking ahead so they can react instinctively to the situations presented.

The middle man should come to a complete stop when making the pass to either wing. This will usually occur somewhere

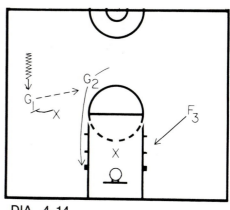

DIA. 4-14

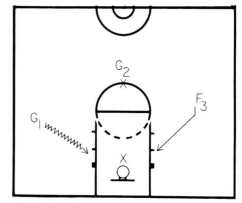

DIA. 4-15

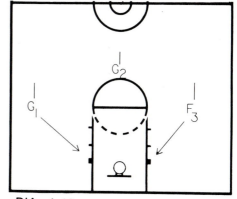

DIA. 4-16

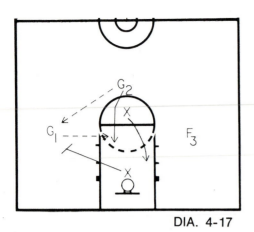

DIA. 4-17

between the top of the key and the free throw line, but will depend primarily on the actions of the first defender. After making the pass, we ask the middle man to step toward the receiver in anticipation of a return pass or a possible give and go cut down the lane. The give and go cut is precipitated by the back defender stepping out wide to cover the first pass and the first defender dropping quickly to cover the weakside (Dia. 4-17). This can lead to a wide open lane down the middle. The middle man, in stepping to the ball, delays his cut to insure the proper timing and make sure the give and go is open and available. Once the opening is evident the middle man must explode to the basket to take advantage of a quick return pass from the wing. This is the play we are looking for before any thought is given to the trailer or the fourth man down the floor. The reasons for this are twofold. First of all, the first three offensive players can never be assured that the trailer has been able to make the transition as quickly as they had. He may not be in the right place at the right time. Secondly, the only time a fourth offensive player is needed is when there are three defenders. If he can take advantage of a clear opening in this type of situation, we will certainly expect him to cut through the lane and expect the ball handler to make the proper pass. The option must be wide open, however. If it is not, we prefer the trailer to stop outside the key area for reasons we will elaborate on shortly.

If the give and go cut is not open, the middle man remains in position for a return pass at about the vertex of the free throw lane and the free throw line. He should stay out of the lane area to avoid a three second violation, but should be ready to go to the basket for a possible offensive rebound if a shot is attempted by one of the wing men. The non-shooting wing and the trailer should also be ready to get to the offensive boards. The man trailing the play can sometimes see a clear path to the basket and can anticipate the direction of the rebound from his position on the floor. He should be poised to "knife" through the congestion and rebound aggressively. The time after a fast break attempt is when the rebounding positions and chances for possession are relatively even. All of the players are moving and the defense is usually unable to establish clear cut inside position. Further, the offense may be at a numerical advantage and will usually have better vantage points from which to anticipate the rebound.

The Secondary Break

After our initial fast break attempt the defense enters another period of transition. From hustling back on defense to stop the fast break, they must now set up their half court defense in an organized and efficient manner. Adding to this problem is the fact that some of these players may not have made a successful or hustling conversion into the defensive end. Even if all the players have converted quickly, there is still the possibility of momentary relaxation after having thwarted the fast break attack. If the defense relaxes or fails to quickly pick up their men, they are quite vulnerable to an aggressive team that places an emphasis on the secondary break. Mismatches are the least that can happen and these can quickly be taken advantage of by the offense. We certainly want to take advantage of any breakdowns that can occur during this transitional period. Ours is a simple, quick hitting attack. The players know they can get into the offense at any time depending on the possibilities that are raised by the defense.

The secondary phase of our fast break attack involves reversing the basketball quickly and looking for the possible breakdown in the defensive transition. The trailer stops outside the key area in a position where the ball can be reversed back to him quickly and safely from the wing or wing to baseline areas. The safety does the same thing on his side of the floor. He is in a reverse pass position in relation to the trailer. We now have a 2-1-2 set up from which we can reverse the ball with the man in the middle following each pass (Dia. 4-18).

If G_2 has cut to the basket, he posts up momentarily and G_1 look inside before reversing the ball (Dia. 4-19). As the ball is reversed G_2 moves to an open spot looking for the inside pass. He follows the ball around the horn (Dia. 4-20). If the man playing the middle receives a pass, he immediately faces the basket and looks for his shot or a pass to a weakside player moving to an open area. If the trailer has made a cut to the basket, he will become the man in the middle with G_2 stepping out to make himself available for the reverse pass. In other words, G_2 and C_5 will have exchanged positions.

The opposite wing man (F_3 in these diagrams) always has the option to fill the spot that has just been vacated by the middle. He will be breaking in behind the defense on the premise that they may have relaxed momentarily and are vulnerable to a quick cut into an open area. Once the ball has been reversed to the weakside G_1 will have the same option.

Additional Points of Emphasis for the Fast Breaking Team

1. Speed part of the fast break is at the outlet and the middle.
2. Poise at the scoring end. Be under control.
3. Recognize when the break is not there.
4. A tough, aggressive defense will key a successful fast break. There are not many break opportunities after a made shot. Force your opponents into error; then take advantage.
5. Any time the defense tries to intercept, be ready to release to receive the pass further up the floor.
6. Talk. Communication is essential.
7. Move the ball up the floor and into the open areas as quickly as possible.
8. Big men never handle the ball when a guard is available.
9. Don't force the fast break, but read the defense and be alert to take advantage of the slightest opportunity.
10. Be mentally and physically prepared to handle the basketball on the move.

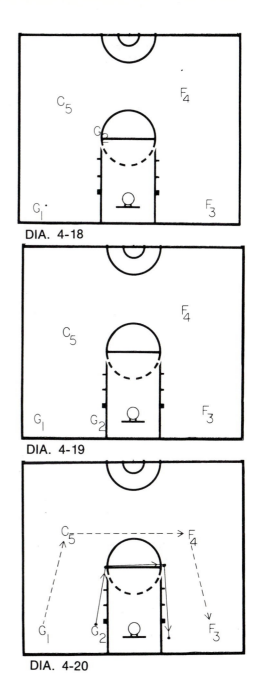

DIA. 4-18

DIA. 4-19

DIA. 4-20

Drills for Teaching the Fast Break

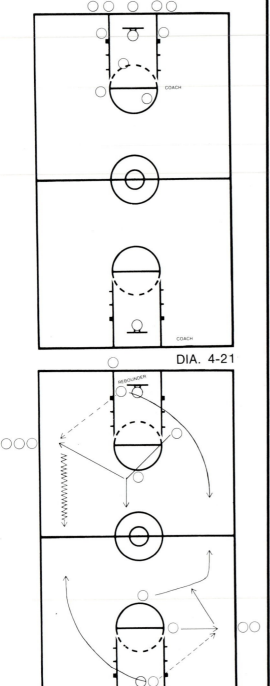

DIA. 4-21

DIA. 4-22

As in most of our teaching we utilize a whole-part-whole method with the fast break. We want our players to see the entire picture so they can better understand the purpose and thinking behind the breakdown drills. Generally, we will begin fall practice with two weeks of strict emphasis on the fundamentals as discussed in Chapter Two. These will include much drilling on the team's ability to handle the basketball while moving up and down the floor, and these should serve as lead up drills to the development of the fast break. During the second week we will spend a good part of an entire practice on the organization of the fast break. From that time on, we will incorporate the fast break attack into our daily practices to develop that aspect of our offensive system. We begin teaching of the fast break with a five on none dummy drill and give our players a farily complete overview of how our fast break is to be organized. We also come back to this drill at least once a week during the season as a means of repetition for our fast break organization. We try to include some competition in many of our drills and the fast break is no exception. A final point is important in the running of many of these drills. We never let a player shoot the ball when we want to miss intentionally. The coach or a manager will always do the shooting in this type of situation.

Five on None Fast Break Drill (Dia. 4-21)
Objective: To teach and emphasize in a repetitive situation the overall organization of the fast break attack.
Organization: Three squads of five players. Coach at both ends of the floor. Coach shoots ball. Players rebound missed shot and initiate fast break. Each squad makes two trips (up and back).
Points of Emphasis:
1. Outlet areas (introduce floating technique).
2. Quick, accurate outlet (turning to the outside).
3. Fill the lanes properly.
4. Run hard until reaching the scoring area.
5. Emphasize execution at the end of the break.

After introducing our five man fast break organization we will begin our breakdown drills from the defensive end of the floor. This is where our fast break will be initiated so it is certainly a good place to begin. Blocking out and defensive rebounding will be discussed in a subsequent chapter but we should note their obvious importance in seizing a fast break opportunity. The first breakdown drill we utilize involves three men without a defense. It is simply called our Three Man Outlet drill. We not only place a great deal of importance on the quick outlet but also on the quickness of all our players in filling the lanes. Those first few steps will be extremely important. For this reason, we continue the drill until half court. We do not let the players simply make the outlet and go to the end of the line.

Three Man Outlet Drill (Dia. 4-22)

Objective: To develop the proper outlet technique in our rebounders and the proper "floating" technique for those who will be required to fill the outlet positions. Also, to emphasize to all the players the importance of moving quickly to fill the lanes for the break.

Organization: One rebound line under each basket and one outlet line at each end. Two players from the outlet line position themselves out on floor in defensive position. Coach throws ball off board. Rebounder outlets to that side or middle and fills the third lane. Fast break continues to half court. One end rebounds to right, one to left. Players must avoid each other at half line. After completing drill each time, players go to end of line at the opposite end of the floor.

Points of Emphasis: 1. Quick, accurate outlet.

2. One quarter turn to the outside.

3. Proper floating technique in outlet areas.

4. Proper technique in catching the outlet pass (can add defensive player).

5. Diagonal cut or ball up sideline.

6. Quickness in getting three players to half court.

Outlet and Over the Top Drill (Dia. 4-23)

Objective: To further emphasize the proper outlet and floating techniques. To teach our frontline players to get out and run on the break. To teach our guards to make the over the top pass to a player out in front of everyone on the break.

Organization: Two lines; a rebound line and a guard line. Coach throws ball off board. Rebounder makes proper outlet and turns opposite his pass to sprint for the basket at the other end. Guard receives outlet, dribbles to the half court area and passes the ball to the rebounder in stride for a lay up.

Points of Emphasis: 1 thru 4 in previous drill.

5. Rebounder runs hard until he begins gathering himself at the free throw line extended.

6. Guard comes to a stride stop to make pass. Must come to a stop and lead the receiver so he catches the ball without breaking stride.

7. Guard follows pass and rebounds shot.

Outlet Recognition Drill (Dia. 4-24)

Objective: To develop the ability of the rebounders to recognize the open outlet area. To teach the guards to read

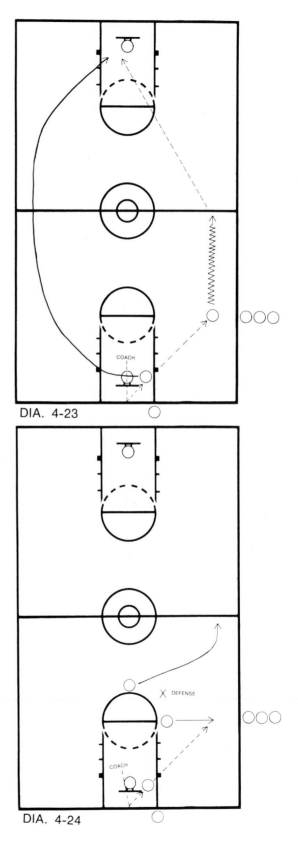

DIA. 4-23

DIA. 4-24

The Fast Break 125

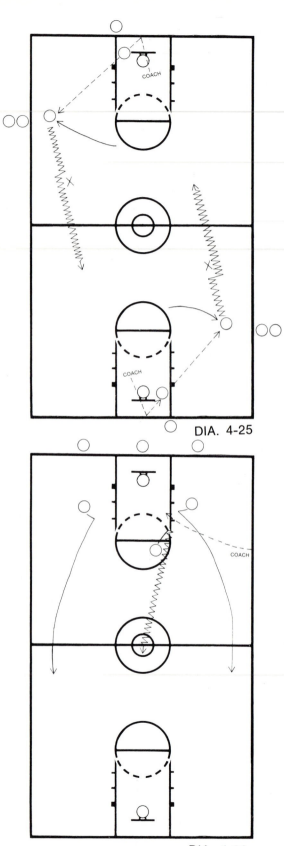

DIA. 4-25

DIA. 4-26

and react to the position of the defense.

Organization: Rebound line, outlet line. Place defensive man in position to pressure outlet. Rebounder outlets to the open area. Outlet men execute the break to the half court line. Rebounder becomes defensive man; next man steps in.

Points of Emphasis: 1 thru 5 in Three Man Outlet drill.

6. Make the open pass.

7. Guards read the defense and make themselves available (coming back or on the fly).

8. Diagonal cut after outlet pass.

Dribble Quickness Drill (guards and ball handling forwards only) **(Dia. 4-25)**

Objective: To teach the guards to blow by a stationary or slower defender on the dribble without delaying the fast break.

Organization: Both ends of the floor. Rebound line and outlet line at each end. Coach is with rebounders and they are working on aggressive rebounding and proper outlet technique. One guard steps out to assume defensive position. Next guard receives the outlet and advances the ball up the floor going by the defender and all the way to the basket. Offensive player hustles back to become defender. Defender goes to the end of the line. (Coach at opposite end can deliver token pressure on the drive to the basket).

Points of Emphasis: 1. Quick, accurate outlet utilizing proper technique.

2. Guard uses proper technique in positioning himself for and receiving the outlet pass.

3. Guard sees the whole floor and recognizes the actions of the defense.

4. Guard must blow by the defender with one quick move.

Loose Ball— Fast Break Drill (no defense), **(Dia. 4-26)**

Objective: Develop the players' ability to react to a loose ball or steal and make the quick transition to a fast break opportunity.

Organization: Line of three off end of floor. First three step out and simulate defensive basketball. Coach rolls, throws, or puts the ball wherever he wants to. Three players must get the basketball and quickly fill the lanes.

Points of Emphasis: 1. Quick reactions.

2. Get the ball first—then go.

3. Fill the lanes properly.

4. Execution at the scoring end.

Three Lane—Two Ball Drill (Dia. 4-27)

Objective: To develop the players' passing skills while on the move.

126 The Fast Break

Organization: Three lines at end of court. Middle line and one wing line have balls. The middle man passes to the wing man without a ball and immediately turns to receive pass from the wing man with the ball. He returns that pass and repeats this manuever with the opposite wing man. The same procedure is repeated up and down the floor. First three players return to the end of the line—next three in.

Points of Emphasis: 1. See the floor ahead while moving.

2. Crisp, sharp passes leading the receivers.

3. No dribbling and no traveling.

As we have emphasized, execution is vitally important in the offensive end of the fast break. We stress simplicity and the fundamentals. Early in the practice sessions, we will develop our methods of running the two on one and three on two situations. After our players understand how we want the break situations to be executed, we will combine the drills and give them some continuity and diversity. We do not run a two on none drill because we feel it is unnecessary, but we do run three on none to give our players practice in pulling up for the short jump shot. We want each and every player to develop extreme confidence in this shot because it will occur quite often during any given game.

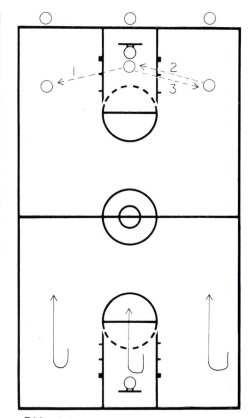

DIA. 4-27

Three on None Fast Break Drill

Objective: To develop the proper spacing and timing for the three lane fast break. Further, to develop the ball handling abilities of the middle man and the running techniques of those in the outside lanes.

Organization: Players form three lines at one end about the free throw line extended or top of the key. Middle man dribbles to free throw line at scoring end with wing men filling the lanes. Middle man passes to one of the wings for the short jumper. Opposite wing and middle man both rebound.

Points of Emphasis: 1. Middle man head up. Develop speed.

2. Wing men running. Wide until angling their cut at the free throw line extended.

3. Wing men running hard until gathering themselves in the scoring end.

4. Middle man makes accurate, crisp pass at the end of the break.

5. Proper shooting technique and angle on the shot attempt by the wing man. "Fluff" the ball off the board. Come to a stop and have legs underneath body.

*Remember—this drill is for teaching the execution at the scoring end of the fast break. This can be combined with the

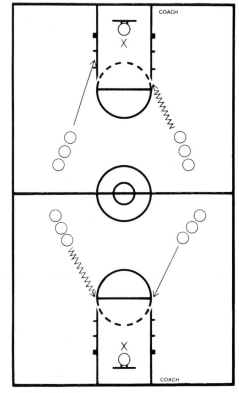

DIA. 4-28

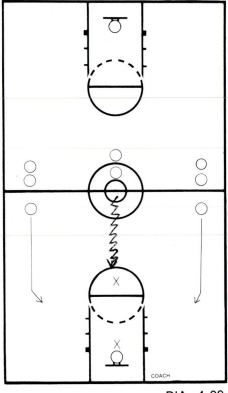

DIA. 4-29

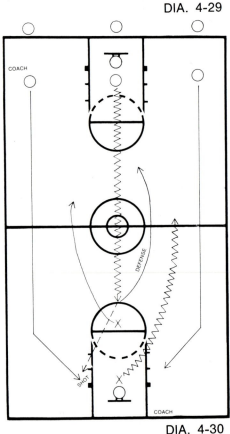

DIA. 4-30

Three Man Outlet Drill to include the three lane break from end line to end line. It is also very similar to the loose ball drill but the emphasis there is on making the quick transition rather than the execution at the scoring end of the break.

Two on One Drill (Dia. 4-28)

Objective: To teach proper execution of the two on one fast break opportunity and the principles behind that execution.

Organization: Two lines at half court. Going both ways. One defender in the lane area. Player who shoots lay up replaces defensive man.

Points of Emphasis:
1. Players in driving lanes just outside lane area.
2. Man without ball slightly ahead of ball handler.
3. Driving lane **or** passing lane.
4. Hard drive to the basket.
5. Take the flash (see Fig. 4-5).

Three on Two Drill (Dia. 4-29)

Objective: To teach the proper execution of the three on two fast break opportunity and to practice the various situations that can occur in this type of alignment.

Organization: Three lines just beyond half court. Ball starts in middle line but we also bring the ball from both of the outside lanes. Two defensive players are back in a tandem or a split defense. The defense rotates every five scoring attempts (this can be adjusted to stress competition or to stress the defense in the drill; ie., defense must stop offense three times in a row).

Points of Emphasis:
1. Middle man tries to make the back defensive man commit or blows by the front defender if possible. Must have body under control.
2. Wings get under control at free throw line extended.
3. Wings make their cut at the proper angle.
4. If middle man gets by first defender, wing on that side pulls up to take himself out of the play.
5. Wings have hands up, ready to catch the ball and gather themselves for the shot.
6. "Fluff" the ball off the board.
7. Middle man move toward pass and look for possible give and go opening.
8. Middle man must be prepared to pull up and hit the jumper from the free throw line.
9. Both non-shooters go to the boards.

128 The Fast Break

Three on Two—Two on One Drill (Dia. 4-30)

Objective: Same as three on two and two on one drills with the exception of some added continuity and full court transitional work. Fast break defense can also be worked on once this has been taught.

Organization: Three lines at one end line. Three offensive players step out and bring the ball. Two defenders attempt to stop scoring thrust at opposite end. After a made shot or rebound the two defenders make the transition to offense and fast break the other way. The middle man in the three lane attack must always convert quickly from offense to defense, thus establishing the two on one break. The wing men will remain as the defenders and this procedure will continue until action is stopped.

Points of Emphasis: Same as three on two and two on one drills.

Three on Two Continuous Fast Break Drill (Diagrams 4-31 and 4-32)

Objective: More three on two work with continuous action. Also utilized as a conditioning drill. Most of the full court fast break drills can aid in conditioning and this is especially true with this drill. Fast break defense can also be emphasized.

Organization: Players are divided into two teams or two lines of players at the half line. The players will always return to the same line. Two players from Line A step out and assume defensive positions after touching the center circle. The first three players in Line B bring the ball on a three lane break. To simulate actual game conditions a third defensive player races out to touch the center circle and hustles back to aid his teammates. He cannot leave until the fast breaking team crosses half court. As soon as the defense rebounds the ball or the shot is made, the next two players in Line B touch the center circle and become the defenders. The players from Line A now fast break in the opposite direction and the drill continues in this manner until action is stopped.

Points of Emphasis: 1. All areas of the fast break execution in our system.

2. Special emphasis on remaining under control. If not corrected, some players can tend to get out of control during this drill.

3. Talking! Both on defense and offense.

4. Defensive positions and strategies (discussed in Chapter Six).

Five on Three Fast Break Drill (Dia. 4-33)

Objective: To drill on the proper execution of the fast break with some defensive opposition involved in all three areas of the break; outlet, middle, scoring end.

Organization: Five players simulate defensive positions. One

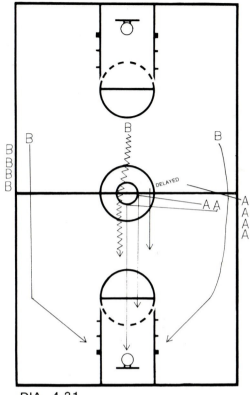

DIA. 4-31

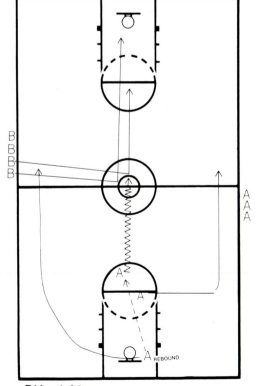

DIA. 4-32

The Fast Break 129

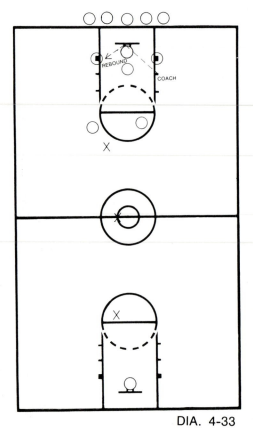

DIA. 4-33

defensive player plays the outlet, one the middle of the floor and the third plays the basket. Coach shoots the ball and the five man team rebounds and executes the fast break. Three of the fast breaking players hustle to replace the defense. Defenders now become part of the third breaking team. The second five man team steps in and the drill continues. Each team returns to the original end around the outside of the court.

Points of Emphasis: All areas of the fast break execution in our system. We especially watch our players for their reactions to the defensive pressure.

Five on Five Fast Break (Dia. 4-34)

Objective: To develop the fast break attack under actual five on five game conditions. To instill in the players the ability to recognize when a fast break opportunity is available and when it isn't. This is where we work on our Secondary Break.

Organization: Team A on defense, Team B on offense. Offensive players are stationary at first. Coach shoots ball, defense rebounds and initiates the fast break. Each fast breaking team makes three trips up and back and then they rotate. A goes to offense, B steps off and C comes in to run the break. Offensive players can be allowed to move to set up different rebound positions for the defense.

Points of Emphasis: 1. All areas of the fast break execution.

2. Getting out and running the lanes. Don't get involved in any congestion.

3. Special emphasis on reversing the ball and pulling it out when the break is not there.

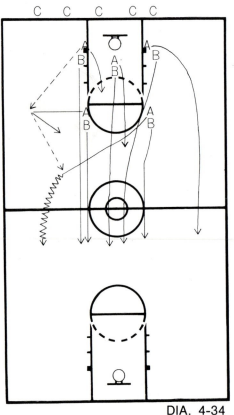

DIA. 4-34

An emphasis on strong individual defense will be the basis for a more effective team defense. We try to instill in our players a pride in their ability to control their offensive opponent. We want them to accept the challenge of stopping their man or holding him under his scoring average at that particular time. There is a tremendous amount of satisfaction that is derived from this type of effort and accomplishment. The importance of this type of effort cannot be over-emphasized or oversold to your team. Since we are almost exclusively a man to man defensive team, it is easy for us to stress the importance of individual matchups. We don't wish to infer that team defense is any less important; only that a great team defense must start with sound individual defense.

From the standpoint of motivation, defense can be more difficult to teach than offense. This is not always true, especially in some individual cases, but much more often than not, the players are offensive as opposed to defensive minded. This is somewhat natural and yet we as coaches must do a better job of emphasizing the balance that must be maintained between the two if a young man is to develop into a complete player. Concentration is perhaps a vital first step in developing a good defensive attitude. We have carefully studied our players and discussed with them the extent of their concentration at the defensive end of the floor. Those that were making costly defensive errors were found to be lacking completely in defensive concentration. They were actually thinking ahead to their offense or the team's offense the next trip down the floor. Naturally, this led to lapses in their defensive adjustments and sometimes in their defensive effort.

The players must be made to realize the part that their individual defense will play in determining the outcome of a game. Comparative scoring totals can sometimes serve as excellent examples. For instance, if one of our players scores eighteen points, but allows his man to score twenty-six, we are getting hurt at this position. If another of our players scores a total of six points, but holds his man scoreless, we are gaining a definite advantage. These statistics can be misleading, too. Our best defensive player may be limited with regard to his offensive abilities. If he is guarding a big gun on the other team, the scoring totals will not be entirely indicative of the outcome of that matchup. In preparing for a game, we make our players aware of the scoring averages of the particular people they will be assigned to guard. The idea is to hold that player somewhere below his scoring average. If our opponent's best player is averaging twenty-five points a game and our man holds him to fifteen, it is obvious that a good job has been done defensively.

The next factor that the players must recognize is that their defense by its nature will be a more consistent weapon than their offense. It is inevitable that a player will have a few off nights offensively. Defensively, however, an off night can only

5 Individual Defense

occur through lack of concentration and/or lack of effort. **Defense is more mental than physical and requires heart more than talent.** The mental aspects of the game and what is inside the player should not be subject to the variables and thus the inconsistencies of the aspects that require pure physical talent. That is, if the players are totally prepared mentally and have developed the proper defensive attitude.

We tell our players that defense is just that—an attitude. It is an attitude that says, "You can't beat me. I won't let you beat me. You may have better talent, but I've worked harder and it's going to pay off right now." It is not going to pay off every time. There are going to be players who are better on a given night or who have exceptional talent and have worked hard to develop that talent. The player's attitude does not lose its validity when this occurs. It merely takes on a new shape; "Next time I will be better prepared. I will work harder and play smarter. Next time I will not be beaten." It is hard to defeat a man who will not give in to defeat. We want our players to possess just this type of attitude, especially with regard to their individual defense. We want competitors. We want players who will not give in to any situation, no matter what the odds. These are the players that ultimately will come out on top.

We feel it is important to get our players thinking about defense right from the moment they begin playing for the University of Missouri. As far as we are concerned, that moment starts as soon as the players begin spring and summer workouts after deciding to be a part of our program. With that in mind, we counsel the players as to what will be expected of them in the fall and make suggestions regarding their individual needs so that they can best meet those expectations. Defense is always a main topic of discussion. We never hesitate to use John Havlicek as an example to our players, both in this and many other areas. We tell the young players of Havlicek's ideas upon making the transition from the college game to the pro game. He knew that he would be going to camp with rookies and veterans who had just as much, if not more, natural ability than he had. His plan was to make the team with his defense, feeling that the rest would fall into place with some experience and much hard work. This is exactly what he did and his record speaks for itself.

These same ideas can be applied to a player coming out of high school and making the transition to college basketball. All of the players that he will be competing with and against have been stars at the high school level. All will have varing degrees of natural ability, but the player would do well with the attitude that he is going to have to work harder to make his presence felt. Defense can very often be the difference in a young player making the team, making the first five, or becoming a top player.

Right from the start, our players realize the importance we place on defense in developing a winning program. They recognize that to compete at this level, to play for M.U., to win in the Big Eight—they are going to have to improve on and place a great deal more emphasis on their individual defense. We feel that with this recognition half of our battle is won. All of the players that are able to successfully make the transition from high school to college basketball have the quickness and the ability to play very good or excellent defense. A willingness to learn and some capacity for hard work are all that are needed now to develop sound defensive habits and skills.

As we alluded to previously, however, a tough defensive attitude can be difficult to encourage and maintain. Constant motivation and stimulation is necessary to successfully teach defense. After the players are made aware of our defensive emphasis, we try to further make them aware of the competitive nature of defense. Defense is a man against man proposition. A special kind of pride and sense of accomplishment can be derived from this type of confrontation. It is our job as coaches to make this feeling of accomplishment even more special. The great defensive player is not going to get the public acclaim that he deserves unless we work hard at educating the media people and everyone involved with the game on the importance of defense. We feel that we made great strides in this area during the 1975-76 and 76-77 seasons and subsequently, the last few years. During those seasons, we had a young man playing for us by the name of James Clabon. James is the finest defensive player we have ever had at the University of Missouri. He is 6'8", and has the defensive quickness and speed to cover the guard position. James always took our opponent's best offensive player, no matter what position he played, and thus gained a great deal of notoriety around the league and outside the league for his defensive prowess. James deserves all of the credit for the recognition he received, but his efforts were something we stressed whenever discussing the strengths of our team or the success we enjoyed during that period.

While it is hard for us to control who gets the credit in the media, it is easy for us to distribute credit where it is due in our practice sessions, team meetings, etc. Any chance we get, we praise a good defensive play, especially when it involves a great deal of hustle. We encourage our players to acknowledge fine plays by a teammate. **We will praise a hustling play even if it does not end in success. This is vitally important because hustle is an essential ingredient in the makeup of any great defensive player or defensive team.**

The pride we talked about earlier can become even more important when a player develops into the best defensive player at his position or the best defensive player on the team. The knowledge that he will be assigned to the opponent's top guard or top forward leads to a feeling of confidence and a further arousal of the player's competitive instincts. Additional motivation is supplied when the opponent has a particularly high scorer that must be stopped if we are to defeat rather than be defeated. The simple act of going to one of our players and discussing the importance of his task has high motivational value. We make sure that our player is aware of any All-American, All-League, or other honors that this player might possess. We refer to him as a "so-called big name" player and expect our defender to either prove this player is overrated or make him earn his honors. We don't underplay the opponent's abilities, but we build our player up, because we want the proper balance of respect and confidence going into the matchup. If our defender is able to come out on top in this encounter, the sense of accomplishment and his confidence continues a snowballing effect. Defense is fun now. It has become a matter of pride.

We have applied these same ideas to our weaker defensive players at the right time and have had outstanding results. We have assigned players other than our top defenders to certain high scoring opponents because they matched up better with regard to height, weight, and position. Many times, they have accepted the challenge and responded with an excellent job defensively. Again, the snowballing effect takes place. The defender becomes more sure of himself and finds that playing outstanding defense can be just as gratifying as excelling offensively. Defense may not be as exciting as offense, but it can give a player an inward feeling of extreme satisfaction because he has accomplished something through sheer hard work and effort rather than pure physical talent. We further believe that this discovery of the value of defense can lead to greater effort in other areas of individual play that will make for a more complete ball player. All players today, especially younger players, must realize the significant part that all of the fundamentals play in developing the outstanding basketball player at any level. Offense is not the only criteria. This realization is especially important for those players who are not as gifted offensively as some of their counterparts. Development in the other areas of the game can serve to offset this disadvantage.

In emphasizing the value of strong individual defense, some great offensive performers are hard to reach. Many can be reached through the means we have already discussed. Others are still unable to extend themselves at the defensive end of the court. We have found that many of these players have lacked what we discussed earlier in this chapter — concentration. Their offensive creativity is still at work in the defensive end. Their formative years in basketball have been spent perfecting their offensive skills and creating new and better ways to attack the basket. There has been no emphasis on the complete game. They have not been forced to play both ends. We not only force them to play defense, we expect them to excel defensively, because of their creativity and their natural ability and quickness. We tell them that if they want the ball back, they should get it. Why wait for the offense to miss a shot, or, worse yet, make a shot before getting back to offense? Make the steal, force the turnover, force the bad or hurried shot and then get the rebound. Use some of that creativity on defense. Make the great defensive play; then go down and create something on offense. Score. Then get it back. Aggressiveness—that's the name of the game. Making something happen—offensively and defensively.

Competition among our own players can lead to an improved defensive attitude. We stress in practice situations the same things that will be stressed in defensing an opponent. A defensive one on one drill is man against man. In the organization of most of our individual defensive drills, the players will be competing against other players at their particular position. Each player should be intent on impressing the coaches with his effort and success against his competitors for that position on the team. We wholeheartedly encourage this type of competition. We don't expect our players to be content with a certain place on the squad. We want everyone to be pushing someone else. Those that are not among the starting five should be pushing the starters. The starters should be pushing each other and working hard to keep their positions. When two players of equal ability are competing for the same position, we will go with the best defensive player every time. We make the players aware of this philosophy so there is no doubt as to the significance we place on defensive effort and improvement. This type of emphasis leads to a great deal of intensity and enthusiasm in our drill situations.

Competition in the practice sessions is essential because the players are going to be competing in a much more pressurized atmosphere on game day. If the players cannot accept the challenge of competing for a spot on the squad, they will certainly not be able to compete when facing an opponent under game conditions. This has important implications regarding a player's defensive attitude. No one can loaf or not extend full effort on defense in practice and expect to play good defense in a game. Defense is an attitude and your players cannot just turn it on or off. Much of a player's success will be determined by the habits he develops in practice. It is obvious then that the habits that are developed must be based on sound defensive principles and maximum individual effort.

Full Court Individual Defense

The first step in teaching sound individual defense is the introduction of the proper stance and correct sliding technique as discussed in Chapter Two. We teach these fundamentals in a group formation and demand accuracy before moving on to the more advanced drill situations. Once these skills have been perfected, we begin teaching our players defense from end line to end line. During most seasons, we will utilize some full court and three-quarter court pressure. Our purpose in learning defense all over the floor also involves a continuation of our philosophy of totally aggressive basketball. Furthermore, a player who has learned to cover all over the floor and who has confidence in his one on one defensive ability will be a tougher defensive player within the half court or scoring area.

We first divide the court in half and slide at forty-five degree angles from one end of the court to the other. The sliding technique of all of our players is viewed and corrected. There is no ball and no offensive opponent. To review the proper sliding technique, we stress a good, balanced defensive stance with the head directly over the midpoint between the two feet. The feet are staggered with the knees bent, rear low, and back straight but not stiff. This is an excellent time to develop good habits in the position of the defensive players hands and arms. There is no inclination to steal the ball or pressure of any type from an offensive player. Insistence on the proper position of the hands and arms in this drill will make it easier for the player when an offensive player and a ball are added. We coach our players to keep their hands about waist high with the palms up. They are taught never to reach in for the steal. We sometimes call this ''slashing''. We want to pressure the ball handler into making his own mistakes and then we will capitalize on the error. We take a lead step in the direction of the slide and simultaneously make a strong push-off with the back foot. The lead foot points in the direction the defender is sliding. This technique holds true throughout any sliding action. The player is always pushing off with his back foot and stepping with the lead foot. The feet never come together. As soon as the back foot (push foot) comes within six to nine inches of the lead foot, it executes another push-off and this footwork continues. The head remains level throughout the sliding movement. If the head is bobbing, the player is slowing himself down through wasted motion. The rear end of the defensive player does not protrude as this would cause the back to bend too far and a wider stance to develop. An unbalanced stance would be created and this is not recommended.

In dividing the court in half, we establish an imaginary line down the center of the floor. We tape the line for practice purposes. The players are required to plant their foot on this line and the sideline when changing directions on the sliding angles. Our objective in guarding a man full court or in the half court area will be to make that player turn or change directions as many times as possible in attempting to advance the ball toward the basket. We feel this type of pressure will lead to forced errors. There are several reasons for this. The offensive player will be prone to mistakes because: 1) he will not be able to see the whole floor and his teammates very well; 2) he will not be able to see his defensive man or the other defenders. This defensive method will also offset some of the offensive player's quickness and take away many of his one on one moves. Finally, this type of pressure will wear down the ball handler as the game progresses. To accomplish this the defensive player must completely seal off any route the offensive player is trying to manuever in bringing the ball. The defender cannot attempt to cut his man off at the sideline and leave some space for the ball handler to drive through. The same idea applies when trying to cut a man off in the middle. The outside foot must completely cut off the dribbler. He must be forced to change direction or commit a charging foul. Even though there is no imaginary line in a full court game situation, our players must apply the above idea to completely overplay the offensive opponent. For our drill purposes, the lines will simulate a change of direction by the offensive player and as a result, the defensive player will follow suit.

There are two ways to execute the change of direction defensively. Each will be determined by the actions of the ball handler. The first involves a drop-stepping action with the inside or back foot as shown in Figure 5-1. The defender plants his outside foot and drops the inside foot to a position to become the lead foot in the other direction at a forty-five degree angle. The defender must stay low throughout the movement so as to facilitate a quick change of direction. This type of execution is required when the offensive player changes direction by the use of a reverse dribble or a behind-the-back dribble. The defender must give a little ground and select the next angle at which he will cut off the dribbler. If the defender does not give ground in this situation, the offensive player will have the opportunity to gain a step on the defensive man and take a more direct route to he basket. Failure to give ground could also lead to contact and a foul on the defender if he was not completely set before the contact was initiated.

The only other way the offensive player can change direction is by the use of the crossover dribble. When this occurs, the defender should close off the area between he and the dribbler rather than drop step to give ground. This defensive manuever is shown in Figure 5-2. Again, the defensive man plants his outside foot in cutting off the ball handler. As he sees the opponent begin to execute the crossover dribble, the defender shifts his momentum in the opposite direction, but does not open up or drop the back foot. The defender keeps his hands low and stays in tight forcing the offensive player to pick up the basketball or risk a turnover. The hands are kept low for a possible deflection, but the defender must never reach in causing an unbalanced stance and an improper shift in momentum.

We teach the drop step first and then introduce the technique used in defensing the crossover dribble. Accuracy in executing

FIG. 5-1

FIG. 5-2

all of the aforementioned principles is again the first order of business. We run the drill at half and then three-quarter speed, correcting bad habits and reinforcing the good habits. Once a satisfactory level of accuracy has been attained, we begin to stress quickness. While it is debatable whether the actual quickness of a player can be increased, it is certain that an improved sliding technique and an improved effort can lead to a quicker movement on the part of the defensive player. Before we even put in an offensive opponent and a ball, we want the players working on their lateral quickness and speed in getting from end line to end line. We want a lot of enthusiasm from our coaches and squad in running this drill, especially when we are working on quickness. The enthusiasm we generate will encourage the players to develop some pride in their defense and will indicate the emphasis and importance we place on improvement in this area.

We must admit that if we have an exceptionally quick player who is excellent defensively, we will not be overly concerned with his defensive form or his sliding technique. We will be if we think some corrections will make the player a better defensive player, but the bottom line is results. With the exception of some of the basic principles mentioned previously, we don't care how a great defensive player gets the job done. Some very smart defensive players use unorthodox techniques in confusing and controlling their offensive opponent. The single most important individual defensive concept we teach our players provides the basis for our thinking in this regard. We will be discussing that shortly.

The next step in our first full court individual defensive drill is to add an offensive player. This drill still does not include a ball. We ask the offensive player to run at forty-five degree angles for the length of the floor at half speed. He runs back and forth from the sideline to the imaginary middle line. There is no faking or stopping and starting. The defender is to slide with his offensive opponent, keeping the proper distance and spacing in relation to his body position. The defensive player should be close enough to the man he is guarding so that he can reach out and grab the man's shirt at the chest level. If he is just able to touch the offensive player, he is giving him too much room. Not enough pressure will be applied. He must reach out and grab the shirt. Once the slide begins the defender's head should be aligned with the ballside hip of the offensive player until he is ready to cut him off and make him turn the other way. In other words, the head is in line with the left hip if the ball handler is going to his left and the right hip if he is going right.

We next allow the offensive player to utilize fakes in running the drill. He still must run at forty-five degree angles but he doesn't have to reach the lines to change direction. He can change direction at anytime within the contained (sideline to imaginery center line) area or he can fake a change of direction and continue to one of the lines. The offensive player is still running at half speed. The defender is required to react to the moves of his offensive opponent, maintaining the proper relationship with regard to distance and spacing. Quick reactions and quick movement are a must for the defender. We are placing him at a decided disadvantage because the offensive player does not have to worry about the ball or the pressure applied by the defense. The next aspect of the drill involves the offensive player with the basketball. We have the ball handler again move at forty-five degree angles from line to line the length of the floor. We start the offensive player at three-quarter speed and progress to full speed. The defensive men are working on the same ideas as mentioned previously, but we will further emphasize the quickness of the feet by requiring the defenders to keep the hands behind the back. The defenders must continue to concentrate on quick movement because the ball handlers, while having to control the ball on the dribble, still do not have to worry about the active hands of the defense. We really highlight a mistake or turnover by the offense in this part of the drill because we sell our players on the fact that the quickness of the feet will apply more pressure and cause more turnovers than will any hand or arm action. We feel that the offense will make the mistakes through us forcing the action. We don't need any reaching or slashing or continued attempts for the spectacular steal. After drilling with this emphasis on quick feet, we allow the defensive players to use their hands, but only in the prescribed manner. The palms should be up so that any deflection or steal will come from underneath or, at worst, the side of the ball. This will greatly limit the chance for contact and a foul on the defender. We want the hands to be active, bothering the ball handler, but not reaching in to try for a steal. We want the ball handler to feel the pressure from our defensive quickness and active hands. He will make the mistakes if we don't make them first. Our philosophy in this regard should not indicate a total lack of appreciation for the defensive steal. We do not rule out any individual initiative when the opportunity for a steal presents itself. We do feel, however, that a player must have an excellent chance of stealing the ball if the effort involved is going to leave him off balance or out of position.

The drill now progresses to a live one on one drill within the contained area. All restrictions are off the offensive player with the exception that he must stay within the previously mentioned boundaries. The defensive man is free to apply any and all defensive pressure with the objective of turning the offensive man as many times as possible or keeping him from crossing the half line within the ten second time limit. Perhaps this is the time to introduce and explain the individual defensive concept we alluded to earlier as being so important in our defensive scheme of things. As with most areas of basketball, it is not a new concept. It was not invented here at the University of Missouri and we are certainly not the only

Defensive Overplay

program in the country that incorporates it in its defensive system. We do place a great deal of emphasis on this concept in our teaching of individual defense and we do feel that it fits in quite well with our aggressive style of basketball. This element of defense has been successful for us and we think everyone would do well to consider it in theory. The idea again is to make something happen.

Generally, defensive players are taught to overplay their offensive counterpart one-half man to his strong side. The idea is that the offensive player is forced to use his weak hand, limiting his effectiveness and increasing the possibility of a turnover. It is our contention that those "on the defense" can take this philosophy one step further and neutralize an offensive player with a greater amount of ability. The average offensive player can at times be completely dominated utilizing this defensive concept. What we are describing is a philosophy of defense that takes the offensive away from the team that is in possession of the ball. The opponent has the basketball, and by definition he is the offensive player, but we tell our players to take the offensive away from the ball handler. They are taught to make him react to their pressure and their moves, rather than vice versa. Why let the offensive player make the first move and then try to react? Then we are truly on the defensive. The defender is extremely vulnerable to a second or third move by the offensive player, especially when the first was used to decoy or set up the defensive man for the additional moves.

Active use of the hands on the part of the defender is the first vehicle by which the offensive and defensive roles can be reversed. However, to completely take control of the opponent, we advocate giving him an avenue to advance the basketball and then taking it away. Instead of just overplaying the ball handler, we completely take away either the inside or the outside route to the basket. In a full court situation, we will usually force the player to use his weak hand. By playing an opponent head up or with a slight overplay you are giving the offensive player two directions in which to maneuver. Using our method, the offensive player has only one way to go and the defender knows which way that is and is able to anticipate the movement. While the defender is forcing the man to one side or the other, he must already have picked out a spot on the floor where he will cut him off. Many a charge can be drawn by this simple maneuver of giving the offensive player an avenue for advancement and then quickly beating him to a predetermined spot in that direction. Obviously, the defender cannot go for the charge every time, but a smart player will pick his spots.

The offensive player is now reacting to the defense rather than the defender waiting until the offense has made the first move and then trying to adjust. Let's envision a one on one confrontation with the defender playing head up on the offensive player who still has his dribble. This type of situation puts the defender at an extreme disadvantage, especially if the offensive player is quicker and if there is quite a bit of open floor. How many times have you seen the offensive man make a fake and blow by the defender with a quick move while he was reacting to that fake? The defensive player cannot give the ball handler two ways to go and expect to react in time to apply any pressure. This is vitally important when the offensive player has not used his dribble. The defender is very susceptible to a breakdown because the offensive player is much quicker going into his dribble than off the dribble. **The defender must force the offensive player to put the ball on the floor.** His second objective is still to turn the offensive man as much as possible. The reasons for this have been discussed. Once the ball handler has made the first move, the defender has to react. Inevitably, the offensive player will advance the ball and the defensive man is forced to make up that reaction time, beat the dribbler to a (now undetermined) spot, and make him turn or pick up the ball. The offensive player, since he made the first move and forced the defender to react may have already planned his next move (i.e. a reverse) and the defensive man is again reacting or has possibly been beaten.

Now let's envision a player using our defensive method. In Figure 5-3, the defensive man is completely overplaying the ball handler, allowing him only one direction in which to manuever. The line shows that the defender has picked out the angle and the spot that he will be able to cut off the progress of the dribbler. The correct angle is important. If the defender tries to cut off the offensive player at too sharp an angle, contact will be made and the defensive man will probably be whistled for a foul. At the same time, if the angle is too wide, the offensive player will have the opportunity to gain a step or two on the defender. The dribbler has only one way to go and that is to his left. Our defender has made the first move, the offense has reacted. Now the defensive man will slide quickly to his predetermined spot, overplay the dribbler to that side and again give him only one direction to go. The offense must now react again to our defense rather than the defense trying to react to his offensive movement. An argument might be that the offensive player could start to his left with one or two dribbles and then reverse or cross over in the opposite direction while our defender is moving to cut him off. The answer is that we have now met our two main objectives. The offensive player has put the ball on the floor and he has been forced to turn or change direction. Furthermore, the crossover dribble would be extremely hard to execute if the defensive player has maintained the proper spacing. On the reverse or behind the back dribble, there should be no problem in drop-stepping and again beating the offensive player to a spot to cut him off. We expect our players to be intelligent when using these methods and encourage them to develop their ability to

FIG. 5-3

Individual Defense 141

anticipate. These characteristics will be essential in the success of this defensive concept.

After our players have developed the skills we have described and attained a certain level of achievement in their one on one abilities, we expand the drill situation to include the entire court. Giving the offensive player the entire court to work with is extremely difficult for the defender so this is a great drill as far as defensive preparation is concerned. If a player can learn to pressure his offensive opponent in this type of wide open situation, he will be ready to face anything that can occur during game conditions. This drill progresses into two on two work and on up to five on five, which we will discuss later in relation to team defense.

Individual Defensive Techniques in the Half Court Area

Our fundamental drill for teaching defense on the ball in the half court area we refer to as **Driving Line One on One.** We can place the driving line at any angle on the floor and work on our one on one defense. The two primary angles are from the guard and the wing positions. The corner position is also very important because we teach our players some different ideas on how to use the baseline. The stance, sliding technique, and defensive principles are basically the same as we have already outlined. There are three differences which we discuss right from the beginning of fall practice. First of all, there can be a slight differential in a player's stance when guarding the ball in the scoring area. Some players, in defensing the ball full court, assume a relatively low stance in an effort to aid their quickness. This can be a detriment in the scoring area because the defender is sometimes too low to properly contest a quick shot by his offensive man. Additionally, we ask our players to not only stop their man from scoring, but also to stop him from throwing a pass that will lead to a score. By assuming a low stance the defender will give his offensive counterpart an unobstructed view into our defense and into a potential scorer. If we can obstruct the vision of the ball handler or congest a potential scoring area, we want to do so as long as we don't leave ourselves vulnerable in other areas. As the defensive man on the ball, all of our defenders must learn to play in a good, comfortable position at all times but to adjust to the level of the ball handler. If the offensive player is attempting to drive the defender must assume a low stance to insure maximum quickness. However, if the offensive player is playing straight up looking into our defense the defender must make the adjustment. The second difference involves the position of the hands and arms. In the half court area, we want one hand up and one hand down (Figure 5-4). The photo shows the offensive player looking for his shot. In this situation we want a hand up on the ball side to discourage the shot. The opposite hand is down in case the ball handler decides to drive. When the offensive player is utilizing the dribble we want the hand on the ball side in a down position about waist high, still with the palm up. The hand opposite the

FIG. 5-4

ball is up in an effort to discourage a direct pass to one of the opponent's teammates.

The third difference has to do with the direction we want the ball handler to take in any attempt at driving to the basket. In our full court defense, we want the offensive player to start out dribbling with his weak hand so we overplay him on his strong side. Depending on the floor position and the dexterity of the ball handler, this could be to the inside (middle) or to the outside. **Once the offense crosses half court we want to force everything to the outside.** There are a couple of reasons for this and there is also an occassion for an exception to the rule. The exception occurs when there is an offensive player at the wing position and there is no help below him. That is, there is no offensive player in the corner. Thus there is no defensive help or any player congestion to aid the defensive man on the ball. In this case, the man on the ball should force the wing player back into the middle where there should be considerable player congestion and ample defensive help.

One of the reasons we force to the outside is because we will have a better chance of keeping the ball on the sidelines. Many offenses can be neutralized by keeping the ball on one side. Better weakside help develops and the offense can easily become lax at reversing the ball. The offense will make mistakes by trying to force the action on one side. Another reason we force to the outside is because of the breakdown possibilities when a ball handler penetrates the middle. The penetrator now has passing angles in every direction by which he can deliver the ball to a teammate whose defensive man has dropped off to help (Dia. 5-1). Two of these passing angles can lead to an uncontested lay up. This is a dangerous situation, especially with an excellent scorer and/or excellent passer handling the basketball. The help in this situation can come out from the basket area or in from the outside. There can be no organized manner for rotating to provide help.

Contrast this to the action shown in Diagram 5-2. The offensive player is forced to the baseline and all the help is rotating in the same direction—**toward the basket.** The passing angles are nowhere near as sharp or well defined because of the position of the ball handler and the position of the defense. The top defenders drop to clog the middle or pick up the man of a teammate who has helped. The weakside defenders are further congesting the area and forcing the ball handler to pass the ball back out or take a bad shot. Finally, by forcing the ball handler to the outside, we are moving him laterally—away from the basket, and reducing his area of manueverability. It is vitally important that the defender control his man. He cannot give the offensive player too much room to the outside or breakdowns will result.

In the driving line drill, we encourage a lot of competition among our players. We compete according to size and

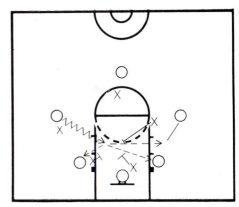

DIA. 5-1

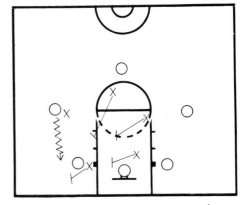

DIA. 5-2

Individual Defense 143

position, so it is again a man against man proposition that will be important in selecting a starting five and determining the status of all the players. We want to sell our players on the value of defensive intensity and the competition factor is one of the ways we can accomplish this. The driving line again provides a wide open one on one situation that is much more difficult than our players will face in a game. The players learn that if they can control their man in this type of situation, they can be much more aggressive and confident when playing defense under five on five conditions.

The one on one defensive techniques are the same as we have discussed. We still want to make the ball handler turn as much as possible (this will vary in a game depending on who we are playing) and we want to continue our attempt to put the offensive player on the defense. Each player must accept the individual responsibility for controlling his man, but he must also be confident that help will be provided when needed. A good team defense will do much to encourage further individual aggressiveness and an increased pressure on the offense. These ideas are discussed with the players in developing the one on one skills and are emphasized when we begin teaching team defense.

Individual Tactics When Guarding the Ball

1. Be confident in your ability to hold your man and confident that your teammates will provide help.
2. Anticipate your opponent's moves. Make him go one way and then cut him off. He cannot run over you—he must find an open avenue to the basket. Don't let him have it.
3. Study your man the first few times down the floor. Read his movements (applies when guarding man without the ball also).
4. Overplay your opponent. Force him to the outside, but keep a relative position between your man and the basket.
5. Know the areas on the floor from where your man likes to score.
6. Take advantage of the offensive player's weak hand.
7. Don't reach in. Pick at the ball, bother the ball handler, but don't get off balance.
8. Talk to your teammates and listen for their communication.
9. Be aggressive. Try to completely control your man. Force him to make mistakes.
10. If the offensive player puts the ball over his head, belly-up to him and apply pressure to the ball. Apply extreme pressure if the ball handler has already used up his dribble.
11. Remember the scouting report. Have an idea of where the ball handler wants to go with the ball, by dribbling or passing. Try to block that option.
12. Do not allow an uncontested shot. Get the hand up and on the ball. Jump straight up when contesting the shot. Do not leave your feet until your opponent leaves his or the ball has left his hands.
13. Get off your man and toward the direction of the pass when your man passes the basketball. Jump to the ball immediately, but do not turn your head to follow the flight of the ball. Use your peripheral vision to see the ball and your man. Never turn your back on your man.
14. On a shot attempt, make contact with your man and go after the ball. Don't allow the second or third shot.

Pressure the Ball When Picked Up

Any time an offensive player puts the ball over his head, we want our defenders in a belly-up position as shown in Figure 5-5. Both hands are up and jamming the basketball. The knees are bent with the legs outside the offensive player. The ball handler must be forced to make a quarter or half turn to bring the basketball back down. When this happens, the defensive player can readjust to his regular defensive stance in anticipation of a one on one move. As long as the defender is jamming the basketball and the offensive player, that player will be unable to execute a dribble drive without turning to bring the ball down safely. Thus, there will be sufficient reaction time for the defender to assume the more conventional stance. This defensive technique increases in importance when the ball handler has already used up his dribble. In this situation the defender is free to not only jam the offensive opponent, but to apply extreme pressure, knowing that the ball can only be advanced by means of the pass. The defender should apply pressure with his hands and arms, but should be careful that he does not commit a foul by being overly aggressive. There must be no contact and the potential for contact must be avoided. Many times in this type of situation the defender can be whistled for a foul, when in actuality, the ball handler caused the contact.

Contesting the Shot

We require a hand up on all shots attempted in our defensive end. The thinking behind this is based on the study at Ohio State on the percentages for success of the contested and uncontested shots (see Chapter Two). The defensive player must get off his feet, get his hand up, and force the shooter to change his shot to avoid a block or deflection. The defender cannot merely raise his hand in an effort to distract the shooter. The good shooter will recognize a half-hearted attempt and will not be concerned about the defensive pressure being applied. We ask our players to get up quickly and to try to get a hand on the basketball just before or just after it leaves the shooter's hands. Even if they are unable to get a hand on the ball, the shooter might have to change his shot or at least lose a little concentration due to the defensive pressure. The correct way to contest a shot is illustrated in Figure 5-6 while an incorrect method is shown in Figure 5-7. The incorrect method is sure to lead to a foul on the part of the defender. In contesting the shot, the defender must jump straight up in the air and try to place his hand on the ball. There can be no slapping at the ball or an over-extension of the hand in attempting to block the shot. The defender must also wait for one of two things to happen before he leaves his feet to contest a shot. Either the offensive player must leave his feet for the shot or the ball must be in the air heading for the basket. The defensive player cannot react to the fakes of the shooter.

FIG. 5-5

FIG. 5-6   Correct

FIG. 5-7   Incorrect

Individual Defense 145

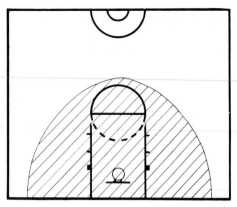

DIA. 5-3

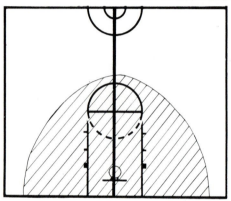

DIA. 5-4

Defense Off the Ball

There are two important ideas that we convey to our players when we begin to teach individual defense on a man without the basketball. The first is simply that the man cannot score if he does not have the basketball. The more the defender can keep the ball from his offensive opponent, the better chance he will have of holding the opponent under his scoring average. This is an obvious defensive concept that is taught universally, but that does not limit its importance. The second idea follows the same general thinking. It is not as widely taught as the first concept, but we feel it is even more important when you consider the defense under game conditions rather than on paper. The offensive player is going to handle the ball. There is no way a defensive player can keep his opponent from getting the basketball for the entire game. This goal becomes more difficult as the relative ability of the offensive player increases and is especially difficult if there are special screens and plays designed to free a particular offensive performer. The key then is to follow our second idea, which states that when the offensive player does catch the ball, make him catch it in an area outside his shooting range. The defender should know his man and should never let him catch the ball where he is most dangerous. Every player has his favorite shots and favorite positions on the floor from which to manuever. The trick is to make that player play from an unfamiliar or uncomfortable position. This is easy to accomplish when a player has let himself slide into predictable moves and patterns. It is not so easy when the player has developed a more complete offensive repertorie. The individual and team scouting report should help and the player should try to study his man the first few times down the court to get a feel for his offensive movements.

We ask our players to envision an area inside twenty-one feet to the basket and an area outside twenty-one feet (Dia. 5-3). Our players are to deny the basketball inside that twenty-one foot area. They should make it as difficult as possible for their man to receive a pass that close to the basket. Ideally, a pass would never be completed within that area. We are attempting to push the offensive players and the ball out beyond the twenty-one foot mark. The farther out on the floor we can push the ball, the less effective the offense is going to be.

After establishing our twenty-one foot denial area, we next divide the court in half to develop our ballside and helpside rules (Dia. 5-4). Bobby Knight, while at Army, popularized the terms "ballside" and "helpside" to add further meaning to the still widely used terms of strongside and weakside. The strongside or ballside is defined as the area of the court (divided by our line down the middle) in which the ball is being played. The weakside or helpside refers to the area that is opposite from the ball. These can change quickly and often, depending on the movement of the ball by the offensive team. Coach Knight feels, and we agree, that the ballside term places more emphasis on the fact that the ball is the focal point of your defense. Likewise, the term helpside will aid the players in remembering their responsibilities when the ball is away from them on the opposite side of the floor. We place a great deal of emphasis on a helping defense, so we feel this is an improvement in our defensive terminology. The defensive responsibilities are made simpler because of the floor diagrams we issue to our players to facilitate their understanding of our rules. The ballside defenders will deny all passes into the twenty-one foot area. The only exception can occur when an offensive player is within that area but is more than one pass away from the ball as shown in Diagram 5-5. The defensive men one pass away from the ball (X_2, X_3) are overplaying their men in a denial position. The corner player is two passes away, so X_4 can afford to open up toward the ball, splitting the differences between a denial position and a position of help. He should still be in a position to pick off a pass to O_4, should the offense choose to skip a receiver. We should mention that this situation will not occur often in most offenses because of the floor balance that must be maintained. Our general rule, then, is that the defenders are denying the pass to their man when the ball is on their side of the floor and they are within the twenty-one foot area.

Denial Position

Our denial position is illustrated in Figure 5-8. This position is very basic and extremely important to our defensive system, because it is used extensively when guarding a man without the basketball. This semi-crouched stance remains relatively the same, whether the defender is denying the lead pass to the wing position, defensing a cut down the lane, across the lane, or up the lane, or trying to keep the ball out of the post. We ask our players to keep the arm and leg nearest the ball in the passing lane to totally deny the chances for a completed pass. We do not align the head in the passing lane, because this will decrease the defender's ability to split his vision between his man and the ball. With his head slightly back off the passing lane, the defensive man has a wider angle by which he can utilize his peripheral vision. We teach the players to pick out an estimated point of vision on the floor (see photo) that will enable them to see their man and the ball with equal emphasis. Many players make the mistake of maintaining light body contact with the offensive player, thinking that this is the way to offset the offensive advantages. This will only lead to foul trouble and defensive mistakes caused by being too close to the opponent. There are angles to play in any sport and basketball is no exception. Notice in the illustration that the defender is approximately three feet off his man and up toward the point where the ball is being played. He is playing the angle of interception. There

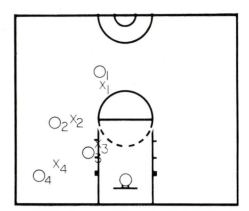

DIA. 5-5

FIG. 5-8   Tom Dore denies a lead pass versus San Jose in the 1980 NCAA Tournament.

Individual Defense 147

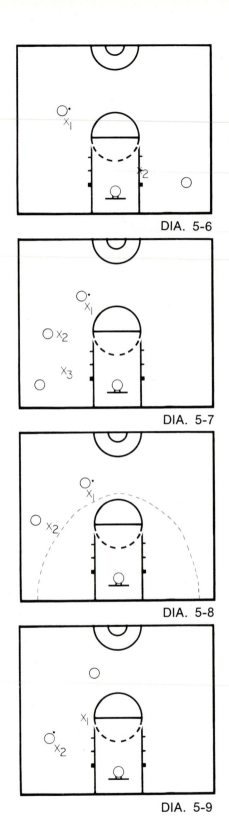

DIA. 5-6

DIA. 5-7

DIA. 5-8

DIA. 5-9

is no advantage to guarding the offensive player tightly, unless he is in the post position or lane area. The defender should maintain this distance from the offense until the potential receiver is in a position near enough the passer that this angle is no longer advantageous. We advocate the use of an armbar as illustrated in the photo, to avoid contact with the opponent. The armbar is to be used only as a deterrent in keeping the offensive player away from the defender's body or to gain some feel for the offensive player's movements if contact is unavoidable. Our players must learn to play defense in this position and to totally deny the basketball in that twenty-one foot area.

Helpside Positioning

There are four defensive situations that call for an individual defensive player to assume helpside positioning. These are shown in the accompanying diagrams. The first and most obvious is when the defender is away from the ball and clearly in the area designated as the helpside (Dia. 5-6). A ball side defender two passes away from the ball should also be in a helping position somewhat closer to his man as explained earlier (Dia. 5-7). As we mentioned, this does not happen often, but can occur a few times a game, so there should be some rules and preparations for handling this type of situation. The third possibility for helpside positioning will depend on our scouting report or defensive strategy for a particular team and particular individuals. In some instances, we may want to apply pressure outside the twenty-one foot area. We also may want to keep the ball away from a particular offensive opponent at all times. We would then be denying this individual all over the floor. For the most part, however, any defensive man on the ballside whose opponent is outside the twenty-one foot area, will be in a position of help, as shown in Diagram 5-8. Finally, the ballside defender out front will be required to help any time his man does not have the ball (Dia. 5-9). This will usually be one of the guards. The pass to his man will not be a penetrating pass, so we will give that up to concentrate on additional help. We will see in describing the technique and body position of the helpside defender that they will only be one step off the line of the ball, so they should still be in a position to discourage a direct pass.

These thoughts are equally applicable under the heading of team defense, but we feel they are important in introducing the stance and responsiblities of the helpside defender. Whether you classify defense away from the ball as individual or team is unimportant—the principles are the same. We feel there has to be an excellent balance between the individual responsibility of holding a particular man and the responsibility toward a team effort. Again, the scouting reports and defensive strategy will help in this regard because there will be an emphasis on who will need help and who can afford to give help according to our defensive matchups.

Figure 5-9 shows the stance and relative physical relationship to the ball that the defensive man will assume in the circumstance we have diagrammed and described. The player in the photo is demonstrating a helping position. The defender in these circumstances should position himself one step below the line of the ball. The line of the ball refers to a direct line drawn between the offensive man the player is guarding and the ball. The defensive player will generally be just below the mid-point between his man and the ball on this line. The distance of this ball-you-man relationship will depend entirely on how far the offensive man is from the basket and the ball. The greater the distance the more the defender can float toward the middle in a helping position. Our defensive man must be careful not to get too far off his man or he will, in effect, be extending his own area of recovery.

FIG. 5-9

FIG. 5-10

The defender should open slightly in the direction of the ball by dropping his foot nearest the ball back toward the goal. He should still be looking at a spot on the floor that will enable him to keep an eye on his man and the progress of the ball. This will be crucial in maintaining the proper ball-you-man relationship one step off the line of the ball. Anytime the offensive man moves or the ball moves that line will change and the defensive player must adjust accordingly. If the offensive man without the ball makes a cut toward his teammate with the ball, the defender must react in time to deny the pass and, if necessary, close off the distance between himself and his man. This type of awareness and quick reaction can only be accomplished by the use of split vision. A player who turns his head to concentrate on the ball will be continually getting beat by a smart offensive player. By the same token, a player who turns his back to the ball will be of no help to his teammates and will undermine our concept of team defense. To encourage the use of split vision and to help our players remember the correct relationship, we require them to point to the man they are guarding and to the ball (Figure 5-10). This is emphasized early in the practice sessions when we are teaching our defensive system. As the players learn proper positioning and the proper use of split vision we discontinue the requirement for pointing man and ball.

We have a series of defensive drills that cover all of the individual defensive situations that can occur in a half court situation. For that matter, the same cuts and the same defensive principles can be somewhat applied to defense in the full court area. There are only so many options or cuts that the offensive player has at his disposal. These options are futhrer limited, depending on whether the player is with or without the basketball. We have already discussed our Driving Line One on One Drill and we are primarily concerned here with defense away from the ball. There are basically six cuts or situations that the defensive player off the ball is going to have

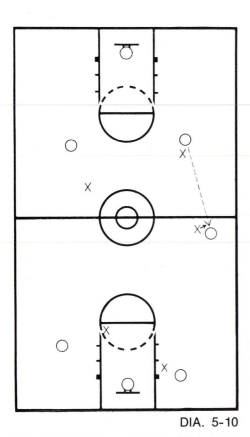

DIA. 5-10

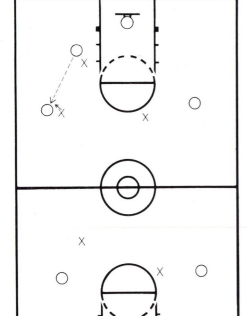

DIA. 5-11

to contend with under game conditions. We introduce these one at a time and explain the defensive coverage involved. Once the coverage is understood and the players have demonstrated some ability in properly defensing the individual cuts, we put the drills together in different combinations. Ultimately, when defensive execution has reached our high levels of expectation, we will combine all of the cuts into one all-encompassing defensive drill. From the start, however, we stress the importance of learning the proper defensive technique for each individual cut. As far as we are concerned, these are the fundamentals of defense. Our players' attention to these fundamentals will shape the success or lack of success with regard to their individual defense. As we stated in the beginning of this chapter, strong individual defensive players will serve as a solid foundation for an effective team defense.

Lead Pass Defense

It is the nature of most offenses that the guard to forward or guard to wing pass is the initiating pass most often used during the course of a game. This, then, is the first offensive cut we are concerned with in defensing a man off the ball. We have already described the denial position we will assume in defensing this cut (see Figure 5-8). We refer to this movement and the attempt to deliver the ball as the lead pass. We should note that the lead pass can be made from just about any position on the floor and certainly is not limited in direction to the wing area. The coverage involved remains the same for all areas so because of the frequency of passes to the wing position, we teach the defensive technique from that angle. The following diagrams (Diags. 5-10 and 5-11) should serve to further clarify our point. The passes being attempted are identical in movement and action to the guard to forward pass at the wing position. They too are referred to as lead passes and the defensive coverage required is the same as at the wing position, if we are pushing the ball to half court or all over the floor.

The organization of our Lead Pass Drill we will delineate at the end of the chapter. To breifly review the defensive technique involved, we stress:

1. semi-crouched stance.
2. inside arm and inside leg in passing lane.
3. pick out estimated point of vision on floor.
4. play the angle of interception—maintain distance from offense.
5. use armbar to avoid contact.

In running the drill at the wing position, we teach our players to maintain their distance (approximately three feet) from the offense. They must continue to play the angle of interception. This principle is especially important when the offensive player is trying to take the defender up the lane before breaking out to the side. If the offensive player can get into the defender's body, he will be able to push off slightly and make the quick cut to receive the pass. The players are taught to give ground only to the foul line extended, however. An angle of interception at this point would leave too much room for a possible backdoor cut or a pass behind the defender. The armbar must still be utilized, especially when our defender stops giving ground at the free throw line extended. Our stated objective is to deny any pass going into that twenty-one foot area. The defensive technique described is utilized to accomplish this goal, but can be adapted to fit the philosophy of any defensive system.

Defensing the Back Cut

The backdoor play or back cut is the next offensive manuever we cover in teaching individual defense off the ball. This cut can be very effective from the wing position, but again, is an offensive movement that can be executed from any point on the floor. We are mainly concerned with defensing the back cut in the half court area because this is where the lack of a proper technique can lead to a quick basket by the opponent. Out on the floor (full court situation) the defensive player needs only to move with his man or sprint to find his man if he is beaten momentarily.

Our players are taught to maintain their denial position so that they can see the man and the ball for as long a time as possible. In this way, the defender will not be susceptible to a backdoor fake and the offensive player stepping back out to receive the ball within the twenty-one foot area. If the offense does attempt a genuine backdoor play, we want our defensive man to retreat quickly, trying to maintain a ball-you-man relationship with the arm and leg in the passing lane. When an offensive man reaches the middle of the floor or basket area it is impossible for the defender to see both his man and the ball. In this situation the defensive man is taught to open to the ball because he can feel his opponent to try and read his intentions or movements. The defender must stay in a position between his man and the ball to discourage the pass into this dangerous area. We teach the defender to open up only when he can swing his inside leg into or right on the free throw or three second lane. The outside leg or leg nearest the basket is used to pivot. The pivot is made with the inside hand down and the outside hand being used to "feel" the opponent. The inside hand is down in the pivot because the most likely pass out of this action is the bounce pass leading the cutter. The defensive man should continue to feel the offensive player with the outside hand. The defender must be ready to assume a defensive post position should the offensive player try to post up or to trail the offensive man across the lane in a ball-you-man relationship. The defender must also be ready to reassume his denial position should the offensive player break back out to the same side.

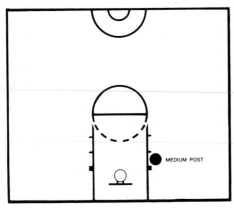

DIA. 5-12

FIG. 5-11

FIG. 5-12

Defensing the Post

The next step in teaching our individual defensive system is in defensing the post position. The high post, medium post, and low post responsibilities are somewhat different, so to simplify things and for our drill purposes, we start with defense on the player in the medium post. This is an area just outside the lane and anywhere from eight to twelve feet up from the baseline between the blocks (Dia. 5-12). Figure 5-11 shows the defensive posture and position in denying the ball into the post. The stance is basically the same as when we are denying the ball at the wing. The defensive player is just a little more upright and playing his man a little tighter. The leg and arm are still in the passing lane and the defender should be splitting his vision between the ball and his man. We like the players to use the armbar, but allow them to place their rear hand (right hand in this case) on the back of the offensive player to gain a feel for his movements. The pressure being applied by the hand is minimal. We do not want to get in a shoving match with the offensive man. We want to use our head and our feet to play position defense. It is vitally important that the defender keep his back foot behind the offensive player as shown in the photo. If the defensive man gets too far out in front, the offensive player will have inside position in the event a shot is attempted by one of his teammates. By keeping the back foot behind the opponent, the defender is able to deny the pass to the inside while still being able to box out, using a reverse pivot method (discussed in Chapter Eight).

The photograph depicts the defender playing on the high side of the offensive man with the ball out front at the guard position. When the ball is passed to the wing area or lower, we want the defensive man to re-establish his position on the low side of the man in the post. The defensive man cannot be content to go behind the offense because the ball can then be passed inside quickly from the wing. We utilize an X-move that calls for quick thinking and quick footwork on the part of the defender. As soon as the ball is passed the defensive man reacts according to how he has been taught. The time to move is while the ball is in the air, not after an offensive player has received the ball in a position to make a play. The X-move is illustrated in Figures 5-12 and 5-13. The defensive post man takes a short lead step with his front leg. As he plants his front foot, the back leg is swung between his body and the offensive post man (Fig. 5-12). The back foot then plants itself on the opposite side of the opponent and the front foot is swung in a reverse motion to a spot behind the post player (Fig. 5-13). The defensive man has simply reversed his position from the high to the low side. The defensive posture is the same except that the left side-right side relationship has been reversed. The defensive man should keep his body away from the offensive player as he executes this manuever so that the offensive player cannot get the defender on his hip on the high side. The defender must also be sure to re-establish the back foot upon completion of the X-move. Sometimes, it is impossible to place the back foot in the proper spot with one step. An additional step or movement of the leg is all that is required.

We feel that defensing the post position is one of the most important aspects of defensive fundamentals and considerable time is devoted to the teaching of and the proper execution of the necessary skills. All players should be able to play defense in the post because at one time or another, they will all find themselves in a posting situation. The offense won't ask which defensive players have had extended experience at that position before deciding who to post up. The front line players, especially the big men, get extra work in this area. They will, of course, get most of the action in this defensive situation. Additionally, these players are somewhat less skilled when it comes to the quick footwork and agility involved in the X-move.

The technique for defensing the low post (Dia. 5-13) is essentially the same as we have just described. The only difference involves the rules for playing the high side or the low side. When an offensive player is set up in a low post position, we will play him on the high side until the ball is moved to the baseline or corner area. The X-move is again utilized to keep the ball away from the offensive post man. We should mention the gray area that sometimes comes into play in this type of situation. There can be doubt and hesitation on the part of the defensive player when the ball is passed or dribbled a few feet below the wing position, yet is not really in the corner or baseline area. Actually, there is no problem because both the high side and the low side defensive positions can prevent the pass from this angle. The defensive player only has to make a small adjustment to the new passing lane. We explain this to the players and also encourage them to look for the right moment when they do have to execute the X-move. When the ball has just left the passer's hands or when a player is dribbling to the baseline are the best times to make the move. In this way, the defensive player cannot be caught off guard or beaten while making the defensive adjustment. The relative passing ability of the offensive player with the ball and the defensive pressure being applied on the ball are other areas to be considered in appraising this situation.

There is an occasion when we will completely front the medium or low post offensive player. We teach our defenders to recognize when the offense is set with only two men on the ballside. That means that there are three teammates playing helpside defense away from the ball. With this type of help behind him the defensive post man can afford to completely front his man without fear of the lob pass. The helpside defenders will be responsible for any lob pass attempted into the middle of the floor. The defensive player on the post must

FIG. 5-13

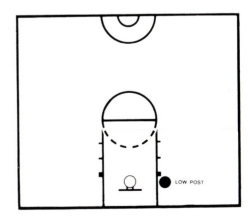

DIA. 5-13

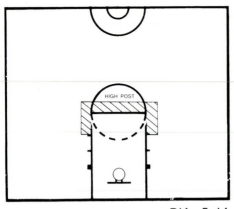

DIA. 5-14

be quick to reassume side positioning should the offensive set change. He must also react quickly to get his man off the boards if the shot is attempted.

Before discussing our ideas on defensing the high post, we would like to point out the ease with which we can combine these drills to cover more than one defensive fundamental. We start a player at the wing position with the ball out front. There is no defense on the ball but we have a defender attempting to deny the lead pass within the twenty-one foot area. If the pass is completed, a one on one driving line situation develops. If the defender is able to discourage the pass, the offensive wing man breaks backdoor. The offensive player then establishes himself at a medium post or low post position at which time the ball is moved to the next man in line at the wing and then to the corner. Depending on the area of emphasis at the time, we can eliminate one or more of the options. For instance, if we need work on our lead pass pressure, we can eliminate the one on one matchup. Now if the pass is completed to the wing player, the ball goes back out front and the lead pass option is repeated until the defender gets it right. We now have a three in one or four in one drill that can include; lead pass defense, one on one defense, defensing the backdoor play, and post defense. We feel these types of continuous drills are essential for developing the players' ability to react instinctively when playing defense under game conditions. There is still no substitute for repetition. These drills not only provide the repetition for each individual fundamental, but also teach the players the reactions involved in moving from one defensive fundamental to another.

The high post position can be on either side of the lane area from just above to slightly below the free throw line (Dia. 5-14). The player defensing the high post will be in a denial position always on the ball side of his man. His responsibility is to keep the ball out of this area, but he must also be alert to give support on a possible back cut by the ballside wing or any cut through this area by the outside offensive men. We do not require the high post defensive player to stay between his man and the ball when he changes from one side of the offensive player to the other. The defender must move quickly behind the offensive player upon movement of the ball. The idea is to beat the opponent to a particular spot on the floor that will satisfy the ball-you-man relationship. Anticipation and quick reactions are vitally important. Any time there is movement of the ball or his man the defender must adjust accordingly.

Defensing the Diagonal Cut

A widely used cut in any offense is when a player takes a diagonal path from the offensive weakside (our helpside) to the basketball in an attempt to receive a pass in or around the lane area (Dia. 5-15). Our four man coming across the lane (see Chapter Three—Team Offense) would be termed a

DIA. 5-15

diagonal cut. We usually run this drill from the positions and cutting angles set up in the diagram. As mentioned previously, however, this cut can be executed from different positions on the floor.

The offensive player is approximately three to five feet off the lane with the ball on the opposite side of the floor at the wing position. The defensive man (X_2) is in a helpside position one step below the line between his man and the ball. The defensive man uses his judgement as to how far he can play off his man with the idea of help in mind. This will depend on the distance his man is from the basket and the ball, but will also vary according to the relative abilities of his offensive man and the offensive player with the ball. The game situation can also have a direct bearing on this defensive relationship. The defensive player must always be in a defensive position with knees bent, ready to move. As the offensive player begins his cut the defender must react quickly to close off the distance between himself and his man. As the cutter enters a point almost to the middle of the lane area, he is now one pass away from the ball handler and is about to assume strongside (ballside) positioning. The defender must have already closed off the distance to totally deny this attempted pass into a very dangerous area. We want the defensive player to use his armbar in an effort to keep the offense away, but we also have the defender attempt to bodycheck the cutter up high where he does not want to go. There is generally some congestion at the high post area. Usually, one of our guards will be in a helping position in that area. We tell the defender on the diagonal cut to run the offensive player right up the back of our guard. There is no way the cutter should be allowed to come directly to the ball and receive an uncontested or unmolested pass in the middle of the floor. **The lane area is no man's land.** Ideally, the player should be totally denied the basketball until he continues out past the twenty-one foot area. In defensing this cut, our man has again assumed a denial position—semi-crouch, arm and leg in passing lane, etc. As we pointed out earlier in this chapter, the denial position is used extensively in executing the proper defensive coverage on the various offensive cuts.

Defense Versus the Lateral Cut

The fifth cut that can be executed offensively we define as a lateral cut. This movement is very similar to the diagonal cut, but is made more on a parallel line in relation to the baseline and the basket (Dia. 5-16). This very often involves a post man or frontline player moving from the weakside into a strongside post position so the defensive frontliners must be well drilled in this situation. Defensing this cut in the medium post and low post areas is especially important because of the offensive player's close proximity to the basket.

We run the drill with the ball at the diagonal position and with

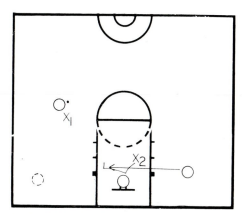

DIA. 5-16

the ball in the corner. It is obvious that the offensive player must be totally denied the basketball in this area. When an offensive player receives the ball this close to the basket he becomes a tremendous offensive threat. The threat increases relative to the offensive abilities of the receiver. Additionally, breakdowns can occur because our other defenders are forced to help out on the offensive player with the ball.

The defender is again in a helpside position one step below the line of the ball. On the lateral cut the defender does not have to be concerned with closing the distance between himself and his man because the offensive cutter will be coming to him. Essentially, the denial or lead pass position is again in effect. We do allow for more body checking and contact in this very critical area of the floor. As with the diagonal cut, we want to push the offensive player where he doesn't want to go. If the defender can discourage the offensive player from making a straight cut to the ball, we are one step ahead of the game. This is aggressive defense—making the offense react to our moves rather than merely trying to assume defensive position once the offensive player executes his cut. By then it will be too late.

Ideally, we would like our defensive man to force the cutter to the baseline. The passing angles that will result will be difficult when the ball is in the corner and extremely poor when the ball is at the wing. This will also allow the defender to open up to the ball and establish himself directly in the passing lane while the cutter is under the basket area. In this situation, there is no way that the defender can see both his man and the ball. Therefore, we want our players to open to the ball and feel behind them for the position of the offense. Once the offensive player is through the lane and trying to establish a post position, the defender must play him according to the post defense we have explained previously. If the ball is at the diagonal and the cutter continues out to the corner, the defender needs only to execute an X-move as the offensive man vacates the post area (see Fig. 5-13). From there the defensive man is applying lead pass pressure until the player is pushed beyond twenty-one feet. The X-move is made easier by the defender allowing the offensive player to go behind him. As he does, the defensive man feels behind to make sure the cutter is continuing to the corner and then adjusts to lead pass position between his man and the ball.

Reacting to the Give and Go Cut

The give and go cut is one of the most basic and one of the most successful manuevers in the game of basketball. There is a tendency on the part of all defenders to relax momentarily when their man passes the basketball. The offense is simply taking advantage of this tendency in the hope that it will lead to a lay up or an uncontested shot. Our players are made to realize that they can never relax on defense, especially just after their offensive opponent gives up the basketball. We constantly drill our players on getting off their man and toward the basketball as soon as the ball passes through their line of defense. This off and toward technique has to become an immediate and instinctive reaction to the movement of the ball. The quick, instinctive reaction is especially important in our defensive system because we require the defender to jam the ball when it is picked up by his offensive opponent. In the event of a successful pass, the defender cannot react slowly and allow his man to get between him and the ball. The ball-you-man relationship must be maintained.

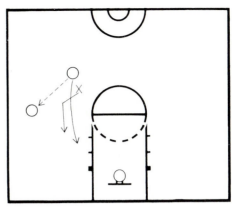

DIA. 5-17

We drill on defensing the give and go cut from various positions on the floor. An example is diagrammed to the right (Dia. 5-17). The players are taught to jump to the ball as soon as they feel it pass their fingertips. Their eyes immediately pick up the flight of the ball and then they focus on an imaginary spot on the floor that will enable them to see their man and the ball. The defensive man forces the cutter to go behind him and then maintains lead pass pressure as the player continues his cut. If the offensive player cuts through to a weakside offensive position, the defender stops in the middle of the floor and assumes a helpside position one step off the line of the ball. He does not follow his man out on the weakside. If the cutter tries to post up, the defensive man must be prepared to play post defense as we described earlier. Finally, if the cutter continues to the corner, the defender utilizes the X-move and assumes the denial position on the opposite side.

The players must be drilled from different spots on the floor so that they realize that the give and go cut can be executed from any position and from just about any pass. It is not limited to any one area, nor is it limited to the penetrating or lead passes. When a reverse pass is made, such as from the corner to the wing, the defender must still jump to the ball and force the offensive player to go behind.

We feel that the mastery of these defensive fundamentals along with the ability to play defense on the ball will prepare our players for the individul situations that will occur under game conditions. By our determination, the techniques described are the best methods for defensing the cuts that are available to the offense. The challenge is to develop in the players the proper execution of those techniques with enough repetition that the reactions become instinctive. Coaches today are placing a great deal of emphasis on movement without the basketball in their particular offensive systems. As seen in Chapter Three, we stress the importance of purposeful movement without the ball. It is obvious, then, that the individual defenders must be able to react properly and without hesitation to the movements of their offensive counterparts. The defensive effort that is extended while the offensive player is working to free himself will make the defenders job that much easier when and if the offensive player is able to receive the ball. The defender must force his opponent to work extremely hard to get open and must never let him receive the ball in a favorite area or spot from which he is particularly dangerous.

To further develop in our players the ability to properly respond to these offensive manuevers, we combine the aforementioned drills into one drill involving all six offensive cuts. Each defender must now learn to keep the ball away from his opponent in every situation in a continuous action type drill. This type of action can occur in any given trip down the floor so it is imperative that our defenders learn to make the proper adjustments. The **Six in One Drill** will be explained thoroughly at the conclusion of this chapter along with the organization of all of our individual defensive drills.

Additional Pointers Regarding Individual Defense

We also teach the following principles to our players regarding the habits they should develop to improve their individual defense. These are issued in a handout and stressed throughout the season. Some have been mentioned previously.

1. You can never relax on defense. When your man does not have the basketball, you must be alert and ready to help or adjust your position.
2. With proper concentration and effort you should never have a bad night defensively.
3. Learn to control your man defensively. Try to take the offensive away from him.
4. Stay low with the hands moving. Active hands.
5. Do not underestimate your opponent. Play him hard and use your head.
6. Develop a positive defensive attitude. Have confidence in your ability to stop your man.
7. Improve your peripheral vision so you can develop the ability to see your man and the ball at the defensive end.
8. Anticipate at all times. Be aggressive. Make something happen defensively.
9. Take pride in your defensive ability, effort, and improvement.
10. Keep the head level. Do not bob up and down.
11. Do not allow the feet to come together or cross.
12. Execute the drop step when presented with a behind the back or reverse dribble.
13. Close up the distance on a crossover dribble. Keep hands low.
14. Change up your tactics. Confuse and thus control your offensive opponent.
15. Force your man to start out with his weak hand when guarding full court. Force to the outside in the half court area.
16. Make the quick transition from offense to defense. Pick up your man as quickly as possible once the transition is made, but don't give up the basket.
17. Do not rush a player who has the ball and has not used his dribble. Be sure you can contain him.

18. Deny all passes in the twenty-one foot area. Try to keep the ball from ever entering the lane area.
19. Force your man to take the low percentage shot.
20. If you lose your man, go to the basket and work your way out.
21. Any loose ball has to be ours. The aggressive, hustling team that is not afraid to mix it up will pick up the majority of the loose balls.
22. Always be ready to draw the offensive charge. This can be a difference of four points in the game situation and can generate momentum for your team.
23. Avoid fouling. Keep the hands off and play defense with your feet and your head.
24. **All it takes to play defense is hard work and the right amount of effort. Are you up to the challenge?**

Defensing the Three on One and Two on One Fast Break

Every team member and especially the guards must be prepared to play defense in a fast break situation where the offense has the decided advantage. Invariably, this situation is going to come up a few times during the course of a game. The team that is prepared and has some sound ideas on how to combat this advantage is going to save a few points that quite possibly could mean the difference between victory and defeat. In a game between two fast breaking teams, chances are that this situation will crop up more than a few times at each particular end. Drilling in this area will be of great value if your players can hold off a few of these attempts while the opponents may be resigning themselves to what they determine to be a hopeless disadvantage.

Stalling tactics can, at times, be all that is needed to hold up the offense and allow the rest of the defense to make the proper transition. A steal, turnover, or offensive charge would be especially demoralizing to the opponent and can lead to the same advantage at the other end. We stated earlier that the game of basketball has been said to be ninety percent mental and ten percent physical. This is one of those areas that requires quick thinking and alertness on the part of the lone defender. A smart player can turn the tables completely on an overconfident and overzealous fast breaking team. Careless ball handlers and passers are also likely prey.

We again stress to our players that they must make the offense react to their defense rather than waiting for the offense to make the first move and trying to react accordingly. Why should we let the offense create additional advantages when we are already at a numerical disadvantage? When an offensive or defensive player is able to make the initial move it is impossible for the opponent to read his true intentions. On the other hand, the player making the first move can tell what his opponent will do by watching his reaction. We want our defender to make a purposeful move that will lull the offensive player into a false sense of security. By closing off or covering one of the possible lanes to the basket, the defender can probably note that the offensive player has made up his mind

DIA. 5-18

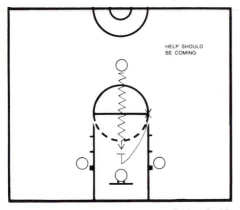

HELP SHOULD
BE COMING

DIA. 5-19

to take the other option. We are, in effect, accomplishing the same principle or concept that we explained previously. We are giving the offense only one way to go and we are prepared to close off that opportunity as soon as it becomes necessary.

We would much rather face the three on one fast break than the two on one for the reasons we explained in Chapter Four. When one of our players is forced to defend against three opponents, we want him to stay on a level or just below the level of the two wing men. If one wing man is ahead of the other, he should align himself with the wing man that is out ahead. If either one of the two men running the outside lanes are able to get behind our defender there is a good chance they are going to score. We want to keep all three players out in front unless they take themselves too deep and out of the play. The defender should fake at the man bringing the basketball and retreat. When the ball is brought into the twenty-one foot scoring area, the defensive man should drop to a position directly in front of the basket with the arms spread. He should be ready to react to a pass in either direction. The man with the ball should be forced to take the outside jumper or to try and bring the ball closer to create something that is not there. If the defender has been able to stall the offense even momentarily, his teammates should be able to hustle back and apply pressure from behind. If the middle man has not put the ball up, he will be very susceptible to a hustling opponent making a steal from behind. If the ball handler does try to advance the ball into the lane area, he will allow the defensive safety to play three men by causing too much congestion.

Another way to slow up the three on one break and to force the offense into an error is to seal off one side of the lane as shown in Diagram 5-18. The defender must remain open to the ball so that he can react once the middle man commits himself. This is a somewhat dangerous ploy, but it is worth a try condidering the advantage that the offense has gained. Any defender in these situations must be able to play games with the ball handler in his effort to stall for help or force an error. The idea, of course, is to win the battle of the minds. It is imperative in this defensive manuever that the offensive wing man being left open does not gain a step on the defender. The result will be a quick pass and a lay up. Additionally, the defender cannot play this game indefinitely. As long as the defender has the angle to cut off the open wing man he can continue to close off one of the passing lanes. However, at a certain point, there will be no angle of recovery and the defensive man must readjust his position before reaching that point. The defender in this situation is trying to make the ball handler commit himself to a drive down the lane or a pass to the open wing. Once one of these options has been selected, it is basically a one on one match between the middle man or the wing and the defensive safety. We should note that these defensive manuevers should only be attempted by those players with enough quickness and enough savvy to allow them to be effective.

It has been our experience that the ball handler will take as long as possible to commit himself either way. This allows us to accomplish our objective of stalling the offensive thrust. In Diagram 5-19 the middle man elects to take the ball all the way and the defender moves over to cover. The defensive player has again forced the three offensive players into a small area of the floor and should be able to cover all three in these close quarters. If the ball handler puts his head down and attempts a hard drive to the basket, the defensive man must react quickly and position himself for the charge. The offensive charge is the defender's best weapon in these situations and he should always be looking for the opportunity to draw one on a player who is not totally under control. Diagram 5-19 shows the defensive adjustment required to draw a charge on the middle man driving the lane while Diagram 5-20 illustrates the movement required on a pass to the wing. If either player dishes the ball off the charge can still be drawn after the pass has been made and before the shot.

Another variation is for the defender to move into the middle as if to give up the pass behind him to the wing man on his right side. If the middle man takes the bait, the defender readjusts into the passing lane and picks off the intended pass (Dia. 5-21). If no pass is made, the defender should be on balance ready to set up directly in front of the basket.

We advocate essentially the same type of deceptiveness in defensing the two on one break. The defender must fake and retreat in attempting to slow down the offensive players. Again, he must keep both offensive players out in front. He is the last line of defense and no offensive player can be allowed beyond that line or an easy lay up will result. As all three players enter the scoring area we want our defensive man to run with the offensive player without the ball. He will be directly in the passing lane, facing the ball and faking at the ball handler to throw him off stride (Dia. 5-22). This will completely close off the passing lane and force the ball handler to commit himself to a drive to the basket. As soon as the offensive player commits himself, the defender must readjust his position quickly to cut off the drive and possibly draw the offensive charge. If the ball handler is able to pass off at the last moment, he will still be hard pressed to bring himself under control before making contact with our defender. Additionally, the pass will have to be made in a very limited area of the floor, making it easier for our man to defend against. The key, again, is for the defender to play the proper angles in attempting to cut off the ball handler or draw the offensive charge. The defensive man cannot wait too long or the man with the ball will gain a step and will have a clear path to the basket.

DIA. 5-20

DIA. 5-21

FAKE AT THE BALL HANDLER

DIA. 5-22

Likewise, if he makes his play before the ball handler commits, the ball can easily be dished off to the wing man he has just left. The defender must do a good job of reading the offensive player with the ball as he decides on his course of action.

Another defensive manuever in this type of situation is for the defender to step into the driving lane of the ball handler and force the pass to the opposite offensive player. The defender then recovers to the opposite driving lane and looks for the charge. This is especially effective when the two offensive players are attacking the basket parallel to each other. The defender must allow enough time to recover back to the ball as the pass is attempted and completed. The defensive man can also be looking to step into the passing lane for a possible steal or deflection.

The preceding defensive thoughts will be primarily important to the guards, because they will be responsible in most cases for getting back first on defense. All players must be familiar with the tactics, however, because anyone can find themselves in this type of defensive situation.

We have some different ideas on these situations when we have a shot blocking type player as our lone defender. Most teams will want the ball in the hands of their best ball handler when executing the break. In most cases, the best ball handler will also be the smallest of the players involved in the break. We want our shot blocker, in this situation, to invite this player to the basket by completely opening up his driving lane. When the offensive player attempts the drive, we ask our defender to go up and sweep the ball away. This requires excellent timing on the part of our shot blocker and is something we work on in practice situations that we will detail at the end of this chapter. If the ball is in the hands of a big man on the break, then we want our defender to play him head up and force him to make a play. Many forwards and centers have not been taught or have not developed the skills to handle the ball or deliver the basketball at the end of the fast break.

Any defensive player caught back in a two on one or three on one fast break must play intelligently and must have had some preparation in defensing this type of situation. We are teaching our players to keep the offense guessing as to their defensive intentions and to take away one offensive opiton without giving up his own opportunity to recover to the other option, or options, that are available.

Drawing the Offensive Charge

One of the most effective defensive weapons in the game today is the individual player's ability to draw the offensive charge. We like all of our players to have the courage and to develop the knowledge for drawing an offensive charging foul. The responsibility for imparting the knowledge is up to the coaching staff. The courage must come from the player himself. It is important that the players be shown how to draw the charge so they will realize that the chance for injury is not very great.

We stress to the players that a charging foul can be drawn anywhere on the court. We encourage our individual team members to look for the player who has his head down, who leaves his feet often, or who has a tendency to get out of control. It is our belief that there are many players that fit into those categories. The one on one oriented teams and the run and gun teams are especially vulnerable to a defense that is very much aware of the possiblities for drawing charging fouls and is adept at setting itself for those charges. It is very improtant to stress to the players the difference between looking for a foul that they hope will be charged on the offense and being in the proper position to draw a sure offensive foul. If our players can't take the contact full in the chest area, then we don't want them attempting to draw the charge. We have seen too many teams and individuals that are constantly trying to draw the charge when the opportunity is simply not there. This type of misguided effort offsets the advantages of the play, even when a legitimate offensive foul is drawn. The officials will begin to ignore the play when it is continually used unsuccessfully. When this occurs, it will be easy for them to overlook a legitimate charge, because the attempt has been overused. By the same token, it is impossible for the officials to ignore full contact charges taken in the chest area by a set defensive player.

The first drill by which we teach the technique involved in drawing the offensive charge is run at half speed. It is a driving line drill with the players matched up according to size and position. The guards execute the drill from the guard position out front while the frontliners start at the wing or just below the wing area. It is simply a one on one drill with the offensive player required to drive to the baseline from the wing and to the sideline from the guard position. The defensive player must slide to the boundary line at the correct angle to draw the offensive charge. The defender must place his foot on or outside the line. He can leave no room for the offensive player to continue advancing the basketball. We discussed earlier the idea of the defender selecting the proper angle to cut off the ball handler at a predetermined spot on the floor. This is a very important principle when attempting to draw the charge on the dribbler. Too sharp an angle will almost invariably result in body contact and a foul on the defensive player for being overly aggressive. If the angle is too wide, the defensive player will not be applying the pressure that we require. The offensive player will have plenty of room to manuever and could possibly gain a step or two advantage on his defensive opponent. The defender must select an angle by which he can slide quickly

FIG. 5-14

to cut off the offensive player from any further advancement. He must be able to plant his lead foot completely on the other side of the ball handler and position his body all the way in front so that if the dribbler continues, he will be unable to avoid an offensive charge.

Quickness of the feet will again be very important as it always is in our defensive scheme of things. The defender must react and move quickly to beat the offensive player to the predetermined spot. A player who cannot develop the reactions and the proper sliding habits to slide quickly will never be a good defensive performer. As we emphasized earlier, however, effort will be the main factor in determining the development or the improvement of the individual defensive player. If the player can extend the effort, he can develop the correct habits.

The defensive player must plant his foot on or outside the respective lines to insure that the offensive player's route to the basket is completely closed. In addition, the defenders get an idea of how we want to play defense at the sideline and baseline areas. Remember, we are forcing to the outside. At the baseline, we will force back into the middle if we think help is needed. However, we give the players the option of forcing to the baseline with the idea that they will always cut the dribbler off at a particular spot on that baseline. Many times an offensive charge can develop because of this philosophy and we can also trap the ball at the baseline if the dribbler picks the ball up when cut off by the defender. This defensive idea will be discussed further in Chapter Seven on Team Defense in the Half Court Area. The baseline and sideline will obviously not always come into play when we are attempting to draw the charge. However, the defensive player will always be required to plant the lead foot out ahead or on the other side of the ball handler to get his body in front. The planting of the foot on the line teaches the players exactly what will be necessary in establishing the proper body position anywhere on the floor.

As contact is about to be made in a legitimate offensive charge, we teach our players to expand the chest, pull the rear back slightly and distribute their weight evenly on both feet. In this position, the back will be arched and with the rear pulled back, the player should definitely be protected from injury. The shoulders and hands are thrown back to avoid any contact that could be initiated by the defensive player. As contact is made, the defender should rock back on his heels and take the contact with the offensive player full in the chest area. By rocking back on the heels and continuing to the ground, the defensive man will be avoiding most of the force of the contact. The defender will be giving with the blow. The player then is taught to land on the rear which is the best place to absorb the shock of the landing. Figure 5-14 shows a player in the proper position to draw a sure offensive foul.

It is vitally important that the players not shy away from this type of contact. By utilizing the technique described above there is very little chance for injury in a well conditioned athlete at this level. The injuries occur when the player tries to avoid the contact by turning to the side or trying to draw the charge with the shoulders or the legs. Not only will the defensive player be susceptible to injury in this situation, he will also be whistled for the foul because of improper positioning. Nine out of ten of the attempted offensive fouls that are taken in the chest area will be called on the offense. When contact is made with any other part of the body, the reverse is going to be true.

The final teaching point involved in drawing the offensive charge takes place after the contact has been made and the defensive man has hit the floor. We want our defenders to scramble back to their feet and hustle to assume the proper defensive positioning on their man. In the event that the official does not blow the whistle it will do no good to lay there and complain. The defender must get back into the play and look for a better opportunity the next time. If the official did, in fact, miss the call, you can be sure that he will be ready the next time a legitimate offensive foul occurs.

Once the players have developed a certain amount of skills with regard to technique, we progress to a full speed drill. We will run this drill at the beginning of practice and come back to it during the season when we think it is needed. It is not an everyday drill. We will run it any time we feel the players are not taking advantage of the possibilities for an offensive charge.

We think that our emphasis on drawing the offensive charge fits in extremely well with our principles on giving the offensive player an avenue for advancement and then taking it away. Furthermore, it fits in well with our philosophy of hustling, aggressive basketball. It can be especially demoralizing for an offensive team to lose possession by a well timed defensive play that results in a charging foul. The momentum generated by the play and the temporary demoralization that may take place could carry over into the opposite end of the floor. Thus, **the drawing of the offensive foul is one of the best ways to make something happen at both ends of the floor.**

Full Court Sliding Drill (Dia. 5-23)
Objective: To teach the players the proper sliding techniques and proper sliding angles that will be required in our full court defensive system.
Organization: Taped line down center of floor. Two lines in each corner of the court. Players face baseline and slide, one after the other, forty-five degree angles the length of the floor. When placing foot on line, players execute a drop-step in beginning their slide in the opposite direction (technique for defensing crossover introduced later). Players remain on same side of the floor. As soon as last player in line finishes, first

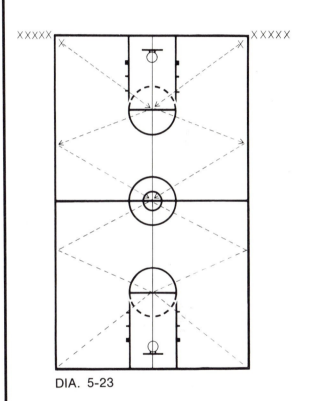

DIA. 5-23

Drills For Developing Our Individual Defense

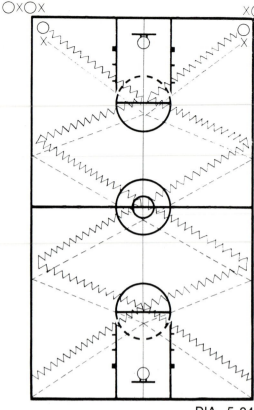

DIA. 5-24

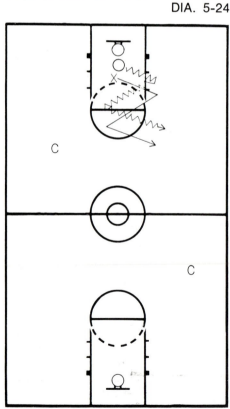

DIA. 5-25

166 Individual Defense

player in line starts them back the other way. Coaches are on sidelines in position to instruct and correct.

Points of Emphasis: 1. Proper sliding technique (feet, knees, hands, head, etc).

2. Must place foot on or outside line. Never pull up short.

3. Introduce the technique to close off the distance in defensing a crossover dribble.

4. Accuracy, then quickness.

5. Once accuracy is attained really emphasize quickness!

Full Court Sliding Drill—Add Offense (Dia. 5-24)

Objectives: To further develop the proper sliding techniques and angles and to teach the correct relationship between the defensive player and his man.

Organization: Same as previous drill, except that players match up according to size and position and execute the drill with their partner. (We usually run the drill with the guards on one side and the forwards and big men on the other).

Points of Emphasis: 1. Same as previous drill.

2. Defense able to grab opponent's shirt at the chest level.

3. Head aligned with what would be the ballside hip of the offensive player.

Full Court Sliding Drill—Add Offense—Add Ball (same as diagram 5-24)

Objective: The same as the previous drills with an emphasis on playing defense with the feet rather than the hands.

Organization: Same as previous drill except the offensive player is given a ball and the defender is required to keep his hands behind his back at first. Hands added later.

Points of Emphasis: 1. Same as previous drills.

2. Quickness of the feet.

3. Completely cutting off the offensive player. Forcing him to change direction.

4. When hands are added for the defense — NO REACHING — PLAY THE DEFENSE WITH THE FEET. Active hands but no slashing.

One on One in the Contained Area (see previous diagrams)

Objective: To teach full court one on one defense. A side benefit is the full court one on one offensive work for the ball handlers.

Organization: Same as in the previous drills. All restrictions are now off the offense and the defense with the exception of the court still being split in half.

Points of Emphasis: 1. Turn the man.

2. Force the mistake without reaching.

3. Active Hands.

4. Quickness!

5. Enthusiasm! Defense is fun! Accept the challenge! (We are still mindful of the defensive fundamentals, but the emphasis here is on getting the job done).

Full Court One on One Drill (Dia. 5-25)

Objective: To further develop each player's full court one on one defensive skills. Provides a situation that is more difficult than will be faced under game conditions so is excellent preparation. Again, the offensive players are benefiting as to their ball handling improvement.

Organization: Players are again matched up according to position and size. (Ability can also be a factor depending on your level and the depth of your squad). If offensive player beats defense, whistle blows and players come back to the point where the offense gained the advantage. Players resume drill and this procedure is repeated until defense does an adequate job or receives an adequate workout. Players reverse roles and come back the other way. Two new men in when first two complete drill.

Points of Emphasis: 1. Same as previous drill.

2. Select proper angles to cut off and turn offensive man.

3. Get the body around — completely in front to force the change of direction.

4. When beaten, select proper angle of interception and sprint to catch up. Never give up.

5. Once this aggressive defensive style is learned, we can change drill emphasis to control or contain the offensive man or force him down one side of the floor. Players must be able to play each style. The style will change according to our defensive philosophy for a particular team or a particular player.

To decrease the dead time for each player, the squad can be divided in half with one group at each end of the floor. The drill would only go to the half court line. Another possibility is to use the side baskets as shown in Diagram 5-26. We like to use the full court to conduct an intense individual drill that involves the whole team. We encourage a lot of enthusiasm and we think this helps our defensive outlook. When time has been a factor, we have gone to the other uses of our space.

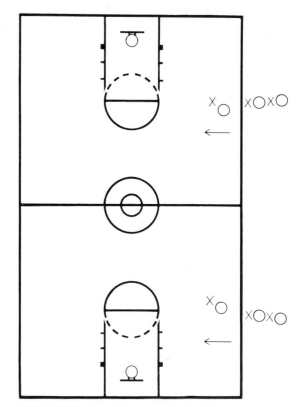

DIA. 5-26

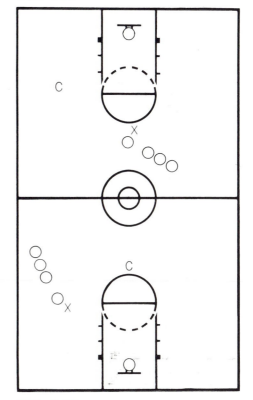

DIA. 5-27

Individual Defense 167

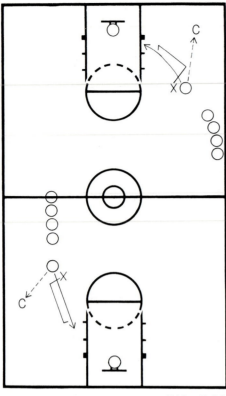

DIA. 5-28

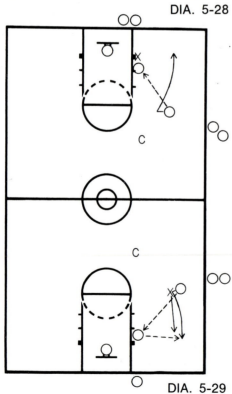

DIA. 5-29

Driving Line One on One (Dia. 5-27)

Objective: To teach and develop the one on one defensive skills in the half court area. We will run the big men in this drill at times, but it is primarily for those that will play out on the floor.

Organization: Team divided in half. Guards at one end. Forwards and big men at the other end. Players form line, one player steps out on defense. Defender stays in until he stops the offensive man. Offense goes to defense, defense goes to the end of the line. Can be run from any position on the floor.

Points of Emphasis: 1. Good defensive stance and fundamentals.

    2. Eyes look through the chest of the offensive player.

    3. One hand up, one down.

    4. Force player to the outside. Turn him.

    5. Contest every shot.

    6. Player puts ball above his head—belly up!

    7. Compete. Accept the challenge.

Off and Toward Drill (Dia. 5-28)

Objective: To teach and develop the proper technique of getting off and toward the basketball every time the ball is passed. Further, to develop the proper reactions in defensing the give and go cut.

Organization: Squad divided at each end of the floor. Guards at one end, big men and forwards at the other. Guards run the drill from out front, frontliners from the wing position. Pass is made from the offensive player to the coach or manager and he executes a quick give and go cut, trying to beat the defender. Defensive player must react quickly off and toward the ball once the pass is made. Rotate after three passes or when the defender executes satisfactorily. Offense to defense, defense to the end of the line.

Points of Emphasis: 1. Get off and toward as soon as the ball passes your fingertips. React!

    2. Do not let the cutter get between you and the ball. He must go behind!!

    3. Assume the denial position as the cutter continues to the basket. Deny the pass!

    4. Avoid contact.

Post Pass Defensive Drill (Dia. 5-29)

Objective: There are two parts to the defensive objective of this drill. One, to teach and develop the defensive skills for guarding a man in the post once he has received the ball. Two, to teach and develop the defensive skills for guarding a man who has hit the post and is now a cutter. This is the same drill as we have shown in relation to our offensive breakdown drills and it will progress, as we will see in the next chapter, to a three on three situation. The emphasis has merely been shifted from offense to defense.

Organization: Same as in **Post Pass Offensive Drill** (Dia. 3-138). The single defensive man is placed on the post or on the wing, depending on the objective of the drill. With the defender on the wing, the ball is passed into the post and the defensive man must play the cutter. The post is a feeder and a rebounder. With the defender on the post, the pass is made and the offensive post man tries to score. The passer works on his cuts without a defense (same principles as in offensive drill). Guards remain at wing or diagonal position. Big men work mainly in the post, but also get some work out on the floor. Forwards alternate lines. Three times and out.

Points of Emphasis: **Post Defense**

        1. Deny pass.

        2. Play upright. Don't get too low.

        3. Play defense with the feet and head.

        4. No fouls.

        5. Contest every shot. Do not slash.

        6. Block out. Go get the ball.

Defense on the Wing

        1. Get off and toward the ball, maintaining vision with your man.

        2. Bother the post man with your back hand.

        3. Be alert to get back to your man if he receives pass.

        4. Stay low. React quickly. The defensive technique involved here will be further illustrated in the next chapter when dealing with the three on three situation.

Post Defensive Drill (Dia. 5-30)

Objective: To further teach and develop the defensive skills for guarding a post player once he has received the ball. Covers all three post positions.

Organization: Big men and forwards at one end. Guards at other end working on **Driving Line One on One** or related drill. Utilize side baskets to get more work. Coach or manager passes ball into offensive post man who tries to score versus defensive coverage. Emphasis is on the defensive coverage, but gives players an opportunity to perfect offensive moves. Three passes, then offense goes to defense, defense steps out. Work all three post positions.

Points of Emphasis: Same as Post Defense in **Post Pass Defensive Drill.**

Lead Pass Drill (Dia. 5-31)

Objective: To teach and develop the techniques involved in denying the pass to a man who is one pass away from the ball.

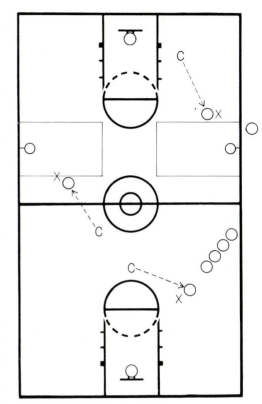

DIA. 5-30

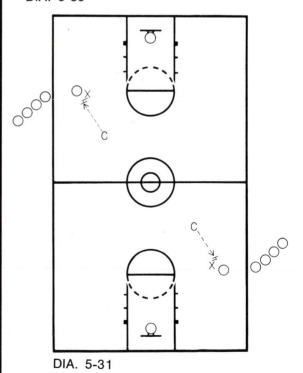

DIA. 5-31

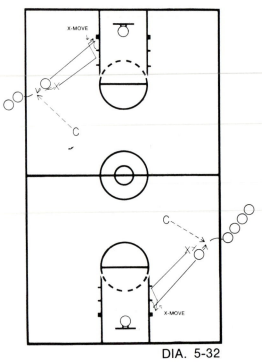

DIA. 5-32

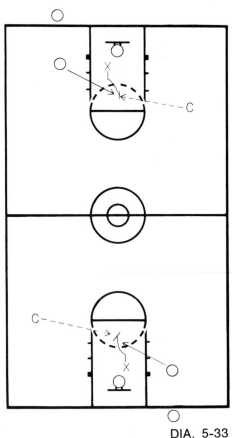

DIA. 5-33

Organization: Squad divided in half and positioned at each end of the floor. Line forms outside the sideline at the wing position. First player assumes defensive responsibilities and denies the pass to the wing area. Pass can be attempted by a coach or manager at the guard position. Defense stays until he does an adequate job and then goes to the end of the line. Offense moves to defense and a new man steps in.

Points of Emphasis: 1. Arm and leg in passing lane.

2. See both the man and the ball.

3. Maintain distance from offense. Armbar if needed. Avoid the contact.

4. Totally deny the pass. Quick feet.

Backdoor Drill (same diagram as previous drill).
Objective: To teach and develop the technique involved in defensing a back cut or backdoor play.
Organization: Same as previous drill. Offense is now faking the lead pass and attempting to create a backdoor opening.

Points of Emphasis: 1. Retreat quickly. Quick feet.

2. Open up to ball only at lane area.

3. Inside hand down. Feel your man with the outside hand.

4. As you open to the ball, maintain a position directly in the passing lane. Reassume denial position as soon as possible, according to the further movement of the offensive player.

Three in One Drill (Dia. 5-32)
Objective: Combines three defensive skills (lead pass, back cut, and post defense) into one continuous action drill. Further develops the three defensive techniques plus develops the reactions from one area to another that will be required under game conditions.
Organization: Same formation as previous drills. Offense looks for lead pass first, then cuts backdoor. Finally, he sets up at the medium post. The ball is then moved from the coach or manager to the next player in line requiring an X-move on the part of the defender. Defense must use proper technique in covering all three situations. Same rotation.

Points of Emphasis: 1. Must work hard to deny ball in all three situations.

2. Proper defensive fundamentals as mentioned in previous drills.

3. Quickness. Especially on the X-move.

4. Keep back foot behind offensive player.

5. Avoid contact.

Diagonal Cut Drill (Dia. 5-33)
Objective: Primarily to teach the proper defensive technique on a diagonal cut in the lane area. (This is where the cut is most

widely used and where it is the most effective.) The diagonal cut and the defense required is not limited to this area of the floor, however.

Organization: One line at each end of the floor. Coach positioned at wing area with ball. Offense lines up three to five feet off the lane and attempts to catch the ball in the lane area, utilizing a diagonal cut to the ball. Defense must deny the pass with the proper fundamentals. Rotate after three attempts or when defense responds adequately. Offense to defense and defense to the end of the line.

Points of Emphasis: 1. Helping position, knees bent—ready to move.

    2. Close the distance as the cutter initiates his move to the ball.

    3. Utilize armbar.

    4. Keep the ball out of the lane area. Deny.

    5. Run the offensive man up high.

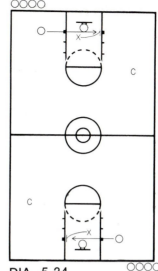

DIA. 5-34

Lateral Cut Drill (Dia. 5-34)

Objective: To teach and develop the proper technique involved in defensing a lateral cut with special emphasis on the cut into the lane area.

Organization: Formation is the same as in the diagonal cut drill. The offensive man now makes his cut in a direct line across the lane and the defender denies the pass, utilizing the correct technique. To simulate two different defensive situations, the coach (passer) can be positioned at the wing or in the corner. **This drill is especially important in the defensive development of the big men.** The rotation is the same as in the previous drill.

Points of Emphasis: 1. Alert—ready to move. Able to see man and ball.

    2. Must totally deny the pass.

    3. Do not give ground in this area. There will be some body contact.

    4. Force the cutter to the baseline.

    5. Open to the ball when the cutter is behind you.

    6. Be alert to establish post defense or continue to corner.

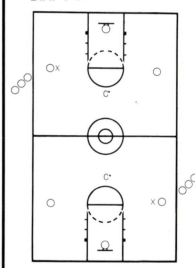

DIA. 5-35

Six in One Drill (Diagrams 5-35 thru 5-38)

Objective: Combines all of the basic offensive cuts into one continuous action defensive drill. Teaches the defenders that they must be ready to react to different situations as quickly as they occur.

Organization: Squad divided at each end of the floor or can be run with the entire team because of the continuous action involved. Line forms outside the court at the wing area the same as in the **Lead Pass Drill.** Coach is at the top of the key with the ball. One player is positioned at the opposite wing for

DIA. 5-36

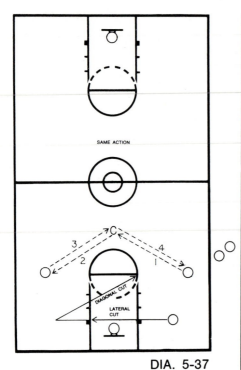

SAME ACTION

DIAGONAL CUT

LATERAL CUT

DIA. 5-37

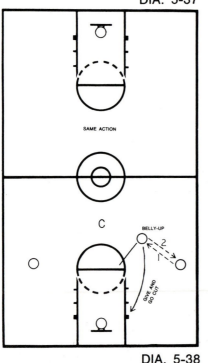

SAME ACTION

C

BELLY-UP

GIVE AND GO CUT

DIA. 5-38

Miscellaneous Drills Covering Individual Defense

the drill purposes. He will move to the end of the line upon rotation. The first offensive player tries to catch at the wing position (lead pass). If the defense denies the pass, he cuts backdoor, still looking for the pass from the coach (backcut). The offensive man then establishes himself in the post and the defense must react properly while the coach has the ball. The ball is then passed to the next player in line who has moved to the wing position. The defender must execute the X-move to re-establish himself on the low side (post defense). These first three cuts are shown in Diagram 5-36. The offensive man then steps out away from the lane just as in the lateral cut drill. The ball is moved to the coach and then over to the opposite wing. The offensive player must step out the correct distance to allow for the proper timing of the drill. When the ball is at the opposite wing, the offensive player exectes a lateral cut. Again, the defender must respond properly (lateral cut). Now the offensive player steps off the lane in the opposite direction and the ball is moved to the coach and to the original wing position. The cutter moves to the ball on a diagonal path, thus requiring the defensive man to defend against the diagonal cut. These are shown in Diagram 5-37. The offensive player now steps out to a position outside the top of the key and receives the ball. Immediately he brings the ball above his head and the defensive player plays him belly-up. The pass is then returned to the wing and the offensive man tries to beat the defender on a cut to the basket (give and go cut). The belly-up requirement and the give and go are illustrated in Diagram 5-38. The defender stays in until he gets it right. Offense goes to defense. Defense replaces opposite wing. New man in.

Points of Emphasis:
1. The offense should not try to force the passes. Player must definitely be open.
2. Looking for proper technique from defender on all the cuts. Denying the basketball at all times.
3. Defender must react **quickly** to the different situations.
4. Stress defensive intensity.
5. Enthusiasm! Each player should accept the challenge.

*The defender is not shown in the accompanying diagrams so as to give a clear picture of how the drill progresses.

The drills explained in the preceding pages are the individual defensive drills that are basic to our entire defensive system. We feel that the drills shown cover virtually all of the individual skills needed to play the tough man to man defense that is required at the Univeristy of Missouri. Furthermore, the drills and the skills involved are taught in a progressive manner that will eventually lead to the development of our team defense.

These drills serve as a consistent teaching pattern from which we can build our defensive system and are where we place most of our emphasis during the preseason and in-season practice sessions. Interspersed with these, however, are some other, different drills that we introduce at various times during the practice sessions when they are needed. The important thing to remember in devising more and different drill situations for the players is that while the drill may be different, the technique involved in executing properly will remain the same. Following are some of the additional drills we have used the past few years in developing our players individual defensive skills.

We should point out that the drill we use in relation to defensing the two on one fast break has already been explained in our chapter on The Fast Break (see Dia. 4-30). The emphasis in the **Three on Two—Two on One Drill** is simply shifted from the offense to the defense. We will also change the drill slightly to incorporate a three on one situation which we will work on a relatively short period of time compared to our other drills.

Slide—Run—Slide Drill (Dia. 5-39)
Objective: To teach and develop the correct sliding technique. Also beneficial for leg and overall conditioning. Team drill with which pride in defensive intensity can be encouraged.
Organization: Squad lines up off the court in the corner area. Can split the squad to give more individual attention and/or to group according to size and quickness. Players follow one after the other. Start out in a defensive slide facing toward the half line. At every intersecting line, they alternate from a slide to a run or vice versa (see diagram). Can go as often as necessary and can vary the required speed of the run. Defensive sliding is always full speed.
Points of Emphasis: 1. Correct sliding technique (feet, knees, hands, head, etc.)
2. Intensity! Quickness!
3. Enthusiasm!!

Lane Drill (Dia. 5-40)
Objective: We use this drill both as a method for improving defensive quickness and as a conditioning drill.
Organization: For defensive purposes, two players in each lane area and in a lane area at a side basket. Coaches at all three stations. Players slide from one side of the lane to the other as quickly as possible while still utilizing the proper defensive fundamentals. Coaches should watch closely the defensive positions that are being maintained. Drill is to develop quickness in the correct defensive position not to develop bad habits. Thirty second to sixty second intervals.
Points of Emphasis: 1. Correct sliding technique. Especially

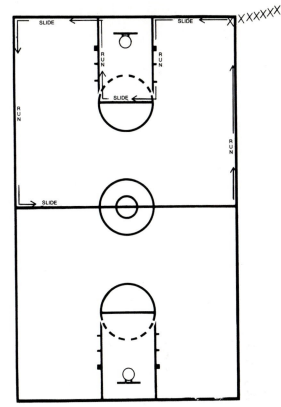

DIA. 5-39

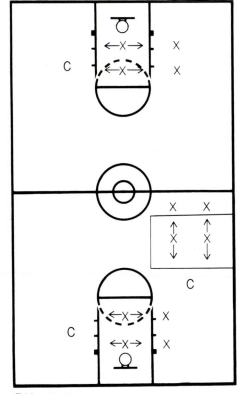

DIA. 5-40

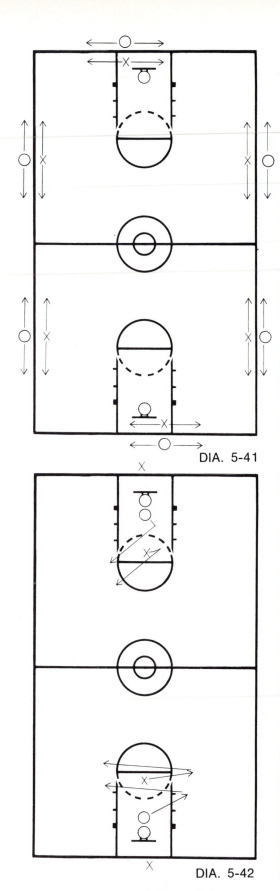

DIA. 5-41

DIA. 5-42

feet and hands. Feet do not come together.

2. Intensity! Quickness!

3. Enthusiasm from players outside the lanes!

Mirror Drill (Dia. 5-41)

Objective: To teach the defensive player to slide quickly when he must react to the offense and to keep his head aligned with the ballside hip of the offensive player. Can also aid in teaching players how to draw the charge.

Organization: Players match up with a partner. Offensive player lines up outside the court, defensive player inside. Offensive player runs the sideline (at varying speeds). Defense must slide with offensive man and maintain proper alignment on the ballside hip. To work on drawing the charge, coach blows whistle and the offense steps into or moves into court area. Defense must get in front and draw charge.

Points of Emphasis: 1. Correct sliding technique. Feet do not come together.

2. Quick feet.

3. Get out in front of the offense with quick reactions. Head on ballside hip.

4. When drawing charge, must take full in chest. Do not back up to avoid contact. Get in front, take it in the chest, and hit the deck.

Tag Drill (Dia. 5-42)

Objective: To teach our defenders how to use the angles in playing good position defense. Also, to try to get the defenders to make a move on the offensive man rather than always waiting for his move.

Organization: Players match up according to size and quickness. Line forms off both ends of the floor under the basket. Offensive player has the entire half of the floor (no ball). He tries to get to the half line without being caught by the defender. Next time up, partners reverse roles. Keep the drill moving.

Points of Emphasis: 1. Think.

2. Don't run at the offensive player, especially if he happens to be quicker.

3. Make him react to your moves.

4. Play the angles.

Driving Lines—Draw the Charge (Dia. 5-43)

Objective: To teach the players the angles that can be played from their particular positions on the floor and to teach and develop the proper technique for drawing the offensive charge.

Organization: Guards set up driving line at guard position on one side of the floor. Forwards and big men at opposite end with driving line at the wing or just below the wing area. Both defenders forcing to the outside. The offensive player drives and the defensive player must cut him off at the baseline (front liners) and the sideline (guards). The defender must plant his foot on the line and take the charge. Offensive players go at half speed at first while defenders pick up technique. Once the technique is learned, drill is run at full speed. Ball handlers must take the ball right to the boundary lines. They cannot pull up short or reverse directions. The idea is to work on taking the charge. Defense stays in until he gets it right. Offense to defense. Defense to the end of the line.

Points of Emphasis: 1. Force outside.

2. Quick feet. Beat the offensive player to the predetermined spot.

3. Plant foot on line.

4. Take charge full in the chest. Chest out, hands and shoulders back.

5. Must get all the way in front. When contact occurs rock back on heels.

6. Land on rear. Be ready to get up in case the whistle is not blown.

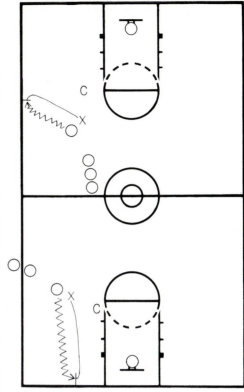

DIA. 5-43

Shot Blocker Drill (Dia. 5-44)

Objective: To teach and develop the shot blocking skills of our frontline players. Additional benefit is the development of the driving skills of all of our players. Very competitive drill that the players like.

Organization: One driving line or a driving line at each end of the floor to increase participation. Place the shot blocker in the basket area. Players drive to the hole. Defensive player must block or discourage the shot without fouling. Shot blocker takes two drives from each man and then goes to the end of the line. New shot blocker in. Drivers alternate lines.

Points of Emphasis: 1. Shot blocker gives the offensive players an open lane.

2. Must time the jump. Delay until just after the driver releases the ball.

3. Sweep ball away without goaltending.

4. Avoid body contact and do not slash. Sweep the ball away. Keep it in play.

5. Offensive players must make a hard drive to the basket.

Loose Ball—One on One Drill (Dia. 5-46 and 5-47)

Objective: To develop aggressiveness in obtaining possession of a loose ball and to provide a very competitive loose ball and one on one situation.

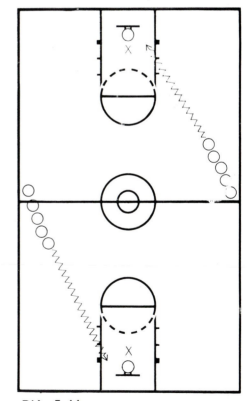

DIA. 5-44

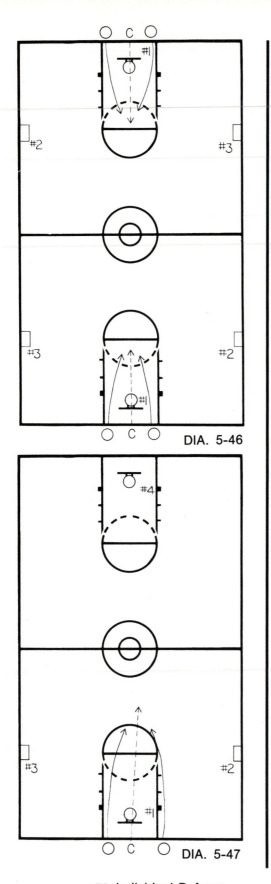

DIA. 5-46

DIA. 5-47

Organization: Big men and forwards at one end of the floor. Guards at the other. Two players line up on baseline. Coach stands in middle and rolls the basketball into the court area. Players hustle for possession of the ball and the coach calls out a number that corresponds with a particular basket. Player who comes up with the ball attacks that basket and the opposing player must play defense. Each group has the use of three baskets. Drill can also be run with the entire team at one end to facilitate some full court defensive work and conditioning. Four baskets would come in to play in this aspect of the drill; the two side baskets on the end the players started and the main baskets. At times, we will divide the squad in half and then bring them together for the last portion of the drill.

Points of Emphasis: 1. Be aggressive.

2. React to the ball.

3. React quickly either offensively or defensively when the coach designates the basket.

4. Tough defense!

Whether we begin to develop our team defense in the half court or full court area will depend basically on the material we have returning. The great majority of the time, we are going to begin teaching our system from end line to end line. Most of the players at this level have the quickness to play full court defense and our philosophy is going to incorporate defensive pressure all over the floor at times. There are two other reasons for our thinking along these lines. Even if we have determined that our material is not suited to a full court pressure defense, there are going to be times we will be forced to come from behind and some type of pressure will be absolutely necessary. We have used some zone defensive pressure which we will show at the end of this chapter, but we have already expressed our preference for matching up man to man. The final reason follows the same idea we applied to individual defense. If the players can be taught to play defense in a full court situation, they can surely play tough defense when the court is divided in half. If you decide that your material warrants concentration on half court defense, you may want to begin developing your defensive system in the half court area. The advantage of teaching defense beginning in the half court area lies with the mental attitude of a particular group of players. You will want them to fully understand that the scoring area is where the defensive emphasis will be placed. Their mental approach can now be geared toward learning and developing their defensive skills in the half court. The pressing defense can always be added at a later date once the players have developed some expertise in your primary defensive set.

In our defensive system, we designate six objectives that we want our players to understand and apply when the opponent is in possession of the basketball. These are the objectives on which we base our entire team defense. It is imperative that the players recognize exactly what we are trying to accomplish defensively. Our goal is to regain possession of the ball, but the objectives are the means by which this goal can be accomplished. It is much the same as teaching offense. The ultimate goal offensively is to put the ball in the basket as many times as possible during the course of a game. To meet this goal, we want our players to have a thorough understanding of our offensive system. This includes not only the offensive plays we utilize, but the principles behind those offensive ideas and the scoring opportunities that they should generate. There can be no less emphasis placed on the defense. The players have to be taught the objectives behind any successful defense. The first four defensive objectives we teach are more applicable to a half court situation, so they will be outlined more thoroughly in the next chapter on Team Defense in the Half Court Area. The remaining two objectives, however, have much to do with the philosophy behind our full court defensive

6 Pressing Defenses

Objectives of Defense

system. **The objectives of our defense are to:**

1. **Guard the basket area against all lay ups.**
2. **Prevent all unguarded shots.**
3. **Force the offense to take a poor percentage shot.**
4. **Prevent the offense from gaining possession for a second or third shot.**
5. **Break up the continuity or timing of the offense.**
6. **Force the offense to make mistakes.**

It is easy to see how these last two objectives have influenced our thinking in regard to playing defense the full length of the floor. Full court pressure is the first and probably the most effective means by which we can break up the continuity or the timing of the offense. It is undoubtedly the most effective method for forcing mistakes on the part of the offensive team and individuals. Pressure is a very important element for disrupting the overall efficiency of any offense. Any time you can force the offense to free lance or force them to lose confidence in their normal pattern, you will have gained an advantage defensively. When applying full court pressure, it is not unreasonable to set a goal of forcing twenty turnovers per game. The actual number of turnovers will be subject to many variables, including the tempo of the game, the opponent's inclination toward the fast break, their ability as ball handlers, and the formation and execution of the defensive game plan. Through the individual game plans, we want to exert our influence and even control most of these variables. If the opponent is a poor ball handling or poor fast breaking team we may want to speed up the tempo of the game to force them to play toward their weaknesses. The opponent's ball handling ability and their quickness will have much to do with determining the extent of our defensive pressure as far as our game plan is concerned. A team that is lacking in these two areas we will want to pressure at every opportunity. Against a team with excellent ball handlers and/or excellent quickness, we may want to drop back and pick up in the half court scoring area. The players must understand our different philosophies for each particular team, but must always put into practice our objective of forcing the offense to make mistakes. These mistakes often come in bunches and can add significantly to our offensive output if we can capitalize on them at our own scoring end.

Communication

As you could see in studying the preceding chapter, we try to introduce and develop all of our individual defensive drills in a progressive manner. The progression, then, continues into the introduction and development of our team defensive drills and our philosophy of team defense. Many players and teams, when they think of playing together, think only in terms of teamwork in the offensive end of the floor. Teamwork is just as important on defense as it is on offense. Team communication is even more important in defensive as opposed to offensive execution.

After developing the individual pride necessary to play tough man to man defense, we now want to channel that pride toward a team defensive effort. The first thing we insist on in working to achieve this effort is effective communication. The players must talk to each other if we are to be successful defensively. It is up to the coaching staff to make sure that this communication is taking place. This idea must be constantly emphasized during the practice sessions so that it becomes a habit by game time. One of the tenents of our program is that everything is done with a purpose in mind. We do not want to waste time or energy just to be doing something. This was evident previously when we discussed our ideas on offensive movement. We stressed the idea of purposeful movement. The same principle holds true when we are teaching our players to communicate on defense. There is no need to keep up an endless stream of chatter just to be talking on defense. Our purpose is to communicate with each other: 1) what the offense is doing and; 2) what position we are in defensively. There is no way a defensive player can concentrate on his man and listen to four voices behind him. At the same time, when all this talking is going on, the player is sure to miss much of the communication that is immediately important to his defensive situation. The process of learning how to communicate as a team is simply something that will take time as the players play together and get to know each other's habits.

As mentioned above, the time to develop the right habits for communicating as a team are in the practice sessions. In any defensive drill that involves two or more defensive players, we want this communication to be taking place. Each player must concentrate on his man while tuning in to the voices of his teammates. We also have done something a little different at times to further emphasize the importance we place on talking on defense. We have required the players who are not in the drill to talk and communicate with their teammate or teammates. For instance, in a five on five drill situation, we would require the players on the sideline to talk to whichever group is on defense. In a two on two drill, the players in line would be required to talk to the two defensive players. This is a teaching method that we have used early in the practice sessions so that the players understand what we are trying to do. We will come back to it whenever we feel our players are not communicating enough on defense.

We have identified for our players the basic situations that will necessitate some type of communication. We have also offered suggestions as to the words that can be utilized to communicate effectively. Those situations are listed below with the possible advice to be given shown in parentheses.

SITUATIONS REQUIRING DEFENSIVE COMMUNICATION

1) When your man is setting a screen either on the ball or away from the ball. (Pick Right or Pick Left or Watch the Screen)

2) When a switch has to take place. We do not switch as a rule, but when it is necessary, the man switching must let his teammate know. (Switch! I got him. Take mine.)

3) To let a teammate know his side has been cleared or help has been taken away. (All Alone! Force to the middle.)

4) When you want to let a teammate know you are in a good position to provide help. (Help Right or Help Left)

5) To let your teammates know when you have been beaten momentarily and help is needed. (Help!)

6) When we are employing full court pressure, the man guarding the inbounds pass will let his teammate know when the ball is in the air and when the inbounder is running the baseline. (Ball! Baseline—Right Side or Left Side)

7) When we are pressing, the fifth defender will let his teammates in front know the movement of the offense. All players should be tuned in to his voice.

8) To call for additional help from the weakside if you are being posted up on the inside. (Help Inside!)

9) To let a teammate know you have picked up his man during the transition and to ask him to take yours if that is the best line of defense. (I've got yours. Take mine. Identify by number or by name.)

10) To identify whether you are going to take the ball or the basket or a side when retreating back to stop the fast break. (I've got the ball. Take the basket. I've got the right side.)

Developing our Full Court Team Defense

In the preceding chapter, we stressed the individual situations that occur on the ball and away from the ball. The individual reactions and defensive techniques were explained according to our coaching ideas. As we stated, strong individual defense will be the basis for a successful team defense. This is because each player must extend the effort and have the ability to meet his defensive responsibilities first. Once this is accomplished, our teaching of and emphasis on team defense will provide us with a very formidable defensive system. After our players have developed the individual defensive skills we require, we now begin to emphasize that the real strength of our defense will be that which we accomplish as a team.

We begin developing our full court defense by showing our players the five methods of defensive pressure that we will employ on the inbounds pass. This is the first of three stages of our defense. Next, we need to turn our attention to the type of pressure that we will apply once the initial pass is completed and the offense attempts to advance the basketball. Thus, we will be into our second stage of defensive pressure. Our basic defense will be a straight man to man with pressure on the ball. This is a pressing defense, so there should be no question about the intensity required or the amount of pressure that we want to apply. In addition to this straight man to man, we will also employ a trapping and run and change defense to facilitate maximum pressure. The key thing to remember and a crucial aspect of our defensive coaching is that either of the two full court defenses mentioned above can be combined with any of the five methods of pressure on the inbounds pass. For example, when we deny the inbounds pass with a single defender, the basic defense that will follow is the straight man to man. We can very easily make an adjustment if we think we want to trap or run and change the offense. By the same token, we can double team the inbounds pass but go to straight man to man once the pass is completed. This is one way we can change up the defenses according to what is working at the time. In disrupting the offense, we think it is very important to vary the defensive pressure. We want to keep them guessing and keep them thinking about our defense.

Many coaches will use numbers or color code their defensive system for organizational purposes. We do not do this because we feel it is unnecessary in our defensive scheme of things. If we used colors or some other form of code, the players would have to memorize the colors and then apply the colors to the different defenses. To us, this is just confusing the issue. The only advantage to a coded defensive system is in calling out and continually changing defenses from the bench. We prefer to prepare the players in the practices leading up to a particular game as to what defenses we think are going to be effective against our opponent. For example, we will go into the game with a definite defensive plan that has been drawn up and explained in the practice sessions. The last thing we will tell our players before they take the floor is what type of defense we will employ at the various stages. We will communicate through our basic defensive terminology. We might start out by denying the inbounds pass with single coverage and employing a straight man to man defense once the ball is inbounded. Or we could begin with all-out pressure in the first two stages of our defense by double teaming the primary receiver on the inbounds pass and executing the run and change and trapping defenses as the ball is advanced. We would then instruct the players to play a straight, helping man to man in the half court scoring end, which is the third and last stage of our defense. By dividing the court and referring to the three stages of our defense, the players develop a thorough understanding of our defensive organization. The fact that we are using basic basketball terminology to designate the defenses at the various stages serves to further simplify our system. The preseason practice sessions will be crucial in that we must successfully impart to the players our ideas on playing an aggressive team defense. We stress to our players that if they have any questions about what we are doing, they should ask during or immediately after the practice sessions. We also utilize chalk talks at various times before or after practice. Once the games are underway, each player has to have a complete understanding of our defensive system and what we are trying to accomplish. If we can lay the proper groundwork through the drills and techniques we have been describing and will describe, the player's natural and acquired instincts should do the rest. The players at this level have been playing through grade school and through high school and most all of them started out with some natural instincts for the game. Coaches sometimes give the players too little credit for what they do know and what they can create on their own. Over-coaching can be just as much a problem as under-coaching. This is not to say that the players should be given complete freedom. If the players are taught properly and are able to absorb our defensive ideas, then they are given a certain amount of freedom within the system. If a player insists on going outside the system, then we have to have a serious talk with him concerning the role of the player and the role of the coach. The freedom that each team will be able to handle will vary according to the ability and the natural instincts or basketball intelligence that the team has developed.

The freedom we allow our players is another reason for not instituting a set code for our defenses. Even when we are employing a straight man to man, we allow our players to execute the trap if the offense has entered one of the trapping areas. When we are trapping, the players do not have to form a trap if they do not think it is advantageous in that particular situation. We leave room for our players to use their judgement. Keep in mind that we can always give the players instructions as to the exact type of defense we want. We can give them wide freedom or we can instruct them to stay with a particular defense with no variations. To do this, the players must learn to play together and the coaches must communicate effectively.

Two On Two Defense (First Stage)

Our full court teaching drills progress naturally from a one on one confrontation to two on two, three on three, and then five on five team defensive situations. We organize these drills to include the inbounds pass because this is where our pressure defense starts. As we have stated, we will guard the inbounds pass a number of ways over the course of a game. The method prescribed will depend on the amount of pressure we want to apply and the relative ball handling abilities of the two opposing guards. We start our two on two drills by totally denying the inbounds pass with one defender. The second defender applies as much pressure as possible to the offensive player making the inbounds pass. We teach our defensive player denying the pass to turn his back to the ball and focus full attention on the potential pass receiver in this situation. We want our player to watch the other player's eyes because they will often give away the direction of the pass as it is made. A defender in this situation must be careful to ignore the fakes of the receiver. The defensive player's hands are off the offensive player and about shoulder high in anticipation of a steal or deflection. Once the offensive player commits as to the direction of his cut, the defender can turn his head slightly toward the ball and extend the lead hand to assume a position of lead pass pressure. Peripheral vision should now be utilized to try and pick up the ball while still maintaining vision on the man. We are still closing off the passing lane in a strong denial position. The defensive man playing the inbounder should be waving the arms and moving with the defender and attempting to disrupt the pass in any manner possible. It is very important that the defensive man move with the inbounder if the passer has the freedom to run the baseline. By being directly in front of the passer at all times, the defensive player will be obstructing his vision and not giving him the opportunity to see the floor. If the potential receiver does break open the inbounder may not be in a position to make the pass. This is our first effort at breaking up the timing of the offense. Maybe that effort will lead to a forced mistake.

The disadvantage of this type of defense lies with the defender being unable to see both his man and the ball. The player is susceptible to a lob pass being executed beyond his line of defense. We place the responsibility for this pass on our second line of defenders as we will show in discussing our five on five pressure situation. For two on two drill purposes, we start out by making this pass illegal. Eventually, we add it to our two on two drill at certain times because we want the man denying the pass to be able to react effectively when called upon in this situation. As we mentioned, our defender is to watch the eyes of the receiver for any signs that the ball is in the air and headed in a certain direction. If the offensive player raises his eyes and his hands, the defensive player can be thinking about reacting for a steal. He must be careful, because the offensive player is naturally going to be attempting to fake the defender into overcommiting himself. The defender on the ball again has some responsibilities that are designed to help in this situation. By using his arms, our defensive man must force the inbounder to put an extreme arc on the lob pass. This will obviously give our other defender more time to react to the pass. We also instruct the defender guarding the inbounder to yell ''ball'' as the pass is made and penetrates his line of defense. This should alert the man on the receiver that the ball is indeed in the air and should be heading in his general direction. When this action occurs, we teach the man denying the ball to turn as quickly as possible with the head, eyes, and hands up. The eyes must be quick to pick up the flight of the ball and the hands have to be ready to react once its direction is determined. When the ball is in the air like this, it is much the same as a loose ball—it belongs to no one. We want our players to gain possession of the majority of loose balls and balls that are up in the air. If the player is not in a position for outright possession we want him to make every effort to deflect the ball. We feel that a deflection is worth almost as much as a steal because a loose ball will result and all of our players are taught to anticipate and react quickly to a loose ball situation. Furthermore, all of our players are mentally prepared to react quickly to the ball because we are playing pressure defense and thinking ball. The offense must make a quick transition when a deflection occurs and this should give us a slight advantage.

If our defender was not able to get a hand on the ball, he should still be looking for a possible loose ball caused by our next line of defense (shown in five on five drill) or he should be quick to re-establish defensive positioning on his man. We can run the drill with varying degrees of difficulty to insure adequate defensive work for specific areas. First of all, we can limit the pressure applied to the inbounder so as to make it harder on the man denying the basketball. Secondly, we can instruct the defender on the ball not to let his teammate know when the pass has been thrown to help the defensive player inbounds to improve his reaction to the lob pass. The organization of this drill, as well as all of the drills to be explained in developing our full court team defense, will be detailed at the end of this chapter.

Our next method of defensing the inbounds pass involves some pressure, but basically calls for the defenders to direct the pass away from the center of the floor. It is important in our defensive thinking that the initial pass is not made into the middle of the floor. We want to force the player and the ball to the sideline or corner area where he will be easier to trap if we so desire. We must always use the sideline to our advantage in applying full court pressure defense. If we allow the offensive player to catch the ball in the middle we will be giving him the entire court in which to manuever. By forcing the ball to be inbounded in the corner, we can better control the ball handler on one side of the floor. Once the inbounds pass is completed, our defender can force the offensive player directly to the sideline and cut him off at the proper angle. His objectives now become to turn the man as many times as possible and to keep him from using the whole floor. If the defender wants to make the offensive player use his weak hand and that hand does not correspond to the sideline area, he simply forces the ball handler to the middle, but cuts him off at the proper angle and sends him back toward the sideline. His defensive objectives remain the same as stated above. These are the reasons we like to force the inbounds pass away from the middle. The methods that will be utilized must come from both defensive players.

Most teams are in the habit of inbounding the ball to the right side as they face their offensive basket. We use this tendency to help us direct the ball to the corner. When employing this defensive strategy we want the man guarding the inbounder to apply just as much pressure as before. The difference is that he will shade the left side of the passer to try and direct the pass into the corner. We feel that this defender can exert a lot of influence on where and when the pass is attempted. We tell him that in this situation it is his responsibility to keep the pass from being made into the left side of the floor (his right side). Diagram 6-1 shows the relative position of the four players. The shaded area indicates where we would like the pass to be made. Notice that both defenders are overplaying their offensive counterparts attempting to encourage the pass into the right corner. At the same time, the inbounds defender must force the offensive receiver to the baseline. There is no way we should allow the pass to be made to the free throw line extended or beyond. We want our defensive man on the inbounds receiver to assume a position on the side of the offensive man with his back to the opposite sideline. His eyes will be focused so that he can see his man and the basketball. His job is to force the receiver to catch the ball as deep as possible in the right corner. The deeper the man catches the ball the better off we are going to be defensively, especially if we are looking for or trying to create trapping situations. The defender must remember that he is to allow the pass into the corner but is denying a pass into any other area. Until the potential receiver moves from the middle into the corner he must be completely covered and forced to continue his cut into the open area. The defender will have his right hand up denying the basketball and should be careful not to get in a shoving match with his opponent. The officials are very aware of the defense when defensive pressure is being applied. This is especially true when the defense is denying or overplaying the inbounds pass.

We have found that most teams are content to make this initial pass into the right corner area. Our players must be prepared, however, for a team that will run the baseline and make the effort to inbound the ball to the left side. When the inbounder runs the baseline, it is extremely difficult for the defensive man to direct the pass into our original corner. When this situation develops, we simply instruct our baseline defender to communicate effectively with his teammate. He yells, "Baseline—Left side". The inbounds defender now knows that the passer is running the baseline and that we are going to force to the left corner instead of the right. Remember that our objective is to keep the offense from starting in the middle of the floor. In most cases, it makes no difference to us to which side of the floor the initial pass is completed. To change up our strategy we will sometimes try to force the pass to the left corner from the outset. In fact, starting the ball on the left side can be advantageous to us as long as the ball handler is righthanded. The right hand is the strong hand of the majority of players and by initiating the ball to the left corner, we can force the dirbbler to use his weak hand and force him to the sideline at the same time.

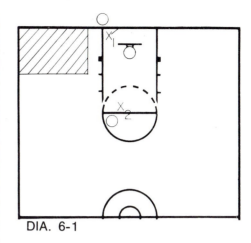

DIA. 6-1

A third strategy that we will utilize involves a combination of the two previous methods. The defensive techniques are basically the same with a few minor adjustments. This calls for our player to force the play to one side or the other (usually the right) and then totally deny the pass when the offensive player has entered a particular corner. This is an excellent surprise manuever, especially after we have been directing the ball to the corner but allowing the completion. Once the offensive player commits himself to a particular corner, his defensive man should keep him on that side of the floor while still denying the pass. The man on the ball should apply extreme pressure head up on the man out of bounds, but he should still be ready to shift to an overplay position. If we can keep the ball and the receiver on one side of the floor the offense will be limited as to the space in which they can manuever. The inbounds defender will be required to deny the pass in a much more limited area than before. Additional pressure can be applied as a result.

To exert maximum pressure on the inbounds pass, we will double team the potential receiver with our two defenders and leave the man taking the ball out alone. This method can be employed when we want to keep the ball away from a particular ball handler, as a surprise tactic, to force a front line player to handle the ball, or as we said, to apply maximum pressure. Our second line of defense must be aware of the strategy involved because the offense is invariably going to bring a third man up as a potential receiver. For right now, however, we are concerned only with the two on two defensive techniques. Figure 6-1 shows the exact alignment of our two defensive players setting up the double team on the inbounds pass. We want one man in front and one man to the side of the offensive player. The defensive man assigned to the inbounds offensive player should be at the side. Both players should be in a defensive position ready to move quickly and totally deny the pass in bounds. The defensive player on the side can see both the man and the ball, so he should be talking to his teammate when necessary. Both players should have their right hand up and ready to pick off or deflect the intended pass. Most important of all, the defenders should not allow any room between them by which the offensive player can split the defense and come to the ball. Notice in the accompanying photograph (Fig. 6-1) that the defenders have their feet together. The defensive players must try to move in unison to keep this relationship intact throughout the play. If the players do leave a gap, they should be prepared to close quickly if the offensive man attempts to cut between them for the ball. It is crucial that the defensive players do not allow the potential receiver to split them.

A determination has to be made whether our second defender will return to his man or continue the double team once the defense has been penetrated and the pass completed. We

FIG. 6-1

designate areas of the floor that we feel have excellent potential for our double teaming or trapping defensive tactics. We issue the players a diagram (Dia. 6-2) explaining these areas and expect them to use them to our advantage when we are employing this type of full court pressure. We will not be applying this type of pressure at all times, so the players must have a good understanding of what we are trying to accomplish against a particular team or at a particular point in the game. Communication is essential, both from the coaches to the players and among the players themselves. We will allow the players to change tactics on their own to try and confuse the opponent. How the individual opponents are reacting to our pressure will dictate the type of pressure or tactics that we will employ.

When we are applying maximum man to man pressure in our full court defense, we will usually be looking to trap the ball handler in the areas designated in the diagram. Therefore, if we are successful in defensing the inbounds pass, the receiver (if he can even catch the ball) should be forced into one of our trap areas for the reception. The second defensive player then should continue to apply the double team, making sure that the offensive player doesn't make a quick return pass to the man stepping in bounds or that he doesn't escape the trap into the middle of the floor. The defensive man assigned to the ball handler must prevent him from advancing the ball up the sideline. Both players are again responsible for stopping the offensive player from splitting the defense. This double teaming relationship is shown in Figure 6-2. The players should apply as much pressure as possible without initiating any contact that could result in a foul being called. We like our players to make themselves big in this situation and apply a lot of pressure with the arms without slashing. We are trying to force the offensive player to make the mistake, not make an outright steal every time. If the offensive man has used his dribble we teach our players to stand straight up, crowd the offensive player, and apply maximum pressure. In this situation, they do not have to worry about the offensive man driving by them.

We do not have any hard and fast rules in these defensive situations, especially under game conditions. We want our players to play aggressively and intelligently and expect them to use their basketball instincts to capitalize on the various defensive opportunities that will develop. Those basketball instincts, of course, will be sharpened in the two on two drills that we will use to teach the defensive principles and techniques we have just been describing. The point is that we will allow the players the freedom to utilize their defensive creativity. For instance, in the double team and trapping situation we have just explained, the second defensive player does not always have to remain in a trapping position. As we have mentioned, we encourage our defensive players to mix

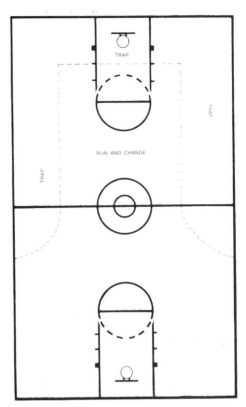

DIA. 6-2

FIG. 6-2

Pressing Defenses 187

FIG. 6-3

FIG. 6-4

FIG. 6-5

it up. The players must learn to work together if this type of freedom and initiative is to be effective. We have experienced outstanding results when we have had excellent defensive players who took pride in their ability to apply pressure and in their ability to read each other's intentions. This is something that comes only from hard work and practice at the defensive end of the floor. We feel that our emphasis on aggressive defense and our emphasis on playing intelligently will lead to this type of defensive effort and teamwork.

A defensive ploy that we teach our players, and have found to be extremely successful, involves the trapping strategy that we have discussed above. The ideal situation that we can develop through our defensive pressure is to trap a player, who has used up his dribble, in the corner or sideline area. The two defensive players, by working together, can induce the offensive player to commit himself and make himself vulnerable to the sideline or corner trap. The sequence of photos shown on the side depict one of the techniques that we can utilize to lure the offensive player into position for the trap. We have been double teaming the pass receiver, but he breaks open and catches the ball on the right side of the floor. In Figure 6-3, our second defender helping on the ball (#25) starts to leave the ball handler to pick up the inbounder stepping into the court. The defensive man on the ball (#24) overplays the ball handler, encouraging him to advance the ball up the sideline. The defender should already have picked out the point on the sideline at which he will cut off the dribbler and force him to pick up the basketball. As soon as the dribbler commits himself to the sideline, #25 will chase him down from behind (Fig. 6-4) and apply the trap when he is stopped (Fig. (6-5). #25 had no intention of leaving the ball handler, but he wanted to lure the offensive player into a false sense of security before springing the trap at the most opportune time. Notice also that the offensive player has turned his back to the second defender. This is always the best time to execute a trap or a run and change manuever in any pressing defense. With his back completely turned the offensive player cannot see the defensive pressure that is about to be applied, nor can he see his teammate or teammates, one of whom might be able to help him out of the double team situation. We go over these tactics very briefly at this stage because our players must learn to cover in the straight man to man before we progress to the run and change and trapping pressure.

The final defensive adjustment that we will utilize on the inbounds pass is simply a straight man to man defense with a very limited amount of pressure on the offensive receiver. Both defenders will have responsibility for covering their own individual assignments. The first defender will allow the player inbounds to receive the basketball and will pick him up as soon as the catch is made. He will still encourage the potential receiver into the corner, but with a limited amount of pressure.

The idea is to make the offensive player receive the basketball in front of the defender. The second defender will take the man out of bounds and will prevent the long pass. He will still be attempting to direct the pass away from the middle of the floor. Once the pass is completed, we want to play straight up defense with no trapping or changing. The defender off the ball will be in a position to help and recover, but should not leave his man to go for the steal. In playing this straight man to man we are emphasizing individual responsibility while providing help if needed. Our objective is to apply enough pressure to allow the offense to make their own mistakes.

To review the different methods for playing the inbounds pass and the possible full court defenses we can apply, we issue the following handout to our players. Again, we must emphasize that guarding against the inbounds pass is our first stage of defense. The full court pressure that is applied after the initial pass is completed is our second stage of defense. The third and last stage is our defense in the half court scoring area.

METHODS FOR DEFENSING THE INBOUNDS PASS	FULL COURT DEFENSE THAT CAN FOLLOW
1. Assigned defender denies the pass to the potential receiver.	1. Straight man to man with pressure.
2. Assigned defender forces receiver to corner and allows the pass in that area.	2. All-out pressure utilizing traps and the run and change.
3. Assigned defender forces receiver to corner and then denies the pass.	3. Combinations of the above.
4. Assigned defender and defender assigned to the in-bounder double team the potential receiver.	
5. Assigned defender plays behind potential receiver. Encourages pass to corner but with limited amount of pressure. Picks up man on completed pass.	
FIRST STAGE OF DEFENSE	**SECOND STAGE OF DEFENSE**

DIA. 6-3

We will incorporate the aforementioned defensive strategies according to the scouting report and the game plan we have devised. During the course of the game we can change our tactics from the bench or we can allow the players to communicate with each other and change up the defense as they see fit. The coaches will have the final say in any defensive adjustment, but sometimes the players can develop a feel or a rhythm of just how to play a particular offensive opponent. We encourage a certain amount of freedom and individual initiative in this regard.

Two On Two Full Court (Second Stage)

The pressure that we will apply in our straight man to man defense comes from the skill we have developed in our individual defensive drills. The defender on the ball will now have a defensive teammate to help discourage the offense from advancing. His first responsibility is to force the offensive player to put the ball on the floor. The second defender should drop to the level of the ball and maintain a relationship between his man and the basketball at all times. We drop to the line of the ball to provide maximum help and because there is no advantage to playing defense beyond the depth of the ball. This relationship is shown in Diagram 6-3. We want each of our defensive players to be aware of where the ball is and what the offense is doing at all times. This does not mean that a defensive player off the ball totally disregards his man in favor of helping out on the ball. The second defensive player must maintain a helping position where he can still recover in time to cut off his man if the guard to guard pass is made. Notice in the diagram that our defender (X_1) is in the helping position. He should be slightly open to the ball. The dotted line represents his angle of recovery in case his man receives the pass and starts up the sideline. Any time the ball moves or his man moves, the player in position to help must react accordingly. Initially, in our two on two drills, we require the offensive player without the ball to stay even with or behind his teammate. As the players progress in their defensive development, we allow the second offensive player to play in advance of the ball but he cannot run off and leave the action. We also start by executing the drill at half speed. We want the defensive players to learn the defensive positioning first and we can better teach and correct that positioning in a half speed drill. After a few times down the floor we increase the tempo.

If the dribbler advances the ball toward help, we want our player in the helping position to fake at the offensive player to discourage easy movement. His first reaction should be to fake and retreat so that he maintains an angle of recovery on his offensive counterpart. We are not looking for a double team or run and change manuever. We are simply playing a straight man to man with helping principles. If the defensive man on the ball is doing his job, the fake and retreat motion by the second defensive player should be a sufficient deterrent to the offensive player continuing up the middle. Our first defensive player should be able to overplay his opponent and turn him to the sideline. As always, anticipation will be of great benefit to all of the defensive players. As our man cuts off the dribbler, he has to anticipate a change of direction. He should have no trouble then in planting his foot, executing the drop step or closing in on the ball, and moving to cut off the dribbler to force another change of direction. Quickness of the feet is extremely important, but anticipating and playing intelligently are equally important in our defensive scheme of things.

In the event that the dribbler beats his defensive man to the middle, the second defender should continue to fake and retreat as long as the initial defender is in a position to recover to his man. If the ball handler attempts to pass over or by the help to the second offensive player, the helper must try to force a lob or a slow pass so that he can generate some additional time to recover to his own assignment. The only time that the second defender should leave his man is when a total breakdown occurs on the ball. He must then pick up the advancing dribbler and stop the ball as quickly as possible. The defender who has been beaten should recognize this situation immediately and should hustle to pick up the open man. These type of forced switches will lead to breakdowns in our defense, so we do not like to see them happen often. If they do, someone is not doing his job and an adjustment needs to be made.

The dribbler advancing up the sidelines should dictate similar reactions on the part of our helping defender. Remember that we always want to drop to the line of the ball. The ball handler, in this case, would have his back to his teammate so a pass back to the opposite guard will be relatively slow and will allow for quite a bit of reaction time on the part of our second defender. When the dribbler commits in the direction of the sideline and has gained a slight advantage on his defensive man, we want our second defender to turn and sprint to the line of the ball as shown in Diagram 6-4. He should be moving toward the sideline at an angle to intercept the dribbler if a total breakdown occurs. For now, his responsibility is to show himself to the offensive player in an effort to discourage any further advancement. This is much the same idea as his responsibility to fake and retreat when the offensive player is dribbling in his direction. In this situation, however, our defensive man can leave his offensive counterpart because he will have time to recover if there is a reverse pass attempted. This will be a much slower and more difficult pass for the offensive player to make. As the defensive man is moving toward the sideline he should watch the play developing. If our defensive man on the ball gains control of the ball handler, the second defender will need to reassume help and recover position in relation to his man and the ball. However, if a

DIA. 6-4

breakdown seems imminent, the helping defender should anticipate its occurrence and should move to intercept the dribbler and stop the ball at the proper angle. The initital defender should move quickly to pick up the vacated offensive player. This defensive ploy is very important to our press coverage because we are able to stop the ball without the second line of defense coming up to help. As we will see in the five on five drill work we do not allow a player on the sideline to come up to stop the ball except under extenuating circumstances. It would be too easy for the offense to pass the ball ahead in that situation. This type of play serves as the reasoning behind our philosophy of a total team defense with pressure on the ball. Our players can play tough individual defense with the knowledge and confidence that help will be provided should a breakdown occur. Our guard in this situation has been able to apply pressure and even though he was beaten momentarily, we are not hurt in any way. These are the plays that need to be made in a truly successful team defense.

Any time a guard to guard pass is made in a two on two pressing situation, the two defensive players must reverse roles instinctively. The guard who has been in a helping position must move quickly to cut off the new ball handler and the initial defender on the ball must get off and toward the basketball as soon as the pass is made. It is very important that the new defender on the ball does not overextend himself in trying to cut his man off. He must try to read his man while on the move and react accordingly. The danger in rushing to the sideline area is that the offensive player can feint that way and make the hard drive into the middle before our first defender has a chance to set up properly in a help position. If the defensive man on the ball has overreacted to the outside drive a breakdown is going to occur. The angle of recovery is also extremely important in this regard. If the player angles too sharply toward the man who now has the ball he risks the possibility of the offensive player escaping up the sideline. By the same token, if the angle is too wide he is not applying enough pressure and he could be vulnerable to a drive up the middle of the floor.

In executing our full court pressure defense we want to continue to keep the ball out of the middle of the floor. Once an offensive player commits himself to one side or the other we want our defenders to work hard to keep the player on that side. By forcing the ball away from the middle, we are limiting the floor area of the ball handler and his passing options. Not only are the offensive player's passing options reduced, but his passing angles are not as clear or as well defined as they would be from the middle of the court. This will allow each of our defensive players to play closer to the ball and will increase their ability to anticipate the movement of the offense and the basketball. The added congestion should produce additional interceptions, deflections, or turnovers on the part of the offense.

The individual fundamentals that we discussed in the preceding chapter do not become any less important when developing our two on two drills and our full court team defense. We especially stress our emphasis on the hands being active, but never reaching in to try for the steal. We want to continue playing defense with our feet and with our heads. If we apply enough pressure the offense will make their own mistakes. The one play in which we will allow the players to reach for the ball is when they have been broken down and they are hustling from behind to catch up with the ball handler. A defensive player can never stand and watch if he has been beaten by the offense. He should turn and sprint to catch up to the ball, looking for an opportunity to deflect the ball from behind without fouling. Help should be coming from the opposite guard but if it is not, the guard who has been beaten should try to re-establish his position between his man and the basket. If the opposite guard has helped out properly (as shown earlier) the first defensive player must now react quickly to pick up the vacated offensive player.

Our straight up man to man places a premium on tough, individual defense. Although we want to provide as much help as possible it is still a man to man confrontation. Each player has primary responsibility for stopping his own man. Intensity and conditioning will be of vital importance in successfully executing this type of full court defensive pressure. Conditioning will be discussed in full in a later chapter. Suffice it to say that the pride that goes into excelling defensively must also be applied in the area of conditioning if we are to obtain maximum results. We have to be in better condition than our opponents. If we are not, we will break down before they do. That our players are required to play intensely has been evident throughout this book and, hopefully, it is just as evident in watching our players during the course of a game and during the course of the season. Defense is the one area in which intensity can equalize talent. All we are talking about is developing in our players an attitude that refuses to accept second best. If we can accomplish that, defense will be easier to teach than first imagined.

The Run and Change and the Trap

We will utilize the two on two drill to begin developing the principles for executing our run and change and our trapping defensive tactics. We have already discussed a few of our ideas with regard to the sideline trap. In Diagram 6-2 and in Diagram 6-5 shown here, we have designated certain areas of the floor as areas in which we will be trying to trap an offensive player advancing the basketball. In the remainder of the court area, we will run at the offensive player and change

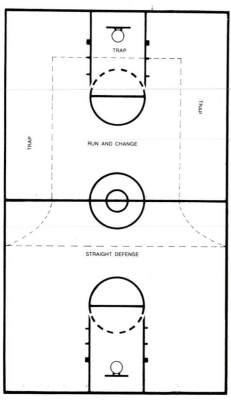

TRAP

TRAP

TRAP

RUN AND CHANGE

STRAIGHT DEFENSE

DIA. 6-5

defenders in an attempt to confuse him and disrupt the offensive flow. The designation of these areas are primarily for organizational and teaching purposes. They are suggested boundaries for applying the various defensive tactics that we have at our disposal. Remember, these are situations in which we do not have to adopt a set pattern or a rigid set of defensive rules. The players will continue to have the freedom to change up the defense. The areas designated will, however, give each of our players a good idea of what we are trying to accomplish with our pressure defense. The players will be able to read each other better. They will have an idea of what the other defensive players are doing or are about to do when the ball is in a particular section of the floor. An excellent team defense will be the result.

In our defensive system the boundaries for the run and change and the trap terminate just over the half court line in our defensive end of the court (Dia. 6-5). The run and change will usually be executed at or beyond the center line, but when utilized in the forecourt area, it can be a very disruptive influence on the opponent's offensive set. The two defensive guards must work extremely well together for this manuever to be truly effective. When applying full court pressure, the trap just over the half line will always be in effect because this is an excellent area for a well executed double team. Once the offense penetrates these boundaries into the half court scoring area, we are immediately into a straight man to man defense with pressure on the ball and an emphasis on help from those players situated on the helpside. This defensive philosophy in the half court area can change according to the game situation and according to the amount of pressure we want to apply. But more on this later. Right now, we are concerned mainly with developing our full court pressing defense.

In the two on two drill, we will introduce our trapping technique but will concentrate principally on our straight man to man pressure and the run and change. We will do most of our work with the trap in the three on three and five on five drills because of the importance of the rotation that is involved. The technique for setting the defensive trap or double team has already been discussed in the preceding pages. The two most important elements for setting an effective trap are anticipation and recognition. We mentioned that the best time to set the trap is when an offensive player has his back turned to the second defensive player and he is dribbling toward the sideline. Our defender must recognize when this situation occurs and he must anticipate the point at which the offensive player will be cut off so he can execute the trap with proper timing. If our defenders do not learn to recognize when a trap will or will not be effective, our entire defensive system will break down. This is why the diagram above is so important to our teaching procedure. In the run and change area, we do not allow a trap to be set when the ball handler is facing the second defender. This relationship is shown in Diagram 6-6 with the defender reacting improperly. The offensive player with the ball is clearly in the middle of the floor and has much of the court area in which to manuever. More importantly, he is dribbling toward the second defender with both the defensive player and his offensive teammate in his line of sight. We do not want to apply a trap in this situation. One of our biggest advantages in setting the trap is the element of surprise. This not only comes into play when trapping a dribbler who has turned his back but it is also one of our reasons for varying the defensive tactics. There is no element of surprise in the action we are describing now. The offensive player should have no trouble in advancing the ball to the open man as soon as he sees the double team coming. We do allow the players to run and change in this situation, although we prefer the blind run and change for the reasons we have already stated. We will further elaborate on trapping and the rotation involved when discussing our three on three work.

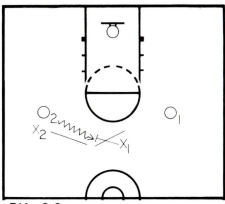

DIA. 6-6

To clarify our terminology and our reasons for execution, we must explain the different techniques and the different defensive options that will be available in the run and change and the blind run and change. The blind run and change is the most potent defensive weapon so this is the opportunity we want our defenders looking for most of the time. The run and change can serve to disrupt and confuse the offense, but the timing on the part of the guards has to be excellent or the play could result in a breakdown. The two players executing the run and change must work extremely well together. The action described above and shown in Diagram 6-6 is, in part, a simple run and change manuever. The run and change is started by the helping defender leaving his man to apply pressure on the man with the ball. With the ball handler dribbling toward the second defender, our man must look for exactly the right moment to make his move. The offensive player might be preoccupied with his defender or he might be looking up the floor and disregarding the helping defensive player. The best possible time to spring this attack is when the offensive player has momentarily lost control of the ball. In this situation, the player is not ready to deliver the ball to his vacated teammate, which is the most advantageous play for the offense to make. An offensive player who has fumbled the ball and is now being attacked by an unexpected defensive manuever can easily become flustered. We want to take advantage of this uncertainty, however momentary. When a defensive player does decide to execute the run and change in this situation, it is very important that he move quickly and that he makes his move directly in the passing lane between his man and the man with the ball. The hands should be up and ready in case the dribbler does react in time to attempt the pass. Obviously, an interception or deflection would be the primary goal, but failing this, the defender must force a lob or a bounce pass that

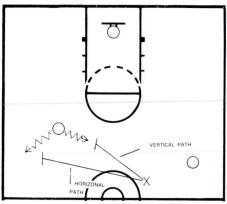

VERTICAL PATH

HORIZONAL PATH

DIA. 6-7

will allow his teammate time to make the change. A direct pass will be disastrous for the defense.

The defender on the ball must recognize immediately that the run and change is in effect. As soon as his defensive teammate moves into position to apply pressure to the ball handler, the change must be made. Unless the dribbler is completely vulnerable, there is no thought of staying for the double team. We are simply trying to force a mistake by attacking an unsuspecting ball handler from a different angle. Only by changing quickly can we permit this manuever when the offensive player is dribbling toward help. We cannot leave the opposite offensive opponent unguarded and any rotation by our second line of defense (in a team situation) would be too dangerous. In making the change, our defensive man should turn and run directly toward the opposite offensive guard. His vision should remain on his original man and the ball. An attempt should be made to play the passing lane in the event that the offensive player tries to pass the ball ahead. If the pass is completed ahead, the defender must select the proper angle in which to cut off the offensive player now handling the ball. If the original ball handler is forced to pick up his dribble but does not make a pass, the man making the change should be all over the opposite guard, totally denying the passing lane. If the ball handler handles the pressure well and continues his dribble, our two defenders have merely switched men and reversed their defensive roles for the time being. As emphasized, the players must be extremely careful in their use of this defensive manuever. We like it as a change of pace but we much prefer to run and change when the ball handler has his back turned to the second defender.

The blind run and change is so named because we expect the offensive man with the ball to be unaware of the attack by our second defensive player. This second defensive man initiates the blind run and change when the ball handler has completely turned his back on the defensive help. His techniques for running at the dribbler are exactly the same as we described before. His path to the ball will be on a little more of a horizontial plane than a vertical one because the dribbler will not be coming directly toward him (Dia. 6-7). The big difference now lies with the technique of the man on the ball. He does not leave his offensive man until the dribbler is forced to pick the ball up. If the timing of the play is such that the offensive player has entered a trapping area then the double team is in effect. If the ball is in the run and change area, we want the initial defender to make the change immediately after the offensive player is forced to stop his dribble. The new defensive man will now apply extreme pressure on the ball handler to force the turnover. In making the change, our original defender will move quickly into the passing lane between the two offensive guards using the same techniques we outlined before. Many times, the ball handler will try to make a quick pass to the vacated guard without recognizing the defensive adjustments taking place. We want our defender looking to take advantage of this type of mistake. A quick basket at the other end will be the result if we can pressure the offense into an error in judgement. If the pass is not made, the defensive man adjusts to a position completely overplaying the off guard. Any time a ball handler is forced to pick his dribble up we want to cut off the passing lanes before he can find an outlet for his dilemma. This must be accomplished quickly and instinctively or the pressure that has caused the offensive player to use up his dribble will go for naught. We will see in our three on three and our five on five work that all of our defenders must react quickly and apply this defensive principle.

When we are having success with the rotation of our second line of defense we will allow the original defender to stay with the trap. This will actually turn our run and change defense into a run and jump situation. We incorporate this into our defensive system but for reasons of simplicity, do not include the run and jump in our terminology. The manuever is merely something that evolves from our trapping and run and change defenses.

Teaching Three On Three Defense (First Stage)

We begin our three on three drill with the offense taking the ball out of bounds and the two potential receivers lining up at the free throw line area. The offense can use any means available to free themselves for the inbounds pass. The defenders again start out denying the pass to their respective men by turning their back on the ball and completely fronting each of the potential receivers. The defender on the ball is pressuring the inbounder and shading one side or the other in an attempt to influence the pass to a particular corner.

Each defensive player has sole responsibility for his man unless the two players attempting to get open cross in any way. In this case, our two defenders are to come together and then switch men. When the offensive players cross there should be no indecision on the part of our players. We are going to come together and switch. By coming together we can discourage either of the receivers from making a straight cut from a crossing position. This is the offensive move that causes the most trouble for the defenders in this situation. In Diagram 6-8, you can see that the offensive players have come to a position as if to cross but the player in front (O₃) makes a straight cut to the ball. If not prepared properly this can create some confusion in the defenders as to whether to switch or stay with their man. Our players are not to switch until an actual cross is made. When the offense moves into a crossing position our two defenders know that their first concern is to come together (Dia. 6-9). The defensive man on the right side (X₂)

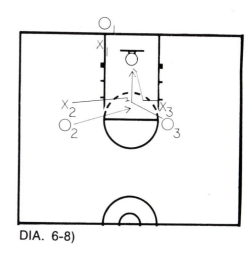

DIA. 6-8)

DIA. 6-9

now has responsibility for the first player to cut to that side. The player on the left (X_3) has the responsibility to pick up the first cutter to the left side. What that means is that if the offensive players do actually cross then the switch will be made. If the receivers come to a crossing position and then cut back to their respective sides, our players know that their responsibility is to stay with their men. Once an offensive player makes the first cut from the crossing position, the defender opposite his cut immediately picks up the remaining offensive man. This covers the same side cut by the offensive players.

In the above diagram, a crossing pattern is shown but the first offensive player makes a direct cut to the ball. Remember, our players are coming together to discourage this play. If the offense attempts the manuever anyway our players know that they are to stay with their men. We must identify and our players must recognize the difference between this play and an actual screen set by the offense. Any time a screen is set and the cross takes place, we are going to switch. If the screen is set but the offensive player breaks back to the same side or holds while the screener cuts to the ball, there is no switch. These techniques follow the same rules we stated before but the players must be taught to recognize the different situations. The players must talk to each other. If they talk and come together properly, then they should be very effective in pressuring the inbounds pass.

If the offensive players start in a tandem set (same as Figure 6-9) then our players immediately come together and the same rules apply. One final point on our idea of coming together defensively. We think that this principle helps our players to avoid a well set screen by the offense. Obviously, a solid screen set by an offensive player can be very effective in opening up a receiver for the inbounds pass. By coming together our players make it extremely difficult for the screener to set a good pick on the side of the defender. We feel that the application of this principle has led to much of our success in this defensive situation.

Our next method of defensing the inbounds pass is to force the ball as deep as possible to a particular corner. We have already stated that most teams like to throw in to the right of the basket so we encourage the ball that way. The important thing is that the player breaking into the corner area is forced as deep as possible to catch the ball. The defensive man on the inbounder is shading the offensive man on his left side to discourage the pass to the left side of the floor. As this is taking place the third defender must totally deny the pass to his man with the same defensive technique that we showed earlier. If we can successfully direct the ball deep into the corner, then we will have gained some definite advantages as we begin our defensive pressure in the full court area. The advantages are psychological as well as physical. The defense will get a big boost by knowing that they have forced the offense to play into their hands. Again, the offense has had to react according to the defense. Furthermore, the defensive players will get the idea that the pressure being applied is effective and this will help to motivate them toward even greater defensive effort. The physical advantages are: (1) the greater distance the offense must advance the ball to cross the ten second line; (2) the limited area the defensive player on the ball will have to cover, if he executes properly; (3) the limited area in which the offensive player will have to manuever; (4) the poorer passing angles that are created when the ball is on the sideline or in the corner area. The players off the ball should especially be aware of the poor passing angles. They should be able to cheat closer to the ball and play the passing lanes looking for the interception or deflection.

If the offense wants to start the ball on the left side of the floor our two inbounds defenders will simply reverse roles. The player on the right side of the basket (facing our defensive end) will deny the pass to his man and the player on the left side will push his man deep in the corner. The man on the ball will shade the opposite side of the passer. We do not want to fight the inclination of the offense to start the ball to one side of the floor or the other. We do want to get them into a pattern for one side or the other because this will make our defense that much easier.

The next form of defensive pressure that we apply is very similar to the one we have just described but adds an element of surprise that can be very effective after a pattern has been set. The three defenders have the same responsibilities that we have outlined above. The difference comes when the player we want to receive the ball is influenced into the corner area. When this happens, we want the defender on this potential receiver to suddenly shift to a denial position between his man and the ball. After allowing this pass for a period of time the offense may have become lackadaisical in their movement and in their concentration. Now they may find themselves in a real dilemma with only two or three seconds to complete the inbounds pass. As soon as the defender on the receiver readjusts to deny the pass, the defensive man on the ball should move to a head up position on the inbounder. From that position he should apply extreme pressure with whatever resources he has available. We like our defenders in this position to wave the hands and arms and to occasionally leave their feet for a purpose. We want them to jump quickly so that they can get their feet back on the ground and continue moving. The third defender must be continuing to deny the basketball to his assigned man. We are working for a five second call in this situation or a lob pass that can be intercepted or deflected to a teammate.

At this point, we should introduce a rule that we follow that is somewhat similar to the above defensive method. We can introduce this practice in relation to our two on two situation, but it involves a circumstance that happens much more often when there are two offensive players working to get open. The inbounder sometimes gets a little overconfident in his ability to make the initial pass. Or he may take a little too much time in deciding which way to go with the ball. At any rate, if, for any reason, the inbounder has not made the pass within three seconds, we want to adjust to a denial position no matter what type of defense we have been playing. We want to apply this concept even if we have been playing behind the offense and allowing them to catch the ball in front. The passer will be hard pressed to make an accurate pass within the time limit if we can adjust quickly and exert maximum pressure. The man on the inbounder can again lend great support by the amount of pressure he is able to apply. All of the players must recognize the time that has passed and must react to overplay their man. If one man is left open the entire effort is wasted.

We next begin to develop the double team method in a three on three situation. The man on the ball will drop off to cover the opponent's best ball handler. In this way, we can force the pass to go to the weaker ball handler and hopefully can apply enough pressure to cause a turnover. The technique for the double team we have already discussed. The third defender can use any of the five methods for defensing the inbounds pass. Which one will depend on the amount of pressure that we want applied or the strategy that we are employing. If we want to exert all out pressure our defensive man utilizing single coverage will totally deny the pass to his man. If we merely want the ball to go to this offensive player, we can tell our defender to execute any one of the other four defensive methods. We can allow him the freedom to change up his tactics or we can specify exactly what we want from the bench. These decisions will again be based on the game situation, what has worked for us in the past, and what is working against this particular team and individual.

The man we double team does not always have to be the opponent's best ball handler. We may want to double team the quicker player who has had the most success in getting open for the inbounds pass. If we put our top defender on the opponent's best ball handler, he may be able to control the offensive player all by himself. Maybe our other defender will need the help. These are all adjustments that will be easy to make if we have prepared the players properly in the development of our defensive system of play.

The final defensive tactics to be employed on the inbounds pass involve both defenders playing behind the potential receivers. We are encouraging, by our defensive position, a pass to the corner, but we are applying practically no pressure. The man playing the inbounder is to prevent the long pass and the pass into the middle of the floor. The full court defense that will usually follow this method is our straight man to man but remember that we can combine our strategies to take advantage of any lapses in concentration or intensity by the offense. Many times we have lulled the offense to sleep with a very limited amount of pressure and then sprung a surprise attack after the ball has been inbounded.

We actually prefer for the offense to use three people in attempting to make the inbounds pass. We feel that our defenders will have less area to cover, that it brings one additional helper into the play, and that the congestion will limit the freedom of the offense. Any time there is congestion, there is less pressure on the defense. By bringing the third player up from the start, the offense has now placed four or five men in the same amount of area that would be occupied by two or three men in a clear out situation. We stress these points to our players in preparing them to play aggressive pressure defense from end line to end line. We want them to be confident in their ability to play this type of defense without giving anything away to the offense. Many teams and individual players never reach their full defensive potential because they lack the confidence and the freedom to play aggressively. They are trying to keep from getting beat rather than trying to do all they can to force the action. As we have stressed throughout, we want our players to be creative. We want them to make something happen on defense as well as on offense.

The three on three defenses shown in the preceding pages explain the coverage involved when the offense does utilize three players in bringing the ball in from out of bounds. Some teams will rely on one individual to break open under pressure and will bring the third man up only when necessary. In that case, we need to identify the offensive player who will most often be the third man up. All of our defenders should be prepared to stay with their men if they break back to help relieve pressure. We insist that our front line players or our second line of defense apply the same type of pressure that we expect from our guards. Anything less is unacceptable in our defensive system. How many times have we all seen an offensive player break back from half court to receive an uncontested pass when a five second call was imminent? We cannot have the guards extending total effort in denying or pressuring the inbounds pass and let our second line of defense waste that effort through their lack of defensive intensity and hustle. The offense will designate a third ball handler and we want to make our defensive assignments with this in mind. The probable alignment that this type of press offense would produce is diagrammed to the right (Dia. 6-10). Most of the time the third offensive player will line up opposite the ball so he can break up on the open side if needed. If he does line up on the ballside, this should help

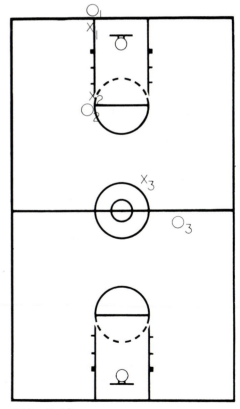

DIA. 6-10

our defensive situation because of the additional congestion.

The two front men in our press are back to a two on two situation and would utilize the same defensive tactics we outlined earlier. The third defender is to play one to two steps off a line drawn between his man and the basketball. He should be on the inside of that line facing the sideline and in a position where he can watch both his man and the basketball. We like our players to point man and ball in this situation because it is very important that they do not lose their men while we are applying pressure. One open man will cause a breakdown in the entire defense, especially if the ball is delivered to an open man somewhere in the half court area. The third defensive player has to be slightly open to the ball and focusing his attention on what is taking place as the offense is attempting to make the inbounds pass. He must be watching his man out of the corner of his eye. In a team situation, both the third and fourth defensive players in the half court area will be tuned in to the defensive player behind them. He can help trememdously by communicating to his teammates the position and the movement of their offensive counterparts. More on that later.

The one or two step relationship to the line of the ball will depend on the distance the third offensive player is from the ball and whether or not the offense is apt to attempt a long and relatively dangerous pass from behind the end line. The defender's relationship to his man will also depend, in part, on the above variables. We want our defender in this situation to cheat as far as possible in the direction of the ball. He should be just close enough to his man to discourage the inbounder from making the long pass. At the same time, if the pass is thrown, he must be able to recover in time to get a hand on the ball. Each player must correctly gauge his own ability and quickness to recover in this situation. We will help them but good judgement is absolutely necessary. We want to provide as much help as possible to our first line of defense but under no circumstances can we allow a long pass to the half court area to be completed. We encourage our players to stretch this area of recovery in practice sessions so that they will increase their ability to recover under game conditions. The players are made to realize that this is an extremely difficult pass for the inbounder to make. The man taking the ball out of bounds has to contend with the basket, his defensive man applying pressure, a five second time limit, and a limited area in which to set himself for the pass. Our third defender must, of course, be fully aware of the defensive method the first two defensive players are employing. If the double team is in effect, there is no immediate pressure on the passer. Furthermore, with the primary receiver being double teamed there is not as much need for help at that end. In this case, the third defender would play closer to his man and should be ready to move into lead pass position if the offensive player breaks back to receive the ball. He must react quickly to deny this pass.

If our first two defenders are employing individual coverage and denying the inbounds pass, then our third defensive man must be able to provide adequate help. We mentioned earlier that our second line of defense would be responsible for any lob pass thrown over the head of our inbounds defender. This is where he will be most vulnerable when turning his back on the ball so we give the third defender primary responsibility for discouraging or interrupting this pass. The tough denial by the inbounds defender and the pressure being applied by our defensive man on the ball should influence a high lob pass. In recognizing this type of defensive employment, the third defensive man should be as far off his man as possible. He should be ready to react to the lob pass or a loose ball caused by a deflection. The ability to anticipate will again be very important for our players in playing this aggressive, pressure defense. We need to anticipate the movements of the offense as well as anticipate and read the intentions of our defensive teammates. The same responsibilities will be in effect when we are forcing to the corner and shifting to deny the pass at that point. The emphasis will change somewhat when we are allowing the inbounds pass to be completed. Because the inbounds defender will be playing behind his man, our third defensive man does not have to be as concerned with the need for help. This does not mean, however, that our defender moves closer to his man and has sole responsibility for individual defense. We still want the defender to get off and toward as much as possible without jeopardizing his relative defensive position to his man. We feel that the additional help provided and the increased congestion will be very beneficial to our defensive effort in the full court area.

Three On Three Full Court (Second Stage)

We start our three on three full court work with some of the same rules that we utilized in beginning the two on two drills. The offense is required to stay at half speed and they are not allowed to clear out for the time being. We again must be concerned with the proper positioning of our players before we expect them to control the offense in a pressing situation. We want to review and make sure that they understand the defensive principles that we have been introducing. We begin by teaching the straight man to man in a three on three situation. As mentioned, the offensive players cannot run off so the offensive and defensive sets should look something like we have diagrammed (Dia. 6-11) after the initial pass is completed. Foremost in our minds, at this point, is making sure that everyone drops to the line of the ball and that the players away from the ball handler maintain a help and recover

DIA. 6-11

position in relation to the basketball and their man. The player two passes away from the ball should remember that the farther his man is from the ball, the closer he can cheat to provide help. As the basketball changes positions, the players must adjust to maintain the correct relationships between man and ball. If the ball handler advances by dribbling, the two defensive players away from the ball must change their line accordingly. If the basketball is passed from one offensive player to another, everyone must make the proper adjustment. The original man on the ball must get off and toward the direction of the pass as soon as it passes his fingertips. The new man on the ball must recover to his man without overextending himself and should assume proper defensive position on the ball. It is very important that all defensive players maintain complete control of their body in advancing toward an offensive man who still has his dribble. It would be defensive suicide to rush at the opponent because a quick move by the ball handler would leave the defender completely off balance and out of position. The idea again is to give the offensive player only one way to go and to anticipate the move in that direction.

When playing the straight man to man, the defensive positioning for the three on three full court work is much the same as we taught for the two on two drill. We like to repeat our principles with three people because we understand the value of repetition, especially with regard to our defensive habits. We are also continuing to build toward the development of our team defense. The players are learning to work together and are finding out that teamwork is just as important on defense as it is on offense.

The one point that we emphasize more in the three on three situation is that additional help is provided and there is further congestion. Therefore, more pressure can be applied to the man with the basketball. Any time a team uses three people to bring the basketball we feel that our pressing man to man defense can be extremely effective. After developing the straight man to man in a three on three situation, we now begin to teach the movement and the rotation that will be involved when applying all out pressure.

The run and change and the trap areas have already been explained fully. Each player must be totally aware of these areas on the floor if we are going to have any type of consistency in our defensive teamwork and effort. Furthermore, the players must recognize and anticipate the movement of the ball into a specific area. The players cannot lose their vision on the ball or they will be lost as to their proper defensive positioning. Defensive rotation will be extremely important in the successful execution of a trapping and a run and change defense. When an effective trap is being set, we want all of our players to rotate toward the ball. We want the defenders closest to the ball to completely close off the passing lanes. The defensive man farthest from the ball is taught to rotate toward the ball, but he does not completely leave his man if he is our last defender. But we are jumping ahead of ourselves to the five on five situation.

We start teaching the proper rotation in the three on three drill. We must again emphasize the importance of teamwork and anticipation in our defensive scheme of things. All three players are aware that we are looking to set the trap in the sideline or corner areas. The player that is not involved in the trap knows that he is to change position as soon as an effective trap has been established. If he is reading his teammates properly, he should be able to make his rotation in time to cut off the primary passing lane. We feel that the offense has the best chance to beat the trap by recognizing the situation immediately and making the pass to the vacated offensive player. This is why the rotation is so important when employing this type of defensive pressure. We define the passing option to the vacated offensive player as the primary pass and we expect the third man involved to move quickly to discourage its attempt. When any double team occurs, the idea is to push up toward the ball and leave the man furthest away from the basketball with the best chance of receiving the pass. In a three on three situation, the third man rotates because his man is furthest from the ball. Obviously, in a five on five situation, we would have people rotating to cover the third offensive player, but we will get to that later. We want to encourage the player being trapped to attempt the long pass and the players executing the trap should apply enough pressure to force the player to throw the ball high. A long, high pass can be picked off easily by the defensive players off the ball. This is especially true if the defensive players are taught to anticipate properly. We instruct our players to be totally aware of the movement taking place but to watch the eyes of the man with the ball. They should try to anticipate the direction of the pass and cheat toward that area without giving up anything in another area.

We mentioned above that the offense has the best chance to beat the trap if they recognize quickly what the defense is doing. This is why we prefer for the trap to be set when the ball handler has turned his back to the second defensive player. We always want to take advantage of the element of surprise. If the dribbler is surprised by the trap and then tries to make a play too quickly, our rotation should put us in possible position for an interception. This happens most often with the rotation involving the third defender. At times, the ball handler will panic and make a blind pass back to his vacated teammate. This is the best chance for our defender to pick off a pass and head for an uncontested lay up. If the offensive player with the ball starts to make this pass but recognizes the rotation taking place, this is the time to apply extreme pressure

DIA. 6-12

DIA. 6-13

and try to force the long pass. In our three on three drill, we want the third defender to leave his man completely and totally deny the pass to the offensive player closest to the ball. We do not worry about the third offensive player at this point because he will be picked up by our fourth or fifth defender when playing five on five. The third defender assumes a position of lead pass pressure on his new man and maintains that defensive posture until the offense beats the trap or commits a turnover.

The rotation we have explained is illustrated in the margin (Dia. 6-12). The trap is developing on the sideline. From the start the third defender (X_3) recognizes the vulnerability of the offense and the intentions of his teammates. He is already moving in anticipation of his responsibilities once the trap is set. As the trap is set the third defender rotates toward the ball and denies the pass to the vacated offensive player. As mentioned, we do not worry about the third offensive player in this drill.

It is crucial in executing any pressure defense that the defenders recognize when they have been beaten. This is no time to stand and watch the action at the other end. If you are going to press, you cannot give up the easy basket. We teach our players to turn and sprint toward the defensive basket as soon as the ball passes their line of defense. Every player must hustle back and size up the situation on the move. The players on the ballside can look to deflect the ball from behind if the offense is being careless. The weakside players must hustle back to the middle of the floor and move out to pick up their men from there.

The third defender's responsibility in the run and change manuever is to provide as much help as possible. This relationship is shown in Diagram 6-13. The second defender (X_1) moves over to execute the run and change. As soon as the offensive player picks the ball up, the initial defensive man (X_2) completes the change by moving into the primary passing lane and picking up the vacated opponent. X_3 is off and toward the ball and as he sees the run and change developing, he moves even closer to the middle to provide help and to add congestion. If the ball handler is able to complete the pass to O_1, X_3 must first discourage the drive up the middle and then react quickly back to his man. The defender on the ball must then try to direct the dribbler to one sideline or the other. We have to keep the ball out of the middle of the floor if we want to apply maximum pressure. We do not want the third defender to switch in this situation. The first defender (X_2) is responsible for making the change quickly and efficiently. If the defensive manuever is a straight run and change, X_2 must start to change as soon as X_1 moves to head off the dribbler. If it is a blind run and change (shown in diagram) X_2 must move quickly to pick up X_1's man as soon as the ball handler picks up his dribble. The help that will be provided by X_3 should discourage easy movement of the ball. He would only switch in case of emergency. Each player must know his responsibilities in any type of rotation or breakdowns will result. If the third defender moved over to pick up O_1 or to look for the interception, we would have two players playing this same area and would be leaving the third offensive player completely free. This type of confusion cannot exist if our defensive pressure is to be effective.

We expect our players to maintain proper positioning throughout the execution of our defense. The tactics will change once the offense moves the ball into the half court scoring area. Until that time, the defensive players pressuring the ball are utilizing the principles we have been explaining. They must learn that they are to react quickly each and every time the ball changes position and that there is not time to let up in our defensive system. We are not going to pressure the ball for a few seconds and then let the offense take control. Whatever amount of pressure we are applying is to be applied the entire time the offense is attempting to advance the ball.

Too many teams let up defensively after the first few seconds. We insist that our players sustain their intensity. The best time to play the tough defense is when the offense is in danger of exceeding a specified time limit. If the offense has used five to eight seconds and is still in the backcourt area we want to apply extreme pressure and force the ten second violation. Our players should be motivated to play excellent defense in this time span and the offense may lose some poise or even panic in their haste to advance the ball into the frontcourt. These ideas are in keeping with our philosophy of a totally aggressive defense; one that will break up the continuity or timing of our offensive opponents and force them to make mistakes.

Five On Five Full Court Pressure (First Stage)

The five on five work is what we have been building for throughout the development of our full court defensive system. While we have controlled the individual and the two on two and three on three drills, they have actually been more difficult than what will be faced in a game situation because of the lack of congestion and defensive help. After our players have developed the necessary skills, we will go more and more to the five on five drill work because it most closely simulates actual game conditions. Working five on five will also give our players the opportunity to get to know each other better. The team defensive effort and pride will be continuing to grow.

At this point in our full court defensive drills, we will allow the offense to execute at full speed from the outset. The first line of our defense should be well versed in their defensive responsibilities. We will teach and demonstrate to the second

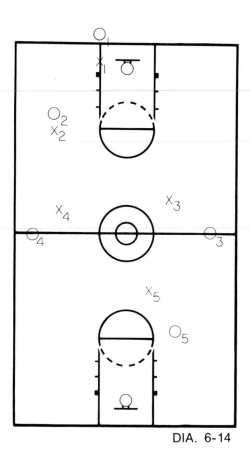

DIA. 6-14

line of defense exactly what will be expected of them when we are applying full court pressure and will make the necessary corrections as the drill progresses. We have the offense bring the ball with a two man front because this is the set we will most often face in a game situation. We still do not allow the second guard to run off and clear the floor. The forwards are lined up at half court with the third best ball handler ready to come back if help is needed. The big man or weakest handling frontline player plays in the offensive end of the court. These positions are shown with our proper defensive alignment in the accompanying diagram (Dia. 6-14). All of the offensive players have some flexibility in their positioning and the strategy with which they attempt to advance the ball up the floor. We are concerned here with the defense and we want them to see all kinds of offensive alignments.

We have stated previously the importance of the off and toward principle in all facets of defensive play. This comes into play again as we want our second line of defense to push up toward the ball as far as possible to aid in the defensive pressure. This also puts them in good position to apply lead pass pressure should their man break back toward the ball to receive a pass. We pointed out the importance of this responsibility earlier, but it is well worth repeating in developing our five on five defense. Regardless of the type of pressure the guards are employing on the inbounds pass, the second line of defense will deny their respective passing lanes unless they can force the pass to be made in the corner area. In other words, if we are forcing the first pass to be made in the corner area the ball should be denied to any player who is in an area other than the corner. This will almost always apply to the third, fourth, and fifth offensive player. They will very rarely come all the way to the corner to receive the pass. If the guards are denying the inbounds pass, then we will want to apply the same tactics with our second line of defense. We cannot let up the pressure on the offense by allowing a man to break back from half court to receive the initial pass. This not only breaks down our defense, but it can be damaging to team morale. We expect everyone to work extremely hard to meet their individual defensive responsibilities. If those responsibilities do not come as easily or as naturally for some players, they must work harder to attain the desired results. We have already emphasized that defense is ninety percent intestinal fortitude.

The three defenders in our second line of defense are off and toward the basketball and applying the same rules that we discussed earlier in relation to the third man up offensive strategy (see Dia. 6-10). Each defender plays just off a line drawn between his man and the basketball. They are playing on the inside of that line, facing their respective sidelines so that they are in a position to see man and ball. We like them to point man and ball in this situation so that they do not lose track of either. The defensive players should be slightly open to the ball and watching their offensive man out of the corner of their eye.

Perhaps the most important aspect of this defensive relationship is the distance each man is able to play off and toward the basketball. We want them to push toward the ball as much as possible, but they should be close enough to their men to discourage the inbounder from making the long pass. The farther their man is from the ball, the longer the pass is going to be in the air. Thus, there is greater recovery time. Each player has to know his own ability and quickness to recover back to his man. While we want to provide as much help as possible to our first line of defense, we cannot allow a pass to be completed into the half court area. We showed earlier the relative difficulty of completing this pass from out of bounds. Obviously, our fifth defender can play farther off his man because of the distance he is from the ball. By the same token, he must remember that he is our last line of defense. He cannot let the ball be thrown behind him. The fifth defender does not go for an interception unless he is absolutely sure of obtaining possession of the ball. If he goes for the ball and we do not come up with it the offense will be breaking behind for a sure two points. Where our fifth defender can help immensely in anticipating steals is by communicating effectively with our third and fourth defensive players. The last defender has practically the entire court area in his vision and the play is being made in front of him. By talking to his defensive teammates, he can allow them more freedom to concentrate on the ball. The fifth man must let them know as soon as either of the offensive players makes a movement that should change the defensive relationship. He should especially be quick to point out a quick cut to the ball or the basket. The defensive player assigned to that cutter should then react accordingly. The fifth defender should also be ready to help on an offensive player breaking to the basket from the half court area. It is the responsibility of the third and fourth defensive players to tune into the voice of their teammate behind them. They have to block out the external noises so they can concentrate fully on the matter at hand.

Recognition and anticipation are, as always, extremely important for our players. Each player must recognize the amount of defensive pressure that is being applied and the ability of the offense or a particular offensive player to handle that pressure. Proper recognition will make it easier for us to anticipate the movement of the ball and the movement of the offensive players. Anticipation is the key to interceptions.

As we have shown, the first responsibility for our second line of defense is to get off and toward the basketball in a position where they can help but recover to their man should the long pass be attempted. They have to stop this pass or a pass to their particular offensive player breaking back toward the ball.

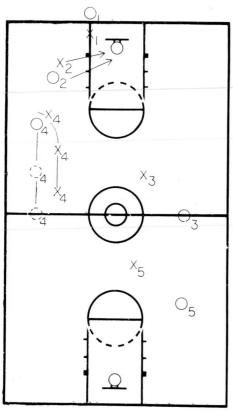

DIA. 6-15

An offensive player breaking back from half court to receive the pass calls for lead pass pressure on the part of the assigned defender. As soon as the offensive man makes his cut, the defender should continue to get off and toward until which time the offensive player can receive a direct pass from the inbounder. When this occurs, the defender should close the distance between himself and his man and assume a position of lead pass pressure denying the pass completely. This defensive relationship is shown in Diagram 6-15. We see that the defender (X_4) maintains his off and toward principle as the offensive player starts back to receive the pass. As soon as the offensive player is in a position to receive the ball, X_4 closes off the distance and denies the pass.

The next responsibility for our second line of defense is to prevent the lob pass thrown over the head of our first defender or defenders. This responsibility is always in effect, but is especially important when we are denying the pass inbounds by totally fronting the potential receiver or receivers. The man defending the inbounds pass will be very vulnerable to this type of pass, so the second line of defenders must be alert to react quickly to the ball when it is lobbed beyond the free throw line into the key area. As far as we are concerned, that ball is up for grabs. We want the third or fourth defender, whoever is closer to the play, to come up quickly for the interception or deflection. The player on the inbounder is taught to call "ball" when the pass is made, so this should help to cue all of our defensive players. The defensive man inbounds can even yell "lob" if he recognizes quickly enough the type of pass thrown. This should further help our men to react quickly and to find the ball. If our defensive man has anticipated and reacted quickly enough he is to look for the outright interception. However, a deflection can be just as effective because our other defenders should be alert to react to any loose balls. The defensive man on the intended receiver should especially be ready because he will be at the center of the action. If we do come up with the ball, our players must learn to convert quickly from defense to offense. The ball handler should find the open man nearest the basket or take the ball to the hole himself. The other players should make themselves available in an open area. These type of scoring opportunities can come in spurts if the defense applies enough pressure and takes advantage of the mistakes made by the offense.

A different type of conversion will be necessary if we fail to come up with the ball despite our defensive effort. Any time the ball is in advance of our defensive players we want them to get to the level of the basketball. If the offense is advancing the ball quickly the defenders must turn and sprint toward their defensive basket. They can be looking to steal the ball from a careless ball handler, but mainly they should be concerned with getting back to their original men. The players have to have the ability to think on the move and this is one of the reasons we spend considerable time with our five on five work. It is imperative that the players talk and that they work together in protecting the basket and stopping the ball.

The defense of the first two players will determine just how much help the second line of defense is to provide. When we double team the primary inbounds receiver the second line of defense should be more concerned with their individual defensive assignments. The two front men should be able to handle the one immediate inbounds receiver. This is one of the times the offense will most likely bring a man back to receive the initial pass. We want our players to understand this and be prepared to anticipate this type of offensive movement. If we are forcing the ball to the corner or allowing an uncontested initial pass the need for help will also not be great. We still want the players described to push up as far as possible to congest the floor and to be in position in case the opposition tries a lob. If the initial defender is forcing to the corner and then denying the pass the second line of defense definitely has to be responsible for any lob passes that may be attempted. We have already explained that this responsibility is in effect when we are utilizing single coverage but denying the initial pass.

Five On Five (Second Stage)

We feel that we can get a tremendous amount of work done within the framework of our full court five on five drill. The players must put into practice all of the individual fundamentals and the team defensive principles that we have been teaching in leading up to a five on five situation. The team aspects that we are looking to solidify include:

1) Defensive positioning—especially with regard to providing help and recovering to their men.
2) Teamwork—working together, reading each other's intentions and communicating effectively.
3) Aggressiveness—we want our players to have confidence in the pressure we are applying and to go all out toward making the press successful. This means aggressive play with a nose for the ball.
4) Intensity—probably the most important element of a good defensive team. We feel that all of our players can play excellent defense if they will learn to play hard.

Individually, we will be looking at the quickness of the feet and the ability of each player to get the job done defensively. We will still correct the fundamental mistakes but at this point we are concerned primarily with each player learning to control his man. Quickness and/or intensity will have much to do with how well each individual accomplishes this goal. The players should be well grounded in the fundamentals of our full court defense. A few corrections and minor adjustments will be necessary during the drill to remind the players of these fundamentals.

Conditioning and some offensive work against the man to man press are side benefits that will be gained from our full court

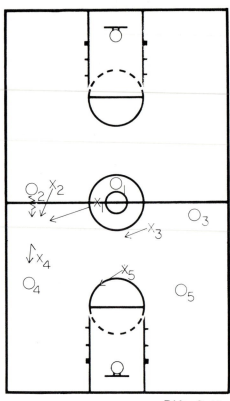

DIA. 6-16

five on five work. We expect the offensive team to play with poise in handling the defensive pressure. To do this, they must have confidence in their ability to beat their man one on one. When speaking to the offense, we tell them that they are in control of the ball and the situation. The offense cannot let the defense dictate where the ball is to go.

Once the ball is inbounded, we teach our three defensive players up the floor to work for the opportunity to push even closer to the ball. Their first responsibility is still to their man, but we want to again provide as much help as possible to our teammate on the ball. We think that this congestion helps to discourage easy movement of the basketball. When the inbounds receiver puts the ball on the floor, the defenders off the ball should edge slightly in that direction. When the dribbler has his back turned the defenders on his blind side can look to move even closer. Remember, we are not telling our defensive players to leave their man. They still must be in a position to recover to their man if a pass should be attempted. We are merely looking for opportunities to cheat in toward the basketball to further inhibit offensive movement. The relative abilities and the movement of the offensive players off the ball also enter into this defensive relationship. One of our defenders will be guarding a player who may not be used very often in the opponent's press offense. That defensive player will be able to cheat closer to the ball. If the offensive player is stationary, the defender can concern himself a little more with the ball. If the offensive player is working to get open the defensive player has to be more man oriented.

We again start the second stage of our defense by developing our straight man to man principles. The offense attempts to bring the ball up the floor while the defense applies man to man pressure with no run and change or double team tactics. Each player has individual responsibility for guarding his own man along with responsibility for helping to stop or discourage advancement of the ball. The second line and last line of defense will be called on to help and recover just like the guards. They must know the technique and what will be expected of them in a help and recover situation. The best example that can be used to illustrate the proper technique is when an offensive player is advancing the ball up the sideline versus our defensive pressure (Dia. 6-16). The helping defensive player in this situation (X_4) cannot allow the pass to be made over his head or through his defense to his assigned offensive opponent. At the same time, adequate help must be provided to slow down the dribbler and allow the man on the ball to reassume proper defensive positioning. We teach our players to fake toward the dribbler to help slow him down. They must fake and retreat back to their man to stop the dribbler from passing ahead. The offensive player without the ball is likely to cut to the basket if his defensive man gets too far off so we want our defender to continue faking and retreating until the ball is stopped. We can see in the diagram that help should be coming from all angles. Every player must change his position according to the movement of the ball or his man. As we discussed earlier, X_1 will be dropping to the line of the ball and showing himself to the ball handler. X_3 will be getting off and toward the basketball and should be adding to the congestion in the middle of the floor. X_5 is very important in this situation because he should be off and toward the ball in a position to help discourage the pass up the sideline. X_4 cannot leave his man to stop the ball unless it is absolutely necessary. If this situation does occur, X_2 must sprint to pick up the vacated offensive player while X_3 and X_5 clog the middle in an attempt to slow down or stop the offensive thrust. We have already shown that X_1 should be in a position to make this play because he is dropping to the line of the ball as it is advanced.

The above defensive technique and alignment does not just apply to the play up the sideline. Any time a dribbler advances the ball toward a defensive man, we want that defensive man in a position to help. If the ball handler has gained an advantage on his defensive opponent our helping defender must make an effort to slow down the dribbler or stop the ball. This can occur anywhere on the floor and the defensive technique is still to fake at the ball handler and retreat back to cover the assigned opponent. During our five on five full court work we constantly stress to our players that their first responsibility is to their man. We emphasize that we are playing a man to man defense with helping principles. If this is not stressed to the players, they begin to concentrate too much on the ball. They lose vision on their men and the offense is able to pass ahead to the open man. There is a fine line here because we certainly want to pressure the ball handlers and react to the ball. The idea is to force the offense to put the basketball on the floor and from there we want to apply maximum pressure on the dribbler and provide help off the ball. When the offense advances into the half court area the ball becomes the focal point of our defense because the offensive players are all in a position to score. When we are applying all out pressure, we become more ball oriented. When we are playing our straight man to man, we want each player to understand his individual responsibilities to his own man.

There are two very important full court defensive principles that we wait to introduce until this time because their development is more conducive to a five on five situation. The first involves the defensive strategy we employ when the offense elects to clear out the pressure and bring the ball up the floor in a one on one confrontation. Until now, we have required that at least one offensive player stay back with he ball handler to help bring the ball. We did this primarily to show

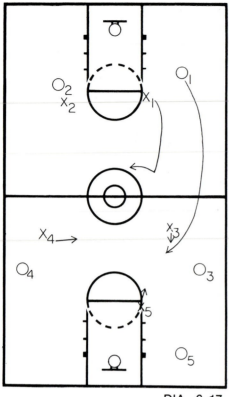

DIA. 6-17

our players the proper defensive positioning but also so that help was provided and we could build confidence in our ability to apply this type of pressure. Some teams will clear out to bring the ball and we want to be prepared to handle this situation when it does occur. We will handle it in such a way that help will still be provided. Our principle states that the second defensive player in our press alignment will never clear past the center circle when the offense attempts to clear out the floor. Usually the offense will bring the ball with two guards back to handle the pressure. If one guard clears out, his man will remain in the backcourt area to provide help and discourage easy movement of the ball. The frontline defensive players will help out with the vacated offensive player without losing their own men. This offensive alignment and the defense that will be required is shown to the left (Dia. 6-17). Our second defensive guard (X_1) maintains his relationship just off the line of the ball as his offensive assignment (O_1) moves up the floor and changes that line. As soon as X_1 recognizes that it is a clear out situation he moves to the bottom of the center circle and opens to the ball. If possible, he should re-establish vision on his man and the ball or maintain some type of defensive relationship to his man. The main concern, however, is to provide as much help as possible to X_2. As we mentioned, the frontline players will be responsible for helping out on O_1. Communication is of the utmost importance in defensing the clear out. X_1 must let X_2 know that the clear out is in effect and must also let X_2 know how much help he (X_1) will be able to provide.

All of the guards and the forwards must learn to make this play because of the different press offenses that we will face. Some teams may bring the ball with a guard and a forward or some teams may send the guard long and bring one of the forwards back from half court to handle the pressure (Dia. 6-18). In this situation, the defensive forward (X_3) came back to the ball. As O_3 then executes the clear out, X_3 would be responsible for staying in the backcourt to provide the help. We do not require our big man to make this play and because of the nature of most press offenses, he will not be called on to do so anyway.

The second principle that we introduce at this time is precipitated by two offensive players (one with the ball) crossing in a full court pressure situation. This is a dangerous move and one that we do not allow our players to execute when facing defensive pressure in the backcourt. It is advantageous for the offense to keep the floor spread as much as possible when facing pressure. Our defensive philosophy is to keep the areas of the floor congested, so by crossing two offensive players who will be closely guarded by two defensive players the offense is playing right into our hands. When this situation develops, we want the two defensive players involved to double team the ball. We tell the defenders to, "Nail the ball

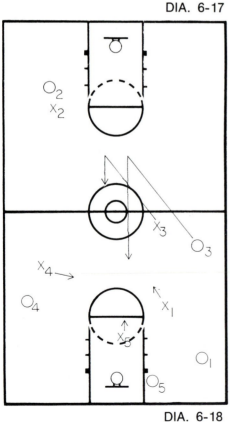

DIA. 6-18

handler!'' This defensive strategy is automatic no matter what type of defensive pressure we are employing at the time. If the offense crosses we are going to nail the ball handler and the next line of defense should look to rotate toward the ball as the double team is set. We will be discussing the rotation shortly. The double team should occur slightly before or just as the offensive players enter into a crossing position. If the ball handler goes behind the second offensive player the trap is set just as they cross (Dia. 6-19). If the second offensive player cuts behind the ball handler our second defensive player (X_1) should anticipate the cross and nail the ball just before the crossing action takes place (Dia. 6-20). The idea is to set the double team while the two offensive players are too close together to make an effective pass. Most of the time, the vacated offensive player will try to move to an open area and the time span allows the two defensive players to apply additional pressure on the ball. As with most of our defensive maneuvers, the double team will be more effective if the offensive player has used up his dribble or if we can force him to pick up the ball after springing the trap.

The final element we will teach and develop in our full court man to man defense is the rotation involved in the execution of our run and change and trapping defenses. There has to be a certain amount of organization in any press defense or breakdowns are going to occur. While we are attempting to apply maximum pressure with these defenses, we don't consider them to be of a gambling nature because we expect our players to use good judgement at all times. The players must recognize when the trap will be effective and must learn to sprint back and protect the basket when the offense beats the pressure. Our second and last line of defense must learn to recognize when and where to rotate. We tell these players to anticipate the effectiveness of the trap and to rotate or react to the ball accordingly. If the offensive player does not react well to the double team, our back defenders should rotate up and should be looking for the interception or deflection. On the other hand, if the ball handler escapes or minimizes the pressure of the double team, the back defenders must be very cautious in their rotation. The last defender must be especially careful not to leave the basket totally unprotected. If our first defenders have exercised good judgement in applying the trap, there should be an element of surprise and we should be able to push up toward the ball without too much danger.

In our rotation, we try to let the last defender split the distance and guard the two offensive players furthest from the ball. This allows the third and fourth defenders the freedom to rotate. Because of the different offensive alignments that may be in effect we are not always able to put this idea into practice. In Diagram 6-21 to the side we can see how the above rotation works on paper. It is obvious, and we emphasize this fact to our players, that the deeper the double team is set, the easier

DIA. 6-19

DIA. 6-20

DIA. 6-21

Pressing Defenses 215

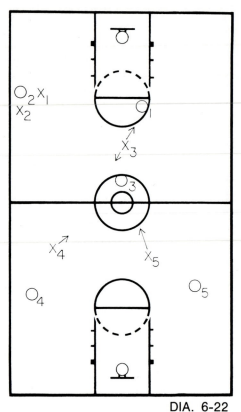

DIA. 6-22

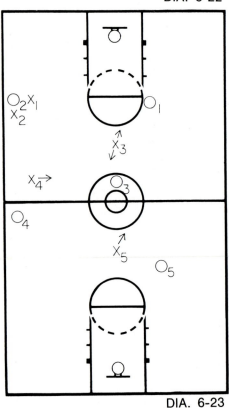

DIA. 6-23

it will be for our back defenders to rotate. In the diagram, X_2 and X_1 have executed a successful trap relatively deep in the backcourt. X_3 anticipates an effective double team and rotates up to cover O_1. X_4 plays his same passing lane because O_2 can theoretically make a direct pass to O_4 on the sideline. X_5 pushes up to cover both O_3 and O_5, the two offensive players the greatest distance from the ball. X_5 must be careful not to push too far. He must be able to recover back to O_5, if the long pass is attempted. The two defenders applying the double team must effectively discourage this pass or force a high lob if it is made.

The above illustrates the basic rotation that we would like to see develop. Our second line of defense (X_3, X_4) has sole responsibility for rotating into the backcourt. The last defender (X_5) will never move into the backcourt area unless all five offensive players are in front of him or another defender assumes safety responsibilities. This simplifies things because X_3 and X_4 know that one of them must move up quickly to cover the vacated offensive player. This is determined by which side of the floor the ball has been trapped. The defender opposite the ball will rotate to cover this horizontal pass. The defender (X_3 in Dia. 6-21) must read O_2 as he comes up to cover. As we mentioned, the effectiveness of the trap will have a lot to do with how much we rotate. The only problem area in this rotation is if the newly vacated offensive player (O_3 in the diagram) breaks back to the middle to receive the pass. When this occurs, we want the defensive players off the ball to apply some zone principles. X_3 would still have primary responsibility for O_1, but would open to the ball and drop back slightly into the middle to help discourage the pass. X_4 would edge toward the middle of the floor, especially if O_4 is making no effort to come back for the ball. X_5 would push up slightly, again depending on the effectiveness of the double team. Anticipation is always a vital key. All of the defensive players should be reading the eyes of the ball handler to try and anticipate the direction of the pass. These same responsibilities will be in effect if the offense starts with a man in the middle (Diags. 6-22 and 6-23). The back defender on the ballside (X_4) will never be expected to rotate all the way up. X_3 has to stop the pass to O_1 while still giving some attention to his man in the middle. X_4 and X_5 will be providing help and should be communicating effectively with the players in front to insure proper coverage.

The more players the offense needs to bring the ball, the better off we are going to be defensively. We mentioned earlier that the last defender (X_5) would not be involved in any rotation into the backcourt area unless under certain conditions. This is to avoid confusion when the offense brings the ball in a two-three set (Dia. 6-24). X_3 would still have responsibility for O_1 and O_3 while X_4 and X_5 would be pushing into the middle to help. If O_5 started in the middle and O_3 on the side the responsibilities would still remain the same (Dia. 6-25). X_3 would now be guarding O_1 and O_5 in the middle. X_5 would assume back responsibilities in case O_3 cut for the basket and would still be required to help on O_5 in the middle. X_4 would make the same move to help on O_5 in the middle. If the double team is timed so that it is extremely effective, X_5 may be able to concentrate most of his attention on O_5. He must use good judgement, however, so that he is able to get a hand on a long pass if attempted.

We will not, as a rule, trap the ball on the sidelines with a front defender and a back defender (Dia. 6-26). We have already stated that the trap will be most successful when there is an element of surprise. In this situation, the dribbler will be looking right at the second defensive player so the element of surprise is not there. As we showed earlier, the responsibilities of the back defender will be to fake at the offensive ball handler and retreat back to his man. There is still the possibility that the dribbler can be forced to pick up the ball or that the original defender can get around in front and look for a possible double team from the other front defender.

We cannot stress enough the importance of the last man talking to his four defensive teammates, especially the two back defenders. He must help direct his teammates by verbal communication. They must tune in to his voice and play their positions accordingly. The more the last defender can help with their men, the more the second line of defense can push up to help on the ball. This becomes even more important when the offense is shifting their men in the front court. If at all possible, we want our big man to remain as the safety in our pressure defense. He should be the most adept at protecting the basket area while the quicker forwards should do a better job of denying the passes or pressuring the ball. If the deep offensive player comes up to screen for or merely shift positions with one of the players at half court we want our defenders to switch men. The back defender would take whoever cuts to the basket and the defender in front would cover the man in the half court area. If both offensive players remain at half court the original assignments would still be in effect. If both offensive players broke long the last defender would help to guard both while the defender in front would look to play the ball. Effective communication must take place if we are to handle whichever situation does develop. A problem can arise when the deep offensive player breaks to the half line to receive the pass and one of the forwards delays before breaking to the basket. The back defender is required to deny the pass at the half line so each of his defensive teammates must be ready to assume safety responsibilities depending on which opponent cuts to the basket. There is no switching in this situation.

The rotation we have shown involves the play developing with

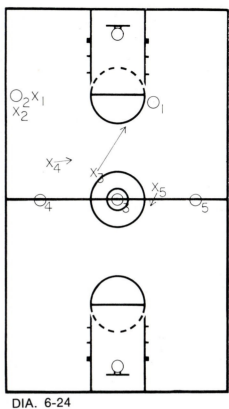

DIA. 6-24

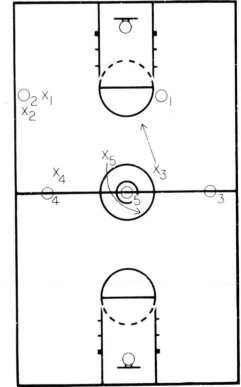

DIA. 6-25

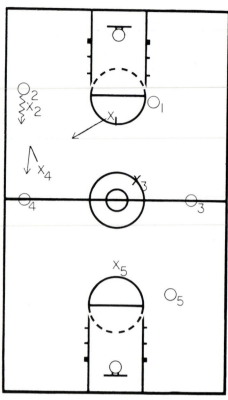

DIA. 6-26

the offense bringing the ball up their right side of the floor. If the ball is reversed or the offense brings the ball on the opposite side, the defensive adjustments remain the same. The roles are just reversed. Diagram 6-27 shows the same offensive alignment and double team situation that is illustrated in Diagram 6-21, only with the ball on the opposite side of the floor. The double team is now being formed by X_2 coming over to trap O_1 on the sideline. X_4 now has responsibility for rotating up because he is away from the ball. X_3 maintains his defensive positioning on O_3 and listens for directions from X_5. If O_4 breaks into the middle, X_3 and X_4 must both open to the ball and to the center of the floor. X_3 would then be utilizing zone principles to stop the pass to O_3 and to the right hand side of O_4. X_4 would be responsible for the pass to O_2 and the left hand side of O_4. X_5 pushes up to help and to provide direction but he cannot totally disregard O_5 and the basket area. Everyone reads the effectiveness of the trap.

In closing out this section on the man to man press, we should re-emphasize the importance of the players' getting back and protecting the basket as soon as the offense penetrates our defense. Failure to accomplish this goal can quickly lead to the press becoming more of a liability than an asset. If we can apply pressure in the backcourt and still get back to stop the easy baskets, the press will eventually take its toll on the offense. We realize that there is always the possibility we are going to give up some early baskets but they have to be kept to an absolute minimum. The turnovers forced and the opportunities gained through our pressure have to outweigh the defensive mistakes that may be committed. Consistency is a very important and sometimes overlooked characteristic of a successful pressing defense. It will do no good for the defense to give up a lay up or easy basket for every time they steal the ball. We want to capitalize on the mistakes of the offense. At the same time, we want to limit our own mistakes or cover them up by all of our players quickly retreating to guard the basket area. This defensive principle receives a great deal of emphasis in our five on five drill work.

Two-Two-One Zone Press

We are almost exclusively a man to man team but we have used some two-two-one zone pressure in the past and will continue to do so when we feel it can be effective. Our two-two-one press is a combination of many presses that we have researched but it probably most closely resembles the two-two-one employed by John Wooden for many years at UCLA. We don't think that is too bad of an example to follow. We evaluate our personnel each year to determine whether or not we can be successful with this type of pressure. Our first priority is to look for two key people that we feel are essential to the make-up of a two-two-one press. First of all, we want a big man or a forward with great instincts for protecting the basket area. We can develop a player for this position, but that player is going to have to have some native intelligence and it certainly won't hurt if he has some natural shot blocking ability. James Clabon and Clay Johnson have been excellent players for us in this position in years past. Curtis Berry is a player off our present team who is ideal for this spot. James and Clay were very valuable at other positions also so there has to be some flexibility with regard to the shifting of players. This player also has to be a talker. He is going to direct his teammates because of his excellent vantage point. The play will be developing in front of him so he should be communicating to the rest of the players the movement of the offense. This made James especially effective in this back position because no one ever accused James of being a non-talker. In all seriousness, James was exceptional at this position because he had great defensive instincts. Our only problem was that James was our best defensive player at just about any position.

The second position that we need to fill is that of an interceptor. We want to make sure that we have at least one player who has a nose for the basketball. He has to possess good quickness and a great ability to anticipate. We will place this player at one of the positions in our second line of defense, usually on the side where we are influencing the ball to be inbounded. Whenever possible, we like for this player to be our best ball handling guard. When he does make the interception or steal we have the ball in the hands of our best ball handler as we go on the offensive. If anyone else gains possession of the ball in the half court area, they are to look for this man and he is to work to make himself available. Good judgement must be used in making this pass. Walt Hazzard filled this role for Coach Wooden's 1964 championship team and was very effective. Larry Drew has done an excellent job for us when we have utilized him in this position.

After identifying the two players who can fill these positions we have to determine if we can adequately fill the other spots in the two-two-one zone press. If our big men cannot handle the back position and is not mobile enough to move up front we will have to make a substitution. A press is no place to try and hide a weak, slow defender because the offense is going to attack that area and breakdowns are going to result. The two front men in our press must be quick enough to pressure the ball and to make the necessary adjustments as the ball is moved. We like to use one of the forwards in a front position to free up our guard to play the interceptor.

It is very important in setting up the zone press that the players make the quick transition from offense to defense. Each player must set up quickly and adjust to the offensive alignment or the location of the ball. We will never press after a missed shot because we feel the transition is much too quick and the players have too much ability at this level. We

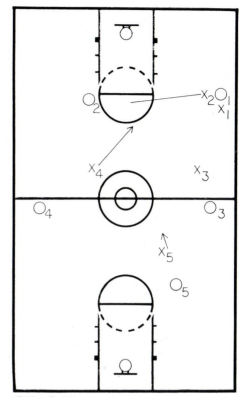

DIA. 6-27

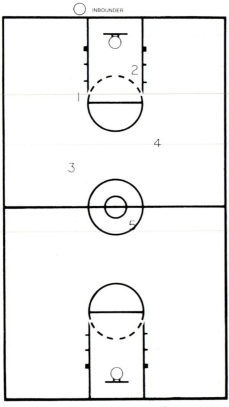

DIA. 6-28

will utilize zone pressure after a made field goal or a made free throw. After a made free throw is an excellent time to call for the zone press because we can make the change from the bench and make sure that each player is aware of the change. During a time out is another good time to change up the defense. We time the players in practice to insure that they are making the quick transition and also appoint a defensive captain to encourage the players to get back quickly after the made basket. We want each player to be moving in his area so he is covering as much ground as possible. This will help to discourage the offense from making the direct pass into a specific area. We also ask the players not to set up parallel to a teammate across the court. This relationship is shown in the diagram to the left (Dia. 6-28). By setting up at different levels, our defense will appear to be covering more ground and thus will appear to be more formidable to the offense.

We apply some general rules for all players to follow when executing the zone press. These are issued in the form of a handout and the players are expected to understand them completely and apply them in a game situation. These rules are listed as follows:

1. Do not reach in to attempt to take the ball away from an opponent. We are playing position defense. We want to force errors as the offense loses their poise.

2. If the offense penetrates our defense and is advancing the ball toward our defensive basket all players are to hustle back immediately. Every player should size up the situation and look for a possible steal from behind. The ballside players chase the ball. The players away from the ball get back to the middle of the floor looking to intercept a pass from behind.

3. When the offense has successfully entered our defensive end of the floor every player with the exception of the man playing the ball must get a foot in the lane and pick up defensively from there.

4. If you intercept or steal the ball in the center of the floor or farther back you are to look immediately for our best ball handler (usually in the #3 position). #3 is to get open as quickly as possible. All others should convert quickly from defense to offense.

5. If you steal the ball in our offensive basket area immediately look to the basket. If you have an open lane, take the ball yourself. If not, find the open man.

6. If there is no offensive player in your area, drop back toward the basket and the middle of the floor watching for someone to flash in from behind. If there is no one flashing in, cheat toward the area that is being attacked.

7. If you are guarding the dribbler, put pressure on the ball but contain the dribbler. Do not allow the offensive player to make an easy pass or movement up the floor.

8. The deep or back players must watch for the long pass and any movement into their area.

9. A deflection can be as advantageous as a steal so always look to get a hand on the basketball. Try to deflect the ball toward a teammate or at least keep it in the court area.

10. If the man in your area has the ball, guard him with man to man principles. If he does not have the ball, use helpside (line of the ball) principles depending on his distance from the ball handler.

11. Results from an effective press often come in bunches so be ready to apply immediate pressure after a forced error by the opponents. We might be able to shake their poise.

12. ANTICIPATION IS THE KEY TO ANY PRESS!

Zone Press Responsibilities (2-2-1)

Diagram 6-29 shows our initial press alignment and the direction in which we want to influence the pass. After the pass is made into a specific corner the arrows indicate the movement of our defensive players. We will always designate a side of the floor where we want the ball to be inbounded. In keeping with the tendency of the offense to go to their right this is the side we will usually designate. The specific responsibilities for each position are listed below. We always place a guard in the #1 position because he will be called on to pressure the ball and contain the dribbler much of the time. We will place a front line player in the #2 position. If our big man is active and mobile enough he can be extremely valuable in this spot. His height can be a definite factor in setting an effective double team. Now this does not mean that we will place just any big man in this position. An immobile player would be completely out of his environment, but we have had some centers who were completely capable of handling this assignment. As we mentioned earlier, we like to fill the #3 spot with our best ball handler and passer. Many times he will also be our best interceptor. We can also position our best interceptor at the #4 spot if this player is someone other than the ball handling guard. If the guard has great anticipation and is a ballhawk, the fourth spot is filled by another frontline player. The all-important fifth spot will be handled by a shot blocking forward or an intimidating big man. When issuing the following responsibilities to our players we designate which players will be assigned to each position so that they know which area they must be responsible for in learning the press. Some players will be required to learn two positions.

#1 Position

1. Invite the pass into the corner area on your side. Make the receiver catch the ball as deep in the corner as possible.

2. If the ball is not inbounded in three seconds jump in front of your man and try to force a five second count.

3. When the ball is inbounded, play the receiver one half man to the outside utilizing man to man principles with special emphasis on containment.

4. If the receiver **starts to dribble**, contain him so that #2 can come over for the double team.

5. If the receiver **does not dribble**, advance on him cautiously or hold position while faking at him. Try to make him put the ball on the floor.

6. If the receiver is trying to throw a forward pass, apply enough pressure so that he will have to throw a lob or a bounce pass. Prevent him from throwing a straight, hard pass.

7. Do not let the offensive player escape up the sideline. If he dribbles to the sideline, cut him off. #2 will immediately apply the double team from the blind side.

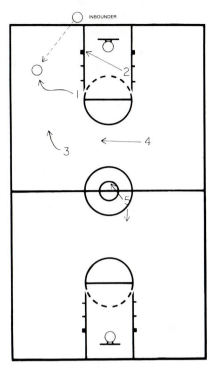

DIA. 6-29

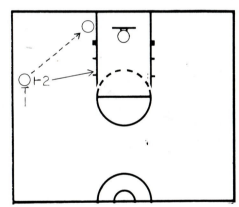

DIA. 6-30

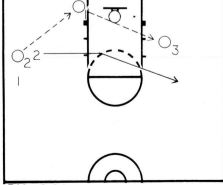

DIA. 6-31

Pressing Defenses 221

DIA. 6-32

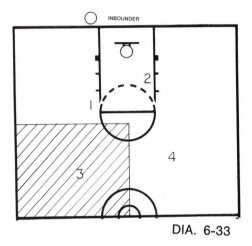

DIA. 6-33

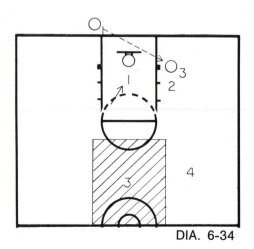

DIA. 6-34

8. If the dribbler does escape up the sideline, chase him from behind and try to deflect the ball on toward a teammate. If a teammate slows the dribbler down or forces him to stop, look to apply the double team.

9. If the offense is able to inbound the ball on the opposite side of the floor you would reverse roles with #2.

#2 Position

1. **Must prevent pass from being inbounded on your side of the floor.**

2. When the ball is passed into #1's area, move over quickly to prevent a return pass to the inbounder stepping into the court.

3. Look for the double team on the man guarded by #1. The best time to apply the trap is just after the player has started his dribble but before the first bounce hits the floor.

4. If the offensive player dribbles toward the sideline (away from you) immediately apply the double team from behind.

5. If the offensive player dribbles toward the middle, it is your responsibility to stop him from splitting you and #1. If he is dribbling hard, stop him right away and set the trap. If the dribbler is sizing up the situation, the inbounder will likely move away toward your sideline. Without allowing the split, stay with the inbounder for an instant and then spring the double team. Vary your tactics.

6. If a pass is made out of the double team back to the inbounder you must hustle to re-establish your position. Select the proper angle to contain (Dia. 6-30). **Don't run at the man**.

7. If a one-two pass is made to a man below the free throw line extended, we want you to cut him off on the sideline. You must select the proper angle and turn the man back to the middle for a possible double team (Dia. 6-31).

8. If the one-two reverse pass is made to a man above the free throw line extended you should chase the ball and look for a double team with #4 who should be in a position to cover the man with the ball (Dia. 6-32).

9. If the offense **is** able to inbound the ball on your side of the floor you must quickly re-establish your position one half man to the outside of the offensive player with the ball. You would then reverse roles with #1.

#3 Position

1. You are responsible for the area behind #1, from the center line to the key area when the ball is out of bounds or on your side of the floor (Dia. 6-33).

2. Prevent anyone in that area from receiving a pass either from the inbounder or the inbounds receiver. You must intercept or deflect any lob or slow passes made into that area. If a receiver does catch the ball in your zone cover him with man to man principles.

3. If a dribbler gets by #1 up the sideline, you should fake at him and retreat. You are trying to slow him down. Then look for the right opportunity to double team with #1 who is running the play down from behind.

4. If there is no man in your area, look for someone flashing in and then cheat toward the center of the floor or the area that is being attacked.

5. If the ball is inbounded on or reversed to the opposite side of the floor, your area becomes the middle of the floor (Dia. 6-34).

6. Should the ball be advanced up the opposite sideline so that #4 moves up to double team with #2, you would rotate to #4's position and play the sideline area looking for the interception. #1 rotates back to the middle of the floor (Dia. 6-35).

#4 Position

1. Responsible for the middle of the floor to your left as you face the inbounder and for the area on your side from the center line to the foul line or deeper in case #2 is pulled over (Dia. 6-36).

2. As soon as the ball is inbounded to the opposite corner you become responsible for the middle of the floor area between the foul circle and the center circle (Dia. 6-37).

3. With the ball in #1's area, you should be aware of the offense bringing a third man back to receive the pass. You should force this man to catch the ball below the free throw line extended or intercept any pass to him beyond that point.

4. If the one-two pass is made to this player below the foul line extended you are to fake at him and retreat. It is the responsibility of #2 to get over and cut him off at the proper angle. Your job is to slow him down. You again assume responsibility for the sideline area behind #2.

5. If you are unable to intercept the one-two pass made above the free throw line extended, you are to cover that player and #2 is to run him down and double team from behind.

6. If the dribbler (on the opposite side) advances the ball up the sideline so that #3 moves up to stop him, you would rotate to the #3 position and play the sideline area looking for the interception (same as diagram 6-35 with the players reversing roles).

7. If the ball is inbounded on your side, you maintain responsibility for the sideline area around the half line (see diagram 6-36).

#5 Position

1. You must convert quickly from offense to defense as soon as the ball goes through the basket. Sprint to the center circle (or farther) as fast as possible and direct the defense from there.

2. Must talk to the people in front of you.

3. Push up as far as possible without giving up the basket.

4. Shade the side of the floor that the offense is bringing the ball.

5. Be alert to intercept any long passes.

6. Guard the basket. If a guard is driving, invite him in and wipe the ball off the backboard. **Keep the blocked shot inbounds**. If a big man is coming, pressure him to make a play or slow him down until help arrives.

The idea of keeping the ball in play is very important throughout the execution of the press. When our players are able to get a hand on the ball, we want them to make every effort to deflect the ball away from the sidelines. If possible, they should try to tip the ball in the direction of a teammate. Even when a ball has been deflected toward the boundary lines, we want our players to react quickly and try to keep the ball in play. This idea is stressed constantly while working on our press in the practice sessions. It applies to both the zone and the man to man defenses. We work not only on deflecting the ball to a teammate or into the middle of the floor, but in saving the ball when it is heading out of bounds. We want our players to become adept at making the save back in to a teammate. This idea takes on even greater importance with regard to a blocked shot by one of our defenders. It is just as easy to block a shot inbounds as it is out of bounds. There is no difference in timing or in the height needed on the jump. If we block the ball out of bounds the offense retains possession. If we keep the ball in play, we have an excellent

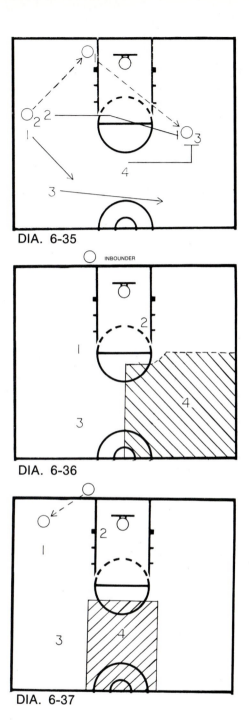

DIA. 6-35

DIA. 6-36

DIA. 6-37

chance of obtaining the loose ball and initiating our own offense. This is especially true if our players develop some expertise and some consistency in applying this principle. The shot blocker can sometimes direct the ball to some teammates. The players other than the shot blocker can see the play developing and should position themselves near the action and react quickly to the location of the ball.

Drills For Developing Our Full Court Pressure

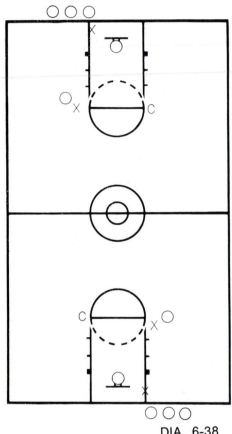

DIA. 6-38

In introducing our full court defensive system we want to give our players an overview of what the defense will look like and what we will be trying to accomplish under game conditions. The fundamental sliding drills and the individual drills we have already shown are our primary emphasis for the first week of practice. During the second week, we set aside a section of a practice for a chalk talk and a walk through our full court defense. From here, we begin to develop our breakdown drills. We are basically talking about two breakdown areas (two on two, three on three) from which we will build to a five on five situation. We are teaching many different things in the two basic drill situations and we do this in a day to day progression which we will outline shortly.

For the most part, we will run all the players in the various drills. At times, we may break down into different areas of specialization or we may separate the big men from the two on two pressure drills, but as a rule we do not. We feel it will help develop our system if all players learn to play the entire ninety-four feet. We also feel that this work will help to improve the overall quickness and agility of our big men. In executing the drills, we carry them through the first and the second stage of our defense teaching the various strategies. We can always break the drills down further if we feel that extra work is needed in a particular area. For instance, we can work the guards at one end solely on playing the inbounds pass while we work with the big men on playing off and toward the ball (see Dia. 6-42). There are numerous ways you can break down the drills to fit your needs.

When first running the two on two drill, we apply the five methods for defensing the inbounds pass with a straight man to man once the ball is inbounded. We want to develop a certain amount of expertise in the straight man to man before concentrating on the run and change and the trap. We do show a little of the run and change and trapping strategy when we introduce the double team on the inbounds receiver. This is so that we can begin to build for what will come later. As we will see, the full court defensive drills remain pretty much the same with just a change in the defensive emphasis for the various methods we will teach.

DIA. 6-39

Two On Two Full Court Drill (Dia. 6-38)

Objective: To each and develop our full court pressure defense starting with the inbounds pass and continuing to the half court line (first and second stages of our defense).

Organization: Squad divided in half. Guards and small forwards at one end. Big men and big forwards at the other. Match up according to size and position. Offense attempts to bring the ball, first at half speed then full. Defense pressures the ball utilizing the inbounds method prescribed by the coaches and continuing with the straight man to man defense. Drill starts again when offense reaches half court or when the defense steals the ball and converts for a basket. Defense stays in three times or until adequate results are derived. Offense rotates to defense. Defense goes to the end of the line.

Points of Emphasis: These will vary according to the defenses we are teaching at the time. The points we emphasize for the various defenses have been fully explained in the preceding pages of this chapter.

Three On Three Full Court Drill (Dia. 6-39 and 6-40)

Objective: To teach and develop our full court pressure defense in a three on three situation and to continue building toward our five on five defense.

Organization: Entire squad at one end of the floor. Again match up according to size and position. Offense first brings the ball with the two inbounds receivers working to get each other open in the lane area (Dia. 6-39). Next alignment involves the third man up starting at the half court area (Dia. 6-40). Defense pressures the ball according to the dictates of the coaches. We start with the straight man to man in the second stage, but begin to further develop our run and change and trapping tactics. From here, organization and rotation is the same as in previous drill. Drill starts at half speed and progresses to full.

Points of Emphasis: (See explanation for previous drill).

Five On Five Full Court Drill (Dia. 6-41)

Objective: To teach and develop our full court pressure defense in a five on five game situation. We place special emphasis on the development of our back defenders in our five on five work.

Organization: Squad divided equally or into a first and second unit depending on how far along we are in evaluating personnel. Offense brings the ball. Defense pressures the ball utilizing the different defenses dictated by the coach. Drill starts again when defense steals and scores. Drill ends when defense gets back with a foot in the lane and forces the offense to set up or when the offense shoots or scores. Teams reverse roles and go the other way. Drill starts at full speed.

Points of Emphasis: (Same explanation as previous drills).

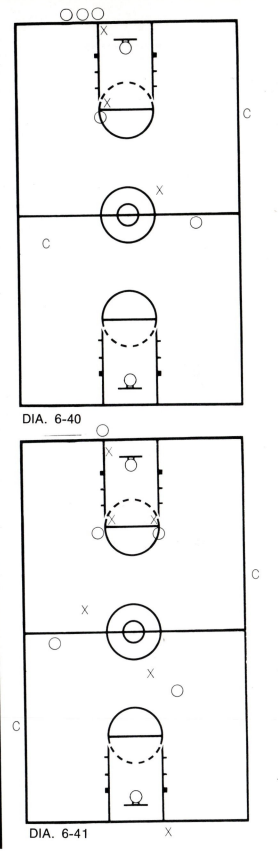

DIA. 6-40

DIA. 6-41

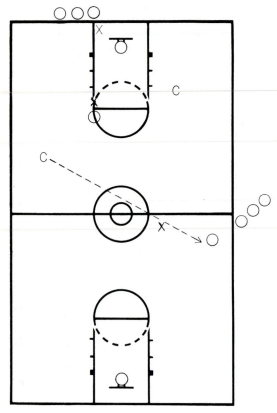

DIA. 6-42

Drill Variations

Two on Two Drill—First Stage—The two on two drill covering only the first stage of our defense. Defending against the inbounds pass.

Two on Two Help and Recover Drill—The two offensive players bring the ball at half and then full speed. They are required to reverse the ball at least twice. Defensive players must maintain proper positioning to help and recover. Offense cannot run off.

Two on Two Run and Change Drill—The two offensive players bring the ball at half and then full speed. The defensive player on the ball must turn the dribbler and the defensive man off the ball looks for the right opportunity to execute the blind run and change or the straight run and change. Offensive players remain parallel.

Three on Three Drill—First Stage—The three on three drill covering only the first stage of our defense. Defending against the inbounds pass. We do a lot of work in this area because of the screening and different offensive manuevers that the offense can utilize to get open.

Three on Three Drill—Prevent the Lob—Offense places third man at half court. Third defender must push up to protect against the lob. Inbounds defender is totally denying the pass. Offense attempts lob. Defense must generate loose ball and convert quickly to offense if possession is gained. Must recover quickly to men if ball does not change hands.

Off and Toward Deflection Drill (Dia. 6-42). We use this for both our zone and our man to man pressure. It is designed to help the players (especially the frontliners) determine the distance they can play from their man and still recover in time to intercept or deflect the ball. It is also beneficial for working to keep the ball in play. We instruct the players to deflect the ball into the court area. Defensive player gets off and toward the coach with the ball. Offensive player holds position at first and then is allowed to move. Coach throws the ball and the defensive players must intercept or get a hand on it and then react to the loose ball. Offense to defense, defense to the end of the line. We will run this while the guards are at one end working on the inbounds pass.

We do most of our work on the two-two-one press in a five on five situation but we do have some breakdown drills which we utilize for different areas of specialization. We run a drill for defending the inbounds pass at the same time we work with our safetys on the long pass. We also run two transition drills that we feel are very important if we are to be successful with our zone press.

Drills for Teaching the Two-Two-One Zone Press

Zone Pressure Drill—Inbounds Pass (Dia. 6-43)

Objective: To work with the front people in our two-two-one zone press in properly defensing the initial pass by the offense. Especially important to work with the frontliners playing the front position.

Organization: Three on two drill with coach inbounding ball. Offense attempts to inbound the ball to the middle of the floor or the left corner facing in from out of bounds. Defense must force the pass to the right corner. No lob or long passes. Defense stays in until they do the job. Offense goes to defense and defense steps out. Two new players in.

Points of Emphasis:
1. #2 player does not allow the pass to be made on his side of the floor. Must deny the pass to O_3.
2. #1 player denies the pass until O_2 is forced deep into the corner area.
3. When the inbounds pass is completed #2 must react quickly to stop the return pass to O_1 stepping in.
4. #1 must force the ball handler to put the ball on the floor.

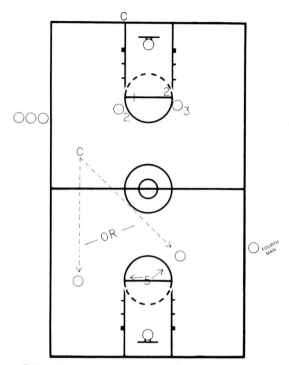

DIA. 6-43

Safety Drill (Dia. 6-43)

Objective: To work with our deep defenders in anticipating the direction of the long pass and to improve their ability to react for the interception or deflection.

Organization: Will usually have three players who are capable or have the potential to play this position. If you have four rotate him in. Coach stands in the backcourt and makes the long pass to one of the two offensive players. Defensive safety must react to the ball. Defensive player gets a good workout and then players rotate from left to right. Everyone reacts to a loose ball. Offense attempts to score if pass is completed. Safety looks for the return pass to the coach (assuming the role of the #3 position in the press) if he intercepts. Must work both sides of the floor.

Points of Emphasis:
1. Shade the ball side.
2. Read the eyes of the passer. Anticipate.
3. Fake the passer.
4. Deflection as good as a steal. Keep the ball in play and then react to the ball or protect the basket. Use good judgement.
5. First responsibility is to protect the basket.
6. On the interception find the #3 man (the coach) immediately.

**The shot blocking drill we discussed in Chapter Five is also important in relation to this man's safety responsibilities.

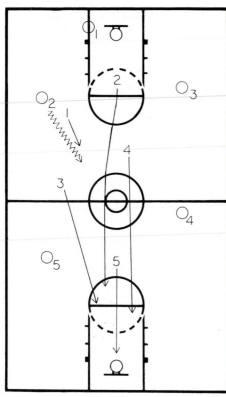

DIA. 6-44

Five On Five Transition Drill (Dia. 6-44)

Objective: To develop the player's ability to hustle back after defensive pressure.

Organization: Five on five zone press situation. Offense is allowed to beat the defense. Defense must hustle back to force the offense to run set offense. Teams reverse roles going back.

Points of Emphasis: 1. Turn and sprint for the basket as soon as offense breaks us down. Think on the move.

2. Ballside players chase ball looking for the opportunity to knock it ahead. Weakside players get back to the basket and the middle of the floor.

3. All players get a foot in the lane with the possible exception of the player who is stopping the ball.

Quick Conversion Drill

Objective: To develop in the players the concentration to set up quickly in our press defense.

Organization: Offensive team shoots a made free throw or a made basket. They must then quickly set up in the press defense. We time them and give rewards to the team with the quickest time that day. This drill, as well as the previous drill, are run for a very short period of time and are used as lead up drills to the live five on five zone press situation.

Points of Emphasis: 1. Safety must get out quickly.

2. Players should talk and encourage each other to set up in a hurry.

3. No player can be parallel to a teammate.

4. Drill and timing device stops when everyone is in position.

The diagrams that we issue to our players (see Dias. 5-1 and 5-2) designating the ballside and helpside areas are very helpful in beginning to develop our defensive system in the half court area. Through the diagrams, the players can understand the emphasis that we are going to place on a **helping defense**. There is nothing more discouraging to an opponent than a team that is able to apply defensive pressure and yet provide help if the offense escapes the pressure momentarily. This is one of the essential reasons **we will employ tough man to man pressure on the ball and the ballside** and a **sagging helping defense on the side away from the ball**. A second and more obvious reason is the necessity of a helping defense. When an individual defensive player is applying pressure there are times when he is going to lose his man if only for a moment. This is when help is needed. With each player fully understanding our philosophy of a helping defense and fully capable of carrying out the methods prescribed these breakdowns should be kept to a minimum.

An effective team defense takes a special kind of team unity and pride that will require constant stimulation from the coaching staff. Each and every player must be willing to help a teammate at all times. In accomplishing this goal a player may have to sacrifice the defensive position or defensive control that he has gained on his particular man. It is surprising the number of players who are hesitant about leaving their man open to provide help when an offensive player has gained an advantage. **When the offense moves the basketball into the half court scoring area, the ball must become the focal point of any team defense.** An offensive player cannot score unless he has the ball. Therefore, the position of the ball is of extreme importance to all of our defenders. If the ball has been manuevered into a dangerous scoring area we want some help by our defenders off the ball. If one of our defensive players is beaten we must have someone in a position to stop the ball. All of the players must be reacting to the movement of the ball and rotating to help if a breakdown occurs. Before the breakdown does occur, the helpside defenders, if they are properly aligned off their man and toward the ball, should be discouraging the offensive players from penetrating our defense. If we can motivate each and every player to think along these lines, then an attitude toward team defense will have been established. Furthermore, we will be creating situations that will force the offense to play three on five. With all five of our players packed in toward the ball and the middle of the floor, the offense will, in effect, be pitting their strongside players against our entire team defense. The scouting report and pre-game preparation will again be important in setting the defense. There are teams we will face for which we will really emphasize packing it in on the

7 *Team Defense in the Half Court Area*

helpside. This could be prompted by the type of pattern our opponents will run, the fact that they are poor outside shooters, or the fact that they go to only two or three scorers. We feel very strongly that a helping defense that places the proper emphasis on individual pressure and individual matchups will be especially demoralizing to the offense.

In the previous chapter we listed the six objectives we designate as extremely important in playing our team defense. The first four objectives receive a much greater emphasis in the half court area so we will discuss them more thoroughly below. We require the players to know these six objectives from the day we have our first defensive chalk talk. They will form the basis for our entire defensive system.

1. Guard the basket area against all lay ups. This has to be the first concern of any defensive individual or defensive team in making the transition from offense to defense. The basket area must be guarded to prevent an easy two points by any offensive player attempting to get behind the defense. The first man back is always responsible for the basket and he directs the defense from there. The first man back after a missed shot will usually be a guard. It is important that he play intelligently and that he communicates effectively with his teammates. As soon as a frontline player is able to retreat to the basket area the guard should be ready to come out to pick up the ball or his man depending on the situation. He must let his teammates know what is developing (situation #8 requiring defensive communication—Chapter Six). When an opponent is attempting the fast break we want our players to sprint to the lane or basket area and then move out to pick up their men. The basket area must be guarded first. If the defense is content to pick up their men on the outside there will be no help available on an offensive player who may have beaten his man downcourt. This situation can vary according to how the break is developing. It is important that the players be able to think while on the move.

The objective of protecting the basket against unguarded lay ups continues as the opposition enters into their half court offense. Each individual defensive player has the responsibility of stopping his man from making a drive all the way to the basket. The helpside players and the ballside players off the basketball should realize that one of their responsibilities is to help should any offensive opponent attempt a drive into our defensive basket area. The ballside players have less responsibility in this area but we want everyone to be constantly aware of providing help when a breakdown occurs. The players must develop a very team oriented attitude toward the goal area. We expect each player to be willing and eager to step in front of a driving player to draw the charging foul whenever possible. We drill on this from a team aspect which we will discuss later on in this chapter.

More on the Objectives of Defense

2. Prevent all unguarded shots. We touched upon this objective in relation to individual defense on the ball in Chapter Five. The importance of this objective cannot be underestimated. Each individual defensive player is responsible for contesting any shot attempted by his offensive counterpart. If our defender is off balance or just getting back to his man we still want the hand up in an effort to distract the shooter. The previously mentioned study at Ohio State is all the evidence that we need to continue our insistence on this defensive objective. There are too many good shooters at the college level for our defense to continually allow unguarded attempts at the basket. A shooter's individual range will have a lot to do with the application of this objective but basically we want a hand up on every shot. An offensive player is generally going to know his limitations and will shoot only within his particular range. If a shot is attempted from outside a player's range, he may get lucky if we don't apply some pressure.

At times, a defender will lose his man and an unguarded shot may develop if one of his teammates is not quick to provide help. Any time a defender is in the area where an unguarded shot is being attempted he should leave his man momentarily and at least make an effort to bother the shooter. This can be accomplished by faking at the shooter, hollering and/or throwing up the hands in an effort to distract the shooter's concentration. When there is no reason to worry about his man, the defender should make an all out effort to stop or discourage the shot. This can occur when there is another defensive player in a position to pick up the vacated offensive player or when a defender is sure the shot is going to be attempted. We feel very strongly about the effect that this type of defense will have on the shooting percentage of our opponents. The shooting percentage will obviously have a great impact on the outcome of the game so we place a great deal of emphasis on this aspect of our defensive system. We never want to see an unguarded shot when we have a player in a position to distract or discourage the shooter.

3. Force the offense to take a poor percentage shot. This idea follows right along with our two previous objectives. We do not want any lay ups, because the lay up is an extremely high percentage shot. We do not want to allow an unguarded shot because we can lower the percentages by applying pressure on the shooter. Now we are trying to make the offense attempt a shot that they would never attempt by design or under normal conditions. The first means by which we can force the poor percentage shot is by pushing the offense outside the twenty-one foot area. The farther the ball is from the basket, the better off we are going to be defensively. Once the ball is within the twenty-one foot area, the defenders must try to apply enough pressure so that the offense cannot move comfortably. Each defender must try to keep his man from catching the ball in an area where the offensive player is most effective and we must have a lot of help from the defenders on the helpside. If we play tough, aggressive defense the offense is going to get impatient at times and force the bad shot. This is what we are striving for. We especially like to encourage a poor percentage shot by a player in an off balance position. Some offensive players can be a detriment to their own team because of the types of shots that they might attempt under adverse conditions. A smart defensive team will recognize a player's reluctance to pass the basketball and will take advantage of this selfishness. When we do force a poor shot, we still want our defenders to apply pressure to the shooter without taking a chance on committing a foul. When we meet all three of the aforementioned objectives, the chances for a basket by the opposition has been kept to an absolute minimum. We now need only to fulfill our fourth objective.

4. Prevent the offense from gaining possession for a second or third shot. This objective pertains to blocking out the offensive players and rebounding and therefore will be discussed fully in the following chapter. We must stress, however, its importance in maintaining defensive intensity and overall defensive success. A team can play excellent defense and yet if they continually allow the second or third shot, their defensive intensity is ultimately going to break down. The opposition will benefit both from the defensive letdown and the additional attempts at the basket. It is imperative that the defense, after extending maximum effort to force a poor or low percentage shot, continue their effort by blocking the offense off the boards and gaining possession of the basketball. Defensive rebounding must be included in any emphasis on total team defense.

The fifth and sixth objectives we discussed in relation to our full court pressure defense but they certainly do not end when the offense crosses half court, so they are just as important for our defense in the scoring area. The fifth objective is especially important with regard to the set offense that the opposition will employ.

5. Break up the continuity or timing of the offense. This objective takes on added dimensions in the half court area. The opposing team will have some type of offensive set or offensive pattern that is adapted specifically to fit their personnel. Anything we can do to disrupt that pattern will pay dividends for us both at the defensive and the offensive ends of the floor. This is because the meeting of these final two objectives should generate scoring opportunities if we are able to gain possession of the ball and convert quickly from defense to offense. The scouting report and the coaching preparation prior to the day of the game will certainly have a significant impact on the meeting of our fifth objective. We want our players to have a good understanding of what the opponent's offense looks like, as well as a knowledge of the particular strengths and weaknesses of each individual player. Our defensive aggressiveness and intensity is also going to be an important factor in breaking up the continuity of the offense. We have already discussed the emphasis we place on aggressive individual defense and this philosophy is equally important when teaching team defense. A passive defense will do nothing to disrupt the continuity or timing of the offense. It will only serve to stop the offense from penetrating and then only part of the time. An aggressive defense forces the offense to react to pressure from each individual defensive player as well as the defensive team as a whole. The offensive execution cannot be as smooth as when facing a defense that lacks aggressiveness. Remember, we are attempting to make the offense react to our defense and our defensive moves rather than waiting for the offense to make the first move. The sixth defensive objective also highlights the importance of aggressive play and can stem directly from the realization of our fifth objective.

6. Force the offense to make mistakes. The meeting of this final objective will, of course, have a great effect on the outcome of any game. Just as it is defensive suicide to continually allow the second and third shots, failure to generate a legitimate scoring attempt a good majority of the times down the floor will eventually take its toll on the offense. We want our players pressuring the ball handler and the players one pass away from the ball in an effort to force an offensive mistake. By sagging toward the ball and the basket, the helpside players will also be forcing the issue. We especially want to apply defensive pressure to those players that are inexperienced or unable to cope with this type of situation. We will not, as a rule, use any stunting or all out pressure defenses in the half court. We can go to some run and change tactics in the forecourt area around the half line and we may have to resort to all out pressure to come from behind. We want to force the offense into committing their own mistakes by packing the defense in with five people on the ballside. From these positions, all of our players will be looking for the opportunity to draw the offensive charge. This will be one more defensive strategy the offense will have to worry about in executing their pattern.

There is a seventh idea we do not include in our objectives, but we do encourage our players to apply in pressuring the ball in our defensive end. We feel that by stressing this idea we greatly benefit our concept of a total team defense. We want each player thinking along the lines of how he can help a teammate be successful. The idea states that each defensive player is not only trying to stop his man from scoring, he is trying to stop his man from making a direct pass that leads to a score. This should improve our pressure on the ball and the added pressure on the ball handler should help make it easier for our defenders away from the basketball.

The whole-part-whole teaching method is again used in beginning to develop our half court defense. Through a chalk talk and a walking through of our five man defense we give the players an overall picture of what our defense will look like. The objectives will give the players a thorough understanding of what we will be trying to accomplish. The players will then have a better idea of how the breakdown drills apply to our defensive system. They will see what purpose the drills have in the overall picture. We think that this helps in the concentration and the effort that the players display in the drill situations. As we begin to develop our defense, keep in mind the emphasis we place on communicating effectively. Communication on defense is vitally important in the scoring area.

Halfcourt Situations

After we have explained the defensive philosophy we will employ and have developed the individual skills we discussed in Chapter Five, we begin to teach our team defense through a progression of drills. We start by introducing some two man defensive principles that are best explained in a two on two drill situation. These two man plays are easily applied to a three on three situation once the players learn the techniques required. Therefore, after the first few days, we move away from the two on two defensive drills. As the season progresses, the same can be said for our four on four drills. We will introduce some defensive techniques that are well suited to a four on four breakdown drill. Once the techniques are learned, we apply the same defensive possibilities in our five on five work. In this way, we can simplify our practices so that we are running most of our team defensive drills in a three on three or five on five situation as the season progresses. This does not mean that we will never come back to the two on two or four on four drills. If we feel the players are doing a poor job in one of those areas, we can come back to a specific drill at any time. We keep a master list of drills which we refer to often in finalizing our practice plan. We can also revert to a specific drill, depending on the offensive tendencies of the team we are going to face in a particular week. We will explain these ideas further when discussing our practice organization and planning.

Two On Two Help And Recover

The initial team situation we want to cover is the basic help and recover responsibilities for both the guards and the frontline players. The players should be able to absorb this quickly because we will have already spent some time on it in developing our full court defense. The players should also have a good grasp of our philosophy behind the help and recover principle and the helping defense. In the help and recover from the guard position, the player away from the ball should be in a position off and toward the basketball ready to discourage easy movement by the offense (Dia. 7-1). He is just off the line

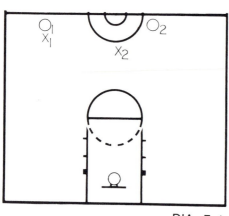

DIA. 7-1

drawn between his man and the ball handler and is slightly open to the basketball. In this drill, we allow the offensive player to beat the initial defender so that help is required. It is up to the off guard to see that the offensive player does not split the defenders. The helping defender must slow the dribbler down so that his teammate can reassume proper defensive positioning. At the same time, he must be able to recover quickly to his man if the guard to guard pass is thrown. When the guard to guard pass is made the initial defender on the ball must now react quickly to a helping position. The players are not only developing their ability to help and recover, they are learning to play together and they are becoming more and more aware of the importance we place on a helping defense.

We run this drill from the positions shown in Diagram 7-2 to teach the fundamentals involved to our frontline players. In this situation, the helping player may have more responsibility for denying the pass but he must still be able to help if a teammate loses his man. Remember, the ball is the focal point of our defense. If X_1 is beaten, X_2 must recognize that and open quickly to the ball to stop penetration. When the ball is picked up or the initial defender recovers X_2 can get back to his man. If the dribbler is out of control or attempting to drive all the way to the basket X_2 should look for a possible opportunity to draw a charge. It is important that he use good judgement in looking for the charge. He still has responsibilities for recovering to his man so he must not get off balance or out of position without the offensive foul being called. In executing the help and recover, we like our players to fake at the ball handler and to maintain a position where they can recover to their man. In faking, we teach the players to show themselves prominently and to throw up their hands to try and distract or discourage the dribbler. Both defensive players should be talking so that we are communicating effectively. The initial defender should call for help (situation #5 requiring defensive communication) to alert his teammates that help is needed.

One Man Removed Principle

The second defensive technique we introduce in the scoring end we refer to as our one man removed principle. This defensive principle should be applied when two offensive players cross outside the twenty-one foot area (or outside their shooting range if that range exceeds the twenty-one foot area). We discussed the offensive maneuvers that can be executed off this play in Chapter Three. The defense must slide through one man removed or problems are going to result. Diagrams 7-3 and 7-4 show the relationship we want to occur when the offensive players cross. Our defensive player (X_1) should be off and toward the basketball in a position to help. When O_1 starts in the direction of the ball X_1 must read the cut and slide through accordingly. If O_1 goes

DIA. 7-2

DIA. 7-3

DIA. 7-4

behind his teammate X_1 slides between X_2 and O_2 maintaining a one man removed distance (Dia. 7-3). If O_1 cuts in front of the ball handler (for a possible inside steal) X_1 slides behind X_2, again utilizing the principle of being one man removed (Dia 7-4). After the cut is made, O_2 dribbles out to the guard position and O_1 sets up wide on the wing. O_2 can now cross by the use of the dribble or he can pass to O_1 on the wing and execute one of the same cuts we have described. The drill continues in that manner until the defense does a satisfactory job. The technique remains the same whether the players dribble cross or cross on a cut as long as the offensive players are outside shooting range. There is no need to fight over the top or for the second defender to influence the cutter because the screen should be ineffective from outside shooting range. The player making the cut or dribbling off a screen is not going to attempt a shot from behind his teammate so there is no defensive urgency to staying with him throughout the play. This type of play will call for different defensive tactics when executed inside shooting range. The twenty-one foot area will usually be an accurate point for determining whether a player is inside or outside his shooting range. This, of course, will depend on the player and highlights the importance of our scouting report.

Two On Two Influence

The next defensive technique we will teach is utilized when there is a screen on the ball within the twenty-one foot or shooting area. When the offense is within shooting range tight man to man defense must be provided. The first thing that we stress when this play develops is communication. The defensive man guarding the screener must let his teammate know that a screen is coming and from which direction (situation #1 requiring defensive communication). As the ball handler moves into a position to use the screen, we want our man on the screener to step out and influence the dribbler to change his path or pick up the ball. Figure 7-1 shows a player executing this defensive tactic to push the ball handler wide. We ask our players to step all the way out exactly into the intended path of the dribbler. If we only step out part of the way, it will not be enough to influence the player with the ball. The ideal defense is for the man stepping out to completely stop the ball handler. We are not switching, however. X_2 in the photograph is to step out and at least force the dribbler wide. From there, it is the responsibility of the man on the ball (X_1) to get over the top of the screen to maintain or regain his defensive positioning. If O_1 picks up the ball, X_2 immediately recovers to his own man as long as X_1 is in position to contest a possible shot attempt. We cannot leave the shooter unguarded. X_2 will also recover to his man whenever the pick and roll is attempted. As soon as the screener rolls to the basket X_2 would drop back, playing the passing lane and still giving some attention to the man with the ball (Fig. 7-2). In a

FIG. 7-1

236 Team Defense

five on five situation, we expect the helpside defenders to be in a position to discourage the screen and roll. With the help provided and proper defense on the screen this is an extremely difficult pass to make.

We mentioned previously that the man on the ball is to fight over the top of the screen and we show the players what we feel is the best way to accomplish this task. This can sometimes be a tough proposition and is one of the reasons defensive intensity is so important. The player is warned of the impending screen by his defensive teammate. As soon as he becomes aware of the pick situation the man on the ball tries to force the ball handler to make a wider cut. The offensive player is taught to rub shoulders with his teammate so there is no room for the defender to slide through. If the defensive man can force the dribbler to take a wider path around the screen he should have no trouble getting his body between the two offensive players and limiting the effectiveness of the offensive manuever. In fighting over the top we teach our players to get the lead foot around the screen and to arch the back to avoid getting hung up on the screener (Fig. 7-3). By arching the back the defensive man creates a space between himself and the offensive player setting the screen. Many times the rear end is the section of the body that catches the screen and slows down or stops the defender from sliding. In the photograph, you can see that because the player has arched his back the rear end is not protruding and the defensive man should not have any problem continuing over the screen. A probelm can develop when the officials allow the offensive players to set moving screens. This simply requires more intensity and more effort on the part of our defensive players.

It is very important in this pick and roll situation that the man on the ball does not overreact to the initial direction of the ball handler. When the defender slides the lead foot around and is on top of the screen he must be in a balanced position prepared to slide either way. A clever offensive player can quickly change direction and catch the defensive man on the opposite side of the screen if the defense overreacts to the play. We tell our players that once they get to the top of the screen, between the ball handler and the screener, they are in a good position to go either way. There is no need to get all the way across the screen unless the dribbler commits himself fully to that direction.

Western Roll

We also introduce a variation of the above offensive manuever which calls for the same technique on the part of the man being screened but without influence. This occurs when the screener has the ball and is looking to hand off to the cutter while screening the cutter's defensive man. We refer to this situation as a western roll. The man guarding the screener can obviously not step to influence or to help on the cut because he will be leaving the ball. The defender off the ball has sole

FIG. 7-2

FIG. 7-3

responsibility for getting through the screen and maintaining proper positioning on his man. This will not be difficult if the defensive man is in the correct position off and toward the basketball. As soon as he sees the play developing, he should close the distance between himself and his man and force the offensive player to go wide. From there, he fights over the top of the screen and discourages the player with the ball from making the hand off. While fighting over the top of the screen we want our player to use his hands to find the ball but we do not want him slashing at the ball attempting to make the steal. He is merely pressuring the ball handler to stop him from making a clean hand off that could lead to a basket. The players should be made to understand that when defensed properly this is a tough play for the offense to make because they are attempting to exchange the ball in a congested area. We emphasize this point because we want our players to have confidence in their ability to stop this play even without influence. Remember that this is the technique we employ when the offensive players are within the twenty-one foot area or within their particular shooting range. When they are outside that range we apply the one man removed principle.

Reaction Drill

Our drills now progress to three on three situations. The first drill we utilize many coaches refer to as a shell drill. We call it a reaction drill because our players are going to react to the movement of the ball by the offense. All we are looking for at first is proper positioning of our players in relation to their man and the ball. We place two offensive players at each wing and an offensive player on the point. They pass the ball back and forth without changing positions or putting the ball on the floor. The defense reacts to the movement of the ball utilizing the principles we have discussed in relation to individual defense. When the ball moves, we want our men to move. The coaches are very vocal in encouraging quick movement in these reaction drills because we are trying to develop the players so that the proper movement becomes instinctive. When the ball is passed each player is required to jump to the ball (off and toward) and assume a helping or denial position depending on the situation. Diagram 7-5 shows the alignment of the offensive and defensive players. When the ball is at the point X_2 and X_3 are pushing the passes at the wing but allowing the pass to be completed for drill purposes. The defense is not attempting to deflect any passes. We are working strictly on our defensive positioning. X_1 is pressuring the ball handler and forcing the play to one side or the other. In a live situation a man guarding the ball handler in the middle of the floor will generally try to force the offensive player to use his weak hand. We want to give the ball handler only one way to go without giving up the drive to the basket. When the ball is passed to the wing (O_2 in Dia. 7-6) X_1 gets off and toward immediately and assumes

DIA. 7-5

DIA. 7-6

a helping position in case O_2 attempts a drive to the middle. X_2 shifts to the outside of his man to force him back to help since there is no help below him in the corner. X_3 reacts off and toward the ball as soon as the pass is made. He is one step off the line of the ball in a position to close off the passing lane if a pass is attempted. Both helping defenders are slightly open to the ball and maintaining a bent knee defensive position. Too many players, especially when they first come to us, are in the habit of standing up or resting when their man is away from the ball. This is a habit that must be broken if we are to have a successful team defense. We do not rest in this situation. We want our players to be looking for the opportunity to make a play defensively. We want them trying to do as much as possible rather than looking for opportunities to rest. We really encourage the players to stay down and be prepared to force something on defense. We especially want them to be aware of any loose ball situations that may develop.

We introduce a defensive rule at this time that will further improve our players' understanding of their helping responsibilities away from the ball. The rule also gives the players a specific idea of where they should be in relation to the basketball. This principle applies only to the helpside players two passes away from the ball. If the ball is at or above the free throw line extended, we want the helpside players to be off and toward the ball with at least one foot in the lane area. In Diagram 7-6 the ball has not penetrated the free throw line extended so the helpside defender (X_3) is required to have one foot in the lane area. The defensive man can be even more inclined toward help depending on the distance his man is from the basketball, but this is the minimum requirement we establish. If the ball is advanced below the free throw line extended (Dia. 7-7) the helpside defenders must have two feet in the lane area. The application of these defensive relationships follows right along with our emphasis on getting off and toward the basketball and changing our position according to the movement of the ball. Again the players must understand that these are the minimum requirements we establish. We want our players to sag toward the ballside as much as possible without jeopardizing their defensive positioning on their own individual assignments.

When the ball is passed back to the point the defensive players assume their original positions. When the ball is moved to the opposite wing (O_3 in the diagrams) the same defensive adjustments take place with X_2 and X_3 reversing roles. In the first stages of the drill the offensive players do not shoot the basketball. After we are satisfied with the defensive positioning of our players we will allow the offense to shoot the basketball so we can work on contesting the shot and blocking out defensively. We will go over our rules for blocking out and going to the boards in the coming chapter on Rebounding. In

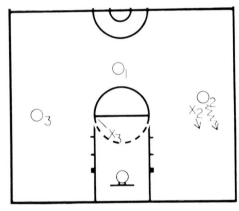

DIA. 7-7

all of our defensive drills where a shot is taken, we will require the defense to block out. Play will not be stopped until the defense gains possession of the ball or the offense scores. We want to emphasize totally the importance of blocking out and going to the boards strong in defensive and offensive rebounding. In contesting the shot, we teach our players to go straight up in the air trying to get a hand on the basketball without slapping or coming down with the hand. If the defensive player cannot place his hand on the ball at the peak of his jump we are satisfield that the shot has been contested and that the shooter's concentration will be somewhat affected. This is all we are looking for in attempting to block or contest the shot. We are sure to experience foul trouble if we have players who think they must block every shot or are in the habit of slapping at the ball when it is released. See Figure 5-6 and Figure 5-7 for the correct and incorrect methods for contesting the shooter.

The final change we will make in this first reaction drill is to allow the offensive players to shift their positions slightly by putting the ball on the floor. This is still a very controlled situation. The wing players are allowed to take three dribbles to the baseline and three dribbles back out to the wing. They are not trying to beat the defense. The defenders are now required to adjust their position according to the movement of the ball by the pass and by the dribble. They must maintain a defensive position where they can see their man and the ball so they can react as soon as the ball is dribbled to a different point on the floor. If you will remember from Chapter Five, we teach the players to pick out an estimated point of vision on the floor where they can see both man and ball. We want an equal emphasis on each and we must stop the players from continually turning their heads to watch one or the other. We watch closely during this drill to try and break the players of this habit and to make sure they are maintaining a defensive position just off the line of the basketball.

Inside Cut

The next defensive situation we want to cover in a three on three drill is the inside cut or give and go cut. Keep in mind that we are still running a reaction drill. The defenders now must react not only to the movement of the ball but to the movement of the offensive players. In the first part of the drill, the cut can only be made from the point position. The wing player who is opposite the pass will rotate to the point and the cutter fills his position. In this way all of the players will receive some work on defensing the inside cut from the key area. As we have taught previously, the man on the ball is to jump in the direction of the pass as soon as the ball passes through his line of defense. This must become an immediate and instinctive reaction on the part of all defensive players. We stress to our players that they do not have to be concerned with the initial movement of their offensive counterpart. As the offensive player continues his cut the defender must adjust accordingly, but by jumping to the ball, the defensive man makes the proper adjustment for any movement by the offense. There are four things an offensive player can do after he passes the basketball. One, he can cut to the basket. Two, he can cut in the direction of his pass or screen on the ball. Three, he can go away from his pass or screen away. Four, he can hold position. All of these possible movements are properly defensed by getting off and toward the basketball. This is very important for our players to learn because many of them have been waiting for the offensive player to make his move and then trying to react. This is the type of defense that is picture perfect for the inside cut, especially when the cut is preceded by a jab step or fake in the opposite direction.

When our defensive man jumps to the ball his job is to force the cutter to go behind. He cannot allow the offensive player to get between himself and the basketball. In defensing off the basketball, a ball-you-man relationship must be maintained at all times. As the cutter continues to the basket, our defender assumes a position of lead pass pressure denying the pass on the ballside. As the offensive player continues out to the helpside to fill the opposite wing, the defender stops in the lane area and establishes a helping position one step off the line of the ball. The defensive player does not follow the offensive player out to the weakside. When the pass is made back to the point, the man who has defensed the cutter must now close the distance to his man and push the pass to the wing area. During this cut the original helpside defender has been maintaining his relationship just off the line of the basketball and trying to provide as much help as possible. His man is rotating to the point position so he must adjust slightly up the lane and to the ball as the rotation is made. If the inside cut is successful and the pass is made we want this defender to immediately drop to the ball to try and jam the middle of the floor. Needless to say, the inside cut should have no chance to be successful if we are jumping to the ball as it is passed.

The next step in this drill is to allow the inside cut from any of the three positions on the floor. To keep the drill from becoming frantic the offensive players do not execute the inside cut every time they pass the ball. We want them to hold position at times. The receiver looks for the pass to the cutter and waits to make his pass until the offensive players are back in their original three man alignment. If the inside cut is executed from the wing position, that player fills back to his original spot if the pass is not made. Defensive concentration in this drill is extremely important. Even more important, that concentration must carry over into a game situation. Players have a tendency to relax when their man gives up the basketball. We have stressed to our players that this is no time to let up defensively. There is no time to rest in the defensive end of the floor. The problem we are trying to avoid by working

FIG. 7-4

on the above fundamentals is that the players especially tend to relax when their man makes a reverse or non-penetrating pass. The principle of getting off and toward the basketball remains in effect no matter what type of pass is made. The players must remember that this cut can be made from any position on the floor. Figure 7-4 shows a player making the inside cut from the wing position after a pass back out to the point. The defensive player did not jump to a position off and toward the basketball and the offensive player is able to gain a step advantage between the defender and the ball. There is not as much movement required in this play as on a forward pass because the defender does not have to be concerned with dropping to the line of the ball. He does have to jump toward the ball and stop the offensive player from gaining inside position on the cut. The ball-you-man relationship must be maintained. If the wing player holds position, the defender plays just off the line of the ball denying or pushing the possible return pass. The three on three drill is a great situation for the players to learn to defense this cut properly. When the ball is at the point, both defenders on the wing have to be primarily concerned with their individual assignments. There is not much help provided so the players must react correctly or a lay up will result.

Screen Away

The screen away from the ball is a very important defensive situation to cover in the game today because of the great popularity of the passing game offenses. At the present time, seven out of eight teams in the Big Eight Conference incorporate a form of the passing game in their offensive system. We are the only team that does not. Of course, the screen away can be just as prominent in offenses other than those that are based on the passing game. At any rate, we place a great deal of emphasis on the technique required to defense this offensive manuever. We feel that defensive effort will be a primary factor because of the number of screens that may occur away from the ball and because of the contact that will take place when the screens are set. Offensive players are being taught to screen the defensive player rather than a spot on the floor. As a result, good, hard screens are being executed and sometimes hard, moving screens are going to occur. Both situations are tough for the defense, but are made easier by our ever present principle for playing off and toward the basketball.

We are still teaching from a three on three drill situation. In the drill we have the point player pass to either wing and then screen away. The offensive player accepting the screen tries to set his man up and catch the ball at the free throw line area. If the defender reacts properly and stops this pass the offensive player continues out to the point and receives the pass at that position. The drill then continues in the same manner.

The defensive technique of our man guarding the screener is very important in limiting the effectiveness of the screening action. He must let his teammate know that the screen is coming and he must give him room to slide through as efficiently as possible. The defensive man being screened is below the play so he should realize what is coming but we still want the communication to take place. Diagram 7-8 shows an incorrect method of defensing the screen away. Instead of getting off and toward the basketball and playing the line of the ball X_1 has followed his man on the helpside. X_1 is now, in effect, forming a double screen with O_1 on his own defensive teammate. The correct method for defensing this offensive manuever is shown in Diagram 7-9. X_1 has jumped to the basketball. As O_1 starts to screen away X_1 must maintain his line, but he must also maintain proper distance from his man because he is now a helpside defender. He does not follow O_1 away from the ball. By maintaining this distance, X_1 creates a lane for his defensive teammate to slide through in coming up to deny the pass in the middle of the floor. We even ask the defensive player on the screener to help his teammate by pushing him up through the screen. This is not so much a physical push through the screen as it is some more defensive communication and help. By lightly pushing his teammate through, the helping defender is letting him know that the lane is there. He is saying, "You are open, now get through." This takes the defensive worry out of the screening action. The player that was to be screened can now concentrate fully on his man and the ball. He still has to deny the pass and push the player outside **twenty-one feet**, but he has to have some confidence in the knowledge that the screen was ineffective.

The man being screened certainly has his own responsiblities for properly defensing a screen away option by the offense. As always, his first reaction when the pass is made to the opposite wing is to get off and toward the basketball. If the ball is at or above the free throw line extended he is to have one foot in the lane area. If the ball is below the free throw line extended we want both feet in the lane. The offensive player accepting the screen should be taught to take the defender to the base line or basket area to set him up for the downscreen. The defensive player must maintain his position just off the line of the ball as this action occurs. His vision must be on his man and the ball and he must remain in a slightly open stance in case he is called on to help on the baseline drive. When the player recognizes that a screen is going to be set, he must decide if he is going to fight through the screen on the man side or slide through on the ball side. We establish some general principles that help the defensive player in this decision making process. The closer the screen is set to the basket area and the middle of the floor, the more responsibility the defender will have for closing the distance to his man and fighting through on that side. This relationship is shown in

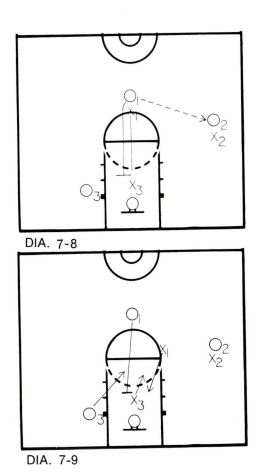

DIA. 7-8

DIA. 7-9

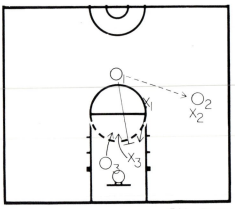

DIA. 7-10

Diagram 7-10. The defensive player must become more man oriented because his man is closer to the basket area. The offensive player (O₃) also has more of the floor to work with in this situation. If X₃ were to try and slide through on the ballside, O₃ would merely step out to the weakside and have a nice twelve or fifteen foot jump shot. To fight through the screen in this manner, the defensive player must first close the distance between himself and his man. You might say that this conflicts with his responsibilities as a helpside defender. The defensive player in this defensive situation is not required to maintain a helping position. There are a couple of reasons for this, one of which we have already mentioned. That is the fact that his man has moved closer to the basket and thus the defender must become more man oriented. The second reason is that the offensive player coming off the screen is now only one pass away from the basketball. Remember that a helpside defender must be two passes away from the ball. The final reason stems from the fact that the man on the screener (X₁ in the diagram) should be opened to the ball and providing help in that area of the floor. The offensive players coming together in this situation allows our defensive players to shift responsibilities smoothly and efficiently. After our defensive player closes the distance to his man, we want him to get his body between the screener and his man coming off the screen. He cannot allow the offensive players to rub shoulders sealing off his path on the man side of the screen. We are, in effect, fighting over the top of the screen just as we did when the ball was involved. From this position, the defender should be able to deny the pass as the offensive player comes off the screen or defense the back cut if the offensive player goes to the basket. We continually emphasize to our players that the term "fight through" means exactly that. There are some very effective screens set in the Big Eight and we have to be prepared to handle them with a great deal of determination and effort.

When the screen is set away from the basket and the middle of the floor, the defensive player being screened should slide through ball side. Good judgement has to be used in making this play defensively in the lane area. Any time the screen is set outside the lane area, the defender automatically slides through ball side. We have already shown the defensive positioning that is required in Diagram 7-9. X₁ must get off and toward the basketball to create a lane for X₃ to slide through. X₃ is maintaining his line and his distance from O₃ because they are still a good distance from the ball and the basket. As O₃ starts to use the screen X₃ should read the play and either slide through or defend against the back cut. If O₃ is coming up to catch the ball, X₃ needs to slide through the lane created by X₁ and beat the offensive player to the ball on the other side of the screen. He is now employing lead pass pressure to deny the pass into the lane area. It is imperative that the defender utilizes his quickness to beat the receiver to a spot where he would like to catch the ball. We emphasize our rules for keeping the ball out of the lane area in this drill. We do not want to allow the offensive player to catch the basketball within the most dangerous area on the floor. Ideally, we want to push him out past twenty-one feet to catch the pass. We should note that the majority of the time the defender should be able to slide through the screen on the ball side. We never want our defenders chasing an offensive player around a screen away from the basket area. The easiest and most direct route is up through the lane.

It is imperative that the defenders away from the ball maintain a good defensive position with the knees bent. This is absolutely essential in defensing the above offensive manuever. We have already mentioned our requirements for staying low throughout the execution of our defense and we watch this closely throughout these three on three drills. We constantly remind our players to stay down when they are away from the ball. Every time a player takes a moment to rest, he is giving the offense an opportunity for a quick basket. It is important that we do not allcw our players to get into this habit.

Influence (3 on 3)

After introducing the influence technique in a two on two situation, we apply the same defensive work in our three on three drills. The two on two drill is an excellent learning situation. Once the players are taught the proper technique, we progress to three on three to make the drill more difficult and better simulate actual game conditions. We can and will come back to a two on two breakdown if the players become lax in their execution.

The drill starts with the ball at the point in the same three on three alignment we have used previously. The two wing players are to step in tighter as the man with the ball starts his dribble. The ball handler has the option of going in either direction and trying to rub his man off one of the screens set by the two wing players (Dia. 7-11). We want the screens set within the twenty-one foot or scoring area because that is the area in which the influence must take place. We have to provide help when the offense is screening for each other within shooting range. Remember that a screen outside the twenty-one foot area calls for the application of our one man removed principle. The players must learn to recognize which defensive play will be required.

While the main emphasis of our drill is on the influence, we also want to make sure that the helpside player is off and toward the basketball providing as much help and congestion as possible. The helpside player (and players in a five on five situation) are going to be instrumental in discouraging a pass into the middle off the screen and roll play. At the same time,

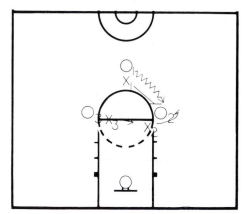

DIA. 7-11

the two wing players in this drill cannot commit too soon to helpside positioning or they will be vulnerable to a play made to their side of the floor. The players will be continuing to improve their ability to react to the movement of the ball and the offensive players. Proper reaction on the part of the helpside is also shown in Diagram 7-11.

We teach the technique for influencing and fighting over the top of the screen in our two on two breakdown drill. Now the players have to apply this technique in a live, continuous drill. The offense is trying to score. They are not going half or three quarter speed while the defense develops their technique. The offense is limited to trying to score off the screen or the screen and roll play. If the defense reacts properly and stops the initial play, the offense balances the floor and the drill continues. The screens are repeated until the defense does a satisfactory job of influencing and fighting over the top. Corrections are made where needed. When a shot is executed, we want a hand up (to contest the shot) and we want all three offensive players blocked off the boards. We cannot allow the second and third shots off the offensive rebound. As we mentioned earlier, a live defensive drill never stops until the defense gains possession of the basketball or the offense scores. The defense can gain possession by forcing a turnover or a steal or by blocking out properly and gaining control of the rebound. To emphasize the block out, we will not change the defense if all three players do not block out properly, even if they do get the defensive rebound. Everyone must do the job or breakdowns are going to occur. Breakdowns in our defensive rebounding will cause problems in our overall defense.

Forward Cut

The forward cut is almost identical to the lateral cut we explained in Chapter Five on Individual Defense. The difference is that the wing player or forward executing the move can either come to the ball (lateral cut) or break to the basket (backdoor cut) Therefore, we designate this manuever as a forward cut in our defensive terminology. The defender has to be concerned with both possibilities in properly defensing the play. This situation is very conducive to a three on three drill because the most important defensive requirement is that the defender maintain his position just below the line of the ball. He must change his line when the ball is passed from the guard (point) to the wing. If the defender is too high on the line, the corresponding offensive player will be able to break behind him on the backdoor cut. If the defensive player is positioned more than one step below the line of the ball, his man will be able to break into the middle and catch the ball in the lane area. We cannot allow either of these two cuts to be successful. The three on three alignment also makes it very tough on the defender because there is much less congestion than there would be under five on five game conditions. Remember we want our breakdown drills to cover situations more difficult than we will actually face during the course of a game.

Diagram 7-12 shows the two cuts that the offensive wing players are allowed to take for our defensive drill purposes. Again they are trying to score, but only off of these offensive manuevers. If the pass is completed at the basket or in the middle of the floor, the receiver is looking to shoot. If the defense reacts properly to deny either pass the wing player making the cut pops back out to his wing or to the point position. We try to have the offense pop back to the wing from the cut to the basket and to the point position from the cut to the ball. The point player then rotates to fill the vacated wing. With this rotation all three defensive players will get some work in covering the forward cut. If the initial cutter pops back out to his original wing position, the ball is reversed to his side and the opposite wing executes the forward cut. If he fills the point position with the point rotating to the wing the ball can be reversed or it can be passed to the point and returned back to the same side.

When the guard to wing pass is made the defender who is now on the helpside (X_3 in the diagram) must get off and toward the basketball. As mentioned above, he is just off the line drawn between his man and the man with the ball. Whenever his man moves, that line is going to change and therefore the defender must readjust his position accordingly. On the backdoor cut by the wing player, the defensive man must drop back as the cut is executed to maintain his position just off the line of the ball. He does not run to the offensive cutter. The defender is still in a helpside position two passes away from the ball so he merely needs to drop straight back providing help in the lane area. As the offensive player nears the basket area our defender needs to become more man oriented but the cutter will, in essense, be coming to him. If the cutter tries to break across the lane to set up on the ballside, we want our defender to deny the pass in lead pass position and to establish a post defense if necessary. We also encourage our players to body check this cut without fouling. The technique is to block the intended path of the offensive player. The defensive player does not initiate any contact but he forces the cutter to take a different route or risk an offensive charging foul away from the ball. The defensive player attempting to defense the backdoor cut must always be aware of his man faking to the basket and breaking back toward the ball and the middle of the floor to receive the pass in the lane area. This becomes a lateral cut or a cut to the ball and the defender must deny the pass as the offensive player enters an area only one pass away from the basketball.

In defensing the cut to the ball we want our players to maintain their relationship off and toward the basketball until just

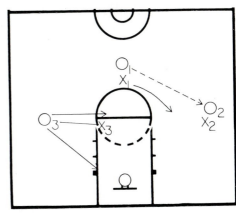

DIA. 7-12

before the offensive player is in a position to receive the pass. At that time, the defender must close the distance to his man and assume a position of lead pass pressure denying the ball completely. Ideally, we want to keep the offense from making a pass into the lane area. At the very least, we want the pass contested with a great deal of intensity. Realistically, the offense is going to be able to complete these passes at times, but we want them to earn everything they do get. The defensive player at the point position will be providing some help and some congestion so we want the defender on the cutter to force his man as high as possible to catch the ball. We tell our defender to run the player up the back of his defensive teammate, or teammates, if there is a two guard front and both guards are holding. Once this is accomplished, we want to push the player outside the twenty-one foot area or force him to step back out away from the ball.

Help And Recover (3 on 3)

This is a normal progression from the two on two help and recover situation we discussed earlier in this chapter. The purpose of the three on three drill is to further emphasize the importance of helping on the ball while still recovering back to your man to contest the shot or stop penetration. We are putting the offensive players in scoring position and conducting the drill under live conditions. The help and recover play is a difficult one at the very least. Good judgement must be used and each player must develop the quickness and the intensity to make this play when necessary. The helper has to get back to his man when the original defender assumes proper positioning or if the ball handler makes the pass to the vacated offensive player. The technique that we teach we feel will help our players to provide a great deal of help and yet allow for a quick recovery in case of the pass.

The drill starts with the ball just outside the key area and with the wing players on each side between the baseline and the free throw line extended (Dia. 7-13). We spread the players to make the play more difficult and more urgent for the defense. The defensive man at the point allows the ball handler to beat him to either side. The offensive player is to drive hard to the basket. The defensive player providing the help must jump into the driving lane or a sure basket will result. In the drill alignment the vacated offensive player is close enough to shoot the ball or drive to the basket if he feels that is open. Therefore, if the pass is made, the helping defender has to recover quickly to stop either option.

When the helping defender recognizes that a breakdown has occured, his first move is to fake into the driving lane or toward the ball handler in an effort to slow him down or make him pick up the ball. At this point, the helper must recognize immediately if the offensive player with the ball intends to

DIA. 7-13

continue his drive. If penetration has been stopped or slowed down, the defender on the ball should be able to reassume proper positioning. The second defender will still provide some help, but he can now pay more attention to his own man. If the driver is not diverted by the initial fakes of our helping defender, the driving lane must be closed immediately and a more difficult help and recover situation presents itself. The defensive player providing the help is now required to jump into the driving lane to completely stop penetration or draw the charge. There is no way the offensive player can be allowed to split the two defenders. We instruct our players to jump into the driving lane and throw up the hands in an attempt to further distract the ball handler. We want him to be concerned with the defensive pressure and a possible double team rather than give him a clear path to the basket and hope for the best. We want to put him on the defensive. The defensive helper should be poised to recover to his man if the driving offensive player elects to make that pass. We tell our defender in this situation not to plant his feet or continue his momentum into the middle of the floor. As soon as he gets in a position to stop the drive, he should shift his body weight back toward his man so that a quick recovery can be accomplished.

A development that we want our players to especially watch for in this situation and one that will call for the defender to plant his feet is the possibility of the offensive charge. A good defensive team will always be looking for an offensive player to get out of control, especially on the drive to the basket. If our defensive player determines that the driver is out of control or susceptible to an offensive charging foul, we want him to set his feet and square up for the contact. The defender must take the charge full in the chest or risk a defensive blocking or moving under call. We can't stress enough the importance of meeting the offensive player head on and receiving the contact in the chest rather than the shoulder or the side of the body. When the contact is made in the shoulder area, the majority of the calls are going to go against the defense or there will be no call at all. If the defensive man turns to his side, you can bet the official is going to call him for moving under the offensive player. When drawing the charge inside the scoring area (especially this close to the basket) we want our players to use good judgement before letting themselves fall to the floor. If there is a minimum amount of contact and there will be some question as to whether a foul was committed, we want the players to fall backwards, but we do not want them to hit the floor. By falling to the floor, the defensive player is taking himself completely out of the play. If there is no whistle the offense could be in a position for an easy two points. If quite a bit of contact is made and the defensive player draws the charge properly with the feet set, we encourage him to hit the floor and to make a little noise when the contact is initiated. This sometimes causes the official to see the play more clearly because he may have been watching some other area just prior to the development of the possible offensive charge. The original defensive man on the ball handler should recognize if his teammate is attempting to draw the charge and should immediately drop (sprint) to the vacated offensive player in case there is no whistle. All players will be dropping to the ball and to the basket when a breakdown occurs which we will dicusss later on in this chapter.

We think that the techniques just described can do much to discourage the drive to the basket in our defensive end. The final technique is perhaps the most difficult for each individual defensive player and is why we place a great deal of emphasis on this drill and this help and recover situation in teaching our team defense. A good offensive player will stay under control at all times. When defensive help is provided he will recognize the situation immediately and will look for the opportunity to hit the open man. We constantly stress to our players that a play does not end with our defensive help. A quick recovery must be made whenever the ball handler attempts a pass to his open teammate. As we mentioned earlier, the helping defender is to shift his body weight back toward his man as soon as he is in position to stop the drive. This does not mean that the defensive man should lean completely in that direction. He merely has his weight on that side and is on the balls of his feet ready to react in case of the pass. If the defender anticipates the pass, he should play the passing lane with his hands, but should not give up the driving lane until he is sure the pass will be attempted or the original defender has regained his position. In making the proper recovery, anticipation and effort are the two primary prerequisites. There is no set footwork to teach for getting back to your man after helping on the ball. The idea is to get the job done whether by sliding or sprinting or a combination thereof. We do ask our players to continue playing the passing lane with their hands. We want them looking for the deflection as they are making the recovery. The defenders are not to lunge into the passing lane because this could leave them further out of position. Many times, however, a deflection or an interception can result when this play is executed properly by the defense and the offense becomes careless. This is especially true when the play develops in close quarters. Any time there are a number of people in a limited amount of space the defense has an advantage and the offense must be careful with the ball.

An important part of recovering effectively back to the offensive man is not to overextend in that direction but to recover in a balanced position ready to slide either way or go up to contest the shot. At the end of the recovery, the defensive player must slide into position rather than run up to or by the offensive player as he catches the ball. The defender must especially cut off the baseline drive to the basket in this drill alignment (Dia. 7-14). If it looks like the offensive player

DIA. 7-14

250 Team Defense

is going to go up for the shot, we want our defensive man ready to contest, but again, he cannot overextend himself. The defender does not go into the air until the ball is in the air or the offensive player has left his feet for the shot. We discussed this earlier in our section on contesting the shot, but it is especially important in this situation. The defensive player, in his effort to recover to his man, may become overzealous and he can be very susceptible to a shot fake and a drive to the basket. This defensive idea must be emphasized in any help and recover situation. When contesting the shot, the defender must also be careful not to run by the shooter as shown in Figure 7-5. The defensive player in the photograph is completely out of position for the defensive blockout. The offensive player will have a clear path to the basket in which to follow his shot. The defender should contest the shot in a balanced position in front of the shooter so he can execute the blockout as soon as he returns to the floor. In running the drill we expect the offense to make every attempt to score. The defense must make the play properly, block out, and gain possession of the ball. We leave the defense in until we are satisfied with the effort and execution.

FIG. 7-5

Post Split Coverage

These days, we do not meet many teams that split the post as a regular part of their offense. Again, this is because of the great influx of the passing game offenses. We do feel that it is still important to cover this situation in teaching our team defense in the half court area. While we do not want to waste precious practice time, we want our players thoroughly prepared for anything that will come up under game conditions. Also, this situation is excellent for teaching the players our philosophy of collapsing to the ball whenever it goes into the middle of the floor. This philosophy follows right in line with our theory of a helping defense that is ball oriented in the scoring end of the floor.

We split the post extensively in our offensive system. Because of this, we introduce the defensive coverage involved early in the practice sessions. Once we have introduced the technique involved and run it for a brief period of time, we will get most of our defensive work accomplished in the split the post offensive drills and against our set offense. We will concentrate totally on the defensive aspect of the drill only when we are going to face a team that utilizes the post split or when we need to go back to a breakdown drill on collapsing to the middle. Until then, we will correct the defensive mistakes as they are made against our offensive pattern. The split coverage must be introduced both from the low post (Dia. 7-15) and the high post (Dia. 7-16). The defensive technique remains pretty much the same, although the closer to the basket the play is being made, the tougher the defensive players must fight through the congestion. Also, the high post defensive player is able to give

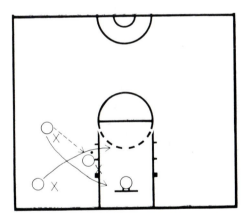

DIA. 7-15

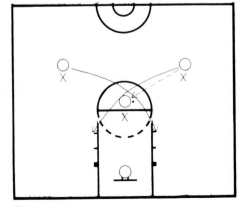

DIA. 7-16

FIG. 7-6

a little more help than if he were guarding the ball down in the low post position.

Remember that the first reaction on the part of all of our defenders is to get off and toward the ball as soon as the pass is made. This fundamental holds true when the pass is made into the post. The immediate reaction of the outside players when the post pass is executed is to open to the ball and drop back on top of the post player. The defenders should then attempt to bother the post man by picking at the ball with the back hand. This relationship is shown in Figure 7- 6 . The two defensive players do not disregard their offensive assignments in making this drop to the ball. They are still picking out an estimated point of vision on the floor where they can see both man and ball. There are two times we allow a defender to turn his back to his man in this situation. The first is when the post man brings the ball down and there is an opportunity for a steal. This play must be made quickly and instinctively and the defensive man must be ready to recover to his man on a cut or a pass back to the outside. The other time we will allow this defensive play is when the post player turns to face the basket for the shot or the drive. We want our defenders to try and play the ball from behind without fouling when this occurs. We want to completely jam the ball from the outside when the post player turns it in to the basket. At this point, we want to force him to throw the ball back outside. That is a very difficult play to make for most post men after they have already turned to face the basket. More times than not, they will force a low percentage shot.

We teach our players to cover the post split from these positions on top of the feeder. It is very important that they do not drop to a position below or at the side of the offensive post man. There will be enough congestion on the split without getting in too tight and allowing the post man to use his body as a screen. We do not switch on this play. We want each man fighting through the split maintaining proper defensive positioning on their own individual assignment. In this way, there is no confusion as to the responsibilities involved. Each defender is required to stay with his man as the splitting action is executed. They must maintain their defensive position between the ball and their man to keep the post man from handing off to an open cutter. This defensive relationship will also insure that the defender is between his man and the basket as the cut is made. Any defender placed in this situation cannot trail his man as the splitting action occurs. He must get his body in front of the offensive player as soon as the cutter commits to a particular direction. If not, the defensive man is sure to get hung up in the traffic around the ball. We instruct our players to get on top of the feeder as soon as the ball goes into the post. From there, the defensive men can play the cutters in either direction. There are only two ways to go and there is just as much congestion for the offense as there is for the defense. At times, our defensive coverage is going to break down and a switch is going to have to take place. When it does, the two defensive players making the switch have to communicate effectively or further breakdowns will result. We want them to yell "switch" so that the entire bench can hear the call. When this goes into effect, both players must be quick to pick up their new man and remain with him until an opportune time to switch back. A safe time to switch back may not come until the next trip down the floor and again effective communication must take place. **Remember, we are advocating the switch only when absolutely necessary.**

When the ball is in the low post (Dia. 7-15) the defensive post man can help only after a hand-off is made. His first concern is the post player turning the ball in or manuevering for the shot. As the hand-off is attempted, we want the defender on the post to fake at the cutter and try to play the ball without fouling. He does not switch to stop the cutter except as a last resort. It is the responsibility of the defender covering the split to fight through successfully and there should be additional help coming from the side away from the ball. When the ball is at the high post (Dia. 7-16) the defender on the ball can step back and help slow up the cutters as long as the feeder has his back to the basket. The defensive man must move up to cover the high post player as soon as he turns to face the basket. The defender must anticipate this move so he does not get caught off guard. The range and the shooting ability of the offensive post man must be taken into consideration when applying these defensive rules.

If the offense does not execute the split but pitches the ball back to the outside players the defenders are merely in a help and recover situation. They drop back to help on the ball when it is passed inside and recover quickly to their men on the pass back to the outside. The methods for recovery are the same as we discussed in relation to the three on three help and recover situation. The defensive helpers must get back to their men in time to stop or contest the shot and yet they cannot overextend in that direction or they will be vulnerable to the drive.

Three On Three Situations Drill

One of our final two three on three drills that we run we refer to as a Situations Drill because it covers quite a few of the situations that can occur against our half court defense. It is a combination drill that includes, guarding the post, helpside defense, defensing the diagonal cut and the backdoor cut, and the influence and pick and roll play. In this drill, we also introduce and work on our defense versus the lob. Any time a lob pass is attempted into the middle of the floor our helpside defense must be in a position to deflect or intercept the ball or draw the offensive charging foul. We cannot allow the opponent to complete this pass

DIA. 7-17

DIA. 7-18

near the basket area, especially when they are throwing to a post player or a front line player with excellent offensive ability. This defensive rule is particularly important when the offense sets with only two men on the ballside and are looking to go into the post with the ball. In this situation our post defense will completely front the offensive player and force the offense to lob over his head. The helpside defenders have full responsibility for disrupting this pass.

The drill alignment is shown in Diagram 7-17. The coach has the ball and will make the initial pass depending on the defensive coverage. The first look is into the offensive post player. The defensive post man (X_3) denies the ball from the side position. We are not fronting the post because the fifth offensive player could be aligned on the ballside. The defensive guard (X_1) is in the off and toward position ready to help or recover to his man if the guard to guard pass is made (coach to guard in this case). The defensive forward (X_2) is just off the line drawn between his man and the ball ready to help in the middle or close the distance to his man if the diagonal cut is attempted. All defenders must be maintaining vision on both their man and the ball.

The next pass that the coach looks for is a lob to the baseline side of the post man. We want our defensive player in the post to deflect or intercept this pass if at all possible. This is a very difficult pass for the offense to make. We want our defender to realize that he should be able to stop this pass completely. Everyone will be rotating to the ball as the pass is made so help will be provided. The defensive forward rotates to help on the ball and will pick up the offensive player if the post man goes for the steal and does not come up with the ball. If the post recognized early that he can't get a hand on the ball he should readjust his position immediately to cut off the drive to the basket. The defensive forward would then maintain a helping position as would the defensive guard dropping back into the middle. If the defensive forward is pulled over to pick up the ball the defensive guard must drop to the basket to cover the offensive forward away from the ball (Dia. 7-18). The basket must be protected when the ball is at the baseline. If the post player pitches the ball back out to the coach or the weakside guard all players must recover to their men immediately.

If the post defense and the helpside positioning is correct, the coach will look for the weakside offensive forward coming to the ball on the diagonal cut. The responsibilities for X_1 and X_3 remain the same until a pass is made. X_2 must deny the pass into the middle of the floor using the techniques described in Chapter Five on Individual Defense. If the offense is able to complete the pass, the offensive guard immediately cuts backdoor and the defensive guard must react to stop this play. He merely closes the distance to his man and assumes a position of lead pass pressure denying the pass all the way down the lane. Upon completion of the pass into the middle,

X_2 must readjust his position to play one on one defense. If the ball handler does not face the basket X_2 can play a step or two off the ball and look to help on the cutters. He cannot disregard the offensive player with the ball. As soon as the offensive player turns to face the basket, X_2 must move up with caution to stop the shot or the drive with tough man to man defense. Our defensive player in the low post position readjusts his position slightly toward the ball as the pass is made into the middle. He must continue to deny the ball to the offensive post man because his man is still only one pass away from the ball.

If X_2 is defending the play properly he should be able to deny the pass to the forward on the diagonal cut. The coach then executes the guard to guard pass and the offensive forward steps out to screen for the new ball handler (Dia. 7-19). X_2 must step all the way out to influence. X_1 has to force his man wide and fight over the top of the screen. X_3 readjusts his line and as the guard dribbles off the screen he assumes helpside positioning in the middle of the floor. He must provide help on the pick and roll play, especially if the guard tries to lob the ball to the forward rolling to the basket. There is no way we can allow this pass to be completed.

As you can see, this all purpose drill covers many of the team defensive principles we have discussed throughout this chapter. It is an excellent breakdown drill that involves a lot of players. We run the drill at both ends of the floor so the entire team can achieve the work desired in a very short period of time. We keep the defense in until we are satisfied with their effort and the results of that effort. We then switch the offensive and defensive roles and repeat the drill. When all four groups have been through at least once, we trade a group from each end so the defenders are working against different people.

Three On Three Survival

The survival drills are our favorite means of working on our defensive effort and intensity. They are perhaps our favorite defensive drills because of the competition that is involved. We divide the team into four groups of three just like the three on three situations drill. The difference is that the coach is not a part of the offensive alignment. The offense is to try to score using any and all manuevers at their disposal. The defense has to stop the offense and gain possession of the ball through a mistake by the offense or a defensive rebound. The catch is that the defense must stop the offense three times in a row for the ball to change hands. Early in the practice sessions we run the three on three survival drill at both ends to provide the maximum work for our players. As we get into the season, we utilize half of the floor and the teams come out of defense to wait on the sidelines. The offense goes to defense and a new team comes in. Each defensive team has to stop the offense three times in a row. Every player is required to play tough,

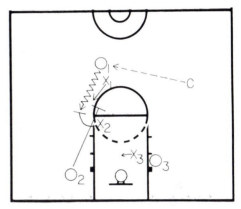

DIA. 7-19

aggressive, individual defense and to help his teammates when help is needed. If one player lets down in a particular group of players, that group is liable to end up playing defense for long periods of time. In addition to developing the necessary defensive intensity, the survival element helps us to install our philosophy of emphasizing both individual responsibility and teamwork in the defensive end. Peer pressure also becomes somewhat of an impetus in the execution of this drill. The only vocal peer pressure we will allow has to be of an encouraging, positive nature. If we are not getting sufficient effort from someone in the drill the coaches will provide some pressure of a somewhat stronger nature. We insist that our players play hard at all times and this drill is an excellent means of getting our point across.

We feel that we help ourselves offensively as well as defensively in the survival drills. The offense is learning to work together and they are also further developing their individual moves within the team concept. The concentration of both the offense and the defense is at a peak because of the competition factor and the resulting defensive intensity will help our offense to improve their efficiency.

Reaction Drill (4 on 4)

The following defensive situations are conducive to four on four breakdown drills and are conducted in that manner when introduced. As the techniques are learned, we include the same situations in our five on five work.

The reaction drill involving four players is run much the same as the Three on Three Reaction Drill. In the first stage of the drill the offensive players are not allowed to move but merely pass the basketball around the horn. Again we are watching the defense to make sure they are reacting quickly to the movement of the ball and that they are establishing the proper helpside and ballside positions. The defensive reactions we are looking for have already been discussed in relation to the three on three drill. A defensive principle that receives additional emphasis in this drill alignment is the objective of protecting the basket. The drill alignment is shown in Diagram 7-20 with the ball at the forward position near the basket area. The players out on the floor must drop to the ball and to the basket to help discourage the offense from further penetration. This is a help and recover situation but it is the responsibility of the defense to protect the basket first. There is no advantage to guarding an outside man closely when the ball is below your line of defense. We want our players to learn to pull back in toward the ball and to force the pass back to the outside. Once the pass is executed, the sagging defenders must quickly recover to their men without overextending themselves.

The reaction drill now progresses to where we allow the

DIA. 7-20

offensive forwards to make the diagonal cut when the opposite guard is in possession of the ball (Dia. 7-21). The defender must close the distance to his man and deny this pass into the middle of our defense. To assure continuity in the drill the offensive players must return immediately to their original position if the passing lane is blocked effectively by the defense. The defensive guard away from the ball should be able to provide some help in discouraging this pass. If you will remember from Chapter Five and the forward cut, the defensive man on the cutter is to try and run his man up the back of this off guard. The offensive forwards do not have to make the diagonal cut. They can merely hold position as in the first stage of the drill and look for the right opportunity to break into the middle. In the meantime, the guards are holding position and moving the ball around the defense. When the ball does go into the middle or after it has been passed at least six times, we want the offense to put up a shot. The shot must be contested and each defensive player must keep his man off the boards and go after the ball.

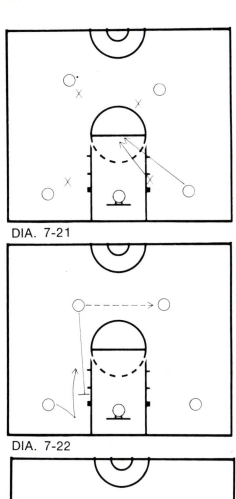

DIA. 7-21

DIA. 7-22

Vertical And Horizontal Screens

We feel that the four on four alignment is excellent for developing our defensive techniques against any vertical and horizontal screening executed by the offense. These two screening actions are very much a part of the passing game offenses we discussed earlier and therefore will be very important in our defensive preparation. When we refer to a screen as a vertical screen, we are talking about a downscreen as shown in Diagram 7-22. A horizontal screen involves a player on a path parallel to the baseline and is usually set somewhere in the lane area so it can also be referred to as a screen across the lane (Dia. 7-23). We combine these two movements in one four on four drill situation but the drill can be broken down further if we feel it is necessary to concentrate on one or the other in our defensive work. This can depend on the success we are having with each particular technique or on the offensive tendencies of our upcoming opponent. Some teams will employ the vertical screens almost exclusively while others will utilize both screening methods throughout the execution of their offense.

DIA. 7-23

For our drill purposes, the different screens are keyed as shown in the diagrams. When the guard to guard pass is made (Dia. 7-22), the guard making the pass will set the vertical screen for the forward on his side. If the defensive forward denies the pass properly, the two offensive players merely exchange positions and the drill continues with the ball at the opposite guard. To key the horizontal screen the guard dribbles at the forward on his side and the forward screens across for his teammate on the opposite side (Dia. 7-23). If no pass is made, the guard dribbles back out, the forwards have exchanged positions and the drill continues.

The technique for defending against the vertical screen is almost identical to that which we taught on the screen away action in one of our initial three on three drills. The slight difference is caused by the new offensive spacing and the position of the ball out on the floor rather than on the wing. If you will remember, the defensive man guarding the screener is to get off and toward the basketball as soon as the pass is made. As his man leaves to set the vertical screen he should remain in an off and toward position slightly open to the ball. This will create an open lane for the defender being screened to slide through and deny the basketball. As shown in Diagram 7-8, if the defensive man on the screener does not get off and toward the ball he will, in effect, be setting a double screen on his own defensive teammate. The defender being screened has to read the situation to determine if he should slide through the open lane on the side of the ball or fight through the screen on the man side to keep his opponent from receiving the pass. This is where the offensive spacing and the position of the ball comes into play. When the ball is at the point or on the side of the floor where the screen is being set the defender may need to fight through on the man side of the screen to properly deny the pass. On the other hand, if the ball is positioned on the opposite side of the floor, the defender should almost always be able to slide through ball side and still beat his man to the ball utilizing the proper angle. This is the situation that usually develops in our four on four drill. The exceptions will occur when the forward attempts to take the defender all the way into the basket and then receive the screen near the basket and the middle of the floor. As we have previously shown, the defender is now required to fight through the screen on the man side as his opponent breaks back to catch the basketball in the lane area. Another exception that can take place in a game situation occurs when the ball handler dribbles in the direction of the potential receiver to improve his passing angle. This play is shown in Diagram 7-24. The defender must recognize immediately that the position of the ball has changed and therefore his angle of interception has been decreased. Obviously, the defender must maintain vision on both his man and the ball if he is to react properly as the play is executed. The defensive man now has to make another split second decision as to which route to take to avoid the vertical screen and maintain defensive pressure on his opponent. Practice in making the correct decisions is the purpose of these breakdown drills. Remember, the players have to learn not to chase the offensive player around the screen. As we continually preach to our players — defensive intensity (or determination, or effort, whatever your terminology is) — will many times make up for lost ground if a mistake is made momentarily. Increased intensity is always a goal of ours in practice situations and in the game itself.

DIA. 7-24

The horizontal screen in the lane area is a very tough manuever to defense because of the proximity of the potential receiver to the basket. If the offensive player accepting the screen gains even a step on the defender he will be open for the inside pass into the heart of our defense. If we are to be successful defensively we must deny this pass off the horizontal screen a good percentage of the time. The first principle that helps us make this defensive play is our rule for being off and toward the basketball when positioned on the helpside. A defensive player who is guarding his man too closely is very vulnerable to this screening action because he is unaware of where the ball is and what the offense is doing. Furthermore, the middle of the floor is left wide open allowing the offensive player ample space to cut to the ball or to the basket. By playing off and toward the ball the correctly positioned defender is congesting the middle and will be able to provide help or close the distance to his man depending on the movement of the offense. Once the defensive player is aware of the screen about to take place he should read his offensive counterpart to determine the direction of the cut. The defender then closes the distance to his man (or allows the offensive player to take up the gap) and assumes a position of lead pass pressure completely denying the pass into the middle. The defender must keep his shoulder and body between the screener and the offensive man accepting the screen as the cut is executed. If he allows the two offensive teammates to rub shoulders he will have lost a step defensively and may be screened out of the play entirely. The defensive man will always fight through on the man side of the screen when faced with a horizontal screen in the lane area. The offensive player is too close to the basket and to the ball to allow the defense time to slide through and still deny the pass. The defender must be ready to play his man in either direction off the screen. Body contact will be inevitable in this situation and we want our player to hold his own keeping in mind exactly what the referees have been allowing.

The man guarding the screener again has some responsibilities regarding defensive communication and teamwork. As his offensive opponent starts away to set the screen he has to remain in a position between his man and the ball. He should open slightly to the ball but should call for his teammate to watch for the screen. As the screen is being set, the defensive man on the screener must be careful to avoid picking off his own teammate. Just as in the vertical screen, there is the possibility of a double screen if the initial defender turns to trail his man. The defender on the screener should look to help discourage the pass into the middle if his teammate is beaten momentarily. Therefore, his two major responsibilities on the horizontal screen are to communicate effectively and to help jam the middle of the floor. Obviously, he still has primary responsibility for his own individual assignment. We are

DIA. 7-25

DIA. 7-26

definitely not looking to switch in this situation but will allow for the switch to take place as a last resort. The players have to communicate effectively with each other to successfully execute the switch.

Collapse On the Post

Continuing our emphasis on a helping defense we introduce at this time a drill which requires the players to collapse to the ball each time a penetrating pass is made into the post. The drill alignment is the same as our four on four reaction drill except a fifth offensive player is added in the middle with no defense (Dia. 7-25). The offensive players on the perimeter move the basketball and put the ball into the post every third or fourth pass. The post man follows the basketball but the pass can only be made on the side of the lane at the medium or low post positions. This is because the defensive strategy is altogether different when the offense has the ball at the high post position. The defensive guards would drop to the ball at the high post (see post split coverage) but the front line players would have to apply lead pass pressure to their respective men to deny further penetration. Once the post player catches the ball in the middle, he is to turn and play the basket or play the ball to an open man.

Diagram 7-26 shows the correct positioning of each defensive player as they drop to the ball and jam the post man. Our philosophy is to force the post player to make a play back to the outside because of the pressure being applied from all angles. We don't think too many big men have the ability to make this play consistently. Many will force the shot or attempt to put the ball on the floor which should lead to a loose ball situation or an outright steal. The defenders are in a help and recover situation so if the pass is made back to the outside the players must respond back to their men in time to stop or contest the shot or deny the next pass. The defenders cannot totally disregard their man to concentrate on the ball, especially when the post player still has his back to the basket. Once the post man turns to face the basket, the outside players can turn to play the ball but must make the play quickly and without fouling. The helpside players, especially the forward, must pay closer attention to their individual assignments because the post player can still execute a pass to the weakside after facing the basket.

Reaction Drill (5 on 5)

In beginning our five on five work we will add an offensive and defensive player at the post positions and run a reaction drill involving all ten people. We do not spend a lot of time on this but we can come back to it at any time if we are not satisfied with our team defensive positioning. The offense moves the basketball with the post player following the ball in the middle of the floor. The four perimeter players hold position but look for their shot at all times. We are mainly concerned with defensive positioning, blocking out, and rebounding aggressively after every shot when running this drill in a five on five situation.

Baseline Help

We discussed in Chapter Five our philosophy on forcing the ball to the outside rather than to the middle in employing our half court defensive strategy. We stated a number of reasons for our thinking behind this philosophy. One of the most important of these reasons involves the passing angles that are created when an offensive player penetrates into the middle of the floor. There is no organized pattern for rotating to provide help on penetration into the middle. The help can come out from the basket area or in from the perimeter positions and this is where the clear passing lanes are developed. We attempt to force the offense to the sideline or to the baseline where all the help will be rotating in the same direction when it is needed. Diagram 6-2 earlier in the book shows the proper defensive adjustments that are required in providing help along the baseline. As we pointed out at that time, the offensive player does not have near the passing options or clear passing angles that are available from the middle of the floor.

We teach this rotation through the use of a Baseline Help Drill in a five on five situation. Again the objectives and the mechanics of the drill are building on our philosophy of a total team defense. The players are repeating the process of getting off and toward the ball each time it is moved. At the same time, we are working specifically on providing help to a teammate in need and guarding the basket area against all lay ups.

The initial drill alignment is a basic two-three offensive set with the corresponding defenders. The ball is passed from the guards to either forward with each defender on the ball forcing his man to the outside as we have discussed. The defensive players off the ball position themselves according to the relationship of their man to the basketball. For our drill purposes, the forward or wing defender guarding the ball will allow his man to beat him on an outside or baseline drive to the basket. Normally, in this position, the defender would force his man back to the middle if there is no help in the corner area. We have had excellent defensive players who were able to continue forcing their man to the outside in this situation. They utilized their quickness and anticipation to cut the driver off at the baseline and many times were able to draw the offensive charge. The secret again is to give the ball handler only one way to go and to anticipate the drive in that direction. We will see below that help will still be provided in case the offensive player gains an advantage. If our defenders away from the ball are thinking help and if we get proper rotation the offensive player should not reach the basket area without additional defensive resistance.

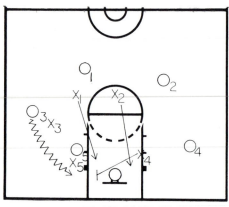

DIA. 7-27

Diagram 7-27 shows the defensive rotation we are looking for in providing help along the baseline. It is obvious that the helpside defenders must be sagging toward the ballside and that they must have the ball in their vision to react quickly enough to the driving offensive player. To aid in our defensive teamwork it is very important that the beaten defender lets his teammates know that help is needed. He merely calls for help as soon as he feels the offensive player has gained an advantage (situation #5 requiring defensive communication).

The first important aspect of this defensive rotation is the responsibility of the post defender to stay home rather than to leave his man to provide help on the ball. The helpside forward (X_4 in the diagram) should be the first defensive player reacting to stop the ball. He has to maintain vision on the ball and must react quickly and instinctively to cut off the driving lane to the basket. Ideally, we would like the helpside forward to meet the offensive player before he can take a step into the lane area. This is what we are striving for in the execution of this drill. The reason we want the forward to make this play rather than our post player is because of the proximity of the offensive post player to the basket and to the ball. If the defensive post man drops off to stop the ball the other defenders may not be able to rotate or drop to the ball quickly enough to guard the offensive post man rolling to the basket. The driver would then be able to dish the ball off as the defensive post cuts him off on the baseline. With the post man staying home and the helpside forward coming over to cut off the drive we have this offensive possibility completely covered. The weakside offensive forward will be left open for an instant but this is a much more difficult pass to make and our players should have no trouble dropping quickly enough to discourage its attempt. We do want our defensive post man to react to the ball if there is no help coming from the forward but only as a last resort. If the offensive player is able to lay the ball up then our helpside defensive players are not reacting properly to the movement of the ball.

The helpside forward in sliding to cut off the drive should be looking for a possible offensive charging foul. He must be sure to square his body exactly in the driving lane and to come set before contact is initiated. The defender has to have the courage to take the charge full in the chest with the hands up and out in case the ball handler pulls up short for the jumper. We want the defender to adequately contest the shot should this occur. The defensive helper does not return to his man until the ball is passed back out and then effective communication must take place to insure that each offensive player is covered.

It is the responsibility of the helpside guard (X_2 in the diagram) to drop to the basket to cover the vacated weakside forward (O_4). He also helps out on any other movement or cutting action into the middle of the floor near the basket. The guard should try to anticipate and intercept the pass across the lane from the driver to the weakside forward. If our defensive forward has reacted properly in providing help the ball handler will sometimes attempt to make the pass across the lane without considering the rotation of our guard. The guard must maintain his position on the forward until the ball is forced back to the outside or the shot is attempted. On the shot the guard (X_2) assumes responsibility for keeping the weakside offensive player away from the boards. He must be prepared to block out very effectively because the offensive player will usually enjoy a considerable height advantage and the weakside rebounding position is extremely important in gaining control of the defensive boards.

The ballside guard (X_1) will drop to the ball and jam the middle of the floor. The additional congestion should serve to help discourage the offense. His first responsibility is to help on the post and he should be prepared to recover to either guard on the pass back to the outside. With this in mind X_1 should not drop too far into the middle of the floor or the congestion and the extended area of recovery could hurt his ability to react back to the guards.

The original defender on the ball (X_3) should not give up on his man after he is beaten momentarily. We teach our players to try and regain proper positioning without fouling. If the offensive player drives all the way to the baseline or lane area and then meets opposition the trailing defender can either double team or look to play the passing lane on the pass back to the outside. The double team is the most effective manuever, especially if the driver is not utilizing his peripheral vision to see the whole floor. From the double team we can also continue our rotation in the most organized manner once the ball handler is forced to pick up the ball. Defensive communication will still be of the utmost importance in making sure that each offensive player is picked up quickly and with the least amount of confusion. Diagram 7-28 below shows the new rotation once the ball is stopped and forced back to the outside. X_4 must react quickly back to his man and X_2 must hold on the weakside forward until X_4 is in a position to discourage a pass into this area. Keep in mind that X_4 cannot leave the ball until it is most definitely on its way back out to the guard. X_3 reassumes defensive positioning on O_3 and X_5 continues to deny the basketball into the post. The guards now have the most difficult task in reacting back to their men to stop or contest the shot from the outside. In this situation we teach the ballside guard to pick up whichever player receives the first pass. The majority of times, the ball is going to be passed back to the strongside guard (O_1). In coming out to defend against O_1, X_1 should shade the passing lane over to O_2 to try and discourage easy movement of the ball. This will give X_2 additional time to recover since he has the most area to cover in getting back to his man. Both guards must be careful not

DIA. 7-28

Team Defense 263

to overextend themselves in hustling back to their original assignments. If the ball should be flared out to the weakside guard (O_2) X_1 would be required to stop his shot. X_2 would recover back to O_1 once X_4 regains his defensive positioning. X_1 must learn to fake at the offensive guards, seemingly playing both, until X_2 can recover to the outside. The double team should cause the initial pass to be lobbed or thrown around the defense. We are counting on a good double team to slow down movement of the ball.

Another possible rotation is effective because the basket remains guarded and there is less movement required. We do not like this rotation as well because the defensive switches allow for too many mismatches and changes in assignments. If X_3 was not able to form the double team, this is the rotation that the defense should try to put into effect (Dia. 7-29). X_4 would remain on O_3 while X_2 would continue to guard the weakside forward (O_4). X_5 continues to defense the post and X_1 reacts to pick up the first pass to the outside. X_3 would then hustle to find and pick up the open man. This places much of the responsibility for rotating on the shoulders of X_3 and while this is not a bad concept we prefer the first rotation for the reasons we mentioned above.

In the organization of our Baseline Help Drill we simply rotate the defensive players so that they play each position twice. After this is accomplished, we switch the offense to defense and the drill proceeds in the same manner.

Congesting The Middle

We emphasized at the beginning of this chapter our philosophy of implementing tough man to man defensive pressure on the ballside and a sagging, helping defense on the side away from the ball. This philosophy has been stressed throughout the chapter and is indeed thoroughly stressed to our players in developing our defensive system. We feel very strongly that there is nothing more discouraging to an offensive player than beating his man, only to find too much congestion or a blocked driving lane as a result of excellent helpside defense. This type of play can be especially demoralizing when a good offensive move and drive to the basket ends with a charging foul rather than the intended lay up and two points. This is the thinking behind our next drill which emphasizes drawing the charge against any offensive driver who has left his feet or is out of control. We want every player on our team capable and willing to take the offensive charge in stopping penetration to the basket. We work on this drill only once a week or less in preseason practice and then infrequently during the season. We can come back to it if needed but basically we are setting the tone for what we expect from our players under game conditions. With proper emphasis, the players quickly understand that we want to jam the middle and look for the

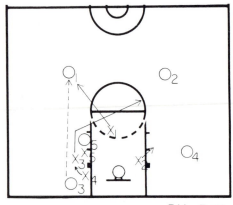

DIA. 7-29

charge whenever an offensive player takes off for the basket. The concept is really the same as on the baseline drive except that the rotation and help will be coming from different angles. The most important aspect of the drill is to develop in every player the willingness to take the offensive charge. We never want to have a player avoid a situation that could lead to contact and a definite offensive foul.

We refer to this drill as the Jam the Middle Drill and run it from the same two-three alignment we showed before. Instead of allowing the drive to the outside from the wing, we have the offensive players drive to the basket from all the positions and angles. We point out that the first defender in a position to draw the charge or stop penetration is the player nearest the ball in the direction of the drive (Dia. 7-30). We explained earlier in the chapter that this player cannot allow the offensive player to split he and his defensive teammate. He must drop quickly from the help and recover position to cut off the drive. For our drill purposes, however, we will allow the offensive players to split the defenders so we can work on congesting the middle and drawing the charge on the inside. Diagram 7-31 shows the type of helpside positioning that we are looking for in the execution of this drill. The post can even help to jam the middle by faking at the driver while staying home to guard his man. We will also work on the post stepping over to stop the drive at the last possible instant. Basically, the defensive post man must concentrate on his man for the same reasons we discussed on the baseline drive. However, there is no reason to watch another player lay the ball up while remaining glued to the offensive post man. As a last resort, we want the center willing and able to draw the charge also. If the post player is a shot blocker he may be able to play the shot, but many times the charging foul is a better play to make. This does not mean that we will limit or discourage the abilities of a true shot blocking center. This is obviously a great defensive play also. If the big man has both defensive manuevers in his repetoir he will be invaluable in our team defensive system.

One of the primary reasons we utilize this drill only infrequently involves some habits that could develop if good judgement is not used in the execution of these principles. The players cannot become so intent on drawing the charge that they neglect their responsibilities for recovering back to their man or going to the defensive boards. The players must be able to distinguish between a player who is out of control and susceptible to the charge and one who is under control and may be looking to hit the open man or pull up short for the jumper. The latter situation could precipitate a help and recover reaction because the beaten defender should be hustling to regain control of his man.

Five On Five Survival

Our final defensive drill utilizing only the half court area can include all of the aforementioned defensive situations. We

DIA. 7-30

DIA. 7-31

Converting From Offense to Defense

have built our defense from the ground up and the players should now be ready to play with the defensive knowledge and intensity that is required in our program. We have already discussed the importance we place on the survival drills in developing the proper intensity and this should be evident as we place the players in a very competitive five on five survival situation. This drill is run in the half court and the defense is required to stop the offense and gain control of the ball three times in succession before the teams reverse roles. The offense attempts to score with the knowledge that they remain on offense if they are successful. Some very competitive action develops in these survival drills and we encourage the competition as long as it is of a positive nature. This is still a defensive drill and the coaches concentrate on correcting the defensive reations and techniques that we have been teaching up until this time. All of the situations have been covered and the players should have a good understanding of what we are trying to accomplish at the defensive end.

The next phase of our defensive system that we introduce and develop is our conversion from offense to defense. In the game of basketball today, the importance of conversion cannot be underestimated. We have already mentioned in Chapter Four the emphasis that Coach Knight at Indiana places on proper conversion. This is another very important area of basketball that requires only effort and hustle on the part of the players. We emphasize the effort and hustle aspect with a few very simple teaching points. While conversion takes place over the entire court, we include it in this chapter because we are actually getting back to set up our half court defense as quickly and efficiently as possible.

We will utilize two methods of conversion depending on the quickness of our opponents and the particular organization of their fast break attack. The first method emphasizes our half court defense and is incorporated when we need to stop penetration at the end of the fast break. There is no effort to disrupt the opponent's fast break but we completely protect the basket area to prevent deep penetration and the easy baskets that can generate momentum to the other side. The players must simply sprint to the defensive end as soon as the ball is rebounded by the opposition. They should run the quickest route to their general positions in the lane area. In other words, there is no requirement to run on the ballside or the weakside in making the conversion. As the players cross the half court line we want them to look over their shoulder to pick up the ball. Their attention is focused on the ball as they hustle back to protect the basket from half court. The first man back (usually one of the guards) does not leave the basket until there is a frontline player in a position to replace him. The basket must be guarded at all times and the ball handler must be picked up as he nears the twenty-one foot mark. It is important that the players communicate very effectively, especially if a switch has to take place, to insure proper coverage. All of the players are required to plant at least one foot in the lane before working to the outside to pick up their individual defensive assignments. In this way, we can completely jam the lane area and effectively stop penetration at the scoring end of our opponent's fast break.

Our second method for stopping the opponents' fast break is of a more aggressive nature and is employed when we are as quick or quicker than the team we are playing. It is also effective against a team that likes to outlet to a particular player or a particular side in initiating a patterned fast break. This method can also be advantageous if the team we are facing is not particularly skilled in the execution of their fast break. If they are not a very dangerous fast breaking team we can afford to be more aggressive in defensing the outlet pass and the middle of the break. Finally, we can employ this method if we need to come from behind or if we wish to speed up the tempo of the game.

The first means by which we will attempt to disrupt the opponents' fast break opportunity is to apply immediate pressure on the rebounder as he comes down with the basketball. This pressure will usually be applied by the man who was being guarded by the rebounder. His job is to swarm the rebounder to prevent him from making a quick, effective and accurate outlet pass. We teach the man swarming the ball and the rebounder to get the hands high and play the ball with no slashing (fouling). Our defender is to react quickly to the outside of the rebounder to hinder his vision to the outlet areas. Once the ball passes his fingertips, the defender should turn and sprint to the other end looking to play the ball from behind or set up defensively in the half court area. In making that conversion, our defensive man should shade the side of the floor that the offense is bringing the ball. This is very important in congesting the areas of the floor that are under attack.

The second line of defense in stopping the break is set up by one of our guards (usually the biggest or best rebounding guard). His initial reaction when the shot is executed is to block his man off and, if possible, to get to the free throw line area and look for the ball to be tipped out or the long rebound. If the ball is rebounded by the opposition the guard must immediately react to deny the outlet pass, so his responsibilities are one-half rebound and one-half defense. We want our defender in this position to try and read the rebounder and his outlet possibilities and to try for the interception when the pass is made. Good judgement must be used so that the player can readjust his position if there is no chance for the interception or a deflection. If the outlet pass is completed the guard is now to try and delay the ball handler as much as possible or stop the ball completely. We teach the players to fake and retreat in delaying the ball and also work on drawing the charge if the offensive player gets out of control. If the ball penetrates his line of defense, the guard is to turn and sprint to the basket, playing the ball from behind or getting set defensively depending on the situation. While this guard will usually have responsibility for the long rebound and playing the outlet, he should always be ready to exchange positions with the opposite guard in case his teammate is caught underneath the basket or unable to get back.

We designate a particular guard as the safety with responsibility only for getting back to protect our defensive basket. As mentioned above, however, the second guard should cover for the safety in case he is caught under the basket or out of position. We do not want this to happen often as mix-ups will develop. The safety must play back as far as the deepest offensive player as the ball comes off the boards. He does not let an offensive player get behind him until our frontline players get back to protect the basket and pick up defensively. The safety must talk to his teammates because he can see the entire floor and he should be able to read the situation very well. As soon as we have some frontline players in a position to protect the basket, the safety should come out to stop the ball as far out on the floor as possible. The further out we can stop the ball, the better chance we will have of completely stopping the break. There is an exception to this rule. If the opposition has an exceptionally quick penetrator, we may want to congest the lane area and force him to pull up at the top of the key. Moving out on the floor to meet this type of player would spread our defense and create a one on one situation that would not be to our advantage. The player designated as the safety must be adept at protecting the basket when outnumbered as we discussed thoroughly in Chapter Five on Individual Defense. This guard has to be extremely smart and cannot be afraid to step in front of an offensive driver going full speed to the basket. Drawing an offensive charging foul is one of the best defensive manuevers at the scoring end of the opponents fast break.

The key to this defensive method against the fast break is the ability of the remaining two players to make the quick conversion from one end of the floor to the other. These are the two frontline players who are away from the defensive opponent that gains control of the rebound. As we stated previously, the offensive player boxed out by the defensive rebounder is to swarm the ball in an attempt to pressure the outlet pass. All three of the frontline players are responsible for going to the offensive boards. When the opposition controls the rebound, our two players away from the ball are to bust out of the congestion and sprint to the lane area at the opposite end of the court. The players must hustle to clear the congestion near the boards and in the middle of the floor. We tell the players that their first step is just as important as their last in hustling back to set up our defense. There can be no coasting if we are to successfully stop the opponents' fast break. A good fast breaking team will take advantage of any big men that are slow to make the conversion. In converting to the opposite end, these two players should also shade the ballside or the strongside of the court to discourage easy movement of the ball.

In teaching proper conversion we start with a five on five reaction drill with a coach shooting a missed shot after four or five passes. As we mentioned earlier in the book, we never want a player shooting to purposely miss the basket. The defensive players must react properly to the movement of the ball, block out, and look for the outlet pass to initiate their break. The offensive players are to assume the previously explained assignments and react to stop the break if they are unable to secure the offensive rebound. The three rebounders must get to the offensive boards and the half rebounder-half defender must be ready for the tip out or the long rebound. We don't want these players concentrating on conversion at the expense of their rebounding responsibilities. We teach the players the methods prescribed for stopping the opponents' fast break and then designate which method to employ at a given time. For our drill purposes, the players must execute exactly as we have explained our defense against the fast break attack. Corrections will be made as they are needed. Under game conditions, we will allow for some spontaneous reaction with judgement. Many times, a good defensive player can read the flow and anticipate the movement of the offense. A charging foul or an interception can be the result and we certainly don't want to discourage this type of creativity on the part of our players.

From this initial five on five situation we progress to a live drill in which the offense is trying to score. If the offense does score, they get the ball back and keep it as long as they are successful. If the shot is missed and the defensive team gains control of the rebound, they initiate their break and the offense makes the proper conversion. The original defensive team now has the ball at the opposite end and the drill continues in the same manner.

Five On Six Conversion Drill

The half court defensive drills that have not been fully explained in the preceding pages will be outlined at the conclusion of the chapter, but we want to give special attention to our favorite conversion drill. The Five on Six Conversion Drill is very effective because we make the situation much more difficult than what will be faced under game conditions. The drill also highlights the responsibility of the safety to hustle back quickly to protect our defensive basket. We feel that the

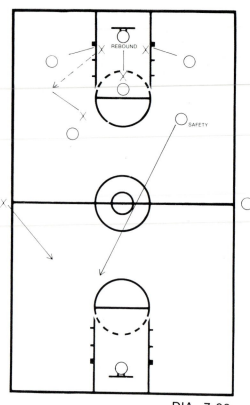

DIA. 7-32

Five On Five
Defensive Game

pressure we are applying in a repetitive situation will make the players aware of the importance of hustling back at all times. The players can never relax in this aspect of the game because a breakdown will usually result in an uncontested lay up.

Diagram 7-32 shows the initial alignment in beginning the Five on Six Conversion Drill. We can execute the drill from a purposely missed shot or we can run our offense live and have the defense break off the missed shot and rebound. If we run the drill live the players are concentrating on all aspects of the game, but we emphasize that the primary purpose of the drill is to develop our conversion game. The players in the half court area play the five on five game and react to the boards when the shot is executed. On a defensive rebound the sixth man on that team (positioned on the sideline) takes off for the basket at the opposite end. The original defensive team now looks to push the ball up the floor as quickly as possible. The opposing team must stop the break utilizing whichever method the coaches have designated. Obviously, this break situation places a great deal of pressure on the defense, especially the defensive safety. The safety must get back to cover the player released from the sideline and the frontline players and second guard must hustle back to defend against the break.

The last offensive player to come to the half line drops out to become the next sixth man because the drill runs continuously unless we stop for corrections. The fast breaking team sets up their half court offense while the defensive team looks to gain control of the ball and run their fast break in the opposite direction. Their sixth man (O on the opposite sideline) breaks behind the defense just as before and the drill continues in that manner. We caution the players that we do not want them to get out of control in executing the break. With the exception of the streaking offensive player we want to use the same fast break principles we discussed in Chapter Four.

The defensive game we are about to describe falls just short of a controlled scrimmage and is leading up to that element of our practice sessions as well as the full scale scrimmage. It is the culmination of all of the teaching and principles that go into the development of our defensive system. The players enjoy this full court game because of the change of pace offered in the scoring system and the competition involved between the teams. In playing the defensive game, the teams can be split into two even groups or the first unit can go against the second unit. In the preseason practices, we will divide the squads evenly to help us determine a starting five. As we near the opening game and get into the season, we will play the first six players against the second six to set our personnel.

The game begins with an offensive team trying to score against the defense. The defense is allowed to break off the missed shot or steal but they must have a legitimate fast break opportunity. A bad shot or turnover off the break will cost the defensive team points. Except for the fast break opportunity the defensive team will remain on defense for the entire game to twenty or thirty points. At that time, the teams will reverse roles and play another game. The total point outcome from the two games will determine the winner. There are four ways the defense can score and the maximum point total they can achieve per possession is also four. If the defense stops the offense without a shot being executed, they are immediately awarded two points. This can be accomplished by forcing a turnover, drawing an offensive foul, or making an outright steal. The ball does not change hands after a turnover or offensive foul. The defensive team is merely awarded the points and the offensive team enters the ball again from half court. If the defense steals the ball, they look for the fast break opportunity and bring the ball to the opposite end. A fast break basket results in two more points for the defense. If the fast break does not generate a good scoring opportunity, the team with the ball should pull it out as if to set up the offense. The ball is then handed back to the original offensive team and they initiate the offense at that end. The fast breaking team must use good judgement and not force the action at the scoring end of their break. If a turnover is committed or a poor shot is attempted, the defense loses one point.

The defense is awarded one point on the defensive rebound and they can again execute the fast break with the same possibilities as explained above. The fourth and final way the defense can score is by forcing a jump ball situation. The jump ball does not take place in this defensive game. The defense is awarded one point and the ball returns to the offense.

The offense can score three different ways in this game. A foul on the part of the defense results in two points for the offensive team. We feel this is an important element of the game because the players must learn to play tough, aggressive defense without fouling. An offensive rebound gives one point to the team in possession of the ball. A made basket, of course, is scored as two points for the offensive team. It is important to remember that after each of the above developments, the ball remains in the possession of the offense. The same holds true for a turnover, an offensive foul and a jump ball situation. This places the pressure on the defense to dig in and make something happen. We feel this is an excellent game for developing a spirited and team-oriented defensive attitude and this is why we call it our Five on Five Defensive Game. The players show a great deal of enthusiasm for the defensive game and this adds significantly to our effort and intensity at that end of the floor.

We mentioned that each of the games are played to twenty or thirty points. These are the point totals we have found to be most useful in organizing our practice sessions. The thirty point games are utilized when we want to concentrate on these controlled semi-scrimmages for an extended period of time. The shortened versions are sometimes more practical as our practices are cut down over the course of the season. A manager keeping score is a must to properly organize the defensive game and the players always have more awareness and enthusiasm when the scoreboard is used. The sixth player for each team can be inserted by the coaches or can enter the game at designated point intervals in the contest. The point system for the Five on Five Defensive Game is repeated below:

Defense	Offense
No Shot = 2 pts.	Defensive Foul = 2 pts.
Fast Break Basket = 2 pts.	Successful Basket = 2 pts.
Jump Ball (no jump) = 1 pt.	Offensive Rebound = 1 pt.
Defensive Rebound = 1 pt.	

A few of these defensive drills have been explained somewhat in detail and yet we want to delineate them here at the end of the chapter for quick reference. Those that have been described completely are listed without further explanation.

Half Court Team Defensive Drills

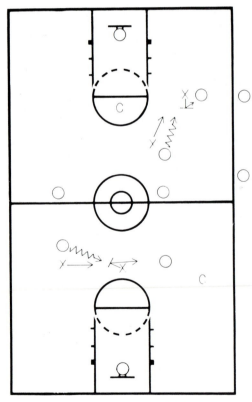

DIA. 7-33

Two On Two Help And Recover Drill (Dia. 7-33)
Objective: To teach and develop in the players the ability to help on the ball and yet recover back to their men as quickly and efficiently as possible.
Organization: The squad is divided in half. Guards at one end of the floor, frontline players at the other end. The guards run the drill from out front while the frontliners utilize a player at the guard position and one on the wing (see diagram to left). Two players step out on defense. The ball handler is allowed to beat his defender and the defensive man off the ball must provide help. Each defensive player gets an opportunity to provide help until the respective coaches are satisfied. The offense moves to the defense and the defense goes to the end of the line.
Points of Emphasis: 1. Proper helping position. Slightly open to the ball.

2. Fake at the ball handler.

3. **React quickly** back to your man when the ball is stopped or the pass is made.

4. **Do not** let the offensive player split your defense.

One Man Removed Drill (Dia. 7-34)
Objective: To teach and develop in our players the defense we want to employ when two offensive players cross outside the twenty-one foot area in our defensive end of the court.

Organization: The division of the squad and the initial alignment of this drill is the same as we explained for the previous drill. The two offensive players now cross each other by use of the pass or the dribble but outside the twenty-one foot area. The defense utilizes the one man removed principle each time a cross occurs. When the coaches are satisfied the offense moves to defense and the defense goes to the end of the line.

Points of Emphasis: 1. Talk.

2. Read the cut or dribbling action and know your position on the floor.

3. Slide through one man removed.

4. Stay low throughout the slide.

Influence Drill (Dia. 7-35)

Objective: To teach and develop the proper technique in defensing a screen on the ball within the twenty-one foot scoring area.

Organization: The squad is divided evenly with guards and frontline players at each end of the floor. Initially the frontline player sets the screen in the key area for the guard. When the defense executes properly the guard comes down to the wing area to screen for the frontliner. Both players are coming off the screen utilizing the dribble. The rotation is the same as in the previous drills.

Points of Emphasis: 1. Talk.

2. Man on screener must influence. Step all the way out.

3. Man on ball must fight over the top of the screen. Force the ball handler wide.

4. Get the lead leg across the screen.

5. Arch the back.

Western Roll Drill (Dia. 7-35)

Objective: The same as above except the screener is in possession of the ball and has not used his dribble.

Organization: We will often run the Influence Drill at one end with the Western Roll Drill at the opposite end and then switch players (see diagram). In the Western Roll Drill the pass is made from the point to the vertex of the free throw line and lane. The passer then cuts off the ball looking for the hand off. The players rotate from offense to defense and switch lines.

Points of Emphasis: 1. There is very little help provided.

2. Man being screened must anticipate and force his man wide.

3. Key is getting off and toward the ball as it is passed.

4. Fight over the top of screen. Arch the back. Lead leg across.

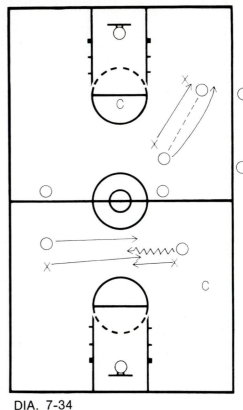

DIA. 7-34

DIA. 7-35

Team Defense 273

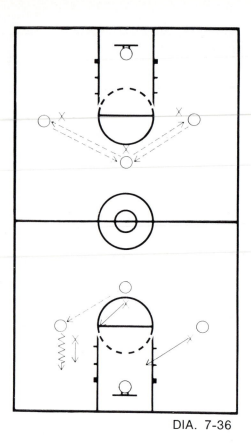

DIA. 7-36

Three On Three Reaction Drill (Dia. 7-36)

Objective: The primary objectives of the reaction drills are to work on defensive positioning, maintaining basketball position, and proper vision. Secondary objectives are contesting the shot and blocking out properly when the shot is executed.

Organization: Squad divided evenly with six players at each end. The initial defensive team works on the above until the coach is satisfied and the teams then reverse roles. At first, there is only movement of the ball by the pass. Next the offense is allowed to shoot. Finally the offensive wing players are able to dribble to the baseline and back out to the diagonal.

Points of Emphasis: 1. Bent knee position.

2. Off and Toward the ball.

3. Pick out spot on floor. See man and ball.

4. Helpside player has at least one foot in the lane when the ball is at or above the free throw line extended.

5. Both feet in lane when ball is below that point.

6. On the shot everyone blocks out and goes to the boards.

7. The man on the ball contests the shot.

Inside Cut Drill (see Dia. 7-36)

Objective: To teach and develop in our players the proper reaction for getting off and toward the basketball to prevent the inside or give and go cut.

Organization: Same alignment as previous drill. Point man now makes the pass to either wing and tries to cut to the basket on the ball side of the defensive man. The opposite wing rotates to the point and the cutter fills that position. The drill continues in that manner with the ball going to each wing so that every defensive player is required to guard the cutter. After some time on this, the offensive players are allowed to execute the inside cut from any position.

Points of Emphasis: 1. Jump to the ball as soon as it is passed.

2. Stay between the cutter and the ball. Force him to go behind.

3. Assume lead pass pressure down the lane. Do not follow the cutter out on the weakside.

4. Helpside player is off and toward the ball providing help in the middle.

Screen Away Drill

Objective: To teach and develop in our players the technique required to defense a screen away from the ball.

Organization: Same as previous drills. Offensive point player now passes to either wing and screens away for the opposite wing. The player accepting the screen is to set his man up by taking him into the basket and coming back off the screen attempting to catch the ball in the middle of the floor. He fills the point position, the screener fills the wing and the drill continues.

Points of Emphasis: 1. Talk.
2. Defender on screener must get off and toward the ball and let his teammate through. Help him through.
3. Man being screened must fight through man side or slide through ball side depending on his relationship to the ball and the basket. Most of the time, it will be ball side.
4. Beat the cutter to the ball. Deny the pass.

Three On Three Influence Drill (see Dia. 7-11)

Objective: To further develop each player's ability to defense the screen on the ball within the twenty-one foot scoring area. This is a continuation of the original influence drill under live conditions.

Organization: Same three on three alignment except that the wing players are in tighter to set screens for the ball handler. The point man can dribble off the screen in either direction and the offense is to try and score. They can reset the alignment by use of the pass or the dribble and the drill continues.

Points of Emphasis: 1. The players must recognize whether an influence play is required or the one man removed principle should be applied. They must then execute properly.
2. The helpside defenders must be in position to discourage the screen and roll play.
3. On the shot everyone must block out and go to the boards. The man on the ball must contest the shot.

Forward Cut Drill (see Dia. 7-12)

Objective: To develop in our players the ability to deny the pass to an offensive player breaking to the ball or to the basket from the wing position.

Organization: Same three on three alignment. On the pass to the wing the opposite wing player makes a cut to the basket or to the ball. The defensive player must work to deny either pass into the lane area. The cutter rotates to the point position if he cut to the ball and pops back out to his original wing position after a cut to the basket. The ball is then reversed so that the opposite wing has the same cutting options. The point player will rotate to fill the wing on the cut to the ball. Each defensive player takes the forward cut twice and the three offensive players change to defense.

Points of Emphasis: 1. Get off and toward the basketball. Establish position just off the line of the ball.

2. Maintain that line on a cut to the basket.

3. Assume lead pass position on a cut to the ball. Push the cutter up high where there is congestion.

4. Deny all passes into the lane area.

Three On Three Help And Recover Drill (see Dia. 7-13)

Objective: To further develop in our players the ability to help on the ball and recover back to their men in the half court scoring area. The offensive players are all in shooting range so the defenders must learn to recover quickly without overextending.

Organization: Three on three alignment with the wing players positioned about fifteen feet from the basket between the baseline and the free throw line extended. The point player is allowed to beat his defender on a drive to the basket. The wing defender must help on the drive and recover to his man if the ball is dished off. The play is run twice in the same direction and then the players rotate clockwise so that each player is required to help and recover. The offense then changes to defense.

Points of Emphasis: 1. Fake at the driver in an effort to discourage his drive.

2. If he continues, close off the driving lane. The ball handler cannot split two defenders. Look for the charge.

3. Throw the hands up at the driver.

4. Play the passing lane back to your man with your hands.

5. Anticipate the pass and keep your body weight and momentum back toward your man as much as possible.

6. Do not overextend in making the recovery.

Post Split Drill (see Diagrams 7-15 and 7-16)

Objective: To introduce to the players the proper technique for defensing any offensive splitting action off the post. We run this drill early in the practice sessions and come back to it only when needed.

Organization: Squad divided evenly at each end. We can run a high post split at one end and a low post split in the other and switch the players or we can switch the drills. The two outside offensive players as shown in the diagram make the pass into the post and execute the split. The defense must cover the splitting action until the coach is satisfied and the teams then reverse roles.

Points of Emphasis: 1. Drop to the ball when the post pass is made. Pick at the ball with the back hand.

2. Fight through the split. Do not switch unless absolutely necessary.

3. Keep your body between the post man and the cutter. Do not trail the cutter.

4. If a switch has to be made, yell "switch."

5. High post defensive man looks to help on the cutters as long as the post player is facing away from the basket.

6. The low post man can help only after the hand off is made and then only to fake at the new ball handler.

Additional Defensive Drills

The following are the half court team defensive drills that we have outlined completely in explaining the technique and the teaching points involved in each drill situation. The Conversion Drills and the Defensive Game employ the full court area but the emphasis is on the defense.

Three on Three Situations Drill
Three on Three Survival Drill
Four on Four Reaction Drill
Screening Drill (Horizontal and Vertical Screens)
Four on Five Drill (Collapse on the Post)
Five on Five Reaction Drill
Baseline Help Drill
Jam the Middle Drill
Five on Five Survival Drill
Conversion Drill off Missed Shot
Five on Six Conversion Drill
Defensive Game

Rebounding ⑧

We feel very strongly that rebounding is much like defense in that it requires heart more than talent. The aggressiveness that we constantly try to instill in our players will be very important in developing our board game. This type of aggressiveness has enabled us to outrebound our opponents in all of the last ten seasons at the University of Missouri. We place a great deal of emphasis on rebounding in our early practices and continue to emphasize its importance throughout the development of our offensive and defensive system. In all drills where a shot is attempted we want both players or both teams going to the boards hard. The drills remain live until the defense gains possession of the ball or the offense makes the basket. In this way the players will realize the importance we place on rebounding in developing our overall game. We don't want them to develop the habit of standing or turning to watch the ball going to the basket. Every time a shot is executed we want to see some aggressive rebounding on the part of all players involved in the drill situation. The only exception would be the designated safety in a five on five drill. He has sole responsibility for dropping back to protect the basket at the opposite end.

The following are the six areas we feel we have to be concerned with in developing our indidivual and team rebounding:

1. **Anticipation**
2. **Position**
3. **Aggressiveness**
4. **Timing**
5. **Strength**
6. **Jumping ability.**

Anticipation is important to almost all phases of the game of basketball. We coach the players to follow the flight of the ball and anticipate the direction of the rebound. The players have to assume that every shot will be missed and they also have to develop an understanding of the rebound percentages that can occur from a missed shot. We stated previously that approximately seventy percent of the shots attempted from one side of the floor, with a medium or high arc, will rebound to the opposite side of the basket. Since most shooters today employ at least a medium arc, the majority of the missed shots from the side are going to rebound to the opposite side. In the event of a line drive shot the players should be ready to play the ball back to that side or to the middle of the floor depending on the touch applied. A shot executed from the center of the court can bounce to either side or come back toward the shooter depending on the touch applied and which side of the rim the ball hits first. An understanding of the above percentages and a knowledge of the shooters will help in developing the proper anticipation required in rebounding. By far the best teacher will be the experience gained in drill situations and under game conditions.

There are two types of positioning we are concerned with in developing our rebounders. First and foremost is inside positioning (between your man and the basket) for gaining control of the rebound. This is the single most important element in becoming a good rebounder. All of the other areas of concern can be negated by a lack of attention to this critical detail. By the same token excellent inside positioning can offset any and sometimes all limitations in the other five areas. The players must be taught to react quickly to block out each time a shot is executed. Again this is why we never allow a drill situation to end unless the basket is made or the defense captures the rebound. The defensive block out or avoiding the block out at the offensive end has to become instinctive and natural. The first step is many times the most important in gaining inside position. Once the ball leaves the shooter's hands it will only be in the air for two to four seconds at the most. After the ball hits the rim it will normally be touched or controlled by a player in less than one-half second. As long as they do not allow themselves to be pushed under the basket the players who have inside position will have the best opportunity to gain control of the basketball. We will be discussing the block out and more on inside positioning shortly.

The second type of position we are concerned with is the position of the body, especially the hands and arms. John Wooden popularized the idea of bringing the hands and the arms to shoulder height and we go along with the theory that the player in this position will be able to react quickly to the ball as it comes off the rim. By raising the hands and arms quickly this player will also avoid some possible resistance in going after the rebound. Figure 8-1 shows a player in the proper position with his hands and arms up and a player on the opposite team trying to bring his own hands up to go after the ball. With all the congestion underneath the boards this type of situation can be a common occurence so we want our players to get the hands up quickly to place the opponent at a disadvantage. The fingers of the hands should be outstretched but relaxed and the palms should be facing the basket as shown in the photograph. We stress this rebounding position from the beginning of our practices and continually correct the players throughout the preseason sessions. It is a new fundamental for most of them and one that we must constantly reinforce if we are to be successful in our teaching. Usually we will designate a coach to watch for this aspect of our rebounding and make the necessary corrections during each particular practice.

As far as the rest of the body is concerned we want our players to maintain a position of strength throughout the rebounding process. The players should establish a wide base on the block out so that they are on balance and in a good strong stance at the start of their jump. By a wide base we mean the feet should be set shoulder width or slightly wider. Each individual

FIG. 8-1

Rebounding 279

player should determine a stance that is comfortable and will enable him to go after the ball quickly and with strength. An exaggerated base should be discouraged because the player will be making himself smaller than normal. This is not advantageous in the rebounding area. We will have our players drop the rear even lower in starting their jump so we don't want them beginning from a relatively low position. The knees will obviously be flexed to facilitate a good jump to the ball.

We have already mentioned briefly the importance we place on aggressiveness in gaining control of the offensive and defensive boards. We will delineate later some aggressive rebounding drills that we feel are essential to the development of our individual players and our team in the area of board play. Many of our young players come to us with no idea of the aggressiveness that they will need to acquire to be successful at this level. This is most evident with regard to rebounding and play underneath the boards. The players have been able to dominate at the high school level because of their superior size or ability or a combination of both. At this level of play there will be too many players of equal ability for any individual to compete successfully without being aggressive.

The final three areas we are concerned with in rebounding are interrelated. Timing, strength, and jumping ability all have to do with the actual leap to gain control of the basketball. The proper anticipation will have much to do with timing the jump correctly in going after the ball. Experience will also be of great value in developing the timing necessary to be an outstanding rebounder. The players must learn to recognize quickly whether a shot is soft or hard. This will determine the distance of the rebound and greatly influence the timing involved in gaining control of the ball. A player's chances for possession are greatest when he is able to time the rebound perfectly and reach the ball at the peak of his jump. This will allow the player to be in a balanced position as he makes a play for the ball and will also enable him to make his play with strength. Jumping too early will result in the player being on his descent when the ball comes off the rim. It is difficult to generate any kind of power or strength while returning to the floor. Usually, a player will only be able to tap or slap at the ball. Timing the jump too late will obviously allow the opponent time to reach the ball first.

An excellent rebounder has to develop his strength and he has to be able to utilize that strength throughout the process of rebounding the ball. The action underneath the boards and in going after the ball can get pretty physical and the players have to be prepared to ignore the contact. Toughness, both mental and physical, will be of great value in this area but a player's toughness can be greatly enhanced by some added strength. We will explain our conditioning program later on in this book but it should be pointed out that we very much advocate the use of weights for our players. We feel that our attention to strength development has been a primary reason for our success in the rebounding department over the years. We also teach our players to use the body to their utmost advantage in controlling the rebound. Once the ball is grasped we teach our players to bring it into the body and to turn the body away from the opponent's pressure to protect the ball. The one-quarter turn to the outside we discussed in Chapter Four is important in regard to defensive rebounding. Most of the pressure and congestion in the rebounding area will come from the inside so this one-quarter turn should help the rebounder to protect the ball with strength. We further teach the players never to make an extended reach for the ball without using the body to protect the area around the ball. Many times the body can be used to seal off an opposing player. While strength is important here, the proper aggressiveness can sometimes be an even more important factor. An aggressive player will not reach in to attempt to gain control of the rebound. An aggressive player goes after the basketball.

Defensive Rebounding

There is no way that we can overestimate the importance of controlling the defensive boards. As we stated in both of the previous chapters, one of the objectives of our defense is to prevent the offense from gaining possession of the ball for a second or third shot. In many cases we cannot prevent the first shot but since we have position we should not permit the second and third attempts. It is impossible for a defensive team to be effective if it continually allows the offense two and three attempts at the basket. There are a couple of important reasons for this in addition to the obvious one of giving the offensive team more chances to score. On an offensive rebound the rebounder is usually in very close proximity to the basket and has an excellent opportunity to put the ball right back up for an easy two points. An offensive rebound also affords the rebounder a good opportunity to draw a possible defensive foul in going back up for the second shot. There is a lot of congestion, the defense is broken down, and the offensive player is already at the basket so it can sometimes be easy for a defensive player to commit a foul in attempting to stop the second shot. We feel very strongly that an offensive rebound will also serve to inspire the offensive team. There is a surge of confidence when a team is able to turn a missed shot into two points or at least another opportunity at the basket. If the offense pulls the ball out after the rebound there is a feeling that this time the shot that is executed will be successful. A confident team does not feel that they will miss twice when given such a golden opportunity. At the same time the defense has to feel a letdown because they failed to capitalize on the missed shot by the offense. This does not mean that every offensive rebound will turn the game around

DIA. 8-1

DIA. 8-2

for the offense or be disastrous for the defense. What it does mean is that repeated rebounding mistakes and a failure to control the defensive boards will eventually take its toll on any team. We want our players to understand this idea as we begin to teach the techniques necessary for gaining inside position and rebounding aggressively.

In designating the six areas we feel are important in developing our rebounding game we have already stated that inside positioning is the most crucial. The defensive team should always have an advantage in this regard because each player should be aligned somewhere between his man and the basket. The helpside players are off and toward the basketball but they are still between their man and the basket and should be in a position to maintain that relationship once the shot is attempted. We have mentioned previously that some seventy percent of the shots attempted will rebound to the opposite side of the basket. This points up the importance of solid rebounding on the helpside of our defense. For this reason and because blocking out away from the ball is sometimes a more difficult proposition than executing the block out on the ballside, we will begin teaching this fundamental from the various positions in our helpside defense.

Diagram 8-1 shows the ideal rebounding positions we will hope to acquire under five on five game conditions. The three frontline players are set in a rebound triangle with excellent inside position and a good chance to gain control of the ball off the rim. The rebounding guard (X_2) has his man off the boards and is positioned around the free throw line and the middle of the floor in anticipation of a tip out or a long rebound. Our ball handling guard (X_1) makes sure his man is out of the play and then positions himself at the top of the key where he can best initiate a possible fast break off the defensive rebound. He is prepared to go after a long rebound or a loose ball that may result from the primary rebounders. We explain this alignment to our players to facilitate our whole-part-whole teaching method. We want to show them the end result of everyone doing their particular job so the breakdown drills will have added meaning and purpose.

While the diagram shows the ideal rebounding positions the players must be cautioned to first block their man off (get inside position) and then go to the board or react to the ball. If O_3 were positioned on the right side of the floor facing in, X_3 would not immediately go to the weakside rebounding areas upon execution of the shot. His first responsibility would be to keep his individual opponent from getting inside for the rebound. This does not mean that we want to ignore the weakside rebounding area. All of the players have to be aware of the floor balance and they should develop a nose for the ball. Diagram 8-2 shows the relationship we are discussing. The players should pick up the flight of the shot as soon as possible after the release. They should then anticipate the direction of the rebound and shade that area without giving up the inside position. With the shot executed from the right side X_5 may want to move slightly to his left to cover the weakside without giving up the middle. Further movement will depend on the proper anticipation. X_2 may also want to come up to position himself in the weakside rebounding area. He can do this as long as he has his man blocked off and he is following the flight of the ball. If he anticipates a long rebound he may want to retrace his steps and react to the ball taking a hard bounce off the rim.

There is one more point we make to our players at this time regarding the rebounding triangle and the defensive rebounding positions. Again it is an ideal goal but we feel it is an effective teaching point. On our home floor at the University of Missouri the lane area is completely gold contrasting to the grey color outside the lane areas. For positioning purposes on the rebound we tell our players to keep the offense out of the gold. If this can be accomplished or even nearly accomplished the defense will be assured of gaining control of the rebound. Mainly we are setting an easily recognizable standard for our players; a standard that is more difficult than what is actually necessary. If the players concentrate on accomplishing this goal, good block outs and excellent rebounding position should result.

The Block Out

The first point we want to get across in teaching the block out is that there is no need to stay in the block out position for an extended period of time. The idea is to get your man off, keep him off for an instant, and then react to the flight of the ball and the anticipated direction of the rebound. We have already discussed the short period of time that will elapse between the ball leaving the shooters hands and rebounding off the rim. Usually a very brief block out is all that is needed for the player who has developed a nose for the basketball. We instruct our players to make contact with their individual opponent by the use of a front pivot or a reverse pivot. The contact will be made with the rear and the lower back (Fig. 8-2). We do not want our players to push the opponent back once inside position is gained. This is a sure way to incur a foul on the block out. We teach the players to apply the same amount of strength or pressure that is being applied by the opponent. If the opposing player is trying to push our man under then he must use the same amount of force to hold his position. If there is no pressure from the opponent; if he is content to stay behind, then we do not want our player to apply any type of pressure to drive him further back.

The player executing the block out must be in a strong, balanced position and he must be pepared to move in any

FIG. 8-2

Rebounding 283

FIG. 8-3

FIG. 8-4

direction to continue the block out or go after the ball (see Figure 8-2). A good offensive rebounder will try to avoid the block out and find an open avenue to the basket. The defensive player has to be able to slide in either direction so that his inside position is maintained. To accomplish this the defensive rebounder must have his weight evenly distributed over both feet. The heels should be touching the ground for balance and to facilitate a position of strength but the weight should be up on the balls of the feet. The player does not go up on the toes because his weight will be too far forward, eliminating his strength on a push from behind. There is always going to be contact in the rebounding area. The players have to maintain a stance that will enable them to handle the usual give and take without losing their balance or positioning.

We teach the front pivot and the reverse pivot early in our practice sessions and show the players exactly where each method of executing the block out will be most effective. We want to develop some fundamental soundness in the players early in the practices. After introducing and working for a few practices on the fundamental pivots we will allow the players to utilize the techniques that are most comfortable to each individual. There now must be an increased emphasis on getting the job done. We tell the players very honestly that it doesn't matter how their man was blocked off as long as he stays off the boards long enough for the defense to gain control of the rebound. We are talking only about techniques within the rules and within the game of basketball. We are not advocating, nor will we allow, unfair play to gain an advantage. We have already discussed throughout this chapter the contact that will be inevitable and the aggressiveness that is necessary to be an excellent rebounder and a successful rebounding team. A certain amount of contact and aggressive play is very much a part of the game of basketball.

The front pivot can be executed off of either foot and is illustrated in the photos to the left (Figures 8-3 and 8-4). The front pivot is most effective in blocking out the shooter and the players outside the post area on the ballside. The defensive rebounder is merely crossing his leg in front of the opponent and establishing contact with his rear or lower back. The player must be sure to initiate contact with the offensive rebounder. If the defender makes the pivot without getting his rear into the opponent, the offensive player could slide by on either side before he has time to react. The slight contact made on the block out allows the defender to feel the actions of the opposing player. If the opponent is attempting to avoid the block out the defensive player can tell which way he is cutting and can slide to maintain inside positioning. Another technique we teach our players is to utilize the arm bar while the pivot is being executed. This allows the defensive player to feel the offensive rebounder until the contact is initiated with the rear. As soon as the shot is attempted the arm should go to the opponent's chest but with only slight pressure. We work with the players until this becomes a natural movement while executing the front pivot. Once the rear makes contact with the opponent's body the hands and arms are up ready to react to the ball. The use of the arm bar is especially important in blocking out the shooter. While only slight pressure is applied with the forearm there is an element of distraction that can sometimes affect the shooter's concentration. Certain players can't help but react to what amounts to an elbow placed in their chest every time they finish their shot.

The reverse pivot on the block out can also be made off of either foot and is used most effectively on the helpside and in the post areas. It is also effective when an offensive player has made a quick move to the basket and is on the defender's side before the defensive player has time to make the front pivot. This relationship is illustrated in the accompanying photographs (Figures 8-5 thru 8-7). The offensive player has made the first move to the basket and has the initial advantage. It would be ridiculous for the defensive player to execute a front pivot while the opponent is already at his side. However, a reverse pivot off the left foot leaves the defender in perfect inside position. The pivot is executed by swinging the leg opposite the opponent back toward the basket and reversing into the block out position. The pivot foot is determined by the direction the offensive player takes in attempting to avoid the block out. In the sequence of photos the offensive rebounder has cut to the baseline side so the defender makes the reverse pivot off the foot closest to the baseline. If the offensive player was to make his move in the opposite direction the defender would pivot off the outside foot and reverse with the leg nearest the baseline.

The reverse pivot has to become fundamental to the post players because they will be required to play on the side of the offensive post player much of the time. When the shot is attempted the reverse pivot must be utilized or the defender will be blocking out air while the offensive player has a clear path to the basket. We mentioned in Chapter Five that the defensive post man has to keep his back foot behind the offensive player (see Fig. 5-11). If this condition is not met the reverse pivot will be rendered just as ineffective as the front pivot because the opponent will already have inside position. We work very hard with the post men on the footwork involved in blocking out properly.

The defenders on the helpside will be positioned in the middle of the floor slightly open to the ball. When the shot is attempted they can usually get back to their man and follow the flight of the ball by using the reverse pivot. A front pivot can be utilized on the helpside but the defender will be turning his back to the ball and will have no way of anticipating the rebound. Keeping

FIG. 8-5

FIG. 8-6

FIG. 8-7

the opponent off the board is the most important consideration, however.

We encourage the players around the basket and on the ballside to execute the front pivot. The advantage lies in the fact that we are making the first move and immediately setting ourselves up on the inside. We feel that the initial reaction after the shot goes up is very important in determining the rebounder. The reverse pivot is necessary if the offensive player has made the first move or in the situations we mentioned above but the front pivot allows the defender to set the ground rules. In executing the reverse pivot the defensive player is reacting to the actions of his opponent instead of vice-versa. We want to be the aggressor in every phase of the game, especially the rebounding phase. To accomplish this, we must make the first move and force the opposing players to react to our position. Again, the bottom line is getting the job done. The above fundamentals will be stressed early and the players should develop each technique and the instinct to select the right technique for the right situation.

We do not set a hard and fast rule as to the direction we want our players to take the offensive rebounders. In other words, we don't teach them to block out toward the baseline or force the offense to the middle of the floor. Basically, the defender is to read the intentions (through the body contact) of the offensive player and slide to cut off his movement to the basket. We want to keep the offensive rebounder out of the gold no matter which direction he takes to the basket. We feel that it would be a mistake to try and force a player into the middle when he is attempting to get to the boards on the baseline side. A defender trying to force this type of action will end up fouling or blocking air while his man gets to the basket. The reason we bring this up, however, is that we do make our players aware of the advantages if the offensive rebounders do get bunched in the middle. We tell them that if the opponent tries to move to the middle we merely want to force him further into the middle while still maintaining inside position. The congestion in the middle should help keep the offensive players out of the play. There are a lot of bodies in that type of situation and since the defense should already have inside position it will be extremely tough for an offensive rebounder to get through to the boards. The other important advantages have to do with the quarter turn to the outside and the outlet pass of the defensive rebounder. With the players bunched in the middle the rebounders should be sure to make their quarter turn to the outside in going up for the ball. This will keep the rebounder's body between the ball and the opposing players. He will be turning away from the pressure on the inside to maintain a very strong rebounding position. There should also be a clear lane for the quick outlet pass because of the congestion in the middle. Finally, the opposing team may have trouble making the quick conversion because of the congestion. We want our players to be aware of these things because the situation may arise during the game. We will not purposely force the offense to rebound to the middle but we will take advantage of any tendencies on their part to become congested in that area. If an offensive rebounder insists on going to the baseline side for the rebound the defender should maintain contact and push the opponent further under the basket. Inside position must be maintained in this situation. If the defender has executed properly the offensive player should be too far underneath to be a factor on the rebound. It is important that the defensive man follows the flight of the ball so that he can react back for the rebound at the proper time.

We emphasize a final point with regard to the block out and rebounding position that has to do with the individual responsibility of each player to keep his particular opponent off the boards. We stress to the players that if each player does his job properly and efficiently we are going to control the defensive backboard. If one player lets down or if a different player fails to do his job each time down the floor we are going to allow the second and third shots that will cost us the game. Every player must concentrate on his own individual responsibilities if the team is to benefit.

Helpside Rebounding

We have already mentioned that the first priority as far as developing our defensive rebounding will be the helpside positions. Diagram 8-3 shows a defensive guard (X_1) and a defensive forward (X_2) positioned on the helpside with the ball situated on the right side of the floor facing in toward the basket. When the shot is attempted from this alignment the helpside players have to hustle to maintain inside positioning for the rebound. This is especially true if the opposing player is adept at going to or crashing the offensive boards. The responsibilities of the forward in this situation are very crucial. He must keep his man off the boards and establish himself opposite the shot as part of our rebound triangle. The guard must first keep his man off and then position himself around the free throw line for the tip out or the long rebound.

This is the alignment from which we will run our first live rebounding drill. Up until now we have concerned ourselves with very fundamental drills involving the blocking out and rebounding techniques. We like to break down our rebounding into helpside and ballside situations. During a segment of practice set aside for rebounding, we will usually run the helpside rebounding at one basket and the ballside rebounding at the opposite end. At the proper time we will combine the drills to include both.

In the above alignment the coach will shoot the ball with the two defensive players reacting properly to their rebounding responsibilities on the helpside. We must stress again that the main concern in keeping a man off the boards is getting the

DIA. 8-3

job done. We want the players working on the footwork we have taught but we are not going to insist on exactness if the player is executing successfully. X_2 in this situation should, ideally, follow the flight of the ball as he moves to the side of the lane to intercept his man going to the boards. He should pick up and watch his man out of the corner of his eye. As the offensive forward (O_2) nears the lane area X_2 should reverse off of his right foot swinging the left leg back toward the baseline and making contact with the advancing offensive player. By utilizing the reverse pivot method the defensive player should be able to give adequate attention to both his man and the ball as it nears the basket and the rebound area. The defensive forward must react quickly to get to the side of the lane for the block out. If you will remember our goal is to keep all offensive players out of the gold or the lane area in going after the defensive rebound. From a position at the side of the lane our rebounder can block his man off or go after the ball if the opposing player has not responded back to the boards. For our drill purposes we want both offensive players crashing the boards so that the defenders are required to block out properly. At times during the practice sessions we will have the offensive players hold position rather than going to the boards each time. The players must be able to recognize this development and should not waste time waiting for the block out. After a defensive player recognizes that his man is out of position and away from the boards he should assume his regular rebounding position and react to the ball and the direction of the rebound. The helpside forward would go to the rebounding triangle position opposite the shot. The helpside guard would move to the middle of the floor for the long rebound if he is our rebounding guard. During this drill all of the guards will have long rebounding responsibilities. It is important for the players to move to these positions when their individual opponent is out of the play so that another offensive player does not slip into the inside of our triangle. Remember, the ball will be rebounded in less than a second so it is unnecessary to go to the outside area to execute the block out. The idea when this situation occurs is to go after the ball aggressively after anticipating the direction of the rebound.

The helpside guard (X_1) should be in a position slightly open to the ball as the shot is executed. His responsibility then is to drop to the free throw line while watching the weakside guard out of the corner of his eye. If the offensive guard is coming to the boards X_1 must reverse pivot off of his right foot, swing the left leg back and initiate contact outside the gold or lane area. Once contact is made the defensive rebounder must react immediately to the ball or position himself for the outlet it a teammate has already gained possession of the rebound. The guard in this position should also be ready to react quickly to any loose balls that result from the rebounding battle.

The above responsibilities will always depend on the distance maintained between the defender and his offensive counterpart. For the most part, the defenders will be applying helpside principles so should be off and toward the ball and away from their man. In that case the above techniques would be the most effective. However, if an offensive player closes the distance between his corresponding defender as the shot is executed a different approach must be put into effect. This type of relationship will call for the same block out technique that will be executed on the ballside. Notice in Diagram 8-4 that the weakside players closing the distance to their defenders will actually be moving into ballside territory one pass away from the ball handler. In that event the defense must also move to close the distance and assume a denial position.

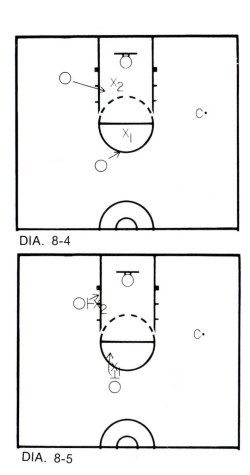

DIA. 8-4

DIA. 8-5

The above means simply that the block out technique utilized will depend on the distance between the two opposing players. If the distance is considerable (Dia. 8-3) the defender will establish position and keep the offensive player out of the gold. There is no need to move out on the floor to make contact if the offensive player does not go to the boards. On the other hand, immediate contact should be employed if the offensive player is in a position close to the defender (Dia. 8-4). The idea is to get the opponent on your back as soon as the shot is executed, thus establishing immediate inside position. Contact is held momentarily and then the defender reacts to the shot and the ball coming off the rim. We discuss these ideas with regard to our weakside rebounding because of the realtionship described above and because of the possibility of a player being out of position on the helpside. This is obviously not a situation we encourage but during the course of the game it is going to happen a few times and we want our players to understand their responsibilities when it does occur. If X_1 or X_2 were caught out on the floor (Dia. 8-5) when the shot is executed they would need to make immediate contact with their man and then come back to the basket for the rebound. The front or the reverse pivot could be utilized and the rear should make contact with the opponent's upper legs or the waist area. Contact is maintained only long enough to pick up the flight of the shot and read the rebounding direction and distance. The player must then make a strong, aggressive play for possession of the rebound.

To add some movement to the drill we will place another coach or a manager in the corner and will move the ball back and forth so that the defense must change position. This will also cause the defense to gauge the rebounding possibilities from two different shot angles and two different types of shots.

Ballside Rebounding

Diagram 8-6 shows the drill alignment we will set up to develop our rebounding on the ballside. A third offensive

DIA. 8-6

player replaces the coach because we want to include in this drill the technique for blocking out the shooter. We place a rebounding ring on the basket because we never want one of our players shooting to miss.

When the shot goes up we want our players to instinctively move for the block out. An offensive player that anticipates the shot and makes the first move to the boards will usually wind up with inside position or at least equal position for the rebound. The defender, however, should already be in a position between the offensive player and the basket. If he acts immediately upon execution of the shot inside position should be guaranteed. We must emphasize again that the contact on the block out will only be maintained for an instant. The closer the player is to the basket, however, the longer the defender will be required to hold his block out. The players around the rebound triangle or the basket area must hold their position until they are able to make a strong, aggressive play for the ball coming off the rim. If they release for the ball too early their offensive counterpart will also be able to go after the ball aggressively. The players must remember that as long as they maintain a body position between their opponent and the ball the offensive player's rebounding effectiveness is going to be severely limited. This is why we want our players to maintain a position of strength even as they go after the basketball. The players are taught to use the entire body throughout the rebounding process. The application of strength and protection of the ball are crucial elements in developing the proper rebounding habits.

We begin our ballside rebounding drill with the shot being executed from the wing position. The corresponding player (X_1 in the diagram) must contest the shot, execute the block out properly, and then move into the free throw line area for the tip out or the long rebound. As the shot passes his fingertips, X_1 should glance the shooters chest with an armbar and should execute the front pivot off of the foot opposite his armbar. In other words, if the right hand is utilized to contest the shot the right arm will form the arm bar as the defender comes back to the floor. Immediately, he will swing his right leg across his body and into the offensive player. The left foot will be the pivot foot. The opposite relationship would occur if the left hand were used to contest the shot. The player must get his rear into the shooter and should attempt to pick up the flight of the ball as he is making his pivot. The defender then judges the direction and the distance of the rebound as he moves into the free throw line area. We should note at this point that the long rebounder does not disregard his man and the ball to set up at the free throw line. He is reacting to the ball after executing the block out on his man. He would not go to the free throw line if the ball looked to be rebounding to his immediate area. The player will also be on his toes ready to move in any direction to go after the ball. Finally, he will not follow a direct route to the free throw line but one which will maintain his position between the offensive guard and the ball (Dia. 8-7).

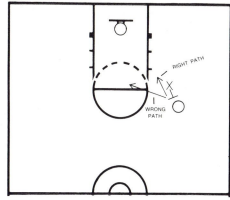

DIA. 8-7

The defensive forward (X_2 in Dia. 8-6) must keep his man off and move to the low rebounding position on the ball side of the basket. X_2 should be denying the pass to the forward with the ball at the wing and the offensive forward within twenty-one feet of the basket. The right leg and the right arm of the defender would be up in the passing lane with the left leg back. From this position X_2 could execute a reverse pivot off of the back foot or he could bring the left leg across his body for a front pivot. The important thing is that the defensive man does not turn his back to the ball to execute the block out. He must keep his man off while picking up the flight of the ball as it leaves the shooter's hands. After making contact with his opponent and maintaining that contact for an instant, X_2 would move to the boards anticipating the direction of the rebound.

The footwork we have been discussing is probably most important for the defensive player in the middle of the floor. He has a difficult task in denying the ball to the post man and yet maintaining inside position for the rebound. We have explained previously that the defensive post player must play on the high or the low side of his man depending on the position of his opponent. The X-move (see Figures 5-12 and 5-13) must be utilized to change from the high to the low side or vice versa. The key to gaining or maintaining the advantage on the block out is to keep the back foot between the offensive post player and the basket when denying the pass. When employing the X-move the defensive man must utilize the proper footwork and excellent quickness so that he can re-establish his back foot before the offense attempts a shot.

When the shot is attempted the post player should immediately execute the reverse pivot off of his back foot. This would be the right foot with the ball at or below the free throw line extended. The left foot would be the pivot foot with the ball above the free throw line extended. Anticipation is of the utmost importance in gaining position around the basket area. The defensive post player cannot allow his opponent to get by him on the inside. The shot must be anticipated and the defender must react quickly to execute the block out and go after the ball. The defensive player again has the goal of keeping the offensive rebounder out of the gold. This is a difficult proposition and certainly not mandatory from a position this close to the basket. The players keeping the goal in mind, however, should lead to excellent rebounding position. We exphasize this idea in the practice sessions because we want to develop some practice situations that are more difficult than what will occur in the game.

In executing the reverse pivot the post player should follow the flight of the ball back over the corresponding shoulder of his pivot foot. In other words, he will follow the ball over his right shoulder when pivoting off of the right foot and vice-versa. This will allow the defender to watch the ball even as he is making initial contact on the block out. When the player feels he has determined the direction and the distance of the rebound he should go after the ball aggressively but with timing. The player in this position should especially be careful to keep his body between the ball and his opponent. The offensive post player is close to the basket and the rebound area and any mistake in timing or positioning can result in an offensive rebound and a quick two points by the opposition.

The second stage of this drill is to execute the shot from the forward position on the baseline and then to move the ball back and forth with the shot executed from either position. The fundamental responsibilities remain the same but the players are required to shift position according to the movement of the ball. The defensive players at the wing and baseline positions must contest every shot before executing their responsibilities for the block out and the defensive rebound. The players will also rotate to the different positions in each of the aforementioned drills so that they become familiar with the different responsibilities and assignments.

After a period of time we will combine the helpside and the ballside rebounding drills into a five on five situation emphasizing the block out and encouraging the players to rebound aggressively. The drill will stop after the rebound because we want all of our emphasis on the block out and gaining possession of the ball. We will usually follow the five on five rebounding drill, however, with our five on five fast break drill so that the players understand the normal flow of our attack after the defensive rebound. Once into the fast break drill the players must continue to execute the fundamentals of the block out or the opportunity to fast break will not materialize. The coaches will be watching closely to see that the players do not neglect their responsibilities in this area.

When combining the drills to form our five on five rebounding drill we must designate one of the guards as our primary ball handler and the other becomes the long rebounder in the middle of the floor. The second guard's position in the middle of the floor will depend on the floor position of his offensive counterpart when the shot is attempted. The offensive guard must be kept off the boards first and then the defensive second guard can look for the long rebound or position himself as close to the middle of the floor as possible. The majority of the time the offensive guard should be somewhere near the free throw line extended or the middle of the floor. This will allow our rebounding guard to execute the block out and then move to the center as shown in Diagram 8-7. If, however, the offensive guard is along the baseline or underneath the basket as the shot is attempted the defensive guard must be sure to keep him out of the rebounding area. The defender would then be able to cheat toward the middle of the floor but he could not leave his man to position himself in the middle. Obviously, if the guard were part of the rebound triangle he would hold his inside position until the ball was rebounded.

By designating one of the guards as our primary ball handler we have defined the guard responsibilities on positioning themselves for the outlet pass (see Diagrams 4-1 and 4-2). The primary ball handler will move quickly to the top of the key after making sure his man is away from the basket or the rebounding area. The corresponding opponent in this situation will usually have safety responsibilities so this will allow a player to get to the top of the key without too much worry about the block out and rebound. The ball handling guard must be certain his man is not going to the boards before he sets up in the outlet area. This is especially true if a shot is attempted while these two players are near the basket or along the baseline. In that case our guard must block his man out and then react to the ball. If the opponent leaves immediately to get back on defense the guard can move for the most advantageous outlet area but he must be aware of the ball and the direction of the rebound. The long rebounder becomes our secondary ball handler in terms of setting up the outlet and initiating the fast break.

An additional point that we will introduce at this time covers the possibility of our defense being spread so that our rebounding and floor balance is altered. All of our players should develop a good understanding of the rebound triangle and an ability to recognize the floor position of our players as the shot is attempted. This will come with repeated drilling in a five on five rebounding situation. We scatter the defense and have them react back to the rebound from different positions on the floor. We feel it is very important that in this, as well as many other phases of the game, the players develop a feel for the floor positions of their teammates. Many times the players must react to cover for a teammate who has been forced out of position by a mistake or by the natural flow of the game. By drilling on these situations in practice our players should be well prepared for their occurrence under game conditions. The idea is to have the rebounding area well protected by forming the triangle as quickly as possible. If the offense has scattered our defense, the players (essentially the front line players and the rebounding or second guard) must find an open position in the rebound triangle or move to the middle for the long rebound.

We feel that offensive rebounding is sometimes a very neglected phase of the game as far as teaching and coaching is concerned. One of the five principles on which our offensive

Offensive Rebounding

system is based is that we end up with optimum rebounding strength on any shot taken. We definitely want our three front line players crashing the offensive boards and we will also send our big guard to the boards against a team that does not employ the fast break as a general rule. Many teams give up the offensive boards because they feel the defense has a decided advantage as far as gaining inside position. While this is basically true the offense does have some very important advantages that we make our players aware of when we are at the offensive end. The first advantage is that of knowing where the shots are coming within our offense. This understanding is illustrated in Chapter Three with the diagrams that we issue to our players detailing the scoring opportunities from each position. While the defense has been taught to anticipate, the offensive team has to have better anticipation because of their knowledge of the offense and the shots that will result off the different options. We teach the players to make the first move toward rebounding position when they feel a shot is about to be executed. Many defensive rebounders will turn their heads to the basket as soon as the shooter releases the ball. This is the perfect opportunity for the offensive player to slip inside the defender for excellent rebounding position. We mentioned earlier that the first step is usually the most important in determing inside position for the rebound. The worst thing that an offensive player can do as the shot is attempted is to stand still or retreat to the other end assuming the shot will be successful. The great rebounders and great rebounding teams always assume that the shot will be missed. Anticipation is the key.

The second advantage that the offensive players' possess is a knowledge of their teammates' shooting abilities and shooting tendencies. This is another strong indication of the importance of teamwork and getting to know each other's strengths and weaknesses. If applied properly, this knowledge will certainly lead to better offensive board play on the part of a hustling, aggressive rebounder. The above advantages go hand in hand and should become second nature by the time the season gets under way.

Movement and split second reaction after the shot attempt are important along with anticipation and the application of the above offensive advantages. If you take a look at all of the great offensive rebounders you will find that they exhibit excellent movement around the basket area. This is an element of a player's aggressiveness that will help in developing in the player a nose for the basketball. They are making something happen rather than waiting for an opportunity to come their way.

After anticipating the rebound and making the initial movement for position we teach our players to get to one side or the other of the defensive rebounder. That is if the defender has already gained inside positioning. We do not want our offensive players standing behind the defenders and attempting to gain control of the ball from this position. The tendency in this situation is to push the defensive player from behind or go over his back for the rebound. The great majority of the time this will result in a foul being called on the offensive rebounder. In fighting for position we want our players to use their body rather than the hands and arms. This is another advantage of bringing the hands to shoulder height in preparation for the rebound. With the hands at shoulder height there is much less risk of a foul being committed while trying to establish a good, strong position for the rebound.

Another method we teach in offensive rebounding is to step back away from the rebounding area to facilitate a running jump as the ball comes off the rim. This will enable the offensive rebounder to gather some momentum thus increasing his vertical jump and his chances for possession. Usually this manuever will only entail a step or two back and the player must do an excellent job of anticipating the direction of the rebound. The player must also be careful to avoid going over the back or crashing into any defensive rebounders as he goes after the basketball. Once he plants his foot for the takeoff, the player should jump as straight in the air as possible in his attempt to gain control of the ball. If there is sufficient contact to warrant a whistle the call will usually favor the player who has gone straight up for the basketball. This is especailly true if the player who has gone straight up does actually gain possession of the rebound.

It is important for the offensive rebounders to maintain vision on the ball at all times. We do not want them to turn their vision away from the ball in going to the boards because the shooter may elect to pass the ball at the last instant. This is sometimes an excellent pass for the ball handler to make because the defenders may have turned to the basket without maintaining vision on the ball. They will be unaware of the additional pass so will have left their man open for the higher percentage shot. By maintaining vision the offensive players will also be able to follow the flight of the ball to the basket when the shot is executed. As we have already discussed in relation to defensive rebounding, this is very important in determining the direction of the rebound and the timing necessary for the jump. The players should continue to keep their eyes on the ball throughout the rebounding process. This idea is similar to the principles involved in the execution of the lay up. In executing the lay up the shooter must keep his eyes on the basket at all times. If the shooter looks away from the basket to a defender or toward a teammate concentration on the target will be lost. The rebounder must focus his concentration on the basketball as it comes off the rim. While the player should be aware of his position around the basket and the position of the other players his immediate goal is possession of the basketball. We tell our players to reach for the bottom of the ball with both hands whenever possible. There are going to be times when an offensive player does well to get one hand on the ball or is able only to keep the ball in play by tipping it back toward the basket. For the most part, however, we want our offensive rebounders going after the ball in a position of strength with both hands firmly grasping the leather. When this is not possible we very much encourage the tipping of the ball back up toward the basket. Through good strength and control in the fingers and wrists the offensive player may be able to tip the ball in for two points. At the very least the ball is kept in play and the longer it is kept in play the better our chances will be for possession if we are rebounding aggressively. We will also encourage our players to tip the ball away from the basket area if they are unable to gain possession and are completely out of position for an offensive tip to the basket. We refer to this as a tip out and it is something we look for extensively when we are at the free throw line. That will be explained fully when we discuss special situations. For now we are looking at the tip out basically as a last resort. We would much rather gain outright possession or tip toward the basket but the tip out is an effective third choice. The man executing the tip out must be sure that he is not tipping the ball away from a teammate who is in a good position for the rebound. Usually the tip out will be attempted when a defensive rebounder is sure to gain control of the ball or when there are a number of defensive players in excellent position for the rebound. The idea is to tip the ball in the direction of an offensive teammate and when that is not possible to put the ball up for grabs out on the floor. If we are playing aggressively and reacting to the ball we should control our share of these loose ball or long rebounding situations. Because of our rebound triangle and the designated responsibilities of our other two players the tipper should have a good idea of the floor positions that his teammates are occupying. This will help in his attempt to make an accurate tip out in the direction of one of those teammates. We mentioned above the strength and control that are needed in the fingers and wrists to insure accurate tipping. The fingers and wrists are extremely important in almost all fundamental aspects of the game that involve the ball. Along with the strength development we will discuss with regard to conditioning we also require our players to do a lot of fingertip push ups. We especially encourage the players to do these on their own during the months out of season. Additional work on the wrists and the fingers is done with a brick drill we discovered this year and with our rebounder. Both of these along with some beneficial tipping drills will be further explained at the end of this chapter.

If one of the offensive players is able to gain control of the rebound we encourage him to take the ball right back up without any wasted motion or time. The key is remaining in a position of strength and exercising good judgement on the shot attempt. There are no percentages in putting up a hope shot from an unbalanced position or shooting too quickly from a position away from the basket. In this situation we would want to pull the ball back out and look for a better shot. The quick second or third shot off the offensive rebound is encouraged when the ball is controlled in immediate proximity to the basket and when the rebounder is in a strong, balanced position. This type of position is another advantage that can result from the player jumping straight up in the air to control the basketball. The player rebounding the ball in this manner will have his legs under him and will be able to put the ball right back up in one motion if the opening is there. At times a ball fake and/or a head and shoulder fake can precede the quick move back up for the shot. This will depend on the defense and the defenders that are in the basket area and on the relative size and strength of the rebounder. Very rarely do we want our players to try and finesse the ball into the basket. We never want them to try and avoid the contact around the basket by changing their shot. What we are basically describing and teaching our players is a power move to the basket. We want them to take the ball right back to the hole. We feel that the worst thing that can happen with this type of aggressive attitude is that the opponent will be forced to foul and we will go to the free throw line with no basket. The best thing that can happen if we execute properly is a successful three point play. When a player changes his shot and tries to finesse the ball into the basket he will likely avoid the foul but he is also liable to miss the shot attempt. The offensive rebound will therefore go for naught. If the offensive rebounder does not have his legs under his body we want him to gather himself quickly for a strong power move or a power move after a good ball and/or head and shoulder fake to the basket. We never want our players in this situation to hurry the shot from an off balance position. The players must show good judgement based on an awareness of the defensive players around the basket area.

One of the most important assets that a rebounder can possess, especially an offensive rebounder, is the ability to jump two, three or even four times in succession without losing his strength or efficiency. The second or third effort is often times the most important in terms of gaining control of the ball. With the congestion around the basket area, and with both teams rebounding aggressively, the ball may be kept alive so that the player who is quickest and strongest on the additional jumps will have the advantage. This is certainly an ability that can be developed or improved with some hard work and diligence. The quickness of the jump must especially be emphasized and improved upon. The player in this type of rebounding situation will not have time to gather himself or bend the knees further in an effort to increase the height of his

FIG. 8-8

jump. All chance for the rebound will be lost while the player is gathering himself. We teach our players to jump quickly by making a quick flex of the knee and extending the plantar flexion of the feet on the jump (Fig. 8-8). Repeated jumping to the rim and to the backboard are excellent for developing the quickness and endurance necessary for this type of rebounding.

Our ideal offensive rebounding positions are shown to the side in Diagram 8-8. We always want at least three players around the immediate basket area in somewhat of a rebound triangle just like the defense. The difference is that the offensive players are looking for an open avenue to the basket if they were unable to gain inside position at first. The fourth player with rebounding responsibilities positions himself in the middle of the floor and is ready to react in either direction for a loose ball or long rebound. This player has one-half rebound and one-half defensive responsibilities. He will play the outlet if the opponent gains possession of the ball as discussed in the section on converting from offense to defense in Chapter Seven. However, we will also give this player the option of going to the boards at least part of the time. This will depend greatly on the fast breaking tendencies of our opponent and on our ability to stop their fast break attack. We feel that under certain conditions we can send four men to the boards without jeopardizing our defensive position at the other end. To accomplish this we must have a very smart protector who has been schooled in defensing the opposition when out-numbered. The other players must realize the importance of smothering the outlet and hustling back as fast as possible once the opponent initiates the fast break. Obviously, we would be cautious about sending four players to the offensive boards against a team that is quicker than we are or one that relies heavily on their fast break attack.

Our philosophy on looking to send four men to the offensive boards evolves from our ideas on aggressive play and continually applying pressure to our opponents. Why should we give up and settle back into defense at the opposite end? The more we can keep the ball in our offensive end of the floor the greater our chances will be for victory. We want to increase our opportunities for high percentage shots and baskets while limiting the scoring opportunities of our opponents. This idea can carry over to a man to man or zone press situation. The goal is to keep the ball in our end of the floor as much as possible. This philisophy again is very much subject to the scouting reports and game plans that we devise for each particular opponent. We must determine and take into consideration their speed and their ability to generate a successful fast break attack.

We will always designate one of the guards as our safety or protector at the defensive end. His sole responsibility on any shot attempt in the offensive end is to get back and protect

DIA. 8-8

our defensive basket. He has no rebounding responsibilities. Even if he has driven to the basket or has taken his own shot from the baseline the designated safety must get out of the traffic and set up as far back as the deepest offensive player. The second guard or rebounding guard should always be alert to cover for the safety in case he is caught out of position but we do not want this to happen very often.

The second guard will generally be the one-half rebounder-one-half defender positioned in the middle of the floor. From here the guard will be looking to fill any open spots around the rebounding area or will crash the boards as the fourth rebounder. We have found that the opposing guards are often very lax about keeping their man off the boards. They have less experience in this area and do not concentrate on the block out as well as the front line players. This is another reason we like to send our big guard in as an additional rebounder. We want to take advantage of the guards failure to block out defensively. We can even take advantage of this situation against an excellent fast breaking team by sending our guard to the boards all the time and requiring one of our forwards to drop back for defensive purposes. All of our rebounders, but especially the second guard (or long rebounder, if other than the second guard) should recognize when the weakside rebounding position is open. We have mentioned previously the importance of the rebounding area opposite the shooter and we always want a player in a position to work that side of the boards. If any one of our players, with the execption of the safety, recognizes that the weakside rebounding position is open, he should get there as quickly as possible while following the flight of the ball to the basket.

The three positions in the rebound triangle will usually be filled by the front line players but this can depend on the relative floor positions of the players at the time of the shot. We work as a team on the rebounding possibilities that will occur according to the shots from within our offense. We do the same with regard to our zone offense (see Chapter Three) but make sure that the players realize that we are only establishing some guidelines that will help them concentrate more on the offensive boards. We also feel that by working on the rebounding possibilities in our practice sessions we are better coordinating the efforts of our players and adding to the general organization of our team We are basically showing the movements that can occur under game conditions and the rebounding positions that can result. In this way the players will be able to recognize and react quicker to their offensive rebounding opportunities in a live situation.

There are two important points that we should discuss before beginning to diagram the offensive rebounding possibilities that can occur within our offense. One is our feeling on requiring the shooter to follow his shot. As a general rule we do not like for a shooter out on the floor to follow his shot for the rebound. The exception occurs when the player immediately recognizes that his shot is off just after release and he has a good idea of the direction of the rebound. It would be advantageous for the shooter to move for the rebound in that situation because of his knowledge of the rebound possibilities and the fact that he has already made his mistake on the shot. We feel very strongly that confidence is one of the most important elements in shooting the ball successfully. Therefore, we want our players shooting the ball knowing that the ball is going to end up in the basket. Their purpose is to shoot the ball down. There is no thought of a miss or a responsibility to follow the shot if the shot is unsuccessful. We want our shooters to be able to return to the floor in a comfortable position and without pressure to move to a rebound area. The shooter (out on the floor) will usually move to the middle of the floor looking to become the fourth rebounder. The rebounding guard looks to fill a spot in the rebounding triangle. Any time the safety takes the shot he still has responsibility for protecting our defensive basket. The second guard will be ready to help whenever he recognizes that the safety is the shooter. Keep in mind that this philosophy involves a shot executed from an area outside the immediate vicinity of the basket. Any shot taken from near the basket area will obviously allow the shooter to be in a position for a possible rebound. We do not want the rebound to enter into his thinking but he is in position in case the shot is missed. A player near the basket area should always be ready to go back up a second and third time to keep possession of the ball.

The second point that we should mention involves a general rule that we like our players to follow so that we have a chance for good rebounding position on every shot executed in our offensive end. For the most part, we do not want one of our players shooting the ball while the other four players are getting to the offset or re-setting the basketball. This does not mean that we can never shoot the basketball in this type of situation. If an opportunity presents itself we certainly want our players to take immediate advantage of the opening. We also want them to have the confidence to act when given an avenue to the basket. The point is that if the shot is not a high percentage one we should continue running the offense and look for a better shooting opportunity and better rebounding strength on the shot. This is just another example of the importance of teamwork in the game of basketball.

Organization of Our Offensive Rebounding

We will show in the following diagrams the rebounding responsibilities that can easily occur from the various shots in our offense. As mentioned these are to be taken as guidelines to make us a more effective offensive rebounding team. These rebounding possibilities are based on the scoring opportunities that we diagrammed in Chapter Three. Please refer back to Chapter Three if there are any questions regarding the offensive options we are describing. We will identify each of the rebounding diagrams in the following pages with the proper offensive series back in Chapter Three. Keep in mind the four series of movements that make up our offense once we are into the offset. These are; the post pass series, the corner pass series, the fourth man across series, and the reverse pass series. The rebounding responsibilities will remain basically the same in each particular series with slight variations depending on the shooter and the shot executed.

Post Pass Series (see Dia. 3-67)

There are several shooting options that can develop off of the pass into the post. Diagram 8-9 shows the post player turning the ball in and executing his shot from the medium post position. The weakside forward (O_3) should immediately recognize that the shot is going up and should move quickly to establish position on the weakside of the rebound triangle. He should continue to read the defense and the actions of his teammate in case his man leaves to provide help. The player at the diagonal (O_4) would be making his move to split the post and would continue his cut to set up a low rebounding position on the opposite side of the triangle. The corner man (O_2) would continue into the middle of the floor and look to crash the boards from that position. Both O_4 and O_2 should veer their cuts slightly when they recognize the post player turning the ball into the middle. They do not want to bring their men into the shooting area to cause additional congestion. The post player (O_5) should return to the floor comfortably after his shot and move into the middle for a possible rebound. O_1 is the designated safety and would drop back for defensive purposes after flaring to the weakside wing position. If O_1 were in the corner with O_2 at the point position the same rebounding responsibilities would be in effect. O_1 always has responsibility for getting back so he would immediately break for the defensive end when the shot is executed. O_2 would look to cover for O_1 but would then move into the middle rebounding position as quickly as possible.

The four remaining options in the post pass series would alter the rebounding action shown in the previous diagram only slightly. Diagram 8-10 shows the shot being executed from the wing position after a flare pass from the post. The only difference from the previous rebounding responsibilities is that the post player (O_5) would move quickly to the basket to fight the boards from the middle rebounding position. O_2 would become the fourth rebounder in the middle of the floor. O_3 and O_4 have the same responsibilities and O_1 would drop back on defense after returning to the floor comfortably on his shot. These same movements would be in effect if the

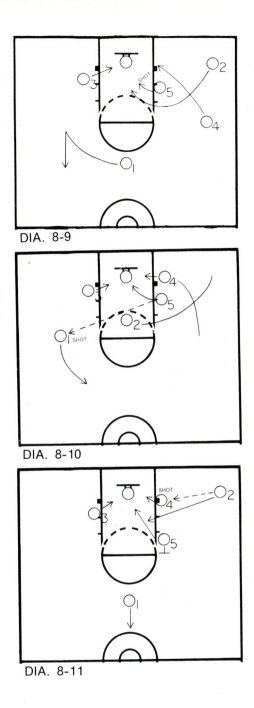

DIA. 8-9

DIA. 8-10

DIA. 8-11

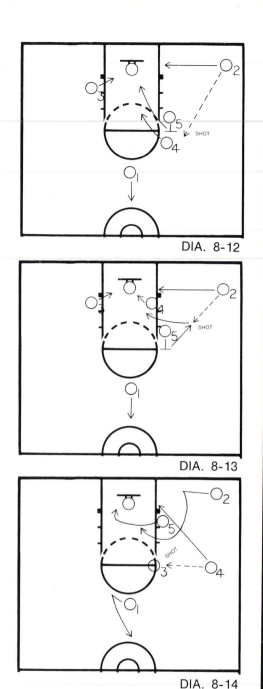

DIA. 8-12

DIA. 8-13

DIA. 8-14

ball were handed to O_4 or O_2 on the splitting action or if the post player dished the ball off to O_3 for the close in shot.

Corner Pass Series (see Dia. 3-73)

The basic cut off of the corner pass series is designed to generate a lay up or close in shot by the diagonal player. The proper rebounding positions that should evolve when this shot is executed are shown in Diagram 8-11. The only difference from the previous responsibilities is that O_5 must crash the boards from a position in the high post area. He and O_2 must really hustle if we are to have the desired rebounding strength on the shot by O_4.

If the cutter (O_4) elects to stop on top of the screen by O_5 and execute the shot from that position the corner player and the shooter must exchange rebounding respnsibilities (Dia. 8-12). O_2 would move quickly along the baseline to set up in the low rebounding position on the strongside. O_4 would return to the floor comfortably and become the fourth rebounder in the middle of the floor. The post player would hold his screen for the shooter and then move quickly to the middle of the rebound triangle as the shot is executed. O_3 and O_1 have the same responsibilities as previously shown.

Another possible option off this corner pass is the shot by the post man stepping to the ball after setting the screen (see dialogue accompanying Dia. 3-73). In this situation O_4 and O_5 would exchange rebounding responsibilities (Dia. 8-13). O_4 would move to the middle of the rebound triangle upon recognition of the shot attempt by the post player stepping to the ball. O_5 would move into a position as the long rebounder after concentration on the successful execution of the shot. All other movements would remain the same.

There are some additional options in the corner pass series that we will run when we have a guard positioned at the diagonal (see Dia 3-78). These involve a pass into the post and a wide angle splitting action that will put into effect the same rebounding possibilities we discussed in relation to the post pass series.

Fourth Man Across Series (see Dia. 3-79)

When we send the fourth man across the lane he is taught to face up to the basket immediately and look for the shot first. While looking for the shot the four man will recognize whether the post player is open rolling across the lane. Diagram 8-14 shows the rebounding action when the shot is executed by O_3 at the vertex of the free throw lane. We teach the post player to look for the pass until the shooter releases the shot and then to turn to the inside to set up at the weakside rebounding position. We want him turning to the inside so he can follow the flight of the ball and better anticipate the direction of the rebound. O_4 would make a

302 Rebounding

rebound cut instead of setting the downscreen for O_2 and O_2 would immediately make his rebound cut into the middle of the triangle upon recognition of the shot attempt. The shooter would look for the possible long rebound but is concentrating primarily on making the shot. O_1 would again be back for defensive purposes. If O_3 did dump the ball inside to O_5, O_3 would crash the boards with O_2 moving into the middle of the floor as the fourth rebounder.

The next option that is available is the pass to O_2 off the downscreen set by O_4. Diagram 8-15 shows the rebounding set up in this situation. O_5 and O_4 should each have a good chance at excellent offensive rebounding positions forming the base of the triangle. O_3 would move to the middle position as soon as he completed the pass to O_2 for the shot. O_2 is the long rebounder and O_1 is the protector. If O_2 is covered coming off the screen, O_3 would then look for the guard (O_1) flaring from the point position. The same rebounding responsibilities would follow with O_2 moving quickly into the middle since he is not shooting the ball. O_3 would crash the middle of the rebound triangle as soon as he made the pass out to O_1 on the wing. He should maintain vision on the ball as he steps to the basket in case he is open for the return pass.

Another option off the four man series is for the wing player to follow his pass instead of executing the downscreen for the corner man. This is a variation that should end up with a fifteen foot jump shot for the wing player because his defensive man may have reacted through habit to cover the downscreen. This option is explained in Diagram 3-87 back in Chapter Three. The corner player would now be responsible for establishing position on the strongside of the rebound triangle. All of the other players would make the same movements with O_3 crashing the middle as soon as he executed the western roll with O_4. O_4 would become the long rebounder on the fifteen foot jumper and our fourth rebounder if he elected to drive to the basket (Dia. 8-16).

If the defense denies the pass to O_3, the guard (O_1) may be open for the lob pass going backdoor on the weakside (see Dia. 3-80). This would be a play that would require the second guard to cover for our safety in protecting our defensive basket (Dia. 8-17). The post player's responsibilities would also differ in that he would be holding his position to keep the weakside cleared for the guard. He would then try to establish rebounding position on that same side of the basket. O_3 would follow the guard down the lane and rebound in the middle. The player who executed the lob (O_4 in this diagram) would move to the middle as the fourth rebounder. All of the players must react quickly to the boards because the shot will be executed very quickly.

We can also lob over the top to our post man if the defense

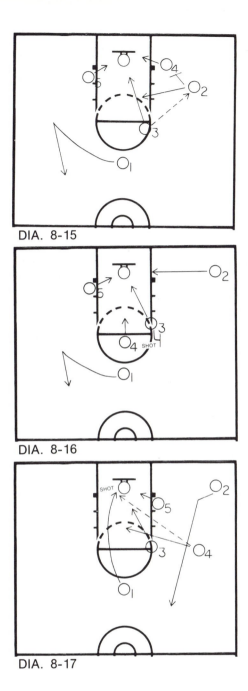

DIA. 8-15

DIA. 8-16

DIA. 8-17

DIA. 8-18

DIA. 8-19

DIA. 8-20

tries to totally front the post position (see Dia. 3-84). The four man breaks across to clear the weakside and the guard at the point holds position. The post player would then pin his man and the lob would be executed from the diagonal. The rebounding positions should resemble those shown in Diagram 8-16. The post player (O_5) remains in a position for a second effort rebound and shot in case his first attempt is unsuccessful. The corner player (O_2) would immediately break for the side of the rebound triangle when he recognized the probability of the lob. O_3 would move to the open spot on the rebound triangle depending on the position of O_5. The shot off the lob can be executed from the side of the basket or in the middle. O_3 must crash the boards looking for the open lane to the basket. After executing the lob pass O_4 would move into the middle of the floor to look for the tip out or the long rebound. O_1 has defensive responsibilities. Again the players must react quickly to the boards if we are to have anyone in position for a possible rebound.

Reverse Pass Series (see Dia. 3-92)

Diagram 8-18 shows one of the first options available when the ball is reversed from the diagonal to the point position. This is referred to as the point pass and the guard (O_1 in this case) immediately looks for his shot in an area around the top of the key. The other players must be reading the actions of the guard to determine their responsibilities. As soon as the weakside forward (O_3) recognizes that the shot is going up he would quickly move to establish his position on one side of the rebound triangle. The post player is rolling to the middle and will fight to control the middle rebounding position as soon as he is sure the point man is going up with the ball. The post man should always maintain his vision on the ball in case the guard decides to make the inside pass at the last instant. The player at the diagonal will screen on the baseline and continue to the basket to form the other side of the rebound triangle. The corner player comes off the screen and becomes the long rebounder in the middle of the floor. The same rebounding responsibilities would be in effect if the guard made the inside pass to O_5 rolling into the middle.

The next option available on the reverse pass series is the two man play on the weakside (see Dia. 3-95). The same basic rebounding responsibilities we have shown will apply if the guard shoots the ball off the screen and if he dishes the ball off to O_3 rolling to the basket (Dia. 8-19). If O_3 brings the ball back to O_2 coming off the downscreen the same rebounding options we illustrated in Diagram 8-15 will apply.

After reversing the ball to O_3 coming up the lane our guards are taught to read the defense and execute the basket cut if the defensive guard overreacts to the weakside (see Dia. 3-96). This is another option where the second guard must respond to the defensive end so that we are assured of defensive balance. This relationship is shown in Diagram 8-20. O_5 must clear the lane to give the guard an open avenue to the basket so he moves to establish position on one side of the basket. O_4 makes the same rebound cut as shown in previous diagrams. O_3 moves in as the fourth rebounder after making the pass to the guard. O_2 comes off the downscreen by O_4 and upon recognizing the cut to the basket by O_1, he immediately drops back to protect on defense.

An additional option in the reverse pass series is the weakside forward (O_3) popping out on the wing for a pass from the point player and a quick fifteen foot jump shot (see Dia. 3-97). The rebound possibilities on this shot are shown in Diagram 8-21. O_5 will be rolling completely across the lane looking for the pass from O_1 and then from O_3. He should fight for position on his side of the basket as soon as O_3 executes the shot. O_4 will make the same rebound cut as described previously. O_2 has the important responsibility of crashing the middle position of the rebound triangle. He must move quickly to the boards after accepting the downscreen from O_4. O_3 would move into the middle and O_1 would drop back as usual to protect the defensive basket.

It is extremely important in designing or selecting a half court offense to consider the rebounding game and the offensive rebounding options. It is easy to see from the previous explanations and diagrams that our offense provides excellent rebounding strength on every shot that we are trying to produce. We also stress continually to the players the importance of the weakside rebounding position. If our players are constantly aware of the weakside and are hustling to the rebounding area we feel we can gain inside position much more often than the normal offensive rebounding team. When the shot is executed out of our basic offset the weakside forward has an excellent chance to beat his defender to the rebounding position opposite the shot (Dia. 8-22). We make the players aware of this situation so that they concentrate on beating their man to the boards when the shot is executed. Any of our frontline players can be in the weakside position and at times a guard may be caught on the weakside with some possible rebounding responsibilities. Notice in the diagram that the weakside or helpside defender (X_3) is required to play off and toward the ball in a position of help. This relationship gives the offensive player a slight initial advantage for setting up inside position on the weakside. The offensive player who anticipates and hustles to the rebound area should be able to maintain that initial advantage. The defensive player will be hustling and he will probably be very much aware of the importance of the weakside rebounding position also. This is why we put some emphasis on our offensive rebounding in the practice sessions. We want our players prepared to win this battle. Over the course of the game it could produce quite a few second and third shots on our offensive end. Those second and third efforts could provide us with the margin of victory.

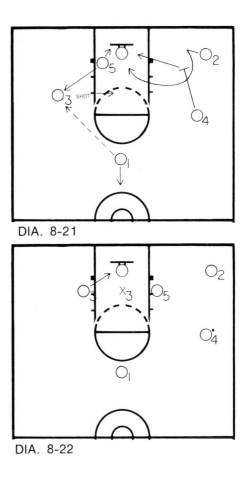

DIA. 8-21

DIA. 8-22

DIA. 8-23

Most of our offensive rebounding work will be done in a five on five drill situation. We will execute the various shots from our offset and show the players the rebounding options we have been discussing. We dummy through it with the defense allowing the offense to get to the boards so that they will recognize the desired rebounding positions. The explanation of these options takes only a short period of time because the players have a basic understanding of the paths they will need to follow to gain rebounding strength but maintain floor balance as shown in Diagram 8-8. We will spend only a few practice days in the preseason on these options. From that point on we run from a live situation with an emphasis on our offensive rebounding. The first emphasis is on executing the offense and producing a high percentage shot. A coach is assigned to make sure the players other than the shooter are anticipating properly and making every effort to get to the offensive boards.

The one offensive rebound area we do cover in a breakdown drill is the weakside rebounding position we discussed extensively above. The same basic alignment and procedure that we utilized in our helpside rebounding drill is used here with the emphasis shifting to the offensive player in the weakside position (Dia. 8-23). The two outside players are not a part of the drill. We have only the weakside offensive player in our normal four man position and an opposing helpside defender. The coach shoots the ball to miss and the two players fight for inside position and the rebound. This drill again is to get our players to concentrate on controlling that weakside rebounding position. This drill can be accomplished in a short period of time by the use of more than two baskets.

Rebounding Drills

Fundamental Block Out Drill (Dia. 8-24)
Objective: To teach the proper technique involved in blocking out defensively. Includes both the front and the reverse pivot. We will teach these fundamentals a few times early in the preseason practices and should not have to come back to this drill once into the season.
Organization: The players are lined up across from each other according to position and height. The coaches instruct the players as to what we want on both the front and the reverse pivot. These are then executed by each line for a short period of time concentrating only on technique. We then designate a line and call for a particular pivot. The players must react quickly and upon initiating the contact and holding it for an instant they make a leap for an imaginary rebound. This is to condition the players to make contact with their opponent and then go after the basketball.
Points of Emphasis: 1. Front pivot first, then the reverse pivot.
2. Arm bar on the front pivot.

3. Make contact with rear into the opponent's waist area or upper legs.

4. Maintain a strong, balanced position. Heels touching ground but weight on the balls of the feet.

5. Do not drive opponent back, but hold position.

6. Hands up.

7. Hold only for an instant and then go after the basketball.

Individual Blockout Drill—With Bricks (Dia. 8-25)

Objective: To develop in the players the habit of bringing the hands and arms to a high position on the block out. The players need some extra incentive to help develop this idea so that it becomes instinctive.

Organization: Two lines of six players each. The players have a brick in each hand which the managers have carted out. The players start with the bricks held at shoulder height and bring the hands and arms up higher while executing a front or reverse pivot blockout on command. This drill should not be done with partners.

Points of Emphasis: 1. Hands up.

2. Maintain strong, balanced position.

3. Weight evenly distributed over both feet.

4. Heels touching ground but weight on the balls of the feet.

5. Maintain this position with hands held high until whistle or other signal from coach.

We run the above drill for a relatively short period of time but will also have the players run from end line to end line in groups of six with the bricks held high. After a few trips up and down the floor in this manner, the players definitely increase their concentration on bringing the hands high for the rebound. As some added incentive we will place the bricks out of the way at the end of the court and move to a line rebounding drill or a half court drill in which rebounding is required. A coach will be assigned to watch the blockouts with special emphasis on the hands and arms. If one player fails to bring the hands up all of the players will have to repeat the running drill with the bricks. This exercise will obviously help our players to concentrate and the peer pressure involved becomes extra incentive.

Circle Blockout Drill (Dia. 8-26)

Objective: To further develop the blockout technique of each player and to teach the players how to maintain inside position.

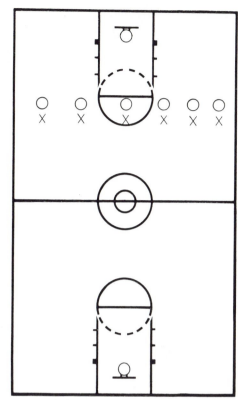

DIA. 8-24

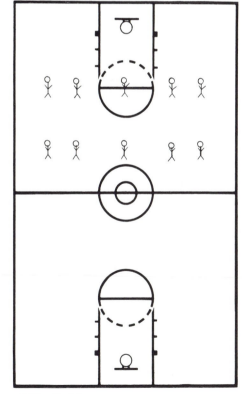

DIA. 8-25

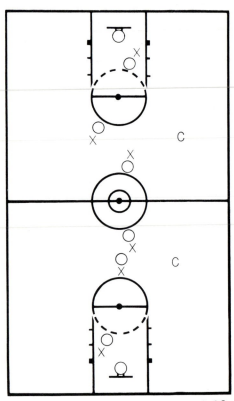

DIA. 8-26

Ogranization: The free throw circles and the half court circle are utilized as boundary lines. The squad divides up according to size and position with four players at each circle. A ball is placed in the center of each circle. Six of the players are designated as the defense and set up directly on the circles. On the command by the coach the six defensive players execute the block out and keep the corresponding offensive player from gaining possession of the ball for five full seconds. The offensive players start from outside the circle. They are required to stay on their feet in going after the basketball. The original defenders go three times or until the coaching staff is satisfied and then the offense and defense reverse roles.

Points of Emphasis: 1. Hands up.
2. Make contact with the offensive player.
3. Be ready to slide in either direction to stay between the offensive player and the ball.

Tipping Drill

Objective: To help develop the tipping ability of our players. Increases the ability to control the ball with the fingers and the wrists, especially in the weak hand. Also beneficial because of the repeated jumping required.

Organization: Players pair off at six baskets if available. A wall can also be utilized but the baskets are preferable. First player up tips the ball off the backboard fifteen times with the right hand on the right side of the basket. The same player then moves quickly to the left side of the basket and tips the ball fifteen times with the left hand and then fifteen times with both hands. The first player rests while the second player repeats the same procedure. Each player repeats the exercise two or three times. We also work up to twenty tips over the course of the preseason practices.

Points of Emphasis: 1. Finger tip control
2. Get as high as possible on the jump.
3. Jump quickly.
4. Work on the weak hand.
5. Keep the hands up.

Control Tipping Drill

Objective: Same objective of previous drill with increased emphasis on accuracy.

Organization: On an open area of smooth wall paint several dots (six if possible) approximately the size of a softball. The players execute the same tipping procedure as the previous drill but concentrate on tipping the ball exactly on the dot.

Points of Emphasis: same as TIPPING DRILL

Rim Touching Drill

Objective: To increase the quick jumping ability of our players so they are able to make the second, third and fourth jumps for the ball with strength and endurance.

Organization: Players pair off at different baskets. Players alternate with each one jumping and touching the rim or his highest target a designated number of times. We start with twenty-five jumps and work our way up to fifty.

Points of Emphasis: 1. Hands remain high.
2. Jump quickly.
3. Flex the knees slightly and execute a plantar flexion of the feet.
4. Stay up around the rim.

Exaggerated Rebound Drill

Objective: To help develop in the players an aggressive attitude in going after the basketball with strength.

Organization: Players pair off on each side of six baskets. Every player has a ball. Each player tosses the ball off the backboard and goes after his own rebound with exaggerated body movements.

Points of Emphasis: 1. Time the jump so you reach the ball at your peak.
2. Grasp the ball firmly with both hands.
3. Spread your legs. Exaggerate your intensity.
4. Turn to the outside as if to seal off an opponent.

Rebound And Outlet Drill (Dia. 8-27)

Objective: Same as exaggerated rebound drill with the additional objective of making the accurate outlet pass.

Organization: Two lines of six players on each side of the basket or at opposite ends. The two playes at the end of the line move to the outlet areas on their side. The first player in each line tosses the ball off the backboard and goes after the rebound. Upon gaining control of the ball the rebounder executes the outlet pass to his side and then follows his pass to become the outlet man. The player receiving the outlet passes the ball to the next player in line and moves to the end of the opposite line. The drill proceeds in that manner with the players exchanging lines so they are outletting to both sides. At the beginning of the drill we require the players to make the outlet after coming down with the ball. After a while we have them make the outlet while still in the air.

Points of Emphasis: 1. Grasp ball at the peak of your jump.
2. Go up strong.
3. Make the quarter turn to the outside.
4. Keep the ball high on the outlet.
5. Hit the outlet man in the head.

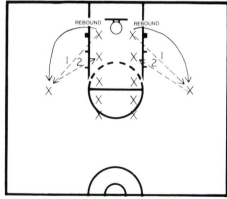

DIA. 8-27

Rebounding 309

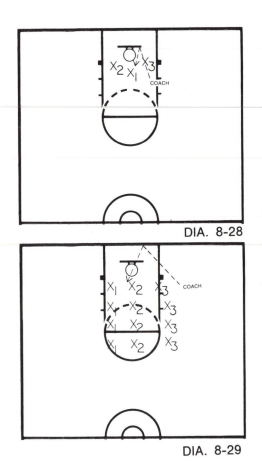

DIA. 8-28

DIA. 8-29

Rebounding Contact Drill (Dia. 8-28)

Objective: To increase our players' rebounding aggressiveness and to develop their ability to withstand the inevitable contact in the rebounding area.

Organization: The players work with teammates of the same size and position in groups of three. Three players at four different baskets. A coach or manager tosses the ball off the boards and the middle player (X_1) goes after the rebound with strength. The other two players sandwich X_1 without causing any dangerous situations. To concentrate on offensive rebounding X_1 can be required to take the ball to the basket with X_2 and X_3 again causing some opposition. The players can rotate after a certain number of rebounds or after the initial rebounder has performed satisfactorily.

Points of Emphasis: 1. Go after the ball strong.

2. Use your body, but not the elbows.

3. Grasp the ball firmly. Ignore the contact.

4. Jump as straight up in the air as possible but do not reach for the ball.

5. If required, put the ball back up strong.

Aggressive Rebounding Drill (Dia. 8-29)

Objective: Same as in rebounding contact drill with increased emphasis on the second and third effort to the basket.

Organization: This is a team rebounding drill. Three teams of four rebounders each are selected and line up as shown in the diagram to the left. A coach tosses the ball up and the first three players battle for the rebound. The successful rebounder becomes the offensive player and attempts to put the ball back up versus the two defenders. The first player to make two baskets moves to the end of his line and a new man steps in. The first team to get through their line is the winner. On a made basket or a ball that rebounds outside the lane area the basketball is returned to the coach. The drill can be repeated as many times as desired.

Points of Emphasis: 1. Go up strong. Be aggressive.

2. Ignore the contact.

3. Put the ball back up strong. Do not try to finesse the shot.

4. Hands are always up.

One On One Rebounding Drill (Dia. 8-30)

Objective: To work on the block out technique required on the shooter and to develop in our players the one on one rebounding skills necessary in the open floor.

Organization: The squad is divided into groups of four players at three different baskets. The first player (O_1) is stationed at the free throw line. The second player (X_1) walks out and hands the ball to O_1. O_1 shoots the ball and the two players battle for the rebound. X_1 remains on defense until the coach is satisfied. X_1 then moves to become the offensive player and X_2 becomes the defense. The drill continues in the same manner.

Points of Emphasis: 1. Contest, but do not block the shot.

2. Plant the arm bar.

3. Execute the front pivot.

4. Hands up. Anticipate the direction of the rebound.

5. Make contact for an instant and then go get the basketball.

Helpside Rebounding Drill (Dia. 8-31)

Objective: To work on the block out technique and the rebounding responsibilities of our helpside defenders.

Organization: We will usually divide the team in half with six players at one end working on helpside rebounding. The players on the opposite end will be working on ballside rebounding. The defensive players (X_1 and X_2) will be aligned in the helpside positions shown in the diagram. The coach will shoot the ball to miss. The offensive players are to crash the boards although they will be instructed to hold position at times. The defenders must block out properly and go after the ball aggressively. The defense must control the rebound three times in succession and the players rotate. Offense to defense, defense to the end of the line, two new players in.

Points of Emphasis: 1. Follow the flight of the ball. Anticipate.

2. Get your man on your back. The reverse pivot should be the most effective manuever.

3. Keep the opponent out of the gold.

4. Hold contact only for an instant and then go after the basketball.

5. Hands and arms up.

Ballside Rebounding Drill (see Dia. 8-31)

Objective: To work on the block out techniques and rebound responsibilities of our players on the ballside of the floor.

Organization: As shown in Diagram 8-31. The shot is first executed from the wing position with all three players blocking out properly and going after the rebound. Next the ball is moved between the two outside positions with the shot going up from either spot. The defense must gain possession three times in a row and then exchange with the offense. The players will also rotate positions.

Points of Emphasis: 1. Defensive player guarding shooter utilizes arm bar.

2. Outside players execute front pivot.

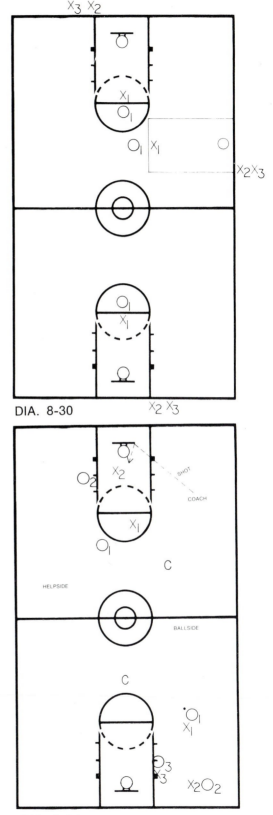

DIA. 8-30

DIA. 8-31

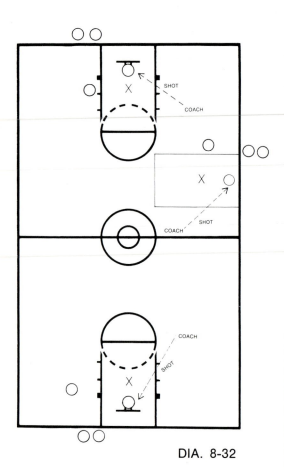

DIA. 8-32

3. Post player keep back foot behind opponent and execute reverse pivot.
4. Hands up. Anticipate. Follow the flight of the ball.
5. Make contact for an instant and then react for the rebound.

Weakside Rebounding Drill (Dia. 8-32)
Objective: To concentrate on the weakside offensive rebounding area from the four man position in our offense.
Organization: Four players grouped together at three different baskets. Offensive player is in four man position between the blocks. Ball is at the diagonal with the defender playing accordingly. The coach shoots the ball with the two players battling for the rebound. Offense goes to defense, defense goes to the end of the line when the coach is satisfied.
Points of Emphasis: 1. Anticipate the shot and the direction of the rebound.
2. React quickly. The first step is crucial.
3. Get inside or to the side of the defender.
4. Hands up. Use the body, not the hands and arms for position.
5. Go straight up in the air.
6. If outright possession is difficult, tip the ball to the basket or to keep it alive.

Five On Five Defensive Rebounding Drill
Objective: To develop our team defensive rebounding in a live situation by combining the helpside and ballside defensive drills.
Organization: A rebounding ring is placed on the basket so the offense is not shooting to miss. For the first part of the drill the offensive players hold position and move the basketball in a two-three set. Every five passes or so the shot is executed and the defensive players must keep their man off and control the rebound. Three times in succession and the offense and defense exchange roles. There is an emphasis here on the rebound triangle and the proper position of the guards in the middle of the floor and the outlet areas as explained in our initial fast break drill. After a while we will allow the offense to move in a truly live situation. The offense is encouraged to go to the offensive boards in both segments of the drill.
Points of Emphasis: 1. Keep YOUR man off the boards.
2. Follow the flight of the ball.
3. Hands and arms up.

4. Make sure there are three players around the basket in a rebound triangle.

5. The fourth player (usually the second guard) is the long rebounder in the middle of the floor.

6. The primary ball handler sets up at the top of the key after making sure his man is out of the play.

Five On Five Offensive Rebounding Drill

Objective: To teach the rebounding options available out of our offense and to place some definite emphasis on rebounding in our offensive system.

Organization: We will walk through and explain the rebounding responsibilities that we have discussed earlier, for a few days in the preseason practices. After that, we will execute our offense in a live situation and emphasize getting to the offensive boards on a missed shot. We will go back to the dummy situation if we are not getting the desired results in our offensive rebounding.

Points of Emphasis: 1. Anticipate the shot out of our offense.

2. React quickly to the basket. Make the first move.

3. Get inside or to the side of the defender.

4. Hands up. Anticipate the direction of the rebound.

5. Work the offensive boards. Keep the ball alive if outright possession is improbable.

Practice Planning And Conditioning ⑨

While recruiting is the name of the game in major college basketball it is also quite obvious that something must be done to develop those recruits once they become a part of your program. Our program at Missouri has been blessed with extremely coachable young men who have worked hard and accepted our teaching in order to develop their potential to the fullest. It has been said that Norm Stewart has had a certain amount of success getting the most out of his players. That goes back to our coaching philosophy and what we tell the players at the beginning of each year. We as coaches are in a supporting role. We are going to do all we can to help our players achieve their full potential. We can help them to get where they want to go, but the bulk of the work they must do themselves. In other words, a player's ability to play at this level and the success he achieves at Missouri will be in direct proprotion to the amount of effort he is willing to expend toward reaching his individual and team oriented goals.

One of the areas that we coaches' can have a very positive effect on a player's development is in the planning and organization of our practice sessions and suggested off season conditioning or improvement programs. We feel these are the most important aspects of our coaching responsibilities. They are not only the most important but also the most crucial in developing and maintaining a successful program. Every practice session must be organized and well planned so that we are using our time and our facilities in the most efficient manner. There must be an objective or a purpose to everything we do during practice time. We feel that by organizing our practices carefully we can avoid extended workouts where little or nothing is accomplished because the players lose concentration. Concentration — the mental aspect of the game — plays such an important part in determining our success. We want our players to maintain a very keen competitive desire. At the same time we want basketball at the University of Missouri to be an enjoyable experience. This does not mean that things won't get tough at times or that the time we do spend on the practice floor won't be demanding. The practices will be extremely demanding, especially during the preseason, because the practice floor is where we can accomplish the most in terms of individual improvement and team development. The point is that we want to budget our time so that it is spent productively. We feel that we can accomplish all that we need to in a two hour practice session if we have planned properly and are well organized before the start of practice until the end.

We tell the players at the beginning of the year that we are going to require two hours of their day for approximately six days a week. All of our practices will be designed to last two hours or less. During that time period we will expect total concentration and effort from each of our team members.

That means intensity and enthusiasm in all of the drill situations. If these characteristics are not evident throughout the practice session then we will reserve the right to extend the time period. We point out to the team that two hours is a very small part out of the day so they should be well prepared mentally and physically to extend full effort during the practices. Those two hour practices will begin at a set time. Because of our class schedules, we will begin most of our practices at 3:30 in the afternoon. Any changes will be posted and discussed with the players at least one day in advance. The coaches will be on the floor fully prepared for the practice at least one half hour before the designated time. This will mean at 2:45 or 3:00 p.m. on most days. In this way the coaches are available for individual work with the players. The players are made aware of our availability and are encouraged to take advantage of the extra practice time but it is entirely optional. We want the players coming early because of their own determination and desire to improve, not because we have made it mandatory. Those that do put in the extra practice time are going to reap the benefits somewhere along the line.

Official practices begin on October 15 for all NCAA Division I schools. We suggest a conditioning program that the players should begin four weeks prior to the first day of practice. Planning for this suggested conditioning program is accomplished in the summer months. The coaches are not allowed to supervise because of NCAA legislation, but we feel it is important to give the players an organized program on what we would like them to accomplish in the workouts. The players are entirely on their own as to how much they accomplish. We will explain fully our suggested off season conditioning programs in the second section of this chapter. Some preliminary planning for our official practice sessions also takes place in the summer months and begins in earnest when we complete our summer camp (for youngsters) around the middle of August. The discussions in June and July are very general in nature. We evaluate the people we have coming back and the new personnel. We discuss changes that may be needed with regard to positions or in our offensive emphasis. We also try to determine how well we accomplished what we set out to in last season's fall practices. We will obviously draw heavily on what we have done in previous seasons. All of us have established some procedures and some teaching and coaching methods that have been successful in the past. The continuity that results from applying these procedures and methods will certainly go a long way toward helping to implement our style of play and overall system. The players will benefit from the repetition and will have a better understanding of what we are trying to accomplish with each year of experience. The experience gained by the older players can aid in developing the knowledge of the younger players at the proper speed. We touched on this in Chapter Two when

Preliminary Planning

discussing our emphasis on the fundamentals. The important thing to remember in utilizing these established procedures and methods is to honestly evaluate their effectiveness from time to time. We don't want to be afraid to eliminate something (i.e., a drill, a practice schedule) that is not accomplishing its purpose simply because we have used it in the past. We have to improve upon an idea that isn't working or if that is not successful, we have to discard the idea in favor of something better. Obviously, we would keep and possibly expand on that which has been successful.

We try to organize our office and our working day so that the planning of our practices and preparation for the games receive full priority. The assistant coaches will be in and out of the office for days at a time because of the necessity of recruiting. This means that not all of the coaches will be at every meeting. We try to follow a general rule that at least one assistant and a graduate assistant will be available for each of our practices. This is not always necessary, so we are somewhat flexible according to the demands of recruiting. We set aside a two hour time period from 9:00 to 11:00 in the morning for the sole purpose of planning and organizing the afternoon practice sessions. Once the season begins this will undoubtedly involve some time spent viewing films of our upcoming opponents as well as our own game film. We will also film some practices and scrimmages as part of our preseason preparation. We will discuss shortly some of the ideas that are brought up and situations that are covered in these meetings. The important thing, at this point, is that we designate a set period of time that we are going to meet to organize our practice plans with a minimum amount of interruption. This is essential if we want to devise the practices to run as smoothly and efficiently as possible.

The coaching staff has until 9:00 to answer mail or take care of any other details that may need their attention. Daily at the designated hour we all know to get together in a special area (we have a meeting and film room that adjoins our offices) to discuss what needs to be done in the way of practice planning and game preparation. We will usually discuss our recruiting efforts at the conclusion of this meeting for whatever time is necessary. The recruiting meeting will occur then around 11:00, depending on how long we needed on a particular day to plan our practice carefully.

During the last two weeks of September, while the players are participating on their own in the conditioning program, we will finalize our plans for the first two weeks of practice beginning October 15. In these first two weeks we will spend approximately fifty percent of our practice time on the fundamentals we discussed in Chapter Two. We will spend about forty percent of our time beginning to teach our offensive and defensive systems. We place a great deal of emphasis on teaching throughout our program but especially concentrate on this aspect in the preseason practices. The first two weeks are very important in this regard because we will be emphasizing the fundamentals and we will be introducing a new offensive and defensive system to the freshmen. We do not introduce or begin to teach our fast break offense until the end of the second week. On the last day of the second week of practice we will spend quite a bit of time showing the organization of our fast break. During the third week we will begin to work on the fast break as a regular part of our practice sessions. Our ideas on rebounding are introduced during the first week making up about five percent of the practice time. The other five percent of practice time is devoted to conditioning. The concentrated conditioning actually comes at the end of our two hour practice sessions. After a tough workout we will spend from six to ten minutes on some intense conditioning. If organized properly and with the players putting out maximum effort we can achieve the desired results within that time span. A typical first week practice plan will be shown shortly. First, a look at some of the ideas and principles that go into our practice planning.

John Wooden, in his fine book, **Practical Modern Basketball**, lists some excellent principles to follow in planning your practices carefully. We have learned from reading and listening to Coach Wooden and ascribe to many of the ideas he has on the game of basketball, so some of those same principles will be covered below. We have also picked up many other ideas from listening and talking with coaches at clinics all over the country and from viewing different high school and college coaches conducting their practices. Our coaching methods usually follow the same basic principle of life. We are all products of our environment. We have learned from our high school and college coaches and from the coaches we have assisted when entering the profession. This is why we feel it is very important to expose ourselves to the different ideas of other coaches so that we are always learning. This does not mean that you should change methods every time a good idea comes along. As we mentioned at the beginning of this book there are many ways of doing things to reach the same objective. The successful coach must develop his own style and he must remain consistent in his methods. The important thing is that we always remain open to new ideas that may fit our particular philosophy.

The first important point that we consider in devising our practice plans is the organization of the drills so that the players are not standing in line for long periods of time. In order to improve the players must get quite a bit of repetition in the various drill situations. Also, the players will lose concentration if they are inactive for an extended time. The drills must be organized into as many groups as necessary to insure the proper amount of repetition. Floor space,

Ideas on Practice Planning

baskets, and coaches must be taken into account in accomplishing this goal. The rotation of the players in the drill must be well defined and understood so there is no time wasted in exchanging positions. It is the responsibility of the players to hustle from one position to the next when the rotation is in effect. It is important from this standpoint that the players learn the drills as quickly as possible so there is no need for the coaches to continually explain their organization and rotation.

The next principle we apply in practice planning involves the sequence of drills and the organization of our practice time. We begin practice with a flexibility period and some station drills which we will discuss later. After the stations we always incorporate a fundamental drill that involves a good deal of movement and is relatively enjoyable from the players' standpoint. We vary the drills from day to day but use some more than others. Our players are especially fond of the Two Ball Lay Up Drill so we use this extensively to get the drill segment of our practice going on a positive note. We encourage a lot of talk in this situation and especially look for some vocal support from our freshmen. This idea is basically some good natured kidding of the new players but it also helps to bring them out a little bit rather than allowing them to follow the lead of the upperclassmen in all drill situations. It is important that the coaches continue to stress the fundamentals that are involved in the drill while encouraging the enthusiasm and intensity.

We will generally emphasize defense before offense in our practice organization because the players should be fresher earlier in the practices and because we want the players to understand our philosophy on the importance of defense. The players should not have any less intensity or concentration during the second half of the practice session but still we are making a statement that defense comes first. We think that an equal amount of time should be spent on offense and defense but there is no question that most players are more advanced offensively and find it easier to learn at the offensive rather than the defensive end. Thus we start with defense and make sure the players understand that everyone in our program will be required to extend equal effort at both ends of the floor.

In setting up the drill situations and the stations we try to follow a very demanding drill with an easier one and vice versa. We also will incorporate two or three tough drills in succession when we want to place some emphasis on conditioning. By the same token we can double up on the less demanding drill situations when conditioning is not a factor or when we are holding a light workout. We have also found it beneficial to run in sequence the same drill that involves some progression. For instance, we will run our full court sliding drill in a dummy situation and then progress to the same drill involving the offense and then the ball. We think that our drills need to be varied from day to day to keep the players from becoming bored but there also must be a good amount of repetition so the proper habits are developed. There must be a lot of thought in this area so a good balance is struck between variation and repetition. The time allotment for each drill can help in establishing this balance. We will never spend more than ten minutes on one particular breakdown drill. If we are doing some five on five work emphasizing a particular area we will sometimes extend that time allotment. Generally, however, if we need to spend more time on a certain area of our game we will come back to it later in the practice for another ten minute segment. Attention to this detail will insure that our drills do not become monotonous to the players. The players have to remain sharp if they are going to absorb what we are trying to teach in each drill or practice situation.

We have already expressed our belief in the whole-part-whole method of teaching. We feel that by showing the players the entire picture they will be better able to understand the purpose behind each breakdown drill and better execution should result. We show them then how each particular drill will apply to the overall picture. Coach Wooden suggests and we agree that the players will respond better when they can visualize the objective behind each drill.

We try to place a great deal of pressure on the players during the week because we feel that more pressure in practice will mean less pressure in games. It has often been said that the games are won on Friday night based on what has been accomplished Monday through Thursday in the practice sessions. We want to do much of our coaching and all of our preparation during that time. On game night we need to make the necessary corrections and adjustments and we need to make sure the players are mentally prepared but most of our work should be done in the weeks leading up to the games. We want the games to be the fun part of the program. We want the players relaxed and confident. This is why we think that practice planning is so crucial to the development of a successful program. The players have to be totally prepared on game night and with that preparation comes the confidence that should lead to success. The pressure we are talking about can be administered in a number of ways. The coaching staff can exert a great deal of pressure vocally. Peer pressure can be developed into the practices as long as it is positive in nature. Both of these elements are considered in developing the right amount of pressure in our practices but our most productive means of applying pressure is through the use of competitive drills. In fact, through the formation of competitive drills, we can easily apply our staff pressure and positive peer pressure. We stress the competition factor in most of our drills involving two or more people. We can also add pressure to simple drills by designating a time and numerical goal that must be reached. For instance we can add pressure to a shooting drill by charting how many shots a player can make in a certain amount of time. Or we can require that a player make a certain percentage of his shots from various spots on the floor. The drills can be set up so that two individuals are competing or the team can be divided to allow for some team competition. There are all kinds of possibilities for including the competition factor in the practice sessions so the players become accustomed to the pressure. Please refer back to Chapter Two and notice how many of the fundamental drills can be developed into competitive drills by designating teams and/or a time and numerical requirement.

We must emphasize that technique must be the first concern in developing any fundamental, especially shooting. The players must not neglect the proper technique in developing quickness for a competitive drill. Accuracy always comes before quickness. You will find, however, that the players concentrate more when both of these elements are a part of the drill. Ask a player to shoot and make five baskets from a designated spot on the floor. Now ask him to shoot and make five baskets as quickly as possible. The player will always concentrate more when fulfilling the second request. Add an individual or a team to compete against and concentration becomes even more intense. The above ideas are always considered when devising our practice plans. We always include some drills that will involve pressure and competition for the players.

We do not scrimmage during the first two weeks of practice. On the Saturday following the second week, we will run a controlled scrimmage involving five on five work at both ends of the floor. We do not teach the fast break completely until the third week so we do not allow the fast break in this first controlled scrimmage. We will have gone over our conversion in the first two weeks of practice so we will simulate the fast break and require the teams to convert properly when we exchange ends of the floor. After the third week, we will hold a full scale or controlled full scrimmage every Saturday. We feel it is important at that time to hold at least one full scrimmage a week in addition to the five on five work that we have progressed to in our workouts. The full scale scrimmages will be held with a regular officiating team and we will film them for observation and evaluation purposes. Before the start of the season we will also hold at least two scrimmages at night (usually on a Wednesday — our conference playing night). All scrimmages during the preseason are charted and the players are given a numerical rating based on their performance. A running count is kept on each player's rating throughout the preseason practices and this gives us a very objective means of evaluation. During the season our scrimmaging will be limited to five on five work in a controlled situation and short scrimmages held at various times in the practices. We don't want to do any long scrimmaging but we have found the short scrimmages to be very valuable in that the players can apply our instructions under simulated game conditions. We might be working at a particular time on executing our offense more effectively. We will work five on five making the necessary corrections and then at the end of the practice we can hold the scrimmage to determine if the players have absorbed our coaching. We like to hold the short scrimmages at the close of practice, but they can be interspersed with the drills depending on our needs on a particular day. Generally, these scrimmages are ten minutes in length.

We will also utilize the scrimmages to help condition the players who are achieving a limited amount of playing time. On the day following a game we will keep these players after the regular practice or allow those with sufficient playing time to leave early so that we can conduct a conditioning scrimmage. The players should understand that the extra practice is not a form of punishment. We merely want them to maintain their conditioning so that when an opportunity for increased playing time presents itself they will be prepared. Over the course of the season there are going to be many opportunities for each individual player to improve his position on the team. We stress this fact to the players because we never want them to become satisfied with their position on the squad.

Player Rating System

The following chart shows an example of the system we use to rate our players based on their total performance in a scrimmage or game situation. As mentioned in the preceding pages we utilize this form to chart all preseason scrimmages and we keep a running total of each player's rating. We post the ratings after each scrimmage and also post the running totals after the completion of our second scrimmage and for each succeeding scrimmage thereafter. By posting the ratings we are giving each player an immediate objective evaluation of his performance during a particular scrimmage. The running total that is posted gives the player an idea of his effectiveness through all of the scrimmages. If the players will study the ratings they can determine through the statistics exactly where their game can be improved. If a player grades out well in one scrimmage and very poorly in the next and this pattern continues, he obviously needs to improve his consistency. On the other hand, if a player is grading at a consistent but relatively low or average level, he may need to be more aggressive in order to make something positive happen. The players must read into the statistics with their particular game in mind. A player who is not a great offensive player but excels in other areas should not try to improve his rating by taking a disproportionate number of shots. The player may determine that he needs to look for his shot more if his field goals attempted (FGA) is low and his field goal percentage (FG%) is high but every player must have a good idea of his role and his limitations.

The player ratings are determined by the following calculations. We feel that this is a very accurate means of evaluating a player's overall contribution in a particular game. Two points are awarded for each field goal made. One point is substracted from that total for every field goal missed. One point is then awarded for each successful free throw and one point is subtracted for each missed free throw. Every rebound, assist, and recovery adds one point to the total while every mistake and foul committed means a loss of a point.

The players can look at each of the areas included in the rating to determine specific improvements that need to be made. For instance, number twenty in the ratings shown has had an excellent scrimmage except for the fact that he made five mistakes. He can look at our turnover chart and determine where the mistakes were made and where improvement is needed. Number forty has shot poorly from the field and from the free throw line, so he obviously needs work on his shooting and may want to take a look at the shot chart and evaluate his shot selection.

PLAYER	MINUTES PLAYED	FGM	FGA	FG%	FTM	FTA	
#42	35	10	14	71	5	6	
(#40)	13	(2)	(7)	(29)	(1)	(4)	
#22	28	4	6	67	4	5	
#54	20	2	3	67	4	4	
#32	30	4	11	36	1	1	
#35	34	1	2	50	2	2	
(#20)	34	8	14	57	14	15	
#44	6	2	2	100	4	6	
A=Assists R=Recoveries							
M=Mistakes F=Fouls							
Team OER=1.14		33	59	55	35	41	

We have our head manager and his assistants keep and maintain all statistical charts. It is up to the manager to see that he has sufficient personnel to chart the statistics at each game and each practice involving a scrimmage. The manager tabulates the figures immediately after the workout or game and makes the ratings available to the coaching staff. The manager then has the responsibility to make the extra copies of the individual scrimmage and tabulate the new running total. These should be posted for the following day's practice.

The coaching staff will take a hard look at these players ratings in evaluating our personnel. Because of their objectivity the ratings can be a very valuable tool but they do not tell the whole story. There are many intangible qualities that a player might possess that do not show up in the figures. At times we will have a player who does not grade out all that well but his team always seems to win. We have to take a long look at the chemistry involved in selecting a starting five. It is important to select a team that works well together and complements each other effectively. It is equally important to develop a starting line-up that is strong at both ends of the floor. For these reasons, the five most talented players will not always make up the first team.

The one area that is not covered adequately in our rating

		FT%	OFF REB	DEF REB	TOT REB	A	R	M	F	PTS	RATING
		83	3	5	8	3		5	2	25	24
		(50)	1	3	4	1	1	3	4	5	-4
		80	0	3	3	3	3	6	2	12	10
		100	0	1	1					8	8
		100	3	2	5		3	2	2	9	6
		100	0	1	1	2		1	1	4	4
		93	1	4	5	3	1	(5)	3	30	23
		67	2	3	5				1	8	10
		85	4 14	3 28	42	13	8	21	16	101	95

system is the overall defense of an individual player. Defensive rebounds, recoveries, and fouls commited touch upon the individual defense but the defensive effectiveness is something we can best evaluate through observation and comparison. The defensive abilities of the players are too difficult to judge only on the basis of statistics because the statistics do not take into account extenuating circumstances. We note the matchups in the scrimmages and games and can evaluate the defense somewhat on a comparison of the opposing player's total points to his scoring average. In the past we would subtract the difference to determine a player's rating. For instance, number twenty earned a rating of twenty-three on the chart shown previously. If twenty's defensive assignment scored two points above his average, we would subtract two from twenty-three to establish a complete rating. We abandon this idea because of the extenuating circumstances that can occur at the defensive end. Because of substitutions, switches, and changes in assignments, it is impossible to keep track of how many times an individual defensive player actually gave up two points. A player may be required to help or pick up a new man because of a teammate's mistake and the helper's man may end up with the basket. This is why we compare the statistics but also rely on our observation to rate the players defensively.

Master List of Drills

Each year we will devise a master list of our drills which we feel is very important in building our program progressively and systematically from the first day of practice. The drills are seperated according to the different areas of our program and are then listed under that heading in a progressive order. These drills will be the basic building blocks for developing our overall program. We refer to this list constantly in organizing the daily practice sessions and we make sure that each area is covered adequately by using the list to check ourselves. The following master list is a good example of what we utilize from year to year. Obviously, we can add to or change the list as we devise or find new and better drills. Keep in mind also that many of the drills are used to teach a particular skill early in the preseason. They are breakdown drills that progress to three on three and five on five work. The list may seem like a lot of drills but once the season starts we will break down the list further so that we can keep things as simple as possible.

Defensive Drills

INDIVIDUAL

Leader Drill
Slide-Run-Slide Drill
Lane Drill
Mirror Drill
Full Court Sliding Drill-Add Offense—Add Ball
Full Court One-on-One Drill
Tag Drill
Driving Line One-on-One Drill

Off and Toward Drill
Post Pass Defensive Drill
Post Defensive Drill
Lead Pass Drill
Backdoor Drill
Three in One Drill
Diagonal Cut Drill
Lateral Cut Drill
Six in One Drill
Shot Blocker Drill

TEAM

Two on Two Full Court Drill
Two on Two Drill—First Stage
Two on Two Full Court—Help and Recover Drill
Two on Two Run and Change Drill
Three on Three Full Court Drill
Three on Three Drill—First Stage
Three on Three Drill—Prevent the Lob
Five on Five Full Court Drill
Two on Two Half Court Help and Recover Drill
One Man Removed Drill
Influence Drill
Western Roll Drill
Three on Three Reaction Drill
Inside Cut Drill
Screen Away Drill
Three on Three Influence Drill
Forward Cut Drill
Three on Three Help and Recover Drill
Post Split Drill
Three on Three Situations Drill
Three on Three Survival Drill
Four on Four Reaction Drill
Four on Five Drill (Collapse on the Post)
Five on Five Reaction Drill
Baseline Help Drill
Jam the Middle Drill
Five on Five Survival Drill
Conversion Drill off Missed Shot
Five on Six Conversion Drill
Defensive Game

ZONE PRESS

Off and Toward Deflection Drill
Zone Pressure Drill—Inbounds Pass
Safety Drill
Five on Five Transition Drill
Quick Conversion Drill

REBOUNDING DRILLS

Fundamental Blockout Drill
Individual Blockout Drill—with Bricks
Circle Blockout Drill
Tipping Drill
Control Tipping Drill
Rim Touching Drill
Rebound and Outlet Drill
Rebounding Contact Drill
Aggressive Rebounding Drill
One on One Rebounding Drill
Helpside Rebounding Drill
Ballside Rebounding Drill
Weakside Rebounding Drill
Five on Five Defensive Rebounding Drill
Five on Five Offensive Rebounding Drill

Offensive Drills

FUNDAMENTALS

Leader Drill
Two Line Passing Drill
Full Court Passing Drill
Machine Gun Passing Drill
Star Drill
Halo Passing Drill
Toss Back Drills
Basic Dribbling Drill
Chase the Dribbler Drill
Dribble Tag
Cock Fight
Two Ball Lay Up Drill
Competitive Lay Up Drill
Individual Cuts

SHOOTING

Combinations
Spot Shooting
Shooting Partners
Two Ball Shooting Drill
One Minute Shooting Drill
Competitive Shooting Drill
Spot Shooting from the Point
Shot Off the Pinch Post
Flare Pass and Shot
Shot Off the Downscreen
Four Man Shots
Individual Moves off the Post

TEAM

Guard to Forward Timing Drill (Add Post)
Post Pass Offensive Drill
Triangle Split Drill
Corner Pass Drill
Point Pass Drill
Point Pass-Post Rolls
Two Man Play
Four Man Drill
Post Pass-Flare Drill
Five on Five Dummy Drill (No defense)
Five on Five Situations (vs. man to man,
vs. zone, vs. zone pressure)

FAST BREAK

Five on None Fast Break Drill
Three Man Outlet Drill
Outlet and Over the Top Drill
Outlet Recognition Drill
Dribble Quickness Drill
Loose Ball Fast Break Drill
Three Lane-Two Ball Drill
Three on None Fast Break Drill
Two on One Drill
Three on Two Drill
Three on Two-Two on One Drill
Three on Two Continuous Fast Break Drill
Five on Three Fast Break Drill
Five on Five Fast Break

CONDITIONING DRILLS

Cone Drill
Lane Drill
Forward-Back Drill
Indian Relay Race
Bench Jumping
Toss Back—Layup Drill

Toss Back—Sliding Drill
Pick Up Drill
10 in 1 Drill
Man-Boy
Basket Drill
Rope Skipping
Running the Steps

At exactly 3:30 every day the players will line up at one end of the floor for a series of flexibility exercises. These will be explained fully in the following section on conditioning. We feel the flexibility program is extremely important to our players because of the role it can play in the prevention of athletic related injuries. We also feel very strongly that increased flexibility will make our players better athletes because they will be able to perform the various skills more efficiently. Finally, we believe the flexibility exercises serve to physically and mentally prepare the players for the practice session that will follow. The physical aspect is obvious. Mentally we try to prepare the players by giving them something different to think about during the time we are stretching. So much of the game is mental and so much of our success in practice will depend on the concentration and the mental approach or attitude of the players. On some days we will require the players to remain absolutely quiet and concentrate on what they can accomplish individually and with the team in the coming practice. On other days we will ask them to concentrate on their strengths and envision how they can better apply these strengths within the overall team concept. Or we will ask them to pick out their weaknesses and determine how they can improve themselves in these areas. On some days we will instruct the players to totally relax. We want them to relax their minds and their bodies and to think of nothing but how good it feels to stretch. We also ask the players to concentrate on the emphasis of the day (a practice idea we will explain very shortly). At times we will play some music the players like during the flexibility period. There are an unlimited variety of thoughts that can be utilized during this time period to help the players with their mental approach to practice. We think some attention to this mental preparation will help the players to practice more purposefully.

During the preseason practices we will follow the flexibility period with six stations drills that incorporate some work in the fundamentals and some individual play and two man plays. We will have a coach at as many stations as possible and the emphasis is on individual attention during the two minute segments. The players will pair off according to a posted practice plan and remain at a particular station for two minutes. On the whistle the players will rotate and we will allow thirty seconds for the rotation and for the coach to explain the station. This gives each group of players a full two minutes of concentrated effort at each station, in a fifteen minute time

Flexibility and Stations

Practice Planning 327

period. The station format provides us with a fast moving means of individual attention and instruction in many areas. The players do not stand around or in lines so the intensity and concentration should be there. The station drills are derived from our master list of drill situations. In planning our practices we change the station drills from week to week so that we are covering many different areas. We have some that are incorporated quite frequently because of their importance to our program. One of these is the station for individual cuts. We think it is extremely important for the players to get to know the habits and tendencies of each of their teammates. In the individual cut station we have the players execute the various cuts in our offense with the pass coming from a teammate. We change the parings every day so the players work with different partners. This is just another way we help the players to familiarize themselves with their teammates and the offense. The players gain a feel for each other through working together. This station also gives the players some concentrated work on their individual offensive moves and cuts. We feel that this is an often neglected aspect of a player's development in organized practice. Because the players today are so advanced offensively, coaches sometimes take for granted the individual offensive moves. We use this time to help refine the moves within the framework of our offense. We try to make the players understand that there are times to take advantage of the freedom inherent in our offense but there are more times when a precise cut or exact execution of the offense will lead to an excellent shot opportunity. The players have to develop an understanding for the natural flow of the game.

Practice Schedule and the Emphasis of the Day

The following schedule is an example of a typical practice session during our first week. Remember that the emphasis here is on the fundamentals and beginning to teach our offensive and defensive systems. Notice also that many of the fundamental drills and a few of the station drills combine the fundamentals with the development of our offense and defense. The practice schedule is typed in the same form each day by our secretary as soon as we complete our plans in the morning meeting. Copies are made for each of the coaches and the managers and a copy is posted in the locker room for the players to view on their way out to practice. Additional copies are made to be kept on file in the office. We encourage the players to look over the daily practice plan so that they have an idea of what we are going to do that day and also so that they become familiar with the names of the drills. The players should learn the drills and the names of the drills so that we do not have to waste valuable practice time continually explaining their organization. The experienced players are again helpful in demonstrating the drills to the younger players. We always ask the players to start at the end of the line if they are unsure of the drill. They should then observe the other players and pick up the drill as quickly as possible. In this way the practices can move smoothly and efficiently from one drill to the next. The copies of the practice schedule are to be distributed and posted by twelve noon each day so that everything can be organized properly. The managers are responsible for making sure that all of the equipment is available at least one half hour before the start of practice. We do not want any last minute preparations that could cause a delay if something goes wrong.

MISSOURI

Basketball Practice # 3   Day Tuesday   Date 10-17-78

TIME

	Pre-Practice: Individual instruction, station drills (lay ups, combination rebounding, free throws, big man drill and guard play)
3:30	Flexibility
3:40	Stations 1. Combinations (Drew-Foster)
	2. Bench Jumping (Wallace-Stoehner)
	3. One on One (Dressler-Berry)
	4. Individual Cuts (Laurie-Droy)
	5. Rebounding (Dore-Drum)
	6. Defensive Sliding (Amos-Frazier)
3:55	Two Ball Lay up Drill
4:05	Full Court Sliding Drill—Add Offense—Add Ball
4:12	Driving Line One on One
4:20	Post Pass Defensive Drill—Defense on the Wing
	Post Pass Defense Drill—Defense on the Post
	Triangle Split Drill
4:35	Forming the Offset
	Guard to Forward Coming In-Timing Drill
	Guard to Post Coming In
4:45	Fundamental Blockout Drill
4:55	Free Throws (each player shoots 50 in a row—chart)
5:05	Machine Gun Passing Drill
5:15	Lead Pass Drill
5:25	Two Ball Shooting Drill (Six Baskets)
5:30	Conditioning
	EMPHASIS OF THE DAY: HANDS UP WHEN REBOUNDING!!

The emphasis of the day highlighted in the practice schedule is an idea we use primarily to stress a particular coaching point to the players. It makes the players think about a very important aspect of the game throughout an entire practice session. Again, we are adding purpose and increasing concentration. The coaches decide daily on an applicable emphasis and it is posted without fail. All of the players must know the emphasis of the day. If a player is asked by a coach to state the emphasis of the day he must do so or the entire team will be put on the line for some extra conditioning. In the drill situations, if a player fails to execute the emphasis of the day the same conditioning will result. In other words, the emphasis of the day in the preceding practice schedule was bringing the hands and arms up for the rebound. If a player fails to do this in any drill involving rebounding or the missed shot the players will be put on the line. We feel that this idea aids us in developing the concentration of the players and in getting across various coaching points. It also helps to encourage the players to look over the practice schedule on the way to the practice floor. Another benefit is that we can use the emphasis of the day to help correct something we have had trouble with in the previous day's practice or we can introduce something that we will be teaching the following day.

We mentioned previously that we try to do everything in a progressive manner. We want to build on what we have done the day before and develop our program as systematically as possible. We want to accomplish this goal without becoming inflexible. We always want to devise our practice schedule according to the progress that we have made up until that time. With this in mind we feel it is essential to keep some flexibility in our practice planning and organization. Changes may be necessary depending on what we accomplished or failed to accomplish on the previous day. Following the first two weeks of practice we do not work far ahead in planning the practices. We think it is beneficial to meet daily and give immediate attention to what we want to accomplish that afternoon. We will discuss on the first day of each week what we need to cover during that week and plan our daily practices accordingly.

For the first two weeks of practice there is always a heavy emphasis on the fundamentals. As we enter the third week the amount of time we spend strictly on the fundamentals is down to about thirty percent of the practice time. This is still a healthy percentage of practice time and we still stress very emphatically the proper execution of the fundamentals. Each week the amount of practice time spent strictly on the fundamentals will lessen. Keep in mind however that many of our breakdown drills and the drills leading up to the execution of the fast break are fundamentally oriented. We have to spend less time on the fundamentals so we can properly teach and develop our offensive and defensive system. The breakdown drills and lead up drills serve to combine the fundamentals with the development of our offense and defense.

The following are typical practice plans leading up to the first game of the season. The last schedule listed is from the final week of preseason preparations. Notice that we have progressed to a good deal of five on five work where the emphasis is on the team rather than the individual. The final week is also very important for refining the special situation areas (out of bounds plays, lay up game, clock situations, etc.) and explaining the pre-game warm-up drills and the organization of the bench during the games and during the timeouts. We will take a more thorough look at the special situations in the next chapter.

MISSOURI

Basketball Practice # 10   Day   Date 10-25-78

TIME

PRE-PRACTICE: Individual instruction, station drills (lay ups, combination rebounding, free thows, big man drill and guard play)

TIME	
3:30	Flexibility
3:40	Stations: 1. Combinations (Drew-Stoehner)
	2. Bench Jumping (Foster-Berry)
	3. Free Throws (Wallace-Droy)
	4. One Minute Shooting Drill (Dressler-Drum)
	5. Control Tipping Drill (Laurie-Frazier)
	6. Toss Backs (Dore-Amos)
3:55	Two Ball Lay-up Drill
4:05	Two on Two Full Court Drill
4:15	Three in One Drill
4:25	Diagonal Cut Drill
4:32	Free Throws (each player shoots 50 in a row—chart)
4:45	Cock Fight
4:50	Triangle Split Frill
4:55	Corner Pass Drill
5:00	Rebounding Contact Drill
5:05	Slide-Run-Slide Drill
5:10	Competitive Shooting Drill—from the Diagonal (Guards vs. Frontliners) winner runs one less sprint during conditioning
5:20	Point Pass Drill
5:30	Conditioning

EMPHASIS OF THE DAY: MAINTAIN BASKETBALL POSITION

MISSOURI

Basketball Practice # 23   Day   Date 11-9-78

TIME

PRE-PRACTICE: Individual instruction, station drills (lay ups, combination rebounding, free throws, big man drill and guard play)

TIME	
3:30	Flexibility
3:40	Stations: 1. Combinations (Drew-Droy)
	2. Rope Jumping (Stoehner-Drum)
	3. Spot Shooting (Foster-Frazier)
	4. Individual Cuts (Wallace-Amos)
	5. Cock Fight (Dressler-Dore)
	6. Toss Backs (Laurie-Berry)
3:55	Star Drill
4:02	Driving Lines—Draw the charge
4:10	Jam the Middle Drill
4:20	Three on Three Survival Drill
4:30	Defensive Game
4:40	Free Throws (shoot 25 in a row, then two sets of ten—chart
4:50	Five on Three Fast Break Drill
	Loose Ball Fast Break Drill (5 on 5)
5:05	Five on Five Dummy Drill (offense)
	Five on Five Offense—concentrate on point pass and four man across
5:15	Aggressive Rebounding Drill
5:25	Competitive Lay-up Drill
5:30	Conditioning

Black—Drew, Stoehner, Drum, Berry, Amos, Droy
Gold—Laurie, Wallace, Foster, Dore, Dressler, Shawver

EMPHASIS OF THE DAY: STAY DOWN ON DEFENSE

MISSOURI

Basketball Practice # 40   Day Wednesday   DATE 11-29-78

TIME

	PRE-PRACTICE: Individual instruction, station drills (lay ups, combination rebounding, free throws, big man drill and guard play)
3:30	Flexibility (discuss pre-game warm up and bench organization)
3:40	Pre-Game simulation—Two Line Passing Drill
	—Two Ball Lay-Up Drill
	—Spot Shooting (six shooting, six sliding)
	—Leader Drill
3:55	Five on Five Reaction Drill
4:00	Five on Six Conversion Drill
4:05	Five on Five Survival Drill
4:15	Five on Five Offensive Situations—work on turning the basketball
	—generate the high percentage shot
4:25	Zone Press Attack vs 1-2-2
4:35	Free Throws (Shoot only one and one—chart how many it takes to make 25)
4:45	Jump Ball Situations
4:50	Lay up Game—handle the basketball
4:55	Defense vs. the Four Corners
5:05	Out of Bounds Plays
5:15	Spot shooting
5:25	Work on Zone Press (2-2-1)—Berry must protect
5:30	Conditioning

Black—Drew, Wallace, Drum, Berry, Droy, Shawver
Gold—Stoehner, Foster, Laurie, Dore, Dressler, Amos

EMPHASIS OF THE DAY: TALK ON DEFENSE

Additional Player Evaluations

Throughout the preseason practices we try to give the players the necessary feedback so they can evaluate their progress on a continuing basis. This feedback and communication in the player-coach relationship is essential if the players are to determine ways in which they can eliminate their weaknesses and develop their strengths. We have already discussed our player rating system which is implemented after our first full scrimmage. Until that time we are always careful to show no inclination toward selection of a starting team. The experienced players all start out on an equal basis and the new players, because they are learning a new system, begin one step behind the veterans. For the first few weeks then, this feedback will consist of comments, both positive and negative, on each player's individual achievements and progress. The players should be shown individual drills that can help them overcome their particular weaknesses.

After the first full scrimmage and subsequent scrimmages thereafter the players will be able to check their performances on the charts posted. The coaching staff will also be carefully evaluating the personnel and beginning to shape possible starting line-ups based on the practice and scrimmage observations and ratings. Certainly nothing will be definitely decided at this point, but we will have a good idea of who to start working together to establish a top eight.

Midway through the preseason practices we will develop a player evaluation outlook that we will hand out to the players as a means of providing feedback. An example of this outlook is shown below. We list each player's strong points as well as areas where improvement is needed. It is important to provide both positive and negative feedback. The coaches have discussed each player extensively to arrive at these evaluations. Every coach has input and our goal is to develop a very complete but concise analysis of each player's abilities. We can now have a unified approach in working with the individual players in areas where improvement is needed.

1976-77 Evaluation Outlook

KIM ANDERSON—**Strong points:** attitude, complete player, good shooting range, aggressive. **Improvement areas:** shooting technique (could quicken your shot), defensively - 1 on 1 need to hold your position, too much commitment, aggressiveness is fine but you need to use better judgment, slapping foul must be omitted.

JAMES CLABON—**Strong points:** good leaper, good defensive player, over-all game and floor game is good. **Improvement areas:** need to improve hands by working in the nets, aggressiveness (particularly on boards) but also in working for shots, need to be able to take the ball strong to the basket on the drive.

JIM KENNEDY—**Strong points:** outstanding potential, good multi-talented player, can play the basket as well as the center of the floor. **Improvement areas:** conditioning that is also tied in with weight control, this will allow you to make an outstanding effort, on defense must slide better and stay in the down position when you are away from the ball.

SCOTT SIMS—**Strong points:** attitude, playing aggressively and providing floor leadership, players will accept you and your guidance, keep asserting good influence, shooting well on the break and on the stop. **Improvement areas:** keep weight at 165, shot release, defensively when you stop or control the man make the effort to keep the hands up and bother him.

JEFF CURRIE—**Strong points:** good understanding of the complete game and good team player, goes to the hole well and defenses well. **Improvement areas:** shooting, particularly FT, work on release.

DANNY VAN RHEEN—**Strong points:** strong player goes to the boards well, has the experience and maturity to play. **Improvement areas:** ball handling, could improve by working on toss back, need to be selective of shots and understand who is covering you on defense.

CLAY JOHNSON—**Strong points:** good competitor, excellent jumper, good complete player with excellent potential. **Improvement areas:** running from FT line to FT line, show intensity on defense, the experience will come for learning what is expected of you.

DAVE STALLMAN—**Strong points:** good 1 on 1 player, excellent jumper. **Improvement areas:** relaxation, offensively - awareness of hitting the open man, working without the ball, defensively - use of hands only when the man is stopped or controlled, still following the man when your man goes away from the ball.

STAN RAY—**Strong points:** good big man, aggressive, keeps hands up around the basket, good high post shooter and weakside player, concentrates on rebounding and playing the boards. **Improvement areas:** defense, staying low, keeping good vision and not following the defensive man away from the ball.

BRAD DROY—**Strong points:** good shooter and has improved ability to put the ball on the floor, aggressiveness has improved on offense, works board well. **Improvement areas:** defensively - conditioning and weight must always be of prime importance, hold 1 on 1 defensive position, jumping and use of hands.

LARRY DREW—**Strong points:** talented player who has good potential, good shooting range, and fine passer with good court vision, good ball handling abilities. **Improvement areas:** shooting (could open your right shoulder to the basket and shot would be quicker and more relaxed), entire game should become more aggressive as you learn more of a new situation and new player.

Player Evaluations

At an appropriate time in the preseason practices we feel it is beneficial to let the players evaluate each other in certain categories. We organize the form shown on the following page and have the players select the best individual in each category and select what they consider to be the top five players and the top eight players on the team. The selections are made in private and we impress on the players that it is not a popularity contest but an honest appraisal of the talent we have on hand. The players are asked not to vote for themselves. The selections are turned in without any identification.

1976-77
Missouri Player List

	Best Attitude	Best Defensive	Best Passer	Best Rebounder	Best Shooter	Best 8	Best 5
Anderson							
Clabon							
Currie							
Drew							
Droy							
Johnson							
Kennedy							
Ray							
Sims							
Stallman							
Van Rheen							

These evaluations by the players are usually conducted around the fifth week of the preseason practice schedule. The players will have had plenty of time at that point to form an opinion on the categories listed. We have usually found that the evaluations by the players fit almost exactly in line with those made by the coaching staff. The results of the player poll are handed out to the team as shown below.

Player Evaluation Results
(1976-77)

Best Shooter
Anderson
Droy
Kennedy

Best Defensive
Clabon
Currie
Sims

Best Passer
Sims
Drew
Currie

Best Rebounder
Kennedy
Ray
Anderson

Best Atitude
Sims
Anderson
Johnson

Best Eight
Anderson
Clabon
Currie
Drew
Johnson
Kennedy
Ray
Sims

Best Five
Anderson
Johnson
Kennedy
Ray
Sims

Final Points on Practice Planning

During the regular season we will limit the time of our practice sessions according to our schedule that week. We will generally hold a light workout or give the players the day off on the afternoon following a game. There will very rarely be more than one two hour practice session per week. During the latter stages of the season we will cut all of our practices down to an hour and a half or less.

A final area we will consider in developing our practices is the implementation of some diversion type drills at strategic points during the season. These drills are fun for the players and can serve to break up the monotony that is inevitable over the course of a long season. These drills will still involve the fundamentals of the game and can aid in developing the individual skills of the players. At certain times in the preseason practices, we will interject one of these drills to relieve some of the pressure and the boredom that occurs as a result of having so many practices without facing an opponent in a game situation. These drills become even more valuable late in the season when the months of practices and games are beginning to take a toll. It is important at that time to schedule some light practices and make good use of some diversion or fun type drills.

Conditioning

FIG. 9-1

In our program, we have a saying that appears on our practice gear and that we continually emphasize throughout the development of our team. It reads simply: **Conditioning, Play Together, Play Hard**. We stress to the players that those three elements make up 85% of the game. The remaining 15% is the organization we have been detailing in previous chapters. The organization is entirely up to the coaches but the players and coaching staff must work together to produce the desired results in the three areas mentioned above. If the talent is there and we are successful in these three areas, then we will be assured of an excellent season. We will be mainly concerned with conditioning here, but we felt it important to include what has become our team motto. Pictured below are the practice shorts we designed to include this saying (Fig. 9-1). This is just another reminder to the players as to what we are trying to accomplish. Playing together and playing hard are crucial in developing a winning program. Our success has been built by emphasizing these two elements as well as conditioning.

At the University of Missouri we want our players to understand that the college game is played from baseline to baseline. The court is ninety-four feet long and the conditioning necessary to play hard for up to forty minutes a game is extremely demanding. There are areas of the game that are harder than others for the coaches to control. Once a game is underway, the performance of the players out on the floor will determine the outcome. The coach still has the ability to give instruction, develop strategy, and make substitutions and adjustments but he cannot **totally** control the performance and execution of the players. This highlights the importance of conditioning in the development of a team. This is one area in which a coach will have total control. There is no excuse for sending a poorly conditioned team out onto the floor. We tell our players that we will not face a better conditioned team. The players will pay the price during the conditioning periods but will reap the benefits at game time. A better conditioned team will have a psychological as well as physiological advantage over their opponents. This will be especially true at the end of each half. Conditioning will be an extremely important factor at the end of the second half when many games are won or lost.

The mental approach of the players is again very important in implementing a successful conditioning program and in maintaining excellent condition. We feel very strongly that our players want to achieve and maintain excellent conditioning. The fact is, however, that the coaching staff must constantly push the players so that maximum results are derived. There are very few players who have the motivation and determination to push themselves to the fullest in the area of conditioning. The conditioning of the team during the season is the responsibility of the coaches and not the individual responsibility of each player. This does not mean that the players do not have any responsibility in this area but the coaches should be accountable for the overall conditioning of the team. The players must be pushed. As we mentioned earlier, the players will find the conditioning periods extremely demanding but they will also find them well worth the effort on game night. With the mental attitude of the players in mind, we will try to vary our workouts and also will include some fun type conditioning drills to relieve the monotony that will be inevitable. These and other conditioning drills will be explained fully at the conclusion of this chapter.

The training rules we discussed back in Chapter One must be adhered to if the players are to maintain peak conditioning. This is where the responsibility rests mainly with the individual. The training habits of the players will show up in their performance, especially during the latter stages of the games and the conditioning segments of practice. Every team member should follow the player training rules to the letter and should give special attention to the general training suggestions outlined by the coaching staff. Please refer back to Chapter One and the section on discipline to re-examine an example of our squad training rules.

In addition to our conditioning during the regular schedule, we suggest both preseason and summer conditioning programs for our players. The comprehensive program that we will outline shortly was designed especially with our goals in mind by Bud Epps, Assistant Trainer at the University of Missouri. Bud worked closely with the coaching staff in incorporating our ideas into his year round format for maintaining excellent conditioning. The players are on their own outside the season, but the suggested program that Bud has devised gives the team members an idea of what will be expected of them and also gives them an excellent workout schedule. The conditioning programs are geared toward increases in three very important areas; flexibility, strength, and endurance or cardiovascular efficiency. As we will see, there are also drill situations that will help to improve the agility and possibly the quickness of our players. It is debatable whether the actual quickness of a player can be increased through anything but the natural maturing process. We are of the opinion, however, that a player can improve his quickness through increased intensity and concentration. Increases in these areas as well as increased endurance will be the goal in drills that combine agility and quickness with conditioning.

Training Evaluation

Below is an example of a training evaluation that Bud will give the coaching staff every spring. Along with the review of the injuries Bud will outline his ideas on how we can improve our conditioning and training for the coming year. Bud will elaborate on these ideas in a meeting with the coaches to discuss any changes that may be necessary for the improved program. The coaching staff will offer our input at this meeting and from there it will be Bud's responsibility to devise a comprehensive program that will best accomplish our conditioning goals. The coaches will have final approval. Bud will also be able to offer his input at this meeting as to the success of our conditioning during the practice sessions or regular season. This is the domain of the coaching staff, but we always want to review our methods to make sure we are effectively accomplishing our objectives.

TO: All Basketball Coaches

After careful review and evaluation of last year's injuries, there are again areas that I feel we must look at in order to improve our program for the coming season.

The following is a short review of last year's injuries:
  1—situation that required stitches (happened at home)
  6—ankel injuries—1 required cast (2 happened at home)
  1—thigh contusion
  1—situation involving the kidney
  3—hospital stays
  1—knee surgery "cartilage"—no patella tendonitis
  2—broken hands
  2—stomach problems
  2—mouth injuries involving broken teeth.

I feel that the suggested spring program, initiated into a summer and fall program, will be a big asset, not only for our overall conditioning, but for the prevention of injuries.

First of all, the stretching program. It takes 10 minutes to do these stretches correctly each day. During this time, the players found that if the gym was absolutely quiet and there was no outside interference, they concentrated better and did them correctly. After last season I could see "first hand" that there was improvement in our overall flexibility as a team, but you must realize that great flexibility cannot be achieved in a few weeks. I have outlined in this summer program the extensive flexibility I want the players to work at. (We should be able to see *good* results when the players return in the fall.) At this point of returning in the fall, I would also like for the players to continue working on a 4-day-a-week basis on flexibility and conditioning (including weights).

Our weight program was one which I feel was a good start for our team. We must continue to *encourage* our kids to lift and work out on weights. Our overall strength *must* be improved from where it is now. It will be time well spent.

The program has aroused some excitement in lifting, and I hope it continues. The flexibility program opened some of the players' eyes on the amount of time it takes to become flexibile, and with the station drills we will continue to suggest, I feel we can vastly improve our strength and condition for the next season.

Sincerely,

BUD EPPS
Assistant Trainer

BE/t

Letters to Players

After devising the comprehensive program Bud will send a suggested summer workout schedule to both the returning players and the incoming freshmen. Further explanation of a suggested summer schedule will follow shortly. Covering the workout schedule will be a brief letter from Bud emphasizing the importance of maintaining proper conditioning. Below are two examples of the types of letters that Bud sends with a personal note at the bottom.

Dear⎯⎯⎯:

Hope this letter finds you feeling good and having an enjoyable summer. I'm sure that you are playing basketball daily and keeping in satisfactory condition.

I was very proud to be associated with a bunch of young men that accomplished what seemed to be an impossible feat. Your team exceeded what I expected of you. We have a great chance to win the Big Eight Championship this coming season. My goal is to help you maintain your health and conditioning to the fullest. And I hope your goal is not only to win the Big Eight, but to advance to the NCAA Finals in Utah.

Your physical conditioning is of vital importance to you as a basketball player. Therefore, what you do between now and the date you return to school will help you considerably.

I have designed an overall program that *will* help you to maintain your condition throughout the summer and will help you be ready to return in the fall. I suggest you read it carefully and stick to it faithfully. **ONLY YOU WILL KNOW IF IT'S BEING DONE NOW—I'LL KNOW WHEN I SEE YOU IN THE FALL.**

Sincerely,

BUD EPPS
Assistant Trainer

BE/t

Dear _____:

Hope this letter finds you feeling good and having an enjoyable summer. I'm sure that you are playing basketball daily and keeping in satisfactory condition.

As an incoming freshman, it must make you feel proud to be associated with such a fine basketball squad that accomplished what it did last season as Big Eight Post Season Tournament Champions. We have a great chance to win the Big Eight Championship this coming season with *your help.*

My goal as trainer is to help you maintain your health and conditioning to the fullest. And I hope your goal is not only to win the Big Eight Championship, but to advance to the NCAA Finals in Utah.

Your physical conditioning is of vital importance to you as a basketball player. Therefore, what you do between now and the date on which you come to school will help you considerably.

I have designed an overall program that will help you to maintain your condition throughout the summer, and it will help you to be ready in the fall. I suggest you read it carefully and stick to it faithfully.

Sincerely,

BUD EPPS
Assistant Trainer

BE/t

Flexibility

Flexibility has become an integral part of the training program in athletics today. We are now recognizing the importance that flexibility can play, not only in the prevention of injuries, but in the total preparation and training of our athletes. Flexibility can be defined as the range of motion of the muscles that span a joint or combination of joints. The greater the range of motion that an athlete has in the areas that are important to his particular sport, the greater are his chances for achieving success. With all of the skills and movements that are required in basketball, flexibility is going to be extremely important and increased flexibility is always going to be one of the primary goals of our conditioning program.

The flexibility exercises that we utilize are pictured and explained fully in the following pages. We begin every practice and have the players begin every conditioning session with a ten minute stretching period. The players are encouraged to repeat the stretching exercises on their own after a workout as a means of warming down slowly. They are also encouraged to stretch whenever they have some free time away from the practice floor. Players who need improvement in this area are especially encouraged to put in the extra time that will be necessary to achieve the desired results.

Key Reminders for Maximum Results

1. Stretch at a smooth and relaxed pace.
2. Relax the mind as well as the body.
3. DO NOT BOUNCE when stretching. Keep the pressure constant but comfortable.
4. Breathe naturally while performing the stretching exercises.
5. Be positive at all times as to the benefits of stretching and how they can apply to making you a better and more complete basketball player.
6. Hold each stretching exercise for fifteen seconds.
7. Be sure to progress at your own pace. Do not strain to keep up with teammates who are more flexible for now. Put in more time, but don't push the stretch to the point where it is painful.

Toe Touch

Fig 9-2
In the initial stretching exercise, we merely ask the players to bend at the waist and hang very relaxed with the arms, hands, and fingers in the direction of the toes. The feet are shoulder width apart and the body is totally relaxed. We will repeat this exercise with more emphasis on the stretch. For now, we want the players merely to hang and let their position and their upper body weight influence the stretching movement.

Cross Toe Touch (Left and Right)

Fig 9-3
The players cross the right leg over the left and again hang naturally with the objective of touching the toes. Those players who are unable to reach their toes naturally from this position should not strain at anytime. The body must be relaxed. Improvement will come through repetition. After holding this stretch for fifteen seconds, the same exercise is repeated with the left leg crossed over the right.

Left Toe Touch

Fig 9-4
In this exercise, the players are to step out approximately six inches to the side with the left foot angled as shown in the above photo. The right hand goes behind the back and

FIG. 9-2

FIG. 9-3

FIG. 9-4

FIG. 9-5

FIG. 9-6

FIG. 9-7

each player bends at the waist and extends or reaches with the left hand for the left toe or beyond. With each exercise, we want to increase slightly our emphasis on the stretch. There is still no straining but the players should be progressing with each exercise in the flexibility period.

Right Toe Touch

The same exercise as explained above except the right leg is extended six inches to the side. The left hand is placed behind the back and the right hand reaches for the corresponding toe or the floor area in front of the toe.

Repeat Toe Touch

We now repeat the first exercise with more emphasis on the stretch. The players should be able to reach their toes as the very minimum on this exercise. The players who are unable to reach their toes at this point in the flexibility period need some extra work in this area. We have some players who are able to touch their wrists to the floor when repeating the toe touch.

Full Stretch

Fig. 9-5

This exercise is one of the very best for relaxing mind and body and preparing for an excellent practice session. It emphasizes just how good stretching can feel if there is no straining and the exercises are done in a progressive manner. In assuming the full stretch, the players position the feet at shoulder width. The heels remain flat on the ground throughout the stretch. Our primary objective is to relax and stretch the upper body so it is important that the players do not go up on their toes. With this in mind, the players reach as high in the air as possible without straining. After seven seconds, we bring the hands down to the side and then reach again to resume the fifteen second stretch. The players are encouraged to stretch the fingers as well as the rest of the upper body.

Side Stretch Left

Fig. 9-6

From the full stretch, the players now bend at the waist and stretch the right side of the body by extending to the left as shown. The arms remain in an extended position and the players should drop the head to the left in order to stretch the neck muscles. It is important not to overextend on this exercise because the players could easily strain a muscle in the right side. We want the body to continue achieving a relaxed state.

Side Stretch Right

The same exercise as explained and pictured above with the players extending to the right and stretching the left side of the body.

Arm Stretch Front

Fig. 9-7
The fingers are interlocked and the palms are turned outward. The arms are then extended and brought to a comfortable position out in front and above the head. As always, a comfortable stretch is emphasized. At seven seconds, the players rotate the neck while still holding the arm stretch.

Arm Stretch Back

Fig. 9-8
The fingers are again interlocked with the palms facing back toward the body. The arms are extended behind the body and are raised to a comfortable position while the chest is expanded and the head remains in an up position. The players hold this movement for fifteen seconds, again rotating the neck when the count reaches seven seconds. Before moving to the next exercise, the players try to extend their arms just a little higher and hold momentarily. This will loosen up the shoulder and back muscles and further aid in increasing flexibility.

Sitting Toe Touch

Fig. 9-9
This movement calls for the players to sit on the floor with the legs extended out in front and the feet approximately six inches apart. The players again bend at the waist and reach for the toes or the ankles to help hold the stretch. The knees must remain locked and flat on the floor. Remember, we are stretching more and more with each exercise so the players should be loosening up pretty well at this point. At the end of the exercise the players should again stretch a little farther and hold momentarily.

Hurdler's Stretch Left Front

Fig. 9-10
To execute the hurdler's stretch as shown above, the left leg is extended straight in front of the body. The right leg is placed behind and slightly under the body with the inside of the foot flat on the ground and the heel against the right buttock. The knee of the left leg remains locked and the right knee and right calf or lower leg maintains contact with the ground. Once this position is assumed, the players bend at the waist and reach with both hands for the left foot or ankle. The players should not rest the head or forearms on

FIG. 9-8

FIG. 9-9

FIG. 9-10

FIG. 9-11

FIG. 9-12

FIG. 9-13

their leg or on the floor. Without bouncing, we have the players stretch to the inside and then the outside of the leg during the fifteen second stretch.

Hurdler's Stretch Left Back

Fig. 9-11

This continues naturally from the previous exercise. The players roll to the floor so that their backs are flat to the surface. They then try to work the right knee to the floor without forcing the stretch. The more flexible the players become, the easier this exercise will be. They should be encouraged not to push too hard to bring the knee in direct contact with the floor.

Hurdler's Stretch Right Front

The same exercise as explained previously except the right leg is extended in front with the left leg placed behind and under the body.

Hurdler's Stretch Right Back

The same exercise as the hurdler's stretch left back with the position of the legs reversed.

Left Leg Tuck

Fig. 9-12

The players lay flat on the floor and bring the left leg up and back toward the chest. The hands then grasp the leg at the knee and pull it further into the chest. The back remains flat on the floor and the right leg remains extended in front with the knee locked. The players concentrate entirely on this stretch for fifteen seconds and then they rotate the ankle along with tucking the leg.

Right Leg Tuck

The same as above with the right leg tucked and the left leg extended in front.

Double Tuck

Fig. 9-13

Both legs are brought to the chest as explained in the previous exercises. The arms now wrap around the legs just below the knees to pull the knees into the chest. At the conclusion of this movement, we will have the players raise the head and back off the floor and hold this tucked position momentarily. This will further stretch the muscles in the back, especially the lower back.

Back Roll-Legs Extended

Fig. 9-14

From the tuck position, we have the players roll back on

their shoulders and pull their legs over until the toes touch the floor behind the head. The legs are extended when the roll is complete and the arms help to support the stretch as shown in the picture above. The players hold this position with the knees locked and the toes touching, but not resting on the floor, for fifteen seconds. They then bring the knees down to the shoulders as explained in the following exercise.

FIG. 9-14

Back Roll-Tuck Position

Fig. 9-15
The knees are brought down as far as possible without straining. The knees come in tight around the head and ears. The arms are laid flat on the floor as shown. We have some players who have no trouble bringing the knees right to the floor just beyond the shoulders. Others can only stretch comfortably to the shoulders. As in all the exercises, we want everyone to progress at their own pace. The key is that we do want to see progress.

Groin Stretcher

Fig. 9-16
In this exercise the players sit up with the knees out wide and the soles of the feet placed together out in front of the body. The players grab their feet and pull them in toward their body while bending forward slightly with the back. The arms do not exert a great deal of pressure in pulling the feet back toward the body. We only want enough pressure to sufficiently stretch the groin area.

FIG. 9-15

Wide Hurdler's Stretch (Left, Right, Middle)

Fig. 9-17 and 9-18
In executing the wide hurdler's stretch the players sit with the legs as far apart as possible. They then bend at the waist and extend the arms down the left leg and grasp the ankle or as close to the ankle as possible without straining. The players hold this position with the head over the knee for the designated fifteen seconds. The same exercise is repeated with the arms extending to the right ankle. After extending in each direction, the players then bend forward at the waist as shown in Figure 9-18. The players should place the hands and forearms flat on the ground to help maintain balance during the stretch.

FIG. 9-16

Defensive Stance

See Fig. 2-2
The final movement we will require for the players in the flexibility segment of practice calls for them to assume an excellent defensive position and hold that positioning for

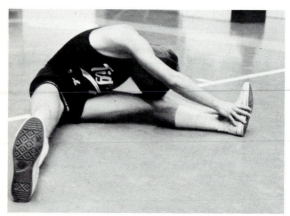

FIG. 9-17

FIG. 9-18

the fifteen second time period. We have the players assume the stance we described in Chapter Two (please refer to Fig. 2-2) including the position of the hands and arms. This takes us naturally into the Leader Drill which we will run immediately after flexibility for at least the first couple of practices. We will also come back to this drill when we need to pay some attention to the basics. When we do revert back, the Leader Drill will always follow the flexibility period.

Summer Conditioning Program

The following is an example of the type of summer conditioning program we have suggested to our players in the past. This program is in addition to encouraging the players to play basketball as much as possible and **against the best competitition available.** Both of these playing requirements are absolutely necessary if the players are to progress and improve as desired during the summer months or during any part of the off season. The fastest way to become a better basketball player is to practice continually against superior players. This idea is especially important for college level players. Too many players go home and work out during the summer months with players of lesser ability because of the lack of competition available. This will hurt them in the fall because, while they may have been dominating the games during the summer, they were not improving their game to any great extent. We impress on our players the need to find the best competition and go where those games are being played.

Suggested Summer Conditioning

First Week (July 17-July 21)
Monday: Flexibility Routine, a.m. and p.m.
Tuesday: Flexibility Routine, a.m. and p.m.
Wednesday: Flexibility Routine, a.m. and p.m.
Thursday: Flexibility Routine, a.m. and p.m.
Friday: Flexibility Routine, a.m. and p.m.
PLAY AS MUCH BASKETBALL AS POSSIBLE. THE SUGGESTED CONDITIONING PROGRAM IS SUPPLEMENTAL TO PLAYING THE GAME.

Second Week (July 24-July 28)
Monday: 1. Flexibility Routine
                      2. Jog 1 mile—walk—jog 1 mile
                      3. Sit ups—set goal of 50 in 70 seconds (2 sets) BENT KNEES
                      4. Push ups—Set goal of 20 in 20 seconds (2 sets)
                      5. Skip Rope—3 minutes (2 sets)
                      6. Flexibility Routine
                          PLAY

Tuesday: 1. Flexibility Routine
                          PLAY

Wednesday: 1. Flexibility Routine
                      2. Jog 1½ miles—walk—jog 1 mile
                      3. Sit ups—2 sets of 50. BENT KNEES
                      4. Push ups—2 sets of 20
                      5. Skip rope—3 minutes (2 sets)
                      6. Flexibility Routine
                          PLAY

Thursday: 1.   Flexibility Routine
                 PLAY

Friday: 1.   Flexibility Routine
             2.   Jog 2 miles—walk—jog 1 1/2 miles
             3.   Sit ups—2 sets of 50
             4.   Push ups—3 sets of 20
             5.   Skip rope—3 1/2 minutes (2 sets)
             6.   Flexibility Routine
                 PLAY

Third Week (July 31-August 4)

Monday: 1.   Flexibility Routine
             2.   **Run** 1 1/2 miles—walk—jog 1 1/2 miles
             3.   30 yard sprints—5 at 3/4 speed
             4.   Sit ups—2 sets of 50
             5.   Push ups (fingertip)—3 sets of 20
             6.   Skip rope—1 four min., 1 three min., 1 two min.
             7.   Flexibility Routine
                 PLAY

Tuesday: 1.   Flexibility Routine
                 PLAY

Wednesday: 1.   Flexibility Routine
             2.   **Run** 2 miles—walk—jog 1 mile
             3.   30 yard sprints—7 at 3/4 speed
             4.   Sit ups—2 sets of 50
             5.   Push ups (fingertips)—2 sets of 20
             6.   Skip rope—1 four min., 1 three min., 1 two min.
             7.   Flexibility Routine
                 PLAY

Thursday: 1.   Flexibility Routine
                 PLAY

Friday: 1.   Flexibility Routine
             2.   **Run** 2 miles—walk—jog 1 mile
             3.   30 yard sprints—8 at 3/4 speed
             4.   Sit ups—2 sets of 50
             5.   Push ups (fingertips)—2 sets of 20
             6.   Skip rope—1 four min., 1 three min., 1 two min.
             7.   Flexibility Routine
                 PLAY

Fourth Week (August 7-August 11)

Monday: 1.   Flexibility Routine
             2.   **Run** 2 miles—walk—jog 1 mile
             3.   30 yard sprints—8 at 3/4 speed
             4.   Sit ups—2 sets of 50
             5.   Push ups—2 sets of 20 (fingertips)
             6.   Skip rope—1 four min., 1 three min., 1 two min.
             7.   Flexibility Routine
                 PLAY

Tuesday: 1.   Flexibility Routines
                 PLAY

Wednesday: 1.   Flexibility Routine
             2.   880 yard run (4), walk 220 in between each
             3.   30 yard sprints (8) at 3/4 speed
             4.   Sit ups—2 sets of 50
             5.   Push ups—2 sets of 20 (fingertip)
             6.   Skip rope—1 four min., 1 three min., 1 two min.
             7.   Flexibility Routine
                 PLAY

Thursday: 1.   Flexibility Routine
                 PLAY

Friday:
1. Flexibility Routine
2. 880 yard sprints (4), walk 220 in between each
3. 30 yard sprints (9) at $3/4$ speed
4. Sit ups—2 sets of 50
5. Push ups—2 sets of 20
6. Skip rope—1 four min., 1 three min., 1 two min.
7. Flexibility Routine
PLAY

Fifth Week (August 14-August 18)
Monday:
1. Flexibility Routine
2. Run 2 miles—walk—jog 1 mile
3. 30 yard sprints (8) at $3/4$ speed
4. Sit ups—2 sets of 50
5. Push ups—2 sets of 20 (fingertip)
6. Skip rope—1 four min., 1 three min., 1 two min.
7. Flexibility Routine
PLAY

Tuesday:
1. Flexibility Routine
PLAY

Wednesday:
1. Flexibility Routine
2. 220 yard run (8)—walk—110 in between each
3. 30 yard sprints (8) at $3/4$ speed
4. Sit ups—2 sets of 50
5. Push ups—2 sets of 20 (fingertip)
6. Skip rope—1 four min., 1 three min.
7. Flexibility Routine
PLAY

Thursday:
1. Flexibility Routine
PLAY

Friday:
1. Flexibility Routine
2. 220 yard run (8)—walk—110 in between each
3. 30 yard sprints (8) at $3/4$ speed
4. Sit ups—2 sets of 50
5. Push ups—2 sets of 20 (fingertip)
6. Skip rope—1 four min., 1 three min.
7. Flexibility Routine
PLAY

Fall Conditioning Program

As we pointed out earlier in this chapter, we suggest that the players begin a specified fall conditioning program four weeks prior to the start of practice. When the players report for school, we encourage them to continue with the flexibility and summer conditioning programs on their own and to continue playing as much basketball as possible. We make sure that the floor is available for games and individual workouts in the late afternoons when the players are through with classes.

The fall conditioning program is outlined in the following pages. In addition to playing, we are going to ask the players to work on three areas of development to attain maximum conditioning for the start of organized practice. We will stay with our flexibility routine so that each individual can work to improve himself in that area. We will implement a weight program for both the lower and upper body to increase the strength of the individual players. Finally, we will include some agility and conditioning drills to improve ourselves in this area.

We will do some running for distance (up to two miles) but for the most part, our running and conditioning drills will be geared toward playing the game of basketball. We feel it is important to condition the players in the fall with the same type of running and movement requirements that take place during practice and under actual game conditions. Basketball is played in quick, explosive sprints calling for much stopping and starting and quick foot movement in confined areas. We want our conditioning in the fall to apply directly to these type of movements. The agility and conditioning will be selected from our master list of drills shown earlier in this chapter. We will include anywhere from one to three of these drills daily depending upon the time and physical effort required. All of the agility and conditioning drills will be explained fully at the conclusion of this chapter.

Strength Development

The weight program we utilize is designed to improve the strength of our players in the upper and the lower body. During fall conditioning, we will work Mondays and Wednesdays on strengthing the upper body. Tuesdays and Thursdays we will concentrate on the lower body. We always want the players to conduct their weight training at the end of the workout because we want the players to play and work on their basketball skills while they are fresh. We feel that it is easier and more beneficial for the players to push themselves on the weights after playing hard rather than lifting the weights and then trying to push themselves to get up and down the floor in a game situation. The exercises we use are listed below with the sets and repetitions listed to the side. We like the players to warm up at each station with five to seven repetitions at a light weight before beginning the regular three sets of ten repetitions with maximum weight. It is very important in conducting a weight program that the strength that has been developed in the off season is maintained during the preseason practices and throughout the season. It is best to get back to the weight room at least once and ideally twice a week during the preseason practice sessions. During the regular season, one workout per week will be sufficient to maintain the strength gained. Brief, intense workouts at the end of a days practice are all that are needed.

Upper Body (Monday and Wednesdays)

1. Bench Press
   —Warm up (5-7 repetitions)
   —3 sets of ten repetitions
2. Military Press
   —Warm up (5-7 repetitions)
   —3 sets of ten repetitions
3. Lat Pulldowns
   —Warm up (5-7 repetitions)
   —3 sets of ten repetitions
4. Bicep Curls
   —Warm up (5-7 repetitions)

—3 sets of ten repetitions
5. Upright Row
    —Warmup (5-7 repetitions)
    —3 sets of ten repetitions
6. Tricep Extentions
    —Warm up (5-7 repetitions)
    —3 sets of ten repetitions

Lower Body (Tuesday and Thursday)

1. Leg Extentions (both legs)
    —Warm up (5-7 repetitions)
    —3 sets of ten repititions
2. Leg Curls (both legs)
    —Warm up (5-7 repetitions)
    —3 sets of ten repetitions
3. Leg Press
    —Warm up (5-7 repetitions)
    —3 sets of ten repetitions
4. Big Blue (Leaper Machine)
    —Include all four days
    —3 sets fast speed (thirty seconds)
    —Every fourth session change to 3 sets slow speed (10 seconds)
5. Ankles (heel raises)
    —Toes straight,1 set of 15 reps
    —Toes in,1 set of 15 reps
    —Toes out,1 set of 15 reps
6. Sit ups
    —2 sets of 50

Typical Schedule for Fall Conditioning

Below is a typical schedule we will issue to the players so that they may implement our suggested program in the fall. Notice that the agility and conditioning drills are the only part of the program that really varies on a day to day basis. The weight program alternates the workouts as to upper body and lower body concentration but there is no other variation in the exercises performed. There is quite a bit of thought that goes into the implementation of the agility and conditioning drills. As we mentioned, these are the movements that apply directly to the game of basketball and we feel they are extremely important in preparing our team for the start of practices and the regular season.

The players should work on all four areas of development for four days a week, Monday through Thursday. We encourage the players to stretch and play on Fridays. Saturday and Sunday are off days, although we still encourage the players to do their stretching exercises and work out on their own. The dedicated players will take very few days off.

First Week (Sept. 18-Sept. 24)
Monday: 1.   Flexibility Routine
            2.   Cone Drill
            3.   Forward-Back Drill
            4.   Skip Rope—4 minutes, 2 minutes
            5.   PLAY
            6.   Weights—Upper body

Tuesday: 1.   Flexibility Routine
            2.   Forward-Back Drill
            3.   Lane Drill
            4.   Indian Relay Race—around Hearnes track

5. PLAY
6. Weights—Lower Body

Wednesday: 1. Flexibility Routine
2. Lane Drill
3. Indian Relay Race—Hearnes track
4. Skip Rope—4 minutes, 2 minutes
5. PLAY
6. Weights—Upper Body

Thursday: 1. Flexibility Routine
2. Forward-Back Drill
3. Cone Drill
4. Bench jumping—2 one minute sets
5. PLAY
6. Weights—Lower Body

Friday: 1. Flexibility Routine
2. PLAY

Saturday: Flexibility and Rest
Sunday: Flexibility and Rest

Second Week (Sept. 25-Oct. 1)
Monday: 1. Flexibility Routine
2. Running (2 miles—outside)
3. Cone Drill
4. PLAY
5. Weights—Upper Body

Tuesday: 1. Flexibility Routine
2. Cone Drill
3. Skip Rope
4. Bench jumping (2 one minute sets)
5. PLAY
6. Weights—Lower body

Wednesday: 1. Flexibility Routine
2. Running (2 miles—outside)
3. Forward-Back Drill
4. PLAY
5. Weights—Upper Body

Thursday: 1. Flexibility Routine
2. Indian Relay Race
3. Forward-Back Drill
4. Lane Drill
5. PLAY
6. Weights—Lower Body

Friday: 1. Flexibility Routine
2. PLAY
Saturday: Flexibility and Rest
Sunday: Flexibility and Rest

Third Week (Oct.2-Oct.8)
Monday: 1. Flexibility Routine
2. Running (2 miles—outside)
3. Toss Backs—Lay up drill
4. PLAY
5. Weights—Upper body

Tuesday: 1. Flexibility Routine
2. Toss Backs—sliding
3. Skip Rope—4 minutes, 3 minutes, 2 minutes
4. Forward-Back Drill
5. PLAY
6. Weights—Lower Body

Wednesday:
1. Flexibility Routine
2. Running (2 miles)
3. Cone Drill
4. Toss Backs—Passing (chest pass, overhead pass)
5. PLAY
6. Weights—Upper Body

Thursday:
1. Flexibility Routine
2. Toss Backs—Passing (chest pass, overhead pass)
3. Bench Jumping
4. Skip Rope—4 minutes, 3 minutes, 2 minutes
5. PLAY
6. Weights—Lower Body

Friday:
1. Flexibility Routine
2. PLAY

Saturday: Flexibility and Rest
Sunday: Flexibility and Rest

Fourth Week (Oct. 9-Oct. 15)

Monday:
1. Flexibility Routine
2. Running (2 miles)
3. Cone Drill
4. Bench Jumping (2 one minute sets)
5. PLAY
6. Weights—Upper Body

Tuesday:
1. Flexibility Routine
2. Cone Drill
3. Lane Drill
4. Toss Backs—Passing (chest pass, overhead pass)
5. PLAY
6. Weights—Lower Body

Wednesday:
1. Flexibility Routine
2. Running (2 miles)
3. Forward-Back Drill
4. Toss Backs—Lay up drill
5. PLAY
6. Weights—upper body

Thursday:
1. Flexibility Routine
2. Indian Relay Race
3. Forward-Back Drill
4. Toss Backs—Sliding Drill
5. PLAY
6. Weights—Lower Body

Friday: Day Off
Saturday: Day Off
Sunday: First Day of Practice

Individual Programs

We stress to the players that the off season, especially the summer months, are the periods where individual players are made. The team will be developed from October through March. It is important for each individual to strive to improve himself in that period from April through September. We will issue some general suggestions and sometimes a complete individual program to certain players so they understand where improvement is needed in their particular game. The complete program provides the players with the specific drills needed to correct their weaknesses. Below are two examples

352 Conditioning

of individual programs we have issued in the past. The first is general in nature and can be followed with a more complete program if that is what is needed for a particular player. The second example shows a complete workout schedule.

Clay Johnson

OFF-SEASON—GENERAL SUGGESTIONS
1. Weight Program—regular workouts with intensity.
2. Finger tip pushups to develop;
   a. fingers and wrists for passing and shooting improvement.
   b. forearms, shoulders, and chest for upper body strength and stamina.
3. Work on improving your **left hand** and going to your **left.**
4. Shooting!
5. Running—must build endurance/stamina.

Tom Dore

OFF-SEASON—INDIVIDUAL PROGRAM
1. Weight Program—regular workouts with intensity.
2. Rope Skipping
3. Toss Back
   a. chest pass
   b. ball over head—outlet
4. Running—must build endurance/stamina (include backward running).
5. Individual Offensive Moves
6. Agility and Conditioning
   a. Combinations
   b. Rim Touching Drill
   c. Bench Jumping
   d. Lane Drill — improve quickness
   e. Pick Up Drill
7. Exaggerated Rebound—Really Get Up
   Move every part of your body. Make quarter turn looking for outlet. Shake—elbows—everything! Grab ball like you own it.
8. PLAY!! (2 on 2, 3 on 3, 4 on 4)

Daily Workouts
Monday:
   1. Flexibility Routine
   2. Rope Skipping
   3. Individual Offensive Moves
      On Post—make yourself big
         —hands up, fingers spread comfortably
         —don't move until ball released
         —READ DEFENSE!
      Turn Around—receive pass a little lower, turn—EXPLODE
         —look to shoot, instinct will tell you when to pass
         —DO NOT look down, **LOOK TO BUCKET**
         —smooth, confident
         —fluff off glass (30-45 degree angle)
      Hook—receive pass, head goes to basket, this will turn shoulder
         —get ball in shooting line
            pivot, knee bent, foot turned
         —leg kick (level)
         —shoulder points to bucket
         —full arm extension
         —index finger turns in
      Counter—start hook, read defense, turn and shoot it down
         —smooth, confident
         —look at the basket!
      Power Moves—on balance, strong
   4. PLAY!
   5. Weight Program!

Tuesday:
   1. Flexibility Routine
   2. Individual Offensive Moves—same as above

3. Toss Back—chest pass, outlet, rebound outlet
4. Combinations—keep ball up, rhythm, bend knee for power
5. Rim Touching—15 left, 15 right, 15 both—increase!
6. Run 1/2 mile—speed
7. PLAY!
8. Run 1/2 mile—speed

Wednesday:
Same as Monday

Thursday:
1. Flexibility Routine
2. Individual Offensive Moves
3. Toss Back
4. Bench Jumping
5. Lane Drill-quickness
6. Exaggerated Rebound—tough!
7. Run 1/2 mile—speed
8. PLAY!
9. Run 1/2 mile—speed (will increase)

Friday:
Same as Monday and Wednesday

Agility and Conditioning Drills

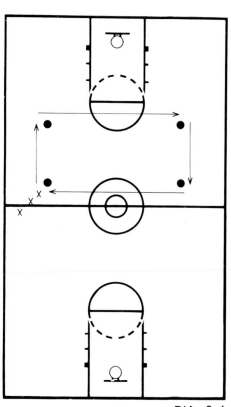

DIA. 9-1

The agility and conditioning drills that we implement during the season and in the off season conditioning are fully explained below. Rope skipping, running the steps, and running for distance are pretty much self-explanatory.

CONE DRILL (Dia. 9-1)

Objective: Primarily conditioning, but we also want to work on the sliding technique and the foot movement and quickness of the players.

Procedure: Four obstacles (we named it the Cone drill because that is what we use to mark the course) are placed in a square area as shown below. The players form a single line and slide in a clockwise fashion around each of the corners. They are facing to the outside. We will start with three trips and then increase the trips to increase conditioning.

Points of Emphasis 1. Proper sliding technique.
                2. Quickness!
                3. Intensity!

Lane Drill (Dia. 9-2)

Objective: Conditioning, quickness, and intensity.

Procedure: The players pair off and line up with six players inside the lane areas or at the center circle. The first six slide from lane to lane making sure to touch outside the line with the hand. The partner for each player counts the number of lines. We will record these periodically. We start the drill at thirty seconds and then increase to one minute. When the first six complete the time requirement, the next six players move in and the roles are reversed.

Points of Emphasis: 1. Stay low.
                2. Touch outside the lines with the hands.

3. Quickness!
4. Intensity!

Forward-Back Drill (Dia. 9-3)

Objective: Conditioning and developing in the players the ability to stop and start quickly, change directions, and sprint backwards. We are stressing the movements involved in basketball.

Procedure: Obstacles are placed on the floor as shown below. The players line up in single file the same as in the Cone Drill. The players sprint to the first obstacle and then sprint backwards to the second, forward to the third, backwards to the fourth and so on. We again start with three trips and increase each time we utilize the drill.

Points of Emphasis: 1. Quick, explosive starts after stopping. Learn to explode.
2. Intensity!

Indian Relay Drill

Objective: Conditioning.

Procedure: The players form a single file line and run at a steady pace around a track area. We have a 220 yard indoor track and this suits our needs perfectly. After one lap, the player at the end of the line is to sprint to the front. As soon as he reaches the lead position, the new player at the end of the line repeats this procedure. This continues so that one of the players is sprinting at all times and the others are running at a good steady pace. Any distance or time requirement can be established. This is a form of Fartlek running which we feel is a very beneficial method of conditioning.

Bench Jumping

Objective: Conditioning (especially the legs) and also to improve the jumping ability of the players.

Procedure: We utilize a rope tied at each end to a cone as the obstacle. Benches can be used, but there is the possibility of injury if a player fails to clear the bench. Non-participating players can hold the ropes, but we prefer the cones so that the drill can move quickly. The players pair off and one player counts while the other jumps back and forth over the rope. The object is to see how many times the player can clear the rope in a set amount of time. We run both thirty second and one minute drills. The players then reverse roles. We usually run for three sets each.

Points of Emphasis: 1. Quickness!
2. Intensity!
3. Do not touch the rope on the jump. Must clear it.

Toss Back-Lay Up Drill

Objective: Primarily to develop the conditioning, intensity and quickness of the players. The drill also includes the lay up shot and passing fundamentals.

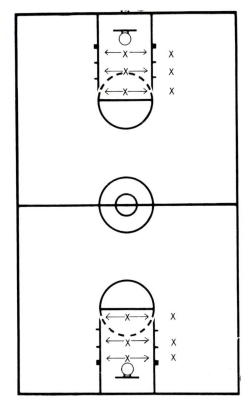

DIA. 9-2

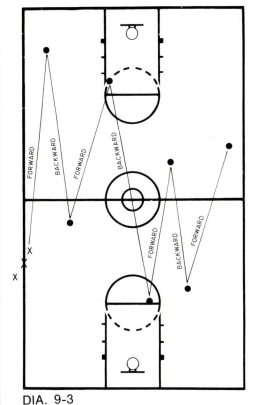

DIA. 9-3

Conditioning 355

Procedure: Toss Back is placed at approximately the free throw line extended. The players are to pass the ball into the toss back and catch the return pass on a cut to the basket. The lay up shot is executed and this continues for a thirty second time limit. The players try to make as many lay ups as possible in thirty seconds.

Points of Emphasis: 1. Quickness
2. Intensity.
3. Pass the ball accurately so the return is accurate.
4. Execute the lay up properly.

Toss Back-Sliding Drill

Objective: To develop the conditioning, quickness and intensity of the players.

Procedure: The players start about 10 feet in front of the toss back and off to the side. The ball is then passed so it is returned away from the player. He must slide and catch the ball and repeat this procedure back and forth.

Points of Emphasis: 1. Quickness of the feet.
2. Intensity.

Pick Up Drill (Dia. 9-4)

Objective:This is a drill we use a lot with our big men to improve conditioning, agility and quickness.

Procedure: The player aligns himself on the free throw line with a coach facing him under the basket. The coach rolls a ball away from the player so that the player must move quickly to recover the ball and return it to the coach. The player returns to the middle of the floor and the coach rolls the ball in the opposite direction of the first recovery. This continues with the coach mixing the throws up to one side or the other as the drill progresses. The coach can make the drill as difficult as necessary.

Points of Emphasis: 1. Intensity.
2. Quickness.
3. The player must make a good accurate return pass.
4. The player must always return to the middle after a recovery.

10 In 1 Drill

Objective: Conditioning.

Procedure: The players run in two groups from the baseline. The squad can be divided according to teams or according to position. The ten stands for the number of times we want the players to sprint the length of the court. The one is a one minute time limit. We like to use the clock for this conditioning drill but a stopwatch or watch is suitable. If the players do not finish the required ten lengths within the one minute time period, then some extra conditioning is required.

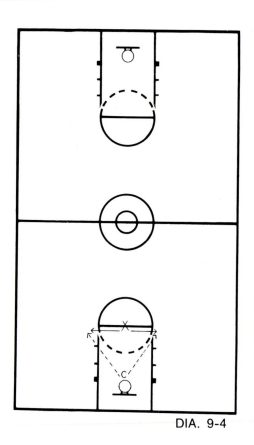

DIA. 9-4

Man-Boy (Dia. 9-5)
Objective: Conditioning
Procedure: This is a rather universal conditioning drill that merely has different names and sometimes different requirements. Ours is a little different. The drill is again run in two groups from the baseline. Each group sprints to the free throw line or free throw line extended and then back to the baseline, to half court and back, and then to the opposite baseline. The drill does not end here but continues with the exact procedure ending where the players started. The players obviously run in a straight line, for organizational purposes, but the diagram shown should give you a better idea of the sequence of sprints.

Basket Drill
Objective: Conditioning
Procedure: The players pair off and the first player aligns himself in the middle of the lane. The second player will count before reversing roles with the first. On the whistle, the players will move quickly to the free throw line and touch the line with the hand. They then reverse and sprint to the basket jumping as high as possible up to the basket. This is repeated as many times as possible in a thirty second time limit. We utilize all six baskets for this drill.

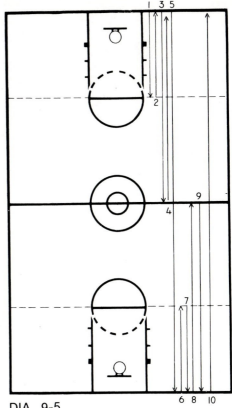

DIA. 9-5

Special Situations 10

It would be a mistake to underestimate the importance of preparing your team effectively for the special situations that can occur during the course of a game. Solid preparation in this area can sometimes mean the difference between victory and defeat. This is especially true in the closing minutes or closing seconds of a close ball game. In our program we divide the special situations plays into five main areas to be included in the organization and development of our team. These areas must be dealt with if a team is to be successful. That means planning, preparation and organization of the practice time to include work on these special areas. The five special situations that we feel are extremely important are: the lay up game (our control offense), out-of-bounds plays, free throw situations, jump ball situations, and situations involving the clock. We introduce the special situations usually about the fourth week of the preseason and will reserve some practice time each week after that for work on the various plays. We will also emphasize the special situations in all scrimmage sessions and will work sometimes at the end of the scrimmages strictly on these aspects of the game. The final week of preseason preparation will be extremely important in finalizing our work in the special situations. At this time the players should know exactly what we are trying to set up and accomplish in every phase of the game. During the last week of preseason practice the emphasis should be on refining the different areas of the game including the special situations. Once the season begins we will set aside some time during the last practice before each game to work on the special situations.

The Lay Up Game

We refer to our ball control offense as the Lay up Game. This is a very apt title considering our philosophy behind the utilization of a ball control offense. In our lay up game we want to continue to put pressure on the defense and the basket area. We are working for a lay up rather than merely holding the ball for long periods of time without attempting to score. By our way of thinking there is no such thing as a stall offense. Only on very rare occasions in the last seconds of a game would we want to hold the ball without any attempt to score. Any time we can produce a sure lay up we want to take advantage of the situation and then convert quickly to the opposite end to set up a tough defense. This has to be the goal of most ball control offenses so the term stall can sometimes be misleading.

Our philosophy on the lay up game fits in with our overall emphasis on aggressive basketball. We continue to try and make something happen rather than merely trying to maintain possession of the basketball. An offense that is designed to maintain possession of the ball without putting any pressure on the basket is much too cautious. The offensive team will actually be playing defensively in their attempt to keep from making mistakes. The defense will be able to apply all kinds of pressure. They become the aggressors and the offense will continue to feel the pressure as long as the goal is merely to maintain possession of the ball. It should be noted that we are not minimizing the importance of possession when we go to the lay up game. The idea is to control the basketball and run time off the clock and we intend to do just that. However, we are still attempting to score if we can produce a sure two points through the movement of our men and the movement of the basketball. As we mentioned above, most teams will take the sure basket because an extended lead will be more advantageous than maintaining control of the ball. The difference is that we are continually working for the opportunity to get to the basket and execute the lay up shot. This is a concept that is certainly not limited to our program here at the University of Missouri. Many teams are running the four corners offense with the same goals in mind and are having a great deal of success. By the same token, we have seen many teams who become too passive and do not execute a sound ball control offense because they do not know how to control the ball and still apply pressure to the basket and on the defensive team. This is something we work on and preach constantly when beginning to teach and then develop our lay up game.

We feel that the lay up game is the most important aspect of the areas that make up our special situations. There are so many things that are important in teaching the game of basketball that it is sometimes hard to establish clear priorities. We are always referring to different areas of the game as the most important element in the development of a successful team. However, there is no doubt that we place a great deal of emphasis and spend a great deal of time on perfecting our lay up game. We think that the proper development of the lay up game instills confidence in the players both in their ability to handle the basketball and in their ability to play with poise during crucial situations. These crucial situations will usually occur at the end of a close game but the tempo of the game, foul problems, or disadvantages with regard to personnel are all factors that can lead up to the utilization of a ball control offense. We want our players to develop enough confidence in this aspect of the game that they believe that the team can go to the lay up game at any time and expand rather than sit on a lead. This confidence will come from continued practice and the proper teaching of the principles involved in our lay up game.

The principles we mentioned above are issued in the form of a handout when we begin to teach the lay up game in the preseason practice sessions. From that point on these ideas or rules are constantly stressed to the players during segments of practice set aside for special situations and our lay up game offense. If the players follow these ideas closely we will have an excellent ball handling team. The ability to successfully execute the lay up game will definitely carry over and add to the efficiency of our regular offense. That is just another reason we place a great deal of emphasis on developing a sound lay up game or ball control offense.

The following principles are shown and explained to the players out on the floor. Each player is then issued a handout as a repetitive teaching device. As we mentioned, these points are continually stressed during practice time. Most of these principles will be discussed in greater detail as we explain and develop our ball control offense in the following pages.

The Lay up Game

1. Play the Basket! Continue to put pressure on the defense!
2. Play the half line if the defense sags.
3. Meet the basketball at all times.
4. Stay out of the corners and off the sideline.
5. **Do Not** set a screen for or cross a teammate handling the basketball.
6. **Do Not** pick up your dribble until you are ready to make a pass to an open teammate. Keep the ball alive.
7. Maintain spacing out on the floor. Stay wide!
8. Always look to break behind the defense but don't go to the basket unless you are open and the ball is in a position to be delivered.
9. If you do go to the basket and the pass is not thrown clear the basket area as quickly as possible. Reset to your original position or fill an open spot.
10. Read your defensive man and the defense. If your man is playing you high, go to the basket. If the defender is playing you low, go to the ball (make yourself available for the pass).
11. Keep your man occupied at all times. Vary your movements within the framework of the offense. Mix it up. Take what the defense gives you.
12. If you are screening away from the ball and a switch occurs, look to go to the basket.
13. If you clear your defender at any time, get to the basket.
14. CUT HARD TO THE BASKET when you do elect to go all the way.
15. Finish or make your cut on the ballside of the basket to improve the passing angle.
16. HEADHUNT ON THE SCREENS. Screen the defensive man, not a spot on the floor. Make sure you come set.
17. Make your passes away from the defense.
18. AVOID THE USE OF THE BOUNCE PASS OUT ON THE FLOOR!!
19. Possession is of the utmost importance. Protect the ball at all times!
20. Play with Poise and Confidence!

Lay Up Game Alignment and Personnel

Diagram 10-1 shows the alignment we will utilize in executing the lay up game. It is a basic two-three or two-one-two set that is designed to take advantage of the entire half court area. This is a very important teaching point in developing a ball control offense. The players must learn to use all the floor space that is available without flirting with danger on the sidelines or along the half court line. We tell our players to keep the floor spread but stay off the boundary lines and out of the corners. As a general rule, the players are told to play approximately three feet in from the sidelines and

DIA. 10-1

the half court line. This gives them a cushion in which to pivot, bounce the basketball, or escape the defense if necessary. We want to use every inch of the floor possible to spread the defense but it would be a mistake to play right near the lines without allowing a margin for error. The offensive players out front are to play at the midpoint between the sideline and the middle of the floor when handling the ball. The front player opposite the ball (O_2) will shift to the ballside of that midpoint ever so slightly in case he is needed to relieve pressure. The weakside wing player (O_4) and the player in the middle position (O_5) will also shade slightly to the ballside but the idea is still to spread the floor so the defense will be forced out wide.

As we mentioned, we put a lot of work and practice time into the perfecting of our ball control offense. We want all of the players to develop the ability and the poise to handle the ball in our lay up game. While we want to work with all of the players in this area there are times when we will want to substitute or adjust our personnel so that our best ball handlers and most poised performers are in the game. When in a situation where the defense may be forced to foul it would also be beneficial to have excellent free throw shooters in the line-up. Rebounding strength and defensive matchups are still important to consider so the insertion of four or five guards in the line up is usually not advantageous. Ideally, all of the players will develop the ability to contribute in the lay up game so that wholesale line-up changes will not be necessary and different strategies can be employed while executing this offense.

In establishing our personnel for the lay up game we try basically to keep the players at familiar positions so that we have the same rebounding strength and we are not hurt in the matchups at our defensive end. We can substitute a small forward or big guard to place a better ball handling player at one of the forward positions. We can also place one of our forwards in the center position to possibly improve ourselves there. The point is that if our normal post player and our normal forwards become adept at running the lay up game, there will usually be no need to make those changes. This is what we are constantly striving for in working with the players on the lay up game. There are different strategies that we will employ by adjusting our personnel but we will never be forced to make an adjustment if our players develop the proper skills. We have found this to be a very obvious advantage when our opponents have been forced to make some substitutions or adjustments in their line-up. For instance, the defense will often substitute a third guard to enhance their defensive ability and add some quickness to the line-up. That guard will usually be assigned to cover one of our forwards. If our forward is not bothered by the increased quickness of his defensive counterpart and if he is confident in his ability to execute the lay up game, then we have gained a definite advantage. The height and strength differential should be beneficial to our player in protecting the basketball and in rebounding at the offensive and defensive end.

The one situation that could necessitate a substitution is while protecting a lead at the end of the game. The defense may be forced to foul under these conditions and we want to take away any opportunity they may have to send a poor percentage free throw shooter to the line. At this level, that should not be that much of a problem. All of the players should have the shooting ability and the poise to handle the pressure of an important free throw late in the game. Still it stands to reason that some players will have a higher free throw percentage and/or a greater ability to handle the pressure in that situation. Again, ideally your best players in the lay up game would all be high percentage free throw shooters and tough under pressure. If a poor free throw shooter is in the line-up, most of the time it will pay to substitute for him at the end of the game. Keep in mind also that just because a player is a high percenage free throw shooter, it does not mean that he will be one of your best shooters in a crucial situation. By the same token, a relatively low percentage free throw shooter may be at his best under pressure. These are all factors that have to be considered in adjusting to a ball control offense and determining the best personnel available for the successful execution of that offense. It is obvious that the players called on to protect a slim lead at the end of the game have to possess poise, a confidence in their ability to handle the basketball, and a great amount of mental toughness.

In keeping with our philosophy on personnel, we think it is a tremendous advantage to have a post player who is confident and capable of handling the basketball in a control offense. Having a big man in the game can be extremely helpful in relieving some of the defensive pressure applied to the primary ball handlers. The big man will be able to step out and catch a high pass from an offensive player who has picked up his dribble or is under extreme pressure from the defense. The height of the post player gives the ball handler an excellent target and allows him to make a higher pass than usual away from the defense. An agile, excellent ball handling post player can be extremely valuable in the middle position. We ask the post player in this position to play just inside the key area in the middle of the floor. He will be facing the sideline on the ball side of the floor with one foot inside the top of the key and one foot outside. In other words, in starting the offense, the middle player will be directly over or straddling the line forming the top of the key. Floor spacing is extremely important in running a successful ball control offense and this teaching point gives the player an exact idea of where to align himself in initiating the offense. The player is facing the sideline so he can maintain vision and eye contact with the ball handler and so that he can get to the ball or to the basket with equal quickness. If the ball were reversed to the opposite guard, the middle man would merely open to the flight of the ball and reverse the position of his feet. The middle man may want to seal his defensive opponent off or take him higher as the ball is reversed to set up a possible cut to the basket or to the ball. These and more options in the offense will be discussed shortly. The important thing for now is the initial alignment and the personnel requirements.

The players at the wing or forward positions will be faced in toward the middle of the floor so that they too can get to the basket and to the ball with equal ability. These players are aligned basically the same as in our half court offense. They are positioned on the free throw line extended and are out as wide as possible while still allowing for a cushion area on the sidelines. As we mentioned earlier, the wing player opposite the ball will cheat very slightly toward the ballside. It will be very important in our offense to utilize all of the floor space available but we also want this weakside player to be able to get to the ball if needed. It will also be very important for him to be able to get to the basket as quickly as possible for a pass from the ballside. The weakside players will, for the most part, be holding their positions or exchanging positions with a vertical screen so a half step or step into the middle of the floor should not hinder our spacing.

The forward on the ballside should be ready to seal his man off and meet the pass from the guard or break to the basket depending on what is open. The player in this position must read the defense and he must work well with the guard so they can determine the most advantageous offensive maneuver. Both forwards must have the ability to handle the basketball out on the floor. The guards also assume the same basic alignment we use to initiate our half court offense. The ball handling guard is at the midpoint between the sideline and the center of the floor. The weakside guard is in a slight reverse pass position and about one half step on the ballside of his midpoint. The guards must be extremely poised and excellent ball handlers. The frontline players will be looking to go to them whenever possible which is the way it should be. In a control offense, you want your best ball handlers to be in possession of the ball the majority of the time. The guards must be confident in their ability to handle the pressure and in their ability to provide leadership, especially late in the game.

Basic Pattern

The basic pattern involved in our lay up game is very simple to execute. We are going to utilize the give and go on the ballside and a simple exchange involving the guard and forward on the weakside. The post player does not move out of the middle of the floor unless he is instructed to exchange positions. **The middle man stays in that lane**. He has three responsibilities or options to perform in the middle position.

One, he can step out to catch the ball and relieve pressure. Two, he can hold position at the top of the key. Three, he can break to the basket for a possible pass and sure lay up. It is crucial that the player in the middle of the floor has the discipline to hold position unless he is needed to relieve pressure or unless he has a clear opening to the basket. There is an art to playing this position and the player who has learned to play it well can make a great contribution in the execution of a lay up game such as ours. We should mention that the middle man, as well as all players, has the opportunity to face the basket and see what develops after catching the ball. He can work to go one on one but the ball must be protected at all times and he cannot force the action. This player can totally frustrate the defense if he utilizes the timing we have mentioned above. Frustration on the part of the defense will lead to lay ups for the offense if the players learn to react and make the proper cuts.

Movement on the Ballside

The guard has three possible passing options from our two-three alignment; the lead pass to the strongside forward, the reverse pass to the opposite guard, and the pass to the high post player stepping out on the floor. His first look is to the forward because that is the shortest and most available pass. Diagram 10-2 to the left shows the cutting action that immediately follows the guard to forward pass. The forward receiving the pass will make a front turn into the middle of the floor or drop step his man if the defense has overreacted to the pass. More times than not, the front turn will be executed. The forward immediately plays the basket making sure that the ball is protected from any defensive pressure. As O_3 is playing the basket, he will recognize if O_5 or O_4 have cut behind the defense for a possible lay up. These options will generally not be open on the first few passes but the opportunities will increase the longer the offense is able to control the ball and keep the opponent on defense. At any rate, by playing the basket O_3 can recognize and take full advantage of any opportunity that does present itself. As is evidenced by the cutting action shown, the four outside positions in the lay up game are all interchangeable. When playing the front positions, the players are taught to play the basket or play the half line. This will depend on the pressure applied by the defense. The guard executing the guard to forward pass has the option of cutting to the basket or holding his position for a return pass back out to the half line. To execute this properly, the guard must read the actions of his defensive opponent. In the diagram above (Dia. 10-2), the defense is applying pressure and maintains that pressure and relative position so O_1 makes a hard cut to the basket for a possible give and go play. In that situation he is playing the basket. In the diagram to the left (Dia. 10-3) X_1 has dropped to the level of the ball so O_1 merely needs to step back out to the half line for the return pass from

DIA. 10-2

DIA. 10-3

364 Special Situations

the wing. That move is referred to as playing the half line. Remember we are in a ball control offense. We want to keep the defense spread and force them to work extremely hard in their attempt to gain possession of the ball. Keep in mind also that X_1 will have to move back out to cover O_1 with the ball. If he rushed out without caution O_1 can possible drive by him and place a great deal of pressure on the basket and the other four defensive players. It is awfully tough to apply pressure to players at this level when the defense is forced out wide. It becomes even tougher when the offensive players learn to play with their heads and apply the lay up game principles we are discussing.

If the offensive team has learned to play with poise and can handle the pressure and react properly, any double teaming tactics by the defense can easily be handled or turned to an advantage by the offense. Notice in the diagram to the right that X_1 has left his man to double team the ball with X_3 (Dia. 10-4). O_3 should have no trouble recognizing the situation and finding the open man. O_1 should immediately cut to the basket and make himself available for the pass from the wing. If the double team is effective, O_1 should make himself available wherever possible. That can sometimes mean a cut to the sideline to create a better passing angle for O_3. From that position the ball can be brought back out to the half line to reset the offense.

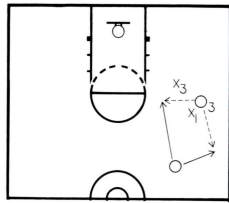

DIA. 10-4

If the guard does execute the hard cut to the hole but the pass is not made, O_3 will continue to play the basket for an instant. If nothing develops O_3 will reset the ball at the half line by use of the dribble (Dia. 10-5). O_1 will empty on the ballside and fill the spot on the wing vacated by O_3. In dribbling to the half line O_3 will be looking into the middle where he can see the action on the weakside, in the middle of the floor, and at the basket. The players must dribble the ball with the outside hand to insure protection from the defense. As O_3 nears the half line he should decide whether to play the ball across the court to O_4 or to make the pass back to O_1 filling the wing position. The pass to the middle man is the last option. O_5 does not step out unless he is needed or the backdoor play is open. If the reverse pass is made, O_3 and O_1 become the weakside players and they look to make the weakside exchange when the timing is correct. If the guard to forward pass is again executed, the possible cutting action and options shown in Diagram 10-2 are in effect.

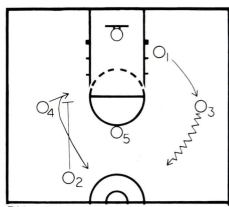

DIA. 10-5

Weakside Action

The weakside players have the option of exchanging positions or holding their original position on the initial guard to forward or guard to wing pass. This will be discussed in detail below but the point we want to make here is the timing that is necessary to maintain the proper floor balance. If O_2 moves to screen for O_4, both players should time the cut so

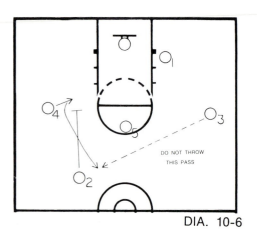

DIA. 10-6

that O_4 is breaking to the half line at the same time the ball is at or near the half court area. This will enable the players handling the ball to make the reverse pass with the proper timing. The pass can be executed by O_1 if he has held position at the half line (Dia. 10-3) or by O_3 if the dribble out is utilized (Dia. 10-5). This teaching point is important in developing the proper timing in our lay up game. It is not crucial because the weakside players can always rescreen which we will discuss shortly. However, the timing must be such that the reverse pass across the floor is never made from the wing position (Dia. 10-6). We want to keep the passes as short as possible while still keeping the floor spread. This pass is entirely too long and offers the defensive player (X_4) a much wider angle of interception and opportunity for the deflection or outright steal. To make this play O_3 would need to dribble out to the half line to improve his passing angle as we have shown in Dia. 10-5.

The action of the weakside offensive players is based on the amount of pressure applied by the defense and the proper timing of the offense mentioned above. It is important in any offense but especially in the lay up game to read the defense and then exercise good judgment on the cuts. If the defense is denying the guard to guard or reverse pass to O_2, he will execute a vertical screen for O_4 coming up to meet the basketball (see previous diagrams). We constantly emphasize in this situation that the man setting the screen must screen the defensive player rather than a spot on the floor. We call it "headhunting" and it is a very important concept involved in the lay up game. We do not want to take a chance on committing an offensive blocking foul so the players must be sure to come set and let the defensive man make the contact. However, the defensive player will be working hard to avoid the screen. Our man must "headhunt" and effectively pick off the offensive player to free up his teammate for a possible pass.

The player accepting the downscreen has the option of breaking behind the defense on the pass to the wing or coming out to the half line to possibly relieve pressure. This is one of the many areas where good judgment has to be exercised in executing the lay up game successfully. As we mentioned previously, the pass to the weakside man or the post player breaking behind is generally not there after one or two passes. In looking to cut to the basket, the wing player in this situation and all players in general must make the cut only if the basket area is wide open and they have an excellent chance of beating their defensive man. We are attempting to spread the defense and open up the basket area. Indiscriminate cutting will only serve to clog the middle of the floor. Take for instance the cutting action shown in Diagram 10-2. If O_1 was able to get past his man on the give and go cut, O_4 breaking to the basket would bring at least two more players into the play. The players have a responsibility not only to read the defense, but also to read the intentions and the cuts of the other four offensive players. We want to keep the basket area completely open for the individual cuts that will produce a sure two points. The offensive players looking to go to the basket are encouraged to fake in that direction and to play games with their defensive counterpart, but the fakes must be made within a one or two step area. Head and shoulder and upper body fakes (including the arms) are effective in keeping the opponent busy. The players do not take their man to the basket in attempting to get open out on the floor. The offense must stay wide.

If the wing player elects to come out on the floor for the possible reverse pass he has some responsibilities of his own in making sure the pass is safe. As with all screening plays, the player coming off the screen must be sure to rub shoulders with his teammate so that there is no room for the defensive man to slide through. In making the cut to the half line, the wing player should angle slightly toward the ball so that he will be meeting the pass and cutting off the angle of interception. If the pass is thrown the receiver will naturally step with the inside foot and do whatever is necessary to seal off the defender without fouling. Possession is of the utmost importance. The ball must be protected at all times. The pass should not be thrown if the defender is anywhere near a position to make an interception. If a mistake is made and the pass is executed in this situation, the receiver should change his cut to meet the ball and decrease the distance the ball has to travel (Dia. 10-7). We continually emphasize that all receivers must move to meet the ball in executing the lay up game. This is a fundamental that is crucial to maintaining possession especially when the defense begins to apply all out pressure.

There are two correct options to consider when the defense is denying this reverse pass. If O_3 is not being pressured, O_4 can merely take his man higher or more to the half line and hold position waiting to see what develops or he can rescreen for O_2. If O_3 is receiving pressure then O_4 would immediately move to rescreen so that O_2 could move out for the possible pass to relieve the pressure.

We mentioned earlier that the action on the weakside will depend on the defensive pessure that is applied. The players away from the ball do not have to execute the weakside exchange. O_2 and O_4 can merely hold position in an attempt to keep the floor spread. This strategy can be effective in one of two ways. The helpside defensive players will be forced to help on the ballside or to continue denying the ball out on the floor. If the defenders sag to help the reverse pass is wide open and should be thrown. If the defenders choose to pressure out on the floor, then we have isolated our remaining players in a three on three situation which places the defense at a definite disadvantage. O_5 is basically holding position except when needed as a safety valve so we are

DIA. 10-7

essentially isolating two players on one side of the floor. The three players holding position must keep their men busy or be ready to move to an open area if their man looks to help. The reverse pass and the pass to the middle will be open if additional pressure or help is applied so this should make it very tough on the defense. As in everything else in basketball, proper execution will be the key.

One of the primary reasons for the success of our ball control offense lies in the simplicity of the basic pattern. We have already shown that pattern in its entirety. The strongside players will be executing the give and go and dribbling out to reset the offense and establish floor balance. The weakside players will be screening for each other or holding position, except to relieve pressure on the outside or break to the basket for the sure two points. The middle man does not move out of the middle lane unless absolutely necessary to make himself available to relieve pressure. This in a nutshell is the offensive pattern for the lay up game. Again, we are playing basic basketball with an emphasis on reading the defense. All of the different options that become available and all of the strategies we employ are implemented from this simple pattern but are based on the actions and reactions of the defense.

Getting Behind the Defense

For every defensive play that the opponent can make to apply additional pressure there is a counter move that if executed properly will shift the advantage to the offense. By spreading the defense out we are opening up the basket area and forcing the opponent to cover the entire half court so we can take advantage of the opportunities that are presented. We are basically talking about backcuts from any position on the floor. We have already discussed a few of these in showing our basic pattern. There are additional options that are basic to the game of basketball and are dictated by the position of the defense. These options will usually open up the longer the opponent is forced to remain on defense. The players get tired, impatient, and sometimes desperate in their attempt to gain control of the ball. This is why an excellent ball handling team can use the lay up game to actually expand their lead rather than sit on a one or two point advantage.

The players are taught to get to the basket anytime they can get behind their defender and the ball can be delivered. If these two conditions cannot be met, the players must stay wide to keep the basket area open. The only exception is the strongside guard executing the give and go cut. He will make a hard cut to the basket so as to generate some movement and create problems for the defense. This type of cutting action may open something else up if the defense overracts. We want to get to the basket to put pressure on the defense. The

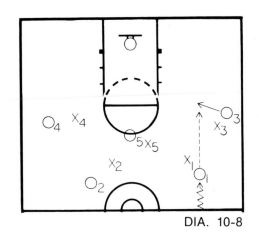

DIA. 10-8

following diagrams will show the backdoor plays that can develop within our lay up game offense.

We should mention that the players executing the backcuts are taught to vacate the basket area immediately if the pass is not thrown. They must get back to their original positions out on the floor so we can reset the offense and maintain floor spacing for the lay up game. Posting up or hanging near the basket will only clog up the middle of the floor.

Diagram 10-8 shows the defense attempting to totally deny the guard to forward pass without much sag on the helpside. Again, this will usually be a play that will be set up after a number of passes. If X_3 gets off balance or out of position out on the floor, O_3 merely plants his foot and makes a backcut on a direct line to the basket. This play must be extremely wide open for the pass to come from the guard or the player out front. He must be aware of the position of the defensive man in the middle (X_5) and the defender on the helpside (X_4). The pass cannot be thrown if either one of these players are in a position to get a hand on the basketball. If the pass is not thrown the backdoor cut has been successful even though it did not result in two points. The offensive maneuver has met our previously stated goals of putting pressure on the basket and on the defense. If the play is wide open, the bounce pass will usually be the most effective pass to get by the defense. This is a pass leading to a score so we will allow the bounce pass if the play is wide open. The player executing the pass must exercise good judgment.

Actually, the most effective play in this situation is for the guard to make the pass into the middle with O_5 making the shorter, safer pass to O_3 cutting to the basket (Dia. 10-9). This is recommended whenever possible. O_5 should step up and seal off his defender after recognizing the situation. O_3 should attempt to take his man as high as possible to set up the backdoor cut.

Diagram 10-10 shows a backcut executed by the middle man after completion of the guard to forward pass. We discussed earlier the responsibilities of the forward to execute a front pivot and play the basket from his position on the wing. O_5 must time the cut properly to make sure the ball can be delivered before X_5 has a chance to recover. Sometimes it is advantageous to take the defender further out on the floor before quickly reversing direction for the cut to the basket.

The wing player opposite the ball also has the option of cutting to the basket on the guard to forward pass. This cutting action is shown in Diagram 10-11. Notice that the defender (X_4) is trying to totally deny the passing lane to O_4. If he loses vision on the ball and does not react back to the basket to change his line of defense, O_4 should make a hard cut to the ballside of the basket. Again, the cut must be timed properly and O_3

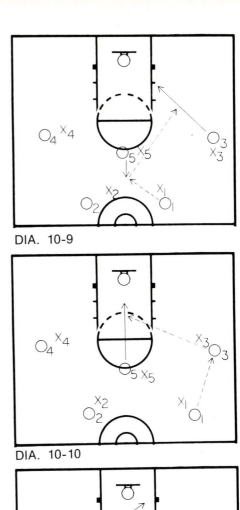

DIA. 10-9

DIA. 10-10

DIA. 10-11

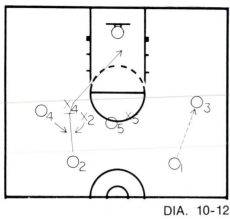

DIA. 10-12

DIA. 10-13

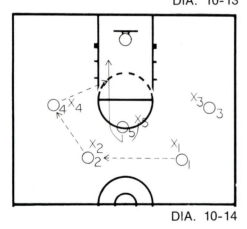

DIA. 10-14

is responsible for seeing the basket and the middle of the floor. We caution our players to execute this backcut only when there is an excellent opportunity for beating the defender to the basket. There is a tendency on the part of the players to overuse this cut from the weakside or to try to create an opening that is not there. The players must learn to be patient and exercise good judgment in getting behind the defense. If indiscriminate cutting is allowed, the effect of our floor spacing will be lost.

If the helpside defenders choose to switch on our weakside exchange, the same cutting action that is shown in Diagram 10-11 can be executed by the weakside guard. We tell our players to look for the opportunity to get to the basket when screening. In Diagram 10-12, O_2 is moving to set a vertical screen on X_4. As the screen is executed X_2 and X_4 switch defensive assignments. O_2 is now being guarded by X_4 and he should look immediately for the opportunity to cut to the basket because X_4 is momentarily out of position. Again, this cut must be wide open and the ball must be in a position to be delivered for the cut to be successful.

The action described above takes place when the defense switches immediately before or during the execution of the screen. The guard can actually make the cut sooner if the defensive guard (X_2) is expecting the exchange and is attempting to stay out on the floor in anticipation of the switch. Notice in Diagram 10-13 that O_2 has cleared his defender. Anytime an offensive player can clear his defensive man, he should get to the basket and look to see if the ball can be delivered. This is basically what has occurred in all of the previous backdoor plays we have diagrammed.

Keep in mind that all of the above options can occur on either side of the floor. When the ball is reversed, O_1 and O_3 will have the same opportunities we have described for O_2 and O_4. Obviously, O_5 will be working the middle of the floor and will be able to exercise his options with the ball on either side. An example is given to the side (Dia. 10-14) because this backcut by the middle man is often created by reversing the ball quickly from one side of the floor to the other. This option has also been used effectively for relieving pressure in our regular half court offense (see Chapter Three). On the reverse pass to the weakside guard, O_5 will attempt to pin his man or take him higher out on the floor. O_2 will immediately make the guard to forward pass on his side and O_5 should look to break for the basket so that the ball can be delivered from O_4.

Additional Points of Emphasis

There were four important principles that we listed at the beginning of this section that were not covered adequately in the preceding pages. The first involves our reasons for not allowing a screen or any type of crossing action on the ball.

In going over our basic pattern and noting the emphasis we place on spacing, it is apparent that there is no reason for two players to come together or cross except on the weakside exchange. When there is a cross involving the ball, you will have four players in a relatively small area of the floor around the basketball and the ball handler. The congestion will cause problems for the offense and will afford the defense an excellent opportunity to double team the basketball.

The temptation to cross the ball handler comes when the defense is applying maximum pressure and this looks to be a way to alleviate some of that pressure. For the reasons mentioned above, this type of movement will increase rather than decrease the pressure. This is why we teach our weakside players to rescreen if the first weakside exchange does not free a man for the reverse pass. The high post player will also be working the middle of the floor and it is his job to be available to relieve pessure out on the floor. When this type of defensive pressure is applied, it is crucial that the offense maintains its spacing and its poise. They can then look intelligently for the opportunity to get behind the defense to the basket. There is no way the defense can apply maximum pressure and effectively protect the basket against a poised team that is well drilled in the lay up game offense.

We also teach the players not to pick up the basketball or stop their dribble until they have a definite passing option. This again ties into the pressure that can be applied by the defense. If the offensive ball handler does not have an open teammate in an immediate position to catch the basketball, he must keep the ball alive. If he uses up his dribble, the defense can totally deny all potential receivers because there is no necessity to provide help. The ball handler is no threat because he cannot get to the basket. The defender on the ball can either swarm the ball handler or look to help a defensive teammate if the offensive player is outside shooting range.

A third principle that is extremely important in providing lay up opportunities has to do with the actual cut to the basket behind the defense. The players getting to the basket must execute or finish their cut on the ballside to greatly improve the passing angle and lessen the chances for a deflection or interception. This is especially important for the players cutting from the weakside but it can also be a valuable teaching point for making sure the strongside players maintain the proper cutting angle. The best examples we can give are shown in the following diagrams. When cutting to the basket from the weakside, the player executing the cut (X_4 in the diagram) must angle so that he finishes on the ballside. In Diagram 10-15, both the wrong cutting angle and the proper cutting angle are shown. Obviously, the passer will have a much better opportunity to deliver the basketball on the cut to the ballside.

It is easy to see the importance of this principle when teaching

DIA. 10-15

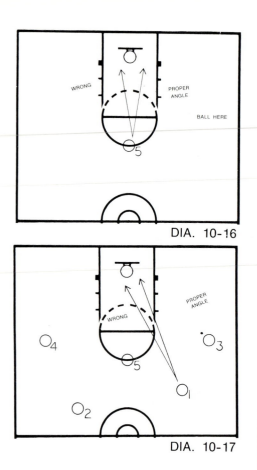

DIA. 10-16

DIA. 10-17

the backcut from the weakside. It would seem that a player cutting from the middle of the floor or the ballside would execute the proper cut instinctively. While this is true most of the time, it is not always the case. O_5 or O_1 in the following diagrams can easily lose a little of their court awareness in their effort to allude the defense. They may think they are open at the basket when in all actuality, they have decreased the chances for a successful pass by ending up on the weakside. We have already stated that the pass should not be thrown unless it is assured of being completed so the ball handler may be unable to deliver the ball in this situation. Diagram 10-16 shows the proper and improper cutting angles from the middle of the floor while the same relationship is shown for the player out front in Diagram 10-17.

Finally, we want all of our players to avoid using the bounce pass when they are positioned out on the floor. This is a good idea to follow at all times during the game, but it is especially crucial in the lay up game where the protection and possession of the ball is extremely important. The bounce pass can be utilized around the basket or lane area as a pass leading up to a score, but the play must be open and the pass must be made with the utmost accuracy. When out on the floor, we want our players to execute a good, firm chest pass away from the defense. A bounce pass is too slow coming up off the floor and can allow the defense time to recover for a deflection or interception. The bounce pass can also be picked off very effectively if it is not thrown to bounce past the defender or defenders in the general area. For these reasons, the bounce pass is relatively inconsistent and very dangerous when maintianing control of the basketball is of prime importance.

The one exception we will allow for use of the bounce pass out on the floor is when a player is trapped and the bounce pass is the most effective means of escaping the double team. The player must be sure to make a firm, accurate pass in this situation and he must be aware of any additional defensive players rotating for the interception. The bounce pass out on the floor is only used as a last resort in this situation and at all other times in the lay up game it should be prohibited.

Strategies Employed in the Lay Up Game

We try to make our lay up game more efficient by making effective use of our personnel which we discussed earlier in this section. There are a couple of strategies that we have employed in this regard that have been extremely valuable in the overall success of our lay up game. At times, we will place our two best ball handlers, regardless of position, on the same side of the floor. They will handle the ball exclusively on that side of the floor through the strongside or ballside action we have previously described. The middle man will hold position and will act as a safety valve only when needed. As always he will keep his defensive counterpart busy by faking to the basket and to the half line without leaving the key area. The weakside players will hold position most of the time with an occasional weakside exchange. They will, of course, always be available if absolutely needed but we want the ball to stay on one side of the floor. The idea is to either lull the helpside defenders to sleep through the lack of action on that side or force them to help on the ball in an effort to gain possession.

Our weakside players can help to lull the defenders to sleep by their seeming lackadaisical effort and lack of involvement in the offensive pattern. At the same time, they should be alert to take advantage of any defensive mistakes. The offensive players should recognize immediately if their defensive man leaves to help on the ball or look for a possible double team. The vacated offensive player should get to the basket or an open area of the floor depending on the ability of the ball handler to deliver the pass. If the trap has been effective he may need to provide an outlet in an open area. This is not always the case, however, because the ball handler may be able to make a pass to a cutter or to the basket area. Also, two passes could be made leading up to the score. If there is relatively little pressure being applied to the man with the ball, the vacated offensive player should get to the ballside of the basket as quickly as possible. His teammate should see the open man and deliver the basketball.

The weakside players should also look to get to the basket if one of the helpside defenders falls asleep or attempts to rest because of the lack of action. We tell the players to explode to the basket when their man stands straight up to rest. A quick, intelligent player can usually get at least one basket a game by catching his man resting at the defensive end.

An extention of the above strategy is employed by isolating an extremely quick player at the weakside wing position who has a knack for beating his man and getting to the basket. The strongside players continue to play but are very much aware of the player isolated at the wing. The weakside player out front widens out and moves slightly back to provide more room for the wing player to work his man one on one (Dia. 10-18). With this player isolated on one side and the other four players looking to get him the ball, this is an extremely difficult situation for the defensive player on the wing. We will take advantage of many mis-matches by adjusting our personnel in this manner. We have even moved our most mobile post players out to this wing position to take advantage of a slower big man on the opposing team.

We will also adjust our personnel by placing an excellent one on one player in the middle of the floor (Dia. 10-19). The idea is to get this player the ball and let him work one on one from the high post area. The four outside players will widen out

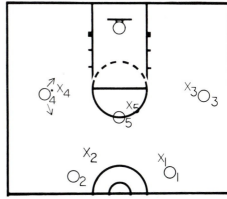

DIA. 10-18

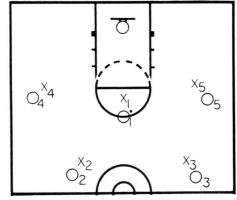

DIA. 10-19

Special Situations 373

slightly to take away the defensive help. We are again isolating an offensive and a defensive player in a one on one confrontation that should place the defender at a disadvantage. The difference in the two strategies lies in the fact that the wing player is working to get open away from the ball on the weakside. The emphasis is on beating his man to the basket for the pass and lay up. The middle man described above will also work without the basketball and can execute the backcut at anytime, but the emphasis here will be on facing the basket to go one on one with the basketball. This concept is almost identical to the idea on which the four corners offense is based. The four corners is designed to allow the offensive teams best ball handler and usually its best player to go one on one and handle the ball the majority of the time. This is what we are attempting to do with a slightly different alignment and philosophy. The player in this position must exercise good judgment in driving to the basket. We do not want to force the action. Remember that possession is of prime importance. We are looking for the sure two points or we will pull the ball back out and go again. We can move any player to the middle to take advantage of a mis-match in our favor. We have had success moving a quick guard to this position, especially when the guard knows how to work without the basketball in the post area. The defensive guard will usually have had a limited amount of practice time in defensing a man in the post area. We can see from the diagram that this one on one confrontation in the middle presents a difficult problem for the defense, especially if there is no help from the four outside defenders. If help is provided and there is no driving lane to the basket, the middle man would need only to find the open man and reset the offense.

Practice Hints

In developing our lay up game we will work five on five utilizing the clock in various time and score situations. To help our players gain a feel for how to play the game, we will specify different areas to concentrate on in executing the offense. The aforementioned strategies are excellent to use as practice situations. The players are thinking and playing intelligently when applying different strategies rather than going through the motions. We will also designate a particular player in the line-up as the man we want to get open at the basket. We will do this without isolating him on the wing or in the middle position. The designated player will learn how to work to get open in the lay up game and the other four players will learn to help him get open and to find him on the cut to the basket. The other four players are not allowed to shoot in this situation. We use this same teaching method for our regular half court offense. Another variation we will use at times in practicing the lay up game is to add a sixth defensive player. This will obviously add to the pressure the defense will be able to apply. There will be a greater number of double team situations and the offensive players will have to learn to handle the increased pressure with poise. The offensive team must continue to play the basket and put pressure on the defense or the defensive team will gain the upper hand. The offensive team can easily put themselves on the defensive when a great deal of pressure is applied. That is exactly the type of situation we want to avoid. We think we can accomplish this goal by continuing to play the basket and looking to get behind the defense in our lay up game offense.

Planning and practice time must be set aside for coordinating out of bounds plays from each area on the floor. That includes under our offensive basket, from either side of the floor in the offensive and the defensive ends of the court, and at the end line or underneath our defensive basket. To simplify things for our players we try to limit the number of set plays as much as possible. We feel it is important, however, to have some scoring plays that have been rehearsed a number of times in the practice sessions so that they are totally familiar to the players. The players will obviously execute better under game conditions with this type of preparation.

We try to devise our out of bounds plays according to the personnel we have each year. It is wise to coordinate what is best for each particular group of players. During the fourth week of practice we will begin teaching the out of bounds plays to the squad. First, we will diagram and discuss one or two plays on the blackboard. We then walk through the maneuvers with the team divided at each end of the floor. Following the practice sessions the players are issued a handout that details the particular play or plays we have covered. At various times, we will also select players to diagram a designated play on the blackboard for the team. This will occur only after we have covered the play and worked on it a number of days in practice. As we mentioned previously, we will work on the special situations, including the out of bounds plays, during all scrimmage sessions. The special situations will also be emphasized the last week of practice leading up to the first game. During the season, we will review the out of bounds plays the last practice before almost every game. Execution will be the key to success.

Under the Offensive Basket

This is the out of bounds area where many coaches will try to run a scoring play each time they are awarded possession of the ball. That is certainly our primary objective also but we don't think the number of times we have the ball in this situation is conducive to surprising our defensive opponent. We feel it is wise, therefore, to refrain from using all of our special scoring plays in case we need a crucial basket and are in this situation at the end of the game. In selecting or devising

Out of Bounds Plays

DIA. 10-20

any out of bounds plays, the alignment and positioning of personnel must be taken into consideration. This is especially important when attempting to score rather than merely trying to inbound the ball safely. In terms of aligning our personnel, we think it is essential to designate an intelligent, excellent passing player to take the ball out of bounds. We refer to this player as the trigger man. He has to exercise good judgment in making the right pass without forcing the action. The shooters must be aligned in bounds and in a position to get open for a high percentage shot. The only exception to this rule would occur when the play is designed to free the player executing the throw in for the shot. Obviously, an excellent shooter would be assigned to take the ball out in that situation. Another important consideration would be the rebounding strength that is produced or maintained as the shot is executed. It would be beneficial to align the best rebounders so that they would be near the basket on the shot and in a position to get inside the defense. The rebounding is often a neglected aspect of the out of bounds plays. In the event of a missed shot, attention to this point can result in an offensive rebound and a second or even third attempt at the basket. That would be particularly advantageous on a crucial play at the end of the game. Maintaining floor balance is also essential, both to allow for defensive coverage and so the players can move naturally to the regular offensive set if a shot is not produced immediately. In most all of our out of bounds plays from under the basket we will have a player who is not directly involved in the screening action or movement. He will have sole responsibility for dropping back to protect the basket at our defensive end. Even if all four inbounds players are involved in the out of bounds play we will make sure one player is in a position to convert quickly to the defensive end. The final consideration with regard to choosing an alignment is the need for a second or even third option in case the primary options are covered. If the initial pass cannot be made we have to have another receiver to go to or a safety valve so there is no danger of a five second violation.

Before diagramming a few of the plays under the offensive basket we have used in the past, we should mention the possibility of designing at least one out of bounds play that would be effective versus a man to man and a zone defense. With many teams today changing defenses in this situation, it can be a good idea to incorporate a few plays that will work against both basic defenses. The straight line and the box plays shown below have both been designed with this idea in mind.

Straight Line (Dia. 10-20)
As we mentioned this simple play can be utilized against a man to man or a zone defense. The trigger man (O_1) is again an intelligent player and one of our best, if not the best, passer on the team. He will signal the start of the play by slapping the ball with his free hand. The first player in the

376 Special Situations

line (O_2) will usually be our big man. His responsibility is to try to get to the basket for a possible quick inside pass from the inbounder. If the pass is not there, O_2 will position himself for the rebound on the weakside of the basket. O_3 will break to the corner area to try and spread out the defense so O_4 can step into an open area. O_3 should be a good corner or baseline shooter so the defense has to honor his cut. Usually he will be one of our forwards. The third player in line (O_4) will generally be our quick forward. We want someone in this position who possesses an ability to get open around the basket area and the strength to take the ball to the hole in heavy traffic. O_4 will be stepping to the basket as soon as O_2 and O_3 execute their respective cuts. Against a man to man, O_4 will be attempting to beat his man for an inside pass and the lay up. Against a zone, he will look for an open gap and move into that area in his attempt to get to the basket. This is the primary option in the straight line formation. If the ball can be delivered to O_2 at or near the basket, that will be an even better option but this cut will usually be covered adequately by the defense. The cuts by O_2 and O_3 are basically designed to decoy and spread out the defense. O_5 will drop back beyond the key area to assume the defensive responsibility and act as a safety valve in case the ball cannot be inbounded to the previous three cutters. The pass to O_3 in the corner is the third option for the trigger man. As a last resort, O_1 can deliver a high, direct pass to O_5 out on the floor. A lob pass should not be thrown because the defense will be able to react back for the interception. Also, the inbounder must make sure that the pass will reach the intended receiver within the five second time limit. If the count is nearing five seconds this is not the pass to throw.

Box (Diagrams 10-21 and 10-22)

In the box formation shown to the right, the play is designed to set up the trigger man for a relatively close-in shot along the baseline. Therefore, we would make sure the player inbounding the ball is an excellent shooter as well as an intelligent player. O_2 set up on the block will be one of the guards because he is going to be required to handle the ball and deliver the pass to the shooter. He will also have defensive responsibilities after completing his pass to O_1 on the baseline. O_3 should be our strongest rebounding forward. He will have rebounding responsibilities on the weakside after reversing the ball to O_2. Our big man (O_4) will always set up on the block away from the ball on this play. He will be valuable in setting the screen for the shooter and will also be in a position to get to the offensive boards as the shot is executed. O_5 will be forming a double screen with O_4 and then rebounding in the middle of the floor so ideally this would be the third front line player. This position could easily be filled by a guard depending on which player we want to place in the shooting role. All of our plays are started by the

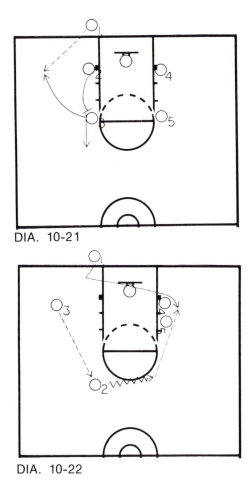

DIA. 10-21

DIA. 10-22

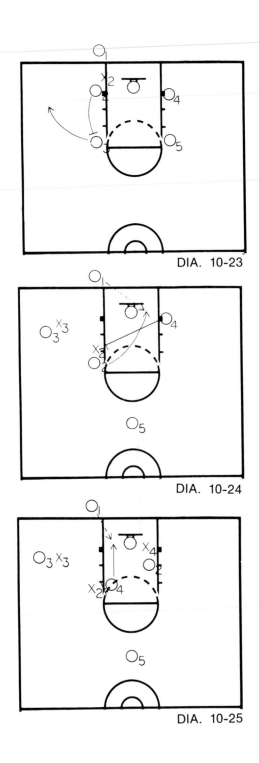

DIA. 10-23

DIA. 10-24

DIA. 10-25

inbounder slapping the ball as we discussed on the previous play. On signal, O_2 will screen for O_3 cutting to the corner for the initial pass (Dia. 10-21). O_3 will delay his cut to receive the full benefit of the screen from O_2. He must make sure to rub shoulders with the screener as we advocate on all screening plays. O_5 will move down the lane to form the double screen with O_4. Both of these players will face the center of the floor making themselves perpendicular to the baseline and they should establish a wide base to insure the effectiveness of the screen. After screening for O_3, O_2 will step out on the floor to receive the reverse pass (Dia. 10-22). The inbounder will start to follow his pass to the corner but will reverse direction quickly and use the double screen for his shot along the baseline. Upon receiving the pass from O_3, O_2 dribbles to the middle to establish a better passing angle and makes the pass to the shooter getting set behind the screen. O_2 drops back immediately for defensive purposes and O_3 moves to cover the weakside rebounding area. O_4 and O_5 must hold position until the shot is executed but both should look to crash the boards at that time. It is obvious that this play would be effective when facing either a zone or man to man defense. Keep in mind also that versus a man defense, the defenders assigned to O_4 and O_5 will cause a lot of congestion in the area of the double screen. This should help the shooter in losing his defensive counterpart.

Screen the Screener (Diagrams 10-23 and 10-24)

This is perhaps the most effective out of bounds play we have seen in the game today. It is an excellent play because of the deception involved and because of the different options that are available depending on the reactions of the defense. We have already stated that the inbounder must be intelligent and that he must be an excellent passer. Those requirements are especially important in the execution of this play. The player taking the ball out will truly be the triggerman. O_2 must be a good all-purpose player with excellent quickness. He must also be able to handle himself around the basket area. This position will usually be filled by our quick forward or a big guard. Ideally, we will position our best pure shooter at the free throw line on the ball side of the basket (O_3). We want the defense to think we are going to this player because he will be acting as a decoy for the primary option. The pass to this player will be our third option so it is also important for O_3 to be a good shooter in case the first two options are covered. O_4 is again our big man. His responsibility is to screen for O_2 and then roll to the basket so it will be advantageous to have a post player or at least a big forward in this position. O_5 will have defensive responsibilities and will act as a safety valve in the event O_1 cannot find a receiver.

On the signal from O_1, O_2 will turn to the sideline and loop up the lane to screen for O_3 at the free throw line (Dia.

10-23). It is important that O_2 execute this screening action along the exact angle we have shown in the diagram. This looping action will help set up the next cut by O_2. O_3 is to fake with one step to the inside and then break to the corner off of the screen. He should make a good but not a great cut. Ideally, we want the defender assigned to O_3 to get over the screen without switching assignments. The play will still be effective if a switch occurs but the above relationship offers our best opportunity for an uncontested lay up shot. We want the defense to know we are going to O_3. He will call for the ball after accepting the screen to help draw the defense in that direction. O_1 will be looking in that direction all the time and will make an excellent pass fake as O_3 comes off the screen. At this point, X_2 will probably have been helping on the screen and generally will let up, thinking that his job is temporarily over. This is where we will screen for the screener. Our big man (O_4) has taken a one and one half count and now comes across the lane to set the screen as shown in Diagram 10-24. The timing of this action is extremely important. On the signal by O_1, we have O_4 count to himself, one thousand and one, one thousand. As soon as he says the second thousand, he opens to the ball and moves straight up and across the lane for the screen. O_4 should look to headhunt on the man guarding O_2 (X_2, or X_3 if a switch has taken place) but the congestion will cause the play to be effective even if he only screens an area. We teach O_2 to "knife through" the congestion to get to the basket on the weakside. O_4 will look to roll to the basket after setting the screen for O_2 (Dia. 10-25). This play will be especially effective if the man guarding O_4 switches to cover O_2 on the primary option. O_4 should then reverse pivot away from the sideline putting the defender (X_2) on his back for the roll to the basket. As we have mentioned, O_5 is back for defensive purposes and as a safety valve for the inbounds pass. It is obvious that this play is designed primarily to take advantage of a man to man defense but it can also be successful against a zone.

From the Offensive Sideline

The same elements that are considered in selecting or devising the out of bounds plays under the basket must be applied here. The alignment, positioning of personnel, maintaining floor balance, and establishing rebounding strength are still very important. The plays diagrammed and explained are again some that we have had success with in the past.

Sideline Box (Diagrams 10-26 and 10-27)

This is an all purpose out of bounds play that can be used as a scoring play or merely to make the inbounds pass safely. We generally designate our quicker forward to take the ball out in this situation. If we are attempting to score we will need someone in this position that knows how to play around

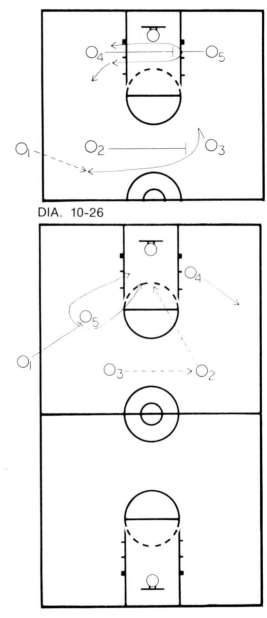

DIA. 10-26

DIA. 10-27

the basket. The guards will be positioned out on the floor (O_2 and O_3) and will be required to handle the basketball in setting up the scoring option. O_4 will be our other forward. He may also be required to handle the ball in setting up the cutter. Our post player will be aligned near the basket on the side away from the ball (O_5). As the play evolves this player will screen for the cutter on the scoring option and will then be in a position to rebound on the weakside. It will pay to have our big man handle those responsibilities. Diagram 10-26 shows the initial alignment and the screening action that takes place to safely inbound the ball. If that is the only objective, we will get to our set offense from these positions. However, if the objective is to score, the play will continue in the following manner. O_5 will step up as if to play with the ball handler (O_3). O_3 must play the basket and that side of the floor to set up the play properly. The ball will then be reversed to O_2 and O_4 will widen out to the wing to open up the basket area and make himself available for a possible pass (Dia. 10-27). On the reverse pass, O_5 will turn to face the basket and the middle of the floor. He will hold position and establish a strong base to act as a screen for O_1. It will be the responsibility of O_1 to run his man off the screen. He has the option of going either way off the screen depending on the position of the defense. The pass made into O_1 for the lay up can come from out front (O_2) or from the wing (O_4) depending on what is open and the timing involved. We face O_5 in the direction shown so that he can get to the basket or to an open area at any time. If his man anticipates the cut by O_1 and switches or moves to help, O_5 should move immediately to make his own cut to the basket.

Sideline Box-Big Man Out (Diagrams 10-28 and 10-29)

This play is very similar to the one diagrammed above but involves a slightly different cut with more emphasis on deception. The alignment is exactly the same except that we place our big man out of bounds and position the two forwards down low. We want to pull the opponent's big man out on the floor where he is not used to playing defense. We are also going to deceive this player into letting up once the inbounds pass is made. The less mobile this player is the more effective our out of bounds play will be. O_2 and O_3 will execute the same screening action we have shown on the previous play and the ball should be inbounded as before (Dia. 10-28). As soon as the pass is completed to O_3, O_5 will break to the high post area on the ball side and will allow the defense to push him out even higher. O_3 will play the basket and look in but will not make the high post pass to O_5. While this action is taking place, O_4 will be walking up the lane and out to the wing as if he is trying to set the offense. He will actually be moving to set a double screen with O_5 as shown in Diagram 10-29. After making the inbounds pass O_1 will walk his man into the middle as if he

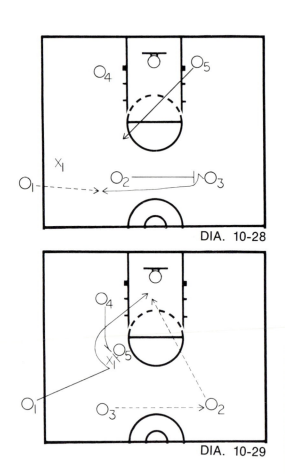

DIA. 10-28

DIA. 10-29

too is trying to set the offense. Our offensive post man is taught to do this in a manner that will cause the defender to let up or at least relax momentarily. O_1 will break to the basket as soon as the defender relaxes and/or he is able to run X_1 off the double screen. O_3 will have reversed the ball to O_2 after establishing the proper timing. The pass to O_1 cutting to the basket should come from O_2 after the ball is reversed.

Misdirection (Diagrams 10-30 and 10-31)

We have used a misdirection play in the past that is designed to produce a short baseline jump shot against a man to man or zone defense. This is not a play to run with only a few seconds on the clock. There must be at least six seconds showing for this play to be effective. The play is run out of the same box alignment as we have shown in previous diagrams. The personnel will be positioned the same as in the sideline box play. The guards will be out on the floor (O_2 and O_3). The post player sets up low on the side away from the ball (O_5) and our strong forward (O_4) is in the same position opposite the post. Our quicker forward will be designated as the inbounder (O_1). He will be required to handle the ball out on the floor in setting up the baseline shot. We will position our best shooting guard (ideally our best shooter) nearest the ball. If the play is executed properly he should end up with an open shot along the baseline. O_2 and O_3 again execute the screening action out front (Dia. 10-30). After screening for O_3, O_2 will continue down to the baseline. O_5 moves across the lane to set up a double screen with O_4. The ball is inbounded to O_3 and he immediately turns and dribbles hard to the side away from the double screen (Dia. 10-31). This is where the misdirection and thus the deception comes into play. We want O_3 to play the basket and play with O_2 as he goes hard to that side. The defense must think we are looking to set up a scoring play in that direction. After throwing the pass to O_3, O_1 will step in bounds and make himself available for a reverse pass. O_2 will now continue his cut along the baseline and use the double screen to lose his defensive counterpart. With timing, O_3 will pull up and make the reverse pass back to O_1. O_1 then makes the pass to O_2 coming off the screen for the shot.

Straight Line (Diagram 10-32)

We will generally implement the Straight Line formation to be used from any area of the floor. From the areas other than under the basket, this play is utilized merely as a means of inbounding the ball safely. The options and cutting action will be exactly the same. This simplifies things for the players and gives us a fundamental yet effective means of combatting pressure when we need only to complete the pass from out of bounds. The following diagram shows the cutting action when the ball is awarded to us on the offensive sideline. There is no change when we are inbounding the ball from the end line or on the defensive sideline. The positions are

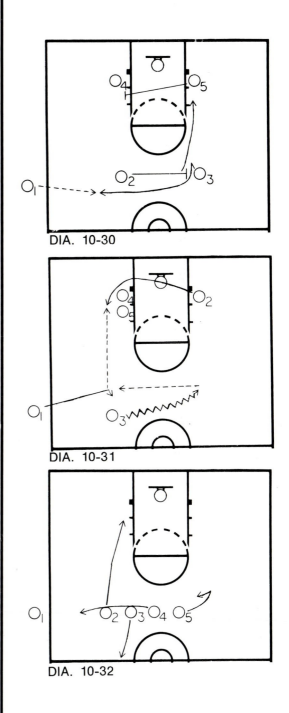

DIA. 10-30

DIA. 10-31

DIA. 10-32

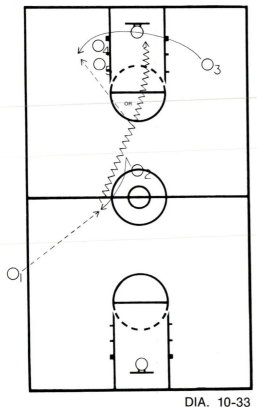

DIA. 10-33

interchangeable but we will ususally place our big man in the first spot followed by the two guards or the two players we want to handle the ball. The post player will be clearing the defense and getting to the basket when the ball is on our offensive or defensive sideline. If we are inbounding the ball from the end line, his cut should serve to clear the defense and open up the area near the inbounder.

From the Defensive Sideline

From this position we will generally run the straight line play if there is pressure from the defense. We will only attempt to run a scoring play when we are in the last few seconds of the half or at the end of the game. To keep things simple, we will have only one scoring play from both the defensive sideline and the end line out of bounds situations. We might change to another play at a certain point in the season but we will never have more than one scoring play in our game plan. Here are two that we have used in previous years from the defensive sideline.

Double Screen-Clear Out (Diagram 10-33)

To attempt to score in the last few seconds in this situation the ball must be inbounded as far up the floor as possible and advanced quickly from that position. This play will produce two excellent options if that criteria can be met. We will place an excellent one on one guard in the middle of the floor (O_2). He must get open as close to our offensive basket as possible without help from a teammate. Once he catches the ball, he will dribble hard for the top of the key. The best shooter available (O_3) will be clearing out one side of the basket and attempting to run his man into a double screen set by O_4 and O_5. As O_2 brings the ball he should look for O_3 coming off the screen or for the possibility of taking the ball all the way to the basket. If O_2 does elect to go all the way, he should be ready to dish the ball off in case one of the defenders guarding O_4 or O_5 drops off to help. The time on the clock is obviously a very important consideration in determining which option or scoring opportunity has the best chance for success.

Sideline Pass (Diagram 10-34)

The following play is effective when the defense is playing man to man with some pressure out on the floor. On a last second play, the defense will generally not spread themselves too far out on the floor. However, if there are from four to ten seconds left, the defense will want to apply a minimum amount of pressure so the ball cannot be advanced uncontested. We are hoping to get the ball to our best ball handler on the fly so he can outdistance his defender and gain a numerical advantage at the offensive end. We position our big man and our best offensive front line player down low near the basket (O_4 and O_5). Our best fast breaking guard

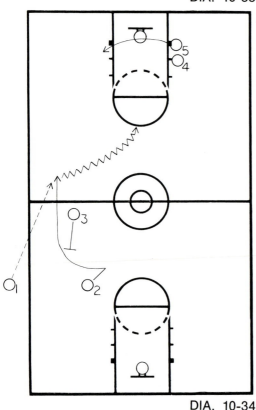

DIA. 10-34

382 Special Situations

(O_2) is aligned near the inbounder as if the ball is to be thrown in and then advanced from that position. The other front line player (O_3) sets himself near the half court area on the side where the ball is being inbounded. The remaining guard (O_1) is the trigger man. There is no signal from the inbounder on this play. O_2 will start the play by faking into the middle of the floor and then cutting back to the sideline and using the advancing screen of O_3. It is important that O_3 looks like he is a threat to catch the ball so that his man does not automatically pick up O_2 when the screen occurs. The defense should not be looking for this type of pass. O_2 must cut as close to the sideline as possible while still allowing himself a margin for error. He should also be careful to avoid a possible charging foul if one of the defenders steps into his intended path. O_1 must throw an extremely accurate and intelligent pass. He must lead the receiver properly but should hold onto the ball if one of the defenders has anticipated and is looking for the charge. As O_2 receives the pass on the fly, O_5 will cross under the basket to balance the floor. O_2 will then bring the ball in the middle of the floor and will look for the opportunity to hit the open man or work for his own shot.

From the End Line

As we mentioned with regard to the out of bounds play from the defensive sideline, we will attempt to score from this situation only if we need some points in the closing seconds of the half or at the end of the game. For the most part, we will execute our scoring plays only at the end of the game. At the half we will throw long or advance the ball as quickly as possible, but will not show any of our last second plays. A prime consideration in aligning your personnel for this type of play is to install a trigger man who can throw the ball long with accuracy. Below are three out of bounds plays that we have attempted to run as last second plays from the end line.

Straight Line Variation (Diagrams 10-35 and 10-36)

This play can be effective because it evolves from the same basic formation that we may have used at other times during the course of the game. The defense must employ a man to man. There is a chance that we can catch one of the men off guard by changing the movement from this straight line formation. The first variation is to form the straight line with only three players and position our big man (O_5) near the half court line. We have to have the post player in a position where he can get to the basket in case we need to throw a high pass in that vicinity. At the same time, we may want him to break back to the middle of the floor to catch the ball and look for O_3 in the offensive end (Dia. 10-36). At any rate, the primary option is for the trigger man to hit O_3 streaking for the other end (Dia. 10-35). O_3 must be a fast

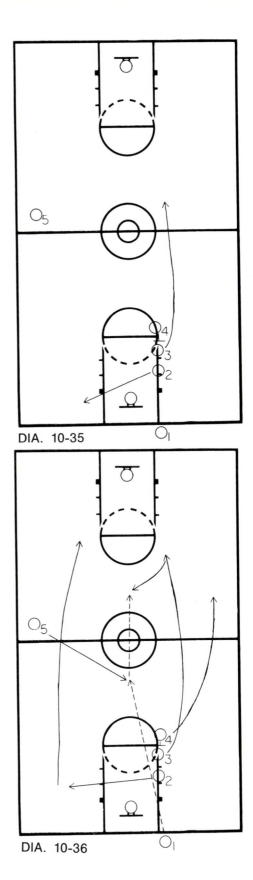

DIA. 10-35

DIA. 10-36

DIA. 10-37

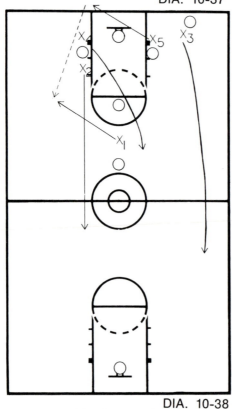

DIA. 10-38

player who is able and willing to go after the ball in a crowd. On the signal from O_1, O_2 will break out to the side just as we have done in our previous plays from the straight line. Instead of breaking opposite, O_3 will turn and sprint for the other end of the floor looking for the long pass. O_4 will screen for O_3 as he breaks long. If the pass to O_3 is successful, O_5 will trail the play to look for the possible tip in or offensive rebound if time permits. On the other hand, if O_3 is not open, O_5 will break back to the inbounder as a second option (Diagram 10-36). He will then look to advance the ball to O_3 still attempting to shake his defender. O_2 and O_4 will also turn and sprint up the floor if there is time left for them to get involved in the play.

Defensive Free Throw

We think it is advantageous to outlet the ball as quickly as possible after a made or a missed free throw and at least look for the opportunity to execute the fast break. While the fast break lay up will not be a common occurence in this situation, our aggressiveness in getting the ball to the outlet area should continue to put pressure on the defense. The quick outlet on the made free throw will also enable us to beat the defense in case they are attempting to set up a press in this situation. Our basic defensive free throw alignment is shown in Diagram 10-37. Many teams are setting an offensive rebounder along the baseline on either side of the lane. We place a player in this position when aligning for the offensive free throw (see Dia. 10-41). In the event our opponents utilize this strategy we will move our second guard off the lane to cover the offensive player along the baseline. The forward remaining on the lane (X_2 or X_3) will then be required to cut off the shooter and rebound in the middle of the floor. The players should be alert and should communicate to each other so that we have a defensive player in a position to cover this situation. The forward mentioned above will line up opposite the players along the baseline. X_1 will not fill the open spot on the lane. We want him in a position to receive the quick outlet on either side of the floor. Our primary ball handling guard will always be aligned in this position at the top of the key. Our big man and strong forward will be in the key rebounding slots near the basket. They will align themselves according to the set up of the offensive team. We want our big man always on the same side with the opponent's big man so we are matching size with size. If we fail to match up with this in mind, the big man from the opposing team may be able to reach over our forward for a possible offensive tip. We make the players totally aware of this possibility so they should be able to establish the proper alignment on their own.

Made Free Throw

We will designate one of the primary rebounders (X_4 or X_5)

to take the ball out of bounds after every made free throw. His responsibility is to take the ball out of the net and step out of bounds as quickly as possible. We will always inbound the ball to the right side of the floor so he should step to the right side of the basket and look for X_1 breaking to the outlet area (Dia. 10-38). We would like to have the designated inbounder line up across the lane opposite the right side as shown in the diagram. It is easier for the player in this position to take the ball out of the net and step out of bounds quickly. Even more important the player can survey the entire floor as he is moving to his out of bounds position. This alignment is not always possible, however, because of the matchups we mentioned previously. We think it is more important to align our men according to the offensive positioning. After receiving the inbounds pass, X_1 will look to advance the ball just like in our normal fast break attack. He can push the ball up the floor to X_2 or X_3 if they are in a position to get behind the defense. X_1 can also advance the ball himself up the sideline or into the middle of the floor. If X_1 elects to dribble into the middle, X_2 must fill to the outside to fulfill our lane requirements. If there is no defensive pressure on the inbounds pass, X_2 and X_3 can release as soon as the shot is made in an attempt to get open long behind the defense. It is very important that the players run the proper lanes as shown because this will be the basis for the possible fast break advantage. There is no organized fast break pattern as such. We are merely making the quick conversion and pushing the ball up the floor as quickly as possible. If the defense is slow getting back or we are able to generate a legitimate fast break opportunity, we will certainly take advantage of the situation. Keep in mind that the ball handling guard must exercise good judgment. He can always pull the ball back out if we do not gain an advantage in our offensive end.

Missed Free Throw

It is obvious in looking at our free throw alignment that X_1 is in a position to get to the outlet area on either side of the floor. He is required to get to a specific outlet area as soon as he can determine the direction of the rebound on a missed free throw. The rebounder should turn to the outside as he gains possession of the ball and should look for our primary ball handler in the outlet area on his side of the floor. If the ball is rebounded in the middle of the floor, X_1 should make himself available wherever possible. It is up to X_1 to find an open passing lane in which the rebounder can execute the outlet pass. If the pass does not open up, the rebounder should protect the basketball or execute the dribble outlet to clear himself as we discussed in Chapter 5. Diagrams 10-39 and 10-40 show the ball being rebounded on each side of the floor and the lanes that should result on the fast break attack. The key to achieving a fast break

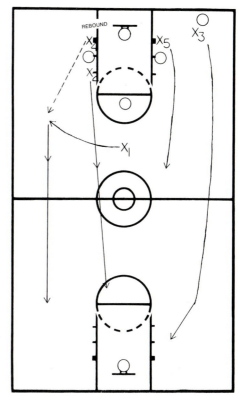

DIA. 10-39

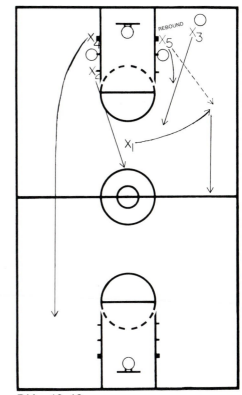

DIA. 10-40

Special Situations 385

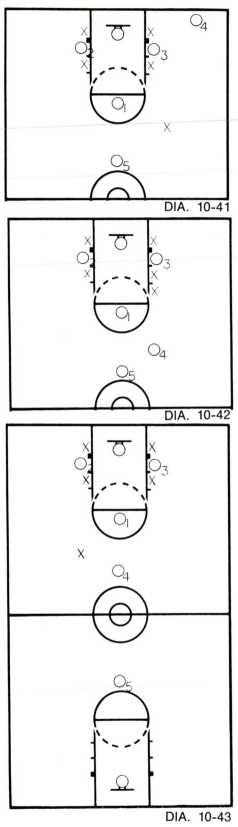

DIA. 10-41

DIA. 10-42

DIA. 10-43

Jump Ball Situations

opportunity is getting the ball out quickly to X_1 with the other players filling the proper lanes. There is no set pattern for filling the lanes but some suggested routes are shown. This will depend on the position on the floor of the respective players and their ability to make the quick conversion. The first two players to make the conversion and fill the proper lanes will form the initial thrust of our fast break with the ball handler. The remaining two players become the trailer and the safety.

Offensive Free Throw

When we are shooting the free throw, we naturally align our two best rebounders nearest the basket. We also make sure one of our guards is aligned between the top of the key and the half court line or as far back as the deepest opposing player for defensive purposes. These relationships are shown in Diagram 10-41. The remaining player (O_4) will have flexible responsibilities. We will position him along the baseline as shown if we feel the opposing players are doing a poor job of rebounding and protecting the basketball. His job in this case would be to crash the boards along the baseline or to attempt to steal the ball from a defensive rebounder making the outlet. We teach our players to come from behind the unsuspecting rebounder and to go after the ball without fouling in this situation. If played properly, this maneuver can result in an easy two points off the steal. We will also position this player around the key area in anticipation of the tip out or long rebound (Dia. 10-42). Notice in the diagram that all of the defenders are aligned on the lane leaving the area out on the floor wide open. We school our players to be alert for this situation and to look for the tip out on the missed free throw. The primary rebounders (O_2 and O_3) should look to get a hand on the basketball and tip it out to the open floor. Because of our floor position, we should come up with the ball on most of the occasions when the tip out is executed. If we are facing a particularly quick or excellent fast breaking team, or if we are trying to protect a lead we may position O_4 with additional defense in mind (Dia. 10-43). He would move to the area between the key and the half court line. The original defender (O_5) would move into our defensive end to completely protect the basket against a fast break attack. At both the offensive and the defensive end we want our rebounders to assume that every free throw will be missed. They must anticipate the ball hitting the rim and react quickly in the direction of the rebound without incurring a lane violation. We require the players to get the hands and arms up as soon as the referee hands the ball to the free throw shooter. From that point the players must be ready to move and rebound aggressively. Anticipation and quick reactions will be crucial in rebounding the missed free throw.

We do not spend a great deal of time on jump ball situations but feel they are important to cover at some point in our special preparations. We go over the situations that can occur in a game and familiarize the players with the alignments and strategies that can result from the different situations. We also cover the techniques that are advantageous for the jumper. These will be very important in challenging a taller opponent for control of the tap. Finally, we will implement one tap play that is designed to create a lay up opportunity. This scoring play will be used sparingly and only from the jump ball situation in the center circle. We should note that during the past season the Big Eight has experimented by using the jump ball only at the start of the game. Thus we are spending even less time now on the jump ball situation.

Defensive Jump Ball

It is wise to employ a defensive alignment anytime control of the jump is doubtful. The only time we will align ourselves otherwise is if we are absolutely sure of controlling the tap. On the defensive jump in our opponents end, it is crucial that we have the basket protected and the opposing players on the circle covered with the proper defensive assignments. We try to place our big man directly between the jumpers and the basket in this situation. If we can establish control of that position our defensive alignment will be much more effective as we will see in Diagram 10-44. Our defenders are taught to line up with their respective men on the basket side. The diagram shows a typical offensive alignment if our player (X_4) is able to establish himself in the middle position. The remaining players would then be able to align themselves next to their assigned opponent. X_3 would be required to shade toward the basket to help on the open side of O_4, but he is still in an excellent position to cover O_3 and break up a tap to that area. X_2 will be shading to help on O_3 but he also has the freedom to anticipate the tap and move to intercept. All players should have their hands up and should be ready to move in either direction to go after the basketball. Anticipation and aggressiveness will again be very important because a jump ball actually creates a loose ball situation. We have already emphasized that we want our aggressiveness to enable us to come up with the majority of the loose balls.

If we fail to gain the middle position on the defensive jump ball, we will need to offer a little better protection in the basket area (Dia. 10-45). X_3 would move closer to the basket and the open side of O_4. X_2 would shift more toward O_3 but would still be free to anticipate and rotate to break up the tap. X_3 must move to cover O_3 if the tap is made in that direction. Keep in mind that we may limit the freedom of X_2 depending on the game situation. Obviously, a smart player with the ability to anticipate can be very valuable in all jump ball situations.

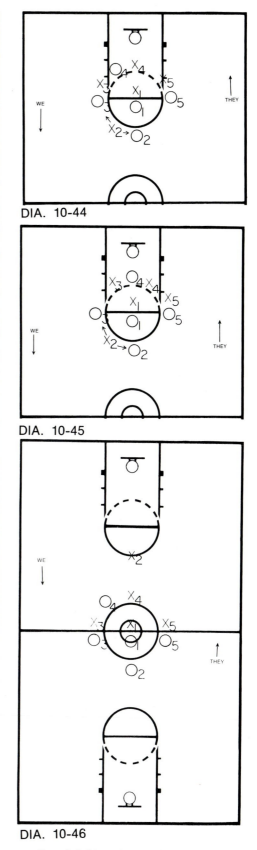

DIA. 10-44

DIA. 10-45

DIA. 10-46

Special Situations 387

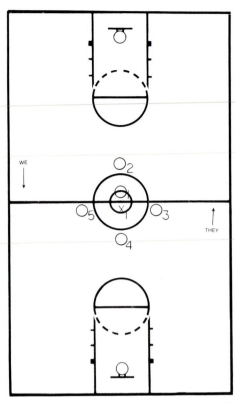

DIA. 10-47

The defensive jump ball from the center circle and in our offensive end will call for the same basic defensive alignment (Dia. 10-46). We may allow for more rotation, however, especially with the jump ball occuring at our offensive basket. We will always place a safety (X_2) toward our opponents end of the floor. He must prevent the ball and an offensive player from passing his line of defense. If the ball is loose in his direction, X_2 must exercise good judgment in going after the basketball or remaining in a position to protect the basket. His primary responsibility is defensive protection but we don't want to inhibit his aggressiveness in going after a loose ball in his territory. The players lined up on the circle should be anticipating the defensive tap and should be ready and alert to go after the ball. We encourage these players to rotate toward the direction of the tap if they can determine the intended receiver on the opposing team. All of the players must be ready to convert quickly to the defensive end if we do not intercept or come up with the loose ball.

Offensive Jump Ball

We mentioned earlier that to set up an offensive alignment on a jump ball we must be absolutely sure that our player will control the tap. Even then we will position our players so that adequate defensive floor balance is provided. If we are protecting a lead or if we want to play it safe, we may go to the defensive alignment and instruct the jumper to tap the ball back to our safety. Our players do not communicate to each other their intentions as far as the direction of the tap. We feel this can only serve to tip off the opponents. We simply have our jumper step back and survey the jump ball area completely. The other players can accomplish this same task while he is out of the jumping circle. All the players should now have a good idea of who will be open and where the most advantageous tap should be directed. At the same time, we want everyone ready and alert to react to the ball.

Diagram 10-47 shows the offensive alignment we will usually set up when we are assured of controlling the tap. O_2 will be required to be our first player back in the defensive end in case we do not gain possession after the jump ball. We again want one of our players (O_4 in this diagram) to move in quickly to assume the middle position on the circle. The two wing players should line up toward our offensive basket to put additional pressure on the opponents. They can always readjust their positions according to the defensive alignment. Once we do gain possession of the tap, we will look for the fast break opportunity or the quick score, but we do not want to force the action or take a bad shot. If an opportunity presents itself we will take advantage of the situation. However, if the defense protects the basket we will look to get into our regular offense. Possession is the most important consideration.

Techniques Important for the Jumper

The techniques we teach our players in the jump ball situation are improtant no matter what the matchup but they will be especially crucial when jumping against a taller opponent. The first requirement is for the jumper to step back and take stock of the situation as we mentioned before. He should make sure all of our players are in the proper position before stepping into the jumping circle. We do not insist that the players assume a particular stance prior to the jump. This is an invidivual area that will vary from player to player. We do encourage the players to develop their jumping from a set position or a short stride step. The players who need to take a long step before executing the leap for the ball are relying on perfect timing with the toss of the official. Different officials will have different habits and tendencies in making the toss so this type of timing is not always possible. The quick jump to the ball from a set position will be more advantageous in attempting to control the tap. Once into the jumping circle, our players are all taught to get ready immediately so that the toss does not catch them off guard. We teach our players to crowd the line on the jump but we do not want them jumping into or attempting to disrupt the leap of the opposing player in any way. We want our players jumping straight up in the air concentrating on stretching as far as possible. As the referee starts his motion to put the ball in the air, the jumper should begin to coil for the leap to the ball. The jumper should reach for control of the tap with his inside hand and arm. This is the side that is closest to the ball so the player should be able to reach the ball quicker and at a greater height than would be possible with the outside hand and arm. The bottom of the ball is the goal for the jumper, again because of the quickness factor. This is the lowest portion of the ball and therefore the easiest and the quickest portion that can be reached. This concept is especially important when challenging a taller opponent for control of the tap. While the taller player may be going for the side of the ball to totally control the direction of the tap, our player may be able to execute the quick jump and tip the ball on the underside in the direction of an open teammate. All of the above are important techniques to cover for the jumper. Just as important is the quickness of the players on the circle to react to the ball as it is tapped. We want all of our players to go into each jump situation with the philosophy that we are going to come up with the basketball.

Scoring Play

At the start of the game or the start of the second half, we will sometimes run a special play that can result in a quick two points if executed properly. The objective is to catch the opposing jumper standing still rather than converting quickly to the defensive end after the ball is tapped. A particularly

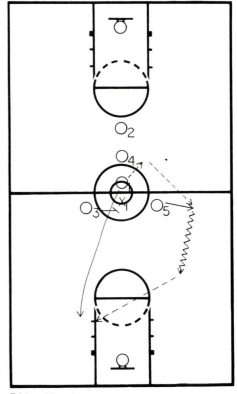

DIA. 10-48

mobil center with the ability and the determination to get out and run will be especially effective in executing this tap play. We will change our initial alignment slightly so that one or both of our wing players are in the offensive end of the floor (Dia. 10-48). We will have designed this play to be run before the game or at halftime so there should be no problem in making the necessary changes. The tap is designed to go to O_4 on his open side. The diagram shows the tap going to O_4 on the side away from O_3. O_3 will step into the middle and screen for O_1 cutting through the congestion to the basket. O_5 will break out to the side to receive the pass from O_4. He will then bring the ball to the basket looking for O_1 hustling down the opposite side. Naturally, if O_4 were open on the other side, O_3 and O_5 would merely exchange roles and the ball would be advanced on the opposite side of the floor. The jumper always sprints to the basket opposite the direction of his tap.

Defense Versus the Four Corners

The four corners offense or delay game has become a very popular tactic in the game today. Coaches are now utilizing this tactic throughout the course of the game rather than only at the end of a game to protect a lead. The idea is to force the defense to cover all over the floor so that breakdowns and excellent scoring opportunities will result. We feel it is essential to go over our defensive coverage of the four corners offense with our players so that we are prepared when we do face this strategy. We will teach our defense versus the four corners briefly during the preseason practices and will review the coverage when we feel an upcoming opponent may employ the four corners. Attention to this defensive coverage will be especially important for very talented teams that can anticipate the utilization of this tactic from weaker teams on the schedule.

The first important point that the players must understand is not to become impatient when defensing against the four corners. That is exactly what the opponent wants us to do. We want to play position defense as long as time is not too much of a factor. We want our players to play the passing lanes and look for the opportunity for the deflection or interception but good judgment and patience must be exercised at all times. It is our intention to let the offense make their own mistakes. It is very difficult to handle the ball for long periods of time without making a physical or mental error. We want to let the offense commit the mistake and then capitalize on it defensively. We will continue to play aggressively, but more with position defense in mind. It is very important to keep from becoming too aggressive. The officials are keenly aware of any type of contact in this special situation and we want to avoid sending the offense to the foul line and putting ourselves in foul trouble. One situation involving contact that our players are taught to always look for is the offensive charging foul. We have already stated that this is an excellent defensive play to make. It becomes even more effective when the offense is attempting to control the ball in the four corners offense or delay game. Our defensive men can look for the charge on the ball handler or on a cutter looking to get to the basket. We do not want to fake the charging foul because the officials will tend to overlook even the legitimate foul when too many questionable charges are taking place. The defenders must anticipate the intended path of the ball handler or cutter and step in front to draw a definite offensive charge.

With our emphasis on position defense, double teaming or trapping tactics are to be discouraged unless time is becoming a factor. At this point, we begin looking for the possible double team if two offensive players cross. This is an excellent time to spring a trap. Our players must be quick to readjust if the offense escapes the double team. When we are forced to get after the basketball, we will also look to double team when an offensive ball handler turns his back. This is an effective defensive maneuver but we will only use it as a last resort because of our philosophy of playing position defense and letting the offense make their own mistakes. Before diagramming some of our defensive positioning versus the four corners there is one final, all important rule that the defenders must follow. The rule states that when the ball is picked up by any offensive player, the defensive players should immediately close off all passing lanes. In other words, if the ball handler has used up his dribble, the defenders should get into the passing lanes. This is the situation where all out pressure can be applied.

Diagram 10-49 shows the defensive position that should be established by the players out on the floor. The defender on the ball (X_1) should play close enough to his man to apply some pressure but his primary job is to contain the ball handler and keep him from getting to the basket. The idea again is not to overextend ourselves and to let the ball handler make the mistake. Our on the ball defense cannot break down. All players must be prepared to handle their man one on one. The defensive players off the ball (X_2 and X_3) should play approximately three to four feet away from their men. They should play close to the passing lanes and look for the possible deflection or interception. X_2 and X_3 must be ready to help in the middle but it is the responsibility of X_1 to contain the ball handler so that help is not necessary.

Diagrams 10-50 and 10-51 help to explain the defensive position that is required of the front line players in the corners. The defenders in this situation must play on the high side of the offensive corner players approximately four to six feet off their men and toward the ball. This distance can increase or decrease depending on the position of the ball. The same off and toward principles that we discussed in

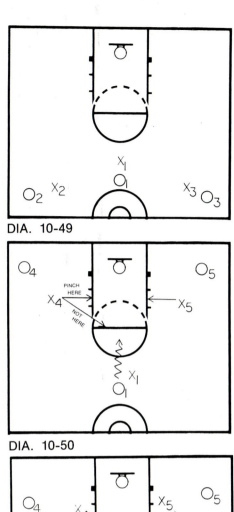

DIA. 10-49

DIA. 10-50

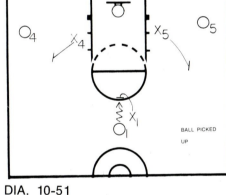

DIA. 10-51

relation to our half court defense are in effect in this situation. These players should play the passing lanes, utilizing the proper angles. If the defense breaks down out front, the low corner players should pinch and help out but only low (Dia. 10-50). We never want to pinch out high and give up the easy lay up. There is no switch or double team in this situation. X$_4$ or X$_5$ must get back to their respective assignments as soon as the pentrating ball handler is picked up by the original defender. The players out front must work hard to contain the ball handlers and keep them from penetrating the basket area. X$_4$ and X$_5$ must remember and be alert to jump into the passing lanes whenever an offensive ball handler picks up his dribble (Dia. 10-51).

The Clock

We will go over most of the aforementioned special areas by developing time and score situations during the practice sessions. We will utilize the clock and even chart statistics in this area. Our purpose is to prepare the players for the different situations that can occur over the course of, and especially at the end of, each game. In concluding this chapter we should list some ideas we give to our players involving strategy or common sense in some of the special situations. Included are some ideas that are especially important in situations involving the clock. A few have been mentioned previously but are well worth repeating.

Special Situations

1. If we have to foul to get the ball, make sure we are not whistled for an intentional foul. Make a legitimate effort to go after the basketball.

2. If we have to foul, be sure to foul their poorest free throw shooter.

3. If our opponent is holding the ball on us in the last few minutes, here are a few key things to remember:
   a. Be aware of the foul situation (1 and 1). No foolish fouls. We can look to go for a steal or foul if we are below the bonus foul situation. They will have to take the ball out if the foul is called.
   b. Look to draw the charge.
   c. Do not gamble for a steal. Play position defense. Our individual responsibility is even more important at this time.

4. If we need a time out at the end of the game and we score, grab the ball out of the net before the opponent can get it, then call the time out.

5. If we are holding the ball for the last shot at the end of the game or at the end of the half, start working for the shot with twelve seconds showing on the clock. Do not let the time run down and then start running the offense.

6. Execute the last shot with six seconds or less showing on the clock. Allow enough time for an offensive rebound and score. Make sure someone is back for defensive purposes and do not foul if a defensive opponent gains control of a missed shot.

7. We want to use our time outs wisely. No one is authorized to call a time out unless directed to do so by a coach.

8. The more enthusiastic the crowd, the more emotions out on the floor. If we are on the road and the crowd goes wild, we need to run our offense and get a basket. This will quiet them down. If we are at home and the crowd is with us, look for every opportunity to keep the momentum in our favor.

9. One of the best ways to stop a 2 on 1 or a 3 on 2 fast break is to draw an offensive charging foul. Fake as if you are going to leave the player with the ball and then square up for the charge.

10. Always protect the basket when the opponent has the ball out of bounds underneath our goal. Our out of bounds defense must be tight and expand as the ball is inbounded.

11. We will usually man the out of bounds play but will go to a zone in special situations. The defensive player guarding the inbounder helps to protect the basket in the man to man defense.

12. When we are awarded possession on an out of bounds play, the inbounder should check the floor before accepting the ball from the referee.

13. On a deadball situation the inbounder cannot run the baseline after the official hands him the ball. Establish a pivot foot. If there is doubt, ask the official if you are allowed to move.

14. Remember—we are looking to score on the out of bounds plays under our offensive basket but the key thing is to inbound the ball safely. Possession is of the utmost importance.

15. We want to stay out of the bonus free throw situation for as long as possible. It is not unrealistic to stay out of the bonus situation for the entire game. To accomplish this goal we must play defense with our feet and our heads—not our hands.

16. On a defensive jump ball situation, the players not jumping should look for the obvious areas where the opponent might like to tap the ball.

17. If you are closely guarded near the basket and know you are about to be fouled (in heavy traffic) go for the shot. Look for the three point play. At the very least, we will be awarded two free throws and the opponent will be charged an individual and team foul.

18. Play hard and let the coaches know when you need a rest. As soon as you are ready to get back in the game, let the coaches know again. Always be ready to give 110%.

19. Do not react or let any teammate react to an official's decision. Our job is to play the game to the best of our ability. The officials will do the same with regard to calling the game.

20. Do not show any negative emotion no matter what the circumstances. Play with poise and intelligence at all times.

FIG. 10-1 Mark Dressler shows our emphasis on the special situations on this defensive free throw. Notice the position of his arms and eyes in anticipating the missed shot or rebound.

The Silent Nine 11

We have attempted in the preceding chapters to present to you our program at the University of Missouri. Each of the ten chapters have covered in detail a particular aspect of the game that we teach in building a complete basketball program. It is our hope that this book will prove valuable in the development of your basketball philosophy and the development of your team and overall program.

This concluding chapter will highlight our 1979-80 Championship Season. This past year, a group of young men came together to overcome injuries and adversity on their way to the Big Eight Title and an NCAA Mid-West Regional Runner-Up Finish. It should have been evident throughout this book, the premium we place on preparation and mental toughness. This team, perhaps more than any other, exemplified those two characteristics. Their preparation leading up to the season indicated to the coaching staff that the players had determined the direction they wished to take and that they understood the hard work that would be necessary to achieve the desired results. As the season began, we stressed constantly that with the proper preparation and attention to each particular game, the overall success of the season would fall into place. The players were able to grasp this idea and did an excellent job of preparing for and playing each game one at a time.

The mental toughness of the individual players and our team as a whole was tested with the depletion of our squad to nine members. Those players became known as "The Silent Nine" because rather than displaying a lot of emotion, they let their actions on the court speak for them. In concluding this coaching manual, we would like to let Mark Fitzpatrick, our Assistant Sports Information Director of the past few seasons, tell you about the 1979-80 Missouri Tigers. We hope you enjoyed the previous chapters and that they prove helpful to you as a reference throughout your coaching career.

Missouri's 1979-80 basketball season had a special attraction to all of us involved with the team. The 25-6 final record, along with the Big Eight championship and outstanding play in the NCAA Tournament, made the Tigers special enough. But there were several teams with comparable records to Missouri's.

What made this team different was its personality—its togetherness and camaraderie. Adversity struck the Tigers in many ways, but they refused to let it spoil their fun.

It was quite a cast of characters. There was Larry Drew, the outstanding senior who left little doubt as to his ranking among the premier point guards in America.

Tom Dore, the 7-2 senior center, was always popular and quotable. He waited patiently for his chance to play, and when it came he made the most of it.

Most of the Silent Nine celebrate winning the Big Eight Championship.   FIG. 11-1

Who will ever forget the third senior—Al Hightower. A former star centerfielder of the baseball Tigers, he used a fifth year of eligibility to help the basketball team in a pinch, and became the "cause celebre" of the fans.

Outstanding play came from veteran all-Big Eight forward Curtis Berry, and center Steve Stipanovich, everybody's choice as one of the nation's top five freshmen. Two other newcomers—forward Ricky Frazier and guard Jon Sundvold-came to the forefront faster than many people expected.

When one of the starters was injured or in foul trouble, Norm Stewart could look to forward Mark Dressler, who went from the Big Eight's best sixth man to a star in the NCAA Tournament.

There were tough, dependable reserves in juniors Carl Amos and Mike Foster. And though his season was cut short, guard Steve Wallace gave us plenty to cheer about with his floating jumpers and fancy passes.

The records came in numbers, with the most outstanding an NCAA field goal percentage high of 57.2. That shattered the previous mark of 55.5 and led the nation by more than two percentage points. Yes, it was quite a year.

"Sometimes it was frustrating to look down the bench and see more coaches than players. But even though our bench was short, it was productive all season long.

"I can't say enough about this team. As young as it was, and with the number of personnel that we lost, it could have quit a number of times. But these players hung in there, giving each other support, cheering each other along. They were a pleasure to be around.

"We may have had the youngest team in the entire 48-team NCAA tournament field. But you work at it, you keep plugging, and when you achieve the things we did—like a Big Eight championship and two wins in the NCAA, you just want to sit back and take it in. You can't be satisfied that you lost that last game, but you can be pretty darn pleased when a group of young men play hard to get where these guys did."

Norm Stewart

Game Three

It was time to take these upstarts on a real journey—short sojourn to Champaign, Ill. that would prove—at least for the moment—whether this collection of Tigers was really a national power or just a passing fancy.

The Ramada Inn in Champaign is about a half-mile from Assembly Hall, an attractive structure that is the site of some fine Big 10 basketball. After the Tigers got done with shooting practice that afternoon they walked the distance back to the motel, in a tight casual group that seemed immune from the expected pressure of the evening.

FIG. 11-2   The MIZZOU coaching staff (L-R) Gene Jones, Norm Stewart, Gary Garner and George Scholz.

The Non-Conference

The Tigers show their unity   FIG. 11-3
after defeating Illinois on the
road.

Ricky Frazier sky-walking   FIG. 11-4
with one of Larry Drew's
assists in the Show-Me Classic.

It was significant that they walked in a "casual group" because that attitude and togetherness would bring victory in a few hours. At times Mizzou looked like it might succumb to the Illini, as suspect Tiger free-throw shooting allowed the home team to come back from a substantial deficit for a one-point lead with three seconds left. Then Curtis Berry who had rebounded Steve Wallace's errand short, hit the second of two free throws. Overtime.

Again Illinois looked in control, leading 63-62 with 1:00 to go in the extra period. But Steve Wallace and Larry Drew used their teamwork to come up with a steal for a Drew layup. Moments later, Mark Dressler and Wallace set up another theft, which in turn set up a three-point play by Drew. Final score—Missouri 67, Illinois 66.

It was perhaps the most important game of the season's first month, as the Tigers outplayed a team which had defeated them in Columbia the year before. The veteran Drew had steadied the young team with a season high 25 points on 10 of 15 shooting, along with three steals, while Dressler's late heroics off the bench gave inspiration to the team when it needed it most.

Game Four

"The Show-Me Classic is our tournament, and we've never lost," said Norm Stewart. "That's the attitude we took into it this year."

The attitude was the proper one, judging by the results. Missouri put on an amazing shooting performance in the opener against George Washington to advance into the finals for the seventh straight year. According to the Columbia Tribune, "Big Stuff had arrived."

Larry Drew was magnificent in setting a school record with 11 assists. His main target was Ricky Frazier, who turned 5 of those fancy passes into buckets, including three slam dunks. Frazier scored 18, Curtis Berry 19, and Steve Stipanovich 14, while Mark Dressler came off the bench for 11. As a team, Missouri shot a staggering 74.1% in the second half, and tied a school record with 66.7 for the game.

"Obviously, they're a good team," said George Washington coach Bob Tallent. "They have thoroughbreds at every position."

One night later, they would be off to the races again.

Game Five

While Friday's shooting was amazing, Saturday's was absolutely spectacular, as Missouri broke its school record with a 67.2 percentage to easily win its seventh Show-Me title, 86-67 over Arkansas State.

Ricky Frazier, as John Hutchinson of the Columbia Missourian wrote, "proved . . . that he is capable of taking a basketball game into his own hands." In a four-minute span of the first half the 6-5 transfer scored 11 points to send Missouri on the way to a 44-30 halftime lead.

The flurry earned Frazier the tournament's Most Valuable Player award over teammates Steve Stipanovich and Curtis Berry, who combined for 47 points on 19 of 22 shooting in the finale, and Larry Drew, who handed out nine more assists for a two-night total of 20. Frazier was not the tournament's leading scorer or rebounder but his ability to control both games left its imprint on the voting committee.

Frazier remained laconic even in his finest hour.

"Well, he said in his post game comments, "it's just something that happened with Drew's help."

Game Eleven

As the New Year began the nation's eyes turned toward Kansas City for some serious basketball between a pair of undefeateds—13th ranked Missouri and number three DePaul.

Despite the snafus that arose in hosting a game at Kansas City's Municipal Auditorium, 9,500 fans packed the ancient structure, and as Dave Dorr of the St. Louis *Post-Dispatch* wrote, "There was electricity in the air."

Television was on hand from the national cable network, from Chicago and from St. Louis. This was a biggie.

It turned out to be a big lesson for the young Tigers, whose winning streak was snapped 92-79 by the Blue Demons, a team on its way to the naton's top ranking.

Mark Aguirre scored 34 points to lead the winners, who held Missouri below the .500 mark in shooting percentage for the first time. It was a frustrating night for the Tigers, who committed 25 turnovers.

"Man, we played a hell of a team" Larry Drew said. "Man, are they good. They've got that killer instinct. It was a lesson for all of us."

A lesson well learned, I might add. One the Tigers would apply well in the NCAA tournament.

Game Thirteen

Missouri tried a different approach to its travel plans for the conference opener at Kansas. The Tigers bussed to Kansas City the previous night, then headed the remaining distance to Lawrence the next day.

The omen was bad when their K.C. motel had little if any

FIG. 11-5   **Curtis Berry**
6-8 Junior Forward

"I've never been on a team that was this close. I've been together with some of the guys for three years. Each year, living with each other and seeing each other every day. We've become very close, as people and as basketball players. Even when I was hurt, I felt a very big part of it."

The Big Eight

Steve Stipanovich dunking versus DePaul.　　FIG. 11-6

Mark Dressler　　FIG. 11-7
6-6 Sophomore Forward

"Everyone on this team was always up for a challenge. Sure, I wanted to start when the season began-everyone does. But if my role was the sixth man, then it was my job to have my head in the game at all times. When I did start, the same thing held true for the guy replacing me. You've got to be prepared to win. This team was prepared."

heat. Towels were not available in quantity, and even a warm guy like Larry Drew had to sleep with his stocking hat on.

It was that kind of trip.

The next night Missouri got its conference season off on the wrong foot in a 69-66 loss to Kansas. The Tigers jumped to a nine-point lead in the first 12 minutes but couldn't hold it and trailed by two at half. Kansas used a pressure defense that kept the ball away from Missouri's powerful front line in the second half, while mediocre free throw shooting and turnovers continued to be the albatross around the Tiger's neck.

"What we need to do," Norm Stewart said afterwards, "regardless of whether we win or lose, is to play a good, solid game."

Game Fourteen

As Norm Stewart said, Missouri was in need of a good game, win or lose. They got a double bonus at Nebraska with a good performance and a notch in the victory column.

In their best game to date the Tigers ran by Nebraska 84-63 before a regional television audience. Steve Stipanovich hit 10 of 13 shots for 20 points and grabbed six rebounds while outplaying Andre Smith, the Cornhuskers' all-conference center.

The Tigers were accurate again from the field with a 64.2 percentage, but this time they also were solid from the line with a 92.3 accuracy. Five players scored in double figures as Missouri won its first game ever at the Bob Devaney Sports Center.

"That's what we've been after for some time." Stewart said, "I would have been pleased with this even if the result would have been different."

It was a win the Tigers could be proud of, but one they wouldn't have long to savor.

Game Seventeen

The press table in the Hearnes Arena is located high in section C, and usually quite removed from the mainstream of action.

But on January 23, the area was a hub of activity during halftime as media across the nation called to confirm the score. Missouri led Colorado 29-4, and wire service, newspaper, radio and television reporters thought there must have been a typo.

The score was right. Colorado, beset with injuries to some key individuals, had tired a slow down game in the first half only to have it backfire. The Buffaloes were icy from the field and Missouri was able to score the last 19 points of the period. It was a Tiger defensive record for fewest points allowed in a half.

The second half was much more sane, but by then it was too late for the Buffaloes to make up ground. Missouri ended up winning 76-45 to keep pace in the Big Eight race. Ricky Frazier, with 17 points, led four Tigers in double figures.

"What did I say at half?" said Colorado Coach Bill Blair. "I told them to score more points."

Game Nineteen

Despite a loss to Oklahoma, Missouri still was in shape to win the Big Eight Title. The Tigers trailed Kansas State by a game, but had the Wildcats in Columbia January 30 to start a string of five home appearances in the next seven outings.

But there's something about K-State and the Hearnes Arena. And the Wildcats, who have ended the four longest homecourt winning streaks in school history, snapped Missouri's 14-game Hearnes streak by a 66-64 count.

The Wildcats played a near perfect game to put Mizzou two games down in the standings. Rolando Blackman with 21 points, was one of four Kansas State players in double figures, which out did a 16-point performance by Curtis Berry, 12 points by Jon Sundvold and 11 by Steve Stipanovich.

"We're still groping, still vacillating," Stewart said. "What we've got to worry about is becoming the best basketball team we can become. Do that, and the race will take care of itself."

How prophetic those words would be.

Game Twenty-Two

With Kansas coming to town, the tickets were scarce at the Hearnes Arena. People were advertising in the local papers for a couple of spare ducats.

Despite bad weather, a crowd of 12,704 hearty souls still showed up February 9 to watch Mizzou face the hated Jayhawks before a regional television audience. They stomped, they shouted, they mocked the opposition and they enjoyed every minute of the 88-65 romp.

"Lovely, lovely, lovely, lovely," said a smiling Larry Drew outside the locker room. Drew had outplayed his old rival, Darnell Valentine, with 17 points and seven assists while hitting nine of nine from the free throw line.

While Drew was magnificent, the day really belonged to Steve Stipanovich, who set a school freshman scoring record with 29 points. Practically everything he threw towards the basket found its mark, as he hit 10 of 11 shots from the field and

FIG. 11-8   **Larry Drew**
6-2 Senior Guard

"We really did some playing. Togetherness. We're like one big family out on that court, helping each other out, complimenting each other. To me, that's the sign of a championship team."

FIG. 11-9   Jon Sundvold working to get open against archrival Kansas.

The Silent Nine 399

Carl Amos   FIG. 11-10
6-9 Junior Forward

"People never gave us enough credit until the end, but we always knew as a team we could accomplish a lot. This team had a winning attitude, but more importantly we had a togetherness that helped us overcome any problems. It was one fun season."

Stipanovich blocks while   FIG. 11-11
Drew draws the charge in Big
Eight play.

nine of 10 from the line.

"Once you get him started," said Drew of his freshman teammate, "it's hard to turn him off."

Said Stipanovich, "We were psyched."

Said a nearby Tiger fan, "So were we."

Game Twenty-Five

Forgetting that this was not just a routine win, Mike Foster and Carl Amos dashed for the locker room after Missouri wrapped up Oklahoma, 81-69.

"Get out there," assistant coach George Scholz told them. "You're missing it."

"It" was the ceremonial cutting of the nets, as seniors Larry Drew and Tom Dore put the finishing touches to a night on which Missouri clinched the Big Eight championship.

At that time all Mizzou knew was that it had clinched a tie. But everyone around the locker room kept steady tabs on the Kansas State-Nebraska game which was well into the second half. And when it was announced that the Cornhuskers had dumped the Wildcats, those remaining players could hardly hold their composure.

Even members of The Silent Nine were forced to let out a little whoop.

If ever there was a team victory in this season of team victories, the Oklahoma win was it. Reduced to nine players by the loss of Curtis Berry, Missouri received outstanding play from a number of individuals to win going away. From a 35-35 halftime score the Tigers survived a wild and wooly affair filled with controversial decisions to assure themselves of their second conference title in five years.

Mark Dressler, stepping into the starting lineup for Berry, scored a career high 18 points. Carl Amos came off the bench to slow down the Sooners' high scoring Terry Stotts. Larry Drew scored 17 and dealt out five assists, while Jon Sundvold had 11 points and Ricky Frazier 10. In the second half Mizzou delighted a crowd of 11,033 with 73.9 percent shooting.

Wrote Kirk Wessler of the *Tribune*, "Missouri . . . pounded the Sooners in the final 13 minutes. Sundvold bombed from the wings. Dressler owned the baseline. Stipanovich dominated the middle. And Drew ran the show with a masterful blend of passing, shooting and gravity-defying flights . . ."

Drew gave much of the credit to everyone around him, including Stewart, who was Stormin' as much as he ever had during some rough play in the second half.

"Man, he was fired up," Drew said. "We got around the

bench during the timeout, and you could see blood in his eyes. It really pumped us up."

Game Twenty-Six

Near the Missouri locker room at Kansas State's Ahearn Field House is a cage-like door that keeps intruders out of the bowels of this ancient arena.

"That," remarked Joe Castellano of the St. Louis *Globe-Democrat* during the post-game press conference, "is where they keep Manley Ray."

Mr. Ray is one of several Wildcats who are anything but gentle in their playing habits. But even though Missouri may have been outmanned physically the Tigers were not intimidated, by human size or a boisterous crowd. The Tigers capped their regular season with a 67-65 victory over the Wildcats to win the Big Eight by three games.

Jon Sundvold, who at 6-2, 170 was assigned to guard K-State's 6-7, 230 Ed Nealy, showed bulk could be outdone by hitting eight of 10 shots from the field for a team-leading 17 points. Sundvold also "muscled up" for six rebounds—his personal high.

Kansas State made life rough in the middle for Steve Stipanovich, but Tom Dore came through with seven points and four rebounds off the bench, while Ricky Frazier and Mark Dressler combined for 27 points and 14 boards. Dressler's six-of-nine shooting from the field gave him a 69.9 percentage for the 14 conference games—good for a Big Eight record.

All that was left was a happy flight back to Columbia, with the Big Eight trophy firmly in hand. Missouri had won it outright, and no one could dare say the Tigers had backed in.

Norm Stewart sat at home, watching the Big 10 showdown between Indiana and Ohio State and awaiting word as to where his Tigers would play in the NCAA Tournament.

There was a lot of conjecture as to whom, when and where Mizzou would play. Even a slight if, since the Tigers had lost out on the Big Eight's automatic NCAA berth when they were eliminated from the Post-Season Tournament and would play without Curtis Berry. But an NCAA tourney without Missouri would have been the greatest rip-off since the Great Brink's Robbery.

So Stewart, his staff and other athletic department personnel went about their business as if there was another game. And sure enough, there would be. Missouri was selected to play as the number five seed in the Midwest Sub-Regional at Lincoln, Neb. against San Jose State. If the Tigers won, they

FIG. 11-12 **Mike Foster**
6-3 Junior Guard

"We stayed cool down the stretch. I took that term 'The Silent Nine' as a compliment. There was no reason to get excited on the court. Just be prepared, do your job—and when it's over do the celebrating."

The NCAA

Jon Sundvold FIG. 11-13
6-2 Freshman Guard

"Our numbers were small, and you know Coach called us the Silent Nine because we don't show any emotion. But inside everyone on this team had the desire to play hard and well when needed."

Al Hightower FIG. 11-14
6-1 Senior Guard

"At times I look back and can't believe this whole thing. I just wanted to help out and I end up as part of a team of this quality. Amazing isn't it? You sit on the bench, and when the fans get the fever you become a celebrity."

would face Notre Dame two days later.

Mizzou, despite its season-long ranking in the top 15, was not judged worthy of one of the 16 first-round byes. But there was nothing that could be changed. It was time to play for keeps.

The trip began on an ominous note as the official party's charter plane had a broken windshield. But a bigger jet came to the rescue, and this one had almost three seats per person. Even 7-2 Tom Dore could stretch out.

That extra room must have had some effect on the big senior. For in a weekend that would result in some of the brightest moments in Mizzou basketball history, he was a man of destiny.

After the initial flight problems, things went normally for the Tigers in Lincoln—a place they were well-acquainted with. There was a touch of flu around the traveling party, but trainer Bud and Dr. Glenn McElroy kept their black bags open to tend to any sickness.

With Curtis Berry resting comfortably in a Columbia hospital, the Silent Nine were a little short-handed for practice on the tournament's eve. So graduate assistant Bob Sundvold donned his practice togs and jumped in.

To the non-Missouri media, what a collection of vagabonds this must have seemed. Teams in the NCAA Tournament are limited to taking 15 players. Missouri could surpass that limit only if all coaches, managers, and trainers were included. And of those nine healthy players, one was more at home in center field, one entered college a year early, one made the team as a walk-on in 1977 and two had barely turned 19. Yes, what a collection. What an impact they would have.

The first half against San Jose State was the lowlight of Mizzou's NCAA appearance. The Tigers trailed 30-23 at intermission, had shot only 42.2 percent from the field and committed 10 turnovers. Worse yet, Steve Stipanovich had four fouls. He never was eliminated by a fifth, because after dehydrating, Dr. McElroy never allowed him to leave the locker room the rest of the game.

Enter Mr. Dore.

Now legend has it that in the locker room, when it was learned that Stipo could not return, Dore walked over to Jon Sundvold and Mike Foster and said, "I will lead you to Notre Dame." In this case, legend is true in two ways. Not only did Dore say it—he did it.

Previous to this night, Dore had not played more than 16 minutes in any game. But, as he said in the post-game interviews, he knew at some time he would be needed. If ever there was a time, this was it.

To put it simply, Dore was magnificent. In the second half he scored 11 points, grabbed five rebounds, blocked five shots and had two steals and an assist. Not only was he a prolific shot-blocker, but his tall presence forced the Spartans to alter the trajectory of several other attempts and hit only 30.6 percent from the field in the second half.

He had help, particularly from Ricky Frazier, who hit nine of 13 shots on the way to a season-high 24 points. Mark Dressler (another man of destiny), scored 11 points with a team-leading eight rebounds. Nine of his points came in the second half, and it was his three-point play with 12:24 left that put Missouri ahead for good.

Entering the final four minutes Missouri was up by 12 and had the game in hand. The final count was 60-51.

Dore, who handled the post-game press conferences with savvy and confidence, had become a favorite of the fans and press. His performance was just one more intriguing adventure in the story of The Silent Nine.

"I'm happy as can be for him," Norm stewart said. "He's a good kid who's been with us for a long time."

"Just look at him," assistant George Scholz said as Dore faced the questions, "He's in seventh heaven."

With San Jose State deposed of, it was time for the Tigers to turn their sights toward Notre Dame. The Irish rolled into Lincoln on their usual plethora of publicity, while Mizzou quietly went about its preparation. Stipanovich had been judged fit and ready to play. The same could be said for the rest of the team.

With Kansas State, which had destroyed Arkansas in its first-round game, facing second-ranked Louisville in the opener of the doubleheader, it was a chance for the overlooked Big Eight to gain some national prestige. The Wildcats played a fine game before losing on a last-second shot in overtime. And if they could come that close, what about conference champion Missouri?

It was that kind of afternoon. A crowd of 14,558 was treated to some great basketball—so great that one member of the press remarked, "I would have paid top dollar to cover these games."

In the second part of the doubleheader, Notre Dame moved to a six-point first half lead as Kelly Tripucka scored 16 points. The Irish held that lead for the first three minutes of the second period, before Dressler went from "former sub" to national hero.

The guy they call "Goober" scored 10 straight Missouri points—six on passes from Larry Drew, and the Tigers tied it at 48. From there until the end of regulation no one led

FIG. 11-15   Tom Dore was the hero versus San Jose State.

by more than four.

And everyone was getting in on the Tiger act. Drew was on his way to a school-record 12 assists. Jon Sundvold's two 17-foot jumpers with eight minutes to play had kept Mizzou within range, and his two free throws at 2:58 gave Missouri its first lead of the half. Stipanovich, playing 44 minutes of inspired basketball, scored 15 points and grabbed eight rebounds. His bucket off a Sundvold assist put Mizzou up by two with 35 seconds to play. Frazier tallied 14 and continued his brilliant play, while Dore, often used in a double post when the forwards were in foul trouble, contributed three rebounds in 11 minutes.

After Stipo's go-ahead bucket, Notre Dame scored with four seconds left to force the second overtime game of the afternoon. But the crowd was with Mizzou—and so was destiny. Drew found Frazier for a dunk and a two-point lead at :49 of the extra period, before Dressler and Stipanovich hit five of six free throws in the stretch to put an 87-84 win under wraps.

Dressler, who never stopped smiling as he hit his last four attempts from the line, finished with 32 points—13 above his previous career high and the most by a Tiger in three seasons. He had his biggest fan along, too. Berry, who was hustled from the hospital to Lincoln as a surprise inspiration to his teammates, was cheering every move by his replacement.

"I was so happy for him," Berry said. "I've been pulling for him all along."

The scene, needless to say, was jubilant. Virginia Stewart had tears in her eyes, while her husband Norm was drenched from the quick post-game shower he received from his charges.

"I don't know how much more of this I can take," said St. Louis Post-Dispatch writer Dave Dorr, who had just returned from the Lake Placid Olympics. "First, the American Hockey team, and now this."

"I constantly hear Notre Dame, Notre Dame," Drew said. "We just wanted to get out there and show them that Notre Dame is not the only team around. We want some people looking at Mizzou."

The plane ride home was a pleasant one. The players were smiling, chatting about some upcoming celebrations in Columbia. Carl Amos sat by himself, occasionally nodding off to sleep, frequently smiling.

"You know," said the 6-9 junior, "there will be some partying tonight. We've worked hard together this season, and there have been some ups and downs. But this makes it worthwhile. Even though we still have a long way to go, it

Ricky Frazier FIG. 11-16
6-5 Sophomore Forward

"We were that good, as good as any of the rest of them. I think this team proved that to all the fans and to the other teams in the country."

calls for a little celebration."

The first celebration came moments later, when the plane touched down and a crowd of nearly 500 greeted the team at the airport. That week, a pep rally was held in the Hearnes Fieldhouse prior to the team's trip to Houston for the regional semifinals. All the while the players tried to remain relatively composed. But finally, when Stipanovich stepped to the microphone for a few words at the rally, he let it out, "Beating Notre Dame was one of the greatest feelings I've ever had."

All good things don't have to come to an end, but even so Missouri's glorious 1979-80 season finally stopped against LSU in Houston. The Bayou Bengals used a second half delay game to beat the Tigers, 68-63. But Mizzou did not go down without a gallant effort. It led 40-39 at halftime before the slowdown, combined with Missouri foul problems, enabled highly-ranked LSU to take control.

In light of all that had happened, in light of the claims that Missouri was to slow to compete with the big boys and too decimated by personnel losses to advance in NCAA play, the Tigers kept plugging. They out shot LSU; they out rebounded LSU; they just couldn't out score them.

"What gets you so upset," Stipanovich said, "is that you know you weren't overmatched. We were so close, we could have done it."

"It's frustrating," said Berry. "The guys went out and played hard. They fought the boards. They played a real hard game of basketball. Unfortunately, we came up on the short end."

Long after the players had departed for their hotel, Stewart still sat talking about the season with a group of area reporters. He said he had never had a team do so well against so much adversity.

Perhaps Frazier summarized it best in a post-game interview: "There's nothing to say, except that I wish it had come out different. I just hope the guys don't get too down about this loss, because there were a lot of good times this season."

Indeed there were, and Missouri's efforts did not go without notice. Joe McGuff of the Kansas City *Star* wrote, "Missouri lost the battle, but won the war." Said John Hutchinson of the *Missourian*, "The Tigers displayed a maturity beyond their years . . . They were the closest, classiest and best-coached team in the regional."

From a pre-season canoe trip, to the beginnings of "Big Stuff", to the final days of the Silent Nine, it had been quite a year.

"The Silent Nine . . . will not forget the experiences of this season," wrote Kirk Wessler of the *Tribune*, "—what was, or what could have been. Theirs is a remarkable story."

FIG. 11-17　**Tom Dore**
7-2 Senior Center

"People were saying how LSU was going to blow us out. But except for that one spurt at the start of the second half, we had them. If they're one of the best teams in the nation, then so are we—and with only nine players."

FIG. 11-18　**Steve Stipanovich**
6-11 Freshman Center

"Looking back at our record, you've got to be satisfied with that. You look at our starters in the NCAA—one senior, two sophomores, and two freshmen—and from that standpoint, the season is good. But don't get me wrong. We're not satisfied with being second best."

The Silent Nine 405